NAM ET PRO EX BPC

VOLUME 1 - MCMXXXIII - MMXX

A Short History of the Bradford Pothole Club first published 2020.

Copyright © John Edwards and Bradford Pothole Club Ltd 2020 www.bpc-cave.org.uk

Printed by;
Book Empire
7, Lotherton Way,
Garforth
Leeds
LS25 2JY
www.bookempire.co.uk

British Library Cataloguing in Publication Data
A catalogue record for this book is available from the British Library.

ISBN 978-1-913319-65-6

A SHORT HISTORY OF THE BRADFORD POTHOLE CLUB

FROM LIMITED COMPANY TO LTD COMPANY –
THE FIRST EIGHTY SEVEN YEARS.

CONTENTS

DEDICATION, ACKNOWLEDGEMENTS, ACRONYMS, INTRODUCTION.

SECTION ONE – A SHORT CLUB HISTORY

SECTION TWO – SOME BPC MEMORIES

SECTION THREE – THE PEOPLE OF THE BPC

DEDICATION

This book is dedicated to the memory of all the past members of Bradford Pothole Club. Those we never met and those we have lost and will never meet again. Their memory might fade from our minds, but we can still find them, their spirit blows through the caves, across the fells, through the Dump and most of the pubs in the Dales. They can be found in every aspect of the modern BPC. They built a caving club that doesn't judge people on their profession or politics. They built a caving club where co-operation, mutual respect and loyalty bond members past and present. They built a caving club where all are included. They built a caving club that feels more like a family - filled with love and trust. *JE 2019.*

A Short History of the BPC

ACKNOWLEDGEMENTS

To write this book obviously took a lot of help, help from the direct contributors, help from every member that filled in the request for personal information, help from all the honorary librarians who over the years have stored and filed away all the clubs documents. Thanks also to the honorary assistant secretaries who published the hundreds of newsletters and bulletins over the years. Help from the book binders of the past who collected paper membership forms and minutes and had them bound into books thus preserving them in our library forever. Help from the 'digital people' for the massive effort, over the years, to convert all the application forms, bulletins and newsletters into downloadable digital form. Not to mention the countless hours spent by people writing the articles, minutes and meets reports over the last 87 years. All that work makes my part look quite small, for all that help I thank them all.

Special thanks must also go to Ian Cross for responding to endless emails about minute details in our records, to Gerald Benn for his contributions, his help and information from his personal diaries and his vast knowledge of the club, to John Robinson for explaining about the various club photographic archives and providing access to shortlisted pictures from the past. Thanks also go to those who responded to my pleas for pictures, some of which have been included. And of course a huge thank you to those who wrote down and sent in articles for inclusion. This book can only be as good as the contributed material, now is the time of regret for all those who didn't send in those personal data forms. *JE2020.*

ACRONYMS USED IN THE BOOK

AAC	Austrian Alpine Club
ACC	Airedale Caving Club
AGM	Annual General Meeting
ARCC	Achille Ratti Climbing Club
ASS	Alberta Speleological Society
AV	Audio Visual [Presentation]
BAR	Bedale & Aiskew Runners
BBC	British Broadcasting Corporation
BCC	Brynmawr Caving Club
BCC	Burnley Caving Club
BCG	Border Cave Group
BCOAS	Bradford College Outdoor Activities Society
BCRA	British Cave Research Association
BEC	Bristol Exploration Club
BITPC	Bradford Institute of Technology Pothole Club
BMCC	British Mountaineering and Caving Club
BOCE	British Overseas Caving Expeditions
BOPC	Bradford Outdoor Pursuits Club
BP	Bottoming Party
BP	Before Present [Day]
BPC	Bradford Pothole Club and Bradford Pothole Club Ltd
BS	Bronte Society
BSA	British Speleological Association
BSAC	British Sub Aqua Club
BSC	Bolton Speleological Club
BSCC	Buttershaw School Caving Club
BSG	Burnley Subterranean Group
BWCC	Bramley Wheelers Cycling Club
CATMHS	Cumbria Amenity Trust Mining History Society
CC	Cave & Crag
CCC	Castleton Caving Club
CCC	Croydon Caving Club
CCG	Christchurch Cave Group
CCPC	Crewe Cave & Pothole Club
CDG	Cave Diving Group
CHECC	Council of Higher Education Caving Clubs
CHGS	Cambridge House Grammar School
CMCCC	Charlotte Mason College Caving Club
CNCC	Council of Northern Caving Clubs
CPC	Craven Pothole Club [Ltd]
CPCC	Coventry Polytechnic Caving Club
CRO	Cave Rescue Organisation
CRG	Cave Research Group
CSCA	Combined Services Caving Association
CUCC	Cambridge University Caving Club
CUCC	Cardiff University Caving Club
Cwt	Hundred Weight [50.8kg]
DCC	Derbyshire Caving Club
DCC	Dudley Caving Club
DCM	Distinguished Conduct Medal
DEFRA	Department for Environmenmt, Food and Rural Affairs

DMMC	Derwent & Matlock Mountaineering Club
DSS	Devon Speleological Society
DRT	Double Rope Technique
EDSS	East Dorset Speleological Society
EGM	Emergency General Meeting
EMRG	Earby Mine Research Group
EPC	Eldon Pothole Club
EPC	Earby Pothole Club
EPS	Electric Picture Show
EUSS	Edinburgh University Speleological Society
FICC	Four Iron Caving Club
FOC	Free of Charge
FRCC	Fell & Rock Climbing Club [Ltd]
FYI	For Your Information
GCC	Grosvenor Caving Club
GG	Gaping Ghyll
GSS	Glasgow Speleological Society
GSV	Group Speleologique Valentinois
HCC	Hyperion Caving Club
HCC	Hallam Caving Club
Hp	Horse Power
HQ	Head Quarters
HSCC	Hampshire Scout Caving Club
HWCPC	Happy Wanderers Cave and Pothole Club
ICRO	Irish Cave Rescue Organisation
JCG	Jackpot Caving Group
KCC	Kendal Caving Club
KMC	Kingsdale Master Cave
KMC	Kyle Mountaineering Club
KRG-O	Karst Research Group - Ontario
LC	Limestone Club
LCC	Lincoln Caving Club
LCCC	Lancashire Caving & Climbing Club
LKE	Long Kin East
LPPS	Liverpool Polytechnic Potholing Society
LSCC	Lincoln Scouts Caving Club
LSCT	Lancashire Scouts Caving Team
LUCC	Lancaster University Caving Club
LUCC	Liverpool University Caving Club
LUCC	Leeds University Climbing Club
LUES	London University Expedition Society
LUG	Lancaster Underground Group
MAM	Midland Association of Mountaineers
MC	Mine and Cave [Diving]
MCC	Masson Caving Club
MCG	Mendip Caving Group
MCS	Marine Conservation Society
MEG	Mendip Exploration Group
MNRC	Mendip Nature Research Committee

MPC	Morley Pothole Club
MRT	Mountain Rescue Team
MSCC	Moorgrange School Caving Club
MUPC	Manchester University Pothole Club
MUSS	Manchester University Speleological Society
NB	Northern Boggarts
NCC	Northern Cave Club
NCCC	North Cheshire Caving Club
NCFC	Northern Cave and Fell Club
NGS	National Geographical Society
NMRS	Northern Mines Research Society
NPC	Northern Pennine Club
NSG	Northern Speleological Group
NUCC	Nottingham University Caving Club
NWCC	North Wales Caving Club
NWCRO	North Wales Cave Rescue Organisation
NZSS	New Zealand Speleological Society
OBJ	Oh Be Joyful [*The name of a beer made by Dutton's of Blackburn*]
OCC	Obertraun Caving Club
OCC	Orpheus Caving Club
OFD	Ogof Ffynnon Du
OOPA	Oldham Outdoor Pursuits Association
OU	Open University
PCC	Padfield Caving Club
PCC	Preston Caving Club
PCG	Plymouth Caving Group
PDMHS	Peak District Mines Historical Society
PMC	Preston Mountaineering Club
PPCC	Preston Polytechnic Caving Club
QMCCC	Queen Mary College Caving Club
QMCMC	Queen Mary College Mountaineering Club
QUCC	Queens University Caving Club
RC	Rucksack Club [Ltd]
RFDCC	Royal Forest of Dean Caving Club
RPC	Raven Potholing Club
RR	Ripon Runners
RRCPC	Red Rose Cave and Pothole Club
RSSG	Royal Society of St George
RDCC	Rubber Duck Caving Club
SBHC	Sherburn Boghoppoers & Hiking Club
SCCC	Shoreditch College Caving Club
SCG	Stockport Cave Group
SFCC	San Francisco Caving Club
SMCC	Shepton Mallet Caving Club
SPCC	Sheffield Polytechnic Caving Club
SOC	Swaledale Outdoor Club
SRT	Single Rope Technique
SUCPC	Salford University Cave and Pothole Club
SUI	Speleological Union of Ireland
SUSS	Sheffield University Speleological Society

TCC	The Climber's Club
TSG	Technical Speleological Group
TC	Tufty Club
UCDCPC	University College Dublin Cave & Potholing Club
UCET	United Cave Exploration Team
UBPC	University of Bradford Pothole Club
UBSS	University of Bristol Speleological Society
UK	United Kingdom
UKMC	United Kingdom Mine/Cave
ULSA	University of Leeds Speleological Association
UNCC	University of Newcastle Caving Club
USA	United States of America
UWFRA	Upper Wharfedale Fell Rescue Association
VMC	Vibram Mountaineering Club
WASG	Western Australia Speleological Group
WCC	Wessex Caving Club
WCMS	Wealden Cave & Mine Society
WRCPC	White Rose Cave and Pothole Club
WSG	Westminster Speleological Group
WVCC	Wharfe Valley Caving Club
YCC	York Caving Club
YGS	Yorkshire Geological Society
YMC	Yorkshire Mountaineering Club [Ltd]
YRC	Yorkshire Ramblers Club
YSS	Yorkshire Speleological Society
YUCPC	York University Cave & Pothole Club
YURT	Yorkshire Underground Research Team
YY	Yorkshire Yetis

INTRODUCTION

Before writing a history of the Bradford Pothole Club one must appreciate how serious an undertaking it is. There are so many aspects, so many people with an opinion of how it should not be done and so many things that have happened over 87 years. Well, it's been talked about for long enough and nobody else has volunteered so I thought I would stand up and put myself out there for the club. On the understanding that this is issue one, so if people don't like it they can do it better for issue 2 'The Centenary Issue' perhaps. In 2001 Dave Ryall produced a wonderful millennium Bulletin which was made up from articles spanning the history of the club. There were some great stories in that bulletin and it nurtured a wave of nostalgia in a few members but not enough for anyone to consider bringing a history of the club together. I know of several institutions similar to the BPC that have printed history books, some with interesting formats. But if a club the size of the BPC can't have a printed history after eighty seven years it's a poor show. To write down the history of the Bradford Pothole Club has long been talked about in shady corners where the idea is usually dismissed as being too big a task or too dangerous to name names if it were to inadvertently wake up sleeping dogs. Well, after eighty odd years it is surely time to have a crack at it. If I leave out certain stories from the past I will hopefully avoid getting some people prosecuted and if I get my facts right I should avoid personal liable charges. People's memories of events vary, we only remember events from the last time we remembered them, so as far as possible, all statements have been verified and agreed by the individuals involved and if your memory differs from this version you can write to the President.

Each person entered in this book has caved with the club at least once and in some cases for well over fifty years. Obviously there would be far too many entries against each name to mention all the UK caves visited by each person, even if records existed. So for brevity, it has been decided to only list the trips recorded in the newsletters and bulletins where the member's name is listed as attending. But not to rely on the records to pass on any tales of bravery and achievement or simple stupidity that indicate a person's character, these have all come from personal accounts. If the reader wants to know more about any or all of the trips mentioned the official trip reports exist within the club's library. There are, in section 2, a number of expanded stories re-telling some of the many famous tales of the BPC attempting to re-tell a story that has not been heard for 80 or 10 years. I did try to select subjects evenly across the decades but obviously there were not as many members in the 30's as say the 90's and the records simply don't exist the further back you look. The style of trip reports in the early days didn't include any of the banter or the events that great stories evolve from. They referred to each other by surname only and were more like a military dispatch than a report about a bunch of friends sharing a great experience.

This book is intended to record a history of the Bradford Pothole Club through its members; it is after all, the people that make an institution such as the BPC what it is. The club publishes bulletins and newsletters that partly reveal how active the club is, both at home and around the World. The Bradford Pothole Club is respected throughout the caving world because of what its members have done, how they behave and the way the club fulfils its obligations as a larger member of the domestic caving fraternity. The published documents produce an accumulating historical document describing some of the club activities and show how the club appears to work. What they don't show are the people, the personalities and characters, their individual and shared achievements, the humour and the friendships and at times the sadness. Trust and respect between members forms as we support each other and develop the lifelong ties that only come from such arduous shared experiences where one regularly puts one's life literally into someone else's hands.

Compiling this book has shown it to be almost impossible to present all the decades of the Club's existence in the same detail. The records simply don't exist and there are not enough living memories to provide the stories that we know must have been laughed about in the pubs over 80 years ago. This just goes to show that we should have commissioned this book 35 years ago when it was last discussed. I joined the BPC in the late 1970's and for the next three decades, I knew the people who were involved with the exploits of the club. Some of the people were older and were from a previous decade and they knew tales from the 60's and even the 50's, but tales from the 50's were rare when I joined. In a similar way tales from the 80's or even the 90's are now seldom heard except when in the company of some of what is now the old guard, [*no longer the tigers we once were*] But we never heard tales from the 30's and 40's because the tigers that did the daft and amazing things then have sadly passed beyond being even the old guard. Every generation seems to think they 'invented' drinking beer and acting daft and were the hard men of caving. Well, that is in fact true; every generation does drink beer and act daft and are the hard cavers. That is the type of people we are.

The image projected by modern young men is that designed by modern commercialism and advertising. These forces slowly change society; we have all seen how our grandparents and parents eventually fail to keep pace with this constantly evolving modern world. We will all reach this point sooner or later in our lives. The young are under pressure to comply with the latest trends seen on TV and in films and especially 'social' media. Social media is now the major force defining which age group one is in, the older might make some limited use of it while the younger element is immersed in its use. The club has rapidly become more communicative due to Facebook and Twitter I know what they are, but 'drop boxes' and 'Tik Tok' mark the point that I pass into the obsolete generation. Modern young men are 'seemingly told' to do nothing except watch football, drink lager and hug each other like heroes meeting after some epic shared victory. They don't understand the meaning of 'adventure' having never stepped out of the safety of society. It is little wonder that a modern young man who says he wants to go underground and make decisions that could endanger his life is seen as an eccentric, somehow different. When this eccentric develops a love of mountains and countryside, it further distances him from his own generation, we are these people. When I talk with the young members of the club there is huge common ground and we talk of experiences we have had. When I talk to my window cleaner or the people I worked with, I get a blank look of someone who has no such experiences other than how to dress fashonably, watch football and drink lager; there is sadly nothing else there. The Dump is full of generations of eccentrics, individuals who are willing to be responsible for their own actions and have a real perspective and expectation of life. There are some who might actually have trouble surviving the modern world so for them the BPC offers sanctuary.

The older members of the BPC are not ignored or pushed out of the club's activities; in fact, these days there are so many older members, beyond serious caving, there is a highly active cycling community and a very successful cave digging group. We no longer look at our past cavers as some sort of chivalric order waiting for the club's hour of need; they are an integral part of a wider club. There is a strong tradition in the BPC of drawing the young tigers onto the committee rather than it becoming a departure lounge for those expecting a position of respect and authority for their years of membership. The shared tasks involved in being on the committee bring the generations together and this is where we truly achieve synergy as the old and new world's work together sharing experience and energy. Having read every trip report the club has published it is clear that these days there is a growing number of 50 – 70 year olds who are still active to a reasonable degree. This was rarely the case up until the sixties and now having a 50 year age span is common on our well attended club meets. I hope this book can show all of the generations of members that they are all the same. We have all drunk beer and acted daft, and achieved great things underground in the UK and abroad and we have formed lifelong friendships in the process, all because we are members of a family of many generations of the Bradford Pothole Club.

This book will not highlight individuals for special recognition as it is all of the people that made, and make, this great club what it is today and show that we are better than we think we are.

This book, it is hoped, will sit on a shelf and draw the owner back time and time again to dip in when a date or a name is missing from a memory or conversation. It will also act as a posterity message to pass down our family lines so that a great, great, granddaughter can perhaps take the book from the shelf and get a real sense of who her ancestor was, and what it was like way back when to be part of such a great thing as the BPC. In this way we are literally creating our future from our past. In the future, institutions such as the BPC might be marginalised as society increasingly believes that interactive virtual reality experiences are actual adventure. Even today it is a word often used to describe a package holiday, for instance, but rarely understood to mean a daring experience where the outcome is, to some extent, uncertain. There will, of course, always be those eccentrics in life that need to walk a different path, one that leads to our front door.

A caving club is only as good as its members; the BPC is a truly great club. - John Edwards 2020

SECTION 1
A SHORT HISTORY OF THE BPC.

SECTION 1.1 – 1930'S

As with many such things, the history of the Bradford Pothole Club starts with a group of seven working men who had grown up together in Bradford. The effects of the Great War 1914-1918 were still affecting people's lives; but the inevitable social changes were slowly becoming visible. Mill workers were taking their wakes week holidays to the coastal resorts with their family for a full week rather than the old day trips in a charabang organised by the mill owners. The railways were adapting from troop carrying and finding their peacetime purpose. As the holiday industry developed they started advertising themselves as holiday resort transport to compete with the motor buses that had been the natural choice of transport for holidays. There was a new mood in the air, ordinary people could now enjoy seaside holidays, but it wasn't until after the events in Hayfield, Derbyshire, on the 24th April 1932 that the possibility of walking the open fells came to the attention of the general public. With the formation of the first National Park and the long distance Pennine Way footpath resulting directly from the Kinder Mass Trespass the ordinary working man could now imagine venturing into the Yorkshire Dales and the underground world of caves. These seven young men were determined they were to do just that. It was in 1933, after the excitement of a few years of marriage had died down a bit, their first contact with caves happened and that was that, they knew a life underground was all they wanted, they were hooked. The rest, as they say is history, and this is that history. But rather than me simply paraphrasing the makers of that history, I will, where possible, let the voices of those pioneers tell their own stories.

It becomes clear, reading the incorporated accounts below, that caving in the 1930's was full of difficulties the modern caver wouldn't recognise. Transport from the towns to the caves had largely been sorted out, as I described earlier, but this still left every expedition starting by walking from the station to the cave. In these early days that also involved carrying the tackle, or at least pushing a wooden wheeled hand cart loaded with the comparatively heavy gear all the way to the entrance, and back before the last train home. Caving in these early days was nothing like the modern experience, they wore tweed jackets and flannel trousers, perhaps two or three pairs at a time. Several woollen jumpers were worn over vests and shirts for warmth and any sort of jacket that might keep some of the water out over the top. Footwear was heavy leather boots with tricouni or cleat nails attached around the edges for gripping, and damaging, the rock. They made a lot of noise and made sparks and then generally fell off. They wore ancient felt hats, or bowler hats, stuffed with newspaper. They mounted miner's acetylene lamps on the front or had torches fastened at the sides. There wasn't a formal dress code, it was considered sensible to wear clothes that can get wet and carry dry gear to change into after the water. [*There were no bin liners or waterproof poly bags to keep gear dry – Ed*] Water in caves was the serious issue; if they were dry they could cave for hours and afford to wait around for a long time. If they got wet, they had to keep moving, as soon as they had to wait their body heat was sapped away very quickly and their body core temperature started to drop and would continue to fall down beyond hypothermic levels. Fred Ackroyd slipped and fell off the roof traverse in Lost John's once, he fell 8' [2.4M] down to the stream way and despite several people dropping down to the stream and even descending the 100' pitch they couldn't find him. With severe concussion he had lost his light and helmet but made his way back out along the stream way beneath his would be rescuers. He blamed the whole incident on his inadequate footwear; he had been wearing plimsolls on the traverse! His boots were in his rucksack presumably keeping them dry for later.

The caving was planned around a 'season', defined as the end of March to the end of October. Winter was for mill and mine visits, evening talks and knot tying nights, probably drinking and planning the next season's trips as well. The winter closed season was possibly initiated by the clubs of the time due to the thermally poor clothing when wet, the addition of more winter rain and colder water with snow melting etc could routinely put cavers in the hypothermia zone or beyond. The caving trips were organised more along military lines than the more relaxed attitude towards the responsibilities of leadership we see today. The meet leader and his deputy held real authority and were respected men as meet leader status was not awarded lightly. They were referred to as the 'Lord or King of the Mountain' and their responsibilities extended outside of the cave and onto the whole fell. Cave leader was a status achieved after performing well underground on many trips, showing resilience and good judgement as well as fitness, stamina and leadership. They didn't necessarily have to be experienced in a particular cave to lead a trip down it; they were more general purpose caving managers. This isn't to say the lads on the trip were marched down the cave, there was a good atmosphere based on camaraderie, or as we call it today Banter and the famous dark humour that always accompanies mishaps underground. When they got to the cave the leader, if there were no volunteers, had to allocate which people were to wait at the top of each pitch to lifeline the 'bottoming' party back up towards the daylight. If the cave had an entrance pitch requiring such a service that man wouldn't even get underground that day. The BMCC tackled the big caves with the same siege tactics that got people to the summit of Everest in 1953. A trip down Lost John's, for instance, could involve several tackling teams and an unfortunately named 'bottoming party' to get 3 or 4 men to the sump before the whole task started again to de-tackle the cave. This meet could take several weekends to achieve. Records show that the length of time tackle was tied up in a cave coupled with the difficulty of moving the huge mass of tackle led to the committee planning several trips in an area before moving tackle to the next area or back to the dump.

The first recorded meets list agreed at a meeting on the 4th March 1934 comprised: Alum Pot, Douk & Weathercote Cave, Newby Cote, Douk Cave Kettlewell, Goyden Pot and Jingling Pot. The committee were presented with a 60' Alpine rope by Milton Shackleton; it is to be assumed they had more tackle at this early stage if their first trip was to be Alum Pot. At the May meeting they thanked Harry Hargreaves, Frank Keigthley and Titus

Illingworth for making and presenting a 45' ladder, which only weighed 14lbs 4 oz [nearly 4.5 kg dry] Regardless what the meets list had said they did Bull Pot on June 3rd and Sell Ghyll on October the 7th. The last decision of the 1934 committee was to sanction the purchase of sufficient rope to make a 100' ladder [presumably 10 kgs dry weight - Ed.]

To add to the difficulties of these pioneer cavers, there were very few guide books. They scanned maps, read old tourism guides and talked to other cavers. The Yorkshire Ramblers had been around since before the turn of the century and the Craven Pothole Club had been around since 1929. It's surprising it took until 1947 for the first issue of Pennine Underground to be published. [It would probably have been a bit earlier if it were not for the interruption of World War 2 - Ed] Having said all that the end of the 1930's marked the end of the first golden age of UK caving when you could still be the first person to climb into an open cave, albeit after pulling a few boulders out of the way. The 1935 season started with a trip to Rift Pot on April 14th. This was followed by an Alum Pot Open Day on May 12th when they expected about 20 visitors. The next trip was June 1st down Lost John's Pot, and Hunt Pot on the 30th. Due to a transport 'issue' [Possibly a CPC problem getting their winch up to Gaping Gill for the August meet – Ed] the next trip wasn't until September 22nd when they were back at Alum Pot.

It was at a committee meeting at the Black House Hotel on February 8th 1936 that it was proposed the club change its name from the Bradford Moor Cave Club to the Bradford Pothole Club, the minutes do not state whether the proposal was carried or not but the empirical evidence would suggest it was. The 1936 trip list was planned as; March Goyden, April Sleet Cavern, June 14th – July 12th Alum Pot, and Sell Ghyll, Marble Steps, Lost John's, Rowten Pot, Stump Cross and Gaping Ghyll with no fixed dates. But when the meets list was issued it was quite different;

1936 - 1st published BPC Meets List.

Regardless of the hardships the available accounts of early BPC, or should I say BMCC, trips reveal the members had exactly the same attitudes as modern cavers. Tolerant of indescribable hardships, in squalid cold, wet conditions for hours on end and can still be relied upon to selflessly risk life to help a friend and then joke all the way back to civilisation. All generations of the BPC will recognise these attributes and remember the occasions when things didn't quite go to plan. But level heads were maintained; the team all worked as one and didn't become another statistic. The first UK caving fatality had occurred in 1936 when Mabel Binks was hit by a falling boulder in Alum Pot. The second occurred at Rowten Pot in 1938 when John Lambert fell down the shaft, the BPC were involved with the rescue/recovery. Although we weren't associated with these sad losses we did have our first rescue incident in 1938. It was not serious in terms of injury but valuable lessons were learnt. The events of the 27 hour ordeal are best described by the leader of the trip, Hugh Browne. His short article, written after the event, is reproduced in section 2 of this book.

For the BPC, the 1930's were the six years from 1933 to 1939 when all caving activity in the BPC came to a sudden stop. The war took people away to fight and those remaining had to work long hours for the national war effort. The only BPC trips underground at this time were simple days out, when time permitted, with a helmet and lamp, no tackle, that was all hanging up at the Cross Streets. That is, of course, not true of all caving clubs in Britain at the time and records show that the start of a second global conflict was not serious enough to deter several groups from caving and digging through to the end of 1939 and indeed throughout the war years. In 1939 Simpsons Pot was explored as far as the bottom of Storm Pot. A UBSS dig broke into GB Cave on Mendips, and the first attempt to dive Alum Pot Sump was made using a garden hose and a car foot pump. In 1940 the 'sump' in Simpsons Pot was enlarged and the connection was made with the bottom of Swinsto. Hull Pot was explored and seven young men got lost in the Alderley Edge Mines in Derbyshire resulting in a 24 hour search. The first volume of the Journal of the Mendip Exploration Society was published. [*In 1947 this became British Caver - Ed*]

In that short time since 1933 the club had come a long way from the lad's first underground experience. They had even moved on from the first 'Dump' at the Crown in Horton. In early 1938 the club moved to the Cross Streets. The club had a significant tackle stock and according to what records we have from this period, there were at least 49 members by the end of the 1938.

SECTION 1.1.1   THE START OF THE BPC   W. GOTT.

Largely because I was a founder member and its first Hon. Secretary, I have been requested by Frank Moulson to tell how the Club came into being. I have very few records concerning the founding and early days of the Club. Just a few menu cards, none, alas pre-1959, and one or two old photographs. What I shall write, therefore, is being dragged mostly from the cluttered attic of my mind. If I am a little astray in my recollections, or miss out the name of one or other of the early members I ask for your indulgence, but my account will be substantially correct, and I will try to indicate the things about which I entertain my doubts. All good fairy stories start with "Once upon a time" so I will do the same. Once upon a time there were five young men. Their names were Milton Shackleton, Charlie Biggin, Norman Middleton *[Norman does not feature in the club records before 1939 – Ed]*, Titus ('Tite') Illingworth and me, Willie ('Bill') Gott. We attended the same church and Sunday school, and at the dances held there we met four girls. Only four? Yes, Norman did not succumb until some years later. This was during and shortly after the 1914/18 war. During 1927/8 the four of us were married, but the five of us kept up our close relationship and became known as 'The Lads'. Parties were held at one another's homes, and at one of these in 1932, and after 5/6 years of wedded bliss, the shackles were maybe beginning to drag a little. It was therefore proposed that 'The Lads' should be unshackled for a day out on their own, and the girls agreed and said they too would have a day out on their own. They never did! But the lads did.

The first question was where to go. At the time, potholing was beginning to get a little publicity in the press. Charlie leach was writing a weekly article in the Telegraph & Argus about outdoor pursuits under the pseudonym of 'Fellman', and potholing began to, be mentioned in his column. Milton, about this time, was teaching Building and wanted to see more of these potholes. One of his colleagues, Harry Crabtree, also a teacher at the 'Tech', knew where one of these potholes was, Alum Pot, and offered to lead a party. Very few people had cars at the time, and certainly none of 'The Lads' had one, so we had to go by train, and it had to be on a Sunday since we all worked on Saturday mornings. No five day week at the time! And so, we met in Forster Square Station on the Sunday in question, at about 6.30am in order to

catch the 6.36am milk train to Morecambe, our destination being Clapham. Harry Crabtree turned up with a sack slung over his shoulder, and diving into it he fished out acetylene bicycle lamps, one for each of us. They were heavy, cumbersome and temperamental. Incidentally, the cheap day excursion fare to Clapham was 4/6d (22.5p)! Arriving at Clapham we walked up through the village, under the tunnels, and along the 'Green Road' and thence along the clints with Moughton Scar to our right hand until we came in sight of the belt of trees surrounding the pot. None of us, I think, had previously seen fell country like this, and we promptly fell in love with it. Approaching the pot I fell and twisted my ankle getting over a wall, and had to hop about on one leg for the rest of the day. At the time I am writing about, there were only two pothole clubs, I believe, in Yorkshire, the Yorkshire Ramblers and the Craven Pothole Club. In Lancashire there was, so far as I know, only the Northern Cavern and Fell club, based in Blackburn, and it was this club which we found on arriving at Alum Pot, to be in "possession". We fiddled about for a while in Long Churn, but as I remember, we did not get very far as one hand was immobilised by the acetylene lamp. But we had had our day out, we had seen a pothole, and we were 'hooked'. Before leaving the pot, we sought out the Secretary of the N.C. & F.C., Cliff Downham, and he informed us that the club would be holding another meet at Alum Pot only a few weeks later, this time it would be an open meet, and we promptly booked our passages. Three more names now appear, Harry Hargreaves, Frank Keighley and Vincent Shackleton, Milton's brother. I believe I am right in saying that these three came with us on the open meet. Harry and Frank were workmates of Tite's, and both were very keen. We were taken down to the sump on this open day, and went home full of enthusiasm.

Now we had tasted blood we had to do something about it, and so a meeting was held in my greenhouse on Cliffe Road allotments, Bradford, and this is, or rather was, the birthplace of the B.P.C. Charlie Biggin opted out, not being as interested as the rest of us, and so the seven founder members were myself, Milton Shackleton, Vincent Shackleton, Harry Hargreaves, Frank Keighley, Titus Illingworth and Norman Middleton. *[Records show that Norman Middleton was not at the inaugural meeting – 4th March 1934 and therefore not a founder member – Ed]* I have a photograph taken in 1958 at the Silver Jubilee dinner, but, sadly Harry Hargreaves is missing and so did not live to have the pleasure of being made a Life Member of the Club as did the remaining six of us. I have the 'illuminated address' which was presented to each of us, hanging up on my wall, and can see it as I write these lines. At his express wish, the ashes of Harry Hargreaves were scattered on the open fell above Alum Pot. We now needed a name for the newly formed Club. Milton lived in Acton Street, Bradford Moor, and so at first we called the Club the Acton Speleological Club, but this was too high falutin' and was soon changed to the Bradford Moor Pothole Club, and subsequently to the Bradford Pothole Club. Charlie Leach ('Fellman') - he later became Editor of the T. & A. was invited to be our first president, and he accepted. He held the office for 3 to 4 years as I remember. At Easter, 1934, we spent the weekend doing a 'recce' around Ingleton, visiting - but not descending Marble Steps, Bull Pot and Rowten Pot. We couldn't, we had no tackle. Sorry, we had one 60ft length of alpine rope! We also poked about a bit in Yordas. Charlie Leach gave us a frequent mention in his column and as a result we had applications from quite a number of people wishing to join. I can't name them in the order of joining, in fact I shall probably miss some of them out altogether, for which I apologise in advance, but I will do my best:- Freddy Crowther, Frank Moulson, ('Dad'), Fred Ackroyd ('Ferdy'), and Jack Ackroyd, his brother, Hugh Browne ('Hughie'), Arnold Patchett (who took over the job of Hon. Sec after the war ended). Henry and Bob Atkin (colleagues of mine at A. & S. Henry & Co Ltd.), Arthur Shepherd ('Shep'), Bert Ambler, Alf Ingham, and two lads from Blackburn whom we ran into one day on the fells and who promptly joined, Bert Ratcliffe and Tom Burgess, both from Blackburn. And later on also from Blackburn, Eddie Hobkirk, and by gosh, I am forgetting Howard Dobson.

The first Annual Dinner was held at the Hermit, Burley Woodhead, and there would be less than a dozen present. I remember we had to run like hell down to Menston Station to catch the last train to Bradford. I never went into the Hermit again until summer 1978 when Milton, Norman and I were having a run around after having been to Nab Wood Cemetery to put some flowers on Tite's grave. We do this every year on July 8th or near. Tite died in 1964. On this evening we were passing along Burley Woodhead road towards Ilkley when Milton suggested that we pop into the Hermit "just for old times' sake". We parked the car and went in. It was packed to the doors with young people and we felt completely out of place, so we drank

up quickly and came out. Moral - let the distant past sleep in peace. I am getting to the point when Frank Moulson can take over the story and fill in the blanks I have left. Dinners after the one at the Hermit were held in Skipton for a number of years, and took on the pattern which they have followed, more or less, ever since. 'Tite' was a natural comic and acted as compere for the entertainment. He did Stanley Holloway Monologues very well indeed and one called "Runt", which was considered very improper in those days by some, but every year there would be cries of "We want Runt" and sometimes he had to capitulate. I usually sang a song or two, and I came across a book of songs written by a Lakeland Composer, mostly concerned with the Lakes and climbing, but there was a refrain as follows:-

Rats, Mice, Rabbits and Moles,
Stoats and Foxes take to their holes
But we go down by ladder and rope,
Deep in the earth to grovel and grope.

For many years this was as much in demand as "Runt", and I sang it for many years. When I gave up singing I turned the books, there were two, over to the Club. They may still be in the archives. I wonder if anyone sings "Rats, Mice" any more. It was 'Tite' who first introduced "The old homestead" and it has been printed on the menu cards ever since. When the war came we put our tackle - we had quite a bit by then - into store, and Godfrey Wilson, a master at Giggleswick School took our library into his safe keeping at Stainforth where he lived. Soon a lot of members were going off into the forces, and it was decided that we should send each one of them the "Yorkshire Dalesman" each month, which I did, and I always tried to write a few lines in addition to tell the lads what, if anything, we were doing. When any of the lads were on leave I would try to arrange a week-end up at Cross Streets and we would go up on the fells and look forward to the day when we could resume our activities. I remember one occasion when Eddie Hobkirk was on leave we decided to climb Ingleborough and Eddie was wearing his RAF greatcoat. We nearly had to drag him over the last bit from the shoulder.

One or two of the lads did not come back. Freddie Crowther fell down the lift shaft on an aircraft carrier in the Mediterranean. One of the Blackburn lads was killed, but I don't remember whether it was Bert Ratcliffe or Tom Burgess *[It was Bert – Ed]* "Shep" was in the Navy, and never failed to call at my office for a few minutes when he was on his way back from leave to Hayling Island. He was torpedoed, but came through all right. A few more have passed on besides the ones I have mentioned. Hughie Brown, Frank Keighley, Bob Atkin, Bert Ambler. Grand lads and remembered for the good times we had together. And the 'Lads' who started it all? Except for 'Tite' we are all still batting, all on the way towards eighty. And we still have happy memories....and now, over to Frank.   **W. Gott.**

SECTION 1.1.2 – THE START OF THE BPC. FRANK MOULSON [1954]

Listed as one of the first to join after the Founders was Dave Wilman, who joined in 1935. A few of the early slides were photos by Dave, although most of the early slides were taken by Milton Shackleton. After Dave came Freddy Crowther, Charlie Leach [who wrote under the name 'Fellman' in the local paper, the Telegraph] Then came Hugh Browne, Howard Dobson, Fred Ackroyd, Jack Ackroyd, Rob Atkin, Frank Fearnley, Roland Robinson, Frank Moulson, Alf Ingham, Arnold Patchett, Graham Watson, Arthur Shepherd, Bert Ambler, Harold Robinson, Edgar Wheatley and from Blackburn, Sam Grundy, Dick Carrysforth, Bert Ratcliffe, Eddie Hobkirk and Tom Burgess. Bill Gott was Hon Sec, Chas Leach was President, Fred Ackroyd was Chairman and Hugh Browne was Hon Photographer. Hugh Browne made stands on which to dry slides, and collated all the photos he could before making them into slides. I purchased an old school projector, oil lamp type, and converted it to electricity, and with the help of Fred or Shep went all over the place giving lectures on Potholing, charging 10/- or 50p to help club funds. The club hired a small room in St Clements Church, and Milton gave instruction in Knots, the geology of limestone, its flora and fauna and what to look for in caves.

In 1936 the Club had a dump behind the Crown Hotel at Horton in Ribblesdale. It was a very dingy little place, but it was a place to store tackle, and would sleep three or perhaps four. We did not have it for long, because, unfortunately, the landlord found a few beer bottles that had not been bought in the Crown and he kicked us out! How the contact was made I don't remember, but we found refuge at the Cross Streets Hotel. It was in the old Harness room over what had been the Stable in the coaching days, and the only lighting was by candles. [It came about when Howard Dobson and Roland Robinson talked to the new landlord, Eric Stead, about his plans after the farm house conversion to a pub was finished - Ed]

The Club held an unofficial meet every fortnight, but we had what might be called a hardy element which met every week for a booze up on Saturday and potholing on Sunday. We used to meet in the Castle Hotel, and after a few drinks would go to the shops and each of us bought something for breakfast on Sunday morning. Bacon, egg, tomato, sausage, kipper.... it all went into one big frying pan. There were some real concoctions, but it all

got eaten. The early ladders had loose rungs with a castle or crown laced through the rope for the rung to rest on. The ends were loose, and the ladders were tied together with reef knots (we hoped); and what a nuisance it was if one was put on upside down! All the rungs moved down, and it very often left a long step between ladders. In the winter of 1936 Fred Ackroyd devised a new way of making ladders, using split wood rungs with four bored holes, bolted to the ropes. The ropes were bought from a firm in Sunbridge Road, in 30ft lengths, with spliced ends. One end had a loop and the other, a spring locked loop. Howard Dobson's father owned a weaving shed, and every night the Tackle Brigade went up to the Mill to use the vices for compressing the rungs before the bolts were put in, tightened up and peened over. We thought they were wonderful; easier to roll and carry, no knots to tie.... this was as big a breakthrough as the introduction of electron ladders. The type of clothing worn then was heavy trousers, two or three roll neck jerseys, climbing boots with clinker nails and two pairs of socks to keep your feet warm. In 1958 Bert Ambler, who was an electrician, wired up the Dump to the electric.

Up to this time the club was looked upon by the CPC and the Yorkshire Ramblers as very much the poor relation in the pothole world, but as the club improved and we descended some of the larger and deeper pots, CPC invited us to a joint meet at Long Kin and Rift Pots. Phillip Tyas and I led from the Long Kin end, and Hughie and Waterfall from Rift. This did wonders for our reputation, and the Club went from strength to strength. Then came the outbreak of war. Bert Ambler immediately volunteered for the Navy, and all the field members clubbed up and bought a Rolls Razor, a real luxury in those days. Bert was surprised and delighted. Designs for a club badge were asked for (one designed by Vincent Shackleton was chosen) and unknown to us all, Bert had about twenty made up in cloth, and Henry Atkin made up the 'latin' motto: "Tacquinarti ego bonus sum" - the nearest to "Beggar you, Jack, I'm all right"! This was on the badge, and he gave one to every field member of the Club.

We listened to the speech declaring war with Germany as we stood round the Bar at Cross Street, and a sad gathering it was, for it meant the end of all potholing. A week later, nails were put in the rafters in the barn, and the tackle was stored for the Duration. Of the members, Bert Ambler won

the D.C.M, Arthur Shepherd was torpedoed in a
ship in the Irish Sea and survived, Bert Ratcliffe and
Frank Fearnley were killed in Action.

BPC Membership at the end of 1938

Ackroyd	Fred		Jepson	Arnold	
Ackroyd	Jack		Keighley	Frank	
Ambler	Bert		Keighley	John	
Atkin	Henry		Leach	Charlie	
Atkin	Robert		Middleton	Norman	
Broadbent	John		Mitchell	John	
Briggs	William		Mitchell	Albert	
Brothers	C.		Moulson	Frank	
Browne	Hugh		Moulson	Arthur	
Burgess	Tom		Nichol	Alan	
Carrysforth	Dick		Patchett	Arnold	
Coffey	T.A.		Palfreman	Bernard	
Coffey	Leon A.		Pevison	J.	
Crabtree	Harry		Prest	Robert	
Crowther	Freddie		Ratcliffe	Bert	
Darwood	C.		Robinson	Harold	
Dobson	Howard		Robinson	Roland	
Fearnley	Frank		Rycroft	R.	
Goldsbrough	H.		Shackleton	Vincent	FM
Gott	William	FM	Shackleton	Milton	FM
Grundy	Sam		Shepherd	Arthur	
Hargreaves	Harry	FM	Thornton	John	
Hobkirk	Eddie		Watson	Graham	
Illingworth	Titus	FM	Wheatley	Edgar	
Ingham	Alfred		Wilman	David	

SECTION 1.2 - 1940'S

Starting amongst the dark days of WW2, the 40's, like the 30's, were not a full decade for the BPC, or many clubs for that matter. The Second World War didn't end until September 1945 and it was clearly going to take a long time for life to get back to anything like normal. Some major progress had been made underground during the War years by some caving clubs that hadn't felt the need to cease all their peace time activities for the duration of the War.

In 1941 the first serious cave accident on Mendip occurred down GB. The entrance to Mossdale was discovered and elsewhere Bob Leakey free-dived through several short sumps.

In 1942 Coleman & Dunnington finished their survey of Pollnagollum after two years, at 3.5 miles it was the longest cave in Ireland. Quaking Pot was explored from the first pitch to the chamber at the bottom of the third pitch where it was decided that further exploration would need explosives.

1943 saw the first exploration of Grange Rigg after digging through a boulder choke to reach the final chambers. The BEC were the first club in Britain to use an Electron Ladder, on the 12m pot in Swildons.

In January 1944 a naked Bob Leakey solo free dived the then sump in Disappointment Pot and dug out beyond it, to convert it into a duck with 1 inch of airspace. Over the next few months the cave was pushed until it joined Hensler's Streamway.

1945 Saw Graham Balcombe diving the Alum Pot sump, as well as Goyden Pot and Keld Head. Clearly with some inertia from the preceding months 1946 saw the Northern Pennine Club (NPC) and Red Rose Cave & Pothole Clubs (RRCPC) formed.

In early 1946, a meeting was called in Bradford to gather together again the widely scattered threads of the BPC membership. It was here, at last that the self inflicted war-time burden Bill Gott had shouldered, was rewarded, for not only was the club in existence, but its members were 'raring to go'. Officers and committee were elected and a programme of meets arranged. At the suggestion of the president, all of the club's tackle was tested and overhauled and replaced where necessary. It is interesting to record that the first post war meet was held on the 7th April 1946 at Rift Pot, and the first descent, appropriately enough, was made by "Dad Moulson". As the year wore on, however, it became apparent that some of the old enthusiasm was lacking and most of the meets were very lean affairs. Transport difficulties to the dales were partly to blame, but the club was not alone in experiencing the uncertain period that lay ahead. Other clubs were similarly affected, the 'Leeds Pennine Club', old friends and neighbours, were disbanded. Six years of war had left a scar which could only be healed by time and the next few years were the most critical in the club's history. On the one hand were the pre-war members, in whom the spirit was willing, but the flesh woefully weak. A full day of hard caving was out of the question. On the other hand were the keen young newcomers, men who could go the whole distance but who lacked an experienced leader. Frustration, on many meets, was often their lot. That the club did survive these difficulties is partly due to Arnold Patchett being elected Hon. Sec. at the 1946 meeting. The BPC Bulletin was produced, the first issue appearing in September 1946 and continuing to do so until the end of 1952 when high paper costs and shortages became prohibitive. There is no doubt that it played a leading part in helping the club through such an awkward phase.

The search for a new Dump didn't take long and on 2nd November 1946 the club tackle was moved, for the second time, from the old milking shed at the Cross Streets to an upstairs room next to the Flying Horseshoe at Clapham Station. Nobody at that time suspected it would ever be moved again.

Club activities were also extending beyond the caving 'season' with the resurrection of the program of talks by learned committee members and invited guests covering subjects such as Palaeontology and reminisces of foreign travel holidays. These talks were in addition to the visits to places of interest organised by the committee. Trips to woollen mills, engineering works and telephone exchanges have all been recorded in the bulletins. The members seemed to get good value from their 10s 6d [52.5P] annual subscriptions.

As with today, if somebody got access to a stock of equipment it was offered to the general members via the bulletins. Possibly because war time stock piles were being disposed of, the club advertised miners helmets [the cardboard type] and knee pads for more than the annual subs [11s 3d] These were probably released as the Bevin boy conscription was coming to an end. Government surplus was becoming available after the war and ex-army boots with steel nails and horseshoe heel plates proved to be the most cost effective footwear for caving, fell walking and climbing[!] in the late 40's and 50's.

Two meets which shine out in these dark years deserve a special mention. In August 1946 the club made a successful descent to the master cave in Lost John's, and on September 7th, 1946 five members conquered Mere Gill Hole. At the time the club had "over 25 ladders" which were probably ranging in length from 15' to 100' and represented an impressive depth capability. The trip down Rift Pot on 7th April was followed by the return on the 28th April and again on 19th May, Rift Pot was a great favourite with the BPC in the early days. This is possibly due to the relative ease that it could be tackled as there is no great horizontal development and tackle hauling is predominantly up and down pitches, and it is dry. When the club took on Lost John's Pot on the 14th July it was a very different story. They had not attempted to get people down to the master cave by the end of the 21st. The tackle stayed in and it was the 4th August before the master cave was reached and the tackle started to move out of the cave.

The 1947 annual dinner and first two meets of the year had to be postponed until April due to bad weather in Yorkshire; the snow had paralysed the county's transport system. The educational talks offered to the members in 1947 reflected the increasing opportunities for foreign travel. Mr H.W. Rhodes gave a talk entitled 'Some Foreign Caverns' during the annual dinner on a Tuesday in February. George Webb told of his adventures climbing in Switzerland and G. Philip Leedal regaled the membership with the tale of his trip to Iceland, including the journey out which involved surviving a four day Atlantic storm in a trawler. There were 2 other BPC members on the trip but they remained un-named!

The club received a letter from member Sam Grundy in which he describes the caving possibilities in Jamaica where he had moved to. This had no response at the time but this letter and a subsequent update was possibly the acorn for a club expedition seventeen years later. There was a trip to Lister & Co to see their facilities the week after the Annual Dinner in February. In May 1947 the club was growing rapidly and reported 11 new members since the previous bulletin [3 months earlier] The club at this time managed to trade a roll of sisal rope and acquired a similar length of manila as there was no longer any confidence in sisal as lifelines.

The 1947 caving season eventually got off after a very cold then wet start, and under the threat of yet more rain, another trip down Rift Pot and Long Kin [East] Pot was attempted on April 19th / 20th. The planned meets list for 1947 went on to include Mere Ghyll [July 6th – 13th] where rain and high water conspired to deny success. Then the Craven Pothole Club Open meet at Gaping Ghyll, 20th July – 5th August, and a trip to High Birkwith Cave on the 24th August just about concluded the years planned trips underground. There was a successful 'scratch' 7 man trip down Mere Ghyll on 7th September when one man [ANP of course] reached the bottom of the 100' pitch [2 men at the top of the three previous pitches were left to life line his return trip] The following notice appeared in the club bulletin in November which does indicate the member's willingness to plan serious drinking sessions.

"It is proposed to arrange a week-end at the Golden Lion, Horton, on 23rd/24th. November next. If conditions are favourable, your Hon. Sec. [ANP] may attempt the Three Peaks, and two men will be needed at the top of each Peak to see that all is above board. If the Three Peaks are done in less than six hours, a memorable evening will follow" [This clearly happened before the Pen-y-ghent cafe cashed in with the clocking in machine and convinced the increasing number of weekend visitors to the Dales that the Cafe was the official start and end of the Three Peaks walk- Ed]

The 1948 annual dinner was held on the 21st February at the Red Lion Hotel in Skipton. There was a talk and slide show of the caves visited by Mr Norman Thornber [Norman had just published the first Pennine Underground in 1947 – Ed] before the dinner which cost 7s 6d [37.5P] Caving in 1948 started with a trip into Ingleborough cave on 10/11th April. The meets list for the year then read as; Alum Pot 20th June with a photographic meet on 11th July, August 1st Long Kin West, 19th August Rift Pot [Open meet] and September 19 / 26th Juniper Gulf with Ribblehead caves on 10th October and a fell walk on the 24th completing the season's activities. It is to be assumed that there were 'private' trips in between the dates of the published meets list but sadly not many records exist anymore.

1949 was to be a landmark year for the BPC, it started with a visit to Hemsworth Colliery, on the 16th of January and ended with a frenzied engineering endeavour that would ultimately define the club. 1949 also saw Stream Passage Pot and the BSA's Bar Pot dig being connected to the GG system. Ireby Fell Cavern and Pen-y-ghent Pot were also discovered.

It was while deciding on the 1949 meets list that the club was informed by the Craven Pothole Club that they couldn't guarantee being able to run their annual open meet at Gaping Ghyll due to insufficient technical support being available. This was initially seen as a disappointment as the chaps enjoyed Gaping Ghyll. This was not seen as an opportunity until a committee meeting in March or April when a member [*Possibly Alf Hurworth and/or Donald Leach – Ed*] suggested making our own winch. See section 1.2.1 for a full explanation and how this came about and changed the BPC forever. There was a knot tying night arranged for the evening of 2nd March before the caving season started. The rest of the list was agreed as follows; Tackle test 20th March, Rift Pot Open meet 2nd/3rd April, Sunset Hole 24th April, Whitsuntide Camp, Sell Gill 4th – 6th June, Lost John's 19th June, Clapham Cave [Ingleborough] 26th June, Marble Steps 27/28th August, Almscliffe Crag 4th September, Derbyshire Weekend 17/18th September, Kingsdale 8/9th October and finally a Fell Walk in the lakes on the 30th October.

The club received an invite to attend an International Caving Meeting in Valance Sur Rhone in August 1949. The objectives were to establish informal links between caving clubs across Europe and begin the creation of an International Caving Congress. Attendance of this could put the BPC at the heart of European caving with the prospect of the use of foreign club facilities and experiencing foreign caves not to mention the exchange of ideas on equipment and techniques...... Nobody went!

And that brought to an end the shortest decade the BPC endured. But in that short time the club not only recovered from the war, it expanded it's activities and membership and made the defining decision to show how a winch should be made and operated. Even in these early days of the BPC it had been recognised that efforts should be made to prevent groups with an agenda forming within the club. The following is an extract from an article by Arnold Patchett in the January 1949 bulletin;

"The members of many clubs frequently form themselves into cliques, or even one clique; new comers are discouraged - perhaps not always intentionally - through their non-admittance to the inner circle. The Club flourishes, but sooner or later the members of the inner circle lose their youthful enthusiasm, become disinclined, or circumstances arise which cause a cessation of activities be it only temporary, and the whole club disintegrates overnight. It has always been one of the endeavours of the BPC to avoid drifting into such a state, and it is the constant desire of the Committee that new members should be fully encouraged, for surely amongst their numbers will be future leaders, future chairmen....... future men who will be described as pillars of strength, and on whose efforts the whole structure of the Club rests.... men who will carry it through periods of adversity and difficult circumstances. It was, in fact, the adherence to this policy and the good spirit which went with it that the Club was kept going through six years of war, during which time neither a single potholing expedition was made nor a new member elected. It will therefore be our duty to preserve this spirit, and the coming year will provide us with the opportunity to do it"

[*Please excuse the 'sexist' tone of the above, there were no female members at the time of this article, it is reproduced here for the message it carries to all our modern members, male and, of course, female. This principle is still very much at the heart of BPC thinking and demonstrated in a contemporary article describing the successful shared experience of the making and assembly of the new gantry in 2014– Ed*]

1.2.1. THE ORIGINS OF THE BPC WINCH. Synthesised from two articles by Frank Moulson
[1965 & 1978]

The most popular event that members looked forward to before the war was the opportunity of going down Gaping Gill on the CPC winch. Their gantry was a very heavy wooden affair with side members made from 10"x 4" and uprights of 8"x 4", all bolted together with huge bolts and handrails made from 3"x 2" section. It took about 8 men on 4 ropes to pull it over the hole, but it did give one a feeling of security. It was powered by a two horsepower Lister water cooled engine. It was kept in the roof of the barn at Clapdale Farm, and Mr Murray conveyed the whole assembly up to Gaping Gill on a hay sledge pulled by his old horse "Dolly". It took Mr Murray about six trips on his own to get it to the pot and ready for them to assemble.

They had a few stalwarts, in particular Jim Hill, Allan Waterfall and John Mitchell of the Craven Herald, who camped at the pot all week and took people down, by appointment. Then came the war, and afterwards though it was hoped that the CPC would put up their winch again, it was not to be. John Mitchell and a member called Proctor had gone abroad, and Phil Tyas and Bob Crunden were not available. Not enough members had the experience to assemble and work the winch. In 1946 Eli Simpson of the BSA group in Settle decided to build one of their own. It was a real Heath Robinson affair, made from two wagon chassis bolted together in the middle, with steel tube uprights and rope guide lines at the sides, and with a Beardmore motorcycle engine and gearbox mounted in a square frame, chain driven to the cable drum. It was a most frightening affair, and you needed three hands to drive it. They let the chair down in free engine and brought it back up to the overhang in second gear. When it was 10ft below the overhang, you had to hold the brake on with your knee, change into first gear, let in the clutch and take off the brake at the same time. They had some very near misses, having the chair run back through faulty gear changing. They had many members who, to our minds, took too many risks but it did what Eli wanted. It made a hell of a lot of money, and they never used it again.

By 1949 the situation was that only about four members of the Craven had sufficient knowledge regarding the erection of their winch, and we, the Bradford Pothole Club, wondered whether or not they would be holding the Gaping Gill winch the following summer. It was whilst the B.P.C. Committee were trying to arrange a Meets list for

the following year that the Craven were approached to see if they would be including the winch meet on their syllabus. We were later informed that they had not the members to do so. It must be remembered that all the senior clubs, of which the B.P.C. was one, were invited and joined in the meets at Gaping Gill, and this point was raised at our next Committee Meeting. We wondered what could replace this annual event. It was while we were discussing this situation that an astounded committee heard an inspired member suggest that we build our own winch! We agreed to think about it, and come to the next Committee Meeting with our conclusions. At the next meeting, and after much discussion, it was decided that we should go ahead with the idea. It would, have to be completely new in design, featuring a lightweight gantry and a modern air-cooled engine to provide the power. We were completely sold on the idea when, at the next meeting Donald Leach brought a scale model of a gantry he had built from 5/16" copper pipe soldered together. The idea of a light weight gantry constructed from alloy tubing was Donald's. The idea was to use scaffold tubing for the gantry. They were building ten storey blocks of flats with it, so why couldn't we use it at GG? There was then, as there always had been throughout the history of the club, and probably always will be, a very active field section, who were all for immediate action. On the other hand, there were those who were more cautious and wished to consider all points, mainly the cost, as at that particular time funds were rather low, possibly as little as £32 in the bank, and our only income was through subscriptions and a small amount from showing Club slides. It was decided to find out how much a winch would cost, and a figure of £150 was expected. We thought of ways of making money, and ran a sixpenny raffle which brought in about £95. It was a bit of a swindle, but we had to have some money. Then we had a Bring and Buy sale, which raised about £20. Now we had a bank balance of £130, after expenses.

The estimated cost was, if we begged many parts and cut back the design, it could be built for £60 - £70 so we got the Green Light but there were some who were against it and thought we were mad. We formed two special winch committees, one with Fred Ackroyd and myself, as engineers, to get some idea of the engine, and one with Don Leach, Hughie Brown and Frank Briggs as the Gantry team. The only parts of the winch that were bought were the aluminium tubing, engine, cable and guide ropes.

Permission was obtained from the Craven Pothole Club for us to examine their winch. Not long after a working party went up to Clapdale barn, where it was stored. After pulling the various bits and pieces out of the barn, the gantry was bolted together and the complete assembly then measured up. We wanted to know the length of the base and the height of the uprights, and the angle and line of the pulley. How far was it from the wall? We knew this was important to get the cable running right in the corner. Scale drawings were made to enable us to obtain the correct length of tubing, but this was only possible with the A frame. All the other lengths would have to be tailor made over the pot.

Since Fred and I had access to trade discounts it was left to us to order the various parts. Fred, through Crofts Engineers, ordered the cables from British Ropes, and the tubes, I believe, from Alloy Tubes Ltd. To get the full discount I ordered the engine from Barfords in Westgate. The Dural rails were in short supply, but we found some in Dewsbury. At this time I was technical sales rep for my firm, and all the metal for the A frames, tie bolts, engine platform, shafts, gears and pulleys were obtained by putting dummy orders through my firm and not through the sales books! The major difficulty was the cable and brake drum. My firm had all welding done on sub-contract, and I persuaded the owner to make one on the quiet and work it out later [We never paid for it – Ed] It was not perfect, but it did the job for three years, and then we had new rims welded on and turned up to make for more even braking.

The next difficulty was the small pinion and the bearings, but Fred got these through his firm, saving further money. Since the gears were standard stock, we had to build the winch to suit the gears, and to get a lift of 100ft per minute it meant a very small bottom sprocket had to be made, Fred got over this. The boring of the metal for the A frames was done by Fred and myself at my Firm's premises one Saturday and Sunday. All the parts were taken to Clive Place, and I built it up in my cellar. I begged the belting from various customers, and made three spare belts, just in case. Other parts, shafts, gears, metal frames, brake bands, tie bolts, pulley, pulley strap and cable drum were supplied by me free of cost. The small pinion and the bearings were supplied by Fred Ackroyd, free of cost. The first Field Telephone and cable were supplied by Don Leach,

free of cost. What all these parts would have cost is anybody's guess, and having to buy them might have made the whole idea impossible.

The building of the gantry was left in the hands of Don Leach, Hughie Browne and Frank Briggs, with of course many other members helping to fetch and carry the tubes up to Gaping Gill. Building began by assembling the A frame at the side of the hole and then pulling it over by means of ropes from the other side. Then began the job of measuring and cutting the rails, which tied the A frame, and the supports under the bottom rails. Credit must be given here to Don Leach, who, although life lined, stood on the frail 2" diameter tubes over the centre of the hole, marking off the rails to be cut, the work of a real sky man! Slowly, as the gantry began to take shape it was found that we were short of couplings. This was quite serious, as they were on priority and could only be obtained for building site work. The deficit was made good, in a way frowned upon by the more godly, but the gantry HAD to be up and ready!

Meanwhile, Fred Ackroyd and myself were busy on the design of the winch, and we came up with something similar to that used by the Craven. The main difference being that the Craven winch had the winding drum on top of the "A" frame, which made it top-heavy, and caused it to sway badly on descents, whereas on ours we intended fitting the drum at the bottom, thus giving it more stability. It was Fred's decision that the winch should have a safety factor of 30, enabling it to run well within its capacity and withstand many years of hard work. Consequently, we proposed to use 3/8" diameter wire rope, which had a lifting capacity of 30 cwt., whereas the normal weight we should be lifting would be just over 1 cwt. The engine used by the Craven was the water-cooled type, and often boiled, sometimes to the point of becoming dry, causing unavoidable and maddening delays. We decided to use an air-cooled Petter engine of a nominal 2h.p. at 2,000 r.p.m. incorporating shafts of 1" diameter to transmit 2 to 3 h.p. A lifting speed of 100ft a minute was decided upon, but later proved to be too fast. So much so that the first time it was used by one of the other members, he over wound, and, to everyone's horror, lifted the gantry 2" from its seating.

All the parts of the winch were brought up to my house and assembly began in the cellar, my mother often coming down and shaking her head at the queer contraption slowly taking shape. At this time of life, my mother, like most potholers' mothers, had given up trying to alter my ways from this (in her opinion) silly sport. At last the winch was ready to be taken to Clapham, but how to get it there was quite a problem. Nobody had a van and we could not afford to pay a carrier. We were finally saved when John Fleming and Arthur Shepherd managed to borrow an Austin Light Van. This turned out to have a very short wheelbase and when the winch was loaded, half of it stuck out of the back. With the weight of the winch and three members, the back was nearly on the floor. I followed in my little Ford with three more members, and to watch the van dipping from behind was really frightening to behold. All went well until John took the little bridge over the stream at Clapham a little too fast, and the rear mounted petrol tank touched the floor when the van bottomed, and partly broke the petrol union on the tank. We off-loaded the winch, and then tried to find a way of repairing the damage. Over a gill of ale, we decided that the best way was for Frank Briggs, who was a motor mechanic, to drain the tank and seal it with chewing gum. As it was after 11 pm and not a garage open I think we all said a prayer of relief as we rolled into the Flying Horse Shoes yard.

The alloy tubes were ordered from Alloy Tubes Ltd in London, with the instructions that they should be delivered to Clapham Station, where we could easily collect them from the Flying Horse Shoes Hotel. Easter was decided upon as the time for erection, with the hope that we would have the winch and gantry ready for a Whitsuntide meet. We expected the tubing to be delivered in February, but by the beginning of March it had not arrived. Many anxious letters were sent to London, but the only information we could obtain was that the tubing had been dispatched three weeks previously. Just when it seemed that we should not have it ready for Easter, it was discovered that the tubes were lying in the Lost Goods Department at Clapham Station - LONDON! The railways then really moved and two days later our order was at Clapham Station, Yorkshire.

Then came Easter 1950, and our attempt to assemble the whole thing as a unit. New holes had to be drilled in the side of the shaft, for the gantry and on the edge of the shaft, for the winch. The winch had to be lined up and secured, and the wire run over the pulley, the wooden flooring for the gantry was obtained from Mr Barton, Mr Farrer's agent, and charged to Arnold Patchett. By an all round effort we had it ready before Whitsuntide, and then we realised that we had no corrugated iron sheets for the dam. Even these were hard to get, but I bought some second hand, and made

some spikes and clips for them at work and had it ready for the day.

The first chair used was an old aircraft ejection seat, acquired from a scrap yard. It was loaded with stones and the first B.P.C. winch descent made. We noticed that the gantry rocked far too much when the chair was lowered fast, and stays had to be made to tie the gantry to the wall, at the side and the top. Many descents, and a bent and buckled chair later, the whole assembly was passed as O.K., and ready for the first passenger. Whoever went down first would have to take the telephone and fasten the guide line, a job nobody really wanted. Frank Briggs was our volunteer, and he was fastened in the chair and the descent started. Nobody expected the cable to twist the way it did, and Frank went down, twisting round and round, and continually bumping into the wall. It had been arranged that he would blow his whistle when he wanted to stop, but as he went through the water coming down the shaft, it filled his whistle, and he was unable to signal as planned. By the time he got to the bottom, after a nasty bump on the ledge, he was really battered and bruised, but, thankfully, able to complete the job he had gone down to do. It may seem an easy thing to do today, but don't forget that this was the first time it had ever been attempted by the Club and much was learned on that first trip. Frank finally had the guide line fixed, and what a joy it was to us, that members of the Bradford Pothole Club would be able to descend Gaping Gill on their own winch. It was going to put the B.P.C. right into the top ranks of the senior clubs. Compared to the huge wooden gantry the Craven used, ours looked really frail, but as members of other clubs made more and more descents, it quickly gained their approval. Here was something completely new, modern in design and with great strength. We were all very proud of it, what a success it was, and when, the following year, we were asked by the Yorkshire Ramblers and the Craven Pothole Club, for permission to join us in an open meet, we felt that the Club had really made the tops. As the years went by, many improvements were made, which added to the safety and reliability of the winch and by operating a regular Whitsuntide Open Meet, the club was helped financially and gained much in prestige. The total cost is estimated at about £125! I hope this article gives our members some idea of the enthusiasm and the effort put in by the early members of the Club, we can be sure that it will be handed down year by year to new generations of club members for them to enjoy many more wonderful meets at GG.

SECTION 1.3 – 1950'S

Of course caving in the early 1950's was very much the same as it had been in the late 1940's. The tackle was the same, the clothing the same and travel arrangements were largely unchanged. By the middle of the 1950's we see more and more private vehicles being used for caving trips. So much so that in 1954 there were repeated calls to all members to use the coach or lose the coach service. The numbers using the bus were falling to a point that the club couldn't afford to subsidise its continued use. The monthly newsletter quite often asked for people booking attendance at a function to say how many spare seats they had in their car. This strongly indicates the demise of the coach based caving trip. It would prove to be a slow, lingering death however. The strongly worded threats in the newsletter and the reducing use of buses continued into the 1960's. These days the only bus trips are the annual walking meet and to and from functions. Some of the early traditions of the club were still evident in the 1950's such as the educational trips and tours to factories, telephone exchanges, etc. In May 1954 there was a well attended tour around Birkshall gas works and in November the same year there was an organised tour of the Bradford Police Headquarters.

The caving scene was changing around us in 1950 Poetic Justice and Eureka Junction were discovered and the connection through to Lancaster hole was established. In 1952 County Pot and Top Sink were dug out and connected to the rapidly growing system.

The most significant difference to BPC caving in the 1950's from that of the 1940's was the Gaping Gill winch. It is clear, from reading the old accounts, that there was, as now, a very diverse skill set within the club. In part due to the very basis on which the club was formed, whatever your academic or employment background was irrelevant to join. This allowed the club to draw a group of specialised people together when a task presented itself. Such was the case when the club set itself the challenge of making it's own winch. Within a couple of years the transport, assembly and operation of the winch, gantry and lighting required much knowledge. This knowledge is slow to learn through experience, but potentially quick to pass on to the next generation if the expert is happy to pass on his knowledge. A relatively small number of people who were involved with the

design and manufacture of the winch had the required skill sets and they were, understandably, the initial experts. But as the procedures for its erection and use were refined through the early 1950's the group of experts got bigger and various aspects of installing the winch could be done by new members after some initial instruction. It is clear the BPC didn't want to suffer the indignity that had befallen the CPC in 1949 when they had to admit they couldn't assemble their own winch. The dedication and enthusiasm of the BPC membership to attending and working at GG over the Whitsuntide meet is as strong today as it was in those early, exciting times when it was all new, largely because of the systematic dissemination of knowledge rather than experts clinging on to their exclusivity based status.

As mentioned before, the new winch was first erected in time for the Whitsuntide meet at Gaping Gill in 1950, as an indication of how successful that was it was decided to transport the winch and gantry to Alum Pot later in the summer of the same year. Here, the weather was at its worst, completely washing out two successive weekends. Transporting the gear up to the pot was a nightmare task for the faithful, and retrieving the last remnants of equipment in a terrific snow storm on December 3rd was another. This venture was never suggested again.

The early 1950's saw the introduction of changes to the published documents produced by the club. The monthly bulletin, which included meets reports, was replaced by an 'information only' newsletter with the intention of publishing meets reports in an annual bulletin. This has proved to be the first step towards what we now enjoy. This newsletter was again changed slightly and the 'New Series' of the newsletter was, confusingly, called a bulletin and number one was distributed in February 1953. One of the last 'Old Series' contained notification of the 1952 Christmas Social on Tuesday 9th December. It describes what was to become the annual evening's entertainment with ladder climbing, a crawl and a mystery item. There were prizes of nylons and sugar, which reflect the times and indicate the post war social and physical hardships and depravations still endured seven years after the end of WW2.

The following weekend the club held the Christmas weekend at the Marton Arms where Saturday evening meal, breakfast and a Sunday evening meal were enjoyed with presumably caving on both Saturday and Sunday, though that is not mentioned in the weekend plans. If these social gatherings weren't enough, immediately after New Year was a fell walk from Bowland with a mixed grill meal arranged at the Ribblesdale Arms in Gisburn. [*The return coach from Bradford cost 12s 6d [62.5P] including the mixed grill! - Ed*]

On February 7th 1951, the club lost one of its staunchest members with the death of Johnny Broadbent, he was one of the first to join the 'Bradford Moor Cave Club'. In the old days, he was a tower of strength and his sense of humour was a pillar on which the whole club leaned for he could turn a joke in the grimmest moment. June 1952 saw one of the strangest meets in the history of potholing; on which nobody went underground at all. A bus from Bradford carried a party to Notts Pot via Leek, whilst their tackle was, due to a misunderstanding, taken via Masongill up the Turbary Road to Marble Steps!

The Hon Librarian, Hugh Browne, noted that the club had in 1952 purchased a copy of 'Underground Adventure' by Gemmel and Mayers. [*Nobody could have realised that it would become such an influence on a nine year old boy who was destined to join the BPC and go on to create another caving epic, in the same style as this original, 65 years later. – Ed*] In the run up to GG53, Arnold Patchet told the committee, we should have a staff tent at Gaping Gill for the leading members to use. This was modified by the committee and we borrowed [rented] a tent from the Queensbury Scout group for quite a few years. There was some sort of issue regarding the winch fees payable by ladies in 1953. It was eventually agreed that lady visitors should be asked for a donation, under Rule 10, at the discretion of the meet leader.

The first of the 'New Series Bulletins' [February 1953] announced the discovery of a rift "a few yards north of Rift Pot, that seems to contain a man made wall". The article went on to name another new BPC discovery 'Xmas Pot. The February bulletin describes the new method of arranging the caving programme for the year ahead. The year is to be divided into four quarters with an area designated to each quarter. This is presumably to minimise the tackle movements by

planning all trips in the designated area and storing the tackle locally.

1st Quarter – Horton Area, including Easter Camp.
2nd Quarter – Ingleborough Area, including Whit Camp at Gaping Ghyll.
3rd Quarter – Ease Ghyll Area, including August bank holiday camp.
4th Quarter – Malham Area.

The reports seem to suggest the Little Hull Trip, led by Arthur Clifford, went very well. The published plans for the Gaping Gill meet involved a bonfire on top of Ingleborough to mark Coronation Day of Elizabeth II. The 2nd quarter [1953] trips included Disappointment Pot and Swinsto before the decamp and move under new arrangements made to camp at Bull Pot Farm for the August Bank holiday. Several trips were successfully carried out in and through Lancaster Ease Gill over the 3rd quarter period. There was some sort of problem with Irvine West's trip down Notts Pot where somebody went missing and the search went on all night before he was eventually discovered in some, undisclosed other person's bed [?] The Lost John's meet in October 1953 had forty five people turn up [*quote*] 'some' made it to the Master Cave as well.

The caving strategy for 1954 was planned slightly differently from the four quarter model of 1953. The first two quarters were merged and planned as being in the Ingleborough Area until the end of June. Attention was then switched to the Horton Area for July and August to include the August Bank Holiday Camp. The last section, September to December was dedicated to Ease Gill and Leck Fell areas.

On the 6th February 1954 the club celebrated its 21st Anniversary at the annual dinner, held at the Red Lion in Skipton. It had been agreed that the Annual Dinner and Annual General Meeting would be on separate dates for the 21st anniversary. We had 75 members and a total of £13 18s 1d to our name. Meanwhile the landlord of the Flying Horseshoe requested that the membership be made aware that the trough adjacent to the Dump is for cows to drink from not for cavers to wash in!

In 1954 Arnold Patchett told the committee that he wanted them to write a letter to the Cave Preservation Society regarding the undisclosed misconduct of members of the Albion Club at Bar Pot. It is unclear if they did or not, but the event hints that the CPS had some sort of authority over caving clubs. [*Bob Leakey was perturbed by the damage done to the floors and formations in caves. As a consequence, in 1952 he established the Cave*

32

Preservation Society - a national organisation dedicated to looking after our caves. It was only active for four years, but in that time was involved with taping routes through caves, clearing rubbish from caves, advising on digs, producing a cave preservation code, writing articles in caving magazines, and lobbying planning departments. It was fifty years before its time - Ed] That authority now only lies with the landowners, Natural England and the CNCC. There were the beginnings of inter club co-operation at this time with each of the larger northern clubs sharing their annual meets lists and then having a get together to re-arrange weekends where any conflicts occurred. The system was extended to inform each other of their dig sites to avoid open warfare on the fells.

The CPC discovered Dowber Gill Passage in 1954 and dug into Providence Pot in 1955, they subsequently connected them together.

There were many successful club trips throughout 1954 with the occasional wash out such as happened in the Autumn of that year. The diving support trip in Clapham cave was over in 15 minutes as the divers reported they were behaving more like surfboards than divers in the beddings. Lancaster Ease gill was similarly affected. Marble Steps was run after a short spell of fine weather which brought out the crowds and 27 people were lined down the entrance pitch. No records tell us what that many people did when they were down, or how long it took to get them all out again. *[It can't have been as bad as the 45 people down Lost John's - Ed]*

The question of public liability was a subject of great debate in 1954, with the club taking the fare paying public down Gaping Gill and other clubs occasionally paying to use our tackle. How would we stand legally if mechanical failure of equipment should lead to a liability claim? The committee took legal advice on this subject and an insurance policy was paid bought.

By 1955 the quarterly move around the Dales was becoming less defined, the published programme for that year shows a clear bias towards Ingleborough from March to the end of May with GG at Whit of course. The meets then move to Lancaster Ease Gill area, but the August camp is back at Chapel le Dale. This is followed by some trips around Kingsdale, then back to Chapel le Dale and Meregil in October before going on a walk in the Lakes and back to Fountains Fell for a couple of meets. The programme seems far less grouped in geographical zones than when the quarterly plan was first introduced.

The weather improved for the Lost John's trip in July 1955 but it still ended up being a two weekend assault to get five men to the sump. The weather was even better for the August Meregill camp but due to the arrival of a second club trip the BPC trip was run overnight. The unsung heroes of this trip were Alf Hurworth and Brian Wainwright who sat at the top of the first two pitches, to lifeline those who went further, for nine hours!

Arnold Patchett and some unrecorded 'associates' joined the 1955 Anglo – French expedition to La Bouiche in the Limoge area. Many extensions were found by him and his team and a small chamber is named after Arnold. He met and was working with the famous Norbert Casteret on this expedition.

The period from the end of 1955 saw some new rules regarding the dump, issued by the committee. They appear strange and somewhat draconian by modern standards but unfortunately the reasons were not explained at the time. There were only four dump keys and members were specifically banned from asking to borrow a key whilst at the Flying Horseshoe *[Which is where the Dump was - Ed]* Another rule emerged at the end of 1955 that is also confusing; no member was allowed to sleep at the dump the night before a club meet was running in conjunction with a bus. This appears to be aimed at increasing the numbers using the bus. *[This rule was repealed in December 1956 – Ed]* But to no avail, by early 1956 in every newsletter the committee was threatening to cease the use of buses if the numbers didn't increase immediately. This situation was saved, temporarily at least, by the Suez War. Fuel prices increased as its availability decreased and the use of the club bus increased to viable levels even though the fares were increased. There was an agreement with the WRCPC to share buses during the fuel shortage. *[Fuel rationing was introduced in 1957 and in the early part of the year all trips were arranged within walking distance of Clapham station. The club had to apply to the Ministry of Fuel in March 1957 asking for 12 gallons of fuel to run the winch over the Gaping Gill meet. Rationing ended on 14th May after 5 months - Ed]* Elsewhere what was previously 'advice' about camping with wives *[No mention of girlfriends - Ed]* was repeated in early 1956 with less of an advisory tone. Members with ladies were told to camp well away from the main camp area.

At the committee meeting on the 24th March 1955 the committee firstly agreed to name the latest dig 'Newby Moss Hole'. The tackle secretary then reported that 2 out of 8 ladders were in usable condition, the other six were in need of repair. The replacing of ladder ropes was an ongoing task for the rope ladder making team. The meeting was then interrupted by the Tackle Sub Committee as it declared it was ready to report. [It was basically set up after the club was shown an Electron ladder in 1951. It had a watching brief to evaluate the implications of introducing new and different types of caving gear. Its members were elected by the committee every year from the newly elected committee members at the AGM. – Ed.] On the day they reported the minutes read like an ultimatum had been given, their recommendations were;

1. All natural rope tackle to be [quote] written off.
2. Two quotations had been acquired for the materials to construct metal [Electron] ladders and their recommendation was that the club purchase sufficient material to construct six ladders for evaluation. [6 x 30' costing 50 shillings each]
3. They also recommended that the club buy 120 feet of nylon rope for evaluation as lifeline.

All recommendations were passed, after much discussion, with the proviso that we did not abandon rope ladders immediately as it takes three weeks to make electron ladders and the cost of complete replacement was excessive. A compromise was reached and the club launched the acquisition of six electron ladders and the repair of the rope ladders. By July 1955 the first electron ladder was in service with three new wire belays. In May, however, the committee had sanctioned the construction of 150 feet of new rope ladder and in August they bought 400 feet of manila life line. [Manila lifeline was about 11mm diameter with a 'new' breaking strain of 1000 lbs [453kgs], 10mm Nylon hawser laid rope has a breaking strain quoted as 4766 lbs [2162kgs] There is a mystery surrounding a statement in committee minutes of May 1953 when Arthur Clifford listed 1 metal ladder among the tackle stock list. Could this be the one shown to the club by M. Railton during the 1951 annual dinner? It is strange that no mention of its use was ever made – Ed]

The club's Annual Dinner in 1956 had 55 people attending, with nine guests that meant forty six members out of less than sixty were attending the clubs formal event. [Remember the Annual Dinner was still a male only event at this time – Ed]

The club records having four new electron ladders in service by September 1955 and approval was given for the acquisition of six more. In April 1956 the committee again sanctioned the purchase of 120' of nylon rope as long as we also bought 240' of hemp line at the same time. A further six electron ladders were authorised in October 1956 but the rope ladder production line was continued, presumably due to a lack of confidence in the new ladders by some unidentified people.

The committee had announced in February 1955 that they would be introducing a small number of 'metal ladders' and would all members kindly remove all of their tricouni nails from their boots to prevent damage to the soft alloy rungs. They said that triple hard hob nails are more than adequate for normal use. They went on to accuse members of standing on ropes and damaging them with the tricouni nails. [Originally 'Elektron' ladders were developed by Robert de Joly before the War, they got their name from the trade name of the Magnesium Alloy used by de Joly for the rungs on his earlier models. Electrolytic corrosion would have been a serious medium term issue with the magnesium alloy and the zinc plated steel cable. These original ladders were made with a rung spacing of at least 500mm [about 20"] and were a problem in narrow pitches. They became standard equipment in France before the War and at least one had, curiously, made it across the Channel during the War as an Electron ladder was used by the BEC in Swildons Hole in 1943. Interestingly the German incendiary bombs used in WW2 were also called Elektron by the Germans for the same reason. They contained a bar of Elektron which was the oxidising fuel for the device. - Ed]

As stated, the first BPC electron ladder was put into service in July 1955, nearly twenty years after their introduction. The committee approved the purchase of yet another 400' of manila rope as lifelines for the 150' of rope ladder under construction.

In May 1956 the committee announced the twelfth electron ladder was nearing completion and funding for a further six had been approved. The club's twelve ladders, presumably thirty foot each, gave the club 360 feet of electron ladder, increasing to 540 feet when the six additional ladders were complete. However, it had also built up the rope ladder stock to 400 feet as well. It is clear that some unidentified committee members that opposed changes to the way things were done still wanted to use natural fibre ladder and lifelines, even after the multiple rope snapping incidents. The original 120 foot nylon evaluation rope is never mentioned and was possibly never acquired. The Westminster had been using nylon lifelines for several years by 1956 but it was to be many more years before the BPC followed suit. The two different ladder production lines continued in parallel apparently oblivious of each other for several years.

However, in the mid 1950's the weight of opinion had pushed the club towards electron ladders and a trip in 1958 down Long Kin West was equipped with electron ladders, but it took many years to fully phase out the old wooden ladders and the methods that went with them. *[The use of pulley blocks, to get all members of a team down, was recorded on a private meet in 1938 but the club didn't buy any pulleys for club meets until the late 1960's -Ed]*

September of 1956 saw the Dump expand, the club took over the room beneath the Dump at the Flying Horseshoe. The new landlord of the Flying Horseshoe had halved the rent so when the ground floor room became available the committee decided to capitalise on the situation. Later in the year the Dump was wired for electricity by the members, it was ready for the following Easter [1957]

In March 1957 the club officially notified a Mr E. Varich of the existence of the new entrance at Flood Entrance Pot, now named Wades Entrance it was discovered by Eric Wade of the BPC. Later in the year the club formally told Mr Norman Thornber [*Of PU fame – Ed*] that the recent finds attributable to the BPC included P5, Wades, Christmas Pot and Newby Moss Cave.

In 1956 following an invitation from the CRG, Bob Powell (CPC) and our Nick Pratchett were invited to join the International Expedition, which reached Sump I in the Gouffre Berger; the first cave to be pushed to over 1000m. The BPC UK caving programme for 1957 had all the usual trips on except in March when a very rare trip down Juniper Gulf was planned. At the last minute however it was cancelled and the trip was changed to Flood Entrance and Bar Pot, two regular favourites. There was a new function in January of this year that seemed to capture the member's needs and the Digger's Dinner went on to become a permanent feature of the club's social calendar.

The Gaping Gill meet at Whitsuntide had a large number of people turnout. The surface camping saw forty tents pitched and there were up to thirty individuals camping in Sand Caverns [*This was a common practice until it was banned by Dr Farrer, for reasons of hygiene in 1965 - Ed*] There were people from fifteen other clubs attending that weekend, including forty from the Westminster Speleological Group and London University Speleological Society. A record 109 descents were made on the Sunday with up to 42 people waiting in the chamber at one point. The only reported concern was when three unidentified youths were found descending the 100 foot pitch in Bar Pot with only one light between them.

On July 23rd 1957, after all the tackle had been removed from the hill there was an accident in SE passage and the CRO suggested that the winch might prove to be the best way of evacuating the casualty. In response, 35 BPC members turned out and began preparations to rush the winch back to Gaping Gill. As things transpired it was eventually decided not to use the winch, but it was a good example of the BPC membership showing its willingness to answer the call, en masse when their help is needed.

The August Bank Holiday camp at Alum pot had good weather and things went well until Don Leach and Derek Jowett went down Rift Pot to recover tackle. When they were moving back from the top of the last pitch, tackle hauling at the entrance dislodged a large boulder that landed and shattered very close to Don Leach. He was very lucky indeed.

August 1957 again saw the committee struggling to to maintain the good name of the club. There was a re-clarification of the rule that forbade women sleeping in the men's dorm at the dump. Complaints were raised at the following committee meeting, but it didn't change the rule.

October 1957 saw the CPC requesting to hire the gantry, the committee decided to lend it them FOC.

Late 1957 was an interesting time; the 1st of November 1957 was the date of the first occasion that the BPC used explosives. Later in the month there was a trip planned down Quaking but the team were informed that the entrance had fallen in. Not wanting to waste the day they decided to run a practice rescue with a stretcher down, or should I say out of Wade's entrance at GG. The volunteer victim was Peter Blackburn. Things went

OK and he got out a little shaken but alive. His next trip was on December 8th and it was one of the first attempts at completing the recently discovered Dow to Providence connection. He went with the Bradford Technical Collage Pothole Club and they were trapped by floodwater. A major rescue followed, which included many BPC members and Peter Blackburn and five students had to be rescued for real. [*Peter's run of bad luck continued into 1958 when everybody left him alone for the night at Gaping Gill prelim. They all went down the hill leaving him to sleep in a 'marquee'. The following week at the member's meet he came with his own tent which he managed to set fire to and it burnt to the ground in a very short time. He then presumably had to sleep in the marquee again – Ed*]

The New Year brought an inquiry from the CPC asking how much we think the alloy tubing to make our gantry would cost? We furnished them with the information needed

April 1958 witnessed a hilarious episode in committee – the club funds were at an all time low and a fundraiser was planned but as there were no funds to draw on the committee members put together a £10 loan so that the club could purchase a typewriter, so they could write a newsletter, where they would advertise the fundraiser, which would raise some money, so they could pay back the loan. The club was at serious risk of insolvency at this time, the accounts were so low that the losses from running an under supported coach for a caving meet could be high enough to push the club into the red.

April 1958 also witnessed a much darker episode in the club's story, John Barker and Bryan Dobson were involved in a tragic car accident in which John survived with injuries but Bryan was killed, aged 26. Bryan, or Moose as he was known, was a very active, leading member of the club and his loss was a terrible shock to the membership. A memorial First Aid box was commissioned by the committee after a fund was started in his name. The box was made by F. Christian of Newby and was mounted in the Dump. The fund went on to purchase the clubs first Neil Robertson stretcher [*Fred? – Ed*]

The 1958 Easter meet was attended by what was described as a record crowd, there were many successful trips carried out to Stream Passage Pot, Flood Entrance Pot, Lancaster Hole and Alum Pot. After 22 members turned up for the Little Hull Pot trip on April 27th there is no record of any caving until the Gaping Gill prelim trip on May 10th 1958.

There had been a technical scare just prior to this trip, when the winch engine was stripped for routine de-coking, it was found that a circlip on the gudgeon pin had detached and scored deep grooves in the bore wall. Frank Moulson saved the day by having the engine re-bored and fitting a new piston to recover the engine; he also riveted new brake linings on the drum brake. The members meet went well with up to forty five tents on the surface, and twenty nine people camping in Sand Caverns. On the Saturday five members of the Kendal Caving Club took ladders to tackle Disappointment Pot and went down at 7 am and were not heard of again for over 19 hours when they rang for the winch at half past midnight. They had come through from Disappointment via Hensler's crawl. On the Monday the BPC sent a strong team [*Paul Stacey, Chris Dufton, Geoff Thorndyke, Barry Wilson, Keith Asquith and Frank Croll also Peter Bury who never actually joined the BPC*] down the winch and they went through Hensler's crawl and up Disappointment Pot to de-tackle the system. All the BPC and KCC members on these two trips, it was said, now qualify for the 'Hensler Star'.

May 18th 1958 saw the BBC transmission from Alum Pot take place, this was the first time such a technical challenge had been attempted. There were many members helping with the fetching and carrying of the heavy BBC equipment and laying cables across the moor and down the various holes. It turned out to be the club's temporary financial saviour, the club was all but broke. Some members were required to speak in an unrehearsed interview live to the nation. The club was paid 10 guineas for their assistance and co-operation, while the five members with a speaking part were paid 5 guineas each. Luckily they all donated the cash to the club and financial disaster was averted.

The August camp was held in Mendips, originally in the WCC hut in Hillgrave, but once they had encountered the Hunter's Lodge they moved camp to the BEC hut to be closer to the caves, and the Hunter's. It got off to a good start in the early hours of Friday in Bradford station when Barry Woof pushed his hand through a train window that wasn't open, the ensuing delay meant he and Keith Asquith didn't get as far as Bristol until the early hours of Saturday. I suspect they were non too popular with the Friday rush hour commuters in Bradford either. Eventually the team arrived and some caving was done. The Sunday teams went to Swildon's with a WCC guide and another team went to St Cuthberts with a BEC member. During the week trips were run down Wookey hole, Eastwater Swallet as well as further trips into Swildon's and St Cuthbert's. A long and difficult trip down Blue Pencil crawl to the upstream and downstream sumps didn't reach the surface until 10pm where they were greeted by U.P. Jones carrying bottles of what they euphemistically called 'healing water', what a gentleman. The only incident over the week appears to be some complaints from locals when Keith Asquith and Barry Woof were drunk in charge of a rowing boat in Bristol harbour.

August 1958 also brought some sadness with the news that Harry Hargreaves, a founder member, had died. Arnold Patchett received an invite to any member of the BPC that wanted to go to the International Congress of Speleology at Bari in Italy, it is assumed nobody went. August also brought a suggestion from Frank Briggs that the club take over the tenancy of Toll Bar Cottage when he moved out. His departure was imminent and the suggestion mobilised the club into all the activities required to move the Dump to this new cottage. It became club policy that we were to acquire the tenancy, drawings were made of the required alterations.

September 1958 saw some great caving with the laddering of Long Kin West again and the exchange trip with the Red Rose CPC between Simpsons and Swinsto holes. The BPC entered Simpsons and the Red Rose went down Swinsto, as the BPC lowered the ladder down Slit Pot the Red Rose lads appeared at the bottom, perfect timing and a great exchange. [*Remember valley entrance was not there then – Ed*] When they exited the cave it became apparent that there had been an accident at Rowten Pot and the BPC lads hurried across. The South Ribble Rovers Crew had suffered a broken ladder and a lad had fallen off. He was eventually recovered on BPC ladders at 9:30pm, with no CRO callout required.

Later that month Chris Dufton and Derek Jowet got very excited about their new find until it was pointed out they had rediscovered Rowten Cave, at the end of October the BPC again rediscovered a fine cave this time it was Gage Gill. The third unfortunate incident was when John Barker led his team in circles in the fog for three hours on the way back to the bus from Juniper Gulf, luckily it was a smaller team than the one that turned up to Marble Steps meet in October. The system was overwhelmed when 59 people turned up for a trip, fortunately there was a communication cock up and people waited at the top to avoid queues at

the bottom, until it was too late to go down. A small team made it to the bottom and had a good trip, the majority just witnessed confusion and disappointment.

The first trip in 1959 was a bit of a shame really, Goyden Pot had been cancelled due to such bad weather and the trip was rescheduled to be at Pikedaw Calamine Caverns, again, and the weather turned out to be a lovely cold January day with clear blue skies and many frozen puddles to amuse the fifty people who turned up for the trip. These huge numbers, by modern standards, were never really seen as a problem by the club as they were transfixed on the bus viability issue and the bigger the numbers the more buses could be justified. The people left milling about tended to wander off and look for somewhere else to go underground. This happened again in February when forty members turned up for Hardrawkin where 17 got to the sump, the over flow went to Sunset hole where 18 reached the bottom and the overflow from there went down Middle Washfold and Great Douk. In March the newsletter says 'Only thirty members turned up for Grange Rigg' the overflow went down Disappointment Pot. Six people got to the bottom of Disappointment and four bottomed Grange Rigg, out of the thirty who turned up only ten reached the bottom of a cave. The rest were presumably left huddled up at the top of pitches in the age old practice of making sure there was someone who could pull up the weary sodden cold people or go for help when the next manila lifeline broke. This situation continued in to June when forty five turned up to descend Meregill!

On a happier note a Mr Feather informed the committee that he would be available to play the piano again at our forthcoming Annual Dinner.

In February 1959, some four years after haviong agreed to do so, the committee finally decided to abandon the use of rope ladders and declared all existing rope ladders to be scrapped and their parts not to be salvaged for subsequent ladder construction. [*Sadly there is no surviving data to calculate the expected service life of a rope ladder even relative to the electron ladders, which did have problems. One electron ladder was once found to have sixteen slipped rungs. In June 1959 a new 45 foot electron ladder was completed to a revised design. The wire was changed from 7 x 19 to a 7 x 7 construction and the pins were increased in diameter from 1/16" to 3/32". This new design, it was declared, was in time for the production line to increase production rates so that the club could hold sufficient ladder to run two simultaneous trips down major potholes, thus relieving the congestion problems – Ed*]

It was March the 22nd that most cavers will remember 1959 for, this was the date that a young philosophy student lost his fight to extricate himself from a narrow pitch in Peak Cavern, Derbyshire. His full name was Oscar Hackett Neil Moss and was on a trip with the BSA. There are several reasons this very sad incident is still so memorable and most people, not just cavers, over a certain age can clearly remember the Neil Moss rescue. Not only was it a tragedy that occurred beyond the means of the rescue services, it happened under the gaze of the nation through the press who sensationalised what was already a drama by inventing elements to boost their readership. This was allowed to happen because there were no official news briefings by the rescue teams to tell the nation of the progress of the rescue, it went on over three days and people who had televisions could see what was going on, it gripped the nation. The final act of the drama guaranteed this accident would be remembered forever. To prevent any more deaths and to bring closure to the drawn out loss of his son, his father, in an act of almost chivalric honour, asked that there be no attempt to recover his son's body and the pitch be sealed with concrete and the chamber named after him. To this day Neil rests in the death grip of Peak Cavern and generations of cavers have respected the ongoing wish of subsequent generations of the family who, for the noblest of reasons, have never been able to visit his grave.

The reason this incident features in a history of the BPC again revolves around the press of the day. The reporting of this accident stirred public opinion against caving and cavers to such an extent that landowners were encouraged to withdraw access, the police, it was suggested should not carry out rescues and parents were told it is their duty to dissuade their children from showing interest in caving. This situation alarmed all UK caving clubs, especially the bigger ones such as the BPC. Full page items were put in the newsletter pleading with members to not antagonise farmers and villagers with behaviour that attracts their attention in anything other than a good light. This situation, due to the degree of the propaganda in the news, persisted for years in some form or other. Even today, after rescues, there is such a fear of access denial, such as occurred after the Mossdale tragedy, that there is almost an orchestrated charm offensive toward the landowners and tenants by the big clubs and national bodies.

April 1959 brought a request from Dr Farrar to fill in Owl Hole if no further activity is planned as foxes were using it as a lair.

The June newsletter in 1959 spelled out the reasons behind the club's ban on abseiling, and the fact that not only was such a practice banned on club trips but any trip using club tackle. The committee's decision was based on the damage done to club lifelines which could then break at a later date. [*No thought that we could be using the wrong ropes – Ed*] Secondly, there was concern over there being only one belay, rather than two if ladder and lifeline had separate belays. This is more understandable in those pre SRT days where there were no thoughts of multiple belays for a ladder.

The caving in June and July 1959 was reasonably successful as the weather was quite dry. A full survey of Ingleborough Cave was started and the club was actually trying, with some success apparently, to use a radio location technique to locate and identify the surface features above Inauguration Aven. The survey work appears to have spawned great interest in surveying and a group within the club had its first meeting in July. The objectives of the survey group were to further the surveying capabilities of the BPC and to co-ordinate efforts. The committee however felt it necessary to start addressing the growing number of complaints about noisy, drunken and untidy people at GG and the Dump. In what can only be called bad timing, Hammonds the brewery that owned the Flying Horseshoes, sent an inspector to look at the pub and more specifically the Dump. He is reported as saying that "he did not like what he saw". It is unsure if he was aware of the further complaints of rowdy, drunken behaviour but the committee decided that we could not afford to be evicted at this stage so gave a sterner warning to the implicated individuals and it was declared that any subsequent offenders would be brought before the committee who would suspend the members from using the Dump. It is unclear if this was the reason why eight un-named members were suspended from the club in December 1959, it equally might have been for non payment of subscriptions.

As a result of several rescues, including the Bradford Technical College rescue, from Dowbergill passage the BPC was asked if it would back a proposal to gate the passage to prevent through trips and subsequent rescues. The committee anguished for a while, but eventually agreed to the gate plan which involves a system of demonstrating competence before being allowed to organise trips through Dowbergill passage. This is another example of managing the public's perception of caving and cavers by limiting the rescues that they hear about and denying the press the opportunity to destroy the good work we had done in public relations since the Neil Moss rescue.

August and September continued very dry and as a result, many caves were bottomed with relative ease. The most significant of these was Diccan Pot. For the first time not only did the club bottom Diccan but an impromptu exchange with Alum was carried out and all participants, including an un-named German professional speleologist, were delighted with the trip. [*Special thanks were given to Messrs Briggs, Dufton, Blakely and Woof for spending the whole afternoon life lining the big pitch in Diccan. Messrs Marston, Benn and Benn were also thanked for giving up their afternoon to life line Dolly Tubs and the 60 foot pitch – Ed*]

The CPC August winch meet in 1959 was when the combined forces of both clubs were used to replace the fencing around Gaping Gill Main shaft. The clubs were used as labour so that the estate retained plausible deniability in the event of a fatal accident at the hole.

The Dump expanded again in September 1959 when we took over what had been the Kendal Pothole Club's headquarters at the Flying Horseshoes. This was to provide urgently needed additional sleeping space but was only agreed on a three month trial basis.

SECTION 1.4 – 1960'S

Caving from the earliest days before the war involved bus meets, after the war caving with the BPC meant catching the early bus in Bradford and caving with up to 30+ members in the same cave. The transport of the time matched the tackle of the time and the clothing of the time. The suffering and frustration of being left at the top of a wet pitch, wearing saturated tweed jackets and ordinary outdoor clothing, for hours on end waiting to lifeline the people who went beyond, must have really tested the dedication of people. The large numbers of people were required to carry the massive amount of heavy tackle; people carried rucksacks with changes of dry clothing, food and stoves on big trips as well as the tackle. The number of people, the amount of gear and the time consuming methods all added to the adoption of siege tactics in the big systems. It was not uncommon to have tackle taken part way through a system by a strong tackling team, only to be overtaken by a second tackling team who, in turn, handed over to the bottoming party. The objective of the meet was to bottom the hole, which could be achieved by as few as one man and that man was usually the leader. If circumstances allowed, more men could be got to the bottom but that relied on time and weather constrictions. The tackle could then be left in the cave until the next week, weather permitting, when de-tackling teams entered the cave to move the tackle back towards the entrance. Several de-tackling teams were sometimes needed to clear the tackle from holes like Pen-y-ghent Pot with many pitches, long distances and lots of water. This whole process could take 2 – 3 weeks to complete.

In the early 1960's there emerged a phenomenon in the BPC called the 'Phantoms'. They were a small group of, at the time, unidentified people who took to tackling the club official meets the night before. They got the experience of moving faster and lighter in the caves, and they didn't have to de-tackle. This led to the immense annoyance of meet leaders as their role had been usurped, they were largely redundant. Bearing in mind that being a meet leader was a traditional indication of respect for their experience and given the number of members there weren't many who the club formerly bestowed with the privilege of such a title. There are two theories about the motives behind the Phantoms. Firstly, there were at the time great frustrations, caused by the rapidly increasing membership numbers and the inevitable increase in time wasted underground waiting at pitches when caving with huge parties and the associated suffering from inadequate clothing. The committee didn't recognise the true nature of the problem and despite committee statements in the bulletins the problem persisted. Interestingly, up until 1959 it was never suggested that the club might try increasing the number of meets on the list to match the large increase in members turning up to go caving. Several trips at the weekends became common practice in later years but the attempts from 1959 and the early 1960's quickly petered out.

The rival theory for the emergence of the Phantoms is reported to be a direct protest against a certain member of the club's committee. The objective was the annoyance of this particular leader. Records, sadly, no longer exist to determine which meet leader was repeatedly attacked by the Phantoms. *[The names of the Phantoms and their victim have been withheld – Ed]*

Eventually the solution to the 'Phantoms' was invented, developed and adopted by the club and its members. Although nobody realised at the time the problem was brought about partly by the need to cave with smaller, faster groups, with less bulk of equipment and less suffering, especially by the life liners left at the top of every pitch. The slow introduction of personal transport, motor bikes or cars now allowed small groups to run their own 'private' meets without a coach but this is, of course, what also enabled the Phantoms to do their work. It was February 1959 when the committee declared we would only use Electron ladders which, along with the widespread use of double life lines to get all men down all pitches revolutionised caving in the UK. There would eventually be an ongoing effort to construct electron ladders for widespread general use in the BPC but it took a long time to get off the ground. In the mean time the technical solution to suffering hypothermic symptoms had been developed and the club members were starting to equip themselves with wetsuits. With these three things together, transport, electron ladders and wetsuits, British caving was transformed and the old wet giants, like Pen-y-ghent Pot, were tamed and could now be done by a handful of cavers, with no specific leader, in a few hours - thus began the second golden age of UK caving.

The 1960's witnessed a step change in British caving, membership numbers rose rapidly domestic exploration had been invigorated by the new equipment and there was a new determination to push wet caves harder. There were also the beginnings of foreign trips, initially with other clubs and having members become part of major expeditions such as Ken Pierces' Gouffre Berger expeditions in 1963 and 1965 and the Provatina expedition in 1967. BPC only trips were beginning to look farther afield as the 60's progressed with regular trips to Ireland and an expedition to Jamaica. But the 60's also brought our darkest hour with the Mossdale tragedy in 1967 when we lost three of our 'hardest' cavers.

January 1960 witnessed a bold statement by the committee; it claimed that their target for the end of 1960 was to have a thousand feet of electron ladder. This is not such an outrageous target considering the committee's declared solution to the overcrowding in caves was now to run two major trips at weekends and still have enough tackle to have the odd ladder in for repair. The published meets lists however, didn't support this directive from the committee; they usually fielded only one trip per month. [*It was as if the committee consisted of two parts, those, younger, elements who wanted unlimited facilities to further caving, and those who wanted things to stay as they always had been – Ed*] It is not thought likely that in 1960 there was any idea of needing 1000 feet of ladder in one cave abroad which is just as well as the target was never actually achieved.

The club news sheet offered members submarine escape suits without the neck seals, presumably for caving, they were available through Peter Hitt at 59/6d [£2.97.5p each] No sooner was Peter's advert announced when a competing advert appeared in the next newsletter by Bob Jarman saying he has exposure suits that are better than submarine escape suits and only cost 38/- [£1.90 each] These were single skin rubberised cotton material, not inflatable, and had substantial feet built in, as a result they didn't fit inside a boot without some paring. Inflatable 'Goon' suits were commonly bought from ex government surplus stocks, these provided a waterproof outer garment to keep the jumpers underneath dry, and they presented a sort of answer to the hyporthermic issues of water immersion, until they filled up with water. They didn't last long without constant

repairs but were better than nothing for those that could afford them. [*F.Y.I. most aircrew immersion suits were made by a firm called Frankenstein's in Manchester - Ed*]

The 1960 Annual Dinner was held at the Devonshire Hotel in Skipton on February 6th which was a Saturday night. Annual Dinners had in the past been held on weekday nights to keep the weekends free for caving, it was also an all male function. We see in the 1960's the formal functions of the club largely taking the shape of the modern format, with the exception of those that were male only of course. There was a very sad loss in the club in 1960, Keith Asquith died in a motor accident and although it was not mentioned in bulletins or newsletters it was somehow decided to commission and erect a memorial seat at the entrance to Ingleborough Cave.

The growing tensions over the issue of tenant farmers resenting the presence of cavers on their land and restricting access to caves stepped up a notch in 1960. Mr N. Scarr, the tenant on Casterton Fell had steel lids put on County Pot and Lancaster Hole and he was keeping them locked. The only access was by postal application to him at Bull Pot Farm. The committee was offering to organise a coach trip to some of the show caves of France in the summer of 1960, along with walking and swimming in the Med, a first meeting was held April 22nd. In the June newsletter the committee announced that British Overseas Caving Expeditions had organised two reconnaissance trips this year [1960], one to Greece and one to Portugal. It was hoped that a full scale expedition could be announced for 1961 by September of 1960. The next newsletter announced that the BOCE were, somewhat surprisingly, organising an expedition to Austria in the summer of 1961. March 1961 saw the beginning of a plan for a road trip touring the Pyrenees as a summer holiday, in July of that year. It was also planned that the sleeping arrangements for the Easter Camp should be at the Dump and, as we were already paying the rent, Toll Bar Cottage, such was the confidence that it was to be the next Dump. It was at this time, however, that an unwelcome and untimely communication arrived stating that the rent payable on the Dump was to double. This was shrugged off with a wry smile at the time as we were already sorted and would be in Toll Bar Cottage before it came into effect.

The idea of taking over the lease on Toll Bar Cottage was still the committee's plan A, but shrewdly, the committee decided to explore other options and approached Hammond's Brewery to see if they would give the club a long lease on the Dump at the Flying Horseshoes as a plan B. To their surprise the answer was that they would only consider a three year lease, which was not nearly enough as the club would have to invest significantly in the building. [*In October the members were limited to eleven people sleeping upstairs, further more they had to sleep in bunks around the walls, no sleeping in the middle of the floor and no boxes to be kept upstairs. This was because the upstairs floor was significantly weakened by woodworm - Ed*] This had the effect of giving the committee a deadline, they had to find another Dump, and soon. The drawings for the alterations at Toll Bar Cottage were completed by John Thompson and submitted to the Settle UDC with a letter from Dr Farrer saying he was happy for the BPC to take over the tenancy of Toll Bar Cottage. The council responded in February 1961 with a rejection of the scheme. It is not clear if the rejection was based on the alterations or the cottage becoming the base for the BPC. They claimed it was due to a concern over access on to the trunk road, which was also a major concern for the Department of Transport. It was decided in committee, under advice, not to appeal against the decision and no formal offer was ever tendered. Now both plans A & B were gone.

The much applauded target of 1000 feet of electron ladder actually only reached 900 feet by March 1961. It was therefore agreed to build another 500 feet of super light weight ladders for use in the more difficult pots where lower numbers are involved. Frank Croll and Geoff Thorndyke were team leaders of the ladder building industry at this time.

April 1961 brought more problems for the committee or rather caving clubs everywhere, as either the landowner or the tenant farmer banned all caving on West Kingsdale on Sundays. This was a particular worry as other major landowners were making noises of discontent and the club looked at its options as to how it could pacify the owners and maintain access. A scheme was agreed with the gamekeepers on GG that members should work with the gamekeepers during the Whit week to help with their increased work load. We sent five members over to help the Gamekeepers in 1961. Then the worst happened, Graham Shaw had an accident down Simpson's Pot on April 16th 1961, when a slab of rock decided that it would join

Graham at the bottom of the pitch. The rapid response by his old schoolmate John Davey, with first aid and care until the rescue arrived saved his injuries from being more permanent. The resulting rescue was seen as potentially just the excuse the farmer was looking for to shut the fell. The committee agreed straight away that the start of our charm offensive would be sending BPC Xmas cards to all the appropriate farmers and landowners.

In an attempt to perhaps shame the Dump dwellers to live more healthily or just clean up a bit in one of the 1961 newsletters the committee announced that they had thrown out all of the cutlery in the Dump and [*quote*] 'as a result the eating habits improved'.

Frank Croll led the Gaping Gill main shaft laddering competition in August 1961, when he confidently predicted he would have the fastest descent and ascent times. The table below shows that he wasn't even close;

Name [In order of Descent]	Down	Up
Frank Croll	12**	07:25
Carl Beaumont	8.5	10
John Michael Barker	8	5
Dennis Wray	08:15	6
Geoff Silson	7***	9
Barry Hopkinson	7	15*
Warwick Pierson	08:25	07:25
Dave Cording	06:25	08:45
Nick Percy	9	00:00
Pete Faulkner	8	07:30
John Davy	7	06:25

* Hampered by unnecessary de-laddering
** Hampered by Great Fat Gut
*** Time in days
Time in minutes and not quite sure how
Nick Percy got back up. [*Not sure how many members could match these times today? – Ed*]

After backing away from Toll Bar Cottage the club was on the search for another suitable building to rent or, increasingly possible, buy. They also resigned to a possibility that they might have to build a Dump and the search for appropriate building land was initiated in September 1961. The committee communicated the status of their efforts to acquire a new Dump in December 1961 with the following statement in the newsletter;
"It is thought that members may like to hear of the efforts made to put the building fund to use. Below

is a list of sites and buildings followed up in the last year.

a) Toll Bar Cottage, Clapham – Planning permission refused mainly because the Ministry of Transport refused to allow access for vehicles.

b) Old Catholic Church and adjacent house at Lawkland. – Outbid.

c) Bungalow on the edge of Newby Common. – Too expensive.

d) Telephone repeater station on Ingleton – Kirkby Lonsdale Rd, - Again thwarted by the Ministry of Transport who refused to allow access for vehicles.

e) Row of Cottages, possibly for the future. [*Ribblehead – Ed*]

f) Site by the Flying Horseshoe to build on – Negotiating.

g) Further possible site may be purchased from Dr Farrer.

h) Possibility of extending and developing in the present building. – Dropped for various reasons."

The WRCPC/RRCPC/BPC Pyrenees trip took place in the summer of 1961, when it returned it was deemed to have been an unqualified success. A letter from the RRCPC was received in November 1961 asking if any 'experienced' cavers, especially any with a Dormobile, would like to join an expedition to France in 1962. Their plan was to liaise with international cavers for three weeks in July / August. It was stated in the letter that 'wives and regular girlfriends were acceptable'.

The question of access to the fells was raised again in March 1962 when Dr Farrer wrote to the club to inform us that he had banned a caving club from all activities on his land for unspecified bad behaviour. This was taken as no light threat and renewed pleas were published to all members asking for good behaviour on all fells and to apply an acceptable dress code when in villages. [*The club's village dress code hit rock bottom in the '70's when Geoff Crossley was nearly arrested for indecent exposure in Clapham – Ed*]

Around early 1962 two farms, Winskill and Winshaw, became available for purchase and advice was taken as to which had the better prospects as a Dump. Winshaw Farm was deemed to be the better, but even that had issues and some were sceptical about its suitability. However, in July 1962 the committee agreed to go ahead with Winshaw Farm. We got permission to study the damp in the walls, any rot and woodworm in the timbers and the required improvements to the water supply. These tasks involved digging holes around the site and lifting floor boards inside. Extensive work was carried out in pursuit of a suitable design scheme for the water supply. By September we had a fire rota in operation which involved people going to Winshaw Farm at agreed times and lighting the fires in the rooms to try and warm the house, before winter set in, and see what happened to the damp walls. At this time another building, only referred to as Hemplans, was brought into the decision making process but when an inquiry was made about its price the club withdrew all interest as it was £3500. In November 1962 the architects involved with designing a water scheme for Winshaw Farm laid out the options and the committee agreed all viable schemes were too expensive so formerly withdrew all further interest. The holes were filled in and we cleared up the mess we had created during our investigations. That was plans A,B,C & D gone. [*Fifty three years after these events a Mr Robinson contacted the club and claimed that his father had owned Winskill farm and the BPC had destroyed the farm and he still got upset at the mess and damage created by the BPC. We responded, pointing out that the farm was used by another caving club after we pulled out, he never came back to us. It seems strange reading the records that we did some work in Winshaw farm and he owned Winskill farm? – Ed*] The club bought 100 Edison mining lights presumably from the National Coal Board, and paid 8/6d for each. [*£42.5 for the lot*]

June 1962 saw the closure of Leck and Casterton fells to all cavers until further notice. August 23rd 1962 saw flash flooding at Alum Pot and the surface entrances, this caught many of our members and other club's members and a withdrawal from the cave was begun. The main shaft had a second ladder put down to speed up the process but several of our less experienced members were very worried and suggested to the Burnley CRO rep, who happened to be there, that they needed assistance. Due to a further misunderstanding a call out was initiated when none was actually requested as, with the help of the Kendal Caving Club, hand lines and life lines were in operation to assist all people from the fast moving water. The whole operation took about an hour but unfortunately the press got hold of yet another story that would not help our situation with landowners.

The club had some unrecognised success in 1962 when Mike Boon passed Sump 7 in Swildon's Hole after an underwater epic through a tight, restricted passage. This sump was not passed again until it was enlarged. Boon was also the first person to use side mounted tadpole cylinders for cave diving. [*Tadpole Tanks were lightweight tanks from aircraft pneumatic systems – Ed*] Frank Salt led the first British expedition to the Gouffre Berger in 1962 which not only bottomed the cave, but one member free dived partway in to the sump and decided that it would be a feasible dive with air.

December 1962 brought renewed access concerns regarding Casterton and Leck Fells. The BPC decided to get involved with the caving clubs discussion groups. All the clubs involved had, their own agenda and it took a lot of wasted time to get them all to agree the approach laid out by the BPC at the beginning. The BPC committee were clearly not full of Christmas cheer during the December meeting as they expelled eleven members from the club for non payment of subscriptions. Though there is no suggestion of a link, the Dump had a fire in the New Year, washing was left drying too close to the fire and it caught fire. The damage to the dump was slight as it was soon discovered and dealt with.

The January 1963 newsletter contained the first reference to Brackenbottom. The building fund was under constant pressure to grow, fund raisers, donations and any lumps of cash deemed available by the treasurer were thrown into the building fund. It was resented in some quarters. Some voices of dissent were heard to say "the club is just a fundraising club" or "money is more important than caving". It was from these mumblings that some were even heard to question the need for a Dump at all. When the committee later went to an Emergency General Meeting to sanction the club getting a loan to purchase a property the mumbling masses broke out in outrage.

There was a diary problem in early 1963 with the solution coming when UP Jones suggested that we hold the AGM on the same day as the Annual Dinner. This has been the default arrangement ever since with just a few exceptions when experiments were tried, and failed. In February 1963 a letter from Colonel Bowering and Lord Shuttleworth, the landowners of Casterton and Leck Fells, lay out their conditions that had to be met if caving was to ever again be allowed on Casterton and Leck Fells. The caving clubs meetings eventually led to the formation of the Council of Northern Caving Clubs to act as a single body responsible for the administration of controlled, limited access to the fells as dictated by the

landowner's letter. It had its first meeting on March 16th 1963 and access was eventually saved.

A second letter received by the committee in February 1963 was from Colin Sharp, a veteran of the 1962 RRCPC/BPC trip to France. He was announcing the potential organisation of another BPC/RRCPC trip to France in the summer of 1963. He had attached an estimate of the shared travel costs at £12.50p. This was to be the third consecutive year that BPC members had travelled abroad. The big foreign news this year was the Ken Pearce led expedition which had dived Sump 1 in the Gouffre Berger only to be stopped by a second sump.

Hammond's Brewery sent the BPC committee a letter in May 1963 asking them to sign a disclaimer that stated if the Dump fell down we would not hold the Brewery liable. It is not known if the committee signed the document, common sense suggests that they did not.

The summer period of 1963 was tarnished by a series of thefts from the Dump, personal equipment was taken on several occasions. The methods are not disclosed but at some point included forcing open members' boxes. The local police were involved. [*It is thought that this is the occasion that Pete Faulkner's camera was stolen – Ed*] In September 1963 the club held a meeting in Bradford where a Mr Don Robinson from the UWFRA came all the way down from Linton to give a talk on rescue techniques. No sooner had he set up in the Church House than he got a call out and he had to leave, in a hurry. To his credit Mr Robinson came all the way back and tried again in November, there are no records of another call out. June saw the BPC reach the bottom of Car Pot and Boon and Livesey were acknowledged as hard men after their epic trip beyond Far Marathon in Mossdale Caverns in September.

September 1963 was also noted for the club showing its more philosophical side by posing seven of the club's greatest thinkers with a more philosophical question to answer. They asked "What is the role of a leader". This task reflected the growing feeling that the days of the 'King of the Cave' type leader were over and with the improved equipment and personal transport available the need of military leadership was gone. However, the combined brain power of the seven reported that they needed to replace the traditional all powerful meet leader with three leaders. A senior leader for the senior trip, a junior leader for the junior trip [*who also had to organise the bus – Ed*] and due to strict rules on routes over the fells and wanderings we now had a surface leader. His role was like a zebra crossing warden [*Lolly Pop Lady*], directing the cavers in groups over the designated footpaths to the entrances of the appropriate holes, and back. [*You can guess how long that lasted – Ed*]

The committee called for an Emergency General Meeting which was held in the Church House in Bradford on August 22nd 1963, the main issue discussed was the need to change the club rules to allow the committee to borrow money from a building society or bank to buy Brackenbottom. It was eventually agreed that the committee could enter into a contract with a bank or building society for a loan up to a limit of £700 at a rate of 1.5% above the bank rate at the Midland Bank. The motion was passed but only after heated debate; subsequently a number of members resigned their membership in protest. The announcement that the BPC actually owned Brackenbottom was made in the November 1963 newsletter; the committee had actually borrowed only £600 of the sanctioned £700. The committee immediately launched into a major fund raising activity with the mortgage repayments and modifications required to the building as a lever to extort yet more donations from the members and to persuade them, to support the suite of fund raising events organised for the period before the end of the year. The Dump fees were put up as rule 1 in a set of new rules for the new Dump, rule 2 was no women are allowed to stay at the Dump. Barry Hopkinson organised a Flying Horseshoes leaving do at the Shoes, with a sit down meal and ladies were allowed to attend [*Oct 26th 1963*] just before the move from old to new. It was also let known that the committee did not approve of the term Dump in association with Brackenbottom. [*There is only one element of the BPC membership's character that is predictable; if the committee says don't call the new Dump the Dump you can guarantee it will be referred to as the Dump forever! - Ed*]

There is no suggestion that subscriptions were withheld by members in protest at the continual fund raising but the committee got tough in November and another 15 members were thrown out for non payment of subscriptions. 1964 started with an eventful trip down Rowten pot, the trip was organised and led by Colin Vickers and there was a sense of anticipation about this trip months before it took place. Sadly the reasons for the anticipation and the eventful nature of the trip are never explained. The club's meets list for 1964 was full of all the usual favourites with a token

weekend in Derbyshire where it was planned to do Giant's Hole. There was an Easter Camp on Casterton Fell where all caving would have to be carried out by arrangement through the new CNCC. There was only one trip per month organised by the meets secretary, except in May of course, which clearly means that the huge majority of the caving, done by the members, was carried out as private trips. The committee couldn't possibly organise enough caving trips to satisfy the whole membership and they were very slow to recognise that the organisation of caving had passed from their control. The committee seemed to be again pursuing the more philosophical aspects of the club when it called a meeting at the Church House in Bradford where the agenda was 'What is wrong with club meets?' The origins for this strange meeting seems to stem from a resurgence of the Phantom problem and the increase in small leaderless private trips and the crisis, as the committee saw it, that the bus attendance was falling. The number of people on the bus appears to have been the committee's only measure of the success of a meet, for all the reasons mentioned before the trend was inevitably towards smaller private meets which the committee and the increasingly redundant Generals had no control over. Whether the committee were told the reasons or if they managed to work it out for themselves is not known but the use of buses for normal caving trips was stopped in 1964.

The year ended with the annual Christmas Dinner again held at the Golden Lion in Horton, now that we were locals. The 1964 Annual Dinner was held at the usual venue, the Devonshire Hotel in Skipton on 1st February and the now regular Digger's Dinner is moved to August 29th and held at the Crown Hotel, Middlesmoor.

March 1964 saw the committee once again heading into constitutional conflict territory when, presumably responding to pressure, agreed to hold a series of meetings to discuss whether ladies should be allowed to sleep at the Dump. Rule 2 was written by the people that were close to the process of buying the Dump, it is not thought that the 'rules' were ever discussed reasonably in committee let alone with the membership. Warwick Pierson arranged a social meeting and debate at the Church House in Bradford and a second meeting was held at the Dump. The April newsletter reported the issue in passing as follows; "The feeling was in favour of this [*Ladies sleeping at the Dump*] as was the case at the meeting held at Brackenbottom on Saturday 4th April. Members

45

are requested to bring their own towels and tea towels to the HQ."

In May another Extraordinary General Meeting was called at the Church House in Bradford, with a single item on the agenda; "It is proposed that members should be permitted to invite females to use the club HQ as their guests, subject to special bye-laws as follows:" There then followed a list of 5 such bye laws stating that members had to apply in writing to the committee to bring a 'female' as a guest, the females have to stay in their dorm and members have to stay in theirs and the Dump warden has special powers to suspend permission should he consider that this is warranted by circumstances. "A date when the bye-laws come into force will be announced soon". [*It took until February 1965 for the announcement to be made, twelve months after the first meetings. – Ed*]

Access became a serious issue again in April 1964 with members being told that they must not walk off the path up to Alum and they must not pay if the farmer asks for money. Permission must be given to descend Alum and separate permission is required to descend Long Churn along with a payment to the farmer if requested. The main footpath was being disputed as a right of way by the farmer. As it only goes to Alum Pot and does not go to Long Churn that requires you to cross his land and a fee may be demanded. The BPC were asked to refuse to pay for walking the main path as that would undermine the Rambler's Association's assertion that it was a right of way. Access to Fountains Fell was becoming fragile and members were asked for volunteers to act as volunteer wardens to help the gamekeepers at their busy time to help foster good will towards cavers, access was eventually lost on Fountain's Fell. The CNCC took over access control for Pen-y-ghent during 1964 such was the feeling amongst landowners.

July 1964 brought some sad news for the BPC, Titus Illingworth one of the founder members died after a long illness at the Cheshire Home in Cleckheaton. Being a real character he was famous for the monologues that he performed at functions as well as being a very active caver in the early days of the club.

The caving carried out by the members on private meets was very successful in 1964, with the first bottoming of Nick Pot. Elsewhere in the UK cavers were officially re-admitted to Dan Yr Ogof beyond the show cave and P8 (Jack Pot) was dug in to by the Manchester group of the BSA. The first edition of Caves of Derbyshire was published.

The 1965 caving got off to a good start with Goyden in January and Marble Steps and Mongo Gill in February, they were both run as a bus trip and were both declared a great success. The Marble Steps trip got 26 people down the cave and the Mongo Gill team numbered 24 underground. Also in February Pen-y-ghent Pot was conquered in fine style. The Gaping Gill meet in May went well even after Dr Farrar wrote to the club to inform them that no further underground camping was allowed within GG. There was another epic push in Mossdale by Mike Boon and Pete Livesey when they investigated the final choke in April. Some of the club members were involved with an expedition to Norway in 1965 and Messer's Boon, Livesey and Stoyles, with a 'Tich' Morris, set off on an eight month expedition to Jamaica. The temporary return to bus meets is not explained, but it was claimed that it was a great success. Another bus was used on the Rowten trip in July which turned out to be a Bull Pot trip due to overcrowding not helped by the leader, Neil Thorpe, who didn't turn up. The Lost John's trip in August 1965 was not recognised at the time as a truly modern trip, a small number, in wetsuits, bottomed the cave in wet conditions and de-tackled in a few hours rather than days.

Construction of electron ladders was evolving in 1965 with the acquisition of a 'Talurit' press to compress ferrules around the folded cable end to form the splice, much quicker, much stronger and no sharp wire ends to fiddle with to form the splice. There seemed to be a distinct lack of standardisation with the club ladders at this time as the rung pitch seems to have varied between 10" and 14", this must have been very distracting when they were mixed up on a long wet pitch. Fund raising was still a popular club activity with Xmas cards and football draw cards being sold as an ongoing fund raising effort.

The caving towards the end of the year was also running well with successful trips down Rumbling Hole and an exchange between Grange Rigg and Christmas Hole. A trip to Ireland at Christmas was very successfull and a return was planned for the Easter of 1966. The Xmas dinner was again held at the Golden Lion in Horton and there was a Grand Social Meeting held at the Church House in Bradford on the Thursday before New Year. The 1966 meets list was issued in the December and showed there was still only one trip per month arranged for the members. This immediately suggests that around 90% of caving trips in the year will be private meets and of those only 10% will be reported and of those that are reported only 10% will mention who went on the trip.

The Dump suffered its second gutter attack in 1965, Bill Frakes had previously been found guilty of damaging the Dump gutters and made to pay for repairs. In Feb 1965 an un-named provisional member repeated the unprovoked attack, he refused to pay for the subsequent repair and was promptly expelled from the club.

The 1966 Annual Dinner was again held at the Devonshire Hotel in Skipton. The Chairman's speech at the Annual General Meeting on January 6th 1966 declared that the Dump now belonged to the club; the £600 debt had been paid off in just over two years. This would have prompted a huge collective sigh of relief had he not immediately followed by saying that the fund raising must continue to pay for the modifications and facilities we now needed. There was another collective sigh, but this was a sigh of resignation.

In February 1966, Dr Ken Pearce, of Berger military discipline fame, was trying to organise the manufacture of waterproof one piece caving suits and was offering them to members at £8 17/6d [£8.87.5p] each. It is not known if any takers were found in the club as this would be about £150 at today's prices. The Dump became a bit of an embarrassment when an unnamed national magazine described the Dump in none too favourable terms and said it needed "sorting out". We had actually been quite proud of the cleanliness of the Dump after a purge the previous September and the setting up of a team of helpers for the warden. By September the new stairs were being made, but a lot of digging was still needed for the completion of the septic tank, volunteers were thin and far between for this job. An uneventful year of caving was passed in 1966 but the dig at Clapham Bottoms was thought to be 'going' imminently which would possibly connect Gaping Gill to Ingleborough Cave, a call was made in March 1966 for fresh digging teams to help in the final push. [If they only knew then what we know now? - Ed] The 1967 Gaping Gill meet was run as normal in May but the committee had a moment of madness when they wrote to the CPC in June and offered to allow them the opportunity to run their winch meet at Whitsuntide in 1968 and alternative years thereafter. Luckily the ever bureaucratic CPC responded with a suggestion that three of their members meet with three of ours and discuss future GG winch meets. It is suspected

that the three members who went extinguished any hope the CPC may have had of getting their winch meets in the spring instead of the rainy season. The committee also heard a complaint from the Dump warden, he pointed out a certain member persisted in carrying an electric fire about the Dump.

These events in committee were soon overshadowed by a fairly long running event coming to a head in July 1967. Four very active members were perhaps letting their ego's get a little too big when they refused to pay Dump fees for the Friday night, arguing that they were caving over Friday night and didn't get to bed until 8:30 Saturday morning. When it was discussed in committee U.P. Jones added that they had raided his locker and stolen food and that J. Pedder's locker had also been bent open. The guilty four [N. Thorpe, P. Livesey, C. Vickers and J. Trott] were called to attend a committee meeting where they had the chance to explain their actions. Somewhat surprisingly, they all attended but failed to explain why they had behaved in such a way. They were asked to leave the room while the committee debated the situation. By the narrowest of votes it was agreed to just give them a caution [Interestingly proposed by Barry Hopkinson – Ed] It was at this point the treasurer, Barry Hopkinson, expressed his dissatisfaction with the committee and its chairman and went on to announce his resignation effective from October 1967. The chairman, Dave Greenwood, then responded with the suggestion that the committee would perhaps be better if the treasurer attended more meetings. That was not the end of this matter in September D. Greenwood also resigned from the committee and no other than Barry Hopkinson took over as chairman. Colin Vickers was subsequently co-opted to the committee to fill the gap caused by his actions in the first instance.

Mike Boon published his famous technical paper on the use of bottled air in cave diving in 1966. In this he not only proposed the use of bottled compressed air but that side mounting them offered great advantages in restricted passages with reduced chance of damage to vulnerable equipment. At this time most cave divers were using early oxygen re-breathers with the obvious inherent limitations and dangers. It had a great effect and within a short time the use of side mounted tadpoles* was widespread. [* Ex- military aircraft air reservoir bottles, they were wire wrapped to reduce damage in the event of an explosion, though it is thought Boon stripped the wire from his tanks – Ed]

The 1967 Annual Dinner was held at the Devonshire Hotel but not in Skipton this one was in Grassington. Frank Croll made his first attempt to get the committee to grant Alan Gill Life membership of the BPC in recognition of his Polar Expedition achievements, this wasn't granted at this time. [*Frank had to wait until the 2000 AGM to get the committee to grant his wish- Ed*] The 1967 caving year got off to a good start with several members going on the joint RRCPC/BPC trip to France at Easter. Back home Ireby Fell was done again and twenty people got to the bottom and back to the surface in just over six hours, which is pretty fast by any standards. Ken Pearce's Berger expedition passed sump 2 but was again stopped, this time by a pitch. Black Shiver was first explored in June and Tatham Wife, Pasture Gill and Smeltmill Beck cave were all discovered in 1967.

The news of Don Leach's death on May 14th 1967 was a very sad event for the whole club. Don was famous for designing and erecting the gantry at Gaping Gill and for always wearing a bowler hat at GG.

Meanwhile, several members were preparing to go to Greece on another expedition, to bottom the Abyss of Provatina in the summer of 1967. Pete Faulkner approached the committee in May of that year to request the loan of 200 feet of club ladders and any that he can make before he goes on the trip in June. The other members going were Carl Pickstone, Russell Cox and Allan Brittain [*See section 2 for full story – Ed*]

The CRO was re-launched in 1967 with a new constitution, no member clubs, only individuals and the freedom to operate as they do to this day. This freedom was demonstrated when they took over the central purchasing of caving lamps from the NCB and sold them on at 25 shillings [£1.25p] each.

June 24th 1967 is still the BPC's darkest day, despite many members desperate efforts the fight to save six cavers, including three of our own, was called off when their bodies were found in the marathon crawls of Mossdale Caverns. The fact is they were dead before the rescue was even called at 11:10 pm on Saturday, but knowing this would never have slowed the unbelievable efforts going into the earthworks on the surface. The initial dam built in the first hours of Sunday morning held the water back sufficiently for the first people to enter the system by late Sunday night. The first five bodies were found in the early hours of Monday by Tony Waltham's team, it took some time to find John Ogden's body but a last chance search team including Derek Castleden, set off at 10pm on Tuesday night and found him up a very narrow fissure where he had forced his body to capture the last available air. The drivers of the earth moving diggers eventually had to be dragged from their machines and made to sleep after days of frantic activity digging massive trenches to divert the flood waters away from the entrance.

The Mossdale victims were as follows;
Dave Adamson, Leader - 26, ULSA
Geoff Boireau - 24, ULSA
John Ogden - 21, Happy Wanderers Club
Colin Vickers - 23, BPC
Bill Frakes - 19, BPC
Michael Ryan - 17, in the process of joining the BPC.

It was a tragedy that can never be forgotten by cavers as it represents every caver's worst nightmare and to this day very few people even go near Mossdale and not many more people have been to the farthest reaches than have walked on the moon. [*See Derek Castleden's account in section 2. The mystery remaining after Colin Vickers' death was why was his motor bike found 30' under water at the bottom of Stainforth Foss? - Ed*]

There was an Extraordinary General Meeting called in October 1967 to authorise the committee to obtain a second bank loan, for £500, underwritten by 19 members who acted as Guarantors, to pay our contribution towards the completion of the septic tank and drainage system at the Dump. [*The total bill was subsidised by a 50% grant from the Government under the 1967 Act. The almost hidden detail behind this grant from the Department of Sport was that as a condition of it being granted the club's constitution had to be changed to say 'person' instead of 'man' IE The membership of the club could not be gender specific. Amazingly it took until the AGM of 1971 to test this amendment to the constitution when our first two ladies applied for full membership. They were duly accepted without so much as a murmur of discontent from the old guard. The application may have had subliminal support as the ladies in question were partners of two of the leading members of the club, at the time – Ed*] This work, by contractors, eventually would allow the flush toilets to work and the 'temporary' Elsans to be removed. There is no record of a repeat of the protests and resignations after this meeting approved the club taking a further bank loan.

The caving activity in the club didn't seem to reduce at all after the Mossdale deaths with Lost John's, Lancaster–Easegill, Notts Pot and Rumbling Hole all being planned before the end of the year. Over the year the club had people on many expeditions, Gouffre Berger again as well as other areas in France, an expedition to Czechoslovakia and the Abyssa Provatina trip to Greece [A *411m entrance pitch of which the expedition got down 217m on ladders. It was in 1968 that the UK Army managed to winch the first man down to the bottom of Provatina, I wonder if he was a volunteer?. See section 2 for the full 1967 story – Ed*]

Closer to home, small teams of members had completed four very successful trips to Ireland during 1967. But more bad news was looming in the UK when in October a Foot and Mouth outbreak was discovered and restrictions were quickly imposed on walking in the countryside which affected caving activity. The epidemic was eventually brought under control, after slaughtering over 400 thousand animals, in June 1968, before the restrictions were eventually lifted.

1968 was another eventful year for the BPC, abroad, Pete Livesey was raising the standard of international climbing in Norway, Urban Jones actually refused three different women's offer of marriage whilst in Ireland and Valley Entrance was opened allowing easy trips into the Kingsdale Master Cave. There were two trips to Ireland in 1968, the second in July/August utilised the frequently used cottage in Lisdoonvarna. At home the Foot and Mouth restrictions had the benefit of allowing more time to be spent working on the Dump, there was a curious scheme to acquire bricks to build the toilet walls. Every member was asked to bring two bricks from home every weekend. [T*his, finally, accounts for those strange walls in the Dump – Ed*]

Whitsun brought the usual Gaping Gill meet, but this year Gerald Benn, Dave Brook, Alan Brittain, John Greene and Carl Pickstone found Whitsun Series at the end of East Passage. It is ½ mile long and was heading straight for Ingleborough cave but alas didn't bring the hoped for connection. Later in the year ULSA discovered Far Country which was also heading in the right direction ending just 200m from Inauguration Series in Ingleborough Cave, this raised hopes of an imminent connection but as we now know it would be many years before the eventual connection, even a temporary connection, was to be made. [*See Section 2 for the full Whitsun Series story – Ed*] The milk marketing board were thinking of setting up a refreshment stand at Gaping gill in 1968 but eventually decided not to bother.

Ken Pearce once again upset the caving world with a letter in the BPC Bulletin suggesting that the BSA becomes the national face of all aspects of caving in the UK. Several members were prompted to reply in writing, I think he got the message from the BPC. This controversy was overshadowed by events on Sa**turd**ay 6th July when the flushing toilet at the Dump was successfully commissioned, only to reveal a leak the day after which rendered it useless again for several weeks. It also became necessary to remind members that the sockets in the walls at the Dump were standard ring main sockets and not to strip the insulation from the ends of wires and poke the bare wires into the sockets. The fire risk alone should have been obvious, let alone the electric shock issue, but there was no immediate improvement and the old gents toilet outside was eventually converted into a charging room with many sockets of different types being wired up for use by member's chargers. [*It is obvious from this that the interpretation of the standard wiring method we all know now was still a little ambiguous in 1968, there were still adaptors available that enabled people to draw power from the light fittings, and it had to be insisted that the plugs used had a fuse in the appropriate pin. The Dump warden had the authority to sell or rent the correct plugs to offenders and remove any dangerous installations. – Ed*] There was an almost unnoticed seismic shift in tackle acquisition doctrine at the back end of 1968, two pulleys were bought for life-lining purposes and a drawing was published which showed how to make a lightweight version. The implication being that for the first time it was officially acknowledged that we didn't have to leave people at the top of every pitch.

The caving towards the end of 1968 included some interesting meets, Langstroth cave, that had been explored by Livesey and his diving friends by diving the sumps at the end of Langstroth Cave and climbing the pitches into what became Langstroth Pot. [*He got into trouble with the committee for leaving BPC ladders in the cave for months on end, but when he explained he was forgiven – Ed*] They got up eight pitches with maypoles and combined tactics before the BSA saw a survey and dug out the top entrance and claimed it as a BSA find.

Swinsto Hole, now including Valley Entrance, could allow separate de-tackling trips to enter from the bottom via the Master Cave. The Christmas Dinner in 1968 was, somewhat predictably, held at the Golden Lion in Horton. The newsletter invitation for this event yet again stressed that this was the only social event held by the club where wives and girlfriends were welcome.

!969 saw the ongoing further explorations in the Whitsun Series in Gaping Gill, with presumably the same activity going on with ULSA in Far Country and their subsequent discovery of Far Waters in 1971. Gary Pilkington was lucky enough to go to West Virginia in the USA and join a trip down a large cave system in 1969. When he got back he was the first to write an article extolling the virtues of SRT, something unheard of in the Dales at that time. His only reservation of the use of single ropes USA style was that they were using Hemp ropes! Later in the same year Gary was off to join the Americans in Mexico and got on an early trip into Sotano del San Augustin and again on his return he told us the way to go with SRT. [*His words fell on deaf ears – Ed*] 1969 also saw Peter Livesey achieve the first descent of EPOS 1 in Greece.

It is clear from an article in early 1969 that the use of wetsuits was still not 100% within the BPC, in Sell Gill hole in winter there was a case of exposure, the unnamed member was dressed in cotton jeans on the lower half of his body and as we all can imagine he got very cold. The article warned of the consequences of not wearing enough wool next to the skin. [*A few years earlier members, not the leader, of a trip were told off, in the newsletter, for letting a chap go down wearing blue jeans, a lightweight Kag and winkle picker shoes. It is not clear if it was just the winkle pickers the committee objected to - Ed*] After the successful annual dinner and AGM in February the now regular trip to Ireland, got off in March, as did the annual Lake District walk. Walking from Borrowdale to Langdale it ran into bad weather.

The Lancaster – Easegill trip in February was noted for a boulder falling from above one of the pitches and hitting Harry Kellet on the head. [*Harry is referred to as a member though no actual record exists. – Ed*] The trip down Lost John's in March was enjoyed tremendously as there were only four people on the trip, it was very fast and exciting with much of the cave visited in high water conditions and only taking 5 1/2 hours. Expectations were high of more discoveries at the Gaping Gill winch meet after 1968's epic discoveries, but alas, it was not to be. The prelim

was almost a wash out and despite valiant attempts no more cave was to be found before the de-tackle meet.

The sleeping platforms in the dorms at the Dump were built under the direction of Frank Croll in the early part of the year and the padding and PVC cover added at a later date. It seems strange today that the members had to be asked to be careful when smoking in bed on the new platforms. New rules were eventually made and smoking was banned in the dormitories all together in August 1969.

Some classic caves were done in fine style with small numbers in the last quarter of '69, Pen-y-ghent, Lancaster, Juniper Gulf and Meregill to name a few. The fact that the trips were written up at all suggests either something went wrong or it was an amazing trip. In all cases the comments were about what a great experience caving in small teams was. "We all knew what the others were thinking when communication up wet pitches was impossible, it adds something to a trip and brings about a bond within the team". They had witnessed being a team, with no particular leader; this truly was the second golden age. It is clear that this message was getting through to people as Peter Faulkner was subsequently moved to propose that there be a minimum number of three people on every trip for safety, it was passed unanimously.

As the year drew to an end the surprise location of the Christmas dinner was released and yes it was the Crown at Horton, again, all in all it was probably the best year the club had experienced in terms of caving trips. Obviously the 1960's started exactly as the fifties had finished, but major technological advances had, against stiff resistance, been introduced and right at the end of the decade the rewards were beginning to be reaped. The members had forced the committee to accept defeat in the first of the equality battles and ladies were allowed to stay at the Dump. Nobody at the turn of the decade was thinking about the next equality battle that without realising had already been won thanks to the small print within Government grant applications.

SECTION 1.5 – 1970'S

Rumour has it that the Annual Dinner held on the 7th February 1970 was the best, most entertaining, dinner ever held by the club to that date. The only words Mike Hartland could use to explain included a reference to a speech by Monty Grainger and that "the festivities were rather prolonged – enough said" So we conclude that the success of the function was directly proportional to the amount of beer consumed, seems about right. The Annual General Meeting was told that the club membership had dropped to 103 paid up members, after a subscription purge over the previous months. The feeling of the meeting was that the 'natural' size of the BPC was around a hundred active members, so there was no problem. The new committee was asked to look into ways of attracting new and younger members. At the Dump the under floor heating had been commissioned and as luck would have it the temperatures in mid February 1970 were well below zero and "there was no need to light a fire except to heat the water". In preparation of 'Decimalisation' the committee raised all the prices at the Dump 'to avoid the use of the current 6d coin'; no explanation is offered as to why this was considered to be a looming problem.

Caving was still going ahead even though ropes were freezing solid, Lost John's and Lancaster – County were done in the dark days of winter. As things began to warm a little plans were made for the annual weekend train trip to Ireland which involved a lot of drinking, driving and not much sleeping but they did get to go underground as long as they were ready to start the return trip by 3pm on the Sunday. They arrived back in Manchester at 5 am Monday morning and had to go straight to work! John Robinson in a very early act in the role of Hon Photographer volunteered to start a club scrap book of black and white pictures showing club life..........

In June the committee agreed that all future jobs in the Dump would be contracted out as finances allowed. This was in response to members wanting to go caving and the same old few were giving up their time and caving to work in the Dump. It was also reported in June that Norman Thornber had died; he was a guest speaker at several BPC functions over the years, but will be best

remembered for producing the famous cave guide – Pennine Underground, first issued in 1947.

There was an incident down Birks Fell in October 1970 when Raymond Lee was leading through a boulder choke when a boulder in the roof slipped out and pressed on his buttocks, pinning him painfully to the ground. His fellow cavers [Gerald Benn and at the time Christine Davies] managed to chock the stone to prevent further movement and after some time managed to break out the floor beneath him enough to facilitate his escape. In April the following year he went through the same crawl after a certain nervous hesitation. He later named the site 'Buttocks Boulder Choke'. The club's digging highlight of 1970 must surely be the 3000 foot extension in Poula Willin in County Clare. The HWCPC digging teams dug into major extensions of Pippikin Pot and opened Hurnel Moss Pot near Gaping Gill in the same year.

The Christmas Dinner in 1970 was held at the Hill Inn, which was a first for the club and must have been a welcome break from the Crown at Horton. The AGM was held on February 13th 1971 at The Golden Lion in Settle, it is not remembered for anything other than the election to membership of our first two ladies, Christine Davies [Later to be; Benn] and Kathleen Faulkner. It is not recorded which was voted in first so which was our first lady is not known. Caving in 1971 got off to a good start with good turn outs for Heron Pot and Crackpot Cave in March and the Birks Fell incident mentioned above. Raymond Lee was clearly very busy in 1971; he discovered a parallel shaft which serves as a safer pitch than the big pitch in Little Hull Pot, when in flood. He also discovered some minor extensions to Disappointment Pot in 1971. It appears that Raymond acquired an 'Inductorphone' in September of 1971, which could be used for location but, as yet, not speech. [*It is not clear if the inductaphone was a device that uses modulated magnetic waves as in the 'Molephone' or some device that induces radio waves, it turns out we also owned an 'Addressograph' whatever that was?- Ed*]

October 1971 was when Jack Coates death was reported to the great sadness of the whole club. Also in October it turned out that an article from the BPC Bulletin had been reproduced in a Descent magazine without the permission of the club or the author. There were many advances and discoveries made in 1971, the Earby PC extensions were discovered in Lancaster Hole and a new permanent ladder had been installed on Stop Pot in the Lancaster/Easegill System. On a solo trip in 1971 Mike Wooding with a mammoth effort discovered and roughly surveyed Far Waters in Gaping Gill. Meanwhile the first Ghar Parau Expedition left Britain for Iran as the last major international expedition using ladders, and Pete Livesey left to be a professional caver in Canada. The Ghar Parau expedition went to the Zagros Mountains and tackled an amazing cave with pitch after pitch, heading for a potential world depth record. Unfortunately the expedition ran out of tackle at the head of a thirty foot pitch and had to come home. A major fund raising effort was set in motion and permission was acquired to return the next year. The Christmas dinner in 1971 was held on December 4th at the Ingleborough Hotel in Ingleton.

After a successful AGM at the Golden Lion in Settle on February 12th 1972 caving got off to a wobbly start when Philip Pendred led a team down Rowten Pot on February 27th. They tackled it at the wrong end and got stuck for a while getting around a car crashed into the rift, they then realised they had rigged the pot wrongly and abandoned the trip and went into the Master cave via Valley Entrance. It was while looking around that Dave Pawson got quite well stuck in the Philosopher's Crawl; it took a long time to get him out. The Lakes Bus meet had 21 people walking in hailstones over Helvellyn at the end of March, followed by a Pasture Gill trip being cancelled due to flooding and the members nearly did Washfold instead. At the end of April another attempt at Pasture Gill was cancelled due to flooding but this time they nearly did Birks Fell Cave instead.

It was with great sadness that the death of Hugh Browne was announced in March 1972, he joined the club in 1936 and was a leading figure for many years and as such was very involved with the design and construction of the club winch in 1949/50. We also lost Herbert Ambler in July 1972; he was one of the great wits of the early years.

The second Ghar Parau expedition, using SRT, was halted by a sump just around the corner at the bottom of the 30 foot pitch which stopped the first expedition in 1971. [*The Zagros Mountains were removed from the International Caving list of places to visit after the Iranian Islamic revolution starting in 1978. Perhaps the time is right to test*

the water and the BPC organise a centenary trip to Ghar Parau – Ed] The fundraising carried out after the first Ghar Parau expedition was so successful that after the failure of the second Ghar Parau expedition there was still a large amount of cash left. With no further trips to Iran possible, the money was used to set up a managed fund [*The Ghar Parau Expedition Fund 1973. – Ed*] to grant donations to the funding of UK based foreign caving expeditions in the future.

Work on the Dump was continuing in 1972 and in June we received the last of the stage payments from the Government Grant which would allow us to finish the planned conversion of the Dump sometime in 1973. Bad behaviour at the Dump was again reported in October but no written complaint was forthcoming so no action was taken.

There was a large turnout for the Swinsto, Valley Entrance trip in September 1972 with people doing all combinations of down, out and up using Valley Entrance. The teams witnessed a solo caver who had just abseiled down the big pitch and was in the process of prussiking up his rope again when the BPC team arrived. No further mention of this incident was made as the BPC was still operating a strict no abseiling rule and prussiking was not even known about so that couldn't be banned. There was one final hint to come, the club couldn't fail to acknowledge this but that was for next year. The Christmas Dinner was held on the 22nd December at the Ingleborough Hotel in Ingleton and was very much enjoyed by the 43 members and guests that attended.

The 1973 Annual Dinner and AGM were held at the Golden Lion in Settle on February 10th 1973. The management of the Golden Lion told the club in no uncertain terms not to book there again [*This was due to an extended food fight involving the throwing of roast potatoes – Ed*] The club had 94 members as of February which was less than the 100 at the same time in 1972. There was growing concern that the Dump was attracting guests rather than members, people who simply wanted to use the Dump facilities rather than join in the club activities. It was not known how to differentiate between the desirable membership enquiry and the undesirable ones.

The caving in 1973 got off to a slow start but Notts Pot was done in January and Juniper Gulf, Birks Fell and Goyden all achieved in March. Preparations for Gaping Gill involved Paul Turner actually obtaining a manufacturer's handbook for the winch engine and fetling the winch to mechanical perfection prior to the prelim on the 12/13th May. There was an unfortunate accident on the de-tackle trip when a trailer overturned and threw several members clear of the trailer but Pauline Shepley suffered a broken leg. As a result of this accident all riding on the trailers at Gaping Gill was banned.

Apparently stemming from a conversation between Raymond Lee and Jim Abbott there was a club expedition to France in 1973. The Chourum des Aiguilles [*Needles Pit*] the third deepest cave in the World was tackled. The experiences of this trip and the witnessing of the Abime Club du Toulon cavers use of single rope technique turned out to be a turning point in the development of the BPC. Not only did it directly bring about the adoption of SRT in the BPC but the research work carried out by members into the safe techniques and equipment it required was publicised in the later Bulletins and was widely regarded and respected as leading edge and probably saved lives in the wider UK caving world. [*This was published in 1976 after David Huxtable died using inappropriate polypropelene rope to abseil GG main shaft. – Ed*] The failure of the 1973 expedition, and the subsequent, successful, 1974 expedition, established the foreign caving holiday as a permanent feature of the BPC calendar.

1973 was the year that Jim Abbott, ably assisted by Raymond Lee and John Bolton, dived Hallucination Aven sump to an airbell, in a 15hr round trip. The dive was a very long way into the system involving a long arduous carry of equipment, which at that time was not being done by divers. [This airbell was later passed by **Geoff Crossley**] It was one of the first dives by a club member since the Mossdale accident after which the committee seemed to assume that as three of the casualties were divers then diving is not to be a supported club activity and it was a taboo subject for a decade.

1973 was also the year that Gerald Benn and his brother Alan jointly developed a new and advanced type of exploder for use in cave digging. The years caving ended with a miserable trip down Barbondale Pot which involved several dead sheep. The Christmas Dinner involved dead turkeys and much good fun, held at the Ingleborough Hotel on December 8th with 57 members and guests.

It was always known that the big effort in 1974 would be learning SRT in time to go back to the Chourum des Aiguilles and tackle it like modern cavers. The committee, ignoring previous rules over abseiling, bought a rope, especially for the learning of SRT. The rope was made the responsibility of Brian Smith and thus began the research needed to make SRT safe in Britain. Much of the conversations in early 1974 were all about jammers, descenders and harnesses. Clothing was also undergoing a review with nylon over suits now being available. What to wear underneath was also the subject of great debate. With Marlow 16 Plait rope being donated by the manufacturer the extensive 'testing' involved indoor and underground SRT practice. Slowly more and more people accepted the potential benefits of SRT, especially for deep foreign trips, and began buying the required personal hardware.

The Annual Dinner in 1974 was held at the Foster Beck Watermill Inn where the afternoon slide lecture was given by Tony Waltham and he talked about his caving trips in the Canadian Rockies. Along the way he mentioned the ongoing exploits of Mike Boon and Pete Livesey who apparently were still taking all the glory on the few trips they were still managing.

The Lakes Walking meet in March achieved a place in history when it was the first club bus to be stopped and boarded by the Police. They had caught up with the bus on the M6 and pulled it in to tell the confused walkers that they had left John Greene at Pooley Bridge, this was after the usual cry, "Is everybody here?" John had been banging on the side of the bus to alert somebody as it pulled out, the bus had to return and pick him up from the Police Station.

There was another spate of thefts from the Dump at this time and the committee pointed out that the Dump is left open at all times even over weekends because people don't lock up when they are last to leave. Not everybody had a key to the Dump at this time so it could have been a bit of courtesy to the next man in and nobody felt they owned the Dump, it was a bit like a B&B you wouldn't lock the front door in day time there either. 1974 was also the year that the CRO bought their base in Clapham and began the conversions.

The Gaping Gill prelim meet was quite memorable in 1974 as just as people were gathering to enjoy the communal food after a long mornings' toil, the pan with four gallons of stew fell off the primus stove, all was lost. The meet report also reveals that the club had bought a new abseiling rope; this is clearly the spreading influence of the SRT expedition to Chourum des Aiguilles later in the year. It is recorded, however, that nobody prussiked back up the main shaft after connecting the guide wire.

The Pen-y-ghent trip in June of that year was tackled with the traditional ladders and lifelines on the Saturday with the intention of de-tackling on the Sunday. Heavy rain on the Saturday night was a worrying feature of the trip that subsequently dropped to twelve people. There were abseil ropes fitted to all the longer pitches which made the bottoming time very quick, luckily. The return trip to the surface eventually became aware that the water levels were rising and that the water was getting cloudier. An exciting and fast crawl out was made; it is possible that if it were not for the use of the abseil ropes on the way in they may have had to retreat back into the cave. At the surface they learnt that there had been a thunder storm and the dam had burst, causing a large pool in the next shakehole.

July 1974 saw the expedition to France succeed with seven BPC members bottoming the third deepest cave in the World in just six hours. This was the first British team to reach the bottom of the Chourum des Aiguilles. The return trip took 14 hours making an amazing 20 hour round trip where the year before, using ladders, they failed completely. The BPC had at last listened to the words of Gary Pilkington and joined what is the 3rd Golden Age of caving. {See *full story in Section 2 – Ed*] We managed a four page writeup, with photos, penned by Brian Smith in 'Descent' Issue 30 November 1974.

Some large turnouts were seen and some good caving towards the end of the year with 23 down Lost John's in August and 17 down Gingling Hole in September. Interestingly the Lost John's trip had SRT and ladder on the pitches, and a lot of congestion was avoided, but it was noted that more people still used the ladders. It was still early days for SRT but the genie was out of the bottle and there was to be no putting it back. It has to be said that the SRT developed in the 1970's and 80's is not what we think of today. Yes we abseiled down and prussiked up but the technical rigging didn't start until mid 80's which is the time when a fair balance between safety and fun was achieved. Up until then the ropes were belayed where the ladders had been, there was very little traversing out to get a free drop, the ropes were pushed over edges and rope protectors put where it touched to save the rope. Deviations came first then load sharing knots and then the traverses. The problem was before the fixed bolts of today, everybody felt that they should put their own bolts in. The more bolts that were put in, the more bad bolts there were. [*Some pitch heads positively bristled with bolts, old, new and bad, I seem to remember seeing a hanger bolted to a curtain/flake with a nut and*

bolt. It wasn't all like that though I still have the hanger and bolt that came out at the touch from the top of the Black Rift in 1977, it was the only bolt and someone had to hold it in while people were on the rope. – Ed] The Black Shiver trip in October 1974 was a purely SRT trip and went well accept for omitting to take a rope for the Black Dub pitch. The Mendip weekend trip went well except for Mick Sharp and his car passengers who somehow ended up in Northampton.

The Christmas dinner in 1974 was again held at the Ingleborough Hotel in Ingleton, where an eleven course dinner was offered. Clearly they valued the BPC custom every year. It is noted that the newsletter before the dinner reminds members that ladies are now welcome at the Annual Dinner. Before the end of the year plans were already afoot for the next big SRT based expedition in 1975. For this we were planning a trip to the Grotta di Piaggia Bella in Italy.

The year started off with some great caving after the Annual Dinner, which was held at the Foster Beck Watermill Inn, with a Flood Entrance – Stream Passage Pot exchange, Tatham Wife Hole, Pen-y-ghent Pot and Birks Fell [to the bottom] all in the early part of the year. It seems that when a good hole is on the meets list there is a resurgence of interest and huge numbers can turn up when it is being tackled for SRT/SRT & ladders. The exception was Birks Fell when twenty two turned up for a ladder only trip. The Gaping Gill meet was the usual success with no major problems. The expedition to Italy was also a success with all three entrances tackled and the sump at -2260 feet below the highest entrance, Caracas, reached. By making the summer expeditions a family holiday as well the club guaranteed good turn outs for future expedition type trips. In the past visits to such caves as the Grotta di Piaggia Bella would have required multiple clubs co-operating and pooling tackle with the old problems of some clubs not pulling their weight on the more arduous tasks like de-tackling.

In September the committee had to consider the future strategy of the club regarding ropes. It eventually decided that they were to scrap the aging polypropylene life lines and replace them with 10mm Terylene [Polyester] SRT rope. This decision recognised the trend to SRT/ladder trips and as long as the ropes were cared for properly could be used as lifelines and self lining ropes as well as full SRT tackle. The major advantage with this strategy was that the club now acquired a huge vertical range for SRT trips.

The caving in 1975, after the summer expedition, continued at a pace never witnessed in the club before. The nucleus of front line active cavers had never been bigger and with the advent of SRT holes like Death's Head Hole with a 200 foot entrance pitch being routinely tackled as big pitches had lost their threat and anything was now possible, this was indeed the 3rd Golden Age. Lost John's, Little Hull and Nick pot, to name but a few, were all done in a few hours, sometimes with quite big teams, in quick succession before the end of the year.

The 1976 Annual Dinner was held on the 14th February at the Plough Inn at Wigglesworth, with Dave Leonard [ULSA] showing 3D slides of caves after the AGM in the afternoon. One of the longer SRT ropes had been damaged and subsequently cut in half. Notices and articles in the newsletter repeatedly reminded members of the best way to carry, handle and rig SRT pitches. [*The newsheet number 149, May 1979, was the first using A4 paper instead of foolscap and marked the return to portrait format which meant they could now be read. – Ed*]

The testing and evaluation of ropes and equipment for SRT was in full flight in the early part of 1976. Marlow was donating different rope types for underground evaluation and testing for tensile strength after increasing numbers of trips. They supplied lengths of 10mm and 12mm dyed strange colours to allow identification. It was through this extensive work that the club was able to determine, to the surprise of the whole caving world, that the ropes were losing half their strength through dirt and grit and the effects of water and SRT. This, it was thought, was due to the microscopic fibres being cut by sharp bits in the mud that was washed into the core by water and the pressure of distortion through abseiling and the pressure of prussiking cams. The good news was that the strength loss levelled off and the ropes carried on maintaining their half strength for a long time. This meant we were using a 1000kg rope with a service life of several years as long as we washed it vigorously after every trip. We have had several rope cleaning machines at the Dump over the years all designed to minimise the embedded mud in the core of the ropes. The major results were published in 1976 with more to follow as ropes finished their exposure cycle underground and were then tested by Marlow.

It is clear that the SRT techniques were not advancing at this time as comments were made about the loss rate of split tubing rope protectors. They sort of worked if you could get them to stay where you put them. The BPC always relied upon friction with the rock to keep the tubes from sliding down when the diameter of the rope reduced under load. The more advanced method that came in later was tubes of tackle bag material held closed with Velcro, these had a string on top to use as a prussik knot above the rub point, a real pain to pass on an abseil. [*In a previous life the club I was in used stainless steel 'R' clips tied to the tubing at both ends, one to hang the tube from and one to act as a slide stop below, much easier to pass – Ed*]

The caving in 1976 continued to tackle all the previously feared classics without any hesitation and although there was a 'leader', his, or her, only real responsibilities were making sure the right tackle was present, checking the rigging was OK and that everyone was accounted for after the trip, as well as writing the report of course. The old ways of even the 1960's were gone, never to return, the post of leader was now more freely offered to almost anyone who would do it. The caving meets list could now include interesting small caves that had never been visited before, such as a party of seven down Scrafton Pot with its amazing fossils followed by a party of four down Black Shiver Pot, with the Black Rift, as happened in April/May 1976. But did this mean the challenge was going out of UK caving? The summer expedition in '76 was an open affair with a pre-determined operating centre declared as Autrans [*Near Grenoble, and the Berger! – Ed*] with no specific objective set. The idea being that they were to organise trips they fancied and liaise with any local cavers as and when possible and with this flexibility they would cave as they would at home but amongst the glorious deep holes of France.

Digging was still a popular pastime in these days of deep exploration, and the BPC's main pastime – Clapham Bottoms dig, rewarded the faithful in 1976 with a relatively big extension, 200 feet including a 50 foot pitch and a horrible crawl. The faithful were again rewarded in 1977 when Strawberry Pot succumbed to their subtle persuasions.

November was a time for the CRO to celebrate as after two years of hard work the depot in Clapham was officially opened, but during his interview with the Yorkshire Evening Post Jack Pickup stated that it was possible cavers would, in the future, be paying a 'tariff' for their rescues. This, along with rumours that the ambulances were to start charging focused member's thoughts about caving insurance. The same month that the above was reported by the Yorkshire Evening Post, the

Guardian reported that no less than Lord Hunt, of Everest fame, had said "the mountain leadership certificates should be scrapped, but the training courses retained. It was felt that the certificates attach leaders with greater authority than is warranted, they reflect little evaluation of performance in difficult or dangerous situations". Presumably the same applies to cave leadership certificates as well.

Cave Divers had several notable successes in 1976, Ireby Fell Caverns and Notts Pot were connected by Phil Pappard and Radagast's Revenge in Ingleborough Cave was found, the significance of this would be realised in the years to come. In the cold days of Autumn 1976 there was a trip down Lost John's that was led by Kevin Murgatroyd, who like all good leaders, was out of the hole first. Feeling cold and wet he soon went back into the cave to see where everyone else was, he met Ted Popham who didn't recognise him. Ted refused to believe Kevin was a member of the BPC and accused him of being a pirate. Clearly the role of leader was reserved for those with a thick skin and not easily offended. The 1976 BPC Christmas Dinner was held at the Brown Cow in Bentham on the 11th December.

The 1977 New Year just had time to settle down before a January trip down, the now very popular, Black Shiver Pot. This was quickly followed by the Annual Dinner and AGM in February which was again at the Plough Inn at Wigglesworth. A new role was created that I don't think went beyond the 1978 AGM, but for 1977 we had a Medical Officer by the name of Norman Brevit. The talk after the AGM was about the summer expedition / holiday and a proposal by Brian Smith that the club tackled the Grotte de Bury [Near Chourum de Bolton? – Ed]

There was a fatal accident in Blayshaw Gill Pot in Nidderdale, a boulder fell out of the roof and trapped a member of Y.U.R.T., who sadly died before the rescue team arrived. There is not a lot you can do about rocks spontaneously falling from the roof in a cave, we have a member [Thirza Hyde] who famously survived a similar case. In October there was a cave diving fatality in Derbyshire; Michael Nelson's body was recovered from 140 feet into the sump at Illam Rising. This happened the same weekend that Phil Smith of the Craven had to be rescued from their Lizard Pot dig on the Allotment with back injuries.

The BPC bought a 500 foot length of nylon Bluewater rope as a hard wearing SRT rope for GG main shaft trips at the upcoming GG meet. The club had also been given a 600 foot length of nylon Interalp SRT rope, for evaluation, by Marlow ropes Ltd, so we could do a direct comparison with the Marlow rope we had now standardised on. It was also reported that the last of the polypropylene life line rope had been scrapped; we now only had SRT ropes, serving as life lines as well of course. The club received 50 meters of Eidelrid SRT rope, donated for testing, from Caving Supplies this was quickly followed by another 30 meter length.

The Dump got it's very own telephone in December 1977 which brought the BPC at least into the 19th Century. The Christmas Dinner was held at the Wheatsheaf in Ingleton on the 10th of December and the Annual Dinner and AGM for 1978 were held on February 11th at the Plough Inn at Giggleswick again. Talk of the summer expedition starts earlier and earlier and this year it was discussed as part of the AGM in February. The plan was to go to the Julian Alps in the Italian – Yugoslav border just north of Trieste. The AGM was also supported by a Slide show and talk by Dave Brook of ULSA where he described the recent British Papua New Guinea expedition where they surveyed 30 miles of cave in three months.

The newly discovered Dale Head Pot was descended after a long period of sustained rainfall, despite some people turning back John Ralphs was able to defecate over the 130 pitch as a form of scent marking his progress. Retreat after this was mandatory.

The Gaping Gill winch engine was a problem this year, it had been re-bored by Paul Turner and awaited rebuild and was set up far too late. When it was tested there were problems which Paul didn't diagnose until after the engine was installed at Gaping Gill during prelim. Paul, in an act of sheer heroism, decided to drive his motor bike up to the hole on the Tuesday night in between prelim and members meets, fit new piston rings and rebuild the engine. What he hadn't taken totally into account was the difficulty in seeing in the dark and he kept plummeting into steep sided shake holes and slithering to the bottom before having to try and drive out again. All the time hoping there wasn't a hole at the bottom and especially GG. Eventually, of course, the shake hole was GG and he did indeed fail to stop in time and plummeted down the side but managed to avoid the void. His mission was successful and after rebuilding the engine in the dark over the hole I would like to say that it ran perfectly for the remainder of the meet. However, the engine mounting failed, the main gear on the drum failed and it sounded like the engine wanted another major overhaul again after the meet.

In the next newsletter there was a paragraph saying there was a plan to go to Marble Mountain in British Columbia in Canada for the annual expedition in 1979! Plans for the Julian Alps were progressing and the date had been fixed as July 22nd to August 5th. That then changed immediately to the Antro Di Corchia instead of the Julian Alps. This trip was planned with a little help from Stan Gee of the Derbyshire Caving Club, who knew the area well. In fact several of the DCC accompanied the BPC on the initial trips to the bottom from the lower entrance. All three of the major entrances [with a vertical range of 950 meters] were tackled and successfully completed in a couple of weeks with only six BPC cavers and up to three DCC cavers.

The caving at home was suffering from too much rain with several trips flooded out and then an attempt at Cherry Tree hole was frozen out with the shake hole full of snow and the walls coated with ice, no way through to the entrance could be found.

Elsewhere at this time Geoff Yeadon and Oliver Statham were pushing hard to connect Kingsdale Master Cave with Keld Head resurgence. After a mighty 3000 foot [914M] dive Geoff brought the gap down to only 600 feet [183M], surely the connection was imminent. Within weeks of this dive he did it again with internationally renowned cave diver Jochen Hasenmayer, when they made a 3300 foot [1006M] dive and discovered 'Dead Man's Handshake'. Geoff Yeadon later dived alone from the Master Cave and reported that he had linked his line with the Keld Head line, thus connecting the two sumps, Oliver Statham and Jochen Hasenmayer were in support. The through dive of 1829 meters [6000'] was done in 1979 and was the longest cave dive in the World. It was filmed as it happened by Yorkshire TV and shown later as the Underground Eiger. Geoff Yeadon had also recently dived and extended Dub Cote to 4000 feet [1219M], bringing it to within a quarter of a mile of Larch Tree hole.

It was with some sadness that the proposed trip to Canada was cancelled towards the end of the year, the reason given was cost, as it would have cost a lot more than the initial estimates. Caving trips in the UK were well attended on the whole, there were exceptions of course. Deaths Head Hole in July had three people turn up and a different three turned up for Giants Hole in December. Whereas the Top Sink to Lancaster exchange was awash with people, there was a two hour queue to abseil down Lancaster. Lancaster Ease gill was extended significantly in 1978 when 'Connection Pot' was discovered by the NPC. With two miles of passage, it dropped into Dusty Junction in Pippikin Pot and another pitch drops into the Earby Inlets down Echo Aven pitch, thus connecting Pippikin to Lancaster via what we now call Link Pot.

The 1978 Christmas Dinner was held at the Golden Lion in Settle and with a record attendance of 78 it was claimed to be 'the best in living memory', which in the BPC isn't that great a compliment.

The 1979 Annual Dinner and AGM were held at the Plough at Wigglesworth on February 10th at which we appointed a founder member of the club to the role of President for the last time. Vince Shackleton was voted in for the second year as club President in 1979 having proved himself as a great magician, equal to Jack McGhee who was the 'lord of the rings'.

The committee received a letter from the Ingleborough Estate in December 1979 warning that the pre-war gripping on Ingleborough was being re-applied and consequentially there would be a faster run off which may have implications underground.

After the Lakes walking meet in April there was an unofficial caving meet in Scotland at Easter. The cave was Scotland's deepest pothole – Uamh nan Claig-ionn [It used to be called the Cave of the Skulls, and although it is the deepest pothole it was not the deepest Scottish cave, that is Cnoc nan Uamh – Ed] The Gaping Gill meet was struck by terrible weather with dam breaches and mud, reducing the weight on the tractors meant extra trips but they were getting stuck in the bogs as well. It was so bad there were no mid week operations. During the previous GG meet a draughting shake hole near Juniper Gulf was found and in the summer 1978 was dug by Brian Lloyd and Paul Edwards to form a tight wet crawl 400 feet long which more than doubled the length of the previously 'uninspiring' Slasher Hole which sadly it went to.

The summer expedition in 1979 was to be the Fighiera on the top of Monti Corchia in Italy. The story of this epic trip is retold in section 2 of this book. The number of people that went to Italy in '79 was limited by the committee's announcement that the Gouffre Berger was already booked for 1980 and as a result only 8 members were caving in Italy in 1979. The Mendips expedition was a very different affair, as it was the venue for the BPC annihilation of the BEC at Sofa rugby with an 8 sofas to two victory at the Belfry, or what was left of it after the game. [*The BEC and the BPC had a deep rivalry when it came to this sport. Originally a Mendip thing the BPC soon picked it up and it used to be played when circumstances allowed. There had to be several things in place before a game was considered, firstly all players must have drunk at least a gallon of beer, there must be an open[ish] space and there must be an old sofa to hand. Sofa rugby is the most violent of ball games imaginable, though there is no actual ball, there are minimal [no] rules and yet it was very much enjoyed by all, participants and spectators alike. There were apocryphal reports of seeing a sofa with attendant group of oafs rolling down the lane, on brass castors, towards Horton in the early hours after a match at the Dump, the sofa was never found. Eventually sofa rugby was banned by committees, wives and girlfriends. There is a contemporary match report in section 2 of this book. – Ed*]

The Dale Head meet in December was a poor turn out so the notable meet in December was Peak Cavern, it was the only meet in Derbyshire that was likely to be supported in number by the BPC. [*Peak Cavern management had just decided to allow the restart of cave diving in the system and there was a great interest in Peak Cavern – Ed*] The week after Peak cavern the Christmas Dinner was held with 86 people attending at the Golden Lion in Settle again. There was a fancy dress theme of 'Facial Deformities' which was won by Phil Rowbotham, though sadly no pictures have been located to support this assertion.

SECTION 1.6 – 1980'S

As we moved into the next decade things remained pretty normal, with the AGM and Annual Dinner being held at the Marton Arms Hotel in Thornton in Lonsdale, where the dress code was dictated as informal but to include dissimilar footwear. This was strange at the time as not even the Christmas Dinner had developed to the now traditional fancy dress code and we still had some die hard formalists who would have had us wearing tuxedos for the Annual Dinner, like a lot of other clubs. We got an unexpected benefit from our guest speaker at the AGM, Stan Gee, of the Derbyshire Caving Club, he checked all of our fire extinguishers whilst he was at the Dump.

The club caving was going well in early 1980 until we tried the dreaded Pippikin to Lancaster trip for the second time. The first trip had some unrecorded disaster and the trip failed. It is a complicated trip with a team abseiling down Pippikin and another team entering via Lancaster carrying the tackle to ladder Maple Leaf pitch and allow the Pippikin team to climb up into Lancaster and onwards through to Top Sink. The second attempt at this trip was going well, the Maple Leaf pitch had been laddered and Geoff Crossley abseiled down the 70 foot Echo Aven pitch he signalled that the next man could come down but instead of Jim Abbott appearing over the top of the pitch, a wall of flood water came roaring into view. Geoff realised nobody would follow him down so he had no choice but to prussik back up, the two teams eventually retreated and vowed to return.

[*The most exciting part of this trip was never recorded in the newsletter, after the Lancaster team had descended, a group of South Wales, pirates, turned up and de-tackled our rope and gave it to some BPC members who were heading back to the cars, having convinced them of their good intensions and then put their ladder down the big pitch. When the Maple Leaf pitch team returned to the pitch they had no choice but to use the, rather inferior looking ladder. All went OK until the last man's turn and 40 feet up one side of the ladder broke, having to climb hand over hand up vertical rungs was not easy. When he reached the surface the life liners pulled the ladder up and reversed a length of ladder to put the failed bit at the very bottom of the pitch. However, what they*

didn't know was they had failed to get the ladder to the bottom of the pitch and it remained hooked on a ledge out of reach from the floor. The pirates ended up having to be rescued after they failed to return. – Ed] The Pippikin to Top Sink through trip was successfully completed on the 13th April 1980 by a team of eight, on the club's third attempt.

February 1980 saw a good eight man team tackle the recently extended King Pot down to the East Kingsdale Master Cave, the trip took 7 $^1/_2$ hours, a very respectable time considering the thrutching and crawling involved. February 1980 was also significant as it was the month that Geoff Crossley did his first Yorkshire cave dive in Goyden pot. The committee issued a formal grumble in the newsletter regarding the slipping standards of the meet leaders. After referring to the good old days when meet leaders were only chosen from the committee members it talked of a recent incident when the 'unnamed' leader didn't even turn up [*This hadn't been recorded since Neil Thorpe failed to turn up in 1965 – Ed*] No sooner than this unacceptable behaviour was denounced in public but we see a grovelling note in a newsletter, from no less than Geoff Crossley, saying that he has also just failed to turn up for the trip down Strans Gill Pot that he was supposed to be leading.

The big Summer Expedition in 1980 was the Gouffre Berger, this was the biggest international challenge the club had ever faced, both in terms of depth and number of people to accommodate logistically. The planning had to include compulsory insurance for the first time as well as underground camps. Club trips carried on up to August when 50 members departed for France and the Berger. The week before departure a trip down Pen-y-ghent was accomplished with a total of 90 feet of ladder short. There was an SRT rope on all pitches but only two people had the appropriate metalwork to use them. [*This didn't bode well for the Berger – Ed*]

The winch and gantry were set up in record time under clear blue skies at the Gaping Gill Prelim meet in May and partly without the experienced eye of Gerald Benn overseeing events. His journey up to Clapham had been interrupted by a motor bike trying to mount the front wing of his car.

Geoff Crossley's driving was also interrupted by someone stealing his car, he got it back but minus his diving gear which he had to carry around in his boot because his mum didn't know he was a cave diver. [*That is until she saw Geoff being interviewed on television after his heroic acts in the Dido's Cave rescue – Ed*]

The August expedition to the Gouffre Berger went exceptionally well, with a lot of hangers on from other clubs 26 people got to the sump, of which 14 were BPC members. The extensive logistical planning had worked very well and the sandwiches in Hall of the Thirteen were still 'edible' back on the surface. The cave was cleared of all tackle, sandwiches and people by the end of the first week.

It was with great sadness that 1980 brought the news of Frank Moulson's death; he had done so much for the club over the years since he joined in 1937. He was very involved with the building of the GG winch as well as being a very active and respected caver. The September trip down Black Shiver was a great success with 9 people entering and only one running away before the Black Rift. An October trip down Bull Pot of the Witches was hijacked by the CRO, after leaving the cave, to help with a rescue at Top Sink. During the process of the rescue however the victim, Tracy Gibson, died from her injuries having fallen down the first pitch. A tragic loss of such a young life, the whole team were shocked and traumatised by these events.

The 1980 Christmas Dinner was held at the Golden Lion in Settle on December 13th and there was a strict, compulsory even, fancy dress code [*no theme was recorded – Ed*] enforced by threat of public humiliation. [*Not a real threat to the average member of the BPC – Ed*]

1981 started with a disastrous caving meet in Kingsdale, the Swinsto team suffered light failures immediately and when they reached the master cave they came across Derek Castleden with a smashed hand. An ammunition box had fallen down the big aven pitch and landed on Cas's hand, there was much blood apparently and it must have been a real laugh getting out without using the hand, or getting it in the cave water. Swinsto had been left tackled for another team following later to de-tackle. What wasn't known at the time was that the driver of the car bringing the next team [*The Motleys*] had demolished 17 yards of dry stone walling on the way and failed to complete the journey. On the up side, however, the driver

[*Martin Coulton*] was made President Elect of the prestigious 'Hole in the Wall Club'.

The 1981 Annual Dinner and AGM were held at the Marton Arms Hotel, Thornton in Lonsdale on February the 14th, where the chief guest was Harry Long. It was a very rowdy AGM with numerous 'points of order' so much so that it was subsequently proposed that all future AGMs were held somewhere without a bar. Meanwhile the committee formed a sub-committee to make all the arrangements needed for the approaching 50th anniversary of the club [*1983 - Still two years away – Ed*]

The preparations for Gaping Gill 1981 were well underway as the 'Supremo' [Colin Gates] had been up to confirm it was still there and to measure up the plot for the new beer tent. This was to be positioned in the favoured camping spot of several members who were un-ceremonially evicted as a result. The new beer tent was fifteen feet square and required guy ropes which, when one was drunk and in the dark, were to become the reason most people had at least one incident that involved rolling in mud or over someone else's tent.

Back at the Dump the locker room was to be asphalted by a local man, Derek Bainbridge, who also pointed the chimneys and some of the walls. The Dump warden also demanded that the habit of peeing in the fire buckets was to cease immediately so that when the buckets are thrown over the sleeping members again it will be just water. There was an argument put forward by a wit stating that the buckets would have been empty if it weren't for the night time contributions and should there be a fire the Dump would burn. [*This was denied by the Dump warden, the standoff was only resolved with the eventual introduction of fire extinguishers – Ed*] The carpet tile experiment in the common room was officially abandoned and deemed a failure, in their place was put an actual carpet. Also in the Dump it was reported that several things had been stolen from the drying room, including Andy France's new wetsuit.

The BBC was at Gaping Gill prelim in 1981, they were filming for Blue Peter and had the privilege of capturing for posterity the lines of members heaving on ropes trying to pull the tractor through deep mud with an over active producer shouting don't look into the camera. They returned the following Tuesday to film our 'Luvvies' Mendip Jim, Long John and Buzby who led their entourage through to Mud Hall. It went out [*as they say*] on Thursday May 21st 1981, [*And to this day I don't know how Buzby got a real Blue Peter Badge, we only got stickers – Ed*]

The club had a significant breakthrough in Keay Hole in Littondale when Brian Lloyd and Brian Judd with other members supporting, broke through a very unstable boulder choke to find 'Brow Narse Chamber' [*Due to the frighteningly unstable nature of the choke – Ed*] which was a respectable size – 40 feet [12.3m] long, 50 feet [15.3m] high and 10 feet [3m] wide. During the winch meet 'Biff and Benn chamber was discovered near South East Pot by Brian Smith [Biffo] and Gerald Benn using a lasso.

The committee in June 1981 decided it was time to act against all the tackle being 'lost', the tackle store could now only be opened by a committee member and all tackle had to be signed out and in by a committee member. If the person wanting the tackle was a committee member they had to get another committee member to sign for it. On a brighter note the committee bought a job lot of paper for printing the newsletters on, they saved 60% and claimed it was gold, yellow or green [*It turned out to be orange, yellow and blue but it was cheap because it was foolscap not A4 and they had bought three years supply – Ed*] The committee was also asking for suggestions for the 1983 [50th Anniversary] expedition while the expedition for 1981 was simply a loose holiday in the Vercor region of France with no published objectives, starting on the second week of August.

Around the World at this time the UK Borneo expedition had returned and showed they had been very successful by finding many massive World class caves including Sarawak chamber. This was so big that when they first entered it they thought it was night time and they had found another entrance to the cave and were outside on the hillside. The chamber turned out to be 100 times the size of Gaping Gill [*15 million cubic meters and you can now go inside as a tourist, how the World has shrunk. – Ed*] The French and Spanish were doing much good work pushing the World depth record to -4773 feet [-1469M] in Gouffre Jean Bernard, while in Spain they had discovered BU56 which at -3920 feet [-1206M] they entered the long sought after Saint Georges River, they left exploration wide open. This whole area was widely considered for the 50th Expedition.

The engineers announced that the winch would have a proper hydraulic oil cooler fitted, instead of wet rags, in time for the hot weather we would obviously be having at the 1982 winch meet. A team of walkers, led by Max Koval and Bob Booth 2, walked Offa's Dyke footpath in August of 1981 taking a week to cover the 122 miles. [*I never did get my Offa's Dyke Guide book back - Ed*] The annual bonfire party was planned for November 7th 1981 and to be held at the Dump as usual, this was our one opportunity to impress our neighbours in Brackenbottom but we never did.

The Little Hull trip in October narrowly averted disaster when a diving bottle was dropped down a 20 foot high rift. [*Geoff Crossley was at the bottom of the rift and I was jammed half way down, Tom Clifford had the bottle in a tackle bag and was pushing it along the hands and knees crawl to the pitch head. Behind Tom were Julian Griffiths and Jim Abbott. I was suddenly frozen in shock as the bottle slipped out of the bag and went past me base first down the pitch, in slow motion. The base thumped into the ground and appeared for a microsecond to be staying vertical; it then started to fall over towards the wall, again in slow motion, A quick calculation instantly told both Geoff and I that the tap would hit the wall, hard, before the bottle would hit the floor. In the following milli-second I managed to thrutch up the rift about a centimetre and in that same time frame Buzby was now above me! The bottle tap did indeed hit the wall hard and bent about 20 degrees, but luckily didn't vent the tank. Julian Griffiths went on, with this tank, and dived the first four sumps without touching the rock. – Ed*] Also in October Geoff Crossley and Jim Abbott dived through the two entrance sumps into 920 feet [280M] of new passage [*Later named Manningham Lane*] in Dub Cote.

The 1981 Christmas Dinner was held at the Plough Inn at Wigglesworth on the 19th December, there was a strict fancy dress instruction with Christmas as the theme. [*This was the occasion that Rick Kendall came dressed as a festive Robin, his costume consisted of a chicken wire cage about one meter in diameter with a head hole, arm holes and a body hole at the bottom. It was covered in brown and red feathers cut from crepe paper and glued through the wire cage to a paper backing inside the cage. It looked very impressive but turned out to be impractical as a serious drinking garment. As this was a BPC Xmas dinner It was therefore discarded to the edge of the room in the early stages of the event. Sometime later a very drunk Bob Bialek thought it would be fun to try it on, but first he attached a pair of angel wings previously discarded by Andy France. Once his ensemble was ready it was time to put it on, he first tried to enter the cage with a pint in his hand*

61

and very slowly realised he would have to put what was now only half a pint down first. Once inside, he then realised he couldn't get the beer to his mouth without pouring it over his head. This greatly amused a small group who had been watching. Under cover of the cage several attempts were made to set alight to the brown feathers of the cage but they resisted all attempts. Finally the lighter was slipped to Geoff Crossley who then tried to light the red feathers at the back, Bob had put it on back to front as well. There was an instant reaction as the red feathers burst into flames and consumed the angel wings, not initially realising the smell of burning was him Bob continued to hold a conversation, however when he registered what was going on he threw himself onto the floor and rolled around furiously trying to extinguish the now fully ablaze globe. He eventually extricated himself from the smouldering wire frame that now looked more like the remains of the Hindenburg and started to stamp it flat, with a final flourish he poured his new pint of beer over the scene of devastation and put out the last flickering flames. At this point Max Koval, who had been messing with the piano, burst into song to the tune of 'London's Burning' he sang 'Dalek's Burning Dalek's Burning'.

Now it turned out that someone else had made a very similar costume to the Robin, but this one was actually a Christmas pudding and it had inside Frank Croll. Now Frank considered himself a figure of authority in the club and began telling young Geoff off whilst wagging his finger at him. This surreal vision was more than a lot of people could witness without collapsing in laughter, which annoyed old Frank even more so he tried to shout over the crowd to drive his point home, this of course was the wrong tactic and he eventually had to give up.- Ed]

On another surreal note, in January 1982 the committee felt that a certain issue was important enough to justify a paragraph in the newsletter, with no explanation or reason, insisting that the practice of sawing the handles off the brooms and mops at the Dump must cease, immediately.
[? - Ed]

There was an unfortunate trip down Gingling Hole in the January of 1982 when Bob Bialek's party exited the cave at night there was a serious snow storm in progress, details are vague but they ended up spending the night in a farmhouse on Fountain's Fell. The 1982 AGM and Annual Dinner were held at the Falcon Manor on 13th February and it was decided somewhere that the club's

annual expedition in 1982 was to be in the Picos de Europa in northern Spain. The intention of this decision was to get involved with the Spanish cavers and the exploration of the new deep systems that were being found in the Picos at that time. Only three members actually made it there but it was a worthy challenge and valuable contacts were made. They bottomed the Cueva de le Marniosa which is 724 feet [220M] deep in an eleven hour trip. [*This was reported in our 200th News Sheet – Ed*] There was another trip abroad this year by Geoff Crossley and Jim Abbott who went cave diving on a nudist beach in Greece. [*I am told they didn't just sit on the beach wearing wetsuits and goggles until their air ran out – Ed*]

The club had quite a few ladders and ropes stolen from Little Hull Pot in July, the thieves found we had left the pot tackled ready for a return trip in the morning; they probably used our tackle to ghost the pot overnight then helped themselves to our tackle. This told us all that the days when it was common practice to leave caves tackled, for weekends or even weeks, were now over and social decline had even reached cavers. [*It would seem that you could now trust your life to the hands of a fellow caver, but not the rope he was holding it with. – Ed*]

The Digger's Dinner was held at the end of October at the Sportsman Inn at Dent, [*Some unfortunate people apparently turned up for this event at the Tan Hill Inn as had been advertised before it was changed to the Sportsman, but I had a good pint before being refused permission to sleep on the floor. They had just done the place up with Ted Moult's windows and turned it into a posh eatery. Everest had replaced all the windows in the Tan Hill and made a TV advert with Ted Moult, [See You tube] the local planning people knew nothing of this until they saw the advert on TV. They made them take them all out – Ed]* The tradition of pie and peas was already well established for this event, it is thankful the club is relaxed about the implied requirement to have dug in a cave during the previous year to qualify for entry to this select event. The Christmas Dinner in 1982 was at the Marton Arms Hotel in Thornton in Lonsdale on December 18th, fancy dress was 'obligatory' on the theme of 'Beauty and the Beast'. As 1982 came to an end good club caving continued with the exception of the Derbyshire meet when nobody turned up.

Planning for the 50th Anniversary Dinner was gaining speed and the date had been fixed as the 22nd October 1983 at the Midland Hotel Bradford.

Events were soon to make this a double celebration and a golden year for the BPC. On January 22nd 1983 two parties of mainly BPC members were successful in making the connection between Ingleborough Cave and Gaping Gill [See section 2 for the full story] after 146 years of serious attempts by many clubs the BPC finally did it. February saw a team of BPC enter via Bar Pot and make their way to the connection dig to clear debris and enter Radagast's Revenge in Ingleborough cave where they took photographs. Clearly only the divers could actually exchange and they then reversed the other dive team's way in. It was filmed by club member Sid Perou and was televised nationally on BBC 1 in the 1984 New Year. The first full exchange trip was carried out on the 28th May 1983, with one diving team [*eventually*] abseiling down Main Shaft with a large group of, mainly BPC, sherpas using the winch to carry all the filming gear through to the connection passage called Dr Mackin's Delivery. The other diving team, with another group of, mainly BPC, sherpas to carry the diving gear, entered Ingleborough Cave. Those sherpas that entered via GG in support had to wait for hours before having to carry all the heavy gear all the way back out through Far Waters and Far Country. Along with the diving team that had come through from Ingleborough Cave [*Julian Griffiths and Jim Abbott*] they gave assistance to the film crew.

The connection trip was only repeated once, by the Derbyshire section of the CDG/TSG/EPC, with Sherpa assistance from the Burnley Caving Club. [*The team carried out a reconnaissance trip during the CPC winch meet in August and went into Radagast's Revenge from the Gaping Gill side which Clive Westlake [EPC] found far more exciting than the subsequent through trip as he saw the reappearance of the Gaping Gill stream for the first time. The exchange trip was completed in the October when the GG team abseiled main shaft and the Ingleborough cave team subsequently prussiked out of main shaft. The sherpas, of course, had to do that after a return trip to Far Waters. A total of eight people have done the through trip, far more people have walked on the Moon – Ed*] The dig site was then abandoned and allowed to collapse, it could be done again but it would take a lot of serious digging work before some divers could parachute in and take the credit again.

It seems there was an increase in the magnitude of practical jokes in the club in early 1983, which appears to have peaked when people were being set alight in the furniture at the dump. The committee couldn't reprimand members for the use of fire extinguishers under these circumstances but after a certain pyro-incident occurred the fire extinguishers were found to be empty and the Dump was in danger. This caused the committee to ask the club's resident fire inspector to check the situation, he reported that [quote] "an alarming number of the extinguishers were found to have been tampered with and left empty" The committee re-installed and increased the number of extinguishers and issued stern warnings in the newsletter.

In May 1983 Jimmy Rattray presented the club with its own induction location device for accurate location of underground features. It was not a communication device, but a survey tool, this put the BPC in a very select group that had access to such equipment. [*From memory the transmitter looked like a pink toilet seat. When it was endurance tested at the Dump it induced a pulsed signal that was picked up by the telephone wires in the common room. This rendered the North Yorkshire phone system totally unusable for the duration of the test – several hours. Presumably the signal was also induced into the mains system through the Dump wiring this could have affected any amount of mains signalling systems including early warning systems, luckily the MOD was not set up to triangulate the source of such jamming signals – Ed*]

The April Mendip trip went well considering the transport issues and poor communications between BPC members and the BEC members. But a memorable night in the Queen Victoria had Geoff Crossley chained to a concrete block, which he had to take to bed with him as the key to the lock was thrown into the flames of the pot bellied stove. He managed to release himself in the morning but foolishly locked the block to someone's Land Rover, sadly not belonging to the person he thought it did, so then spent a good half an hour looking for a hack saw to remove it yet again. In 1983 the annual expedition was to the Vercors region of France, all that was arranged before departure was a choice of campsites which the members were free to choose between depending, it seemed, on how many bars they wanted close to their tent.

The 1983 Gaping Gill meet was rather wet but that didn't stop several memorable trips happening. Firstly, of course, was the first full exchange trip through the connection with Ingleborough Cave and all the associated television crews. Then there were several memorable trips by the club, one was Car pot where the Motleys failed to reach the bottom but Joe Olejnik ended up with a suspected fractured skull and a gashed wrist resulting in two hospital trips. Assistance had to be given to another club's party who had descended Bar Pot and failed to find the way through to Main Chamber [?] and after visiting everywhere else in the system twice they beat a weary retreat to Bar Pot where their energy eventually waned. The club was paid a visit by Eric Hensler during the mid week vigil, he wanted to see the Main Chamber flood lit, he was delighted to travel on our 'new' hydraulic winch. [*He was 78 at the time – Ed*]

A day was spent debating the surface features in an attempt to identify where Henslers High Aven reached the surface. [*This is significant to the BPC as we eventually found the elusive Hensler's Pot in 1999 and four years later recorded the first through trip down Hensler's Pot including the high aven and into Gaping Gill in May 2003, twenty years after the initial surface search – Ed*]

The big social event of 1983 was the 50th Anniversary Dinner held at the Five Flags Hotel in Bradford on the 22nd of October. Work was going on in the Dump through the summer of 1983 installing a new fire protection system. This was thought to be a prime target for the pranksters so serious requests to leave the system alone were published in the newsletter. Probably due to genuine concern for our neighbours and the potential for serious implications if the system was damaged the members have shown their honourable nature and no incidents have ever been reported.

The August trip down Hammer Pot was changed to a trip down Quaking Pot due to bad weather. Several of our thin men, and women, went on the trip and reported it in the newsletter with almost the same cool level headed approach that all serious caves demand. It was, at the time, considered to be the absolute limit of human endurance due to its tight nature and yet to the BPC team on that day it was a routine trip. [*I recall in the late 1970's being told by the hard men of the Eldon PC, of grown men literally crying and others praising all that they held sacred when they found a better position in the passage that was at least a whole inch (2.5cm) wider – Ed*] This trip showed the quality of our members which was rarely acknowledged in the wider caving world at the time as we tended to be viewed as a large Gaping Gill centric club.

That was, as may be, but we had been around for a long time and the 50th Anniversary Dinner was

something many clubs would have been envious of. The event was enhanced with the presence of our remaining founder members and Norman Middleton. We heard a speech by Milton Shackleton and had the opportunity to talk with his brother Vincent and fellow founder member Bill Gott after the meal. The founder members and Norman were each presented with a commemorative Goblet, to mark the occasion. The cake was then revealed and Bill Gott lit the candle and after a meaningful pause, cut the cake to a great cheer. [*The events that must have gone through Bill's mind in that few seconds staring at the candle in silence would have been the centre piece of this history, if only we knew what they were – Ed*]

The caving in 1983 continued with some great trips and memories, from Dalek falling through the ice in Meregill's frozen mere to Rick Kendall free diving the Rowten sumps wearing a cagoule full of air, all great memories. [*The yellow plastic ducks in the Rowten airbell were also memorable – Ed*] The divers were active again, after the connection earlier in the year, Geoff Crossley and Jim Abbott went back to pushing Dub Cote and found a 1000' [305M] extension heading under Pen-y-ghent. Attempts were also started to find a surface connection into the new passages of Dub Cote. The club's old friend Jochen Hasenmayer was also in the caving news as he completed dives in Vaucluse [France] to a depth of 720 feet [219.5M]

The inside of the Dump was steadily repainted by Bob Bialek [Dalek] during the latter parts of 1983, which brightened the whole place up a lot, in time for the Xmas day dinner when 22 people sat down for the now traditional Yuletide members meal. The club's official Christmas Dinner was held at the Marton Arms in Thornton in Lonsdale on the 10th December. The traditional fancy dress theme was dialled back a bit and prizes were offered for the best 'Golden Head Gear', Rusty Scooter [R. Szkuta] won, but no record remains, describing what he had on his head.

The 1984 Annual Dinner was held at the Watermill, near Pateley Bridge on 18th February. This was after the return of the an old social feature, the Winter Film Night in Bradford, on the 1st February at the Star in Bradford one of Sid Perou's famous films [Man Bilong Hole, Bilong Stone – exploring the deep holes in the rainforest of Papua New Guinea] were shown to an appreciative midweek audience.

February found the divers Geoff Crossley, Jim Abbott, Julian Griffiths and Geoff Yeadon making more great discoveries in Dub Cote but still falling short of the Pen-y-ghent Master Cave. Other divers Paul Atkinson, Barry Sudell and Rupert Skorupa successfully dived 2000' [610M] in Joint Hole to find open passage heading towards Great Douk.

July 1984 saw the club celebrating the Dump's 21st birthday with a party; it was planned as a barbeque and a few drinks but ended as an all night piss up with a bonfire. There were many casualties who were found still lying in the garden at breakfast time where they had fallen, glass in hand, just a couple of hours earlier. The Dump also acquired a new facility in 1984, the gable end wall was 'bolted' to enable more realistic SRT practice to be done. It was still considered very much a sort of elitist pastime by some. Some of the older members still resisted using SRT and meet leaders were expected to tackle appropriate caves with both SRT and ladder with lifeline, even self lining was considered an act of betrayal [*There are still a few who believe SRT was the downfall of caving and all the fun was taken out of it - Ed*] It was decided that the 1984 summer expedition was to be held in Yugoslavia around a town called Postojna, where they have a very famous show cave. The expedition was a great success with good friendships made with the local Kranj cavers even after the unfortunate incident involving Dalek and the President of the Kranj caving club's daughter.

The club bought a big drill and generator to support the many digs the club members were involved with. This was after the Motley Potty dig went and joined Disappointment pot making another entrance to GG. The epic digging result of 1984 was the re-discovery of Stream Passage Pot. Ian Wilkinson heroically climbed from stream chamber up all the pitches and guided the surface diggers to re-enter the cave after the entrance had been lost in a serious flood the previous winter.

Geoff Crossley and Geoff Yeadon had returned to Hurtle Pot in the August Bank Holiday and found the passage after 1500' [457M] started to rise upwards from the attained depth of 100' [30.5M] This was bad news as they would now require decompression stops on the way in as well as on the way out. Elsewhere the club [Raymond Lee & Chris Smith etc] were working on Nettle Pot, near Car Pot, clearing boulders from a reasonable rift gained access to a 50 foot [15M] pitch taking the depth down to 100 feet [30.5M] Moss pot was also receiving attention from the diggers with their new generator and drill.

The 1984 Digger's Dinner was held on the 17th November at the Cross Streets Hotel, this was almost the only scheduled club activity that took place in November. The weather was sustained heavy rain with all caving trips cancelled due to flooding or risk of flooding, even a drive to a pub in Hawes nearly ended badly because of flooding problems. The Christmas Dinner was held on 15th December at the Golden Lion in Settle. Three Italian cavers were staying at the Dump over the Christmas period and were shown the delights of Leck Fell, KMC, warm beer and darts. They had a wonderful time and made many friends although it has to be said they never came back.

The Annual Dinner was not held in the same venue as the Annual General Meeting in 1985, this was an attempt to prevent alcohol having such an effect on the meeting. The Annual Dinner was held on 2nd February at the Bridge Hotel in Ingleton, while on the same day, at 11am the AGM was held in Horton in Ribblesdale Village Hall, where there is no bar and a record low of only 29 people turned up, is it possible there is a connection here?

The 1985 Gaping Gill meet was subject to a robbery, during the midweek period when nobody was about an organised gang robbed several barrels of beer from the camp up the hill. The implications were obvious, there is a lot of personal gear left in tents up at the hole as well as the thousands of pounds worth of club tackle and equipment and beer. It was easy for them to rob it once and now may realise what else that could be left lying around. Obviously the Craven were warned of our experiences before their meet in August and we started thinking very hard how we could counter another such attack.

The summer expedition was to be held in Yugoslavia again, it was for some people unfinished business from the previous year and the host club was still willing to have us back. [*Even after the unfortunate incident with Dalek – Ed*] Some good caving was done with trips down Brezno, Leska, Babizop Rakov Scojan and the Pit of Bears not to mention the classic show caves of Postojna and Pivka Jama. The Sunday Telegraph ran a large colour photograph and interview with Geoff Crossley and Jim Abbott about their recent successful exploration and through dive of the Glom Dhal River Cave in Arctic Norway [See Section 2]

With no particularly noteworthy events in the club caving the end of 1985 began to look more like a

65

social or luncheon club. The October newsletter [*The last one in 1985! - Ed*] simply listed five social events with the Plot night do at the Dump on November 9th and the Digger's Dinner at the Sportsman in Dent on November 23rd. These were followed by a Film night in Bradford before the Christmas Dinner at the Marton Arms on the 7th December. Ignoring the implied film competition at the Christmas Dinner there were more films to be seen courtesy of the YHA at Cathedral Hall in Bradford where, amongst other films, they would be screening the 'Underground Eiger' filmed as it happened during the epic dive by Geoff Yeadon and Oliver Statham connecting the Kingsdale Master Cave sump to the resurgence at Keld Head. [*The only exciting news at the end of 1985 was that Sandra Webb had done a charity parachute jump and broken her leg – very sad – Ed*]

There was better news on the way as several of our members [*Bryan Schofield, Brian Rhodes, Rick Kendall, Mick Sharp and Chris Hare*] had gone out to Mexico as part of a wider British expedition. They returned in January 1986 with news of great discoveries but no new records.

The 1986 Annual General Meeting was held at the Falcon Manor on 15th February with the Annual Dinner in the same evening. Interestingly concern was voiced at the meeting about the need for more organisation of the club's history, the need for a club archivist was discussed but there were no volunteers. The AGM also tried to kick the contentious issue of a compressor into the long grass as every time it was discussed they could never even get close to making a decision. The Gaping Gill Guardsmen were being mobilised by Colonel Gates prior to the 1986 meet. The plan was to have people, hopefully more than one, camping up at the hole for the two midweek periods when the winch is not in use. [*This, in time, became a popular retreat for some people, one person in particular was a regular midweek GG dweller. for many years he loved the peace and solitude. – Ed*]

The committee meeting on February 27th 1986 was turned into a bit of a fiasco after the meeting put the decision of what to charge for locker fees into the hands of the Warden [PGF] who promptly said £5 including 10 free Dump nights. This meant a net reduction in the locker fees and after noting the lack of democracy and the lack of common sense in the decision Brian Smith declared he was resigning over the issue, effective immediately. The shambles that followed was very emotional and normality was only saved by the level head of Harry Haigh who pointed out a breach in

procedure and the vote was taken again resulting in £1 locker fees and no free nights at the dump. Brian did not leave the club.

In March there was a curious appeal in the newsletter for 'old newsletters for the club archivist' [*what archivist? – Ed*] The plan to build a drop test rig in the garage was given the go ahead and preparatory work begun. The committee also decided to investigate the possibility of purchasing a molephone, while Jim Rattray had just constructed a molephone locator device that worked under water. The initial discussions over what could realistically be done in the event of a winch failure, with members of the public down the hole, came to the conclusion that there wasn't a problem.

The club's divers scored another success when in April Bryan Schofield and Brian Smith dived 140 meters [460 Feet] in Jingle Pot and connected it to the far end of the dive line in Hurtle Pot, thus connecting the two holes. Later they dived the other way and connected Jingle Pot to Weathercote Hole, thus allowing a 750 meter [2461 feet] dive from Weathercote to Jingle to Hurtle to Midge Hole before breathing fresh air again. The whole system was now about 2 km in length. Geoff Crossley and Rupert Skorupa found the way forward from Geoff Yeadon's limit in Keld Head's Marble Steps inlet. It is now a continuous 1 km dive, that's 2 km of diving before you add any line beyond the new limit.

GG86 became a notorious meet in the history of the BPC; World events had conspired, long before our meet started, to ensure it would be remembered. On 26th of April 1986 number 4 reactor at the nuclear power station in an unknown town in the Ukraine, called Chernobyl, blew up. The steam explosion released a cocktail of undesirable radioactive isotopes into the atmosphere, including Caesium-137, radioiodine and Strontium. The path of the ensuing radioactive cloud was tracked over northern Europe, over the North Sea and to Ingleborough, just as we were putting the winch together. It was made worse by the fact that it rained over us during the day and the TV news that night suggested that people would be ok if they didn't get wet by the rain. We were drinking the stuff in tea made from Fell Beck. [*We didn't glow in the dark that night, but it may explain some of the more extreme cases of follicle loss in the club's older members It turned out to be a successful Gaping Gill meet that year thus proving the old adage that 'every cloud has a Caesium lining' – Ed*]

The club expedition in 1986 involved some serious co-ordination, there was a week's caving in the Jura starting at the end of July, followed by a week's caving in the Dordogne which was timed to allow people to go over to Matienzo in Spain for a third week underground. This marked a shift in the club's confidence in caving abroad; we were viewing Europe as we used to view Britain's caving areas. We had the knowledge, the capability and the quality of members to take on such challenges which is why it was so strange that buying a compressor became such a contentious issue. A group of members felt they had to call an Emergency General Meeting [*Held on July 10th 1986*] rather than let the committee's decision to buy one stand. Of course, after some initially heated debate, the meeting sanctioned the purchase of such an essential tool that our club's divers could make excellent use of both at home and abroad and reward all club members with many future discoveries being associated with the BPC. How could a club such as the BPC, that willingly bought drills and generators for the diggers, not support cave divers as diving was at the time becoming the main source of new finds in British caving?

The ceiling in the common room at the Dump was undergoing fireproofing, it had been boarded over, then plasterboard fixed and it was now, after some months, being plastered. Jim Abbott reported on a very successful junior meet where the average age was 45! Meanwhile, Chris Smith led a trip down Birks Fell from the rear and got himself lost. Whilst discussing possible future foreign expedition areas, Albania and Romania were mentioned. We have still never investigated Romania.

The trip down Pool Park in October was an interesting diversion for the 20 members that went, the entrance utilises an old CPC Gaping Gill winch to lower people down the 320 foot [97.5M] entrance mined shaft. The top of the shaft is capped with concrete with a small hole for access [*Thirza Hyde, probably the smallest person on the trip managed to trap her head in the hole – Ed*] The ride down the shaft passes a World War 2 bomb dump before leading to an active natural cave system. [*Entertainment here was laid on by Sharon Kelly who, at the top of a 50 foot mud slide, decided to demonstrate her downhill freestyle slalom skills whilst simultaneously rehearsing for her Wagner operatic debut, sadly without the breastplate – Ed*]

It was with great sadness that we heard of Irvine West's death at this time, he joined the club in 1948 and continued caving well into his 60's when he settled down a bit and earned an Honours Degree at the age of 70.

The clubs donations to the cave rescue organisations were acknowledged by letters from their treasurers in September of 1986. Interestingly the CRO letter mentioned that our donation of £450 was more than all the other caving clubs combined.

The 1986 Christmas Dinner was held on the 6th December at the Golden Lion in Settle with dodgy judgement in the photographic contest, leaving Frank Croll winning half of the categories after an independent judge turned out to be Frank's mate. By the time the bar closed at 6am nobody cared any more. The Dump had been suffering from bouts of thefts, including money from the dorms and caving gear from the drying room, it was suggested that furry suits should now be locked to the rail in the drying room. [*I chose to rely on having the smelliest gear that nobody would steal – Ed*] After the Xmas dinner there was a Mendip trip to survive before the perils of New Year to contend with. Eight members bravely entered the Hunter's lodge to find there were six real ales and they didn't know any of them, it took them all Friday night to decide which was the best but in the morning couldn't remember which one it was so had to do it all over again on Saturday night. Some good caving and diving was done, but it was most remembered for realising the best beer was 'Farmer's Ales' just as they ran out of it and picking mistletoe at Barrington Combe Gorge.

January 1987 witnessed another example of Frank Croll's magic eye for the future, he pointed out that a member of a motor club had successfully sued his own club after an accident. Frank went on to suggest that the BPC should become a limited company to protect against such potential claims against the BPC. It would be another twenty four years before his suggestion was acknowledged and accepted when the club became a limited company in 2011.

The 1987 Annual Dinner and Annual General Meeting were held on the 21st February at the Falcon Manor Hotel in Settle. There were no motions from the committee but a strange statement was made by Pete Faulkner when he mentioned 'the 'commitment' made by older members to vote against female members' should be reviewed [?] There were no casualties recorded so it is assumed the meeting, and subsequent dinner, were the usual sober affairs some will remember from those days. The first President's Meet was organised by Frank Croll for the 13th June 1987. Centred on Alum Pot it was a great success and a template for every President to this day. [*The barbeque held at the Dump afterwards was made more memorable by Andy France's 'Hot shoe Shuffle' when he set fire to the shoes he was wearing whilst casually standing in the glowing embers of the fire pit. The BPC choir continued well into daylight. – Ed*] July continued to be a very sociable month as we also held the Digger's Dinner [*The usual Pie, Peas and Piss up – Ed*] on the 11th of July, at the Crown in Hawes, and there was a wedding celebration for Bryan Schofield and Rowena Hill which was held at the Dump on the 18th of July.

Mike Hartland made a statement to the committee in June 1987 where he claimed that the CNCC were not making their case strongly enough in negotiations and were in fact failing to respond to organisations such as the Countryside Commission and the Sports Council. He went on to suggest that the BPC should take over their role and to this end he would talk to the Sports Council. The committee's response is not recorded.

It was reported in July that the planning application by Mr Jarman of Ingleborough Cave [*and a member of the BPC – Ed*] to build a scaffolding tower all the way down Bar Pot had been refused by Craven Council [*The final say was to be had by the National Parks Committee – Ed*] His plan was to allow him to run ladder less novice caving trips down Gaping Gill, they would have wooden steps down all the pitches with safety bridges over hazards such as SE Pot he intended to create access to the main chamber and beyond. He intended to have up to 20 novices at a time in the system. His application suggested that Gaping Gill was in fact theirs as it connects to Ingleborough Cave and only by allowing this scheme could proper control and conservation of Gaping Gill take place. The controversy carried on throughout the summer of 1987 with large adverts for his 'Bar Pot Adventure Caving Scheme' put up at the BCRA Conference in September gathering lots of interest.

The annual expedition was again a multi-venue event. Starting in the Jura at Ornans in July it then moved over to Annecy for early August before ending in Matienzo in Northern Spain. Great caving and wine was had by everyone who joined in. It took two attempts to get down Magnetometer Pot in October, very wet weather caused the trip on the Saturday to be called off but the following day looked ok and it was on again.

This determination to go down 'Mag' was because Dave Hyde had noticed a great digging site when he was last at the far end of this cave some time before. He had imagined great rewards to a digging team that ventured through so much unpleasantness to dig in a boulder choke. The trip went very well considering the squalid and thrutching nature of the cave and the fact they were dragging with them the required digging gear. The sight that greeted them must have been sickening as someone else had obviously had the same idea and already dug the choke out. They turned round and dragged themselves and the digging gear all the way out again.

The Christmas Dinner in 1987 was held at the Marton Arms in Thornton in Lonsdale, there appears to have been an instruction to wear fancy dress but no record survives of a theme. No sooner was it New Year than we were being told of the impending Annual General Meeting and Annual Dinner to be held at the Golden Lion in Settle on the 13th February 1988.

[*Gaping Gill, 1988 was largely uneventful with the exception of an unfortunate trip by two of the Motleys. Ian Greenwood and Gwyn Bryan decided, as both entrances were rigged, to do a Stream Passage Pot to Flood Entrance through trip. All went well until Gwyn dropped back and lost sight of Ian, and eventually realised he was indeed, lost. He did the only thing he could and went back up the pitces the way he came. Meanwhile Ian had sat down to wait for Gwyn and waited and waited until he eventually gave up and walked back across the moor to GG. He was shocked to find someone had eaten all his biscuits and put a 'For Sale' sign up on his tent – Ed*]

The summer trips abroad were planned around two weeks in either Yugoslavia, based in Kamnik, or France based around Vaucluse. There was no plan to be able to do a multi venue holiday as they were both planned for the first two weeks in August. It was the Dump's 25th anniversary in 1988 and as a special celebration the Dump warden arranged for a working weekend in September. [*There was also a Plot night celebration – Ed*]

One of our members let the team down by having to be rescued from Pen-y-ghent Pot in October which he had entered without a permit, there are details of how this could have occurred but the club was severely reprimanded by the CNCC for this incident. The member identified at the time was Bob Bialek. The Wales trip in November reported some great caving being done, especially by Bob Bialek and his friend Mike Cooper [Not a member] they did a 17.5 hour trip around Daren Cilau, they got into the distant extensions and passed the fabled campsites including the 'Restaurant at the end of the Universe'. They got beyond the Machu Picchu boulder chokes before getting tired and feeling a long way from home so they set off back.

The Christmas Dinner was arranged for the 10[Th] December at the Golden Lion in Settle, it was in the form of a medieval banquet with a compulsory beach party fancy dress theme. There was a picture show arranged for a cold winter's night in January, where the members could bring along their slides of the old days and share the nostalgia. There was another arranged in the Star Hotel in April with specifically foreign caving slides being shown. Slides from the earliest club expeditions to France and Italy were shown to a receptive audience. The Annual General Meeting and Annual Dinner were held at the Long Ashes Hotel in Threshfield on the 11th of February.

This was the age of bolting, some people wanted to fix their own bolts at the top of every pitch which led to 'bolt rash' and many of them were unsafe and in the wrong places. It was a very unsatisfactory time, which allowed a spot of commercialisation to creep in. The normal Yorkshire cavers at the time were debating if the Elliott Red Bolts were, in fact, the right way and there were many discussions about the right and wrong ways to permanently rig a system. Ignoring the liability issues there were obviously great advantages to having permanent bolt belays which would never decay in the best positions with no rope rubbing points. Sadly Elliott's bolts were none of those things and the more cynical would even claim their purpose was financial to promote his guide books. Some people even attacked and removed Red bolts in protest but that damaged and changed the caves and was generally considered vandalism. All the debate and strong feelings eventually led to the introduction of the resin fixed Stainless steel hangers we still see today.

The Annual expedition in 1989 was getting bigger every week; there were some divers and cavers going to Yugoslavia to continue work with the local caving club. There was a group heading for Annecy to visit the classic Diau system and the Tanne de Bel Espoir with a view to the classic through trip. A third group was going to investigate the Trou de Glaz and Guiers Mort systems in the Chartreuse

area. Finally, there was a group heading for the Vercors and the Bourne Gorge to tackle some of the great cave systems in the area. There was also a trip to Tignes or Miribel with flights and all in accommodation in a ski hut for 18 people in the last week of January 1990, all for just £259 each. It's interesting to think back just a few years earlier when the club was just tentatively venturing abroad for the first expeditions to caves much bigger than anything in the UK, the second Chourum trip defined much of the way we do things on caving holidays these days. Though it has to be pointed out that foreign expeditions are clearly not for all members and a significant percentage of BPC members have never been on a foreign expedition.

The 1989 Christmas Dinner was held on the 9th December at the Golden Lion in Settle. The newsletter said it was a compulsory fancy dress theme of Father Christmas; or rather that was what it said in Colin Gates' newsletter everyone else's said the compulsory dress code was a dark cloaked hooded phantom with a face like a skull. This was the description of the figure in Colin's dream that stopped him going down the Tanne de Bel Espoir in the summer. Colin's mistake was telling all the team, as we gathered at the entrance, about the ghostly apparition with it's outstretched hand pointing at Colin saying "don't go down" with some implied threat of dying if he did. The assembled mass, all dressed accordingly, were waiting at the bottom of the stairs in the Brass Cat for the moment when Colin and Pauline came downstairs in their father and mother Christmas costumes to be greeted by a hundred hooded phantoms pointing and moaning warnings about going downstairs. We clearly don't get out enough.

The club funded a memorial bench to the memory of Keith Asquith, who was killed in a motorbike accident after attending a committee meeting in Bradford on the 8th March 1960. After twenty nine years the bench, which was solidly built from oak, fell apart due to weather and vandalism. In 1989 the club replaced it with a teak bench and a new brass plate which had a wider message than just referring to Keith. It reads "In memory of past members and friends of the Bradford Pothole Club who will not pass this way again 1989". [*It is not known what happened to the original brass plate? The replacement teak bench collapsed under the weight of weather and vandalism in 2019, it lasted very slightly longer than the oak bench, a repair was carried out by Ian Wilkinson but we may need to consider our options on this prime site outside Ingleborough Cave – Ed]*

The now annual President's Meet was held as a camping meet in Deepdale in June 1989. There were caving trips and walks organised as well as Buckden Show on the Saturday. A barbeque and Gaping Gill beer tent completed the weekend. An unfortunate exchange took place in Caves and Caving Magazine in August in 1989. A couple of cavers complained that the BPC, and, presumably by implication, the CPC, don't escort people around GG when we operate the winch meets. This was suggested to be the only solution to the graffiti and name carving vandalism in Sand Caverns. The reply was sent by Jim Abbott, as chairman at the time, and he dismissed the possibility of such a scheme and suggested that education would be a better solution to this widespread problem. There was no reply.

We lost two of our oldest members in 1989, Fred Ackroyd who joined in 1937 and Milton Shackleton who was one of our founder members. The caving in the later part of 1989 was as great as ever, though the caves of the UK were, I suppose, losing their challenge a little. One trip however brought a whole new challenge, a Death's Head/Big Meanie exchange trip was arranged for November and Brian Rhodes drove Sharon Kelly and Mick Riley to the fell as the Death's Head team, and he showed Mick and Sharon which rock he had hidden his car keys under in case they came out early. When they reached the bottom of the big pitch, Mick did indeed decide he was going back out the way he had come in and prussiked out. Brian had no worries as he knew Mick would put the keys back under the rock. However, it took a lot longer to get out of Big Meanie than it took to get out via Death's Head and Brian and Sharon eventually got out into a freezing wind on the fell. By the time they reached the car Brian's hands were frozen, Mick had obviously got a lift back with the other team so Brian went to the rock for the keys only to find Mick had left his own car keys under the rock not Brian's. We nearly lost two more of our members that night.

SECTION 1.7 – 1990'S

Virtually all of our 'end of year' social obligations were crammed into the weekend of February 3rd 1990, at the Plough Inn at Wigglesworth. The Annual General Meeting, the Annual Dinner as well as the Annual Photographic competition, which had to be squeezed in as we had run out of time at the Christmas Dinner. The AGM informed us that the district council had decided it was time to do away with dustbins and gave us bin liners to leave out every week. [*I wonder what would happen to them? - Ed*] The tackle secretary reported to the AGM that some ropes had been damaged by melting and it was assumed that the overheating was caused by abseiling too fast on dry rope, a warning followed in the newsletter.

It was announced that there was to be a combined social event at the Golden Lion in Horton, both the BPC and the CPC membership were invited, there was to be a buffet and a band. Almost as rare was the publication of the BPC Bulletin Volume 6, Number 7, not that it said that on the cover, or inside for that matter. The club also announced it had permission to organise a trip to the Gouffre Berger in August 1992, which gave everyone over two years to find an excuse.

As suspected the club now had to build a cat, fox, badger and dog proof shelter for the bin liners that the council had supplied instead of using the dustbins, it was finished in the April of 1990. The tackle store and library were on the move at the Dump in the hope of expanding both facilities. The kitchen and bedrooms were also repainted with lots of help from the members. [*Not so much from Sharon Kelly, who literally fell asleep while painting – Ed*] The Jeff Money studio was finished and bookings were being taken for Christmas 1990 and the main stairs in the Dump were moved in September to comply with fire regulations. Sadly, once again the club suffered from a spate of thefts from the Dump, not only member's equipment and clothes were taken but those of visiting clubs as well. Even now it is hard to know how to tackle this problem.

The dream venue was arranged for the Digger's Dinner in 1990, it started with a tour of Theakston's Brewery in the afternoon then on to Howstean Gorge Cafe for an evening meal a little more up market than pie and peas. They also sold beer, lager and wine etc and to finish camping to

avoid driving, what a day. Christmas Dinner 1990 was arranged for 22nd December at the Bridge Hotel in Ingleton.

The now well established President's Meet was under the control, for the second year, of the second President to run such events – John Clarke. The 1990 event was based in Horton in Ribblesdale and took the form of a triathlon, there was a walk, a cycle ride and a caving trip, a certificate and badge were presented to those that completed all three events. There followed a Barbeque at the Dump with beer of course.

There appeared to be only one plan for foreign caving in 1990 and that was a diving trip to Yugoslavia. To at least make an effort to claim some foreign caving in 1990 Derek Castleden took on organising a 'weekend trip to France'. [*From an original idea by somebody else I should point out – Ed*] The trip was a flying visit to Thorens Gliere in September and then on to the Parmilan Plateau and a through trip down the 3 Beta [β] and out through the Diau system. Threatening heavy rain modified the plan to a down and out of the 3β system, we descended down to Salle Rhomboedres and the lower canals, but water was pouring in from several places by this time and a long prussik out was made.

There was an interesting first in September when a Lakes Walk was officially described as a Bird Watching meet in Eskdale, it is not clear how many birds were seen as it was noted that Sharon Kelly wore the loudest possible colours and apparently talked loudly all the time. As New Year arrived we were given a present of £100 by an appreciative and anonymous old member, he enjoys the newsletters and was very impressed that the committee restored the bench outside Ingleborough Cave.

The 1991 Annual General Meeting and Annual Dinner were held at the Plough in Wigglesworth on February the 2nd and was the occasion of the Presidential Rap where John Clarke, blacked up with a woolly hat on, sang a rap song of his own creation and contrived to mention every member in the club. He didn't even get close to naming all those in the room let alone the 150 other members that weren't there to witness this musical atrocity, it was Rap with a silent C but great fun. This event was also the first time the Member of the Year award was presented. It was made by Frank Croll from the remains of the original Jib, of Jib Tunnel fame, which rotted and collapsed down into main chamber in 1988 after 92 years. He sawed a piece off and left it to dry out for a year or so then had the award, and the little ones, machined up. Frank Presented it to Brian Smith as the first Member of the Year, the idea being that the next recipient is decided by past winners, this obviously would take a few years to get going properly. There was 'entertainment' later in the form of a spoof of a famous TV quiz [*The Generation Game starring Bruce Forsyth*] where contestants were lined up for ritual public humiliation in front of the drunken mob, sadly no longer a feature of BPC events.

There was a Pen-y-ghent Pot trip with a difference in June, the club had volunteered to adopt the entrance of this classic pothole, which meant when it fell in we had to fix it. The trip, led by John Davey, involved a guest with a four wheel drive vehicle carrying half a ton of materials, scaffolding, boards, picks spades and bars etc as far as he could get up the lane. The workforce walked in a lot less time up from the Dump. After much boulder wrestling and scaffolding, and even a bit of landscaping, the surface features of the shaft were restored. There was still work that could be done at the bottom of the entrance climb but that would be for another day.

In July, after a series of inspections by Ian Wilkinson and Frank Croll, the Dump's roof was to be removed and have much of the timber replaced before it could be returned to its rightful place. The dreaded woodworm and various beetles had taken up residency and done their best to eat the roof timbers. This was a major task that the members were not going to get involved with. A contractor was paid nearly £10,000 to do the work, but the members had to prepare the Dump beforehand and clean up afterwards. The garage was cleared of rubbish and unwanted items to make room so we could use it as a dormitory for a couple of months. As part of the job involved taking down all the upstairs ceilings the members were warned that a lot of mess would be made and we were to operate a rolling clear up down stairs. The main problem was the money of course, we didn't have £10,000 and even if we had a successful GG and everyone paid their subs on time we were still a little light. So for the first time since October 1967 the committee was forced to consider taking out a loan to complete what was obviously essential work on our greatest asset. A mock auction was arranged for October as well as increased subs and Dump fees and the need for a dreaded loan was narrowly avoided. [*Though the committee did arrange overdraft facilities and a loan agreement in principle, should it be required during the following months, until we were clear of our cash flow problems – Ed*]

The 1991 President's Meet was an indulgence of nostalgia by John Clarke; his idea was for everyone to dress up as 1930's cavers and walk to Alum Pot from the Dump and then descend the pot still dressed in ganzies with felt hats and carbide lamps. For some inexplicable reason he suggested that the ladies wore long Victorian dresses. [*This was strange for several reasons, firstly the 1930's cavers were only very rarely accompanied by women on the walks and even more rarely underground and on none of the occasions that they did were they wearing Victorian fancy dress. In 1991 some of our hard cavers were women; could you imagine Sharon Kelly, for instance, dressed as Florence Nightingale, laddering Alum Pot? – Ed*]

The foreign expedition in 1991 was to the Chartreuse region of France, meeting at the St Pierre de Chartreuse camp site in August.

The Mock Auction in October was aimed at raising funds for the new roof on the Dump. There have been several of these events over the years and they must rate as the most hilarious night's entertainment known to man. On this occasion we had a framed pair of Sharon Kelly's caving knickers sold for £26 [*That's £48.88 in 2019 money – Ed*] and a set of hand knitted willy warmers, part worn blow up dolls and a fan heater that turned out to be a slide projector on Sunday morning. There was even some blind telephone bidding when the landlord of the Golden Lion was bidding for a rotovator over the phone. It all had to stop for a while when he ran out of coins for the phone but he rang back after raiding the till and secured the deal. There was a determination to make the event a financial success and it eventually raised over £800, which was all collected by lunchtime on Sunday. This, as it was stated at the time, was the BPC at its best. The 1991 Christmas Dinner was held at the Bridge Hotel in Ingleton on the 14th December and was followed by a ceididh with music by a Colonel Custards Country Dance Band.

1992 started with some great caving such as the trip down Nick Pot in February [*The parallel trip down Vulcan pitch didn't go so well as the 8mm bolt placements were largely unserviceable and the* rope for the big drop ended up being held by just one bolt, that knowledge put the Nick pot team off and the exchange was abandoned. That is except for Alan Millward who decided that when Sharon Kelly appeared along the crawl he would rather go down the big pitch on one bolt than de-tackle with Sharon! – Ed,] this was seen as a training meet for the two expeditions happening in 1992, Gouffre Berger in August and Albania in September. By anybody's standards that was an impressive summer meets list.

The AGM and Annual Dinner were held on February 29th but no record shows where they were held!

The Presidents meet happened to fall on the 4th July and the incumbent social secretary decided to have an American and/or independence themed day. The events were centred on Pen-y-ghent which we were invited to venture under, over, and around during the day with a barbeque at the dump afterwards.

The club expedition to the Gouffre Berger involved twenty three members and families setting up camp at La Moliere. Over just a six day period the system was rigged and de-rigged after 14 members had been down to the first sump at -1122 Meters, a very successful trip. [It was rounded off with a classic moment from Ian Wilkinson, who was standing over the entrance pitch, coiling a rope at the end of the final de-tackling trip, and after a moment of reflection said "Well that's Gaping Gill over with for another year." You have to wonder sometimes – Ed]

The British Albanian Speleological Expedition - BASE [Named by Sara Spillett -Ed] comprised 13 members of the BPC and 9 members of the Derbyshire Caving Club. Since receiving permission to organise the expedition in late 1991 the Isolationist, Communist Regime had collapsed and elections held so it was a democratic state when we arrived. [That is true, but the state had been held under communist rule so long that only the very old could remember not living under the tyrannical rule of Enva Hoxha. They didn't know how to be democratic and the villages now had a communist leader and a democratic leader – Ed] There is a short, previously untold, story about the organisation of the expedition in section 2.

In October there was an article in the New Scientist with an alarming message about radon gas in our caves. Measurements had been taken and in certain caves [On certain days – Ed] it would be possible to be exposed to levels 800 times the legal limit for homes, this represented the highest radon measurement in a cave in the World. The 1985 Ionizing Radiation Regulations limit workers to a dose of 15 millisieverts a year. Such a dose increases the chance of contracting lung cancer by 0.05 per cent. This is about four times the chance of being killed in a car accident. With the levels detected in British caves a caver could pick up this dose in 13 hours. We worried about this for a few minutes.

Some classic trips were done in November; one of them was Rowten Pot, a long standing favourite of the BPC. The report was written up by leader Michael Riley who commented that he had only done this pot once before and he remembered seeing a garden gnome on a ledge and reported that it was not there on this occasion. He obviously didn't look in the front garden of the Dump very often as the gnome [Humphrey – Humphrey Boggart, had been liberated from Rowten by Bill Booth and myself – Ed] had taken up residence there for several months before his trip. It was subsequently stolen by unknown miscreants.

The 1992 Christmas Dinner was held at the Bridge Hotel in Ingleton on December 19th with a compulsory 1950's themed fancy dress, there were even some very elaborate drawings in the newsletter suggesting what to wear. There were a few notable moments at this event such as when the reincarnated Pink Tarts made their entrance down the stairs, the Teddy boys singing [Bradfordawaddyawaddy] and Ian Wilkinson, who wore a teddy boy quiff wig, was seen admiring his reflection at every opportunity like an aging Adonis, while inwardly crying over lost follicles. The Rock and Roll band members were taken by surprise by the sheer enthusiasm of the dancing and the demands to keep going. They eventually admitted defeat and accepted that they had failed to keep up with the BPC over 40's.

The AGM and Annual Dinner for 1993 were held on February 27th at the Watermill Inn, Pateley Bridge. Before we got stuck into Gaping Gill the club was volunteered, by Sharon Kelly, to participate in a charity event called the 1993 Horton "Green Label" Tri-Football Competition. This was a knockout competition involving local football teams put up by pubs, Young Farmers and apparently caving clubs. There were to be two local caving club teams but the Craven didn't even bother to turn up, so in a very confusing series of games with three five man teams kicking a ball about at the same time, it seems we lost. The 1993 Champions were the team from the Golden Lion.

The Gaping Gill Prelim meet had a big surprise waiting for the first man to abseil down main shaft, to connect the guide cable. He found an 18 feet tall steel missile in the main chamber. Upon closer examination, it became obvious that the constructers were no other than the Derbyshire Caving Club [Some of whom had come on the Albania expedition with us – Ed], though the reason for all their obvious effort still eludes me twenty five years later. It seems they wanted to provoke some sort of response and the missile was meant to be Thunderbird 3 [from the children's puppet series] as we had called the vehicles we used in Albania - Thunderbird 1, 2 & 3. It had obviously taken many people a long time and some serious engineering to construct. There was a hatch that opened and a model of Derek Castleden's head popped out accompanied with the sound of menacing laughter. Some people thought it should be left for the DCC to remove, others thought we could leave it in situ until detackle but Frank Croll would have none of that. He promptly removed all the safety ballast and pushed it over and tied it to the winch chair to have it hauled up the shaft. It was dumped unceremoniously on the fell somewhat crumpled and bent. It was later dumped in the Dump garden where the DCC carried out a stealth raid and liberated it back from whence it came. The June newsletter carried an anonymous three page cartoon strip depicting a possible back story, there was, of course, no response towards the DCC or about the cartoon [Which I thought was very good, but then I would – Ed]

July saw Geoff Thorndike's Presidential Meet with a five peaks walk [Completed by eight year old Helen Hopkins, who skipped back into the Dump as fresh as when she set off, I wonder if she could do that now? – Ed] There was a five tea shop cycle ride and a five caves trip to cover all preferences.

As a result of the hospitality shown by the Italian caving club on the return journey from Albania, a return visit was planned and a group of BPC did the Spluga Della Preta and a few other caves during their stay. Mountain biking was reaching its peak, of a predictably short life as a club sport, and 1993 saw another coast to coast mud fest being organised for the end of August. It took four days to follow the Anglo-Scottish border, though their support team insisted it could have been done in three days if it weren't for the time spent in pubs along the route. This was timed to be after the

Coast to the Dump walk organised by HRH Max Koval, the weather was against this trip and it suffered from a lot of rain. The walk carried a health warning regarding the sheer volume of beer likely to be consumed in the process. There was also an 'expedition' to climb Mont Blanc at the beginning of August; a small group were intending to spend a week in the area to allow for a weather window. A group of three made it to the top, but the remaining three failed offering a wide range of excuses from nose bleeds to falling Italians.

This year saw the loss of a well know Yorkshire cave feature, the annoying duck at the start of the valley entrance to the Kingsdale Master Cave. Mentioned in the guide book it was a memorable feature but the DCC was digging what became known as the 'Chunnel' and were making many trips into the system and basically got fed up with it. They discovered that by knocking down a small wall, in the chambers beyond, the level of standing water dropped and the duck drained. They never replaced it even when they set up a water jet system and had automatic digging seven days a week and hence made fewer visits to the site.

The Christmas Dinner was held at the Plough Inn, Wigglesworth on the 4th December with the now familiar compulsory Fancy Dress, the theme this year being 'your favourite or most admired or most feared' member of the club. [I went as me – Ed]

After a good trip down Rowten Pot in January 1994 we looked forward to the AGM and Annual Dinner being held at the Watermill, Pateley Bridge on February 26th. The expedition of 1994 was being planned to go to the High Tatra Mountains in the Czech Republic and Slovakia. This was to be a new area for the BPC to explore and good relations had been established with a local club who were to act as guides and hosts. An excellent trip with great caving, walking and cheap beer on offer, it departed at the end of July.

April witnessed an ill fated through trip from Large Pot to Rift Pot; half way through the contortions of the connection route, Des Crowley seriously injured his back. As the symptoms got worse, his ability to complete the trip unaided diminished and at the bottom of the big pitch out of Rift the team split into two. Alan Millward and Martin {Basher} Baines made a rapid exit to alert the CRO, [Well Alan did, poor Basher had trouble passing knots on the pitch and was overheating in his diving wetsuit, the CRO passed him on their way in – Ed] leaving Matt O'Connor and Peter Sykes to share body heat with Des until the rescue team arrived. Des was hauled up the pitch and assisted through the contortions out of Rift Pot by the assembled BPC and CRO teams. A BPC team recovered all the abandoned equipment the following day.

As if the excitement of the Large-Rift rescue was not enough we had another, more embarrassing, incident in Gingling Hole on 18th of June. Sharon Kelly, with a small team of young men, who were probably intimidated by her, jumped down what turned out to be a pitch and promptly found it almost impossible to reverse. Sharon and her young men, who were only obeying orders from their leader, spent fifteen hours struggling with the almost inevitable. They eventually emerged into the cold light of dawn to find the BPC and CRO had been mobilised and the Police were in attendance. One bad decision by Sharon had turned what is normally a routine trip into an unnecessarily difficult marathon. Apologies were made to the CRO and to the club members who had stayed up through the night.

Before the Slovakian trip was due to depart the club received some devastating news, on the 9th of July 1994, Trevor Kemp died in the Dismal Hill-Birkwith Cave sump. At 60 feet [18.3 M] long it had no major technical difficulties and Trevor had dived it before, to this day no real explanation has been given as to why he died with one empty tank and one full tank on that day. The coroner suggested that as both of his valves were right handed, he could have exhausted one tank and with zero visibility taken one gag out and put the same one back. [*Trevor would have had difficulties applying the thirds rule as only one tank had a contents gauge. – Ed*]

On a lighter note Gwyn Bryan used the national press to announce his excuse for not going caving whilst in Slovakia, he said he went walking instead as 'to go underground involved too many administrative problems'. This has been registered as Caving Excuse number 201, well done Gwyn.

For insurance purposes smoking in the Dump was restricted to the common room in August and the Jeff Money studio roof was declared watertight again but the interior decor was still in urgent need of restoration after an inundation.

The club at this time was successfully organising and running eight trips a month, a different hole every weekend day. This, compared to the old days, was a revelation as numbers were lower the trips subsequently easier. On top of these trips members were still organising private meets,

digging trips and walks and bike rides, the club was very active.

The 1994 Christmas Dinner was held at the Goat Gap Inn on December 17th with the customary fancy dress theme being the Wild West. The 1995 AGM and Annual Dinner were held at the Falcon Manor on the 25th of February. There was great talk at this time about recreating Édouard-Alfred Martel's (1859-1938) solo descent of GG main shaft on the 100th Anniversary of the original event on July 8th. Plans were made for Frank Croll to manufacture a rope ladder for the event and Sid Perou was going to film it for posterity. Andy Jackson was considered a near enough likeness to Édouard Martel [*who actually bore a close resemblance to Max Koval but Max wasn't going to ladder main shaft – Ed*], a French man who made the original full descent in 1895, and was therefore volunteered to spend hours dangling over main shaft [*not the same side of the shaft that Martel used – Ed*] As Martel had used candles to get a sense of scale and assist in his sketch survey of the chamber, our plan also included the lighting of candles, a 1000 of them in main chamber.

Few will remember the discovery of Chauvet cave by three French cavers in the Ardeche Gorge. The cave is a remarkably un-special cave with a large chamber. But what they found in the cave makes it a site of Global Scientific interest. The walls were adorned with cave art dated to at least 30,000 years BP, which is 15,000 years older than those at Lascaux cave. These are the oldest examples of art in the world, allowing our remote ancient ancestors to communicate directly with us today.

Permission for the summer expedition for 1995 had been arranged by Phillip Pendred so for the first time the BPC was off to the Complex de Pierre St Martin, appropriately, one of the co-ordinators was Martin Smith. The actual underground stuff was to be carried out in the five day window from July 31st to August 4th. Over the five days set aside for caving forty two members completed the through trip from Tete Sauvage to Salle Verna and out through the EDF tunnel. The thing most members will remember 1995 for is the appearance of the first BPC calendar [*for 1996 – Ed*], originally the idea of yours truly, I mentioned it to Ian Wilkinson over a beer at the Flying Horseshoe, he was chairman at the time, and he pushed it through committee and Ian Lloyd got the job of sorting it all out. What a good job he did as well, the format hasn't changed at all in the subsequent years. [*It was originally conceived as a six sided, stiff cardboard tube that would have a different picture on each side and was to be used as a desk tidy - Ed]*

The date and venue for the 1995 Christmas Dinner was December 16th at the Goat Gap Inn again with 'Way up North' as the fancy dress theme. The venue and date for the 1996 Annual General Meeting was held at the Crown in Hawes and the Annual Dinner was at the Fountains Hotel in Hawes both on the 24th February 1996. After the AGM Sid Perou showed the GG centenary film shot in July and John Robinson showed a slide sound sequence of the making of the film, great stuff.

There didn't appear to be any plans for a full club expedition in 1996 but a few families were planning to re-visit the Maritime Alps and Cuneo on the Franco-Italian border where the 1975 expedition to the Piaggia Bella was based. The group drove to the head of the Col de Tende where they got their mountain bikes off the car rack and donned their over sized rucksacks carrying all their clothes, food, camping and caving gear and rode for 10 miles up a narrow track to the Col de Seigneurs. They then stashed the bikes and walked for a further 3 hours to reach the Piaggia Bella entrance at 22:30 where they camped. The caving after that was relatively easy and straight forward, they got down to -1000 feet [305 M], where the pitches and water were encountered, before turning back. [*The average age of the caving team was 45 – Ed*] The rest of the holiday was spent walking the alpine routes and drinking lots of beer.

The 1996 Digger's Dinner was held in Dent at the George and Dragon on October 4th, various activities were undertaken over the course of the weekend; caving, digging, walking, mountain biking and ending on the Kendal climbing wall. The 1996 club Christmas Dinner was held at the Bridge Hotel in Ingleton on December 14th with a Mississipi Steamboat theme, to enhance the event a New Orleans jazz band played through the evening. The memorable costumes were John Robinson's Steamboat and Sharon Kelly made up as a very stereotypical, blacked up, 'big Momma.

The caving trips on the club meets card were still averaging 1-2 trips per weekend, often two trips on the same day, usually a 'senior' and a 'junior' meet. This was still quite a lot less club trips than a few years earlier. They were well attended and there was a strong element of training with our SRT facility at the Dump and well supported special SRT training meets arranged. The majority of caving trips were 'private' meets and digging was gaining

popularity again. The 1997 AGM and Annual Dinner were held at the Whoop Hall on March 1st.

A memorable event took place in February 1997 during the creation of BPC newsletter number 329, an article by Brian Rhodes, about a trip down Bull Pot, was sent to the editor, Brian Smith, by e-mail. This was the first time this had happened and the newsletter then went on to record that seven club members actually had e-mail addresses. Newsletter 329 also recorded the sad demise of Roy Taylor who had driven our gear up to and back from GG for many years. Predictably Newsletter 331 should be recognised as the first newsletter to be sent electronically, it went to Gerald Benn who had joined the rapidly growing list of e-mail account holders.

A Memorial Service at Coniston Church was held on June 24th 1997 commemorating the 30th Anniversary of the Mossdale tragedy. On a lighter note, there was no 'official' club expedition planned for 1997 but several groups were forming ideas involving travel to Europe. Bryan Schofield was again attending the International Cave Diving meet at the Doux de Coly and welcomed members to join him in the area if not the dives. Three families were intent on mountain biking in the Italian Dolomites and Sharon Kelly arranged a caving holiday to the Vercors.

The Digger's Dinner was held at the Punchbowl at Low Row again and was a relatively sophisticated affair when compared to its origins as a simple pie and peas for the diggers to celebrate their discoveries and exploits over the previous year. November's social event was a photographic evening where members brought along their slides from the previous year to share, have a laugh and drink beer. This led us to December the 13th and the Christmas Dinner which was held at the Goat Gap with a medieval fancy dress theme.

It is noted that there was an increase in walking trips around this time, the three peaks, Ben Nevis, Snowden and Scafell Pike in a twenty four hour period. This had been done a few times before and in 1997 it was again achieved in fine style on the longest day of the year. The coach that drove people from site to site was part of a transport/catering deal where the driver set up under cover eating for the entire party, though the tent wasn't needed on this occasion as the weather at each hill was beautiful. In September the annual, constitutional, walking meet was again run utilising a train for transport from Settle to Wennington where they walked to Lancaster station for the train back. In June 1998 there was a weekend of serious walking arranged which involved climbing every 3000'+ mountain in Wales. It was a 27 mile walk with 13,000 feet of ascent, but for the softies, it was split into two days.

Back at home the AGM at Whoop Hall on February 28th highlighted the massive renovation plans for the Dump, pages of suggestions affecting every room were published for members to peruse. The new stainless steel kitchen was part of these proposals and has shown what good planning and sensible investment can produce; we were keen to maintain our proud position of having the best caving hostel in the country. The 1998 AGM was saddened when it was announced that Peter Livesey had died, as an indication of his fame as a climber his death was recorded in both the Times and the Guardian newspapers. It was just a couple of months later in April that we heard of Bill Gott's death. He was a founder member of the Acton Speleological Club, which was formed in his greenhouse in 1933. A keen underground photographer Bill or 'Willie' Gott, was an active caver all through the formative years of the BPC.

Under advice from the BCRA the club adopted a policy whereby only members of the club can take part in the club's underground and above ground activities. As a result, 1998 saw the introduction of Temporary Membership status, brought about by bureaucrats, we could no longer take a friend or a member of another club on a trip without getting them to fill in a form and get them to pay a pound.

There was a mock Auction at the Dump on June 6th to raise funds for a young Peter Edwards who had been lucky enough to get a place on a BSES expedition to Greenland for the summer of 1998. The club through its amazing generosity raised a staggering £846 of which only £420 was needed for Pete's final payment. The difference, £426, was donated to the Bradford Millennium Scanner Appeal, another example of the great heart within the club. Peter kept his promise and arranged a well attended show of his slides taken on the expedition later in the year.

Gerald Benn's third Presidential Meet was held in Chapel le Dale on July the 4th 1998. The event followed a familiar format with a range of caves and walking carried out during the day and a barbeque and beer at the Dump in the evening.

The club holiday to the Tarn Gorge was a great family success with seven families camped at Pyreleau and a few members passing through on their bikes. The activities included rafting, biking, walking and a token caving trip to the Bramabiau of Martel fame.

The BCRA 'Hidden Earth' Conference was held in Southport and Andy Jackson collected four prizes in the photographic contests. He was competing against the country's best known cave photographers and was clearly up there with the best of them. The BPC was also well represented by Bryan Schofield and Dave Ryall who were both members of the 1998 International Cave Diving Expedition to the Doux de Coly. They gave a wonderful double act performance as they presented an audio visual slide show with the world's longest cave survey in a very well received presentation.

In October the newsletter proposed that for the Millennium Expedition we could organise a multi-activity adventure in Venezuela. There was a challenge within the invite to organise the first ever prussik back up the Angel Falls having previously abseiled down it. There was caving to be done, mountains to climb and canoeing the Orinoco on offer. The members were asked to call John Edwards if they were interested, twelve calls were received and John Duckworth helped with some planning that was done before a major hurricane devastated the north coast of the country. The country suffered complete collapse and foreign aid was required to overcome all of the problems and hardship. A few months after this event I contacted the authorities and enquired about the village we were planning to use as a base [St Luis], they replied 'we think we have found the village you mention but it will take us time to confirm this' we quietly dropped all expedition plans for Venezuela.

There was a very lucky escape from Diccan pot on 21st November 1998, a chap was down this very wet hole on what must have been the wettest day of the year, roads and caves were flooded throughout the Dales. The CRO had set up dams and were waiting to send down a 'snatch squad' before the inevitable dam failure. There were six BPC members along with Police, Ambulance men and scores of other people waiting to help as the ever changing circumstances allow. There were other groups of cavers waiting in their huts all over the Dales, just in case. The event ended with the casualty being snatched and hauled up the first pitch, he had been huddled in an alcove for seven hours, he was very lucky indeed. It has to be wondered if he was ever aware of the number of people who put themselves out and were consequently put in harms way, late on a Sunday night, just because he wanted to go down a notoriously flood prone cave on a rainy day.

The 1998 Christmas Dinner was held at the Bridge Hotel in Ingleton on the 12th December, the theme was 'The simple things in life' and was followed by a Hoe Down accompanied by a band called Witch Hazel. The 1999 Annual Dinner and AGM were held at the Plough at Lupton on the 27th February 1999.

The social calendar for 1999 was pretty well packed with 40th and 60th birthday celebrations at the Dump as well as pubs near the celebrator's houses. It has to be noted that the UK caving done by the club through 1999 was to a very high standard and as a result there were no incidents worthy of note. The clubs digging team was also busy forming and finding their pace, Dave Haigh was the nucleus and as digs closed down there was always another waiting in the wings. In 1999 they had Christmas Cracker and Project X on the go, by the end of the year they were both down to 30 feet deep and still going. Dave Haigh was awarded the member of the year for his work in the various digs.

The 1999 BCRA Conference again saw Andy Jackson winning prestigious awards for his photographs he took down Lechuguilla in New Mexico USA. Famous for its pristine formations the cave is also big, in 2019 it had reached 183 km of surveyed passage. Andy Haigh's photographic entry [Nice Helmet] showing Dave Ryall wearing nothing but a strategically placed helmet in GG main chamber was sadly over shadowed by a picture of two sheep shagging. The BPC contributed a lot to the Hidden Earth event and gained a lot of favourable comments and genuine interest from many people they did the reputation of the club no harm at all.

Many older members remember Reg Hainsworth as the co-founder of the CRO, who sadly passed away in 1999. The 1999 Christmas Dinner was held at the Bridge Hotel in Ingleton on the 11th December.There is no mention of a club foreign trip taking place in 1999 despite many suggestions made at the time.

Caving in Transylvania [Romania]
Caving in the Transvaal [S. Africa]
Caving in the Zagros Mountains [Iran]
Caving in Bhutan.

The above list is an extract from a document circulated in 1998/9 to try and nurture some interest in organising a big trip for the Millennium, no such interest was nurtured.

Early on Millennium eve there was activity at the Dump as people moved towards a celebration of the new Millennium. A group of fourteen members of the BPC crack digging team held a formal dinner down Fat Finger Pot in the afternoon. To say it was a formal dinner is a little understated, the chaps were wearing dinner suits and the chapesses were wearing ball gowns with long gloves and jewellery. Then there was Ragnor, who was wearing an off the shoulder Ra Ra dress with, apparently, matching underwear. After the opening addresses the three course meal was served which was followed by several prepared speeches. Needless to say alcohol featured very strongly in this truly surreal event and a good time was indeed had by all. They had to leave at a reasonable time to participate in the next celebratory event described below. [*Pictures from this hedonistic event were published in January's Descent magazine - Ed*]

There was a drinking session and meal organised at the Dump on New Year's Eve after which everyone had to walk up Pen-y-ghent before midnight where they were given some Famous Grouse to see the Millennium in. Fireworks were set off at the Dump when everyone was back from their drunken stagger up and down the hill.

SECTION 1.8 – 2000'S

Every new Millennium brings change, the arrival of the third Millennium brought the age of President Faulkner and the first newsletter of the 3rd Millennium had a full colour front page, radical times.

In April 2000 a social event with a difference took place at the School in Horton. A group of cavers and divers from the BPC, CPC, YSS and NPC got together and organised a social evening with local farmers and landowners to try and explain why cavers do what they do. Despite a disappointing turn out there were several Audio Visual presentations by Andy Jackson as well as talks by Scoff and members of the other clubs. We received great interest from some families and there was even talk of their kids coming caving and the family coming up to GG. There was a good feeling about the event which can only have done caving's public relations a good turn.

It was realised that GG2000 would mark the 50th Anniversary of the BPC winch, that was first erected at Whitsuntide in 1950 which means it was 50 years since first erected but that meant 2000 was the 51st meet. There was, however a further error in the plan as it would actually be the 52nd meet, as the Alum Pot meet in 1950 must surely count as a winch meet. To mark the 52nd winch meet a plan was made to descend Bar Pot wearing 1950's caving gear, there is some relevance in this plan as Bar Pot had only been dug out in 1949, the year before our first winch meet.

Re-enactments aside GG2000 was very wet indeed, but Dave Ryall managed to dive the Mill Hill sump and gain another 70 meters of passage, albeit cold, tight and full of water. The Fat Finger dig was a work in progress and now known as Ragnor's 'World of Shit Dig' it had a twenty foot shaft which had to have air pumped to the bottom as CO_2 concentrations were getting dangerously high.

July 1st was the date of Peter Faulkner's President's Meet, consisting of a tea table set up at KMC Valley Entrance for the revival of cavers abseiling the various entrances to emerge at Valley Entrance and passing cyclists. The main event was a barbeque at the Dump with beer laid on, a simple yet effective plan.

The location and digging of Hensler's Pot were well under way by GG2000. In the August there was a near miss when the survey team were caught by a 45 minute rain storm and resultant flash flood. The 'evacuate' call was given by Carole White just in time for the rest of the team to pass the rapidly rising duck and exit the flooding cave. A returning BPC Hurnell Moss team was stood at the entrance not fancying a look in; they assisted the end of the evacuation. A retreat was made to the tea tent at the CPC winch meet where they decided to call it a day. To add to the advances the diggers had made in Hensler's Pot, the club dig in Xmas Cracker fell away in August. This revealed a 60 pitch and a draughting boulder choked floor. The 2000 Digger's Dinner was held on the 7th of October at the Flying Horseshoes in Clapham, a place well known to the older members.

At this time another cave in the Dales was digging itself, there had been warnings of the Great Aven in KMC showing signs of collapse. Boulders had fallen and big ones were now hanging, apparently unsupported, mud was being washed out and the inevitable was likely to happen sooner rather than later. On a reconnaissance trip in September it was discovered that the big levitating boulders had dropped along with a huge amount of other rocks and mud and the floor at the top of Great Aven pitch had collapsed. The fallen debris had blocked Philosopher's Crawl and was very unstable and still moving; it now threatened to block the way through to the Master Cave. Pull through trips were not advised as there may be no way out of Great Aven by the time you got there and abseiling the now much longer Great Aven pitch was considered suicidal until things stabilised.

Not wanting the BPC diggers to take all the praise for discovering new cave a few BPC divers went on holiday to Spain, and visited a known sump called El Manadero in the summer of 2000. Described as being only 12M [40'] long before it becomes too tight and as they were camped literally two minutes away Bryan Schofield and Dave Ryall went for a look. To their surprise it was wide open if you are a Yorkshire diver and don't mind a bit of metal on rock noises. The passage went to 6M [20'] wide and 3M [10'] high and went and went. After 400M [1012'] and reaching -36.5M [120'] deep Matt McLaren managed to connect it to a lake in a nearby cave called Cueva del Lago. An impressive feat considering they were supposed to be mountain biking with the ladies.

In the October newsletter Frank Croll presented the case for the recent granting of Honorary Membership of the BPC to Alan Gill. We had granted Alan this status in recognition of his research work in the Polar Regions for the greater part of 32 years. He was also a member of the Wally Herbert team that in 1967/9 walked from Alaska to Spitsbergen via the North Pole a journey lasting 16 months and now recognised as the first team to walk to the North Pole, a feat never repeated. The leader of the expedition, Wally Herbert, was knighted for his achievement and described Alan as the most experienced Polar explorer in the World. He was reported to be delighted with his honorary BPC membership and considered it a great honour.

The Christmas Dinner in 2000 was held at the Bridge Hotel in Ingleton on the 16th of December followed by dancing to a live Rock and Roll band, a tradition now sadly abandoned.

The BPC 2001 social calendar started with the Annual Dinner and AGM which were held at the Plough in Wigglesworth on the 10th of February. Just a week later the caving community was devastated by the news that Foot and Mouth disease had again broken out in the UK. With over 2000 confirmed cases, 6 million animals were slaughtered to stop the spread of the disease and bring it under control [*15 times the number killed in the 1967/8 outbreak - Ed*] For most of the year the fells were closed and access to caving areas held under the strict rules of DEFRA. The Dump was closed until May when it opened for a week before closing again. The only caves in the Dales that were open were White Scar and Ingleborough, all rights of way were closed and all access to caves closed. Obviously the biggest loss was Gaping Gill, there was no winch meet in 2001.

The meets secretary, Simon Froude, was obviously busy trying to arrange trips into all the sites that remained open around the country such as Peak Cavern, Bagshawe Cavern and Carlswalk Caverns in Derbyshire but reports of 60 cavers' queuing to get into Peak didn't raise our hopes much. A programme of Quiz nights and social gatherings was arranged, on a rolling basis, to keep everyone informed. The new President' Dave Brook, held the President's meet at Ingleborough Cave on the 30th of June.

April brought more bad news for the club with the death of John Duckworth [Buzzy Bee] the club treasurer for many years; around 100 members were at his funeral on the 20th April. Grahame Mitchell, who joined the club in 1963 and caved with Pete Livesey, also passed in April; he kindly left the club a substantial legacy in his will.

A reasonable meets list was arranged for June and July with Milwr Tunnel on the 10th of June and Peak Cavern the following weekend. A weekend at Nent Head mines was held in July after the President's meet in Ingleborough and an Auction evening arranged for the 14th of July the proceeds of which were to support the publishing of the next club Bulletin. The Milwr Tunnel trip eventually had to be cancelled through insurance supplier bureaucracy by Welsh Water. Somewhat surprisingly the walking meet managed to go ahead, seventeen miles along the Lancaster Canal towpath, ending at Crookland's where a bus took them back to the Dump.

As the summer progressed more and more areas were re-opening, North Wales in the later part of July, Mendips in August and South Wales was accepting cavers again by September. October 6th saw the successful Digger's Dinner at the New Inn Clapham. Located there to allow people to visit the Xmas Cracker and Hensler's Pot digs that were going so well, before the coming to the event. By the November newsletter many fells were open again, but there was still no access to the Allotment, Fountains Fell, Ireby Fell, Leck Fell or Pen-y-ghent.

The closure of the fells meant a dig in Ingleborough Cave could have almost the undivided attention of the digging crews. Alyson and Dave Brook, with many occasional helpers, succeeded in digging the Time Tunnel through from the end of Long Gallery to connect with Cellar Gallery. This dig was first attempted by the Farrar's in 1838 but stalled very quickly and never got re-started. [*The workmen put to the task went on strike after 3M [10 feet] as conditions were not up to the standards required by USACT – The Union of Sewers and Cave Tunnellers, but, as it turned out, 63 years later it was fine for a 16 year old girl to dig it out. Was this because of her cruel father? - Ed*] Alyson found a tooth in the dig which later proved to be from a Woolley Rhinoceros and was about 17,000 years old.

The diggers were nearly caught out in Hensler's Pot, after successfully locating various features on the surface and dye testing the dig to the Hensler's

High Aven. There was a final task to widen a tight bit at the far end, this required some bang to be used. Unfortunately for Gerald Benn and Mark Slater the resultant fumes engulfed them and were denied their usual venting as a flood had raised the Duckworth Duck and shut off the outward airflow. A rescue bid from the surface by Bob Arkwright, Martin Smith, Dave Haigh and Carole White resulted in pushing a pumped air hose through the sump with instructions bellowed through the water to breathe from the pipe whilst diving the 2M [6.5 feet] sump. Both were saved and the CRO knew nothing about it. [*Another example of the unspoken bond that ties us all –Ed*]

The 2001 Christmas Dinner was held at the Fountains Hotel in Hawes on December the 15th with a traditional Xmas fancy dress theme. It had been a strange year, very little caving but a very close call saving two of our own and the loss of two others.

The New Year brought fresh hope of access opening up all over the Dales and at least one dig going 'big time'. The Annual dinner and AGM were again held at the Plough in Wigglesworth on February 9th 2002. With only 38 attendees and no contentious issues this meeting easily slipped from the collective memory.

For the first time in four years 2002 had an advertised club expedition/holiday, the objective was to be the Dent du Crolles System for the first week before moving on to the Vercors region for a second week of caving etc.

The excitement in the spring of 2002 was the growing anticipation of the return of the Gaping Gill winch meet. Cancelled the previous year due to Foot and Mouth restrictions, plans were developing for all manner of activities at GG2002. The most memorable event, however, turned out to be the GG Olympics [2002] where two very uneven teams competed through a series of challenges to assert dominance. Unfortunately for various reasons, skulduggery, ineptitude and alcohol, the outcome was unclear to the crowd of spectators who were also suffering from alcoholic abuse as well as laughter pains and poor vision through tears.

The Vercors expedition returned with tales of over enthusiasm by Mark Slater and Dennis Wray and the 14 hours wait for their subsequent rescue by the club. They were determined to do a through trip but couldn't be bothered to fully check the resurgence route was open. The team, not wanting

to commit to a pull through, decided to tackle the pitches but were short of tackle, Dennis and Mark decided to get the retreating team to drop the rope from the last pitch and they would pull through with that. Sadly the exit to the resurgence was sumped and they were stuck until enough people were sober enough to arrange a rescue. Terry Devaney, Simon Froude, Sharon Kelly and Carole White had stayed up all night as a result.

After Andy Jackson's success in the 2002 BCRA Conference Photographic Contest there was a BPC slide show arranged at the Golden Lion in Horton on the 16th November. [*Andy had won first prize for his colour print and 3rd prize for his black and white print. He also won the popular vote by conference attendees for his 'Kingsdale Master Cave in Flood' print.- Ed*] On the same night John Robinson showed his hilarious audio visual show "Ladies in Red (and one in yellow) and two in drag" which won first prize in the AV competition at the conference.

After due consideration, the committee published what they thought the Grahame Mitchell legacy should be spent on. A rebuild of the changing room and showers, creating a toilet and private shower upstairs in the workshop area, a full modernisation of the Geoff Money studio and to investigate the purchase of additional land. [*The intention being to have a small campsite and/or additional car parking – Ed*]

The 2002 Digger's Dinner was held on October 12th and Gerald Benn was presented with a unique trophy made to acknowledge his 48 years of successful cave digging. The 2002 Christmas Dinner was held on December 14th at the Fountains Hotel in Hawes, no further details are recorded.

The club was involved with another rescue in January 2003, Brian Simister [Ragnar] slipped on a grassy slope on the walk back from digging down Generator Pot. He heard the bones in his ankle break and attempts by his colleagues were soon abandoned when they realised the seriousness of the break. A callout was made and Ragner was taken to hospital to have nine bolts, a plate and a pin fitted. He was out of action for a long time after that.

The 2003 AGM and Annual Dinner were held at the Whoop Hall on February 8th, despite the January newsletter stating it was to be held both at the Whoop Hall in Kirkby Lonsdale and at the Plough at Wigglesworth, very confusing. Some great photographic caving trips were done around this time with regular examples of the pictures appearing in the newsletters. A real interest was kindled by the efforts of the club photographers especially when they got some great results just using disposable cameras.

In April we held another Mock Auction at the Dump as a fundraiser to assist Emma Bennett to help restore an orphanage in Mexico, a great charitable cause which the club members are usually only too willing to very generously help. The event raised £480. Sadly, we heard of the passing of Jack McGhee in April of 2003, no more magic shows with 'the rings' at the Annual Dinners, he is still talked about and missed.

The 2003 President's meet was arranged to be held at Howstean Gorge near Lofthouse. There was caving with a guide to show the new extensions connecting Manchester Hole to Goyden and the new entrance to the system. The guide was Nigel Spoors, a member of the successful Black Sheep Diggers who found the extensions. This was followed by a BBQ in our own camping field at Studfold Farm.

The 2003 club expedition was to the Felix Trombe in the Pyrenees, it was more accurate to say the trip was to Reseau de la Coume D'Hyouernedo, but nobody knew what that was. The trip was in August, as usual, and camping was arranged in the town of Mauvezin de Prat.

As a sign of the times our BPC e-group had to be changed and became members only from April 2003. Gaping Gill arrived with a new operating procedure [also a sign of the times – Ed] and a BBC film crew arriving mid week to shoot a section of 'British Isles Through Time'. The celebrity [or talent as they liked to be called in the trade – Ed] was no other than professional Yorkshireman Alan Titchmarsh. The main subject was the geology of which he had some knowledge and a genuine interest. When it eventually aired on TV the club was credited as The Bradford Porthole Club, was it worth all the effort?

The digging team, after four years of hard work, finally connected Hensler's Pot to Gaping Gill at 1pm on 29th March 2003, and the first through trip was done by the digging team, and a few interlopers, on 11th May the same year. Not resting on their laurels the digging team were off again in pursuit of Parkinson's Aven. They were digging a rewarding cave for several weeks before Gerald Benn pointed out that the inward draughting rift passage was heading straight for Big Benn Aven in

Hensler's Pot. A smoke test was arranged and sure enough the new dig went straight to their old dig 100 meters away.

It was with surprise that the club heard of the resignation of two of the committee members in August, well one of them at least. Brian Rhodes felt he was no longer sufficiently involved with the club's activities to justify being the chairman. Mark Slater also resigned his position on the committee for an altogether different, undisclosed, reason. The next newsletter confirmed that Jenny Midwinter had also resigned from the committee for the same, undisclosed, reason. Simply following the trend Ruth Castleden later resigned from the committee and Ian Lloyd resigned as our CNCC representative.

The 2003 Digger's Dinner was held on the 11th October at the Helwith Bridge at the personal request of the digging team. The annual slide show was held the following Saturday night at the Golden Lion in Horton. Three members, Dave Ryall, Carole White and Bob Arkwright went on an intensive explosives training weekend in the Mendips. Overseen by the Police [Making sure the attendees were all responsible citizens– Ed] the course was run by a representative from the Institute of Explosives Engineers, all went well until after a night in the 'Hunters' Carole threw up in front of the presiding Police officers.

The 2003 Christmas Dinner was held at the Wensleydale Creameries in Hawes on the 13th December and the 2004 AGM and Annual Dinner were held at the Plough at Wigglesworth on the 7th of February. We were saddened to hear that Roy Dixon had died; he was a long standing BPC member and one of the founding members of the White Rose CPC.

Before the AGM there was discord over the restoration of the Geoff Money studio, the work being carried out by members was not understood or appreciated by the wider membership. There were suggestions that there had been no consultation despite several calls for involvement and invitations to study the plan. It ended with a few heated words and John Davey withdrew his involvement with further work on the studio. There then followed a series of votes on what facilities the studio should have, to say the results were confusing is an understatement. It started with a big majority voting against there being a water supply to the building. That was followed by almost the same majority voting not to have a toilet but then the same majority voted to have a sink! The annual subs were increased from £17 to £22 largely due to a massive increase in the cost of the BCA insurance.

It was with great sadness we read in the April newsletter that Arnold Patchett had died, aged ninety five.

There was a significant dive by Dave Ryall in Deep Well during GG04, he pushed the previous work done by Ian Lloyd and due to the logistics involved suggested a three day dive camp would be required to further extend this site.

Derek Castleden arranged his President's Meet at the Hill Inn during the first weekend of July with traditional BBQ set up at the pub's campsite on the Saturday night with our beer at £1 a pint. [*How did the Hill Inn agree to this? – Ed*] As it turned out the weather, rain and high winds, was so bad the meet was abandoned the event was transferred to the comfort of the Dump. Despite the weather there was a good turnout of 78 members and a great time had by all.

On the 31st July 2004 the club's digging team managed to connect Corky's Pot to Gaping Gill. The new entrance ends with a spectacular 110 foot [33.5 M] pitch landing in Mud Hall. This was the second new entrance to Gaping Gill found by the club's diggers in just over twelve months.

By September we were trying to sell the winch engine [*An old petrol engine we ended up scrapping it a year later though it was salvaged by an engine enthusiast who restored it back to new condition and it now travels around to engine shows and is displayed on a trolley – Ed*] We were also obliged, at this time, to begin considering what would be required to get full disabled access at the Dump. At the same time we were getting unwanted visits at the Dump and decided to fit a dummy video camera to try and deter what we thought were neighbours kids. The situation escalated when we had a dead rabbit pushed through the letter box. At this point words were had with the parents by Ragnar.

September 25th saw the Dump hosting another of the World famous Auction nights, this event was organised as one of a series to raise funds to support Brian Smith and his increasing mobility issues. The club raised £1000 in the auction and a similar amount was required to cover the cost of the various other supported projects. The 2004 BCRA Conference [Hidden Earth] was held on the 1st – 3rd of October in Kendal and the club had

another great stand and featured a lot in the allocation of prizes. Allyson Brook won the fastest ladies' ladder climb while Gerald Benn won the men's. Dave Haigh won the best club T-shirts award, Andy Jackson won the best monochrome print award and Dave Ryall won the best AV award, the Premier Trophy for five prints and the Speleo Technics prize. Martin Baines and Sid Perou won the best video film award with a joint effort.

The Annual Slide show was held on 20th November and heralded a new era, in a packed three and a half hours there were many audio visual shows including original exploration in China, sport caving in the Pyrenees and the Dales, some nostalgic scenes and GG03 all made by club members. There was an AV [*as we call it –Ed*] featuring and called the 'Bradford Girls' which had some disturbing images that somewhat changed the tone of the evening. There followed a couple of DVDs made by Martin Baines and Sid Perou which went down very well. The 'new era' is clearly the digital age as there was not one slide shown, presumably as there were none taken.

The Balls digging team didn't let any dust settle and moved straight from the success of Corky's Pot to start digging out a shake hole near the top of Vindication Pot in Corky's. It was known as Klondyke Pot and got off to a slow start requiring a structural roof building to support things when they had to tunnel horizontally before getting under the roof of the cave. The last midweek trip before Christmas held a great surprise, they found a bottle of single malt whiskey had been left for them by the CPC digging team, what a nice Xmas present.

The Christmas Dinner was held at the Fountains Hotel in Hawes on December 18th with a fancy dress theme of 'cartoons'. The club had clearly matured in attitude over the previous 19 years as the committee was informed that the compressor that caused so much division in 1986 was now knackered and needed replacing. The committee, without resorting to and EGM or even an AGM discussion, sanctioned the purchase of a second hand one that cost £650. Not so much as a murmur from the naysayers on this occasion. The AGM and Annual Dinner were arranged for the 26th February at The Whoop Hall in Kirkby Lonsdale.

The March newsletter brought news of the passing of our longest serving Honorary Member, Ruth Benn, the mother of Alan and Gerald. She was made an honorary member after giving many years of secretarial help producing the BPC newsletters.

Though not a caver she has made several descents on the GG winch, her last being at the age of 89! We also heard of the tragic passing of Colin Pryer despite several of the club's divers being involved in his attempted rescue from Low Birkwith Cave. He was not a member, but he was a friend of the club [He was a member of the YSS – Ed] he was often seen caving and diving with our members, indeed his partner is a member of the BPC.

Terry Devaney called for all interested members to contact him if they wanted to spend the summer caving in the Chartreuse and Vercors regions of France in the summer of 2005. Dave Haigh was the new President in 2005 and organised his Presidential meet for the 2nd July. Based in a quarry outside Ingleton there was a whole range of activities planned before the BBQ back at the Dump. In blazing sunshine the event was a great success with seventy members and families trying all the activities on offer.

The digging team was in the news again in September, their Pay Sank dig went, and they were soon exploring the legendary lost P5 stream through chokes and chambers at the bottom of the entrance pitch. A film was made by Martin Baines, during the second pushing trip with actual real time discovery being captured, which went on to win 2nd prize at the BCRA Hidden Earth Video Competition.

The walking meet was led by Neil Dyson and held in September with a walk from Dufton near Appleby to Garrigill near Alston. Starting up an escarpment the majority of the walk was gently downhill to the finish 13 miles away. The club was, yet again, successful at the BCRA Hidden Earth Conference. The club stand won first prize, for the third year running. John Robinson won first prize in the AV competition and Dave Ryall won the best colour print and the cave life category not to mention the Speleo Technics prize with a picture of Laura Hoggarth in Peak Cavern.

On the down side there were a number of incidents of vandalism at the Dump and the committee tried to gather data to isolate who was responsible. The Digger's Dinner was held at The Station Inn at Ribblesdale on 8th of October and the Plot night celebrations were held at the Dump as usual but it caused big problems with our neighbour who has a large number of Birds of Prey. The committee banned all fireworks at the Dump over Christmas and New Year.

The digging team was celebrating yet again in November when Pay Sank was connected to Grange Rigg Pot. The dig dropped into a passage that had been discovered by Pete Livesey and a BPC team in 1962. After scaling the waterfalls at the bottom of Grange Rigg and free climbing the 22 meters up into Pinnacle Hall they were stopped by a boulder choke at the end of a walking size passage. The Pay Sank dig broke into the handsome passage just 3 meters below the choke. The first through trip was carried out on the 26th of November and found the far reaches of Grange Rigg can now be reached in half an hour of easy caving.

The 2005 Christmas Dinner was held at the Fountains Hotel in Hawes on December 17th with a fancy dress theme of 'Come Dancing'.

To celebrate his 50th birthday Bryan Schofield arranged to complete a sponsored Triathlon on January 6th 2006. He did a 50km bike ride around Ingleborough, he abseiled and prussiked 50 meters down Alum Pot and dived 500 meters into Joint Hole, he raised a total of £1200. With tragic irony, it was all in aid of the Cancer Research and McMillan Nurses.

The 2006 AGM and Annual Dinner were arranged for the 25th February at the Falcon Manor Hotel in Settle. John Schofield was elected as the new President.

The 2006 summer expedition was planned for the first two weeks in August with a trip to Pierre St Martin in the French Pyrenees. Twenty members went and whilst there they did several climbs, some via ferrata routes, a couple of canyons, climbed Pic d'Anie, did several mountain walks, bottomed Couey Lodge and Gouffre Abre Mort then fourteen, in three separate groups, completed the Tete Sauvage – EDF Tunnel through trip. A great time was had by all.

A small group of six BPC members did a charity cycle ride from Land's End to John O Groats and raised an amazing £10,000 for Cancer Bacup.

Once again the BPC featured prominently in the 2006 BCRA's Hidden Earth Conference in Staffordshire. We won the best stand, again, and Dave Ryall won the Cave Life category and the Speleo Technics Prize. Alyson Brook won the ladies ladder climb, John Robinson won the best AV and Tim Sullivan won the free draw for a ticket to the 2007 Hidden Earth Conference.

The 2006 Digger's Dinner was held at The Helwith Bridge on October 7th just a few weeks before the re-located Plot night celebrations. The committee decided that respecting our next door neighbour's predicament, with the wild bird resettlement scheme he operates, would benefit the club's local standing far more than disregarding his request for no fireworks to be let off at the Dump. Dave Ryall was attempting to organise regular social events at the Dump on the Saturday nights after club meets. This was aimed at getting the members to use the Dump more as a social venue rather than just somewhere to meet up before a caving trip. The first of these events was held on February 3rd and was a hilarious success. Given the ingredients – a Dave Ryall caving quiz, two big pans of chilli con carni, frozen cheesecake and beer how could it not be a great success?

The club caving at this time was a wonder of organisation; no other club could produce a twelve month meets list every January. This was due to the requirements of our BPC Calendar which, of course, published the meets on the appropriate days. Most trips happened as per the list, it would require a serious unforeseen circumstance to force a deviation from the master plan. Most trips were organised and permit acquired by the meets secretary who at this time was Terry Devaney. The implication being that most of the trip reports were also written by Terry, several newsletters only had trip reports written by Terry, not that that was a bad thing necessarily, but his Hurnell Moss Pot report appeared in both the October newsletter and again in the December edition. He really shouldn't have gone to such lengths to see if people were reading his reports. But as there was no public humiliation or mocking, related to this event, published in subsequent newsletters we must assume that nobody noticed!

The 2006 Christmas Dinner was held at the Wheatsheaf Inn in Ingleton on December 9th, with an 'Elaborate Headgear' themed fancy dress.

The January 2007 Derbyshire meet went very well underground, the team's problems started when they surfaced from a Maskhill – Oxlow exchange trip, it had gone dark and was snowing heavily. They were staying at the TSG hut in Castleton but with inappropriate cars they struggled to move at all in the thickening snow. They eventually got two cars towed by a 'green-laner' up to the Wanted Inn where the Police gave four of them a lift back to the top of Winnat's Pass. The team then donned their oversuits and trudged down the Winnats to Castleton. That is except the team at this point

decided that Fay Hartley [*aged 60 at the time*] should walk alone, overnight, back to her house in Glossop, some ten miles away, it was -1°C and falling, snowing heavily, no traffic around at all and she had just done a 5 hour caving trip! This appears, to say the least, to be a questionable decision; the fact that she did it shows the stoic character of this hard lady.

The 2007 Annual General Meeting and Annual Dinner were held at the Falcon Manor on February 24th and the main subject of discussion was the proposal to change the status of the club into a Community Amateur Sports Club [CASC] The benefits of such a status are linked to taxation while the disadvantage of this status is there is only one way out of it and that involves giving all the club assets to charity and dissolving the BPC.

Frank Croll finished making six thirty feet long and one ten foot long stainless steel ladders to be left underground for long periods in digs. They were reported to be fantastic and sadly became the last gift to the club made by Frank who did so much for the club for over 50 years.

Although no decision could be made at the 2007 AGM lengthy discussions were held on the contentious issue of the annual Plot night celebration and the emerging conflict with our neighbour and his raptors. The decision was eventually made by the committee and no further Plot night celebrations, involving fireworks, have taken place at the Dump. The 2007 event was a successful 'fire only' event with sixty members present and no complaints from the neighbour, or the birds. This reflects the mature attitude of the club regarding its reputation within the community it lives amongst.

March brought some very sad news that long term member Frank Croll had passed away after being taken ill while skiing in France.

There was looming bad news for all caving clubs with the potential sale of Bull Pot Farm from under the tenancy of the RRCPC. Caving clubs were asked if they could help the RRCPC to purchase the farm, in response the BPC, realising the benefits of the farm being owned by a caving club, organised a mock auction on the 21st April to raise funds towards the acquisition of the farm.

The 2007 President's meet was arranged by John Schofield for Saturday the 30th June. Events included caving in Kingsdale, swimming and diving in Ingleton and cycling and walking all around the

Dales. Sadly, it rained for most of the day and the event suffered as a result.

July 1st was the day that smoking in public places was banned by law in the UK and subsequently the committee banned all smoking within any of the club buildings as of that date. The summer club trip was to the Ordessa National Park in the Spanish Pyrenees. It was planned as a flexible affair with no particular objectives arranged. There were several great pull through trips in the park as well as all the other activities the members got up to in a normal holiday. The main caving activity was the Anonera System with many entrances, a pull through trip was investigated and completed several times before the attempt that ended in a 'rescue' which is best described by Mick Riley in section 2 of this book.

The 2007 summer expedition was to the French Pyrenees and with twenty six members present was a great success. The Hidden Earth BCRA Conference was held in Tewskesbury in 2007. There was a large BPC team in support but sadly, as excellent as it was, the stand failed to win the top prize. [We were getting used to winning that - Ed] There was a call straight away for ideas for the 2008 Hidden Earth stand as it would to be our 75th Anniversary year.

The 2007 Christmas Dinner was held at the Fountains Hotel in Hawes on December 8th with a fancy dress theme of the 'Rocky Horror Show'. It was later in the month, just before New Year, that a rapid flood in Lower Long Churn claimed two experienced caver's lives. This news certainly affected several trips planned by the BPC in the following months, they called off some trips due to the flood risk and in their newsletter reports the leaders refer to the deaths at Alum.

The 2008 Annual General Meeting [the 75th] and Annual Dinner were held at the Falcon Manor Hotel in Settle on February 23rd. All the digging talk at the dinner was speculation about the condition of the digs after the recent earthquake that shook the Dales.

The 2008 summer expedition was again planned to be the Spanish Pyrenees, but not the same area as the 2007 trip by going east of the Ordessa National Park to where the Sistema Alba could be tackled with its eight hour through trip. This expedition was eventually called off due to lack of interest.

On May 11th 2008 we lost our last founder member, Vincent Shackleton, aged 95. It was particularly bad luck as six months later we had our 75th anniversary celebrations and it would have been special if we could have invited Vincent and seen him at the club's 75th anniversary dinner.

The planning for Gaping Gill 2008 was complete, we had even informed NATO of our presence on the hill, but the plan did not cater for the forces of nature we were about to witness. During the prelim meet we had a memorable storm pass through at around 4pm. The downpour caused serious flooding within half an hour and efforts had to be taken, now in glorious sunshine, to prevent the gantry and engine being swept down the shaft. The dam had been completely overwhelmed and a foot of water was washing over the engine platform and the gantry was bent by the sheer force of water. These events rightly caused the club to consider the ramifications of such a flood trapping members of the public down GG after destroying, or at least disabling, the winch system. A rescue dump was subsequently installed in a blue barrel at the end of South Passage with appropriate equipment and written advice. This GG was also noteworthy as the first one to witness the laser scanning of the main chamber being carried out. This project subsequently continued for over ten years surveying the entire Gaping Gill/Ingleborough Cave system. Sadly GG08 was marred by several of the member's camper vans being broken into whilst parked in Ernie's field.

At a discussion after the Gaping Gill meet we had concerns over the new Marlow rope we were using. Its surface glazed very easily, the glazing made for a fast descent, which, in turn, increased the amount of glazing, a viscious, and potentially dangerous, circle.

The post Gaping Gill committee meeting, as usual, discussed the clubs donations to the CRO etc. However, this year we had been asked by UWFRA to consider an alternative to the usual donation. They wondered if rather than the club donating cash, could Dave Brook make them a rope washer?

The President's Meet was held at Usha Gap campsite near Muker in Swaledale on the 5/6th July. As John Robinson had organised a photo opportunistic trip down the local lead mines and the members who were mining enthusiasts were available as guides. The weather was not kind and the inspirational use of a large gazebo really saved the day, and evening.

The 2008 Hidden Earth Conference was claimed, by the organisers, to have been the biggest ever with over 1000 delegate days attending. The BPC again won many prizes including best club stand which was taken down carefully as it was to be re-used at the BPC 75th in November.

The 75th Anniversary Dinner was held at the Stirk House Hotel in Gisburn on November 1st with after dinner entertainment by Mooncoyn, a Ceilidh/Concert Folk Rock Band [?] In excess of a 150 members and guests [*We had about 230 members at this time – Ed*] had a great time helped by two films and an AV running on a loop.

The Plot night celebrations at the Dump were cancelled, permanently, in 2008 as tensions again rose over the previouys year's fire only do. The Christmas Dinner was held at the Fountain's Hotel in Hawes on December 6th with the customary fancy dress theme called 'Carry On'.

The 2009 Annual General Meeting and Annual Dinner were held at the Plough Inn in Wigglesworth on February 21st. As uneventful a day as can be remembered, it was as if it were a prelude to an extremely uneventful year. 2009 must go down as a boring year, the caving was recorded as being as active as any other year but the only thing worthy of a mention at GG was that we had new dam sheets. The monotony of the year's events was temporarily broken in August when we heard the terrible news of Dennis Wray dying from his injuries after a hang gliding accident.

The 2009 electric picture show was enjoyed by the attendees in November and December brought the year end social event. This year the Christmas Dinner was held at the Fountain Hotel in Hawes on December 12th, the fancy dress theme was – Magic.

[With only the fixed social events of the BPC year being worthy of mention amongst some dutifully written meets reports the club year was, at this time, seeming to become a repeating cycle of social events. Starting with the AGM and Annual Dinner, through GG to President's meet and Digger's Dinner then Hidden Earth and back to the Xmas dinner. Nothing happens, in earlier days things were changing, new techniques and clothing had a direct effect on caving. When I started for instance, it was the second golden age; we had recently acquired wetsuits, electron ladders and synthetic ropes. Doing the old wet giants suddenly became easier and caves like Pen-y-ghent were now taking four hours instead of four days and there was a subsequent numbers explosion. The

caving was extraordinary again and was worthy of reporting. Then the same thing happened again with the introduction of SRT, and the extraordinary became the norm again as the deep giants were now vanquished and done with relatively small teams with light weight tackle and the tight depths of Black Shiver, for instance, were now done in a few hours by two people rather than an army of tackle bearers. We had entered the third golden age where caving was exciting again as old challenges were once again dismissed. Now the dry suit technology and modern travel enabled us to tackle deep foreign holes and we did the 'third deepest in the world' rather than the third deepest in Yorkshire. But there lies the seed of our latest problem, we could only go to the big foreign caves when we were on holiday so we were bursting with technical capability but only doing UK caves, over and over again. In the last millennium things used to go wrong and we had exciting times, largely through ineptitude, the odd rescue and people doing daft things. This is no longer the case; young members now train on climbing walls and take the whole business much more seriously than before. The membership used to drink incredible amounts of beer with the accompanying tales of gross misbehaviour and resultant tales to tell. The club drinking peaked in the early '80's* and is now not really abnormal, except that the younger element still drink, in moderation, except in the ale tent. This, I am led to believe is not the norm of today's youth, social media and the phone camera has stifled a lot of poor behaviour as a bad looking picture seen by the boss is a threat no previous generation has faced. As a result of this and many more reasons the club's UK caving, as reported in the newsletters, for the last few years had hardly been of global interest. We await the next innovation that could re-invigorate once again the BPC into ta a 4th golden age – Ed]

[* This statement is a generalisation of course, some individuals continue excessive consumption to this day. The 'peak' of BPC drinking can probably be traced to a weekend at the Burnmoor Inn, at Boot in Eskdale, always known as 'Josie's', where the drunken antics of the BPC caused the club to be banned. The pub was akin to a Wild West bar with climbers crawling around the walls, etc. The saying was "anything goes at Josie's" where the landlady used to catch lit cigarettes behind the bar in between her somewhat over fulsome breasts. To ban anyone was unheard of, but watching the revelry of the BPC and seeing various bodily fluids being passed around and drunk was too much, even for Josie. – Ed]

SECTION 1.9 – 2010'S

Not many members attended the 2010 AGM, only 28 members made the effort. The Annual Dinner was also held at Stirk House in Gisburn in the evening of February 20th. The low attendance to the AGM caused the committee to consider ways of increasing future turnouts. The new committee were also asked to investigate a smell in the member's room at the Dump. It was never announced what the source of the smell was but it went away. A five trip, under sixteen's, meets list was published in March of this year which heralded a new willingness in the club to cater for the younger element.

Also in March there was a trip to Croesor-Rhosydd with 14 on the trip they used a zipline to cross a big lake, at the other side they had to use an inflatable boat to cross another deep pool, one at a time. They used a rusty old chain hanging from the roof to lower themselves into the boat, young Josh Marshall was the last to cross. The team shouted him to use the chain but 'whatever happens don't let go of the chain' and drop into the boat. The bolt holding the heavy chain came out of the roof and Josh fell to shouts of 'let go of the chain' to avoid the chain dragging him to the bottom of the pool.

During GG 2010 the digging team connected OBJ to Flood Entrance Pot creating the 21st entrance to GG. Later that year we became involved in an inter-club dig on Leck Fell which became Shuttleworth Pot. In the course of two months of frantic digging with a large team the entrance was opened up and then finished off with an entrance tube and landscaping to Natural England's satisfaction.

At the end of December 2010 we immediately moved on to do a similar job at The Cupcake which became another entrance to Notts II. The connection was made at the end of January but digging continued on the other side of the shaft in search of the continuation of the passage and this continued sporadically until September 2011 without conclusion. The entrance to The Cupcake was similarly fitted with a tube and landscaped. In the course of these two digs large numbers of bones were recovered especially from The Cupcake where complete aurochs and huge wild boar skeletons were found.

Natural England designated Ingleborough an SSSI before the 2010 GG meet and as a result, we had to have their blessing as well as permission from the state to run the winch meet. Obtaining this blessing involved walking the route with their wild flower expert who asked that some repair work be carried out to erosion of the track. The 2010 GG meet was described as the best ever; well organised, good weather and all went to plan. One of the meet leaders [Rachel Storry] was called on to make an executive decision when she was asked if ferrets can go down on the winch, she said, quite rightly, NO!

In July the President's meet involved caving in Diccan Pot, KMC, Shrapnel Pot, Sell gill holes, and Providence-Dow all in the same day. Followed by butties and cake at the Dump and a BBQ with ample beer in the evening and through until the early hours.

Vincent Cox, son of Russell, started his 18,000 mile, around the World, cycle ride in 2010. In due course he not only completed it but the Guinness book of records has recognised him as the fastest person to do so. But of course 2010 is best remembered for the third BPC Gouffre Berger trip in the first two weeks of August. There were regular climbing wall SRT practices as well at this time in training for the summer expedition. The members were subjected to active fitness and skill assessments prior to departure to France. Several members were subsequently given the hard word and were allocated surface tasks. After some suspect weather we eventually got twelve members to the bottom out of the sixty members and families that made the journey. Young Josh Marshall accomplished a trip down the Berger with his dad and went way beyond Hall of the Thirteen only to be almost trapped by flood water. The club, realising, the developing situation sent a strong 2 man team down to assist in extracting them from the system they were both assisted out under their own steam. During GG10 Josh, at 14 years of age, went on to be our youngest member to do Dihedral, though he did get a bit stuck to a deviation.

The 2010 Digger's Dinner was held on October 2nd at the Bunk House in Clapham with over fifty people attending.

An article appeared in the Chepstow Free Press decrying the number of young people jumping in the River Wye as it was pointed out to be a very dangerous pastime. The final paragraph was "SARA (Severn Area Rescue Association) was called out on Monday evening after a man was spotted swimming underneath the bridge. He got himself out of the water and SARA stood down at 10-40pm".

The man in question was BPC member Jan Karvik who was indulging in his frequent Summer pastime of going for a swim from his back garden which is on the banks of the Wye. He has been doing this for about 20 years. Knowing the current is extremely strong he carries this out around high tide when the water is slack.

According to Jan the SARA chap on the bridge shouted out "What's your name?"
Jan demanded, "Why do you want to know?"
SARA chap said "We are looking for a 16 year old girl"
Jan's reply was "Do I look like a F*****g 16 year old girl?

It was a tremendous shock to all in the club when it was announced that Colin Davenport [Corky] had died. He was a fixture at all GG meets and a great personality and a good laugh, he is deeply missed by all who knew him.

The Electric Picture Show on November 20th had no less than nineteen AV presentations covering a wide range of subjects from fourteen contributors with Pozo Azul from Scoff, Berger 2010 by Roger Saxton, a tribute to corky by his wife Christine [Duchess] with the winner being called 'a year in the life of Andy' by Andy Hainsworth. With so much happening at the EPS it is sometimes difficult to remember this is not the annual photo competition and just a bit of fun. We should, perhaps, have some awards relating to the EPS as so much work is involved.

The 2010 Xmas Dinner was held on December 11th at the Falcon manor, the compulsory fancy dress theme was fairy tales. Only 45 people attended this function which again alarmed the committee and raised the question of how to improve the attendance to this informal function. The committee asked in a subsequent newsletter for suggestions as to why we get 45 members at the Christmas Dinner whilst we get over a hundred attendees at the Electric Picture Show. There were

several obvious differences between the EPS and the Xmas Dinner, firstly the EPS was free, accommodation was at the dump and the EPS was a good laugh and great entertainment, none of which is necessarily true for the Xmas dinner.

Attendance was understandably high for the 2011 Annual General Meeting on February 26th at Crooklands Hotel. There was a proposal to turn the club into a mutual society to limit the liability of the club and individuals within it in the case of a third party liability claim against it. We had BCA insurance, but that only covered up to £2 million, whereas a realistic figure at the time would be at least £5M if not £10M. As one of the UK caving clubs with large annual public events could we risk a massive claim against us? The debate was mainly a Q&A with the people involved with organising the set up. The final decision was to be taken at an Emergency General Meeting in April.

It was suggested that the club's 2012 annual expedition/holiday be organised to take place in the French Pyrenees with Felix Tromme, Henne Mort and PSM as possible caving objectives. This was eventually replaced with a club holiday in the Bauges area of France. In the UK the rain was relentless, so much so that lots of the BPC planned trips were called off due to the risk of drowning. The rain was causing Notts pot entrance to show the initial signs of collapse and the CNCC advised to cancel all trips until it was, or became, safe again.

The Emergency General Meeting on April 2nd was well attended, but after absorbing the facts as explained, that if we became a mutual society we could never revert back to being a club without first dissolving the club and its assets, the proposal was still passed unanimously.

The CNCC was getting nervous about potential access restrictions on Leck and Casterton whose owners were both getting annoyed due to cavers wandering over the fells quite often just to visit Shuttleworth Pot, without a permit.

Presidents meet on July 2nd was based around the Dump making it a much less elaborate affair than those in previous years but it was still really enjoyed and the afternoon sandwiches and cakes were woven into the walking, cycling and caving plans for the day. The evening BBQ and beer was sure to be a success as it remains at the heart of the BPC's social instincts.

The 2011 annual expedition/holiday was to the French Pyrenees and Resau Felix Trombe in particular. It was a very successful trip with many great trips into the system and plenty of other activities going on in the surrounding area.

During the CPC Winch Meet 2011 Jeremy Storry noticed a newly collapsed shakehole in Clapham Bottoms and thus began The Pot With No Name (TPWNN) dig – no one could come up with a good name so this was used as a temporary measure and it's stuck! Between September 2011 and early January 2012 a shaft was sunk through boulder clay [2 shafts actually] until bedrock was reached and access was gained to a small chamber with no obvious way out save sinking a shaft in the floor at the far end. The whole place was fairly unstable and efforts then went into stabilising the shaft and installing a tube before landscaping the shakehole back to its original state. This was done during GG 2012 and now just needed the lid and surround to finish the job. Also during GG12 the entrance to Christmas Pot was stabilised and a tube installed.

The trip to Ogof Llyn Parc [Pool Park Mine] down a 100+m man made shaft on an old CPC winch was last done by the BPC in 1986. Which means the concerns at the time of going down on an 'old' CPC winch were know amplified as the winch must now be 25 years older than it was then.

In March and then again in July 2011 we embarked upon another inter-club dig, again in Notts II. The long crawly passage of Inlet 5 had broken into a large, old phreatic passage, which may well be an older version of the main streamway. Surveying showed that one branch was heading directly for a choked inlet (6.5 & ¾) in the main streamway with possibly only about 30m between the two ends. At the end of July we finally made the breakthrough and there is now a quick, easy way into the Inlet 5 passages which have served to protect the formations along the original entrance passage. A bit of digging was done at the upstream end but it was horrendously muddy and although we had a small breakthrough the general consensus of the pensioner diggers was that life was too short for such squalor and generously left it for a younger generation of diggers. Flushed with success we were immediately directed downstream to Inlet 8. This became a much longer term dig which, unlike 6.5¾, had no certainty about where it was going. The club and the 'Green Men' digging team in particular suffered a great loss when Stu Ingham died in September 2011.

The 2011 Digger's Dinner was held in the Clapham Bunkhouse on Oct 1st and was a great evening, as it usually is. There was talk about the 2012 summer

expedition as Carole White and Martin Smith had suggested that they could arrange a camp in the Bauges area, between the Chartreuse and Vercors, in France. As they lived within two hours drive of the area they offered to tour the area and get the caving information and select an appropriate campsite. The date was set for August 11th – 25th 2012.

The Electric Picture Show was still growing from strength to strength with 18 presenters showing a total of 21 audio visual presentations. There was plenty of beer flowing, possibly too much for Max Koval who fell face down into George Perfect's horse trough. Amidst all the laughing nobody initially realised he couldn't get from under the water and was indeed drowning, fortunately Jekyl pulled him out just in time.

The club nearly lost at least one member down Foul Pot in November 2011, Steph Dwyer and Ben Wright went on an evening trip when flood water started threatening the pair. They began their retreat but Ben approached a tight section the wrong way and got stuck, very stuck. After Steph managed to re-enter the rift headfirst and eventually cut the leg off his oversuit they realised that he was very stuck indeed. Steph had no choice at this point but to lie about the rising water level and retreat out of the rift leaving Ben to release his leg on his own. He managed to reach some bits of wood that had washed into the cave and using some rocks and his knowledge of Archimedes principles of leverage he eventually managed to force his leg out of the jam. In the nick of time they escaped the rising water which was threatening their airspace and they made it to the surface after a tense hour of struggle.

The drive at the Dump had been re-engineered with a block of cast concrete that was designed to prevent road flood water entering the drive and beyond. This involved a ridge on the road side acting as a dam wall. Derek Castleden had to do a clearance test to ensure that car sumps would not be damaged when crossing it at a reasonable speed. During the assessment it was realised that flooding was not a problem as long as a drainage ditch on Brackenbottom Lane didn't get blocked. It was arranged that the club would organise annual drain clearing teams to avoid the risk of flooding at the dump, the first such mission was on Sunday 11th December 2011.

The rope washer in the changing room was refurbished by persons unknown around New Year 2012, it was understandable as I made it sometime around 1990. Later in the spring we had the fuel shortages due to the petrol tanker driver's strike in March 2012. People didn't have the fuel to travel and Dump dwelling suffered accordingly. Not requiring petrol Andy Jackson and Dave Dixon ran the 61 mile Fellsman Run in foul weather and still achieved respectable times [*average age 38½*] The 2012 Annual Dinner and AGM were attended by 91 members on the 3rd February. The funeral of Farmer [Raymond Stoyles] was attended by 71 members and friends from the caving community. The ceremony was conducted by John Robinson and Derek Castleden and was thought to be particularly well done and appropriate.

In March Alf Hurworth thanked the club for bestowing him with Life membership in recognition of his involvement in the club over many years.

There was a masked ball held in the GG beer tent during GG2012. And the President's Meet was held at the Dump on July 7th with over sixty members and friends attending the now traditional sandwiches and cakes available in the afternoon and a BBQ and beer in the evening, always a winning formula. The multi discipline event had to be modified at short notice by President Raymond Lee who changed the caving and walk back to the Dump from Kingsdale to the Hill Inn as the weather was not the best.

The August expedition in 2012 was to the Chartreuse rather than the Pyrenees as suggested previously and members had several trips into the Trou du Glaz, Guiers Mort, Annette and Chevalier cave systems. Though a subsequent trip with John Gardner was successful, the initial through trip from Annette Chevalier to the Trou de Glaz had to be abandoned as the entrance was dangerously unstable. There were also cycling trips, walking, canyoning and some did a few via ferrata's.

We nearly missed Hidden Earth 2012 as of the committee meeting on September 3rd the club was not going to build a stand at all. But after a couple of phone calls John Robinson secured floor space and the team went on to win the Best Club Stand with the prize of a weekend for 10 persons at Penwyllt, the SWCC hut and a free survey of OFD, plus two family tickets to Dan Yr Ogof. Aly Brook won the Women's 10m ladder climb [an

incredible 22 seconds], Martin Baines won the Delegates Choice for the Photo Salon for his Mud Hall Photo. Mandy Fu, won several prizes including some Bed nights at the Dump for the fastest mixed doubles in the Speleo Olympics, women's SRT Assault course and Closed Loop surveying. Chuck Holder and partner came as runner up for the Closed Loop survey. The club was also represented well by all its activities; digging, exploration, diving, GG winch meet, cave conservation, historically, photos, video and just participation. The BPC were part of several of the talks over the weekend as well as in the stewarding of the event, in the AV team and the admin team. Chris Jewell created the Opening AV Presentation which featured the GG winch as well and won the Video Salon Prize. Sid Perou's two films on Eli Simpson and the Formation of the BSA were very well received by the audience and will provide a centrepiece for the British Caving Archive. The BPC was recognised as a major force within British Caving at these events, a reputation only acquired after years of brilliant effort by many members of the club.

The librarian commented in the July committee meeting that Members of the Club have been using the library for inappropriate, intimate, behaviour.

October 6th 2012 witnessed the BPC Digger's Dinner at the Helwith Bridge Inn and the Christmas Dinner was held on December 8th at the Golden Lion in Horton in Ribblesdale with no major or memorable events.

The Annual General Meeting was arranged at Stirk House in Gisburn for Feb 16th 2013, with the Annual Dinner in the evening, which was another great social event, brilliantly organised by the social secretary. 2013 was a celebration year for the BPC as it was 50 years since we bought the Dump and a display of old and new photographs of the Dump were put up at the dump. The weather was not typical for spring the rain was relentless, flooding was common and many trips were cancelled or redirected to other less flood prone venues. The boulders in County pot were noted to be moving and in the far reaches of Daren Cilau there was a roof collapse after yet more significant heavy rain. It was during this period in April 2013 that Bob Leakey's death was announced.

The Pot with No Name and Clapham Bottoms had their caps fitted by the digging team and Natural England. They had plastic tubes and lids installed, then backfilled with rock and concrete. They were then landscaped to prevent frost damage to thinly bedded scar limestone below the top soil.

The committee responded to an insurance conundrum by removing the requirement to attend three club meets before applying for membership. This decision, along with the one to remove the need for all new applications to be accompanied by a passport type photograph, was doomed to fail. [*It lasted just over five years before Gerald Benn raised concerns over the number of abstentions when probationary associates were being voted on [Nov 2018] The conclusion was that they weren't getting to know the committee, to cut a long story short, it was agreed to restore the three trip requirement. No further comment was made regarding the insurance issue – Ed*]

The 2013 Digger's dinner had over eighty people attending at the New Inn Clapham on Oct 5th. The Xmas dinner was at the Wheatsheaf Inn Ingleton where eighty members and friends attended, the fancy dress theme was 'around the world'?

The 2014 Annual General Meeting and Annual Dinner were held on February 22nd at Crooklands with over a hundred people attending. It was suggested at the time to organise the 2014 summer expedition to the Chartreuse area again after the success in 2012. It took place on August 2nd to the 16th later that year.

March brought the very sad news that Brian Smith had passed away after a long and upsetting illness. He will be remembered for his enthusiasm for caving and his work developing safe SRT in the UK by leading the systematic testing of ropes.

The fells have been subject to 'gripping' since the end of WW2 in an attempt to establish a faster water runoff time and subsequently create a dryer fell, this was to facilitate better conditions for grazing sheep. The fells are now under Higher Stewardship Level management, which means fewer sheep per acre and grip filling has started. After several years with exceptional wet periods recently *[no doubt a result of global warming and the resulting climate change – Ed]* the fells were beginning to change. By 2014 grip filling work had already made the fells noticeably wetter and the cotton grass on the fell put on the best display in living memory. The grip filling, theoretically, should allow the fell to hold the surge of water after heavy rain and give cavers more time to escape any subsequent flood as well as, hopefully, seeing more plant varieties flowering in future.

The BPC Digger's Dinner 2014 was on October 4th at the Clapham Bunk House or Beer Emporium and was another great social event which was quickly followed by the Electric Picture Show on November 7th also at the Clapham Bunkhouse. Some members were involved with the restoration of the entrance to Providence Pot which had been significantly modified by floods. With its isolated location the logistics of transporting heavy tools and materials as well as accommodation for the volunteers were serious issues. The work took five days, with many people working long hours, but the entrance should now be protected from future damaging floods.

The 2014 Christmas Dinner was held at the Fountain Hotel in Hawes on Dec 6th and was the usual happy event. It was shortly after the Christmas dinner that the club was informed of the death of Mike Boon, a colourful character who caved with the BPC through the sixties before moving to Canada. He is famous for his work in Castlegaurd Cave in Canada and the exploration of Mossdale Caverns. He wrote two books, the first moved cave divers to bottled air and side mounting of the bottles, the other described his involvement in the famous rescue of Polish caver Josef Kuber from San Augustin in Mexico [1972]

The club has always been aware of its responsibilities in the local community, we bring many tourist pounds to the local area with our Gaping Gill winch meet in May and our increasing presence all year round helps stimulate the local economy, especially the pubs. We sponsor many local causes and in 2014 we bought shares in the Clapham Community Village Store.

There was concern in 2015 about CNCC access arrangements when it turned out that there were still a few members who go caving on Leck Fell and Easegill without permits but then post details about their trip on social media sites. At the time access to these areas was still restricted by the landowners and permits were still required. These events made negotiations, attempting to gain better access, with landowners more difficult.

Just before the 2015 Annual General Meeting it was announced that Geoff Thorndike, a long standing member and past President of the club had died. This news was quickly followed by the sad news of John Thompson's death. John drew all of the architect's drawings for the conversion of the Dump in 1963.

The Committee decided that even after a very unsuccessful experiment in 1985, the Annual General Meeting would be held on a different day from the Annual Dinner. The motivation was different; in 1985 the problem was alcohol and its disruptive influence on the meeting. In 2015 the reason was to free up Saturday for the young, active cavers to get out before the meal in the evening. So on Friday 27th February 2015 the meeting was held at the school in Horton. Only forty three members attended the meeting which was even less than the year before, when forty nine members attended. The Annual Dinner was held the day after on Saturday 28th at Crooklands where Martyn Farr was the guest speaker.

The club had a request from Tim Allen, he was asking if he could fly a drone around GG main chamber with a 3D scanner attached to it. The club considered it but Kevin Dixon objected strongly and resigned from the committee in protest.

John Peter Farrar, one of the Ingleborough estate trustees, had moved back to the estate and was set to take a keen interest in its management. The BPC offered him honorary membership which he accepted and he was subsequently presented with a certificate to prove it.

In July 2015 we heard of the sad death of Ernie Coulthard who had driven so many trailer loads up and down Ingleborough in support of our Gaping Gill meet over the years.

The 2015 summer expeditions went to several places, the first being La Chapelle en Vercors on 1st–15th August during which thirty two members and families took part in a wide range of activities, there were several trips in the Grotte De Gournier, Scialet Micheliere, Grotte Favot, Bournilion, Gour Fumant and Trou Qui Souffle. They also did the top and bottom sections of the Ecouge canyon, the via ferrata above the Col de Rousset, plus lots of cycling and walking. They all had a great time enjoying the hot sunny weather most of the time making good use of the swimming pool and drinking the campsite bar dry on more than one occasion.

The second 2015 holiday/expedition was to Slovenia, a small mixed group of ten members and families for the first week, dropping to six the second week journeyed to the small village of Laze near Postojna in Slovenia. Speleo Camp was their base, run by a local caver called Frenk, who was useful for local information. They enjoyed a mixture of tourist trips to the beach, Lake Bled, Boveck and Ljubljana. Activity days of Rafting, canyoning and walking in the north, 'Go Ape' type activities for kids big and small an hour's drive away. The caving was a mixture of self-led trips once they had received their 'cave licences' by completing; Logartcek, Mackovica, Stota Jama,

Jama za Teglovk, Najdena Jama, Vranja Jama and Skednena Jama.

It was soon discovered that the guidebooks are very sketchy as to the precise location or rigging of many trips! Unfortunately to complete any river cave trips local guides had to be used, at considerable expense, we still visited Planinska Jama and Krizna Jama. This was a brief trip to a new area with a member of Dudley Pothole Club joining the team.

A few BPC members [Rob Middleton, Hannah Moulton and Phil Walker] joined the annual Treviso expedition in Northern Spain. They helped form a thirteen strong team visiting the Eastern Massif mountain range; these expeditions are a continuation of nearly 40 years of exploration in the area, originally undertaken by Lancaster University Speleological Society (LUSS) and latterly the South Wales Caving Club (SWCC).

The ultimate goal of the expeditions has been to try and find a way through the mountain from the deep cave systems at the top through to the major resurgence, Cueva del Agua (Cueva del Nacimiento), creating a potential 1550m+ deep through trip. The past few expeditions have concentrated in Cueva del Agua pushing a series of steep ramps and climbs at the end of the cave. The remoteness of the leads requires multiple days camping underground by small teams and the 2015 expedition over 2 weeks made successful gains in the area. Over 1km of new cave was discovered and explored in 2015. A new traverse and climb high above the current limit of exploration re-discovered the powerful draft in the cave and what appears to be the main way on into the cave. Multiple leads were left in the area for next year's trip. Additionally, a huge new sump was discovered while exploring some pitches down from the main leads.

'Belgian Caving Days', a speleo conference similar to our Hidden Earth, kindly sent the BPC an invite via Matt Maclaren. The event was held at Mozet on September 18-20th 2015. But as Hidden Earth 2015 was arranged for September 25-27th it is thought nobody, except possibly Matt, went.

Christine Benn's second President's meet was held at the Dump, the weather was good and everyone sorted something to do before heading back to the Dump for tea and cakes in the afternoon. Some then managed a bike ride or short walk before the evening when a BBQ with lots of beer and sitting in the garden until the small hours.

The BPC caving reports were continually rolling into the newsletters and a lot of great caving was done, there were an increasing number of trips designed for members' children, who were themselves members. What was refreshing about these trips is that the children were not just accompanied by their parents there were some of our young, hard, single men happy to go along and make sure all was done very safely. As a result, we had some very young members accumulating considerable experience underground before they left primary school, and in at least one case before they were born. Prenatal caving does raise some questions, but there have been no problems in the germinal stage and the foetal stage is probably self limiting.

The 2015 BPC Electric Picture Show happened on November 7th with another amazing night witnessed by at least 90 members and friends. The Christmas Dinner was held at the Wheatsheaf In Ingleton on the 12th of December with a 'respectable' number attending.

January 2016 committee meeting had the first discussion about the future uses of the garage, it was determined that most felt it was not fit for purpose and a re-build was the only way forward. The process that is still on-going was started at that meeting and even if it all goes through the new building will not be built before this book is hopefully published.

The 2016 Annual General Meeting was held on February 27th at the Falcon Manor with the Annual Dinner at the same venue on the same day. It was disclosed at this time that Bernie's Cafe in Ingleton was to close its doors for the last time at the end of March 2016. Such nostalgic memories for some who can still remember the jukebox with a picture of the Bachelors behind the carousel and hairy bacon, with bones in it, for breakfast.

The on-going digital survey of GG by Kevin Dixon was very busy over the winch meet and several interesting areas were covered. The survey revealed a potential connection over the top of the Stream Passage Pot pitches and Leakey's Caverns as they are on the same fault line.

The Craven issued an open invite to the BPC to attend their Summer BBQ in Horton on the 11th of June 2016, some members accepted the kind offer but it is unclear how many members did. The President's meet was held on July 1st – 3rd and was

based in and around the Haggs Bank Hostel and campsite in Nentsberry.

The plan to run the 2016 annual expedition to the Chartreuse area was abandoned in April due to lack of support, people seemed to prefer the easier more family orientated holiday in 2016. The alternative venue became the club expedition and the club again went to the Jura mountains near the Swiss border. The club first went here in 1985 when certain members were involved in the Pesmes incident. The 2016 trip was to camp at the same campsite [le Chanet- Ornans] from July 30th to Aug 13th. It is thought that Le Chanet is still the only appropriate camp site for the whole caving area. A great time was had by all who attended. Several members went on other expeditions, Bryan Schofield went back to the Pozo Azul and Cat Moody went with the Borneo/China expeditions.

The 5th Eurospeleo Congress was being hosted by the UK in August 2016 and the CPC winch meet was a designated meet during the congress. The CPC asked/invited BPC members to camp and stay up at the hole for all or some of the winch meet. The event itself was staged at Dalesbridge and had 1300 delegates, 698 caving trips, 400 trips on the CPC winch, 400 km of prussiking, 110 lectures, 11 field trips, 800 meals served per day and 118 barrels of beer consumed. Ian Lloyd got the task of organising 30 clubs to tackle and detackle all the required Dales caves. This was done with 6000 meters of donated Gold Spanset rope which was given to the clubs that did the rigging and de-rigging. Fred Rattray ran a EuroSpeleo communications field trip and gave demonstrations of the 7Mhz radio comms he and Jimmy had been trialling in the Dales. The BPC stand was set up and at least 51 members were seen at the event, all things considered, it was a massive organisational task but very well done and well worth it. The BPC featured very much in the organisation and running of the event and this can only serve the club well in the future.

The annual walking meet was from New Biggin on Lune to Appleby, a good turnout enjoyed a great day on the fells. The 2016 Digger's Dinner was held on October 1st at the Clapham Bunkhouse with a great time and lots of beer.

October was supposed to witness a joint working party with BPC and CPC members repairing ruts and track damage from tractors on the GG access routes up to the hole. There was beer and food arranged for after work was finished. However for unknown reasons the event was delayed until the

New Year when all the ground was frozen and the task was much more difficult.

Christmas Dinner 2016 was held on 10th December at the Royal Oak in Settle with a fancy dress theme of Pirates. Chris Robinson's fancy dress turned out to be a pirate's galleon with working cannon that fired tennis balls, excellent fun. The 2017 Annual Dinner and Annual General Meeting were held at Crooklands on February 18th. 2017 was noted for being the 50th anniversary of the Mossdale tragedy; it is not recorded if the club was represented at the memorial service.

The 2017 caving meets were well attended and many great trips done with a good number of novice trips mixed in as the number of novices turning up increased through the year. The 2017 Gaping Gill meet was eventful as an eleven year old boy had to be rescued from beyond Sand Caverns. It saw the BPC at its best with a continuous line of stretcher bearers rapidly moving the lad through to main chamber where he was winched to the top and into an air ambulance helicopter. Within a short time, Jim [The Scot] Brown was seen to suddenly grip his chest and sit down at the bottom marshal's spot. He was winched straight up to the surface while the helicopter was contacted, and subsequently returned to pick Jim up and take him to hospital as well. Both patients recovered *[it has to be mentioned that this was the second time Jim had been rescued from GG, it's about time he let someone else have a go – Ed]*

It proved to be a bad year for GG accidents as in August the CPC were still installing their winch lighting system which involves a 6 meter climb up to a ledge with a light and trailing wires. Two members had failed to reach the ledge before Nick Gymer successfully reached it and started to crawl along to the designated spot when the whole ledge collapsed. With several serious injuries to his head

and eleven fractures to his body the team assessed him and was able to sit him in the chair to winch him up. The surface team was mobilised to receive him and transport him to the air ambulance. He recovered well at home. *[it seems the CPC needed to address their H&S processes – Ed]*

It was at this time that the club suffered the sad loss of Bryan Schofield who died in July 2017. He was a larger than life personality and was a dear friend to many BPC members. Bryan [Scoff] loved the BPC as much as many members loved Bryan, he was a very innovative and dedicated cave diver

and much respected amongst many of the world leading divers he often dived with. He was a BPC ambassador through his many activities both at home and abroad. His presence in the BPC will never be replaced and many of us will always remember Bryan.

Dave Brook was interviewed by BBC Radio Leeds as the 2017 President, Carol Castleden, held her presidential meet at Low Mill Outdoor centre in Askrigg. A great multi-disciplinary event with caving, albeit in mines, as well as cycling and walking all before a great meal and social gathering with plenty of beer.

The 2017 expedition/holiday was to the Pyrenees and the Complex de Felix Trombe in particular. With up to 100Kms of passage and forty odd entrances with over 1000 feet of height it was a great playground for the trip. The various trips were done amongst cycling and canyoning and walking in the surrounding area. A wonderful time was had by all who went. The CPC had approached the club about the possibility of them joining us on the summer trip. They went on to suggest that we should run some joint trips in the future, the first of these joint trips was a Swinsto-Simpson's exchange which was a great success.

Universal Studios contacted the club at this time to try and gain assistance and support for them to shoot a new Mummy film down GG. They offered to make their own winch as money was no object. Perhaps they thought the members looked like they belonged in a horror movie. We politely declined the opportunity to get involved.

The quest at home in the autumn was to find a new name for the CNCC, the absence of an obvious contender meant no progress was made. It was at this time that Kevin Dixon reported on the progress of his digital survey of Gaping Gill. This had proved to be a mammoth undertaking involving both the BPC and CPC winch meets with volunteers from many clubs helping Kevin survey the most undesirable locations in what subsequently turned out to be 22 kms of system. 2017 turned out to be his 10th BPC/CPC winch/survey meets, and it was nearing completion. The survey looked an amazing thing of beauty which was just as well considering the quite remarkable dedication from Kevin and all who helped. *[In December the rope traverse in Mud hall collapsed, presumably requiring Kevin to carry out a new survey of Mud Hall – Ed]*

The digging teams were busy in Hartley Quarry Cave but a trip in January found the duck was a deep sump so access to the dig site was denied. Not deterred they found another site in the cave that would justify digging. They now had a rainy day dig.

The 2018 Annual Dinner and Annual General Meeting were held on February 24th at Crooklands Hotel but the attendance was again on the low side with only 40 members attending the meeting.

'Berger 2018 Clean Deep' was an initiative of the European Cave Protection Commission which is part of the Fédération Spéléologique Européenne. A similar event had been organised for 2017 when 500kgs of rubbish was removed from the upper parts of the system. The 2018 event was being held in a three week window in July/August and aiming to clear the deeper parts of the system from -800 to -1000 meters. They were expecting around 300 European cavers to turn up, most of whom would be looking out for a small piece of caving history.

There were several issues occupying the time of members in the summer of 2018, the Dump was having a new lock system fitted with electronic tokens rather than keys. This allowed for greater security as the spring closer means the door is locked without having to turn a key or jiggle a lock and slam it shut. We also got greater flexibility when probationary associate members moved up through to full members their increasing access privileges were modified on a computer keyboard rather than someone having to issue new keys and collecting and tracking the old keys. Similarly, when a member stops paying subscriptions their key or non returned guest keys are simply turned off. The Dump was also being re-wired at this time, Andrew Hainsworth, an electrician, was gallantly trying to make sense of the electrical systems that had evolved since 1963. He was trying to simplify the electrical panels as well as cheat the rats and mice by getting the cables changed in small batches in an attempt to get the new wires safely in the steel conduits before they were chewed.

GG2018 started with Joe Sharp and Josh Marshall abseiling down Dihedral to anchor the guide cable. They found a skeleton in caving gear sat waiting, as if from last year. He, Fred the plastic skeleton, had been planted by Karl Martin, Glen Walker and John Cooper the night before. The remainder of GG18 went well apart from there being another rescue, a chap had a heart attack whilst walking up little Ingleborough. The club assisted in getting him down to the shake hole and subsequently on to the air ambulance, he recovered well. GG18 witnessed

the new lighting system in main chamber. With a stainless steel catenary cable and new light weight supply cable the LED lighting was hailed a great success.

In committee there was still the ongoing debate about the future layout and uses of the garage. The present structure was inappropriate in several ways, not least the fact it had an asbestos roof. The meets secretary [Terry Devaney] had to get used to the new CNCC on-line cave booking system which was being tested on Ingleborough caves before being rolled out to cover other areas.

The 2018 BPC President was Ian Wilkinson and had planned his Presidential meet to be based at Humphrey Head Outdoor Centre on the weekend of 6th – 8th July. The walking opportunity was to repeat the Morecambe Bay crossing on the Saturday, this was done by the club over thirty years earlier and due for a revisit. There was then the BBQ and bar in the evening and Coniston Copper mines and the caves of Furnace for the Sunday, a great weekend.

Fred the skeleton appeared again in August at the CPC winch meet. The camp was raided at the dead of night [excuse the pun – Ed] by some BPC miscreants who actually descended the shaft via Dihedral to position 'Fred' in sight of the tourists. He was discovered at eight o'clock and promptly removed by someone who actually had to abseil down and prussic back up a few feet, not at all what the CPC do.

The Annual BPC Walking Meet was from Cow Green Reservoir to Appleby and was again well attended and enjoyed. The 2018 Digger's Dinner was held on October 6th at the Clapham bunkhouse and was a well attended social function going on late into the night.

Another, more successful joint BPC/CPC Gaping Gill track repair meet was accomplished in October where deep ruts were filled and drained to perhaps allow some grass to grow again when the spring arrived. The 2018 Electric Picture Show happened on November 10th at Horton Village Hall this was a huge success again with excellent presentations covering a very wide range of subjects.

The club was putting its money where its mouth was and spending money on clothing for young children to cave in. There was also an increased training emphasis. The committee understood that money had to be spent on these things if benefits were ever to be realised. The club also bought a Disto-X scanning 3D survey head and case for members to take on expeditions.

The new electronic, token, security system at the Dump went live in October 2018, just as we received an electric bill for £11,000! Dave Ryall approached the committee to see if there was any interest in helping to fund the publication of Scoff's memoirs. Dave had taken the unfinished text and worked very hard to finish the book and get it ready for printing. In a humbling act of generosity they paid £3000 and agreed that any proceeds from the sale of the book were to be given to the cancer charity that cared for Scoff.

As winter approached, Ian Wilkinson, almost as his last act as club President, spent many days repairing and re-commissioning the club's memorial bench outside Ingleborough Show cave.

BPC 2018 Christmas Dinner was again held in Settle's Victoria Hall on December 8th which left a few weeks to recover before the now traditional New Years Eve event at the Dump. This consisted of a massive meal with lots of alcohol going on through the night. The event, organised by Carol Castleden and Sally White even had a fancy dress element with a 'Soft and Fluffy' theme.

The 2019 Annual General Meeting and Annual Dinner were held on the 23rd February at Settle's Victoria Hall. The meeting was again poorly attended with only forty five members attending. The Annual Dinner was a sit down, waiter served, meal but didn't attract the big numbers either.

Over the past few years we had seen a major change in how the CNCC is run and an improvement in how effective it is with the online cave bookings system. This was now working for the Gaping Gill, Newby Moss, Hurnel Moss and the Allotment areas. It was hoped it would eventually include Leck Fell. [*The CNCC abandoned the old access agreement on Leck Fell after repeated attempts to negotiate the use of the new computerised, on-line, booking system had failed. Eventually, though the deal was struck, and time has shown the new system to satisfy both landowners and cavers – Ed*]

The 2019 joint BPC/CPC meet was a Simpson's–Swinsto exchange trip. Both teams were made up from both clubs and a great trip was had by all. These meets show the true relationship between the clubs is in fact very strong and the banter is friendly. The club was saddened in April when it

was announced that Andy Pell had died aged just 65.

The May 2019 Gaping Gill Meet got off to a great start with only one shower and a burst of hail during the prelim weekend. Ben Wright dived lost river chamber sump and he spent time replacing lines in the upstream sump which had been washed downstream by winter floods. He then followed the displaced line downstream pushing new territory and found it amusing to be exploring new cave following a line laid by the cave itself. He followed a handsome passage 3m wide and 2m high at -35m for around 80m with no end in sight, in fact he didn't even reach the end of his 2016 upstream line! After a very cold trip into Spout Inlet Kevin Dixon's survey still remained a work in progress.

The open meet saw rain and in fact flooding of Fell Beck stopped winching a little early after water was washing over Gerald Benn's feet whilst he was driving the winch. This flood of Fell Beck was not as bad as the CPC had endured in their GG meet the previous August.

Mick Sharp's 2019 Presidential Meet was held in Upper Wharfedale It had a good turn out with about 80 members attending with all but 4 camping. On Saturday there were caving trips to Birks Fell, Pasture Gill, Dow cave, Hagg Gill and Buckden gavel mine while the cyclists did a long ride taking in Hawes, Middleham and back via Cover Dale and Park Rash. Several less energetic people ended up doing walks of various lengths to the local Pubs.

The 2019 Electric Picture Show was another well attended fun night, it was held on November 2nd in the Horton Village Hall. There was some food laid on but people clearly brought their own beer.

The 2019 Christmas dinner was held on December 7th at Low Mill Outdoor Centre in Askrigg, it was a one off, never to be repeated, spectacular success. The meal was by far the best Christmas dinner the club has ever been served, anywhere, and it was made by a team of crack volunteer chefs led by our very own Ben Wright.

The increasingly popular New Years Eve party held at the Dump was another great social event with thirty one people sitting down to eat. Once again there was fantastic entertainment with the musical instruments and singing plus the usual super humour and silliness. The fancy dress theme was 'French' and the club turned out with striped jumpers, berets, garlic and onions round their necks, young and old together, a great function. After a busy social calendar the club could now get some caving done, until February at least.

The 2020 Annual General Meeting was held at the Falcon Manor in Settle on February 22nd with 59 members attending. It proved to be a unique experience, with Corky gone and Jekyl elsewhere, there were no points of order and the meeting went very much to plan. In fact, it was over before anybody realised it, just 12 minutes and that was it, done. There was just time to vote Nick Cornwell-Smith in as the new President and that was it. The

Annual Dinner was also at the Falcon Manor and was a nice meal, but nothing near the Christmas Dinner. The meal was followed by an introductory speech by President Nick and we then witnessed a disturbing talk by Dave Haigh whilst some sort of breakdown was in progress. One rarely witnesses such a spontaneous unravelling of a hitherto flawless plan. He first lost half the pages of his speech and as Diane had forgotten her glasses so she failed in her role as prompter. Dave then froze with nerves and began the incoherent mumbling of fragments from a long forgotten speech which went on for far longer than was comfortable. He appeared to be having a conversation with a manikin and at times a stuffed parrot seemed to enter the conversation, a mystifying experience, but a great laugh, poor Dave.

No sooner was the Annual Dinner over than a Global Pandemic [*A coroner Virus, Covid 19 – Ed*] made its existence known; we had no alternative but to stop all group activities including meetings and caving trips and to close the Dump until further notice. That is with the exception of the GG beer tent which was recreated as a shared virtual experience. Set up by Rob Jarvis and Fred Rattray, people sat at home drinking beer whilst trying to imagine they were sitting on a builder's plank on top of Ingleborough in a cold draughty tent, drinking even colder beer. Surely such a wonderful experience could never be simulated even with modern virtual reality. The essence of the beer tent is a totally unique experience that can never be digitised; it is an analogue of the beating heart of the club.

To be continued......

Picture Fred Ackroyd.

1930's – An unknown trip in the late pre-war period. All that tackle and it was probably not much more than 200 feet of ladder and a lot less length of lifeline rope. [*The chap far left appears to be falling over - Ed*]

1934 – NCFC Gaping Ghyll open meet. Milton Shackleton [Centre] and Titus Illingworth [Right] with an unknown NCFC guide. Milton and Titus have torches tied to their heads and the NCFC guy is wearing a school cap. Titus appears to be wearing a raincoat with nothing underneath [!] while Milton is wearing his school uniform. The NCFC chap, judging by the look on his face, seems to have more than just cold hands to worry about. [Picture – Bill Gott with no modern sophistications and using flash powder for lighting. Within seconds of this picture being taken the people were probably engulfed with thick acrid smoke meaning they only had one chance at taking this picture]

Right 1937 - The club spent a lot of time digging and surveying their extension and the passages of Jackdaw hole on Penyghent.

Below - The BPC Headquarters was at the Cross Streets Hotel from 1938 to 1946. BPC members listened to the radio while standing at the bar here on 3RD September 1939 and heard Neville Chamberlain say "I have to tell you now that no such undertaking has been received, and that consequently this country is at war with Germany."

Right - Don Leach's model made for the committee meeting in 1949. It is made from brass tubing soldered together. The concept was the use of simple geometric triangles to create a rigid truss frame, obvious now but without precedent in 1949. The weight reduction compared to a wooden gantry, as used by the CPC, was massive. The pulley visible on the top cross bar was for illustrative purposes, the actual pulley is a standard block attached to the bar.

Picture Fred North.

1946 – Lost John's. The clothing had clearly not improved since the earlier picture in East Passage taken over a decade before. Considering the felt hats and tweed jackets it is no surprise that these hard men were prepared to endure the long periods of numbing cold as required in such a wet hole. The bare legs were in anticipation of moving along the wet passage before changing into dry boots and clothes.

Left - 1940's Home on leave, Fred Ackroyd and Bert Ambler looking out northwards from a cold and cloudy Penyghent.

Below – One of the many club glass slides taken in Clapham Cave before it was more widely known as Ingleborough Cave. The club spent many trips in the 1930's and 1940's searching for the connection with Gaping Ghyll. It was known to exist but many early explorers were convinced it would be found in their life time, sadly this was not to be the case.

Picture Fred Ackroyd.

Looking as if he has just beamed down on a shaft of light, this member was caught by Frank Moulson in the late 1940's looking out over Alum Main shaft. The unknown caver is wearing a school type cap and plus fours which were popular with cavers as they could change wet gear below the knee.

The BPC held a fascination with Alum Pot as indicated in 1950. The club had expended huge amounts of energy creating a viable winch and completing the first demonstration at Gaping Gill at Whitsuntide. The club's first thought after that, was just three months later, to try something never done before and install the winch at Alum Pot. The experience was so bad that it was never repeated.

1953 – The founder members with other long standing members.
Back Row L-R - Harry Hargreaves [*FM*], Charles Leach [*1936*], Milton Shackleton [*FM*], Vincent Shackleton [*FM*]
Front Row L-R - Titus Illingworth [*FM*], Bill Gott [*FM*], Norman Middleton [*1938*], Frank Keighley [*FM*]

The BPC winch as installed at Alum Pot in the summer of 1950. It took until December 3rd [*In a blizzard*] to retrieve all the equipment from Alum.

1954 – An overloaded trailer arrives back in Clapham after another successful Gaping Gill winch meet.

Left – Terry Marsden thrutching up through the squeeze in Bar Pot [*The life line is natural fibre and seems to be about 9mm diameter, not a great fall factor there - Ed*]
Right – Irvine West, 'The Speleologist' possibly after a trip down Pikedaw Calamine Caverns 1953.

Left - Don Leach wearing his eccentric bowler hat that he always wore whilst at the winch. He instigated the construction of the gantry and led the design and development effort through to its first trial at Whitsuntide 1950. Looking less comfortable in his environment is Alf Hurworth with his whistle in his mouth he is clearly anticipating trouble. It is not known when this picture was taken but it was clearly before 1967 when Don, sadly, passed away.

Below left – 1958 - Long Kin West the surface hauling team. Done with electron ladders this trip was early in the second Golden Age of UK caving and would have been a logistical nightmare if done with the rope ladders the club was still using. [*This picture has captured someone taking possibly the World's first 'selfie'- second from left, below the teapot – Ed*]
Below Right – L-R Brian Lee, Geoff Shaw, David Grassy Greenwood, Kenneth Tideswell relaxing at the Old Dump.

Below Left – 1966 - A young Terry Devaney outside Dow cave. Below Right - 1964 – Cas and Swampy in the 'New' Dump kitchen [*In what is now the locker room – Ed*]

South Wales Trip 1963.
Left-Right - Alf Hurworth, Jack Schofield, Paul Dyson, David Hall, Barry Crick, Graham Mitchell, David Brook, Peter Berry, Richard Blackeley, Peter Livesey.

Left-Right – Dave Haigh, Raymond Stoyles and Rod McGhee. [*This bike was later bought by Derek Castleden for £12.50 – Ed*]

Below Left – The classic picture of Alan Gill a famous polar explorer who was part of the first team to walk to the North Pole in 1961.

Below Centre- There have been many controversial acts blamed on cavers over the years, thankfully the vandalism of this dinosaur at White Scar Cave in the 80's was absolutely nothing to do with the members of the BPC.

Below Right – A demonstration of John Bolton's famous party piece, the Dance of the Flaming Arsehole.

1974 – The successful return to Chourum des Aiguilles, seven members to the bottom in just six hours, a first for UK caving and a pivotal moment in the history of the BPC. The EPC followed us and spent a lot longer and had to use underground camps. Back Row L– R Dave Mathews, Brian Sellers, Dick McLindon, Pete Faulkner, Brian Smith. Front Row L- R Ian Wilkinson, Raymond Lee, Brian Judd, John Cooper, Jim Abbott.

Left- 1979 Brackenbottom in the days before Global warming.

Picture - Helen Swift.

Gouffre Berger 1980 – The club's first expedition to what was then still one of the deepest caves in the World and the classic hole that every caver still wants to do at least once in their lifetime.

Back Row L-R Colin Davenport, Jim Hool, Bob Bialek, John Offord, Raymond Lee [Behind], Jill Powell, Alan Charlton, Cedric Binns [Behind], June and Brian Smith [Middle], Mick Sharp, Dick Blakeley [Behind], Derek Castleden [Middle], Angie Sharp, Toni Binns, Jim Abbott [Behind], Bob Booth 2 [Middle], Brian Sellers, Russell Cox, Frank Croll, Unknown, Ian Wilkinson, Pauline Koval, Max Koval, Chris Smith, Peter Faulkner, Malcolm Halsay, Martin Gaffney, Mrs Gaffney.

Front Row – Chris Ellison [Airdale], Sheryl Abbott, Pete Dixon [NUCC], Andy Riley [NUCC], Geoff Crossley, John Greene, Martin Scatliffe, Sandra Webb, Liz Sellars, Diana Croll [& Children], Ruth Halsay, Gareth Sewel [Lying]

Picture – Nick Cornwell-Smith

Picture – Pauline Koval

Above Left 1980 – Ian Wilkinson as the Three Wise Men talking to Frank and Diana Croll moments before Dalek erupted in flames causing Frank to wag his finger at the miscreants whilst dressed as a Christmas pudding!

Above Right – Somewhere in France [possibly 1976], Martin Scatliffe and Max Koval helping Bob Booth 2 back from the bar after the lunch time session.

Picture – Pauline Koval

Above Left – BB2, Max, Martin, Jim Abbott, and others, collapsed after the early evening session the same day.
Above Right – Very subdued at the bar in question [Villard de Lans] – Max, Martin and Sandra Webb.

Left - 1983 Radagasts Revenge - picture courtesy of Julian Griffiths

Right - Geoff Crossley in his 80's diving gear.

Below – 1990, a weekend trip to the Parmilan plateau in France. L-R Chris Speight, Dave Roberts, Geoff Douglas, John Edwards [*with the invisible tray of drinks*], Derek Castleden, Chris Smith.

Albania 1992 – Above Left- Pete and Sara Spillett investigating an entrance.
Above right – Derek Castleden demonstrating how to swim the river Vjose without getting wet.
Below Left – Gwyn Bryan waiting to see if Cas makes it across the bridge before he tries it.
Below right – Discussion in Petranik cave entrance.

Left – Sharon Kelly fettling her carbide lamp whilst at an unknown Gaping Gill meet.

Right – Dave Ryall fulfilling the terms of a bad decision and a lost bet, in main chamber. Clearly this was a shock for Diana Haigh [in the chair]

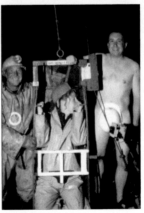

Picture Andy Haigh

Above Martin Grass enjoying a spontaneous alfresco bath on Ingleborough and Left Scoff goes for a walk in the snow.

December 31st 1999 – Fat Finger Millennium dinner. A surreal event with Ragnar creating a particularly disturbing image.

L – R Front – Dave Haigh, Sue Ryall, Dave Ryall, Andy Haigh, Brian Simister with unknown behind.

Rear – L-R Jenny Midwinter, John Duckworth with Gerald Benn.

Below Left – 1993 A present from the DCC, this 18 foot steel rocket awaited the GG rigging team. A miniature version was sent as a reminder the following year. It was never clear what this was all about.

Right – 2013 Matt Setchfield emerging from the entrance of the Tete Sauvage. [*The remains of the 2 meter high snow box are still visible - Ed*]

Picture – Colin Davison.

Picture – Terry Devaney.

110

Above - 2010 – Gouffre Berger team
Back Row L-R Matt McLaren, Sam Allshorn, Andy Haigh
John Robinson, Mick Riley, Roger Saxton, Ian Wilkinson
Al Hartley [Non member], Stuart Hesletine, Deborah Last, Donal O'Byrne, Andy Haisnworth, Steve Smith
Sam Barnes, Fred Rattray, Janet Packwood, Ruth Skinner c/w Emily, Andy Kerman, Matt Jagger
Jimmy Rattray, Gerik Rhoden, Duncan Smith, Brian McGavin, Mike Skinner, Gerald Benn
Terry Devaney, Elaine Hill, Peter Jones, Kath Jones, Peter Davies, Rachel Chattle
Front Row - Carrol Mullins, Derek Castleden, Carol Castleden.

Part of the Corky's Digging Team
Back Row - Dave Ryall, Carol White, Dave Brook, Alyson Brook, Bob Arkright, Jude Harrison, Gerald Benn.
Front Row - Dennis Wray, Martin Smith, Fred Rattray, Tim Sullivan. Jude's dog. Picture – Dave Haigh.

Visits to the local bar [*Autrans*] are always very relaxing, especially when you have just done the Berger.
Clockwise – Jim Rattray, Janet Packwood, Ian Wilkinson, Mick Riley, Donal O'Byrne, Brian McGavin, Gerik Rhoden, Carol Mullins, Gerald Benn, Fred Rattray. [Picture Matt McLaren]

Picture Fred Rattray

Left - Three generations of dentally challenged GG ale tent dwellers L-R Chris Robinson, Max Koval and Amber Storry.

Right – A club meet to KMC for the younger end of the membership June 2018.
Back Row L-R Graham Haydock, Hazel Raison, Jo Hindle, Mike Skinner, Jeff Croston, Will Stewart, Kirsty Stewart, Neil Griffin.

Front Row L-R Erin Raison, Orla Raison, Emily Skinner, Jasmine Du Plessis [back], Jose Rose Du Plessis [front], Ruben Stewart.

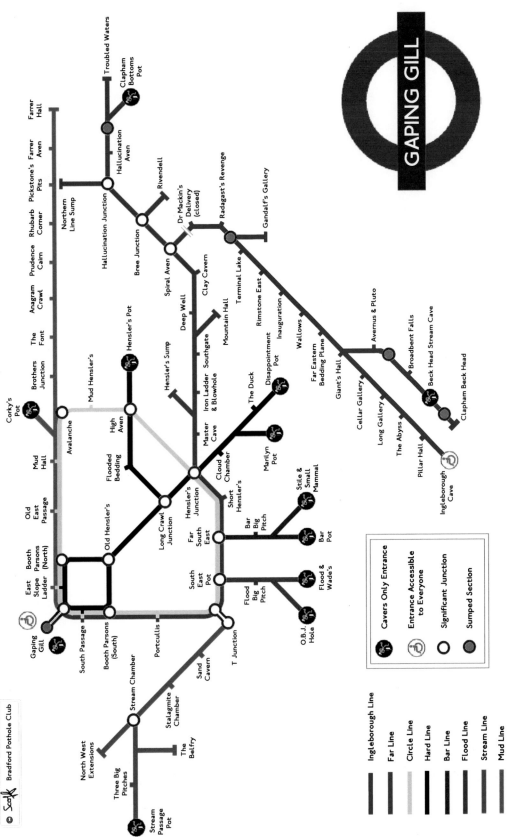

In a moment of creative genius Scoff produced this iconic map of Gaping Gill. It very cleverly serves the caver in exactly the same informative way a London Underground map helps commuters. He went on to create a map of the caves of Kingsdale in a similar style.

Left – May 11th 2003 the first Henslers Pot through trip Clockwise from Bottom – Dave Ryall, Martin Smith, Mark Slater, Rob Ackroyd, Dave Haigh, Sharon Kelly, Gerald Benn.

Above right – May 2018 Gerald Benn, Tim Sullivan, Fred Rattray - GG Whitsun Series. Ged's 50th Anniversary of its discovery trip. [*The average age on this trip was over 68 – Ed*] Picture Fred Rattray.

Left – 2015 Chris Devaney with Terry below on Via Ferrata, Col de Rousett, Vercors.

Above – 2018 Skedena Jama, Slovenia. These two foreign trips were typical of the more family orientated holidays that have dominated the BPC's summers since the 2010 Berger trip. They offered a multitude of activities for families with and without children, not to mention the more solitary members that enjoyed the sociable environment in these larger groups.

Picture – Carole White

SECTION 2
MEMORABLE TALES FROM THE BPC

SECTION 2.1 - PENYGHENT LONG CHURN RESCUE 1938 - H.BROWNE

'Mention has already been made of the setback which befell the members of the club during a meet at Penyghent Long Churn, on the 2nd and 3rd October, 1938. This is an account of what happened in those 27 anxious hours, when the party of six, Herbert Ambler, Alan Nichol, Harold Robinson and myself, of the club, and two friends, Frank Shepherd and Albert Roberts, were trapped by flood waters, which poured down the pot following a thunderstorm. It was not an official club meet, but one of those scratch affairs when members get together to show their friends how they spend their weekends. Our two guests on this occasion certainly were given a most full and practical demonstration. The pot was well known to the members, for in 1937 and 1938 much work had been done there, when the club had extended the lower level and prepared a survey.

We descended at about 10 am on Sunday, Oct. 2nd. 1938, using a pulley block for the last man, and after exploring as far as the head of the third pitch we decided to make our way out and retraced our steps. We realised something was amiss when we reached the short climb at the foot of the second pitch, where several footholds, normally dry, were completely under water. In double quick time we made up the ladder and along the water-course. Here, instead of the trickling drop of water we had left on our inward journey, was a full-blooded, swirling beck, plunging noisily and violently down to the lower level. Dismayed, we forced our way to the bottom of the shaft, finding here that our worst thoughts were grimly realised. A raging cataract filled the shaft, and climbing the ladder was quite beyond human possibility. In fact, the weight of water almost beat one to the ground, merely getting to the first rung. Anxiously, we returned downstream and, leaving the stream, entered the dry traverse and there settled down to wait. Knowing that these moorland becks can rise and fall in a matter of hours, we optimistically anticipated a detention of five or six hours, but of course, we knew nothing of the weather conditions outside. We kept a check on the stream, which showed relentless increase in both depth and noise. Our food, one sandwich, together with our cigarettes and lights, was pooled and rationed and gloomily we made ourselves as comfortable as we could, left with our thoughts.

They ranged from the mixed grill, which would now be ready for us at Cross Streets Hotel; to our wives and parents at Bradford and Halifax, and of course, to the ignominy of having to be rescued, the fact of which we were slowly and unwillingly being compelled to accept.

Time dragged on - we were spared knowing how slowly, for none of us had a watch, until, at last the stream seemed to be quietening down. A trip along the passage, now knee deep though froth was clinging four feet up the walls, proved the ladder to be still unclimbable, and that it was daylight outside. It must be Monday, we agreed, but what time on Monday we could not guess. The stream was now falling steadily, and we made many journeys to the pitch before finally we saw the ladder had been moved. Looking up through the spray we made out a figure descending, which proved to be that of 'Tot' Lord. He was very relieved to find all six of us crowding him. We had been unable to hear and answer the rescue party, whistling on the surface, and they had feared the worst. Vincent Shackleton descended to help, and then we started our ascents. Robinson was the first to climb aided by two lifelines, and when he was about 30ft. from the top, the whole length of ladder came crashing to the bottom. Stranded and weakened by its all night chafing and battering, it had broken near the top but Robinson was safely held by the lifelines and hauled to the surface. The ladder was replaced, to be descended by Graham Watson with further help for those still below, and we continued our ascent greatly assisted by two powerful lifeline teams. It was 2pm. on Monday when I reached the surface, greeted by hot coffee and rum followed by tea and sandwiches at Fawber Farm.

The rescue had started to function at 10.30pm when Mr Stead of Cross Streets Hotel had informed the police of our failure to return. They were handicapped however, by not knowing our location. Things started moving in Bradford and Halifax on Monday morning, where one or two club members, who knew we would be either at Sell Gill or Penyghent Long Churn, passed this information to Settle and gathered a team consisting of Henry Atkin, Milton and Vincent Shackleton and Graham Watson, who left Bradford at about 10.30 a.m., arriving at the pot a few minutes after the C.R.O. Wardens. The debit side of these mishaps is invariably borne by the rescuers who are put to considerable expense and inconvenience. On the credit side, we have our mistakes and misjudgements grimly brought home to us and the lessons they bring should be learned and remembered by all who take part in the sport, but especially by those who have already been rescued. The cause of this incident was the continuous, steady rain which had fallen for a few days before our descent, saturating the whole of the fell. Consequently the heavy downpour, after we had entered the pot, simply ran off the water laden bogs and in no time at all, Long Churn beck was transformed into a torrent. Attention to two details could have reduced the effect of the rain. By fixing the ladders on the opposite side of the shaft by means of a stake, instead of in the bed of the stream, where there was a natural belay, we may possibly have climbed out. Failing this, had we left someone on the surface, he would have realised what was happening and a quicker and less extensive rescue could have been affected. That our club has learned these lessons, and others no less important, is evident'

SECTION 2.2 – FINDING THE LOST TRAVERSE – ARNOLD PATCHETT – 1946/7

The CPC had reported a traverse linking Long Kin East with Rift Pot and the BPC had already carried out several trips in search of the traverse. The following is the contemporary account of their subsequent trips to locate the link.

Rift Pot again - 19th. May 1946. – Arnold Patchett.

In view of the interesting position which had arisen regarding Long Kin East and its connection with Rift Pot, coupled with the fact that Sunset Hole was comparatively difficult of access with tackle, it was decided to pay a still further visit to the Borsber Allotment and endeavour to get to the bottom of the 'missing' traverse.

An early start was made from Cross Streets, and a party comprising Fred and Denis North, Eric Barraclough, Bill Porteus, J. Richer, H. Fielden and G. Charlesworth entered Long Kin Cave at 9-45 a.m. with 350 ft. of ladder, 6 belays and 230 ft. of lifeline. The top of the 180 ft pitch was reached without incident and for once it was a change to report less water running than on the previous occasion, though ironically enough, much traversing had to be done on account of the difficulty of getting all the gear through at passage level because of the narrowness! During the descent Willie Briggs and his son caught up the party and lightened the burden. A thorough search was again made for the missing link out. The party drew blank and could really find no evidence of a ledge or traverse having been broken away, except some soft clay, in a deep bedding cave a few yards up on the right, looked fresh; a crawl along this care was brought to an abrupt end after about 15 ft by a sheer drop down the main hole. After lunch the main hole of 180 ft was attacked, and after 200 ft of ladder had been fed out between two boulders Fred North, who was in charge of the proceedings, descended about 80 ft. to find that the remaining 120 ft of ladder had collected on a ledge. The ladder being displaced, he carried on down a fine pitch with an equally fine waterfall - at least it would have been, had it been viewed from afar. The bottom was reached with 25/30 ft of ladder to spare. Willie Briggs was left in charge of the life lining party at the top and Fred North was followed by Eric Barraclough, Denis North, Bill Porteus and H. Fielden who all reached the bottom - the floor appeared to be about 100ft long by 20ft at the widest part, but no signs of recently fallen rock were apparent. One end of the chamber rises to meet the roof; the other end leads along and down a mud slope to a wet passage until the water meets the roof. Two further passages were then explored - one to a sump. Several smaller openings were entered but they did not appear to 'go'. As it turned out, the 180 ft climb back to Long Kin Cave was not so exacting as it was feared, for it was necessary for each man to stay on the ledge to clear the lifeline for the man below, thus giving all a complete rest 100 ft up.

Over dinner at Cross Streets that evening at 8 p.m. When talking over the day's work, satisfaction was expressed that the bottom had been reached successfully, though no new ground had been broken. What of the traverse? Whilst one was in the Cave it seemed certain that it did not now exist, but with the passage of even a few hours, the first tiny shadows of doubt were forming despite efforts to dispel them. Could it be that the traverse was over the ......Of course, it couldn't. After all the party had explored every possible place. The shadows grew ....

A note was sent to the Recorder, British Speleological Association, reporting the results of our visits to Rift Pot and Long Kin East. The answer came swiftly, and the opinion expressed by him was that there had been no subsidence!

Meet on Ingleborough Allotment, 19th/20th. April 1947 - Saturday, 19th. April was as beautiful a spring day as could be imagined, and the evening sky promised fair weather for the morrow. Eric Barraclough had been appointed O.C. and he and his party had taken advantage of the good weather and had carried up some of the tackle to the Allotment during the afternoon, and rigged up the ladder to enable an immediate descent to be made down Rift Pot first thing on Sunday. During the early hours of Sunday morning, however, the weather, as usual, took a turn for the worse, and at 9-30 a.m. (the time some of the party reached Clapham) the clouds had dropped to an alarmingly low level, though no rain was falling. Undaunted, a party of eleven left the "Shoe" at 10 a.m. and went up into the clouds on the Allotment. In spite of the warm and sunny week immediately preceeding that day, a tremendous drift of snow still filled the hollow just to the South of Rift Pot and a still larger one lay suspended across the Southern end of the Rift itself. No time was lost on arrival for the traverse had to be found, and Eric Barraclough led

B. Porteus, J. Robertshaw and Dan Hutton down Rift Pot. Hugh Browne and Fleming junior doing the lifelining, whilst I took charge of a party consisting of Frank Moulson, Fred Ackroyd, John Fleming and Arthur Shepherd and made for Long Kin Cave. Long Kin Passage was, if anything a little less wet than usual, and easy progress was made. Three 25ft ladders and the appropriate belays, and optimistically enough, a long hand line were taken down. The joint pitch was descended with one ladder, and in the case of the other pitch the ladder was slung over a curtain of rock. I then went on ahead and on reaching the final 8ft fall about 20 yards before one comes to the main hole, I called for a short ladder or rope. Frank Moulson, who was about 10 yards behind me, went back to get the tackle, and I heard no more for some little time; after standing in the blackness for about ten minutes I switched on my light and climbed up as if to follow Frank to see what the delay was about, but on my left, however, I saw a long, low and fairly wide TRAVERSE, which ran immediately above where I had been waiting immediately before. In my excitement, I forgot about the tackle I had called for, and crawled along the traverse, at the end of which I saw a slope consisting of boulders, tufa, large and small black pebbles, limestone scree etc. I scrambled up and at the top found myself high up on a ledge on the left hand wall of what of course turned out to be the main hole. The ledge then descended and so did I - posthaste - and imagine my surprise and pleasure when I saw two lights coming up to meet me.....

Eric Barraclough and party had climbed the wall rising from the chockstone platform from the Rift Pot side and had just crossed the bridge leading to the ledge where I was standing. The traverse at last - it seemed incredible that we could have missed it on the two previous occasions. It was not until Eric and I had exchanged experiences that I realized that we were standing in the middle of the ledge for which we had brought the hand line. The latter was way back in Long Kin! All members who crossed later were, however, experienced men but it was thought prudent to use the hand line, or alternatively lifeline each man across in future, especially if there were any visitors or new members present. Eric and one or two of his party then went forward to locate the rest of my party, whilst I continued over the bridge and descended to the platform by means of a 30ft rope belayed to a large boulder. By this time Frank and the others had been located; it appeared that on seeing Eric's light up aloft they realized that a way had been found across. The occasion called for a few photographs so I climbed the 25ft ladder leading

from the platform to the rocky ledge and then up the steep mud slope by means of the rope which Eric had belayed on the way down. Gaining the foot of No.1. Chamber I tugged at the lifeline and the ladder, whistled and shouted for something like twenty minutes, but there was no response. Had the life lining party gone to sleep in the sun? My patience slowly becoming like that of a one-time dictator, I went back the way I had come and persuaded Eric to carry on right through Long Kin and make for the surface that way in order to see what was happening up above. On returning to the foot of the 110ft pitch (No.1. Chamber) with two others, the three of us managed to attract attention, but on reaching the top, I found to my dismay that conditions were pretty bad - high wind and drizzle - and the two life liners had been driven to shelter in a hollow.

Camera and its attendant clobber in a small rucksack on my back I went down again, glad to get out of the weather, and reached the ledge at the foot of the mud slope nearly an hour after I had first left it. Frank then gave me some assistance in rigging up the camera, and we took what turned out to be quite a reasonable photograph of the bridge. Bill Porteus, and Dan Hutton were both prominent; the latter appears to be kneeling in prayer - thankful of having crossed in safety! After the expenditure of much flash powder on two further photographs, all tackle was cleared and both parties made their respective ways to the surface by 4-0 p.m. All those who made the descent actually did the through trip, except Eric and myself who both did it twice! The drizzle had, by that time, changed into heavy rain and the return to Clapham was made via the Green Road in a veritable cloudburst. The traverse had been found so the weather mattered little. Eric has a good story to tell of this meet - we can look forward to reading it in the next bulletin. A.N.P.

The Traverse leading from Rift Pot to Long Kin East, by E.Barraclough

Meet on Ingleborough Allotment, 19th/20th. April 1947.

We proceeded without incident down the main shaft and the two small pitches in Rift Pot, belaying the tackle in the usual places, and eventually found ourselves facing the base of the natural wall which divides a large cavern and over the other side of which is the 200 ft. pitch. Whilst looking for some signs of the other party, our attention was drawn to some initials of C.P.C. members scratched on the rocks at the top of the wall. As there were more prominent and more easily accessible places on which to carve initials we came to the conclusion that the engravers had not singled out the rocks because of their position, but because they marked an important point and probably led to some other passage. This being the case, I decided to climb up, and after two unsuccessful attempts I reached one of the rocks at the top. On looking around me, I found that I was on the top of a bridge which fell away slightly, from the centre, on each side. It joined the two sides of the cavern and was little over a yard wide. On one side was the 200 ft pitch and on the other was the 12 ft drop to the mass of fallen rocks from which I had climbed, and through which a number of shafts sank to lower depths. Whilst waiting for Jack Robertshaw to join me, I busied myself scraping my initials and 'BPC' beside those of the 'CPC'. Jack brought a line up with him and as we were not sure of the ground I tied one end around my waist and he life-lined me across the bridge which was about 14 ft long. Once across I took my stand behind a large boulder and lined Jack across, and we both proceeded in the direction of Long Kin, leaving Bill Porteus at the foot of the 12 ft wall. After leaving the bridge we turned to the left onto a ledge on the side of the cavern which began to climb rather deeply in a series of rough steps and slopes until near the roof we came to a loose scree slope which formed the top of a hump the far side of which we could not see. Whilst we were testing the scree to see whether or not it was safe we heard footfalls and the clatter of loose stones from the darkness beyond, and a few seconds later a lamp and helmet slowly came into view to be followed by the form of Arnold Patchett cautiously picking his way over the loose boulders. Who was the more surprised, he or us, I cannot say, but we were all very pleased at finding the traverse as two attempts last season had been unsuccessful. Arnold then went down to the bridge and joined Bill Porteus whilst we waited for the rest of the former's party. After joining forces, we took a number of photographs under Arnold's direction and then made our way back to the surface. The Rift Pot party along the traverse to Long Kin East Cave, and the others by way of Rift Pot. On reaching the surface we found that the weather had changed to a heavy drizzle as is its custom, and I, for one, soon found that the pains I had taken to keep dry in Long Kin East were in vain. We lost no time in getting back to the 'Shoe' where a wash and extremely welcome change into dry clothes, and a good meal soon had us back in fine spirits and put the perfect finish to a very successful meet.

SECTION 2.3 – SIMPSONS RESCUE 1959 – TERRY MARSDEN.

On the Saturday Meregill was examined by nameless ones in underpants and pronounced impassable thus the venue for the club meet was changed to Simpson's Pot.

The advance party was up early the following day and thanks to Jonah who provided transport,were ready to start descending the pot just as the coach party arrived on the scene at ll.30 am. The crawl was soon negotiated and a handline fixed down Five Steps Pot and across The Pit. A ladder was used at Chandelier Pot, not a line as stated in P.U. and Camel Pot and Stake Pot were soon followed by Storm Pot and the blasted hole which caused no trouble except to one chap who kept his helmet on and received a soaking. After nearly 300 ft. a small climb up Carol Pot was laddered, which was followed by a nasty traverse and a delicate drop down to two rock projections and the top of Shuffle Pot. The party pressed on to Lake Pot and Slit Pot, the last pitch, was reached at 1:45 p.m. Only three volunteers could be conscripted for Slit Pot Tony Blick, Paul Lake and Dave Cording and the ascent back to the surface started at 2.40 p.m. Graham Shaw was bringing up the rear and everything went smoothly until he reached Shuffle Pot with the rest of the party in front of him and John Davey waiting at the top of the pitch.

John Davey reports:
Since he was one of the most experienced men in the party he set off up the pitch without a lifeline.
However, as he approached the rather awkward take-off, he complained of tiredness in his arms and went back down the ladder. I called for a line and Graham tied on and started to climb again. When he was about half way up (about 10 feet) the boulder to which the ladder was belayed peeled away from the wall and carried Graham down with it. I think the lifeline swung him away from beneath boulder as it fell, otherwise he would have been crushed, for the boulder must have weighed a couple of tons.

Rejecting the idea of abseiling down the pitch, I called for a ladder and, although not too happy with
the only remaining belay, hurried down to find Graham slumped in a pool of water trapped underneath the boulder by his boot sole. Freeing him, I helped him into a sitting position, and when I found he had no bodily injuries, I lifted him onto a broad ledge about 5 feet above the stream.

His ankle seemed badly damaged and he was very badly shocked. In addition the lobe of his left ear was badly cut, and as this was bleeding profusely, I treated this first by tearing up my shirt and fashioning a crude bandage. Then I had a look at his ankle, which was also bleeding, but it was at once obvious that I couldn't remove his boot, for fear of further damaging the ankle, and also in order not to alarm him. By now I knew the accident would require a call-out and Terry gave Dave Cording a message for the CRO and sent him out. Meanwhile, I had made a fairly successful bandage for his ankle with the rest of my shirt. This done, the next thing was to prevent exposure setting in, so I quickly stripped down to my long underpants, string vest and. shirt, and eased Graham into my thick white sweater and exposure suit. My blazer and flannels provided a somewhat inadequate amount of insulation from the cold rock. Meanwhile Terry Marston instructed Gerald Benn to clear the pot of all those not equipped for a long wait underground. This left me at the bottom of Shuffle Pot, Terry and Tony Blick between Shuffle Pot and the bottom of Carol Pot and Paul Lake lining Carol Pot.

Now the action was over, and we were faced with a long wait. I sat on a rock astride Graham and massaged his arms and body to keep him warm, the exercise was good for me too. He was quite calm, but was obviously suffering from severe shock, for his memory was not functioning at all. Every 20 seconds or so he would ask, "What has happened?" I would reply "A boulder fell on you." But it was no use, he couldn't absorb what I was saying for more than a moment. This was for me the most worrying aspect of the whole accident. Still rubbing his arms and legs. I tried to steer the conversation into the future -the hot drinks, which the C.R.O. were bringing, the nurses he would meet in the hospital, the warm bed, and the holiday from work. But always the same question cropped up - "What happened?"

About half an hour after the accident, the bleeding from Graham`s foot stopped. I was constantly warning him not to move it, only to be asked "Why, is it bleeding?" Occasionally Terry would inquire how we were going on but for most of the time I had to go on answering the same questions over and over again.

120

Finally after what seemed to be about two hours, though which I was told would be nearer to three and a half Dave Robinson arrived with hot milk and some food. This was the turning point, and we both brightened visibly. When Dave produced a dry sweater (36" bust) I almost cheered. From now on things moved rapidly. Two Bradford Tech. members brought dates and sweets, followed shortly by Peter Haigh and a medical chappie from the Burnley Caving Club. At this point Dave and I left Graharm in the cave, for we were both inadequately clothed, and doubtful of our ability to get up the ladder pitches. Terry Marston, Tony Blick and Paul Lake had already left since fresh bods were on the way. However, in the event we travelled at an incredible speed yet with an extremely careful eye for any danger. By the time we reached the entrance we were both quite warm and feeling very fit.

In retrospect it is difficult to say why the flake chose that particular time to fall. It may have boon my extra weight which did it, but in that case it is surprising that I didn't follow the boulder down. I myself have no recollection of feeling the boulder go, I only remember the boulder in the air, and then Graham huddled at the foot of the pitch, just as though two stills had been cut from a film. That belay point had been used twice a month ago and on this occasion had born the weight of 15 stoners. As it was, the lifeline probably saved Graham's life, by pulling him clear of the main mass of the boulder. Throughout the long wait, Graham was cool, due mainly I think; to his loss of memory. On several occasions, he was very concerned as to whether anyone else had been injured and never grew despondent. The magic letters C.R.O. were real morale builders all the time, for he rather relished being carried out of the pot.

Shortly after I came out of the pot the bus left for Bradford bearing somewhat dejected trogs homewards and leaving behind those members who were fit enough to help in the rescue operations...

Dave Cording reports:
The scene the bus left behind can well be imagined, the familiar Yellow Land Rover, the. C.R.O. tent, reporters and cavers all milling about near the entrance. The bus left at about 10.00 pm. when the rescue had been in operation for 3 hours. Frank Croll, Peter Haigh and another bod had gone down at 7.00pm with first aid and splints followed by B. Boardman (Burnley C. C.) shortly after. It was indeed a stroke of good fortune that Mr Boardman arrived on the scene so quickly since

he had some good first aid knowledge and was able to help immensely in the rescue.

David and myself followed carrying the stretcher but before we reached Graham that redoubtable Caver Bob Leakey had caught us up and took charge of operations just as john Davey and Dave Robinson withdrew from the scene. After B. Boardman had treated Graham's leg we eased him into the stretcher and with a good hauling party he was soon up the pitch. The traverse following Shuffle Pot presented a severe problem and valuable time was lost on this difficult section. I was with the stretcher party until Storm Pot had been ascended and the whole distance was very awkward. The Blasted Hole went easier than expected; the stretcher went through on its side with sufficient room to allow the patient's mouth to remain just free from the water. Feeling tired at Storm Pot and since there was a large number of rescuers present I went out, arriving at the surface about 1 !.00 p.m. The stretcher-and Graham in it slowly got nearer and nearer the surface. Many willing hands helped on the journey and it is impossible to record the names of all those who helped. Suffice it to say that The Craven. Burnley, B.Tech., N.P.C., N.S.G., Red Rose and other clubs were all represented in some strength or other. Graham himself showed remarkable courage and resolution by helping himself along wherever he could especially along the entrance crawl. He finally emerged in the early hours of the morning and was promptly seized by the ambulance men and whisked away, the reporters getting their photographs as best they could.

The clearing up was a necessary if somewhat unglamorous task, and by the following weekend all the tackle had been withdrawn. The lifelines had turned almost black after their weeks stay in the pot and no doubt will have to be scrapped but that is a small price to pay for a member's life. In closing I should like to thank all those members of the initial exploration party who backed me up so magnificently on this rather tragic meet especially John Davey. Our thanks are also extended to all who helped on the surface or underground, not forgetting the police, ambulance and medical personnel involved.

Initial Party: Dave Cording, John Davey, Graham Shaw. C. Half [*not a known member*], Dick Blakeley, Tony Pester, Rodney McGhee, Tony Blick, Paul Lake, Frank Croll, Geoff Thorndike, Gerald Benn. Terry Marston.

SECTION 2.4 – LANGSTROTH CAVE – M. P. LIVESEY.

Langstroth Cave has gone at last, and with it came the largest British find in the Club's history. The cave was opened by the EPC in the early 60's and 2,000ft explored to a sump. A. Clegg and M. Boon dived the sump to a short section of large passage, leading to a 45 ft. pitch with a sizeable stream pouring down; altogether a most impressive place. Many attempts to scale the aven followed, most of them abortive and ill-planned. The organisation and drive to get the scaling equipment through the sumps and up the aven was lacking until the BPC trip in July, when Bill, Neil, Colin and I took aluminium alloy scaling poles, (9X5ft lengths) through to the aven and scaled it. The ascent of the aven was not without its amusing scenes, for those below, that is. A ladder was rigged on the pitch and soon we were all assembled above in an impressive stream passage. A series of cascades led to a 10ft high passage with a 4ft deep canal and fine formations. 300ft of this were followed by a short section of crawl and a long, high chamber, 10ft wide, 60ft long, with the roof out of sight. A loud crashing noise around the next corner heralded the approach of Pitch Two. A very wet 20ft free climb was Pitch Two, but there were lots more to come. Up a 5ft climb the passage split. Bill and Colin took the smaller, left-hand branch following it up two pitches of 8 and 12 ft, for 400ft. to a chamber containing 15ft straws. The passage continued tight, but they did not follow. Neil and I pushed on up the main way, up a fine ascending stream passage carved through bright yellowish rock. After a few feet we reached a 15ft pitch which we climbed on unstable holds; and along for a hundred feet to a further 15ft pitch. Neil led this and I followed on through more stream passage to a chamber, the stream crashing down a sheer 20ft pitch from a passage above. We did not fancy climbing this - the walls were covered in knobs of black mud stal - a strong deterrent to free climbing. As it turned out later, the pitch would have gone free quite easily, but we had to wait until the following week to find this out. We took 25ft of maypole out with us that trip, running into difficulties a couple of times in the sump, when one of our two diving kits jammed as it was being hauled through. This was freed from an underwater bedding plane half way through the sump after a session of complete confusion with

rope signals through the sump. The following weekend, Bill, Dave, Neil and I dived the sumps and took the remaining 20ft of pole up the four pitches to the final one. The pole was erected and Dave was soon at the top and away, leaving us to belay the ladder. Beyond the head of the pitch the passage continued as a bedding plane, developing after a few hundred feet into a rift passage, high but narrow. Avens and inlets showered trickles of water into the main passage from all sides, but most were tight and only a few explorable. After nearly 1,200 ft we came into a large chamber, 15ft wide and 50ft high and long. Twin waterfalls supplied the noise, spouting from two inlets at the far end. Free climbing was possible for 20ft between the 45ft falls, but there was too much water for the last section to be attempted (although this can be climbed free in reasonable weather conditions). We turned here, descending the five pitches, through the sump and so to the entrance. It was 9.30, Sunday night, the normal finishing time for Langstroth trips. On Sunday, October 16th, a party of six divers and two helpers entered the cave at dinnertime and were soon floundering through the sumps. The water was high and the 45ft first pitch very wet indeed. We moved on upstream, picking up the 20ft of scaling pole at pitch 5 and carrying it the 1,200ft to pitch 6. The pole was erected and slung from a spike 20ft up-pitch which gave a rope climb to 40ft up, then another 5ft of free climbing. A desperate squeeze at the top didn't help matters. 50ft of tight passage led to another sizeable chamber and the inevitable pitch - 35ft this time, very wet and very steep. The pitch was a real "boating" free climb, using small layaway holds up a steep wall. At the top a hundred feet of rift passage was followed to a tight bedding plane. The passage soon became too low, but clearing the floor of pebbles would soon make the passage passable. In front was the noise of Pitch 8!

At this point in the exploration of Langstroth Cave the BPC Bulletin contained a survey of the find along with the above story. With this information another club dug out the surface entrance and 'discovered' the cave. To this day the Northern Caves guidebook credits the BSA, with support from the CDG, for its discovery.

SECTION 2.5 – PROVATINA ABYSS 1967 – CARLTON PICKSTONE.

Mention Greece to anyone and they naturally think of the Acropolis, the Parthenon and countless other masterpieces of the Classical Age which still exist today. Greek mountains too have their place in history, Mount Olympus was the hiding place of Zeus the supreme Olympian deity. Last year the writer visited one of the more remote regions of Greece, which seems to have been in the back of the queue when the pages of ancient history were being written. However lacking in early man-made history it may be it certainly does not suffer from a dearth as far as speleological interests are concerned. The area in question is the North Western portion of the Pindhus Mountains in the Nomoi of Ioannina. The Pindhus extend southwards from Albania to the Gulf of Korinthos, forming the backbone of Northern Greece. It includes tracts of rounded summits and even rolling plateaux some 6,000ft. high, but elsewhere rugged escarpments and deep ravines score the soft limestone. The area visited was dominated by a broad tabular mass of pure limestone, nearly 8,000ft high, named Gamila. This is drained by two rivers, the Aoos and Vikos, which have cut formidable canyons some 4,000ft in depth. The Vikos is a resurgence, emerging in a deep gorge which nearly annexes a minor peak called Astraka from the main block of Gamila. It is Astraka and the Vikos which have aroused interest amongst English cavers, because of the presence of a huge shaft, hitherto unexplored. The shaft is situated on a plateau at an altitude of 5,850ft. and the Vikos resurges some 4,000ft lower down, two miles away. The shaft was first entered upon the European caving map by David Heap whilst with an Oxford University Expedition to the Pindhus. It takes the name of Provatina from the fact that it was located in a place known to the Greek shepherds as "the place of the sheep". Since then the area has been visited by various parties, the only serious attempt being made by a party led by Ken Kelly in 1966. It was on this visit that Jim Eyre of the Red Rose Pothole Club discovered that it was more than "just another hole"; he descended 500ft down the shaft, only failing to reach the bottom because of insufficient ladder. He reported that the shaft was 100ft by 80ft with an estimated depth of 570ft to a snow covered ledge, also that possibly another pitch followed. He resolved to return the following year with an expedition of his

own. The 1967 Provatina Expedition consisted mainly of members of Northern Caving Clubs. The assault was to take place in July/August when it was hoped that the snows would have melted sufficiently to enable a safe descent to be made. Throughout the winter and spring the expedition slowly gathered momentum. Training meets were held down most of the big Yorkshire pots to get the feel of airy pitches. A lifelining winch was constructed to aid in climbing the pitch. It carried 1000ft of wire rope which was thought to be adequate for any pitch which followed the initial drop. It was proposed to use ladders throughout, with an additional 600ft Spunstrom rope for emergency use.

Transport consisted of a hired twelve-seater Bedford Minibus and an aged Diesel Landrover with trailer. The final arrangements were for the Minibus to carry twelve people with as much kit as was possible and for the Landrover to carry four people with the rest of the equipment and food in the trailer. The payload of the Minibus was 25cwt and that of the Landrover 28cwt. At Ostend, however, the Landrover was protesting and more weight had to be taken by the already overladen Minibus. Some of the food in the trailer had to be committed to the still waters of the harbour. The 2,500 mile journey to Papigon, the village nearest to Astraka, was commenced on Saturday the 14th of July, going by way of Belgium, Germany, Austria and the Yugoslavian Autoput. Along its 1000 miles of mostly straight boring road a large number of wrecked lorries spoke of the consequences of falling asleep at the wheel. At the Greek border a two hour delay was incurred whilst unravelling the Greek variety of red tape. The Athens road was followed, through Thessalonica, down the Aegean coast to Larisa, passing close by Mount Olympus. At Larisa the busy highway was left to the hurrying Athens-bound tourists and the quieter route inland was sought. The road to Ioannina lay over the dreaded Metsoven Pass, scene of bitter fighting during the last war. There were 70 miles of unmade road, riddled with potholes and at frequent intervals large sections of the track had disappeared down the hillside. To complicate matters further the pass was crossed in the hours of darkness, with the drivers having to peer through clouds of white dust thrown up by the vehicle in front. After five sleepless hours the lights of Ioannina were seen, twinkling from across a large lake. The party finally turned in at the camp site in the town just as dawn was breaking, only to be driven out at 8 am by the heat of the sun. The journey to Ioannina had taken seven frustrating days - three days longer than anticipated. As Proventina lay in a military zone, close to the Albanian border, permission had to be sought from the Army. This had been done before leaving England. All that now remained was for the general in charge of the area to endorse the necessary documents. Unfortunately the party had arrived at the beginning of the weekend, also the papers were written in English, which to a Greek probably looked as bad as Greek writing does to the average Englishman. Jim Eyre's first sortie did not get him past the "armed doorman" at the entrance to Army H.Q. However, after roundabout parleying, involving the local bookie, a policeman and an army corporal, he managed to get inside, only to be told that it would have to go through the usual channels. It was simply "not done" to go up to a general and say " 'ere mate, can I 'ave yer stamp on this bit of paper", especially as there had been a military coup in which the local Militia were particularly active. The by-now flagging image of Greece was uplifted somewhat on discovering that the local fire-water could be obtained for the equivalent of three pence a glass. Ioannina also possessed a very impressive show cave which was duly visited and photographed. On Monday afternoon permission was finally granted and the last stage of the journey up to Papigon was commenced. After passing through the check point the main road to Albania was forsaken for the dusty unmade road up to the village. It was on this road that Astraka the mountain mass that contains Provatina was first seen. It looked very formidabe with its almost sheer walls, rising nearly 3,000ft to the summit plateau, towering over the village. The arrival of the vehicles caused quite a stir as there was only one other car in the village and that belonged to the doctor. The usual mode of transport is by donkey. By nightfall the vehicles were unloaded and the equipment divided up for transportation up the mountain. Donkeys were to carry most of the heavy gear and individuals their own personal equipment. The night was spent in the scorpion-infested cloisters of the village church. At 5 am the next morning the advance party consisting of Chris Sheppard (Kendal Caving Club), Ron Bridger (Red Rose Pothole Club), Jim Farnworth (Happy Wanderers) and Carl Pickstone (Bradford Pothole Club /Wessex Cave Club), set off up the mountain, their task being to drill the holes for the winch and to find water. An unmade road led from the village to Upper Papigon and from there a donkey track wound its way up through

stunted trees towards a ridge, which afforded access to the plateau. Once above the tree line the donkey track was left and a traverse made across heavy scree under the face of the cliffs, then up steep grass and rock slopes, over the top of a large gulley which cut back into the cliffs. The crossing was by way of smooth, steeply sloping slabs with a high degree of exposure. Once we passed this obstacle the plateau was reached over easier ground. The climb up to the plateau took five hours. Provatina lay at the top of another deep gully in the base of a cliff. The shaft was approximately 50ft wide by 80ft, going back into the cliff face. From a distance it looked like a large cave entrance. However, when a stone was casually thrown down the shaft it was found to be very much a pothole. The stone took six silence-filled seconds before hitting something. Someone started to comment about its depth but was cut off by a further boom, followed after an interval of silence by yet another deeper rumble. Another stone was produced and an accurate timing taken. The stone took six seconds, followed by five seconds, then a further five to a large boulder slope. It was known that a ledge existed at a depth of 570ft so this was presumably the first striking point of the stone. There was a stunned silence and someone suggested heading for the Adriatic Coast, but (alas!!) the plot was foiled by the strident voice of Jim Eyre, urging the rest of the unsuspecting party up the mountain with the immortal phrase "If yer not 'ard yer shouldn't 'ave come!" Reluctantly everyone got down to the job in hand. Bolting the winch down presented a problem as the bedding of the limestone around the entrance was horizontal, in beds of about 1½ inches in thickness. While this problem was being overcome a search was made for water. A small seepage was discovered oozing from a shale bed in another gully, ten minutes away from the camp. After the removal of a few frogs and a little more work it was possible to fill a bucket in a couple of hours. Soon the rest of the party arrived in the searing heat of the midday sun. More equipment was to be brought up later in the evening from the donkey dump at the base of the cliff. Next morning the remainder of the gear was ferried up from the donkey dump and a start made at clearing the ledges at the top of the shaft. 700ft of ladder was put down the shaft and the telephone connected up. Jim Eyre was to make the first descent to the ledge in order to examine the possibilities of laddering the next pitch. He stepped into his harness, clipped on to the end of the winch wire and then began to clamber over the lip of the shaft. The top 20ft of the shaft consisted of ledges and it was necessary to run the winch wire over

124

guide pulleys to reduce friction. Below this the ladder lay close up to the wall for approximately 300ft and then hung free for the remainder of the shaft. The atmosphere on the surface was tense, the silence being broken only by the squeaking of the guide pulleys as the slender wire slowly uncoiled itself from the drum and vanished into the blackness of the shaft. After ten minutes, as the sixth layer of the wire had disappeared into the depths, the handles of the winch ceased to turn. The telephone crackled into life; Jim had arrived at the ledge. He found that it was covered in snow which funnelled down at 65 degrees to the head of the next pitch and this also appeared to be deep. Complications arose because of the extra length of ladder that had been put on to ensure that there was enough to reach the ledge. It hung down the next pitch pulling the main ladder away from the slope. The only place that it was possible to get off the ladder was on the extreme edge of the lower pitch where there was a six-inch wide ledge. Jim managed to pull up the extra ladder and secure it with a piton before returning to the surface. Chris Sheppard went down in the evening, armed with an entrenching tool, to cut a working platform in the 40ft high snow slope. In four hours he managed to cut a snow hole big enough to house three people. On Thursday morning Peter Faulkner (Bradford Pothole Club) and Ian Carruthers (Red Rose) descended to cut a trench at the top of the snow slope. This was to enable Rawlbolts to be driven into sound rock in order to belay the ladder for the next pitch. Later in the day, as more working space became available, Nigel Beattie (Shropshire Mine) joined them. Meanwhile Jim Newton (Red Rose) and Jim Farnworth went down to the village, by way of the gully at the side of the shaft, for more food. They were to return the next morning, as everyone was required for the attempt on the lower pitch. As the Rawlbolting party were being winched to the surface it was noticed that the winch wire had developed an acute kink close to its termination. As this weakened the wire considerably it was decided to reverse the whole wire on the drum and to use the other end of the wire which also had a thimble end. After some investigation the cause of the kinking was discovered. The winch wire had a slight tendency to untwist under load over the 570ft length. The presence of a person on the ladder prevented this but as the length of wire became shorter the degree of twist was increased. The cable was under tension until the top ledge was reached so that the twisting was not noticed since the ladder was against the wall in its upper stage. When the tension was eased off to enable the ladder climber to negotiate the edge of the ledge, the wire quickly relaxed into a large twisted bow. Usually the ladder climber's thoughts were upon other things at this stage and he would not notice this. When the cable again came under tension, the twisted bow remained and the cable became badly deformed. The problem was overcome by using a pulley with a spinning shackle. The circumstances were very similar to those which occurred when an attempt was made to recover the two bodies frozen to the North Face of the Eiger. (H. Harrer 1959). To continue with the plot, the Friday morning saw Jim Newton, Bill Holden (Red Rose), Jim Eyre, Chris Sheppard and Jim Farnworth ensconced in the snow hole and slit trench, busily laddering the lower pitch. A 300ft length of ladder was lowered down the rift, the idea being that Jim Eyre would go down to the end of the ladder and report back. A good ledge would have to be found within the limits of the winch wire. The 1000ft length limited the party to finding a ledge within 400ft of the snow ledge. The snow ledge was not considered to be suitable for good lifelining operations. Up on the surface the weather had taken a turn for the worse. The clear blue skies had given way to heavy, ominous clouds. It began to rain heavily and with the rain came the distant roll of thunder. The underground party was alerted and told to sit tight until the storm was over. As a precaution a couple of hundred feet of the main ladder was withdrawn and the telephone disconnected. The storm grew nearer and nearer and the darkened shaft was being lit up every few minutes by the flashes of lightening which flickered amongst nearby peaks. Thunder also made the fullest use of the shaft's acoustics. The underground party were by this time being subjected to a barrage of stones which had been dislodged by a small stream cascading down the normally dry shaft. The occupants of the snow hole had to bear the brunt of this onslaught as they had no cover whatsoever. It was small comfort to them to hear the stones whining down the shaft for a few seconds before impact. Their period of grace was probably spent in praying!! Fortunately nobody was hurt physically and they were winched out in a somewhat shell-shocked condition when the storm had passed over. It was decided that the bottom shaft would be attempted the following day, weather permitting. In the morning the altimeter showed a drop in pressure so the second lifelining party consisting of Ron Bridger, Bill Bates, Russell Cox, Alan Brittain and Carl Pickstone descended in haste to try once more, before the expected storm could strike again. The writer found the pitch really exhilarating; the top portion was as rigid as an iron ladder, due to its weight, as it hung within an inch or so of the rock. In the roof of the shaft an inlet passage could be seen which possibly connected with a snow cave higher up the mountain. At a depth of 200ft two more inlets of considerable size entered in the gully side of the shaft, unfortunately out of reach of the ladder. At this stage the shaft was much larger, being some 100ft by 80ft. There was a steeply sloping snow covered ledge on the far wall at a depth of 300ft. Here the shaft's tremendous size could be seen in its entirety, giving a very high degree of exposure. Upwards, the squat silhouette of the guide pulley could be seen against the azure Greek sky. The harsh cries of the choughs which nested above the shaft were plainly heard as they wheeled and turned in the narrow patch of sunlight, no doubt annoyed at this intrusion on their privacy. The ladder could barely be seen as a thin silver line against the dark rock of the shaft, whilst the slender winch wire was lost altogether in the gloom. Below, the ladder twisted its way downwards into the semidarkness of the shaft. Far below could be seen a smudge of whiteness, upon which four glow-worms were moving about their business. The muted sound of someone talking floated past but the words were lost in the underground vastness. The blows of a hammer echoed up the smooth black walls as yet another piton was driven into the rock. The descent continued but now the ladder swung free some 15ft from the rock. Another 200ft and things became much clearer and the ladder dropped into the top slit trench. Viewed from above the habitable portion of the ledge looked most uninviting. However, upon alighting in the deep trench and clipping himself on to a handy piton, the latest arrival found things much more comfortable. The ledge was roughly pear-shaped, sloping at 65° down a snow slope towards the small end which formed the edge of the lower pitch, the length being 60ft and the width 50ft. The ladder touched the slope between two buttresses 15ft apart, the left-hand one of which formed the edge of the lower pitch. The narrow trench had been cut in hard packed snow at the top of the snow slope, exposing the rock wall of the shaft. Into this had been driven a number of pitons and expanding bolts, for lifelining purposes. The 4ft high parapet of the trench overlooked the snow hole 20ft below. Access to this was by way of deep steps cut into the face of the slope, down the side of the left-hand buttress. The snow slope continued up beyond the right-hand buttress for another 40ft at the same angle. A few feet below the snow hole the walls narrowed to form a slit, 8ft wide, which looked out into a tremendous rift. The rift ran at right angles to the direction of the major axis of the shaft and in the same direction as the gully. The rift was 20ft wide and extended beyond the limits of vision on either side of the slit. There was a 15ft wide inlet in the far wall, opposite the slit. A stone dropped immediately beneath the ledge produced a bang after five seconds and took another five seconds to reach a large boulder slope. If a stone was flung to the right in the rift a delay of eleven seconds produced a deep rumble on impact. This was presumably a large boulder slope. Whilst Bill Bates and Ron Bridger were being winched to the surface Russell Cox and I attempted to plumb the pitch. The only things available on the ledge were a reel of telephone wire and an entrenching tool. With these a plumb-line was rigged up and lowered down the rift directly beneath the slit. The plumb-line snagged on something a good way down and refused to go any lower. The line was marked and then reeled in, to be measured later. Meanwhile Jim Eyre had descended to the ledge and had secured himself to the additional 600ft lifeline in preparation for a look down. He proposed to go down 300ft to see if there was a ledge within reach. In a few minutes all was ready, the surface winching party were alerted and the descent began. The acoustics of the rift were even better than those of the entrance pitch and every word could be heard perfectly. He descended to a depth of 200ft and could see a further 100ft. He reported that the wall opposite the slit continued straight down, along the whole visible length of the rift, while the wall beneath the ledge began to bell out gradually, giving a little hope of a ledge within reach. The rift curved out of sight on either side of him with smooth walls. He returned as there was little point in continuing. As the party were being winched out of the shaft the long-expected storm broke around the ears of the surface party, causing them to winch up much faster than usual, to the extreme discomfort of the person climbing the ladder. The only time his feet were allowed to climb the ladder properly was when the winching party became tired and another team had to take over. This procedure was repeated five times on the way up. As the last person was hauled out of the shaft, water cascading down the pitch caused some concern by dislodging stones and also by loosening up the snow on the ledge half-way down the upper shaft. After a really foul night Sunday dawned bright but a glance at the "storm predictor" revealed that the same sort of treatment was in store for us later in the day. Ian Carruthers, Peter Faulkner and Dave Stevenson (Shropshire Mine) descended to take photographs and to deladder the lower pitch. They also plumbed the lower shaft to verify the first measurement of 705 ft to a suspected ledge and dropped a flare down it. The flare did not ignite properly so that it did not illuminate the rift as

126

expected. However it did bounce off a sloping ledge a long way down before dropping into the blackness of a huge chamber and going out. During his stay on the ledge Dave Stevenson was hit by a small stone which penetrated his boiler suit and layers of woollens, causing some pain. He recovered the offending object after a search - it was the size of a large pea!! The storm clouds gathered once more and it began to rain heavily, sending streams of water down the shaft. This dislodged huge chunks of snow from the top ledge. These hurtled down the shaft at terrific speed and burst into thousands of fragments upon hitting the ledge. The de-laddering party were all brought out without incident. Scarcely had an hour passed, however, when the malevolent Greek Gods delivered their farewell message in the form of a flash of lightning. It came completely unexpectedly, without any prior warning rumblings, just as the entrance ladder was being hauled up and coiled. It struck the ground a mere couple of hundred feet away, with the earthing currents passing along the 600ft of ladder strewn over the ground around the shaft entrance In doing so ten people received shocks of varying severity, the worst hit being thrown to the ground. Ian Carruthers sustained partial paralysis of his arm and burns to his fingers, which fortunately cleared up after a few hours. That night Jim Eyre and Chris Sheppard bid Astraka their best regards and retired down to the village to organise the donkeys for the morning. A Tyrolienne was rigged up, using the winch wire, to drop gear from the shaft entrance 1000ft down the gully. It took all of the next day to ferry the equipment down through the hazardous stone-racked gully to the village. After a riotous evening, during which Anglo-Greek relations were firmly cemented the party retired very much the worse for wear. On Tuesday evening the nine members of the three-week party set out for Ostend in the Minibus, leaving the remainder to follow in the Land Rover. A thirty four hour journey brought the Minibus up to Ljubljana in Northern Yugoslavia. A leisurely drive followed, reaching Ostend on Saturday night, in time to catch the ferry back to England.

CONCLUSIONS: The unfortunate choice of the Diesel Land Rover for transport completely disrupted the programme of the expedition by causing five days of the three-week visit to be wasted. Its low cruising speed and doubtful reliability told a sorry story over the 2500 mile journey. By arriving in Ioannina three days later than was expected, another two days had to be spent waiting for permission over the weekend. The five days wasted severely curtailed any investigation on the Astraka plateau, other than at Provatina itself. It had been hoped to look at the Vikos resurgence and also to search for other shafts in the area - one report told of a shaft with a fifteen-second drop. However the six days spent up on the plateau were very fruitful indeed. The shaft was found to be far deeper than expected, in fact the 570ft to the snow ledge and the 705ft plumbed in the lower rift, without the unknown portion of the rift being added, proved the shaft to be deeper than the 1135ft entrance shaft of the Pierre St. Martin, the previous deepest known shaft. Tests carried out since returning from Greece puts the eleven-second free drop of the stone in the rift at approximately 1600ft. This makes Provatina Abyss the deepest known shaft in the world, with an estimated depth of 2200ft to a large boulder slope. Every member of the party descended to the Snow Ledge some two or three times. The lower rift was probed to a depth of 300ft and a ledge of sorts located at 705ft. The rift had an estimated depth of 1600ft to a boulder slope. The 1600ft depth could be disputed, as the timing was taken with a sweep second hand of a wrist watch. A one-second error would make quite a difference in depth. The entrance shaft and snow ledge were photographed and the whole of the shaft examined with a view to a further visit. Unfortunately the expedition was not the first to reach the snow ledge. The doubtful privilege of being the first person to reach the ledge fell to Ken Kelly who led a much publicised "do or die" attempt a few weeks previously. They succeeded in getting three men down before retreating as they considered it was "too dangerous". The lower rift was not sounded or probed by them, in fact the only indications of their visit was a pile of ironmongery lying around the shaft entrance and a lot of bad feeling in the village, due to their behaviour. The villagers had to be convinced that the second British party to visit Provatina had nothing to do with the earlier one led by Ken Kelly, before normal relations were resumed.

FUTURE PROSPECTS The depth potential of the shaft is tremendous due to its position of over 4000ft above the only resurgence in the area. The Vikos emerges as a river 20ft wide and up to 6ft deep, welling up through boulders in the 4000ft deep canyon which cuts into Astraka. The area is very heavily faulted and information gleaned from a French geologist conducting field work in the area suggested that Provatina was on a huge fault which ran in the same direction as the gully and the rift in the shaft. The depth so far plumbed accounts for half of the drop to the resurgence. What the remainder consists of will only be revealed after reaching the boulder slope at the bottom of the rift. Being a fault it could drop another 2000 feet and then continue as a huge rift to the resurgence or just end in a chamber like Balinka Pit in Yugoslavia. So much for the prospects, now for the problems! As can be expected the problems associated with a shaft of this size are bordering on the impossible. It will require a very strong team of engineers, rather than cavers, using a motorised winch. For an English party there is the problem of transporting all the equipment 2500 miles to Papigon. This year's expedition came to the conclusion that the route down through Yugoslavia was not the best way. The route through Italy to Brindisi, by ferry across the Adriatic to Igoumenitsa and then to Papigon offers a fitting alternative to the Metsovon Pass and Yugoslav Autoput. A lesson was also learned concerning transport. The Minibus was capable of carrying as much weight as the Land Rover at a much higher speed and could cope with the road conditions without too much difficulty. If time is a crucial factor it is well worth considering using either a 30cwt Ford Transit van or a Bedford Minibus. Then there is the formidable task of getting all the heavy equipment up to the plateau. From Papigon the plateau is inaccessible to donkeys but it is believed that they can be brought up from another village on the other side of the Vikos Gorge. A donkey can carry up to l80lbs. If the load is distributed over its carrying frame. At the equivalent of £1 /donkey/day the expense is justified if only to relieve three men of the gruelling slog up the mountain with packs on. The problem is mainly one of breaking the heavy winch down into packs capable of being carried by donkeys. It may be more easily visualised if the winch wire alone is considered. Without the drum on to which it is wound the cable weighs in the region of 400lbs and can only be carried up in one piece. However there may be a possibility of Greek Army help for any future attempt on the shaft. If helicopters could lift the winch up to the plateau it would save a lot of time and effort and could make all the difference between success and failure.

After managing somehow to convey all the equipment up to the plateau, there remains the problem of getting someone down the shaft and back again in one piece. When the ladder was withdrawn from the lower rift it was winched up in one length from the surface and it gave indications that it may be possible to drop down past the snow ledge to the suspected ledge at 1275ft. To do this it would be necessary to construct a gantry along the left-hand buttress at the entrance to the shaft. This could be done fairly easily as there are ledges on to which the frame could be bolted. An outrigger would be required at -1275ft to enable the cable to pass the ledge and reach the boulder slope at 2200ft. The shaft spirals down in three stages. There are also problems associated with the weather likely to be met during the short period when it is possible to gain access to the plateau. Hazards are caused by the electrical storms which occur very frequently in the area. After all, what better lightning conductor is there than 2000ft of wire rope stretching down inside the mountain? In addition Snake bites have accounted for four deaths in the village in the past few years. A helicopter is on permanent standby during the summer months for medical services! On reflection the writer thinks the visit was well worth all the effort put in by the members of the expedition and hopes that this personal impression of a visit to Provatina will perhaps fire the imagination of caving engineers somewhere, to design a winch capable of dropping someone down the shaft whilst still being portable enough to be transported up to the plateau. Further attempts on the shaft are being made by different expeditions this summer. Meanwhile Provatina waits as it has done for the past few million years. Perhaps it will not yield its very well kept secrets until rocket man-packs have become part of caving equipment!

SECTION 2.6 – THE DISCOVERY OF WHITSUN SERIES – G. BENN

Ever since the East Passage of Gaping Gill was discovered it has been the opinion of many potholers that one of the keys to the passages between Gaping Gill and Ingleborcugh Cave must lie along East Passage. Many attempts have been made to discover these extensions, and some were partially successful in that new ground was broken. Two which spring to mind are the scaling of the aven at the upstream end of Far East Stream passage and the extension of Avalanche Pot, both by the CPC. But in the last 60 years no real headway has been made along East Passage towards the Cave. That is, until Whitsuntide this year. According to Monty Grainger he attempted the sump at the end of the branch passage in Far East Passage before the war but was too large to get through. After the war, during one of the early BPC GG meets someone drained the sump with a hand pump and got through but did not push their success. In 1965, Neil Thorpe and Derek (Cas) Castleden examined the passage, passed the 'sump' which was actually a canal by then, and found a mud slope which led up to a boulder choke through which a strong draught blew. During the two years which followed Dave Brook mentioned this boulder choke to me several times but at Whitsuntide in both '66 and '67 we both had exams and no digging party was organised. Our interest became further aroused in 1967 by a rumour which said that the HWPC had broken through the choke into about 600ft. of stream passage followed by a sump. Rumours of a Clapham Bottoms Master Cave were also flying around at the time. During the Craven winch meet in August, Dick Glover, (CRG) had a look at the boulder choke and it looked to him as though someone had dug through and then replaced the boulders (or it had fallen in) but being alone he did not investigate further.

One night in the New Inn at around Easter time, Dave and I came into conversation with John Hallam of Imperial College Caving Club, who was particularly interested in the GG/Ingleborough Cave area and the branch passage was mentioned during a discussion about the end of Far East Passage. Then a few weeks before our GG Prelim., whilst he was in GG, rescaling the Craven Aven previously mentioned, Hallam examined the boulder choke and told us that it had not been dug before! (We found out later that he had broken through the choke and had found two chambers beyond).

With all these stories and rumours about the place it was obviously the prime objective when the winch was erected. Thus, on the Sunday of the Members' Meet a party of five members set out along Old East Passage, intent mainly on a 'tourist trip' for the benefit of a young lady. I decided to take the opportunity of looking at the ubiquitous boulder choke. When we arrived at Mud Hall no-one, including our female visitor, seemed to want to go back so, rather than split the party, we took her with us. As most people know, Far East is not the cleanest of places and very soon she was plastered in mud, but she seemed quite impressed with her first trip down GG. However, back to the story. I had never been much beyond Mud Hall and John Greene who had been on the BPC scaling party (in Craven Aven) in '65, could not remember the exact layout so we proceeded to the final chamber and worked back from there. We eventually found a passage which led off from behind a mud barrier in the left hand leg of a Y-junction in the stream passage. A very muddy passage brought us to a hole in the floor into a pool. This turned out to be the canal which had a nice comfortable air space. There followed a mud slope up to a low squeeze and a short vertical shaft of 3-4ft of which three sides were composed of mud and boulders - that was the demolished boulder choke. The boulders and mud formed the floor of a small chamber about 6ft wide, 15ft long and about 15ft high. At one end there was a hole in the floor half full of water which was either a sump or a backwater pool. A short crawl of a few feet in length opposite the point of entry led to another chamber of similar dimensions to the first. At the left hand end (S.E.) was a rift which closed down and in the opposite wall near that end was a hole at floor level leading down to the pool. It seemed that apart from one tube in the roof of each chamber (probably phreatic) there was no way out. The mud bank at the entrance to the second pool was undisturbed so I slid down head first to examine it more closely. The pool was only a yard wide and apart from one V notch in the roof there was no air-space. I came out rather disappointed and had a word with John Greene who was with me. It was obvious that the rumour about 600ft of stream passage was untrue. Before we left I had second thoughts about the pool and went down again, this time feet first. There was a hole under water and as I thrust my feet into the opening a small slab fell from the roof onto my feet - if this was the way on no one had been through before. I managed to pull a few more pieces out of the roof and by getting right down into the pool I could see through the triangular hole and between my feet to an upward slope of some kind. I decided not to duck through as the whole thing was fairly constricted and there was little or no room at the other side. It was clear that another trip, this time with a hammer and chisel, was required. We retreated to the main chamber, dispatched the young lady and one of the probationary members up the winch and John Greene, Mick Bycroft, Graham Midgley and myself came out through Bar to de-ladder it. Although there was now the prospect of a few feet of new passage, I thought (being an optimo-pessimist like most cavers - hoping for the best, but knowing deep down that there was little chance) that it would probably close down or choke with mud. But, nothing ventured etc. and on the Saturday of the Bank Holiday a party of four, consisting of John Greene, Alan Brittain, Mick Bycroft and myself, descended and headed straight for Far East with a further party of three (Dave Brook, Carl Pickstone and Chris Davies (M.U.S.S.) to follow later. We left Mick at the beginning of the canal to wait for the other three and John, Alan and I went through to the pool. Five minutes' work on the loose lumps in the roof with a hammer and chisel gave a triangular hole with a maximum of 6ins. Air space. There was then enough room for me to slide through on my back, head-first with my mouth in the roof. At the other side a mud slope started almost immediately and led up to a letterbox slot about 2 ins. high but a yard wide and whistling up the slope into the blackness was a strong draught. About ten minutes was spent digging up the mud slope before I became too cold to continue and after knocking off a few more lumps in the roof I slid back into the small chamber. Alan then took over digging as John hadn't got a wetsuit. For about thirty minutes all we could hear were the sounds of digging and much thrutching, until eventually a shout from the other side announced that he was through. I followed on as quickly as possible and Alan had to drag me up the mud slope through a tight squeeze as there was virtually no grip on the mud. John shouted through that the other three had arrived and that they would all follow on as soon as possible. The hole emerged directly into a large chamber with some very fine stalactites immediately in front. The chamber stretched away to the left with large mud banks on either side. After about 30-40ft a small trickle of water which ran towards us under the boulder floor turned

down to the right and Alan went down to follow it. The pebbly floored passage soon closed down but digging may make it go. Continuing forwards the chamber became more of a large passage with a gully in the floor full of tumbled boulders under which the trickle of water ran. On the mud bank to the left were some very fine stalagmites of varying shapes and there were some straws in the roof. At a kink in the passage were the two longest straw stalactites I have ever seen, the first was about 6-8 ft. long and the second was an estimated 10-12ft long. Around them were many more of 2-5ft! A large mud bank on the left reduced the passage to a narrow gully for a few feet to a small chamber. A series of cracks in the roof discharged a small trickle into a pool whence it flowed down the passage along which we had come. The floor of this chamber was covered in lumps of eroded flowstone the like of which we had never seen before. The lumps were covered in sharp spikes almost as if it had crystallised like that. In front the passage was filled to within a yard of the roof with a big stratified mud bank. Climbing up we followed this for about 30ft to where the mud had been washed away by a stream flowing from right to left to form a Sort of T-junction. The right hand passage curved round to the right and ended in a blank wall.

In the left hand wall was a narrow meandering crawl for 30- 40ft to a small calcited aven. The way upwards was very tight but a good draught was blowing down it. Back at the T-junction Alan went along the left hand branch to an impossibly tight vertical slit. It appeared as if there was no way on at the time so Alan and I made our way back to the Chamber and met the other five on their way along Straws Gallery. The two of us continued on our way back and left them to go and have a look at what had been found. Back at the entrance to the new passage we had a look at the passage to the right behind the big stalactite. This went for a short distance to a small chamber and a smaller passage continuing to a tight squeeze which looked as though it might go with a little digging out of the floor. The others seemed to be away a long time and we went to see what was delaying them. When we got to the T-junction there was no sign of them and the muffled voices did not appear to be coming from the passages we had explored. Eventually we tracked them down in a low crawl which went up the steep mud slope at the left hand side of the narrow vertical slot. Apparently Mick Bycroft (on his first meet as a full member – he was elected the previous Thursday) had gone exploring on his own and had found the low, steep crawl. At the top we found the rest milling around in a bedding plane. To the right was a steep mud slope leading down to a boulder floored passage. The right hand branch sloped steeply down under the way we had come and ended in a boulder choke through which a small trickle of water made its way through the boulders and eventually emerged from under the side wall of a very big rift formed on a NW-SE joint. At the left hand end the small stream entered from a gully about 20ft up. This aven should be climbable and may provide another entrance to the system. I made my way back to the bedding plane where I found that Carl and Dave had set off along it and that the passage was still going. The passage was mainly hands and knees crawling with occasional flat-out and stooping sections. This was later called Anagram Passage after an attempt had been made to form a name from the initials of the party's Christian names. The crawl was mainly along the line of the jointing and although it seemed to bend occasionally it was because the passage stepped sideways into another parallel joint. Large areas of the roof were covered with straw stalactites and helictites; one particular straw had bunches of helictites growing out of it at several points, for all the world like a Christmas Tree. The floor of the crawl was of sand and quite pleasant to crawl on. Shortly after a large calcite pillar had been encountered the passage ended abruptly but we crawled down through a slot at the left hand side and then up again through some boulders into a similar passage as before. This was christened Rhubarb Corner by Chris, whose imagination was taken by a stalagmite at the bottom of the 'U' tube. A little further along, past some nice crystal pools, a crawl was encountered on the left and as everyone had gone round to the right I crawled in, but unfortunately it turned out to be an oxbow (slower than the other route). The passage swung down to the left as at Rhubarb Corner and a flat out section brought us to a beautifully decorated grotto with masses of helictites and straws. Everyone halted for a rest here and, as time seemed to be running out (as far as the lamps were concerned) Carl, who was struggling through a tight bit just beyond, was given five minutes to see if the passage continued. He returned after the allotted time with tales of much larger passages beyond. A conference was held and in view of one or two people feeling tired and the state of our lamps we considered it prudent to return. (Hence Prudence Cairn). The retreat was uneventful except that the duck brought many comments and curses which were often repeated in later trips. It was a tired but excited party that was hauled out on the winch at approximately 11 pm after about a ten hour trip.

Because of the unfinished exploration it was obvious that the discovery had to be kept quiet. Four of us were in camp at GG, but Carl, Dave and Chris. had to go back to Clapham, where their exhaustion and mud-bespattered condition excited a certain amount of comment, especially when told that the trip had been a mere tourist one on East Passage. A return trip was obviously desirable as soon as possible but our lamps were flat and the members of the team needed time to recover from their exertions. The following day (Sunday) I took several lamps down to Clapdale for charging and set about getting another team together for an early start on Monday morning so that the dismantling of the winch would not be delayed. (Little did we know how early on Monday the trip was to be). There were only three 'definites' from the original team (John, Alan and I) with Dave and Carl as 'possibles'. That evening I stayed in camp to help man the winch and John went down to the village, returning with a disturbing story. Apparently whilst down at the 'Shoe' with Dave and Carl, the Brook Brothers and other U.L.S.A. members had been talking quite openly about an extension in GG which they had come across at the end of East Passage. On being questioned they said they had found it accidently and were going to survey it early the following day. The Happy Wanderers and others also knew about the new extension and a 'phantom' trip was obviously possible by any or all of these interested parties. On returning to Clapham, Dave and Co. met up with Dick Glover who said that he would go down with us if no others were available. As a result John set off back to GG to warn us of possible 'phantom' trips, Dave and Bob Jarman parked their vehicles at the bottoms of Long Lane and Clapdale track to make access difficult for would-be phantoms and Dick Glover went back to Carnforth to pick up his gear. On hearing the news, we arranged with Pete Faulkner and Jonah to lower us down the winch when we were ready. They went to bed to get some sleep before winching us down and we went down to Clapdale to collect our lamps. On the way back we removed the ladder from the first pitch in Bar to make entry difficult and Raymond Lee and Mick Bycroft went down Disappointment to take out the top two ladders from there. Eventually we were all kitted up, Jonah and Pete were aroused from their slumbers and at about 3.30 am the four of us (Alan, John, Dick and myself) descended. We didn't know how long the trip would last so we took spare lights and also some food in an ammo box as well as a ladder for the pits which Carl had reported, (Pickstone's Pits). Steady progress was made along East Passage and the Font (so named because it was now my birthday) we passed with little more than the usual curses. Dick was very impressed by the formations as we made our way to the bottom of Bradford Aven. Here he gallantly told us to carry on along Anagram Passage whilst he stayed behind so as not to slow us down. Alan had been behind us on the way to Bradford Aven and, not realising that we were there, had continued along Anagram at a high rate of knots, expecting to catch us up. It was not until John and I had reached Prudence Cairn that we overtook him. The low section just beyond Prudence Cairn was fairly tight and the rocks and floor were very sharp because of a layer of dog-tooth spar. The passage then opened out at a T-junction and the right hand branch continued as a sizeable gulley cut in the enormous sand-mud banks. (The left hand branch was more or less a dead end. The sand floor gradually rose and where the passage was about 3ft high we reached a deep but narrow rift in the floor, running along the passage. It was about 30-40ft deep and at the left hand end through an eyehole was a beautiful circular shaft which connected with the rift at the bottom. The shaft also continued upwards out of sight as an aven. Continuing on over the rift, the floor rose a little and we reached a chamber named Hollow Mountain Chamber because of a large sloping area of thin calcite which had formed on a sand bank before the sand had eventually been washed away. A well hidden aven at the far end was climbed by John to a passage which continued, but fairly small. This was not pushed. The floor kept on rising and eventually we dropped out of the bedding plane into a transverse gulley cut in the deposits by a small stream flowing from right to left. This trickle was the first stream we had seen since leaving Bradford Aven and the sight of this quite large passage going away to the left set my heart pounding. I really thought we had found a feeder which would lead us straight to the Clapham Bottoms Master Cave. However, after going round a couple of bends the stream sank into a boulder ruckle in the floor. Up a mud slope to the left we reached the bottom of a fine aven which both John and I climbed without reaching the top. Following the stream back we found that its source was a spout of water issuing from a small fissure into a natural rock basin. To the left of this another crawl led on past the foot of a boulder-filled rift (some of them gritstone). A little further along, John pulled a few rocks out of a bedding plane and ducked under a ledge to the right, then crawled over a hole in the floor and gained the top of a boulder slope in a large chamber. At the bottom of the slope the dimensions were about 30ft square. An upward mud slope in front had a line of quite good stal

bosses corresponding with a well decorated enlarged joint in the roof. Continuing along the left hand wall in a gulley we reached a continuation of the Chamber (Farrer Hall). A small stream flowed from an opening in front, ran across the floor and disappeared into a pothole against the left hand wall which was full of loose blocks. John and Alan investigated the inlet in front whilst I had a look at the choked sink and also at an alcove to the right of the inlet. All these possibilities drew blanks, although John said that the inlet, which had a calcited floor and ended in a boulder choke, might go with some digging. It was now about two hours since we had left Dick and we decided to return as quickly as possible in case he was beginning to wonder what had happened to us. We made our way back, marvelling once more at the myriads of eccentric formations along Anagram, and found Dick dozing off near the Font. Apparently he had gone along Anagram as far as Rhubarb Corner, made a rough survey of it and then returned slowly to wait for us. After taking one or two photos we collected our gear and returned through the liquid mud of the Font. Whilst returning along Far East Passage we met the Brook Brothers on their way in to survey the new series. When we reached Mud Hall we met a party of Imperial College Cavers led by John Hallam. I have never seen anyone look more dejected than he did after we had told him what he had narrowly missed discovering beyond the pool in the two chambers which he had found. Because of the time of day we were able to be winched out immediately and we finally surfaced at about 2 pm after another ten-hour trip.

Since that time, to my knowledge, there have only been about four trips - all by Club Members - of which only one or possibly two were with the intention of digging. There still remains some work to be done ie. the avens require climbing and one or two digs attempting. Unless the winch is in position an average party can expect to take 10 to 12 hours to reach the end of Whitsun Series from Bar Pot via the main Chamber and Mud Hall, particularly if any photos are taken. Several interesting points have arisen from the discovery of Whitsun Series, not the least being the method of formation of Anagram Passage. Nowhere in the main passage between the Font and Farrer Hall is a solid floor visible despite the dimensions of the latter. It would appear that Anagram could well be at least 10ft square in section. This estimate comes from the size of Straws Gallery, Farrer Hall and in particular from an exposed section of the deposits which occurs at Pickstone's Pits. Here, in a vertical exposure of 10-15ft there is a continuous gradation of alluvial matter from fine sand and silt at the top through gravel and pebbles to sizeable water worn boulders at the bottom. According to the Brook Brothers' survey (who I thank for their permission to reproduce their survey as we saw fit) the roof and sand floor of the passage gradually rise throughout its length. It cannot be ascertained with any accuracy whether the solid floor of the extension rises or falls. Because of the survey, the Brook Brothers suggest that the passage may come to the surface at the dry cove in Clapham Bottoms. However, whilst I wouldn't agree with this theory, until a study has been made of the flow markings and an accurate position and depth measurement made for the end of the extension, it is difficult to decide the part which Whitsun Series has played in the development of GG One final point, not previously mentioned, is that according to the survey the end of Whitsun Series is within about 200ft horizontally and just over 100ft vertically of the Club's dig in Clapham Bottoms. It is possible that this shaft is in some way connected with Whitsun Series and may be the cause of the strong draught through the System. On the final two trips the draught was inwards through the Font but on a later trip the draught was initially outwards and then it reversed during the night.

We were naturally very pleased that the Club had made the first breakthrough in GG for many years but it was with great astonishment (and perhaps a little jealousy) we heard that a few weeks later the Brook Brothers and U.L.S.A. had discovered over a mile of passage beyond the downstream sumps in Hensler's Stream Passage. Thus, in about a month nearly two miles of new passage had been discovered in a system long considered by many to be played out. The 'Far Country' as the Leeds called their extension, ends very close to Terminal Lake in Ingleborough Cave - the separation is variously put at 100 to 600ft. It would appear from this that a connection should be not long in coming. When it does it will certainly be a very sporting trip with at least three Wallows (two in the Cave and one in Far Country) and probably in the region of 2 to 3 miles of passage to negotiate.

Now rumours are flying about concerning an extension from the end of Stream Chamber, presumably towards an old sink on Newby Moss. The story has it that half a mile of large size passage has been discovered without reaching the end. With GG expanding like this in all directions it will soon be back in its rightful position as the longest system in the North. In conclusion, I would like to thank all those who helped in any way to make this discovery possible. In particular, my thanks to Jonah and Pete for winching us down at 3.30 am on the Monday morning.

SECTION 2.7- MOSSDALE-A PERSONAL RECOLLECTION- D.CASTLEDEN.

Mossdale – A BPC Tragedy.

From early in my career as a caver I had a morbid fear of Mossdale caverns. In the early 60s Mike Boon and Pete Livesey from the Bradford had developed a keen interest in the cave with its vast potential and spent lots of time discussing the hole with Bob Leakey the original explorer. Mike and Pete for whom I had the greatest respect were at the top of the pile when it came to cavers and I recall Mike discussing their first trip to the far end in lurid terms.

The fact that the first place to fill in any flood was the entrance and the way into the Marathon crawl was a drop down from the main stream so that if the main stream overflowed there would inevitably be a rapid increase in the amount of water going down the crawl. To make matters worse Mike pointed out that they had found fresh debris on the roof at the far end of the Mini Cow passage and 150 feet above the marathon crawls, a veritable death trap, which I resolved not to enter at any time.

Surprisingly few people realise that half the people who died at Mossdale were BPC members; the oldest Colin Vickers was only 23 and had been a member for 6 years but in those days that was getting on a bit for regular cavers. The next was Bill Frakes who may only have been 19 but had been caving since about 13. I first met Bill, who was caving with his dad Jack Frakes, in Goyden we were at the top of Gaskell's pitch which is about 50ft above the main stream way, and Bill noticed the pieces of green grass on the roof from the latest flood, ironic that a flood would eventually take his life. Mick Ryan was only 17 with limited caving experience but obvious stamina and ability to even consider a trip to the far end of Mossdale.

I caved with both Colin and Bill for several years and knew them very well but by the time of Mossdale I was on sabbatical having decided to get married the following year. This required some attention to my prospective wife and the need to conserve what little funds we had. On the day of the disaster, I was visiting Carol at home in the afternoon, when news came on the television that there had been a storm in the Dales and several people were trapped in Mossdale Caverns. The weather in Bradford at the time was equally abysmal with water running down the street and

my first and immediate comment to Carol was "they are dead" little realising that people I knew as close friends were the cavers down the hole.

Sadly, on the Monday, I had to go to work but then managed to escape and headed for Mossdale, not knowing what to expect. On arrival I was greeted by an amazing sight, vast amounts of earth had been moved and an amazing diversion for the stream away from the entrance. One of the first people I met was Chris Whelan, a pal from the BPC, who had been at the hole from the start of the rescue and had been sleeping on the moor without a tent. Chris told me that since 5 bodies had been found a further flood had forced the bodies through relatively tight sections and they were now further in than ever, increasing the difficulty of recovery. The immediate priority, now that the rain had gone, was to find Hoggy. There seemed little hope, but the possibility was still there that he might just have made it into the high levels.

I immediately offered my services to go and look for Hoggy and was thrilled to be told to get changed and join a small party heading underground to search for our missing friend. By good fortune I was offered the loan of a wet suit which would be infinitely better than woollies and a boiler suit. I dutifully arrived to be the first down the hole. Whilst waiting for the rest of the team I sat with my legs just inside the entrance which was being controlled by one of the Cave Rescue. Whilst waiting this guy was examining a piece of the roof, above the entrance, which came free and then, for some unknown, reason returned it to the hole from which he had extracted it, big mistake. The next thing I knew was the rock dropping onto the back of my hand and crushing and cutting, blood everywhere, idiot!

So that was the untimely end to my best opportunity of a safe trip down Mossdale.

When the team I was supposed to be joining got under way, for what is at best a tough trip, they decided to rest and one of them rolled onto his back and was shocked to see Hoggys boots above him. A cavers worst nightmare bad enough to be drowned but Hoggy had found a narrow rift above the crawl and forced his body into it so tightly that even after he died he was so jammed in that he did not slip out. Having suffered the dreadful fate of the water rising up to him for, heaven only knows how long, hopefully it was quick!

For my part my only claim to fame was that I was the only live casualty that the Cave Rescue had to transport across the moor and off to the hospital in Keighley. Once there the A & E staff appeared with scissors, to cut off the borrowed wet suit, no way! Pain I could stand but the cost of replacing a wet suit was way beyond my financial ability, so I had to grin and bare it!

So that was the end of my Mossdale adventure. I am sure it is common knowledge that after discussion with relatives the decision was made to leave the bodies in the hole rather than risk more lives and the entrance was sealed with concrete. Rumour had it that some cavers did go down an alternative entrance and move the bodies into a side passage but there is no way I could confirm this although it does sound like a worthy enterprise.

We did have a memorial service in Coniston attended by well over 100 people with many from the caving fraternity, one of my final recollections was Mick Melvin a very keen caver from the White Rose saying "that's it I will never cave again, whether he did or not I can't say but I did understand the sentiment, for my part it was all a wake up call which reminded me that however good you may think you are you are neither infallible or immortal.

SECTION 2.8 – REMINISCENCES
– A RUMMAGE THROUGH JOHN ROBINSON'S ATTIC.

Having been a member of the BPC for over half a century, caving seems the most natural thing to do in the whole world, but it is not to many people's liking – very much like Marmite really. So how did I become interested in the subterranean world? I suppose I can trace my early love affair with the custodian of those caves and potholes, the Yorkshire Dales, starting with a family trip to Malham. I was only a young lad, maybe seven or eight years old, and with my mum and dad we travelled by bus from Thornton, Bradford, first to Keighley, then Skipton before catching the Pennine bus with its distinctive black and orange livery to Malham. I recall the walk to Janet's Foss where a dark void in the rock was seen by the waterfall. What lies hidden in the darkness beyond I wondered? (Not much as it happens). We continued along a stream towards Gordale Scar where dad covered my eyes before rounding a rocky buttress, and led me safely round the corner before removing my eye cover. Wow! I was gobsmacked at the spectacle which immediately unfolded before me. Walls of rock soared skyward and a stream splashed down a ravine from what seemed a dizzying height. This was my first introduction to the Yorkshire Dales and to limestone scenery and it sure made a lasting impression.

My next trip to the Yorkshire Dales would have been when I was about ten years old. Again this was with my parents, but this time we took the various buses to Ingleton and stayed there a few days at a local B&B. Ingleton Waterfalls walk was first on our agenda, and what a fabulous wonderland that was. I still never tire of it, and it always remains a delight throughout the different seasons. On the moor top, approaching Beezley falls and looking over to Chapel-le-Dale I noticed the roof of a building with the word "cave" painted upon it. "Dad, dad can we go to the cave" I enthused, so the following day saw us at White Scar Cave. In those days it wasn't as extensive as now, but no matter I was enthralled the moment I stepped out of the sunshine and into the beckoning darkness of the show cave. I wanted to crawl up the several side passages we passed by, and go beyond that final barrier where reluctantly we had to turn round and head back out. Never-the-less, the seed had been sown and the subterranean world of the limestone dales became an ongoing fascination for me. That evening we

visited Ingleton Picture House to see the film "The King and I", but it was the day's visit to White Scar Cave which was firing my imagination rather than the King of Siam.

The years passed and, during my teenage years, camping trips to Stainforth with a group of local afriends became popular, particularly during the Easter and Whitsuntide holidays. We would walk for many miles in the Ribblesdale area and beyond, sometimes not having a clue as to where we were, and during these walks we would pass holes in the ground, some huge and others quite small, and we often would wonder what lies beyond these cave entrances. Someone mentioned that a winch allowed visits to the depths of a pothole called Gaping Gill to take place, so one Easter we discovered where this Gaping Gill was, and walked over there from Stainforth only to find nothing but a great hole in the ground. No surprise there then – Oh the benefits of hindsight! The Internet which we take so much for granted for obtaining information was still a long way off becoming a reality. One particular friend, Barrie Robertshaw, with whom I walked a great many miles with was equally interested in the caves and potholes which we noted on our hikes through the Yorkshire Dales. One Whitsuntide, again whilst camping at Stainforth, we made a more successful visit to Gaping Gill. The two of us paid our ten shillings (50p), a not inconsiderable sum of money at the time, and armed with torches and a copy of Pennine Underground we ventured into the depths of this famous system. We were like young children in a toyshop, fascinated by the myriad of passages which seemed to go every which way. We clambered and crawled, and got lost a few times, we were like the proverbial pigs in shit. We nearly outstayed our welcome though when a couple of "proper" cavers came looking for us as we were the last in the system and the winch operators (the BPC) wanted to close for the day. We had a particular spring in step as we walked back to Stainforth that evening whilst chatting about the events and delights of the day, and our adventures underground.

Barrie and me decided that we wanted to pursue our interest in caving and that we ought to join a caving and potholing club, so we considered how to go about it. We both knew a lad who we went to junior school with, who lived locally to us, and

136

who we understood had taken up potholing. His name was Derek Castleden, and we approached Derek for advice. He pointed us in the direction of the secretary of the Bradford Pothole Club who provided us with a list of forthcoming caving trips and of details of where to meet – a place called Brackenbottom where the club had its headquarters. If we were to become proper cavers then we would need proper caving equipment – helmet, lamp, and suitable clothing. I obtained a book titled Cave-Craft written by David Cons which provided lots of advice for the novice caver. Having recently re-read the book it is very quaint, and oh, how things have changed! The clothing consisted of old woollen shirts, jumpers, and trousers all held together in an outer shell of a boiler suit purchased, together with a pair of Long Johns, from a stall in Bradford's Kirkgate market. Another shop in Bradford, maybe Sports and Pastimes, provided the helmet made of compressed fibre which softened after prolonged wetting, a carbide lamp costing twelve shillings and sixpence (sixty two and a half pence), a steel carabiner, and a waist length; this was a fifteen foot length of light nylon rope, wound round the waist and tied off with a reef knot, a sort of belay belt.

One Sunday was chosen for our inaugural pothole experience with the BPC, and the pothole on the meets list that day was Calf Holes. First we had to get to Brackenbottom, no easy task in the days before we had our own transport (we take so much for granted now). The days of the Hebble bus picking members up from Bradford for the day's caving had come to an end, and so, fortunately for us, Barrie's dad volunteered to take us up to Horton-in-Ribblesdale on his motor bike and side car. It wouldn't go up the lane to Brackenbottom laden with three people and caving gear, so we had to walk the short distance up Brackenbottom Lane to the club headquarters which we later learnt was affectionately called the Dump. Upon arrival we rather nervously knocked on the front door only to be told in no uncertain terms to go round the back! Round the back we were met by someone, maybe Pete Faulkner, and we explained that we wanted to go caving. We were taken inside the Dump to the kitchen area where we were introduced to the assembled throng who were told that we wanted to go caving, whereupon the whole place erupted into laughter and cries of "they want to go caving?" After this baptism of fire things improved, as only they could, and we were introduced to Old Jonah who was the meet leader. He took kindly to us and transported us to High Birkwith in his van for our trip into Calf

Holes. This was the first time that I had seen an electron ladder, never mind used one for climbing, but with Jonah's encouragement, and on a tight lifeline, I soon descended the main shaft in a spray of water to land in a large pool at the bottom of the shaft, rather than use the side shaft most commonly used today. Calf Holes was everything that I expected a pothole should be: a laddered shaft, a stream passage, a crawl and a squeeze, a scramble, a waterfall, and an exit through a cave at a lower level. This was fantastic and I was buzzing. I was also hooked for at least the next half century! Thanks Jonah.

Barrie submitted his membership application a little before me and was immediately accepted into the club. I followed a little later. Soon, however, love proved more powerful for Barrie than the lure of caving, and very soon that was the end of his caving adventure. I, on the other hand, was more pragmatic and realised that affairs of the heart and caving could, and should, survive together.

Club meets were held on a monthly basis and on a Sunday – many people still worked Saturday morning in those days. The only viable way for me to get to the Dump for the Sunday meets was to travel there by bus on the Saturday and stay overnight which inevitably led to my introduction to the Helwith Bridge Hotel. The Crown in Horton was also a popular Saturday night venue with the caving community where we would sing our hearts out and drink copious beers until closing time. There were no twee barstools and tables then, it was mainly furnished with settees and armchairs. By sliding a hand down the side of a chair there was a stash of coins to be found having fallen out of unsuspecting trouser pockets. This helped subsidise the evening's drinking! Since the songs we sang were mainly Irish rebel songs, this abruptly came to an end at the start of the Irish Troubles when army personnel camping nearby and using the pub themselves "encouraged" us to stop singing. Pub singing never returned in such popularity ever again, alas. Bunks at the Dump were either two or three tier contraptions having no mattresses. If you were lucky a sheet of cardboard would be covering the metal frame making it fractionally more comfortable, but woe betide anyone found sleeping on somebody else's cardboard!

Another young lad called Raymond appeared on the caving scene shortly after me. He was a tall, lanky lad and soon acquired the nickname Snake. He lived in Bradford and we often caught the same

137

buses up to Horton. Since neither of us had our own transport and, without the help of those who had, our caving was limited to the area closest to the Dump. As a result Sell Gill became one of our most frequented potholes in that area. John Greene, who had been a member somewhat longer than us and who also came from Bradford but who similarly had no transport of his own often joined us in our pursuits. Between us we decided that since none of us had either transport or a telephone, it would be a good idea to meet up in a pub in Bradford each Thursday night where we could, over a few beers, arrange to get together in the Dales at the weekend and decide upon a suitable caving venue. There was none of this smart phone and facebook malarkey in those days. The pub we decided upon was the Commercial Inn in James Street, Bradford, and here we were able to arrange our future caving trips and discuss all matters caving. Soon, other members would become aware of our Thursday night social, and they too would come along and join us for a few beers and convivial conversation. In its heyday, upwards of thirty people would join us for a Thursday night social, such was its popularity. For whatever reason, we moved to other pubs in Bradford including the Metropole, the Black Swan, and the Fighting Cock, but over time popularity began to dwindle, probably due to the drinking and driving legislation, and ultimately, after a good number of successful years, the Thursday night social fizzled out all together.

A lifelong hobby of mine has been, and still is, photography, and I was enthusiastic about combining this with my caving activities. John Greene mentioned to me that the Heavy Gang used to meet at a pub in Bradford, maybe the demolished White Lion near John Street Market, long before the start of our Thursday night socials, and on occasion would have slide shows where they would be entertained by showing each other's caving photographs. This struck me as being a super idea, and was keen that we should have a go at organising something similar ourselves. Soon I was on the committee, and before I knew it I was Hon. Phot. This gave me the opportunity to put into practice my idea of a midweek slideshow in Bradford (we were the *Bradford Pothole Club* after all, and at the time it was central to where most members lived). Realistically, there would only be sufficient material for one annual show, and late autumn/early winter seemed as good a time as any for such an event. The Star Hotel in Westgate was chosen for our initial slideshows since it had a large function room ideal for our purposes. Over the years we showed each other's slides, Frank

Moulson showed his lantern slides, we had guest speakers, and hired feature length cine films. Once more we had a move, and this time to the Metropole Hotel where we used their function room for our annual winter slide show, and it was here that I had my first attempt at showing an audio visual presentation using an adapted reel to reel tape recorder and two very dissimilar slide projectors. I had to feed each slide manually into the projectors as a small lamp lit up, switched on by a piece of aluminium foil attached to the recording tape passing over two conductors. What could possibly go wrong? As it happened, everything! Very soon the audience lost interest in the slides being projected and concentrated their attention towards the back of the room and on me juggling slides (literally!) trying in vain to keep up with the music track being played. Ah well, we all have to start somewhere.

Over the years the annual Slide Show went from strength to strength, and moved from Bradford up to Horton-in-Ribblesdale since the membership was now no longer centred in the Bradford area, and Horton was our spiritual home anyway. By this time I was Hon. Phot. for the third time, and it coincided with dawn of the digital age in photography. Our slide shows became a mixture of traditional transparencies and digital presentations, and very soon – much sooner than I certainly anticipated – wholly digital presentations. At this point I decided to rename the Slide Show the Electric Picture Show to more accurately describe the nature of the event, and it has become a well established event in the club calendar ever since. I could never in all honesty call myself a hard caver, I think consistent might be a better description. Neither did digging have a great appeal either. Heroic stories of the discovery of caverns measureless to man were very few and far between, and the rest of the time seemed to me to be hard graft and squalor. I do appreciate the camaraderie experienced by these teams and their quest for new cave though.

My interest throughout has been in photographing the caves and potholes of our area and further afield, extending to Europe, but sadly no further. People would disappear in an instant when they saw me approach carrying my ammo box full of photographic gear. Strange how these same people wanted a slide show, but didn't cherish the idea of standing up to their necks in cold water whilst flashguns failed to fire. I think that I've answered my own question there! During the 1970's a group of us consisting mainly of Steve Dudley (Duds), Martyn Scatliffe, Alan Ward

(Gladys), and myself referred to ourselves as the incompetent caving club (ICC) and the incompetent photographic union (IPU) or something very similar. Most weekends would see us involved in some underground photographic activity, with Duds being by far the most competent. Overnight trips into Gaping Gill were a feature of the GG winch meets, where many hours would be spent attempting that special shot. I recall attempting to photograph Mud Hall before the traverse around it was established, and having to use the 60 foot ladder pitch. Numerous failures of the equipment resulted in Martyn having to climb that ladder upwards of ten times. That is 1,200 foot of ladder climbing to get just one photograph! Unlike today's instant digital result of success or failure, we had to wait a week or two before we saw the results of our transparency film.

My first experience of foreign caving was a trip to the Devoluy area of the French Alps. Pete Faulkner had been to that area previously, I believe with the Red Rose, and was aware of a deep pot which at the time had the reputation of being the second deepest in the world. This was the Chourum des Aiguilles, or as we preferred to call it Needles Pit. Pete had made contact with one of the original explorers, Jean Tourres of the Speleo Club de Gap, and with that information a group of us set of to France armed with all of the club's electron ladders and thick, hairy, lifeline rope. I travelled down with Dave Brook in his van, and we met up with the rest of the group at a farm where Pete had camped previously and which doubled up as a bar in the tiny village of Le Villard Joli. We established camp in a field having no facilities, but with the most magnificent views over the Alps imaginable. To have a dump, you took a shovel, dug a small hole behind some bushes, shat, replaced the sod, and returned with a very smug expression on your face. Ah, the simple life. The Millon family who owned the farm were the most hospitable people I think that I have ever had the pleasure to meet. The farm had ceased functioning as a bar, but that was immediately sorted and crates of bottled beer were soon at our disposal in the family's living room. One evening we were invited to a party. Now not being one to turn down a party, I was a little bemused to learn that it would be in a nearby church. Sure enough, bottles of beer were laid out for our consumption on the altar, and before not too long Alan Brittain had donned liturgical vestments — he was quite the part with his beard and staring eyes! Myself, I was keeping a sharp lookout for the bolt of lightning that I felt sure would strike us at any moment.

Whilst Needles Pit was our goal, other attractions caught our attention. L'obiou, a most impressive mountain in Devoluy, and at an altitude of somewhat over 9,000 feet, just had to be conquered. A 4am start ensured we arrived at the summit before the sun got too high in the sky. Equally impressive was the Aven d'Orgnac show cave over in the Ardeche, necessitating quite a long round trip, but the calcite formations were out of this world and exceeded all our expectations. The walk up to Needles Pit, carrying considerable amounts of gear, required another early start since it was quite a hike up to the entrance and the heat from the sun was intense. Once inside the pot we made progress as far as an unstable pitch called the House of Cards. At this point it was decided to retreat and save the continuation for another time. Subsequent trips to this area focussed on completing the descent of Needles Pit. The following year, 1971, I travelled back to Devoluy with Neil Dyson in his van, accompanied with Trevor Kemp. It soon became apparent that a more lightweight assault was required, and that the number and weight of ladders required was too restrictive. A year or two later, Needles Pit was successfully bottomed by the BPC using single rope techniques rather than the much heavier and bulkier electron ladders. In fact I think that it is fair to say that this heralded the advent of SRT within the club and the demise of ladders for general caving. I look back at these times with great affection, and consider that Needles Pit holds a lot of fond memories for those who were around at that time, and was a significant era in the life of the BPC.

I have undertaken many other trips abroad, and many other highlights have been experienced, but without any doubt it is the buzz I get from being with a great bunch of like minded individuals, no matter where I am, that never fades as the years continue to roll by. Lots of other stories can be told, and I'm sure that they will be — I have only scratched the surface here, but from those humble beginnings visiting the Yorkshire Dales as a small child to the less active times of later life, the BPC experience with all its happy memories, laughter, tears, piss taking, celebrations, and of course a few beers, will last forever.

SECTION 2.9 CHOURUM DES AIGUILLES – 1970 TO 1974 – RAYMOND LEE.

Long, long ago in the summers of the late sixties, when Pete Faulkner was, not asleep on the bar at the Helwith, or cavorting in his string vest, he used to explore the High Alps region of South East France, with his friend Jim Eyres of the Red Rose CPC and others. They used Villard Joly as their base, a small Hamlet near St Dizier, a village about 80km from Grenoble. They visited several caves and shafts, including Puits De Bans, a 200m deep pot, which in flood conditions fills up, with water gushing from the entrance, much like Sleets Gill in Littondale.

It was on one of these jaunts that the party met up with Jon Tourres of the Spelio Club de Gap, who, luckily for Pete, spoke perfect Mancunian. He informed Pete that his club, on the direction of a local shepherd, had discovered a cave system in 1963. It was situated in the Vallon des Aiguilles some 23km from Corps by road and a further 3 or 4km walk from La Festre, a small hamlet on the road to Gap. The Aiguilles entrance grid reference was 876,22 269,80 at an altitude of 1995m.

Exploration began in 1964 and after a series of short pitches (the toboggan) Jon Tourres and team were confronted by a low crawl, containing a strong draught (Meandre aux Boutons) where digging was required to make progress. After passing the crawl, the cave enlarged and led to a series of unstable boulder slopes and pitches. In 1967 the top of the Minotier pitch at -510m was reached. Inspite of bad flooding in 1968, the top of Moustique was attained. The team returned in 1969 determined to bottom the system and descended the final pitch of 11m (Deception) to an impassable sump at a depth of -682m. The water resurged at Source de Gillarde, some 400m lower and 11km away.

Encouraged by Pete Faulkner in 1970 a team was assembled including Ged Benn and Chris Davis, Pete and Kath Faulkner, Dave Brook, Raymond Lee, Alan Brittain, Bob Booth 1 and John Robinson. They were shown the entrance by Jon Tourres, who drove them part of the way in his jeep. The club's first attempt, using ropes and ladders, reached a point near the base of the Chateau de Cartes pitch. After this expedition, it became evident that, having only reached a depth of -200 or so metres below the entrance, a much larger party would be required to carry the 1500 feet of ladders and 3000 feet of rope needed to bottom the system. The

camp at Villard Joly was again used and the hospitality of the Millon family were much appreciated, especially by John Robinson. Boisterous evenings were spent in the farmhouse, with the local insects intoxicated by the spilt beer. A devout group of French cavers even arranged a drinking session in a local church, la Mere Eglise.

A further attempt in 1971 comprising Ged Benn and Chris Davis, Alan Brittain, Pete Faulkner, John Robinson, Trevor Kemp, Bob Booth 1, Vince Buckley and Neil Dyson went as far as Puits de Lac.

In 1972, AC Toulon followed an upstream passage below the Chateau de Cartes pitch and after scaling many shafts, including one of 44m, Dalai-Rama, no connection with Tibet, reached a point where soil and roots could be seen, heralding the opening of the Rama entrance. This discovery increased the depth of the whole system to -958m, which at the time made it the world's third deepest cave.

On Friday 27th July 1973 a larger party with Jim Abbot, Alan Charlton, Barry Emmett, Pete Faulkner, Dick Maclindon, John Robinson, Martin Scatliffe, Brian Smith, Chris Vaughan, Ian Wilkinson, Cedric Binns, Raymond Lee, John Bolton, Bob Booth, Alan Brittain, Derek Castleden, Janice Castle, June Greenwood, Sheryl Haynes and Raymond Stoyles set off for France in various vehicles in different states of repair, some breaking down before leaving Bradford, and a wheel bearing failing 60 miles from Southampton.

All arrived safely in the small town of Corps over the weekend and made straight for the bar, where plans were made as to who would do what and with whom. They were somewhat concerned by a rumour that the shifty French had added a further 300m to the depth of the Aiguilles, just to thwart their attempt, but this turned out to be from the Rama entrance, some 300m higher.

The town of Corps, at an elevation of 1000m is about 60km from Grenoble on the Route de Napoleon. It overlooks the scenic Lake Sautet a popular tourist resort as well as supplying hydro electric power from the dam at the Barrage du Sautet.

Finally dragging themselves from the bar on Monday 30th the party made their way to the Col du Festre passing the assumed rising the Source de Gillarde on the way. On reaching the Col du Festre, the large party set off in 90 deg heat following the path over the top of a cliff and dropping down into the Vallon des Aiguilles with a stream flowing across the floor of the valley. The French had kindly left a large marquee at the side of the stream which came in useful for the team. The entrance, a small shake-hole on a path leading up to the summit of La Rama, was eventually found.

On Tuesday 31st, Derek Castleden, Alan Charlton, John Bolton, Alan Ward and Chris Vaughan ferried a large amount of tackle to the base of the Chateau des Cartes. The next day Alan Brittain, Pete Faulkner, Bob Booth and Jim Abbott, after leaving Corps at 4am, staggered up to the entrance and reached the head of the Puits Trempette at a depth of -350m where they left tackle for the next party. Their trip had taken 9 hours. Some tackle had been left in the system by the French but was deemed unsafe to use.

On the Wednesday, the third party comprising Ian Wilkinson, Brian Smith, Cedric Binns, Dick Maclindon and Raymond Lee went down and laddered the vertical sections between Puit du Lac and Trempette. On surfacing and consulting the survey it was realised that little progress had been made in such a deep cave system, progress made slower with the use of ropes and ladders as opposed to the French rope techniques. Ladders and ropes had also been "wasted" on pitches not shown on the survey.

After a short discussion it was decided for the whole party to have a rest day and then the final bottoming trip would happen on the Saturday 4th August with as many as possible taking part. On the Friday evening the festivities in the marquee were disturbed by a Frenchman, a member of AC Toulon, who claimed the tent was his and his three companions who were to arrive later that night. It was their intention to bottom the cave the next day using rope techniques. It then dawned on the BPC party how ungainly their tackle was in comparison with the French alpine equipment.

Saturday saw Brian Smith, Raymond Lee, Ian Wilkinson, Pete Faulkner and Jim Abbot climbing up to the entrance accompanied by the four Frenchmen, with their waist mounted carbide containers and unusual headgear. They went down first and were not seen again that day. Pete then decided to "throw a sicky" and go back down to the valley so the party was reduced to four. The trip as far as the Chateau des Cartes went without

incident but much loose rock was encountered on that pitch. The party then continued down to Puit Jacques where drinks and food were enjoyed. We were feeling the cold at this point and morale seemed to drop off a cliff (no pun intended) It was decided that Jim Abbot and Raymond Lee would press on as far as possible without tackle, but after descending Puit Jacques and a small pitch below they were halted after a few metres by Puit Martine (9m). This marked the limit of the 1973 expedition having reached a depth of -420m and were just six pitches from the bottom.

The de-tackling began and at the top of Puit Trempette, Pete Faulkner, Derek Castelden, Alan Brittain, Bob Booth and Cedric Binns were met and helped to transport the tackle to the Chateau des Cartes where some was left for the next day. The party surfaced at 5am on the Sunday morning after 16hrs underground. On the same day all the tackle was retrieved by another party and brought to the surface. All that remained was to carry all the tackle back down to Le Festre and to drive back to Corps and the bar at the Cafe des Voyageurs from where it all began.

After yet another unsuccessful attempt and clearly being gluttons for punishment there were dark mutterings about returning to France to finally conquer the Aiguilles, even from normally sane individuals. Looking back it was realised it had taken the 1973 BPC team 5 days to cover two thirds of the way while the French, using single ropes, had taken just 18hrs to the bottom and out again including some climbing above the sump. To mount another attempt using ropes and ladders would require a large party long hours in the cave and probably an underground camp. It was decided that realistically the only feasible way for a small party to bottom the cave was using single rope technique in 2 or 3 trips each less than 24hrs duration. Luckily about the same time Brian Smith, Ian Wilkinson and others were becoming interested in SRT and a quantity of rope for that purpose was bought by the club.

To this end many weekends were spent practising the new rope techniques in places like Alum Pot, Bar Pot, Gaping Gill main shaft and crags at Heptonstall and Ilkley. For some reason some members even liked to hang around outside the women's room (on ropes). Many of the members who had enjoyed the "delights" of the Aiguilles the previous year somehow seemed reluctant to return in 1974 however, Dick Mclindon, Dave Mathews and Brian Judd finally offered their services bringing the total team to ten.

The transport arrangements were that Brian Smith, June Greenwood, Sheryl Haynes, Jim Abbott, Dick Mclinden, Ian Wilkinson and Janice Castle would hire a long wheelbase Land rover to transport most of the tackle whilst Dave Mathews, Brian Judd and Raymond Lee would travel in Dave's Mini. Pete Faulkner had discovered his holidays didn't coincide with the expedition so kindly loaned his tent to Raymond Lee, a noted scrounger. Foolishly Brian Sellers then volunteered and somehow squeezed into the groaning Land rover.

The party left Yorkshire on the 19th July for Ramsgate and all arrived in time for the ferry to Calais. After a long drive interrupted by a faulty petrol pump on the Mini everyone arrived safely in Corps eager to enjoy the night life. After a day's rest at the lakeside campsite, Monday saw the tackle and camping gear taken up to the Col du Festre ready for the descent on Tuesday 23rdJuly.

After a 9 am start Brian Smith, Brian Sellers and Raymond Lee entered the cave with the intention of reaching Puit Jacques carrying plenty of food as well as the tackle. They would be followed by Ian Wilkinson, Jim Abbott, Brian Judd and Dick Maclindon a few hours later to bring the rest of the tackle to the top of Puit Jacques. Dave Mathews had allegedly been banned from caving by his doctor. Just inside the entrance "the greasy pole", a dead tree with rungs nailed to it, was bypassed with a ladder for safety. Steady progress was made down to the Chateau des Cartes pitch using the French bolts and split tubing to protect the ropes from abrasion. At this point the food box dropped down the pitch, but luckily for the health of the dropper, the food survived. At the foot of the pitch the second party caught up and continued together. At Puits de Lac a bolt was placed as no belay could be found to back up the French bolt. On reaching Trempette, Brian Sellers, Dick Maclindon and Raymond Lee set off out. The remaining party continued down to Puits Gaulios and Jacques where the shattered limestone defeated all attempts to drill for a bolt for the belay so a 75m rope was wrapped around a large boulder at the foot of Gaulois pitch. What was left of the tackle and food was left at this point and the party exited meeting the other party at the entrance after 12hrs underground.

After so much excitement a rest day was in order, to enjoy the sun and deplete the stock of red wine in the camp. The evening's revelry was disturbed by a strangely familiar voice in the valley which turned out to be Pete Faulkner accompanied by John Cooper. Raymond Lee then realised he'd been tricked into bringing Pete's tent to France. Pete and John had flown to Nice and hired a car, their gear was hidden in the Land rover. The shock of Pete's arrival was somewhat less than the prospect of a night sharing his tent with him.

The next day was also a rest day as the team prepared to reach the sump on Friday 26th July. On the Friday Brian Smith, Brian Sellers and Raymond Lee set off at 10am and reached Puits Jacques in 2 hours. Jim Abbott, Ian Wilkinson, Brian Judd and Pete Faulkner were to follow 2 hours later to start detackling. The end of the 75m rope on Puit Jacques was used to belay the rope for Puit Martine which followed immediately. Puit Versaillais was next with camp 600 near the base, where the food was left for the return journey. The next pitch was expected to be Minotier but a 10m pitch was encountered with no spare rope but a traverse to the right led to a free climb. After some further free climbs the head of Minotier, a well watered 24m deep shaft, was reached. The rope hung down the centre with no way to avoid being soaked. The next pitch Jo, of 20m, was soon reached but with no bolts the rope belay was an eye hole. A passage at the foot of Jo was followed by Brian Smith but became too low. At that point the second party of four arrived and Ian Wilkinson found a short climb which bypassed the low crawl, this led to the Meandre Serrano. Starting out as a walking passage but becoming flat out it suddenly opened out on to the head of the Moustique pitch. Belayed to a bolt and eyehole the 50m rope was lowered down the shaft protected at the top but touching ledges lower down. The dangers of Mustique were realised on the way down with many loose boulders on sloping ledges waiting to rain down on the party. At the bottom a long easy passage with a few formations led to the top of deception the last pitch of 11m.The pitch lived up to its name and at the foot, a short wet crawl led to a miserable sump at -682m. All seven cavers had reached the sump, the first party, in just six hours.

Elated at having finally reached the end the ascent began but Jim Abbott brought the disturbing news that the rope was fraying on a ledge 10m below the head of Moustique pitch. It was decided that some lucky person would prussik up the rope and reverse it so that the fray was near the bottom. To this end Brian Smith ascended the rope only 3m off the floor his carbide lamp failed and he began to descend, a decision that possibly avoided a protracted rescue or worse. Only a short distance from the floor he was struck on the helmet by a large rock dislodged by the rope. Brian was dazed but still in one piece and after being stuffed with food still seemed reluctant to be the first up the frayed rope. It was then decided that the lightest caver should be sent up first and everyone looked at Brian Judd who was hiding in a corner. Brian ascended without incident dodging the shower of rocks raining down the shaft. After the rope was reversed the rest of the party reached the top of Moustique unscathed except Brian Smith whose carbide failed and foot loop snapped halfway up the shaft, he was hauled up with a spare rope. The four de-tacklers were left at the head of Moustique whilst the remaining three made steady progress up Jo, Minotier and Versaillais where it suddenly dawned on them that camp 600, the food dump, had been missed on the way out so all the party had to descend the shaft again or go hungry! Suitably refreshed on hot soup, sausage and cheese etc the party ascended the remaining long pitches until the familiar ground of the Chateau de Cartes was reached. Here the party felt they were nearly out despite still being at the depth of an average Dales pot hole. Through the crawl of the Meandre aux Boutons a few more short pitches and the entrance beckoned. The three emerged at 5am after some nineteen hours underground. The four de-tacklers surfaced about three hours later having de-tackled to the top of Trempette pitch.

Meanwhile the Eldon Pothole Club complete with Clive Westlake, as enthusiastic as ever, had arrived for their Aiguilles experience and helpfully moved some BPC tackle out on their first trip. It was later learned the Eldon had bottomed the hole using ladders and ropes but needed to camp underground. Nine BPC members completed the de-tackling the next day Brian Judd emerging with

bloody knees since he thought shorts were the ideal caving attire. The following day all the gear was carried back down to the Land rover and then to the campsite in Corps where all thirteen members enjoyed a slap up meal in a local restaurant with plenty of refreshments.

Overall, the expedition was a success since the sump was finally reached after several earlier attempts using traditional equipment which had proved too heavy in a system the depth of the Aiguilles and showed that SRT was the future. The system was not extended in any way but this was not the object of the visit in the limited time available.

Personnel:

Bottoming Party:

Jim Abbott, Peter Faulkner, Brian Judd, Raymond Lee, Brian Sellers, Ian Wilkinson, Brian Smith.

Surface and tackling/detackling:

John Cooper, Dave Mathews, Richard Maclindon, Janice Castle, June Greenwood, Sheryl Haynes.

References:

1999 Reseau Chourum de la Rama/Chourum des Aiguilles by Philippe Bertochio

Chourum des Aiguilles 1973 Expedition, BPC Bulletin 1975 by J Abbot

Chourum des Aiguilles 1974 Expedition, BPC Bulletin 1975 by B Smith

Many thanks also to Jim Abbott, Ged Benn, Dave Mathews and John Robinson for all their recollections and advice that went into compiling this article.

R. Lee.

Footnote: *The above article tells the story of the BPC's relationship with the Chourum des Aiguilles but, probably through modesty, Snake has not decribed the effects this drawn out conquest of the system had on the club. After the 1973 trip it would have been easy to simply turn our backs on this 'jinxed system' and move on to pastures new. But that meeting with the French cavers and witnessing the Alpine caving techniques against the direct comparison of the UK's techniques gave an unambiguous message. The ladder and lifeline method was adequate for British caves but was there too much of a leap from viewing the rope as an emergency backup to abandoning the ladder and only having the emergency method? At the time SRT was known about by most British caving clubs but they were developing ideas independently. The 1973 experience fired the BPC with sufficient motivation to develop a viable system using the available hardware. They went on to look at the ropes in detail, they initiated co-operation between the BPC, rope manufacturers and distributers. Testing on a large scale was organised, the results were alarming, and when published were recognised as leading edge research which had implications around the World.*

The BPC were subsequently recognised as being at the leading edge of UK SRT development and the other caving clubs used our work as the basis for their transition to SRT. In 1974 the vindication was when we bottomed the Aiguilles in fine style thus inspiring British cavers as a whole to adopt safe SRT for use in the UK. It is sad to note that the BPC results and developments were published in 1976, too late to stop David Huxtable abseiling down Gaping Gill main shaft on polypropolene rope with fatal consiquences. But how many lives did we save by being so proactive at a time when British caving clubs needed leadership? – Ed.

SECTION 2.10 – ABISSO C. FIGHIERA 1979 – J. EDWARDS

The club had been very successful on their trip to the Antro Del Corchia the year before and Geoff Crossley suggested the Fighiera for the following year [1979] He gave a slide show at the annual dinner where most of the shots were of his old Mk2 Cortina in different locations, there were no pictures of people, this prompted Max Koval to shout out "Did you go on your own?" Without any more persuasion we agreed to go. It was an eventful journey for Madelyn and I, we broke down on the north circular, at the side of the road. It turned out, after several hours, that somebody, presumably after failing to find a bin, had put a condom into my petrol tank, there were no petrol locking caps in those days. Anyway, long story short, the latex was sucked into the petrol lines and shortly afterwards the engine stopped. When we eventually set off again it was rush hour and we crawled what seemed all the way to Dover. Once in France we had to stop in a forest at night to take the thermostat out to aid engine cooling. Cooling was an issue all the way to Italy. I spent one evening picking the remains of thousands of flying insects out of the radiator core, which has not been a problem since we reduced the insect population over the last few years.

I had never even seen a survey of the cave and the only map I had was a European road atlas, which didn't have Levigliani on. I did have some vague instructions of how to get there. These included a strict warning not to miss the Livorno slip road at 'the interchange in the sky' over Genoa and leave the motorway at Massa and head east. Massa turned out to be a huge industrial estate, which really impressed Madelyn. After what seemed like far too many miles, in a very hot car with a leaking petrol tank, we limped into Lavigliani and pulled in to a lay-by to ask directions from a typical looking local who turned out to be John Ralphs. We had arrived at Mama Emma's, the hotel where we were to meet. The camp site was at the back of the hotel on a steep forested hill where a series of small terraces had been cut out for tents.

The next morning we were awakened by the sound of quarry wagons, each carrying two huge blocks of Carrara marble, from the quarry at the top of the hill down the hairpin bends to the processing plant at the bottom. Carrara marble was made famous by the ancient Greeks, the Romans and Michael Angelo and friends who carved all the famous statues from the ancient world to modern times. The problem

with the transport system was that the wagons were not capable of stopping when loaded with several huge blocks and going downhill. They continuously sounded their horns to give notice that they were on the way and everyone had to clear the way or risk being pushed off the precipitous drops at the side of the road. The steep mountain road was liberally decorated with shrines and floral tributes to all that failed to heed the warning horns.

After a couple of days we arranged our first tackling trip into the Fighiera. *[It was originally called the Buca del Cacciatore (Hunter's cave) but was renamed after a famous French caver called Claude Fighiera who, ironically, died in a car that he drove off the side of a mouintain in 1974 - Ed]* We must have been in several vehicles, I was in John Ralph's Cortina, but we had to abandon the cars when the road ran out just after the quarry. The walk from the cars started by watching the quarry at work, they used continuous wires with teeth, like barbed wire, running around pulleys temporarily attached to anything that happened to be in the right place. As the wires cut into the marble they pumped water into the slot formed. The white water washing away from the quarry stained the mountain white and made the quarry visible for miles.

We arrived before the heat of the day at a tin hut, the SGCIF Refugio to use its proper name. We investigated it with incredulity, "How and why would someone go to all this trouble to put this on top of a 5,500 foot hill?" "Why would anyone want to stay in here when they could walk down the road?" But it was there so we may as well get changed in it and it was only a short stroll from here to the cave entrance right at the top of the hill. I say hill, the entrance is at 5,345 feet, which by British standards is..... too high.

At 3pm we rigged the electron ladder down the 35' [12m] entrance pitch and started lowering tackle bags down to the first few of us to descend. As we set off into the cave we all carried large bags as well as our personal gear bags. I remember my bag was in fact two large bags with one enormous 400'+ [122m] rope that filled both bags. We descended many pitches in the traditional 'Yorkshire' method, straight over the edge and lots of hose pipe protectors. We did a large pitch called the Pozzo della Anarchica which took literally hours to rig. We went through some more horizontally developed

144

passages that reminded us of home and there was some whooping as spirits were temporarily lifted. We eventually came to another large pitch where the head was a long, steeply sloping, boulder pile leading to the vertical drop. As we were picking our way down the slope and rigging the drop we couldn't help but notice that the pitch had been rigged by someone else. They had left a brown 10mm rope rigged to bolts leading across the flat roof before dropping clear down the pitch, no hose pipe, no bolts in shear, just nerves of steel. The BPC had been heavily involved in the development of safe SRT in the UK for several years and we thought we knew it all. But seeing that rigging we realised we were in the presence of SRT at an entirely different level.

It was whilst musing over this belittling vision of the future, I realised I was sitting on a rock near the top of the ramp and Chris Smith was sitting 10 meters or so below me at the very top of the vertical pitch. I saw that he was not fastened to anything at all, and as time dragged glacially by, waiting for our turn to go down, both Chris and I started to nod off. After all we had been on the go for many hours by this time and were probably still sleep deprived from the drive from England and the late night the night before. I decided to creep down the boulder ramp with a rope and crab and clip the back of Chris's chest harness to my belay point. By the time I got back to my rock the line was going very tight, he had nodded off and started to slump forward over the drop! I tied him off and shouted to wake him up, we laughed for some time over the thought of someone on the pitch below seeing a sleeping person silently pass them by into the darkness below.

I then started to realise that I had not had even a sip of water in the last 8 hours and as a result I had a headache as well as a failing carbide lamp. We had thought of everything except water and it was a dry cave. I started the trip with an orange drink but that had gone into the carbide hours before. It was whilst musing on these issues that, to my surprise, someone came up the pitch rather than the next man, presumably Chris, going down. There had been a discussion at the bottom of the pitch and all things considered it had been decided that this was to be the limit of the first tackling trip. We split into two groups of four to make our way out. I remember it being agreed that we had got down over 600 feet. To this day I am unsure where we got to. The first team to lead the retreat was Wilky, Snake, John Ralphs and I and progress with no tackle bags was a lot quicker than on the way in.
I think I was the first to ascend the entrance pitch, it was about 2 am on Wednesday and it was a

beautiful clear Moon lit night and I could still make out the Apuan peaks around. In the far distance there were dark overlying clouds and an odd flash of lightning, how pretty, I thought. The first team out assembled at the top of the entrance pitch before walking, very relaxed, the 100 meters or so to the refugio. I was still wondering if we should use it or go back down the hill? We were just settling down on the bunks waiting for the second group to arrive, when Snake produced a one liter bottle of Bacardi from his bag, not my favourite tipple but I thought it would be impolite to leave now. Before long it started to rain, a lot, and the lightning was clearly getting closer. We discussed what we would only accept was a theory of the Faraday cage principle and decided that it might not be a good idea to open the door and look for our mates. Very quickly the full force of the storm hit us, the noise of golf ball sized hailstones battering our tin hut was deafening, but that was just the beginning. Within minutes we were aware that all around the hut the ground was being repeatedly struck by very powerful lightning bolts which sounded like bombs going off. Each strike shattered the rock and fragments flew in all directions and struck the hut like shrapnel, just like a bomb. I was laid on a bunk suspended by steel chains and concerned to see sparks and blue light dancing up and down the chains every time the hut itself was hit. You literally couldn't hear yourself shout for what seemed like hours. The most disturbing aspect of the direct hits was the perception of the hut moving on its dry stone wall foundations. Our initial concerns of our missing comrades soon passed as the Bacardi did its work. I laid there in the dark, still with deafening noises in my ears, watching the almost continuous flashes at the windows, thinking of Madelyn and the other wives, and if indeed we were going to join them a lot sooner than we planned. This seemed increasingly possible as with every strike it felt that we were creeping ever closer towards the cliffs overlooking the campsite 3000 feet below.

As the storm raged on for hours I think we all eventually fell into a troubled sleep, only to be disturbed by Geoff Crossley opening the door of the hut from outside and letting the early morning sun flood in, he immediately compounded our momentary confusion by declaring us all to be dead. Apparently because my arm happened to slide off the edge of the bunk and swing down, as it might in a dramatised film.

They told us of their terrible ordeal in the entrance pitch and how Bones and Chris had been running around at the height of the storm and were both struck by lightning. They seemed relatively unimpressed by our tales of loud noises and alcohol induced indifference. It seems that as they approached the bottom of the entrance pitch there was already lightning above they could hear the thunder echoing into the cave. They assembled on a ledge a few meters below the surface. It was a narrow rift with just enough width to fit shoulders across without touching the walls. If they squatted and sat on their heels with their head resting on the man in front's back and didn't touch the walls they were ok. As soon as one touched the wall they all jumped up having suffered an electric shock. After some time two brave souls, Bones and Chris decided they were going to go for the hut. As they climbed out Geoff climbed up to look out over the scene. He saw quite well under the light of the almost continuous flashes of lightening, the hut getting repeated hits and then in horror saw both Bones and Chris get thrown 'like rag dolls' away from a lightning bolt that struck just in front of them. They came round very quickly and started making their way back on their hands and knees; both reported that the sparking and blue lights were dancing between the blades of grass and their fingers. Confused and panicking Chris stood up and made a dash for the entrance rift where he had seen Geoff and Jim's lights shining out. He made it back and without using the ladder which was also shining blue with St Elmo's Fire he dropped down onto the ledge. Meanwhile Bones had got back on his feet and without the benefit of having seen the other's lights shining out of the entrance he decided to run anyway. Convinced the lightning was being attracted to his SRT metal work he suddenly decided to stop and undo his harness and drop it all to the floor. Whilst doing this a lightning flash lit up the cliff face and he realised he was only a couple of steps away from going over the edge. Turning 180 degrees he ran again and saw the lights ahead, he literally just jumped into the entrance pitch without particularly trying to land on the ledge. As he descended the shaft he managed to catch the end of the ledge with one hand and in one unbelievable act of adrenalin fuelled strength, he pulled himself onto the ledge with the one hand. He was shouting "I've been hit" "I've been hit" and "my beards on fire!"

All four of them spent the remainder of the night squatting on their haunches on that small ledge with water, ice and lightning pouring down onto them with the deafening noise of instant thunder all around they were denied sleep by the random electric shocks and the smell of Bones' burning beard. *[It is interesting that having had so many electric shocks through the night they hadn't lost their short term memories, though Chris did react as though he had had a night of aversion therapy and to this day is terrified of thunder storms – Ed]* As day light began to appear over the mountains and silence returned they dared to venture out and make their way over to where they were convinced the hut contained four dead bodies. Only to find four oafs with hangovers! We began to make our way down and back to the cars only to find the road had collapsed and been washed away by the mass of ice and water the night before. We ended up traversing a tiny ledge for 20 feet [6m] on a vertical wall thanking all we held sacred that we had moved the cars further back down the road before we left them.

It was a quiet drive down the hill that is until we got back to the campsite where we were faced with scenes of apocalyptic devastation. Chris and Pat's tent was a large frame tent pitched on top of a flat roofed garage; it was now in a state of collapse with bent poles and torn fabric. Most of the apparent damage was due to every item of everybody's bedding and clothing hanging out to dry all around the campsite. It turns out that during the storm the ladies, and children were trapped in their tents as the same sparks and blue light we had witnessed up the hill were dancing up and down the tent zips. They eventually tried to get into the hotel but couldn't make themselves heard over the storm. As Pat's tent collapsed under the weight of water and ice she made sure she saved all that was most dear to her and dragged out a suitcase full of tinned food, not her kids.

Members present: Jim Abbott, Geoff Crossley, Chris Smith, Mick Sharp [Team 2]
Ian Wilkinson, Raymond Lee, John Ralphs, and myself John Edwards [Hut Survivors]

SECTION 2.11 – MENDIP 1979 – SOFA RUGBY REPORT – G. CROSSLEY.

Brlstol Exploration Club 2 - Bradford Pothole Club 8

BEC - unbeaten at home this year were looking for yet another Belfry victory. From the push off all hands failed to move the sofa for the first 2 minutes of the match, and a scrum down had to be ordered. From the scrum the BEC pushed forward creating a ruck with the BPC team underneath, good handling from the ruck by the BEC enabled the sofa to be touched down for a try despite brave efforts by the Bradford lads. With the BEC out numbering the BPC by one or two players victory was looking almost certain for the home Mendip team. However, BPC honour was at stake.

From the restart several BEC players were 'taken out of the game' by the Bradford back row, and the tremendous surge forward by the remaining front row sent the sofa crashing over the line for an equalizing try. Again the push off led to a BPC attack, and following a short brawl just outside the BEC try line, the resistance was crushed (literally) and the sofa landed for a second BPC try putting the Northern team 2 to 1 in front.

Yet again the restart signified a Bradford charge and within 30 seconds the sofa was crammed over the line to make the score 3:1. The dispirited Bristol team now took to foul play to try and get back into the game. The foul play came in the form of the 'Flying Whale' alias BEC captain Chris Hatstone. However, after his several attacks simply bounced off the BPC pack he soon rendered the idea useless.

The BPC now scored another superb try after a magnificent run with the sofa left the BEC team sprawled across the floor. With the score at 4 : 1 against them the home team once again turned to cheating. This time the Bristol captain tried to destroy Bradford's concentration by pouring boiling hot tea over them. However the BPC, with so much ale in them, had no concentration or feelings so just went on to smash the teapot and nearly score another try.

Extra players brought on by the BEC led them into a counterattack and a fierce drive forward by them meant that the BPC could had to force them back over their touch line with such force that the sofa crashed through the main Belfry window, taking the score to 5:1. From the ensuing line out a smart Bristol move caused a breach in the stretched BPC defense and the sofa landed for a try to make the score BEC 2 – BPC 5.

With renewed heart from their try the BEC surged forward to within 2 feet of the Bradford line, but a marvelous counter by the Northern lads smashed the BEC attack and sent the sofa, complete with one Bristol player, flying through the air and onto the pot bellied stove, where the poor player was swiftly branded with a mirror image of 'Made in Birmingham' on his bare back.

From the lineout the BPC wheeled the BEC pack and pulled the sofa over the try line to take a 6:2 lead. The BPC team, now growing in confidence, began to control the midfield and from a centre maul the fast Bradford breakaway cut the Bristol team to ribbons and took the sofa over the line for yet another try – 7:2.

With only minutes to go the commanding BPC team won a midfield ruck and trampled over the Bristol team with a devastating run to score yet again, in the corner. With the gong for the end of the match going only seconds later the final score of BEC 2 – BPC 8 signified the first home defeat of the year for the Mendip team. With only cuts and bruises and other minimal injuries this was an excellent, exhilarating match.

"This report is completely without bias"

BPC Team – Biffo, Jekyl, Bowels, King Oaf, Bones, Mendip Turd, Martyn, Dad Smith, Dud, Cow and Gates, Gwyn, Snake, Buzby.

SECTION 2.12 – THE CONNECTION OF GAPING GILL TO INGLEBOROUGH CAVE 1983 – G. CROSSLEY / J. ABBOTT

For countless thousands of years the waters of Fell Beck have wound their way down the upper slopes of Ingleborough only to be swallowed up by the huge abyss of Gaping Gill Hole. Over a mile away and some 500' lower these same waters reappear into daylight at Clapham Beck Head. For hundreds of years the village of Clapham has used the Beck as their water supply but only in the last couple of hundred years did people begin to show any real interest in what lay behind Clapham Beck Head itself. However, early explorations were thwarted when the roof soon came down to meet the water. Attention was therefore turned to Ingleborough Cave, a large dark cleft at the base of a limestone cliff just a few yards away. Ingleborough Cave was found to be dry but progress was barred a short distance inside by a flowstone barrier holding back a large lake. Interest was beginning to be shown at Gaping Gill around this time and it was naturally assumed that the river disappearing there was the same one that re-emerged at Clapham Beck Head. Various objects were thrown down Main Shaft to try and prove this theory although none ever actually re-appeared at Clapham Beck Head. In 1836 the flowstone barrier in Ingleborough Cave was 'removed' thus draining the lake and opening up hundreds of feet of new passages. Within a few years the first serious attempts were made at descending the Main Shaft of Gaping Gill although the first full descent was not made until 1895 by the Frenchman Édouard Martel.

Explorations into the two caves continued over the next fifty years although new discoveries were painfully hard to come by. The Bradford Pothole Club came to have a vested interest in the system when it began to operate a winch at Gaping Gill Main Shaft for a few weeks at Whitsuntide each year. BPC members were also at the forefront of the explorations taking place at the far end of Ingleborough Cave and they were amongst the first to pass the waterlogged areas now known as The Wallows to gain access to the underground watercourse of Fell Beck once again. However, excitement soon turned to disappointment when the streamway sumped a few hundred feet upstream of The Wallows. Over the ensuing years major new discoveries were made in Gaping Gill, the stories of which have been told and retold.

Briefly, however, events unfolded in the following manner:-

1968 - BPC discovered Whitsun Series.
1968 - U.L.S.A. broke through the blowhole above the end of Hensler's Master Cave and discovered several thousand feet of new passages terminating at Clay Cavern. The discovery was named Far Country.
1970 - Mike Wooding dived upstream at the end of Ingleborough Cave. After some 500' he discovered a major new above water extension which he named Quicksand Passage (later renamed Gandalf's Gallery). At the time Wooding thought that the new extension headed towards GG (although it was later found the extension did in fact head away from GG).
1970 - Spurred on by his discovery of Gandalf's Gallery, Wooding made a lone journey to Clay Cavern in GG There he removed some boulders and dug through into ½ mile of new passages which he named Far Waters. However, all ways on at the end were choked due to massive fault collapse, although the discovery did appear to bring Wooding to within an ace of connecting the two caves.
1970-75 - Various digs and discoveries were made although none brought the connection any closer.
1976 - Rob Palmer dived to and surveyed Gandalf's Gallery. He found it to be heading away from Gaping Gill rather than towards it.

Returning to Gandalf's with Geoff Yeadon, the pair continued the dive upstream. Yeadon discovered an above-water chamber, which is still the largest found in Ingleborough Cave to date. This was named Radagast's Revenge and once again all passages leading from it were choked with boulders within a short distance. Further diving upstream of Radagast's led to the discovery of another chamber, Bilbo's Buttery.

On a final dive, Yeadon dived upstream of Bilbo's Buttery whilst Palmer dived from the nearby Shallow Well in GG in an effort to link up with him. However, this attempt was thwarted by underwater silt chokes at each end.

According to the surveys Radagast's Revenge was in fact the closest point to Gaping Gill. However, the inaccuracies of the Gaping Gill and

Ingleborough Cave surveys meant that it was impossible to determine exactly how far apart the two caves were, or which points in the two systems were closest to one another and offered the best chance of a connection. It became obvious that a new and accurate survey would have to be drawn up. An earlier radio location of Clay Cavern by Bob Mackin and Dick Glover was to provide a useful starting point for a new survey of Far Waters. The survey was carried out by Yeadon's brother John and the Kendal Caving Club. By 1978-80 it was beginning to take shape.

1976-79 - Rob Palmer moved away from Yorkshire and Geoff Yeadon turned his attentions to the Keld Head dives. Hence the main activity proceeding in GG/Ingleborough was the Kendal's resurvey.

1980-81 - Although the end of Far Waters was accurately plotted it still needed radio-locating to finish off. In addition, it was still anybody's guess as to exactly where Ingleborough Cave lay, in particular Radagast's Revenge. Obviously, Radagast's would need radio locating and surveying along with Far Waters before the whole thing would fall into place. The elusive connection was not going to give itself up without a fight

Time ran out for the radio-location of the two caves when the two cavers that were the driving force behind the project in 1980, namely Geoff Yeadon and Dave Yeandle, who both left the country. Dave emigrated to Australia whilst Geoff went on the Mulu Expedition at the end of 1980 for several months. Whilst he was away, a couple of other groups made an effort to radio locate Radagast's although these attempts also ended in failure. It appeared that if the connection was going to be made at all it was still going to involve a lot of enormously difficult work. Enthusiasm waned for a year until May, 1982 when once again the Bradford Pothole Club became involved.

I had cave dived regularly with Geoff Yeadon leading up to May 1982. Geoff's role of discovery speaks for itself and I considered myself very fortunate to be diving with someone of such vast experience as he. We'd mainly cave dived together in places such as New Goyden and Nidd Heads (courtesy of Julian Griffiths) in Upstream Hurtle Pot and also in one or two other sumps. When the chance to dive Ingleborough again came around it was immediately obvious that the two of us should have a crack at it together.

A relatively innocent BPC club meet was to take place on Saturday 31st May 1982 that coincided

with the winch meet at GG. Knowing that this trip was to take place the idea of diving the cave was first muted between Scoff and I at the beginning of May. On putting the idea to Geoff Yeadon, the two of us became very excited at the prospects of at last carrying out the long awaited radio location of Radagst's Revenge. We decided without hesitation to go ahead with the project. Geoff agreed to liaise with Bob Mackin over the use of the revolutionary Molephone, whilst I began to pressgang BPC members into helping with the porterage of all the necessary equipment to the back end of Ingleborough Cave. Fortunately, there were many willing helpers (luckily, they didn't know what they were letting themselves in for) and several days of fine weather up to and including the day itself assured that the trip would take place.

On the day some initial problems with the transportation of the equipment up to Ingleborough Cave led to a delayed start, but once the team were underground things began to move swiftly. With the laborious carry behind them the team arrived at Terminal Lake after approximately 1½ hours. Radio contact was made with Frank Addis on the surface after which Geoff Yeadon and I kitted up with the diving gear and headed off towards Radagast's Revenge carrying a second Molephone. The diving guideline in the first 350' long sump was particularly loose, and the problem had to be rectified by tying on a series of lead weights. After passing through a deep water airbell the second 250' long sump was entered. More problems with loose line were encountered before the two of us surfaced into Gandalf's Gallery. Beyond here a third and straightforward dive of 150' led the two of us to the impressive chamber of Radagast's Revenge. After quickly de-kitting we climbed up to a point some 50' from the sump pool and found a suitably flat area where we could assemble the Molephone. When this task was completed we began transmission with a series of tones. Frank, up on the surface, immediately picked up the signals and set about pinpointing our exact position. This was soon done and we switched over to speech transmission. It was evident that Frank was obviously very excited about something and, at one point, he actually thought that we were speaking to him from Gaping Gill! Our position was so close to the known extremities of Far Waters that it was difficult for Frank to believe that we had not made the break through.

Geoff and I then set about the surveying of the lower and middle levels of the Radagast's Revenge complex - a climb up to the large and partly unexplored areas of the higher levels of the chamber was considered too dangerous to attempt without a rope, bearing in mind our isolation. In the middle levels a large passage containing pristine white formations was followed from the radio location base to a point where it abruptly ended at a major boulder choke, almost certainly the other side of the Hurnel Moss Fault to the passages of Far Waters in GG With the survey completed, Geoff and I packed all the gear away, kitted up and dived back to the sherpas at Terminal Lake. Connection fever was rife that evening in the Gaping Gill beer tent! When the Radagast's survey was drawn up it revealed that the two caves were only 6m apart. However, we were not sure as to the levels of the two caves in relation to one another. The level of the various passages in Radagast's was now accurately plotted but Far Waters was not. In addition, the aforementioned new survey of Far Waters didn't include some of the smaller passages below Spiral Aven. Ironically it was these passages that seemed to be closest to Radagast's Revenge. There was nothing else for it but to descend Gaping Gill and make another highly accurate survey of the lower limb of Far Waters. This would be started at Clay Cavern, at the position pin-pointed by the radio location some years earlier. The nearby flooded shaft of Shallow Well was taken as the reference for the level of the passages of Spiral Aven because the water in Shallow Well would be at the same as the water level in Radagast's. We decided to conduct the survey from Clay Cavern down through the Orifice, thus taking the most direct route to the passages below Spiral Aven. This also enabled us to survey down to Shallow Well en route. The survey, when drawn up, would be used in conjunction with the new Kendal survey of the rest of Far Waters. We also planned to radio locate various points in Far Waters and carry out a full surface survey of the area. All this data would finally give us a survey of the two caves and their relationship to one another that would be accurate to within a few inches both in plan and section. The prospect of several long and squalid trips to Far Waters in order to collect the survey data was dreadful. However, because of the three dimensional complexities of the caves, we knew that it was the only way that we could find out where GG and Ingleborough lay and also determine if there was any chance of a connection at all or indeed if there was any likelihood of one that would not involve several months of protracted digging operations. Additionally, more diving trips into Ingleborough would be necessary in order to explore and survey the upper levels of Radagast's Revenge. For all we knew then, there may still have been an easy, 'over

the top' route into Gaping Gill just waiting to be walked into - some hope that was to turn out to be!

Following the success of the Radagast's Revenge radio location, a couple of trips were made down to Far Waters during the week of the BPC winch to see what connection prospects were like from that end. Although one or two digs and discoveries were made it still looked like a daunting task lay ahead of us within the three dimensional maze that made up the Spiral Aven/ Radagast's Revenge complex.

After the end of the winch meet bad weather followed by various expeditions abroad delayed the project until September when surveying began in earnest. With no winch available, we used Bar Pot as an entry point and got to Far Waters via New/Short Henslers. Over the course of several long, tiring trips between September and December, the survey began to take shape. These trips were usually carried out between two or three of us and not always with the use of the Molephone as a back-up. However, on one occasion, when we were using it we managed to obtain an actual sound connection between the surface and Clay Cavern. By using the Molephone for timing we stayed silent in Clay Cavern whilst a boulder was dropped into the shakehole directly above us on the surface. Admittedly it was only a faint, dull thud that issued in the chamber below, but it was definitely there and indicated that maybe a surface entrance could be made sometime in the future following what would undoubtedly be a major digging operation.

On 31st October 1982 another diving sortie into Ingleborough Cave was made in order to explore the beckoning black voids in the high levels of Radagast's Revenge. Upon reaching the chamber the three of us (Geoff Yeadon, Jim Abbott and myself) de-kitted and, with difficulty, using a rope for safety we managed to climb up an impressive ramp for approximately 100' to the start of a huge false floor. Underneath the false floor quickly choked but above it, access was gained to the base of a high and large aven with excellent straw stalactites. Unfortunately there was no way out of the aven and the top of it was hopelessly choked with calcite Disappointed, we began our return to the diving site but were lucky enough to discover a small side passage half way back down the ramp. After excavating a tight boulder filled chute, I squeezed down into a rapid enlargement of the passage. The way on beckoned and tantalisingly headed for Gaping Gill. Geoff and Jim quickly followed and together we explored some 400' of new but relatively small passageways. All ways on choked although digging in the area in the future may pay dividends. One final sandy crawl, which seemingly issued a draught was followed to a point where a way on could be seen upwards beyond a fallen block into a black void. An intense struggle to remove the fallen block ensued for some 45 minutes before it finally relented and we negotiated a way through. Sadly the black void was in fact a small chamber with no apparent way out. The aforementioned draught had also disappeared. Once again we were thwarted and there seemed to be no alternative but to attempt what appeared at the time to be an almost suicidal dig through the boulders below Spiral Aven in Far Waters.

Along with the realization that we were probably nearing a connection came the problems of keeping the operation secret. However, rumours leaked and other 'pirate' parties made their way to Far Waters in an effort to beat us to it. Fortunately none of them had any idea where to look and thus had no success. One party even got trapped for several hours after they returned from a digging trip in Far Waters to find that Southgate Duck had sumped behind them due to rain on the surface. When the water level lowered the following day, the somewhat dejected party almost crossed paths with us making our way in! We ourselves often had problems with high water at Southgate and sometimes had to pass it with only 1"-2" airspace on the way in. We even laid a guideline should the need to free dive back out ever arise. Needless to say we always entered with a good weather forecast and would have never free dived into Southgate if we had found it sumped. After more trips to Ingleborough Cave and Far Waters had taken place, we were at last approaching the final stages of our connection attempt by Christmas week of 1982. During that week the final survey data was collected by making four more radio locations-in Far Waters. Two of them matched up with our new survey and were assumed to be correct, whilst the other two locations seemed to have been deflected by the Hurnel Moss Fault. On New Year's Eve, Geoff Yeadon and I performed a full surface survey of the region of Clapham Bottoms above the connection area taking in all the radio location points. The results of the survey were now awaited with baited breath!

Following a riotous New Year's Eve, a rather hung over Geoff Yeadon drew a line survey from the new data. The results were scarcely believable. An excited telephone call to a very ill me and the news was out. We were only l.2m horizontally and 3.4m vertically from making the connection!! After 150 years it appeared to be ours for the taking.

The Connection

Our excitement at the results of our survey was difficult to contain. Having used the Molephone and put so much effort into creating such a high grade survey, we were pretty certain of its accuracy to within perhaps a couple of feet. Keeping this fact secret was going to prove difficult!

The next stage of the project was obvious. One party would descend Gaping Gill and another party would dive Ingleborough through to Radagast's. If the survey was accurate it would almost certainly be possible for each of the parties to hear each other in the connection area. Logistical, organisational and weather problems delayed the event until Saturday 22nd January 1983. On that day the weather forecast was good but we were a little dubious as to the condition of The Wallows in Ingleborough Cave as it had rained heavily the previous week. However, we decided to give the go ahead and the connection attempt was under way!

To go into organisational details of the trip would take hours but, essentially, the events of the day would take the following pattern -

A party of four cavers (Jim Abbott, Gerald Benn, Mick Sharp and Ian Wilkinson) would descend Bar Pot and make their way towards Far Waters armed with a Molephone. Later in the morning, the main bulk of the cavers would enter Ingleborough Cave with the diving equipment for three people (Geoff Yeadon, Julian Griffiths and myself) and also two Molephones. Using the Molephones, both the Gaping Gill and Ingleborough Cave parties would be able to keep track of each others' progress and also keep an eye on the weather via communication with Bob and Kath Mackin, Frank Addis, Tom Clifford and Fred Winstanley on the surface.

When the Ingleborough party reached Terminal Lake, the divers would kit up and dive through to Radagast's taking one Molephone and a camera with them leaving a Molephone with the sherpas at Terminal Lake. With any luck it was hoped that the sherpas, the divers and the GG party would be able to communicate directly to one another as the distance between them reduced. With all three parties in direct Molephone contact with Bob Mackin et al on the surface, it would make an interesting four way conversation! The divers and the GG cavers would then position themselves on their corresponding sides of the boulder choke and make an attempt at getting actual voice contact with each other. Julian was to record the events with his camera and the sherpas back at Terminal Lake would be kept informed of the proceedings via the Molephone. If we were successful at obtaining a voice contact then a dig would ensue although it was realised that several digging trips would probably be needed before an actual physical connection could be made.

On the day itself, things went as planned until the Ingleborough team reached The Wallows. They were higher that we'd ever known them and with only 1" -2" airspace, proved extremely difficult to negotiate. It was definitely a case of one person through at a time and don't make waves! Eventually we all reached Terminal Lake where more problems followed. It was discovered that Geoff Yeadon's reserve air cylinder had accidentally been turned on and drained during the carry in. With no reserve Geoff would be unable to dive since the consequences of a valve failure whilst diving a sump using only a single set was obvious. With no spanners available to decant air from one of our other main cylinders into Geoff's reserve there was no way of getting around the problem. As Geoff had been involved in the search for the connection for several years, and since we'd both put so much effort into the project for the previous year, there was an immense feeling of disappointment over the fact that he might not be there at what would possibly be the triumphant moment. For a few moments I was toying with the idea of calling the whole thing off but Geoff insisted that Julian and I go ahead with the dive and, considering the massive amount of organisation that had gone into the trip, sense prevailed and the two of us left for Radagast's. Upon arrival there we quickly de-kitted and climbed up to the radio location station. There we set up the Molephone and made immediate radio contact with both the surface (Bob Mackin) and the Gaping Gill team who were already below Spiral Aven. In addition, contact was made with an eager Geoff Yeadon who had stayed behind at Terminal Lake with the sherpas and was operating the Molephone there. Geoff couldn't actually talk to us directly but he could hear us and that was enough.

Julian took one or two photographs of the Molephone in operation before I told him where to go to in order to try and make a voice contact with the others in GG. Amazingly, as soon as he got to the choke he could hear the others only a few feet

away and speak to them quite clearly. Even though our survey had predicted this, we still found it hard to believe that the gap between the two caves was indeed so accurate with Gaping Gill, as thought, being lower than our position in Radagast's.

Immediately, we started a dig going with boulders being tossed all over the place in an effort to make the momentous breakthrough. The first hole we opened up in the boulders appeared to be going well at first and we eventually made a light contact, closely followed by a 2m distant 'face to face' contact with the GG party below. Meanwhile, Jim Abbott was transmitting a running commentary on the events to the surface from Far Waters via the Molephone. This was relayed to Geoff Yeadon who was already listening in at Terminal Lake. Realising that it was likely that a connection was going to be made, Geoff decided to take the calculated risk of diving through the sumps on one bottle to join us. To quote Geoff - "I realised that I would probably rather die than miss out on this!" Whilst Geoff was somewhere in the midst of his dive, the dig that Julian and I were making in Radagast's rapidly became unstable and collapsed. However, moving back towards the radio location point a few feet led us to another promising looking hole in the boulders. Another dig was started here and the area in general seemed to be more stable than the first dig had been. The hole was excavated to a depth of five feet with much of the loose slurry being kicked down into Far Waters. It landed at the end of a low mud logged bedding just in front of the others waiting below, although they could not assist with the dig to a great extent due to the danger of trying to dig upwards vertically through loose boulders with no room in which to manoeuvre safely. After a few minutes Geoff Yeadon appeared on the scene. It was a very pleasant surprise to see him and he was greatly relieved to learn that he had not missed the connection. The dig continued downwards but began to spiral underneath a huge boulder that appeared to be secured in position by a single 1" diameter pebble. The big boulder itself supported tons more rubble and the whole thing looked fairly horrendous. Under normal circumstances I don't think that any of us would have dreamt of digging underneath the boulder, but for something as special as this an exception had to be made. After another hour or so of digging and the gap between the two caves was down to about two feet with the depth of the dig being approximately 9 feet. Working at the bottom of it I managed to kick a hole down through the slurry into Far Waters. A few minutes later, after some furious scrambling from below, my wellington boot was finally grabbed by the outstretched hand of Gerald Benn. Thus at 4.50 p.m. on 22nd January, 1983, the symbolic connection between Gaping Gill and Ingleborough Cave was finally made, nearly 150 years after the first tentative attempts at the same had been made. It must have been particularly satisfying for Gerald as he was one of the first people to explore the back end of Ingleborough Cave some 20 years previously. The news of the connection was immediately radioed up to the surface from where it was passed via walkie talkie to Clapham. Satisfied that the connection had been made, and in the knowledge that a lot more work would be needed to engineer a body sized connection, all of us happily withdrew from our respective caves and retired to the pub where celebrations continued well into the night. News spread rapidly and by the Sunday dinner time it seemed as though the whole of the Dales was aware of the link up.

Events moved rapidly after the connection was made and further trips were made to both Radagast's Revenge and Far Waters in an effort to consolidate and stabilise the dig. On the next trip to Radagast's we managed to remove the final boulders blocking the way before I made an attempt to get through into Far Waters. Unfortunately, I had kicked so much slurry down the dig in front of me that it completely blocked the way forward into GG. By pushing it along in front of me using my feet, I eventually managed to get all my body into Gaping Gill. However, at this point the slurry that I was kicking in front compacted and would not move. There was nobody on the GG side on this occasion, and it was impossible to reach the blockage using our arms, so the trip had to be aborted. Jim Abbott, using the Molephone immediately above the dig transmitted the message ...."Geoff Crossley has now entered Gaping Gill".

It was not long before we were once again sat in the Marton Arms discussing the tactics that we would use for the following weekend. Those took the form of another trip to Far Waters where we dug through the last remnants of the slurry choke and squeezed through the mud logged bedding plane and up into Radagast's. The BPC lads who'd been on the GG side when we first made the Wellington boot connection came with us this time and were part of the first team to enter Ingleborough Cave from Gaping Gill. This trip had the effect of ensuring that a through trip would now be possible. The boulder choke itself could not be stabilized to any extent without many more trips to the area. Therefore we did what we could

and then kept our fingers crossed that it wouldn't fall in before we did the through trip itself.

Since the day of the connection in January we had been involved with Yorkshire Television who wanted to make a film of the through trip. For the next three months they "ummed and ahhed" as to whether or not they would in fact film the event. They messed us about in general, mainly due to the fact that they only had a 20 minute slot to put the film in, which we felt was nowhere near long enough. Finally we began to lose patience with them and this, along with several other complicating factors, led in the end to the dropping of the film completely. We felt a sense of disappointment at this as we thought it was an event well worthy of recording on film. Nevertheless we also felt a sense of relief in so much as we could now go ahead and do the through trip. This didn't turn out to be as easy as it seemed though because it threw it down with rain for the next six weeks and each through trip planned had to be postponed. However, during this period of never ending precipitation, Sid Perou came back to the UK after filming the British Speleo Expedition to Mexico. He more or less immediately decided to film the event for the BBC and the whole thing took off from that point onwards. After one or two more postponements the weather cleared for the last week of May. Everything was organised for Bank Holiday Saturday, a year to the day that we'd started on the project. Sadly on the Friday night it rained heavily and the forecast was for more of the same on Saturday. However, stream levels did not rise and the expected rain did not materialize. At 6.00 a.m. in the morning the go ahead for the trip was given to Sid Perou and the BBC and the masses began to assemble in Clapham Car Park at 9.00 a.m.

The plan for the trip was that Geoff Yeadon and I would abseil down GG Main Shaft, along with our support party and the film crew who would all be winched down. The film crew consisted of Sid Perou on camera and Chris Gibb on sound. The whole team, carrying a Molephone with them, would then make its way to Radagast's Revenge where Geoff and I would meet up with Jim Abbott and Julian Griffiths who were to enter Ingleborough Cave with a support team, also carrying a Molephone, and upon our request would dive through from Terminal Lake to join us in Radagast's. They would give their diving gear to Geoff and I and we would dive out to Terminal Lake and exit from Ingleborough Cave, whilst Jim and Julian would exit with the others from Gaping

Gill. Sid Perou was to film us 'digging' through the already dug out connection to break into Radagast's Revenge after which he would also film the arrival of Jim and Julian from Ingleborough, the swopping of the diving gear, and finally the diving departure of Geoff and me.

During our journey to Far Waters we would make regular weather checks via the Molephone, especially as the weather forecast was bad. If it did begin to rain then we were prepared to call the whole thing off as we could not afford to take any unnecessary risks. Because the Gaping Gill trip would take much longer than the Ingleborough trip, and because Ingleborough was much more flood prone than Gaping Gill, we decided that there would be no point in endangering the Ingleborough team by sending them into the cave before the Gaping Gill team had arrived at the connection area. Therefore we decided to radio the surface from Clay Cavern when we reached it and obtain a weather report from Bob Mackin. If the rain was still holding off we would give the go ahead for the Ingleborough team to enter the cave. This would be done by the surface team contacting them at the entrance to Ingleborough Cave by walkie talkie sets. The BBC film crew were to film the entry of both teams into their respective caves, the surface team as they tracked us with Molephone and finally would film the exit of Geoff and I from Ingleborough Cave. As I say, that was the basic plan; the next question was ... would it all work!?

The Through Trip Saturday 28th May 1983

The first stop that we made was at Ingleborough Cave. Due to the BBC only having one film crew we had to resort to filming the Ingleborough team entering Ingleborough Cave some eight hours before they actually did so! That would then leave the same film crew free to film our entry into Gaping Gill and then follow Bob Mackin and the surface radio team who would be following our progress across the fells towards the mouth of Ingleborough Cave. Once there the BBC would film our exit. Most of the Ingleborough Cave sherpas were camped up at Gaping Gill for the Bradford winch meet but they'd agreed to meet us at Ingleborough Cave at about 9.30 a.m. In the event everyone was assembled by about 10.00 a.m. and the necessary filming was duly carried out. The BBC crew and the Gaping Gill underground and surface support teams then proceeded up to GG, whilst the Ingleborough team began what must be the longest period of time that anyone has spent in a wetsuit without actually going caving! This time

was spent awaiting our radio message from Far Waters that would call them into the cave. Most of the time was spent playing football with the N.C.C!

When we finally arrived at Gaping Gill things quickly turned chaotic. The main problem was that there were not enough people to carry Sid's film gear to Far Waters. Even after press ganging several unsuspecting cavers into helping us do the job there were still not nearly enough but the whole show rolled on regardless. The next problem was getting all the radio and T.V. interviews over and done with after which we found that the Gaping Gill rope was in fact down Jib Tunnel. When the rope was at last pulled out of Jib and put down Main Shaft (belayed at moor level) we then had to pack and allocate all of Sid's gear. Finally, after a couple of hours we were ready for the off. Everybody went down on the winch followed by Sid who was lowered slowly in order to film Geoff Yeadon making the abseil down. Unfortunately, the abseil rope was tangled in the BPC's power cable about 100' down the shaft, and as Geoff's abseil came to an abrupt halt at this point the winch chair carried on down relentlessly taking Sid with it, his protests getting fainter by the second. Meanwhile a telephone message was received on the surface, via the winch phone, from the Main Chamber below - the abseil rope was some 20' too short! Scoff and I had measured the rope a few weeks previously with a surveying tape. It was found to be 393'3" long so how it came to be too short on the day still remains a mystery!

[*The laser survey of GG in 2018 revealed the depth of the shaft from moor to chamber floor level to be 116.6M (383.5 feet) which leaves 11 feet 3" (3.43M) of the rope to belay at the top, run down the slope, rather than run vertically, this is calculated as using an additional 14 meters (45.9 feet) of rope and re-belay at Birkbeck's ledge. This is clearly not enough, probably by about 45 feet (14M), did you actually re-belay at Birkbeck's? – Ed*] [No, we didn't – Geoff]

I eventually joined Geoff on Birkbeck's Ledge and there we both waited until another rope was tied on to the end of the other on the surface. When we received the message that this had been done and the rope was now long enough the two of us at last continued the abseil to join the others in the Main Chamber from where the through trip could begin in earnest.

Once underway the travelling circus slowly made its way towards Far Country, the main delays being experienced on the Mud Hall Traverse and between the Iron Ladder and Southgate Duck. A weather check on the surface was made via the Molephone at the iron ladder. The rain was still holding off so we pressed on towards Far Country. A few hundred feet beyond Southgate we found that two of the party were missing. After half an hour they were located back at Southgate Duck having experienced light problems. In addition, two of Sid's batteries had by now disintegrated to add to our troubles. With all the lighting fixed again we continued slowly but surely on to Clay Cavern. Upon arrival there another weather check with the surface was made. Everything on top was still OK so we took the decision to call in the Ingleborough team. The time was by now 5.00 p.m. Jim Abbott received the message via walkie talkie and the Ingleborough Cave team immediately began their journey to Terminal Lake. Back in Gaping Gill we made another weather check just before the rat runs preceding the connection dig. After that we crawled forward into the twists and turns and boulder choke of the connection area. Our support party didn't know what had hit them as they entered into the squalor of the connection and several were speechless when Sid began filming.

Filming the breakthrough and radio contact with the surface was carried out simultaneously with the BBC crew filming on the surface. Finally the 'second' breakthrough was made (the first breakthrough was the actual connection made in January) for the cameras, and the filming was finished.

Everyone was then subjected to the appalling connection dig itself, which was extremely wet, mud logged, cold, tight and loose (you name it and the connection certainly seems to have it!) It took over 1 ½ hours to move all 13 of us and the equipment through the dig which is only some 20' long! Yet more long, cold hours were spent in Radagast's getting the film gear set up at the diving site. Meanwhile the divers who had also been waiting at Terminal Lake for a long time had been radioed to make the dive and they were now on their way through the sumps. In Radagast's the physical condition of the team was rapidly deteriorating as person after person went down with mild exposure. With all of us through the dig we were extremely worried with regard to the unstable nature of it because, should it collapse, probably the biggest cave rescue in history would ensue. After another 25 minutes, Jim and Julian, to everyone's relief, surfaced into Radagast's Revenge. More filming now took place as Geoff

and I kitted up with Jim and Julian's diving gear. However, the condition of the film crew and the sherpas had deteriorated to such a great degree due to cold and fatigue, that the whole thing was now becoming rather dangerous. Sid Perou could hardly hold his camera and sound recordist Chris Gibb actually fell asleep whilst recording a 'take'. Higher up in the chamber the sherpas' condition had got so bad that finally they did the only sensible thing that they could and began to make their way out with no equipment.

The relatively fresh Jim and Julian soon registered looks of anguish on their faces when they saw the chaos, equipment and destroyed bodies that littered Radagast's Revenge. For Jim and Julian it was too late however; Geoff and I had by now kitted up with their gear and were already in the sump pool. Although we were cold there was plenty of incentive for us to get into the even colder waters of the sump pool and make our escape from the chaos. With cameras whirring, Jim and Julian caught a last glimpse of our grinning faces as we disappeared into the murky sump. Geoff and I did have a sense of guilt at leaving the others but with a fresh Jim and Julian to guide them out and also remembering all the awful trips that we'd had to make to Far Waters and back in order to make the connection, our guilty conscience was eased somewhat. The swim through the sumps was almost idyllic, even in the very poor l-2 foot visibility, with the knowledge that the purgatory was now nearly over. When the two of us eventually surfaced in Terminal Lake our elation was difficult to contain. Now that the dives were over, we both knew that nothing was going to stop us getting out. At the end of Terminal Lake we found that we were on our own. The reason for this was that we'd moved very quickly through the sumps and had arrived at Terminal Lake some five minutes before the Ingleborough support team were expecting us. Thus they were still a few hundred feet downstream at the radio location station when we surfaced. As we were on our own we spent a couple of minutes savouring the moment with a handshake. It was one of the best moments of the project. Soon we took off our fins and wandered off downstream, still fully kitted, to meet the others. We actually met them just coming around the next bend heading upstream to meet us. After the initial surprise of our early arrival it was celebrations all round. These were followed by confirmation to the surface via Molephone that we were both through the sumps safely and everything was OK. Apparently this was greeted on the surface with a cheer, with the tension of the usual 25 minutes radio silence whilst we were underwater now over. Waiting for an OK from Terminal Lake base had become like awaiting confirmation from an Apollo spaceship that everything was OK after the radio silence during re-entry!

Arriving at Terminal Lake was like stepping into a different world! All the support team were in high spirits, totally organised and raring to go. A few hundred feet upstream at Radagast's Revenge, the scene was more one of desperation at the beginning of that team's long haul back to Main Shaft. With all the gear packed away at Terminal Lake base the last message was sent to the surface informing them that we were on our way out and to get the celebrations ready. Time passed quickly as we sped along and it wasn't long before we could see in the distance, the lights of the far reaches of the show cave. We reached the show cave at 10.50 p.m. to a crowd of people nearly all armed with a camera. The crowds grew larger as we made our way towards the entrance which seemed to take an age to get to. Approaching the iron door was like stepping into daylight with a mass of TV and camera lights around the cave mouth. Geoff and I stepped through the door at exactly the same time and exited from the cave. All we could see was a sea of people; it was as though every friend that either of us had ever had was there! Geoff had been through it all before at Keld Head, but for me it was a little overwhelming. After the cheers and applause had abated came the magnum of champagne. The cork popped and amongst more cheers everyone piled in! None of the champagne was wasted as it was all swilled down within a couple of minutes! TV and radio interviews followed before the celebrations finally swept us away into the night. Even so, we still had thoughts of the Gaping Gill team battling it out in their attempt to regain Main Shaft. After a grim journey they eventually made it back at 3.30 a.m. on Sunday. They too were greeted by large crowds and champagne. Some nineteen hours after we had all assembled in Clapham Car Park it was now all over.

After 150 years the underground traverse from Gaping Gill Main Shaft to the mouth of Ingleborough Cave had at last been completed. However, to enable it to happen had seen an incredible amount of effort directed at the project in the year 1982/83. Thousands of man hours had been spent on the project and we had used thousands of pounds worth of the latest caving technology as well as some of the oldest die hard methods in the book in order to make it all happen. It had been a magnificent team effort from start to finish and Geoff and I received an incredible and unforgettable amount of support from everybody involved during our efforts to make the elusive connection. We cannot ever hope to repay our gratitude to all those who helped us. The week after the through trip we had a tremendous celebration at the Marton Arms with everyone together again at last after the traumas of the previous weekend. The connection was named 'Dr Mackin's Delivery' in recognition of Bob's Molephone without which the connection would have been either impossible or, at best, taken many more years to realise.

2020 Postscript
The through trip was repeated later in 1983 by a team of cave divers from Derbyshire. To date, that is the only other through trip which has been completed. The connection choke collapsed not long afterwards and has remained blocked for many years. Who knows, maybe someone will make another attempt in the not too distant future!

The Story of the Back End of a Pantomime Horse – J. Abbott
The connection between Gaping Gill and Ingleborough Cave has been sought by cavers since Birkbeck made his partial descent of the main shaft of Gaping Gill in 1842, and the early explorers investigated the near reaches of Ingleborough cave in 1837. Subsequent explorations by a rich panoply of individuals and clubs have pushed that dream ever closer. The BPC have been involved in that exploration extensively over the years, Whitsun Series was discovered in 1968 by the BPC, which pushed the limits of GG a considerable way towards the connection. The key to the final connection was the discovery by ULSA, in the same year, of Far Country along with LUSS and Mike Wooding's discovery of Far Waters in 1971. At the same time major extensions were made to Ingleborough Cave by Mike Wooding with the discovery of Gandalf's Gallery. Even I had a pop at the connection by diving Hallucination sump in 1973, I had with me two stalwarts of the club Raymond Lee and John Bolton to act as Sherpa's, I couldn't understand why they didn't wait for me up to their necks in water while I thrashed around making a miserable 30 metres of progress. I found them lurking further back in the passage in a much more comfortable spot, "I don't know, you just can't get the staff"! Geoff Crossley eventually passed the sump to discover Troubled Waters in 1985, a fine inlet streamway which was found to lead up the P5 valley and not towards Ingleborough Cave at all. However, a voice connection was made through a choke to Clapham

Bottoms Dig, which was subsequently dug open by the White Rose cavers, including Chris Smith, who had for a long period been a BPC member, to reveal yet another entrance to Gaping Gill. In 1982 a great deal of surveying and radio location then took place in both Far Waters and Radagast's Revenge, this led to a real possibility of a connection between the two with only a few metres separating them. In 1983, after digging in a suicidal choke a connection was finally made by BPC diggers, divers and Molephone operatives included Geoff Yeadon of CDG/Kendal. The through trip was finally arranged for 28th May that year.

The day dawned, to coincide with the winch meet, two teams were assembled, the winch made life so much easier for the operation, the BBC film crew which were to accompany the proceeding's more than detracted from any advantage the winch gave us! The arrangement was, Geoff's Crossley and Yeadon were to enter the main shaft with porters and film crew to arrive at Radagast's at a predetermined time, ably assisted by radio communication, courtesy of Bob Machin and the Molephone. The Ingleborough party consisted of Jim Abbott and Julian Griffiths plus BPC porters. This was a fine tuned operation, what could possibly go wrong, well quite a lot really, for a
start we didn't get the call until late in the afternoon, we had to content ourselves with playing crawl/knee football outside the cave. We were finally called and in we went, a super-efficient carry took place, the only things missing were sedan chairs for the divers. A last call from the Radagast's team was the final bit of information we needed. Off Julian and I went, in the serene silence of the underwater environment through the various sumps that separated us from the incoming GG team. Such pleasure, known territory, relatively benign sumps, shallow and good visibility, as I said before what could possibly go wrong? We arrived in Radagast's, rising from shallow depths to a scene of carnage and despair. Sid Perou was his usual bumbling self, Chris Gibb, the sound man was fast asleep and the Sherpas were on the point of mutiny. Oh Joy! However after a rerun of both Julian, and I, emerging from the Radagast's sump, for dramatic purposes, we swapped diving gear with Crossley and Yeadon. They glided through the tranquil sumps to Terminal Lake, to then be transported by the super-efficient BPC Sherpa escalator to the awaiting adulation of the fawning crowds and fans. "Oh what it is to be a superstar cave diver". Bitter? I should say so!

The GG Sherpas had already voted with their feet and were heading off out through the awful connection choke. Julian and I gathered the stragglers and set off. I had a premonition of things to come when one of the LUSS Sherpas decided to drown himself in the duck at the base of the connection choke. He entered it the wrong way round, head the wrong side, I saw convulsions of a dying man and decided he had to come back out of the duck/squeeze, after all how would I get through with a dead body in the way. After strenuous pulling on his ears, out he popped, a little bit of advice as to the correct way through, and off he went. Hooray, a very satisfactory result [He is probably now a grandfather of many grandchildren] and I didn't have to suffer from indigestion after having to eat my way through him.

The Sherpas, plus Sid and co, had no idea of the complexities of Far Waters, and decided to head for the "Orifice", a hideously tight squeeze leading up into Far Country. Now I did once manage this squeeze in my youth when my shoulders were narrow and guts were slim, but did they listen to me, did they fuck! I took the easy route up into Clay Cavern where we rendezvoused. My lamp by this time was almost non-existent, I was met by the almost comatose party, but they did have lights! My spirits rose marginally. This was now serious; Julian and I nurse maided this party all the way back out through Far Country and Hensler's Master cave, Short Hensler's, and finally Main Chamber, to be greeted by the glorious winch, although, despite the slick operation of that magnificent elevatory device, it took what seemed like an eternity to get to the surface. Three or Four in the morning is not always the ideal time for a celebration, usually it marks the last of the die-hards in the ale tent coming to and realising no one is left. However, on this occasion the BPC and other clubs were there in abundance, champagne was consumed, backslapping took place and a jolly good time was had by all. I was reminded of Ian Wilkinson's oft repeated quote, "Ah well that's Gaping Gill over with for another year." In this case it was for me, unlike Wilky who said it at the Berger in a moment of confusion! This was then followed by sleep and oblivion.

This marked the end of a journey which started in the mid-19th century, by groups of adventurous pioneers, followed by incremental explorations by a whole series of tough inquisitive cavers who were willing to push, dig and dive further into both cave systems. Geoff's Yeadon and Crossley, Julian

Griffiths and I were all beneficiaries of these great men, we stood on their shoulders to finally achieve

that long sought after trip though the Gaping Gill/Ingleborough Cave system aided and abetted by scores of unsung BPC and other Sherpa cavers.

To my knowledge, only a party of four Derbyshire caver/divers, led by Clive Westlake, have repeated this exchange, the unstable connection choke was unable to defy the laws of gravity any longer and has collapsed big time. Whether digging will open

this route again only time will tell. Much more has yet to be found in the system, connections have yet to be found to the Newby Moss area, as Bob Bialek once said, "How many miles of undiscovered passage are there in Gaping Gill?" Quite a few I should think!

SECTION 2.13 DIVING IN ARCTIC NORWAY – J. ABBOTT.

In 1985 Geoff Crossley and Jim Abbott were invited to explore an underground and underwater river in arctic Norway by Andy Ive (Westminster CC). We were to meet up with a team of Norwegian cavers and divers at Mo I Rana led by Stein-Eric Lauritzen. The underwater cave was the full outlet of. The whole escapade was filmed by the BBC and subsequently transmitted under the title "Caves of Marble". After a long drive we eventually arrived to then embark on a long walk through the forest to our base. Although in tents we had the use of a house owned, and built by Mr Glomdahl, for evenings. Exploration took place at both ends of the cave and a middle entrance, visibility was excellent and diving easy, it was about a kilometre long in total with depths down to about 25 metres. The only hiccup involved Mike Pitts the cameraman, who had plenty of underwater experience but no cave diving experience. We were filming a sequence where Geoff was following a line down to the deep point, Mike was filming and I was tracking Geoff with lights, both Mike and I were offline. Mike hit the bottom creating a cloud of silt, being an open water diver he pumped air into his suit to rise above the mirk. He floated up a rift at ever increasing speed, I grabbed his fin and the line, the line stretched like a banjo string but he kept going. Forced to release the line I followed Mike still with fin in hand. We arrived beneath a roof at about -2 metres, attempting to regain my composure I noted a look of concern on his face. He was fine, he was in good hands, I told myself, and I knew the way out. I thought I'd better check my compass, just to make sure of the direction even although I knew it. Bloody thing was 180 degrees out, I kept tapping the glass to free an obviously sticking needle, no, it kept swinging in the same direction. Always trust your instrumentation my mind kept saying, but my instinct said no, wrong way. I followed the compass even though I knew it was wrong, needless to say the compass was right Jim was wrong, daylight appeared in a very short distance, my minds direction suddenly spun 180 degrees back on track and we lived to fight another day, good old Silva.

SECTION 2.14 – THE BPC ALBANIAN EXPEDITION PART OF THE UNTOLD STORY – J. EDWARDS.

It was a conversation with Frank Croll, possibly in 1986 that raised my interest in Albania as a prospective caving opportunity; he waxed lyrical about the wide open shafts and caves that must be there. I started researching the country at Stockport Central Library and found there was precious little known about the country other than its rudimentary industries, how many tonnes of timber and rubber they import and what they were able to export, I also found out what their national holidays were, all interesting stuff. I did however find the name and address of a technical academy in Tirana who seemed to have some sort of responsibility for geography and its name had 'cava' in one of the words. Armed with this mass of, pre internet, information I felt I was an expert on the country so how could they refuse me permission to organise a holiday there for me and twenty odd friends? I had been sending letters to the Akademia Sckencava in Albania three or four times a year for three years before I got a response, I had sent letters to their only embassy in Europe at the time, in Paris and got no response from there at all. Then one day, I was on a course at work and away from my desk when a call came through from an Albanian Government Translator. The chaps who answered the call were very confused but took a message and put the phone down. When I got back at lunch time I didn't believe a word of it, I was convinced they were winding me up. To cut a long story short, he eventually rang again and confirmed permission was possible if I sent lots of information about all who would be going, he also stressed how unlikely this was and that it had never been done before so I was not to get too excited at this point.

This prompted me into action, conversations with friends in the club led to a trip over to a committee meeting where I explained that permission was arranged but I needed volunteers and access to some club tackle the following September. This was agreed although the tackle may be a problem as the club was doing the Berger the month before and it may not all be back. As the names of interested people came in it was obvious that we would only be looking at 10 – 15 people. I talked with Ian Wilkinson and John Perry and we felt that for safety we should aim at 25 people in at least two vehicles, especially as we were taking a few

ladies. I contacted the DCC and they jumped at the chance to fill the empty places.

I contacted the Home Office in London and explained the situation; they said they would need to involve the Foreign Office and the Military planners! [*At the time the Yugoslavian civil war was raging, the Serbs had invaded Slovenia and were now ethnically cleansing Montenegro, Bosnia and Herzegovina and threatening to invade Kosovo, which is 90% ethnic Albanian. The Royal Navy was patrolling the Aegean and blockading Serbia, and Albania was saying if Kosovo is invaded they will also invade from the south*] A team was set up in London comprising people from the Home Office, the Foreign Office, MI6 and NATO. The Foreign Office line was we don't recommend any UK citizen goes anywhere near Albania, the Home Office said they couldn't help very much, they both said as we had no diplomatic relations we cannot contact their embassy in Paris on our behalf. The military said if Kosovo is invaded be prepared to be interred for the duration, at best, we will however arrange for your transport if you want. MI6 asked if we would take a spy with us? So I asked if we could contact the Royal Navy if we had a medical or other emergency, they said No, under no circumstances were we to contact the fleet, whilst at the same time sending me a frequency. I, in turn, politely declined the offer to take a UK spy with us on the grounds that if we were interred and they realised he was a spy we would have been in very deep doo doo indeed. The policy gridlock the Foreign Office found themselves in was threatening to stop the whole venture, without their support and blessing we would have no call on diplomatic assistance should it be required. I needed to remove the gridlock, so I wrote to the Prime Minister John Major and explained how important it was that we got there before someone else did. A few days later I rang my contact who said " I don't know what has happened but it came down from on high and suddenly your expedition is our number one priority and we now have our people in Paris working to contact the Albanians in Paris and establish diplomatic conversations to secure statements of intent to secure the venture" Which I think meant, restrictive processes have been changed and we were initiating the restoration of diplomatic relations between UK and Albania and we were going to get the blessing of the Prime

Minister, the Home and Foreign Offices, though not the Military and certainly not MI6. Two out of four is not bad when there is a war on.

As it happened The Serbians didn't invade Kosovo while we were there, we had no medical emergencies; we managed to make one phone call home and we all got home safely even though the Greek ferry company were threatening to sue because we hadn't paid for the people on the return ferry trip to Italy. We only came close to an international incident when Dalek had to be carried off HMS Gloucester with absolutely no control over his legs, in front of the good people of Brindisi who were out for an evening stroll. Dalek was then carried onto the ferry where he was refused entry on the grounds that he was unconscious.

It turns out we weren't the first cavers into Albania, we weren't even close, we weren't even the first British team to get in. We were however the first BPC team to get in and judging by the straw poll I held on the way home we would probably be the last. [*Only one person in 24 said they would go back*] We were definitely the only team to enter Albania in such troubled circumstances, with dark forces threatening, both within the country and all around its borders.

SECTION 2.15 – BPC DIVERS – THE GREAT ADVENTURE – D. RYALL

After a loud boom the only sound was of birds squawking in alarm, sheep running away, and a whooshing sound as might be made by a wooden door flying through the air and landing in a tree. A few seconds later giggles filtered out of various hidey-holes and Scoff's dulcet tones broke the stunned silence with a Yorkshire Michael Caine impersonation; "you weren't meant to blow the bloody door off!"

At that time - around the mid nineties - I'd been cave diving for a few years, teaching myself how not to kill myself, but hadn't worked up the courage to introduce myself to those I perceived (wrongly it was to turn out) wouldn't give me the time of day. I'd been doing a lot of digging with Bob Mackin and Bob had been approached by Scoff and some others involved in the exploration of the underwater cave network beneath Chapel-le-Dale to remove a troublesome bit of rock obstructing Bargh's Entrance – a potential 'back door' into the passages between Hurtle Pot on Jingle Pot. We'd drilled some holes, put in 'plenty' of chemical digging aid, and retired to what we thought a safe distance. The resulting bang had certainly done the job! Later in Bernies Cafe Scoff and I got chatting about diving; he was a big name, I was a nobody but of course Scoff was his usual cordial self and I was very flattered when he suggested I might be able to help out with some projects he had in mind. Little did I know, but for the next twenty years most of the more dangerous episodes of my life would begin with Scoff saying "I know what we (or you) should do, Dave".

The idea behind opening up Bargh's was that long deep dives in the unexplored passages upstream of the known end of the system would be much safer if divers could avoid having to decompress up to the surface in an air filled chamber called Frog Hall (so called because when first discovered there was a large frog sat on a rock in front of the diver) and then continue back to Hurtle Pot via an almost thirty metre deep flooded section; physiologically this is not good practice. The new entrance would allow a direct exit to sunshine from Frog Hall. The entrance had been dug into and a vocal connection made just as the new CDG Sump Index was going to print and rather rashly the anticipated new entrance had been included as fact, whereas in reality it wasn't actually possible to reach the surface due to a tight restriction. A few years went

by and then guilt got the better of the original explorers and a concerted effort had been made to realise the connection. A wooden door had been fitted to keep sheep from falling in and it was this door, which we closed and piled rocks on to "muffle the sound" (some hope) which had now acted like a giant frisbee and several well known cave divers were trying to dislodge from the tree it was now sat in. Still, the connection was now made and next day we had a trip down to Frog Hall to celebrate. The dive line was tied to a large rock projection above the deep dark lake and Scoff leaned nonchalantly on it and regaled me with stories of how Brian 'Biffo' Smith and he had found the way from Jingle to here. With a big splash the projection detached from the wall and disappeared into the lake taking the line – and very nearly Scoff – with it. "Oh dear" (or something like that) said Scoff, as we had now technically removed a diver's ability to get to Frog Hall rather than extended the cave by creating a new entrance! For the first time, I heard those words "Hey Dave, I know what we should do" before suggesting I get my diving gear on and go find the line somewhere below. This I did, and the connection was finally made, although when I suggested I get the credit for it the answer was a polite "er… NO!"

This incident highlighted a problem in that part of the cave; below Frog Hall is an almost vertical shaft called The Void down which the dive line went. In times of flood a massive volume of water streams trough there which would regularly snap the line meaning it was constantly being repaired and patched up, to the extent it was a series of knots and tangles of old frayed line – a real hazard to any diver. Various options had been tried including a line made of Bluewater caving rope, well known for being 'bombproof'. It may be bombproof but Hurtle ate it up and spat it out in no time. Serious action was called for, and I was to be an innocent dragged into what turned into the usual pantomime comedy of errors (which seemed like a good idea at the time).

A long length of steel chain had been acquired; this was to replace the various lines and ropes, and having a breaking strain of several tons would "last forever"… A cunning plan was hatched to lay the chain down The Void, secured to more conventional dive line in the horizontal passages at the top and bottom. Now, dive line, SRT rope and

162

the like are all basically neutrally buoyant in water; they might float a little or sink a little but essentially are weightless making a bag of rope easy for a diver to transport. Thirty metres of steel chain though weighs pretty much in water what it weighs in air, meaning the diver would by trying to swim carrying the equivalent of a bag of coal. That's not too bad; divers can compensate by adding air into their drysuit or a buoyancy vest to balance this out, although the twenty kilos or so in this case would be at the extreme end of this sort of technique. And so it was that Ian 'Poppet' Lloyd, Scoff and myself found ourselves at the top of The Void having humped in the bag of chain. The plan was that Poppet would swim out over the top of the shaft before releasing a little air from his suit whereupon he would gracefully (and in full control) descend the shaft paying chain out of the tacklebag as he went. Scoff would be above (where the chain had been belayed to a hopefully reliable projection) and I would be below to 'help out' making sure the chain didn't snag on anything. Unfortunately, despite his suit being inflated to Michelin Man proportions, Ian was still a little negatively buoyant and once he got out into the shaft began to sink uncontrollably. Normally this would be a problem, because as a diver descends the air in his suit is compressed, making him effectively heavier, and sink faster, and become heavier etc etc until he lands on the floor in a big heap. In this case though, as he descended, the amount of chain (and thus weight) in the bag reduced, so making Poppet more floaty so he then started to go up rather than down. The chain also started to rattle out of the bag due to the weight of chain not being supported by Poppet (who was now floating backwards up the shaft trying to catch the chain as it ran out of the bag). Stationed half way down, I saw Poppet approach, and then disappear upwards, eyes big in his mask, trying desperately to juggle dumping air from his suit (needs one hand), hold onto the bag (needs one hand) and stop the chain running out of the bag and down the shaft (needs one or maybe two hands). Not being in possession of the required number of hands a runaway 'chain' of events had started which ended with Poppet at the top of the shaft bobbing like a cork on the surface with a surprised look and an empty bag, me halfway down watching the chain whistle past (and trying not to get tangled in it), and finally a big pile of spare chain on the floor. The dive lines were tied on and a relieved exit made to the pub. The dive report in the CDG Newsletter dryly described a chain having being laid down The Void, with no hint of the underwater flying circus which had taken place. At this point I should have spotted the signs and found some more sensible friends to play with, but I didn't.

About a year later I had another dive in Hurtle. At the bottom of The Void was a pile of rusty chain, snapped off somewhere above. So much for "last forever"…

In 1997 Sue and I made our annual pilgrimage to the Vercors where for some years we had joined a French club in the ongoing exploration of Grotte de al Luire. At the same time a team led by a Swiss cave diver, Olivier Isler – then perhaps the most technically advanced cave diver in the World – was exploring a resurgence in the Dordogne called the Doux de Coly. This was currently the longest underwater cave in the World, and the intention was to extend it. A group of UK cave divers were on the support team and it had been suggested that a tourist dive could be on the cards if I happened by. The Doux is a World class site and access is normally forbidden so this was too good an opportunity to miss. Having finished the Luire explorations, a diversion was made on the way home to visit the Dordogne. For me this would be the first visit to the area, justly famous in cave diving circles for the unparalleled number and quality of underwater caves. For a British diver the contrast between Yorkshire pothole diving – cold, poor visibility and dry caving to get to the sumps – couldn't have been starker. In the Lot and Dordogne *departments* the weather is sunny and warm, there are many inviting turquoise pools from which huge cave passages can be followed, full of clear, warm water. A different world and way different to anything I'd experienced. Dictated by the cave conditions, the cave divers here tended to be very advanced technical divers who had adapted to explore underwater caves, whereas in the UK cave divers are usually cavers who have learnt to use relatively simple dive kit to pass flooded sections of otherwise dry cave; underwater potholing as opposed to diving in a cave.

On the continent, cave diving exploration was more akin to being a spaceman, and nowhere was this truer than the Doux de Coly. The specially developed equipment, great depths and long duration dives, coupled with a team approach (in the UK most cave divers operate solo due to conditions underwater), and major financial sponsorship of these big dives which made the newspapers and TV was very different to the low-key, unglamorous world of British cave diving. We were arriving at the tail end of the expedition; all the big dives should have been over and done with. My hope was to get a dive or two in just to visit the cave, probably the 300 metres or so of shallow passage to a shaft which descends from a depth of about 15 metres to a deeper ongoing passage at around 60 metres depth; this continues for thousands of metres but was beyond the abilities and equipment of mere mortals – more people have been to the Moon than have gone beyond a kilometre or so into the Doux de Coly.

The British contingent were camped on a nice campsite with a bar, swimming pool and toilets whilst the Swiss and German members of the team had arranged to use a field on a farm nearby. This was known to the Brits as "The Gobi Desert"; it was a barren spot full of "razor blade bushes and scalpel trees", had no facilities and the only redeeming feature seemed to be that it was cheap, and had an old barn to use for kit. The barn by now resembled a rustic version of NASA; it was jammed full of cutting edge diving kit including Olivier's two massive underwater propulsion vehicles which resembled 8 foot long gold torpedoes, and the RI2000 rebreather system; three independent gas recycling systems which remove the carbon dioxide from a diver's exhaled breath and inject a small amount of oxygen to replace that metabolised. Computers constantly monitor gas levels and vary them depending on the depth. This custom designed and made system was known to the Brits as "the Garden Shed" which is an indication of the size of the thing. Olivier didn't really wear it, he got into it! Coupled with the underwater scooters, gas tanks and other kit he was a quarter ton human mini submarine. This was somewhat hard to control when powering through the confines of a (admittedly large) cave passage and that's why it now had a hole in it.

When we'd arrived the night before it was to the end of a tough day; three kilometres into the cave Olivier had crashed into the roof and badly damaged the primary unit. He'd bailed onto one of the reserve units and had to retreat back, but by now had incurred the maximum decompression penalty and would have to spend nearly nine hours slowly ascending to avoid decompression illness caused by nitrogen dissolved in his bloodstream fizzing and causing severe injury or death. It had been an epic, but successful failure in that Olivier had survived an incredibly serious situation further into a sump then anyone had ever been. This unplanned 'sharp exit' meant that a considerable amount of additional work was required to remove all the equipment from the cave, and many team members were now departing. Poppet and I were promoted from 'freeloaders' to 'essential team members'!

At that time, a 300 metre sump was about the longest dive I'd done; I was now asked to dive the 300 metres to the shaft where there was an ROV (Remote Operated Vehicle) which had been placed in the shaft to monitor Olivier's progress over the nine hours of his deco stops. Called a Hyball, it was the size of a fridge and had thrusters, cameras and lights, and a cable back to the entrance where the operator sat in the 'Mission Control' tent watching activities in the shaft and moving the thing around with a joystick. I was briefed on how to undo the plug from the unit, wrap the delicate plug in a tea towel to protect it (not very space age I thought), hand it off to a couple of others who would take it out, and then hold the end of the cable to protect it from snagging on anything. A surface team would haul on the cable and I would swim along holding the plug. Arriving at the shaft I approached the Hyball. The lights flashed on and off and the camera swivelled up and down, a bit like it was nodding to me which I interpreted as the operator at Mission Control saying go ahead. Locating the plug it had a sticker next to it which read 300v and a warning triangle! Tentatively I unplugged it, wondering if I was about to become the first cave diving death due to electrocution but there was no flash so I guessed someone had turned off the surface supply. Two divers took the unit off me and I deployed the cable protection system (tea towel and a zip tie). After a while the cable gave a jerk and slowly started to head up the passage. I held on, enjoying a leisurely swim and taking in the fine cave scenery. After a little way I realised I was now swimming quite hard to keep up. Shortly after that I realised I could stop swimming as I was being pulled by the cable. Soon I was whizzing along, hoses fluttering in the 'breeze' and having to fin hard on bends to avoid being dragged along the walls. Eventually I decided damage to the plug came second to damage to me and let go; the cable snaked off into the distance. Those guys must be bloody strong I thought. On surfacing I mentioned that I couldn't keep up at which point it was revealed that they had tied the 'delicate' cable to a car and driven up the road!

To aid Olivier on the long decompression stops a 'habitat' had been installed in the shaft; this was akin to an upside down tent which was filled with air so it floated like an artificial air bell 'suspended' by a rope which went to a massive block at the bottom of the shaft. On this rope was a Petzl Stop allowing the habitat to be 'abseiled' upwards to shallower depths as part of the decompression schedule with Olivier sat inside it, out of the water, meaning he could eat and drink and talk to people

164

who visited him on his nine hour wait. Olivier had to do another long dive to retrieve some kit in the deep section, so the habitat had to be moved back down by venting some air out of it to allow it to sink, reset the Petzl Stop and then re-inflate it. And that's how Scoff and I ended up at the top of a fifty-metre flooded shaft on top of a large balloon, letting air out of it until it started to sink. Now, as I've mentioned, when something sinks any air trapped in it gets crushed by the increasing pressure, thus making it heavier, and so sink faster. And that's how Scoff and I, clinging onto the habitat rode it down the shaft desperately squirting air back in to try to slow it down until it was halted by a rope tied to the roof. On surfacing we both admitted to imagining "Ride of the Valkyries" in our heads as we rode it down the shaft. I felt like an aquatic version of Indiana Jones. After the successful failure in 1997 a return was made in 1998 with largely the same team and needless to say more adventures were a part of this; Olivier commented that the reason he valued the British team members so much was because of our adaptability and ingenuity, but most of all our sense of humour. Whatever happened we could be relied on to cobble something together and make it work, and have a laugh doing it. We may have looked like we didn't take anything seriously, but we delivered the goods on time, every time and stuck at it until the job was done. Years later in 2011 a British team attempted to push on from Olivier's final limit of exploration in 1998 at 4100 metres. The attempt was thwarted by bad weather, but Olivier (now retired from diving) turned up to visit and catch up on old times. We talked about the good times we'd had and he confessed that when things got serious and tough, the wise cracking Brits kept him going. After the trips Scoff and I did a presentation at Hidden Earth which was well received, indeed I have at least one friend who still says it's the best lecture he's ever been to. It was a mixture of comedy and education and included a survey drawn on a roll of wallpaper which we unrolled around the theatre along with volunteers from the crowd to demonstrate just how long the sump is. Some CDG members took the mickey by calling us "sump donkeys" but I do believe the trips had a lasting beneficial effect on UK cave divers and diving. We brought back many ideas and adapted them for use on more advanced British dives; in fact these techniques and equipment probably made those dives possible. Perhaps the best compliment paid was from Olivier who when we pointed out that what we do in the UK seems small potatoes compared to exploits like those abroad said "but in France and Florida conditions are so good it's easy; in England the caves are small and the water cold with bad visibility. I couldn't do that". Some of the techniques which so inspired us, Scoff and I were to be put to good use in a resurgence in northern Spain…

At Hidden Earth in 1999 Scoff and I got talking to a Spanish cave diver who talked about endless opportunities for cave diving exploration in his country. At that time there were very few Spanish cave divers and most exploration work had been done by British divers. We arranged a visit to Spain; the initial plan being for Cordoba in the south, but in the end we chose a little visited area between Madrid and the north coast. British cavers and cave divers have been very active in areas like Matienzo and the Picos de Europa, but further inland seemed to have received little attention. There was a cavers' guidebook to the area "Cuevas y Simas de la Zona Centro" which covered a very large area but had comparatively little content. This initial trip was to be mainly tourist diving, but with a view to locating some areas of interest for a return visit. The first area we looked at was near El Burgo de Osma, roughly a hundred miles north of Madrid; an impressive canyon called the Canyon del Rio Lobos. Not far from the campsite we stayed on was a tiny resurgence at the side of the road; this was actually in the cave guide and was called Surgencia El Manadero, also known as Nacimiento del Río Ucero. It was described as being 12 metres long, but given even in summer a steady stream of water emerged, and given it was next to the road and close to the campsite Scoff suggested it was worth a look at least. We'd visited some superb sites that week such as the Fuentona de Muriel; proper holiday diving with crystal clear pools, big passages and gin clear water. By contrast, El Manadero was small and the water coming out wasn't exactly gin clear. Still, just the sort of thing a Yorkshire cave diver is used to so slightly reluctantly I tagged along when Scoff went for a look. Things really didn't look promising, but once Scoff's head was underwater we knew there was at least something there. After a few minutes the bubbles stopped; either he was on to something or was dead! He'd taken a tiny search reel with a small length of line on it, and soon returned with all the line gone; it was more than 12 metres long, and more to the point no end had been found (or any trace of a previous explorer). Game on!

This unexpected turn of events gave us two immediate issues; we needed dive line, and petrol for the compressor to fill dive bottles with. Our local contact offered to sort the petrol; we would go buy some line. There followed a comedy of errors as Scoff and I visited hardware shops and the like on what became known as "the quest for string". Surprisingly difficult thing to buy in rural Spain, string. Eventually we found a shop with a roll of it and bought the lot, having watched the assistant take a nice neat reel of cord and laboriously measure it metre by metre before stuffing it in a shopping bag so we'd have to spend some time unknotting it later. Our Spanish friend came back with a plastic bag too, full of petrol. In 40 degree heat this seemed a bad idea so we quickly decanted it into the compressor before we all got incinerated. We'd learned two things; string and petrol cans aren't big selling items in rural Spain, and there is little concept of health and safety! Now being equipped with air to breathe and line to lay we had no alternative but to go explore.

It became quickly apparent that this wasn't going to be the sort of place British cave divers go abroad to find (ie large passages full of clear, warm water). Beyond the entrance the passage was big alright, but the water was cold and murky and the floor covered in a deep layer of soft brown silt. We could cope – this was more like being at home – but it wasn't exactly what we'd hoped for. It was going though, so no complaining from us. In fact, the nature of the passage was probably the reason that a roadside resurgence hadn't already been explored; the locals had gone somewhere nicer!

Over the next week we both had some epic dives in there; the sump just kept on going in the large muddy passage. It got steadily deeper as well and at 400 metres in and 37 metres depth we ran out of time and suitable equipment. Vowing to return, we headed home at the end of a surprising productive – and difficult - trip to spend the winter making plans and pulling together the gear we'd need to press on.

Assuming the cave kept going in similar style we had two main challenges; the distance and the depth. Depth means the diver breathes more and more air as the depth increases, and beyond around 45 metres narcosis becomes increasingly a factor; the nitrogen in the air at higher pressures becomes a narcotic and impairs judgement; not a good thing in a difficult muddy sump. Longer

deeper dives also required slow ascents to avoid decompression sickness - the bends – which can injure or kill a diver. We needed to be able to travel quickly and effortlessly under water and breathe helium mixtures to avoid narcosis. All this, back in 2000 was pretty cutting-edge stuff; we

knew about such things but had never practiced them ourselves. Time to get learning. Of course, we didn't go shopping or sign up for courses; we did some research, did some practicing, and did some DIY! The Doux de Coly influence kicked in, but on a shoestring.

The underwater propulsion vehicles used by the likes of Olivier are very expensive, unless you have a load of plastic pipe and some creativity. Scoff had developed his own version of the professional Aquazepp, which became known as the Bogozepp (as it was made out of bog pipe) and I now built something similar. Pretty they weren't, but they worked and incorporated some features not available in the shops such as the ability to swop batteries underwater and having switches that could be bypassed in the event of failure. For breathing mixtures, Scoff wrote a spreadsheet which would calculate how to blend the breathing gasses we wanted in the field; I had an account at work for oxygen and I persuaded the supplier to provide cylinders of helium and oxygen on the cheap; this was industrial grade rather than breathing grade, but the salesman assured me it was all exactly the same (apart from the price). Otter Drysuits in Bradford offered us free drysuits as sponsorship and one night Scoff and I along with Matt McLaren who was also coming got measured up and subsequently given nice shiny suits with all the bells and whistles such as special valves you can pee through on long dives. Matt's dad coincidentally worked for a medical suppliers who donated some incontinence sheaths (aka catholic condoms) which you 'apply', connect to the suit and can then pee into the water – as opposed to wetting yourself. I'd used these before and warned the other two that the sheaths were tacky on the inside so they don't come off in use and that it's essential to 'trim the shrubbery' before use to avoid a 'bikini wax' when removing them after the dive. I'd learnt the hard way and it was tempting to let them do the same…

At the start of September 2001 Scoff and I coaxed his overloaded van down through France and met up with Matt at the Rio Lobos. I can remember now, twenty years later, the sinking feeling I got on the first dive that year; over the winter I'd had on rose-tinted diving goggles and had forgotten how grim the sump was. Now I remembered! The line from last year had disappeared, buried in the deep mud on the floor. Occasionally it appeared but effectively we were laying new line from the entrance as opposed to going straight to the end and carrying on. Matt did some sterling work and had similar 'thought provoking moments' to us as

166

he got to grips with the challenge of (re)laying line in such difficult conditions. He also dived a nearby cave, Cueva del Lago, and connected it to El Manadero. This was good, as we'd brought out a sawn-off 45 gallon plastic drum with the intention of filling it with air so it stuck to the roof, forming an artificial airbell which we'd use to get out of the water and decompress in. This was a great idea until we found it wouldn't fit through the entrance! Matt now took it in via Lago. Again inspired by the Doux, we had a 'habidrum' to serve our time in!

As we got towards the limit of exploration I made the dive which would take us into new ground; tying on the line at 400 metres I felt the amount of time and effort which had gone into getting us back to this point, so when after a few metres the mud rose up to the roof I was somewhat worried we had been Ghar Parau-ed! Looking right, in the gloom a black space beckoned; we were off again. A bit like a Himalayan climb, as we got further in progress slowed and incremental advances were smaller than earlier on. Scoff and I were now laying the line with Matt in support and we both had epics. During one dive, Scoff had problems with a line tangle and retreated. On the way back his Bogozepp floatation tubes imploded due to the pressure; to quote him it was "like swimming with a grand piano". On surfacing he let out a long sigh; "that's the hardest dive I've ever done" he said, adding later in the expedition log that a lifetime of experience was what had allowed to fall into the incident pit and claw his way out again. This was getting serious.

Tuesday September 11th 2001 was of course to be an unforgettable day, but not for any good reasons. After a tough day we returned a bit dispirited to the house we were staying in to be shown the images from New York. Matt had work colleagues in the World Trade Centre; suddenly cave diving seemed somehow frivolous and inconsequential so we had a day off. A part of the cave was subsequently named Liberty Street by Matt.

Returning to the fray I had mentally decided on a make or break full on assault so went in armed with lots of gas and lots of line. The floatation on my Zepp was similar in construction to Scoff's which was nagging doubt. What if I couldn't climb out of an incident pit? Full of trepidation I got to the end of the line, ready for the unknown. As I reached the end I took my finger off the switch; the switch which could be bypassed in the event of failure. What we hadn't planned for was a switch jamming on; this had happened previously to Scoff so we'd taken the precaution of applying plenty of WD40, which appeared not to have worked! Losing the line in those conditions is probably the worse thing you can do, but I was clipped to the thing and couldn't stop. Desperately I drove into a silt bank causing a blackout eruption of mud, but at least halted my progress. It was only a momentary glitch; the motor had stopped. I paused for thought. "Well, I'm here now, might as well crack on" so I tied the line on and headed into black void, leaving a diving torch on the Zepp to help me locate it in the murk. I followed the left wall as it curved round to the right for a while before seeing a light coming the other way. For a moment I thought one of the others must have come in, but then realised I'd come full circle and was back at the zepp. Following the line carefully back I spotted a low elliptical space near the roof; water flowed out of it and it was borderline if I could squeeze through. I had a go, but soft mud just spread everywhere and all vision went. I couldn't even see my own lights. This is bloody stupid I thought; time to call it finished. With that I tied off the line and backed out to where there was some visibility, thoroughly shaken by events.

Next decision; use the zepp and risk the switch sticking on, or swim out and incur much more deco time? Answer, use the zepp but don't clip on to it so I can just let go if need be. Turns out the sticky switch was a one-off and there were no problems on the way out. I spent an hour in the confines of the upturned drum, contemplating events. Surfacing I just said "It's finished".

Reading the log now I wrote at one point "the stress of pushing such a difficult site is enormous – there's no such thing as an easy dive here" and now I felt relief it had ended. Matt expressed some interest in having a look at the end with a fresh pair of eyes and I reacted quite badly. The place scared me and we'd all had epics; time to walk away intact. Matt probably didn't understand this and it was no criticism of his abilities at all, I just felt really strongly we should walk away. We both wandered off, and when we got back together the decision had been made – we were calling it a day. It has to be said that even years later the snapshot in my memory of the end of the cave nagged at me; there must be a way on, maybe I'd missed something in the gloom. Maybe I'd bottled it. I semi seriously considered a return, but in the end some things are just best left.

My cave diving days seem to have quietly ended; Scoff was of course diagnosed with cancer in September 2016 and died almost a year after that. It was my birthday in mid August and we'd arranged to meet on the day. In the end he cancelled a few days before saying he wasn't well. I'd arranged to visit him instead but got a call that morning from Rowena saying he was in the hospice and that I should come quickly. I walked out of work and drove and have no recollection of the journey. I ended up standing in the car park outside the place for ten minutes trying to find the courage to go in. We sat quietly; he was asleep but I talked about the old days and our many adventures, and thanked him for both trying to get me killed, and keeping me alive. Next day I went out on my bike in Dentdale; the phone rang and it was Rowena with the sad news I'd been dreading. The year following his diagnosis had been one he was determined to make the most of and he did; some years before, he had introduced me to kayaking and a couple of weeks before he died Rowena and Scoff had joined Sue and I in a beautiful, lonely cottage on Mull and we went out on the sea for the last time. I reminded him that as divers we had avoided the 'salty wobbly thing' all our lives, but now we both loved it – the irony didn't escape us. We sat on a bench overlooking the beautiful Sea of the Hebrides and talked. He was scared of what came next, I was just sorry there was nothing I could do this time. This was one last big adventure, and I couldn't join in.

After that I just didn't have any motivation for cave diving; a bit like the end of El Manadero I guess I knew it was time to walk away and find adventures new. Writing this was really prompted when I was looking for something in a pile of papers; I came across some exercise books which were the old expedition logs. The words jumped off the page and I was right back there; very happy days that I'm pleased we all survived! Looking back, in our own small way we had the 'right stuff'. We did a lot of things, made stuff up as we went along, bodged and adapted, had some rubbish ideas and some good ones, but most of all we had fun doing it. Can't say fairer than that, now can you?

SECTION 2.16 – DAVE HAIGH / BRIAN SIMISTER'S DIGGING TALES

I was ready to put my heart and soul into hunting for new caves – particularly digging on Penyghent and later Ingleborough. Di would come and sit with Beano reading a book and offering words of encouragement and then join us in the pub.

I prospected for new caves solo at first, but soon realised that although I found a few likely "goers", I couldn't dig more then four feet down in them before they started to fall in on me. I tried carrying up bits of old wood and stuff for shoring and to cover up the hole but it wasn't too successful and only solicited lots of piss taking (the foundation of any successful caving club) from my mates and fellow club members. I'm not sure whether it was Basher or Scoff – or both – who coined the verse "shores up his digs with match sticks and twigs" but it certainly stuck.

The very first new cave success was Wrinklies up above the track on the left hand side of Trow Gill going up. I only had to move a few rocks and there was an enterable phreatic tube (there are a few known ones in the vicinity) – I was absolutely ecstatic – partly because I knew it was situated above Terminal Lake in Ingleborough Cave (albeit at least 50 feet down below). On the way home I started to put petrol into my diesel car being as elevated as I was, fortunately I stopped in time for it still to work with a full tank of diesel to dilute it – silly bugger! Unfortunately it proved to be only fairly short. We excavated one or two others up there but they were too solidly choked and we eventually gave up.

Ragnar, now recently retired, joined forces and started prospecting around Penyghent mid week. He was a good companion relating his highly amusing tales of his trip to see the psychiatrist, staying at the dump and getting pissed.

Fat Finger was the first discovery on Penyghent. I'd gone up there after heavy rain the night before, and as it became thick fog at a plateau half way up I decided to prospect there for fear of getting lost. I stood peering around when I
became aware of a

slurping noise at my feet. Upon closer inspection there were two or three finger sized holes in the turf that were slurping down the water from last night's rain. "Bugger me it must be hollow under

here" thought I so I looked around for a likely shake hole nearby. Sure enough there was one only a few yards away – shallow but with smooth water worn sides a metre apart suggesting a filled in rift. Ragnar and I made a start with excavations and after a couple of trips it was looking extremely good – but we were encountering bigger and bigger boulders to extract.

The following weekend Ragnar was indisposed but Andy Haigh and his dad, Harry arrived at the Dump for a walk so I told them of our find – Garth had finished school for the summer holidays and was awaiting a uni placement. I showed them the site and Garth was keen to have a go and Harry was happy for him to stay up for a week. Ragnar was still indisposed but said you and Garth carry on, so Garth and I attacked it with a vengeance – and two crow bars. It was a hot sunny week and most enjoyable – digging by day and down the Lion at night. Andy was very good company and a mighty strong lad who could wrestle out boulders with ease – which is how he came to be named Garth (after a cartoon character of a huge muscle man of the time). We both hurt our fingers, trapping them under the crow bars, so vowed if it 'went' we'd call it Fat Finger. By the end of the week bits of rock and soil were dropping down into what sounded like a decent sized cavity going by the echo and we were very excited. I rang Ragnar to tell him the good news and that a breakthrough was imminent so he needed to be there. He still couldn't make it but very generously said 'don't bother waiting for me - somebody else might muscle in - just get on with it, I'll see it soon enough' – top man. The upshot was we broke through into a decent sized chamber (via a fifteen foot pitch from the surface) with an exciting looking choked descending rift.

Fat Finger was on the map. Garth made the first descent and Ragnar soon rejoined us that summer. We were spending three or four days a week up there, having fun and giving the Lion plenty of good business. At weekends a keen team soon developed with Ged Benn, an already proven cave discoverer who now kept us safe with his brilliant scaffolding skills, and as 'bang master' safely carried out most of the passage widening over the hundreds of very enjoyable digging trips we made, he did come a cropper though in Klondyke Pot – see anecdotes at the end - Andy Jackson, Ian Benn, Ali and Dave Brook, Pete Sykes, Mendip Carol,

Martin Smith (Billy Whiz), Mat McLaren, Ian Lloyd (Poppet), Dave Ryall, Scoff, and Col and Maz Stamp all put a fair bit of time in. Fred Rat appeared on the scene about this time as well, making some useful equipment like the ARSE machine, Air Recycling and Stiring Equipment, which was bloody good.

The rest is history, but I must record that we had a most memorable millenium party down there. The guys wearing suits and the girls wearing dresses for a unique and wonderful occasion. Dave Ryall printed a menu and if I hadn't forgotten the vacuum flask full of peas we would have had pie and peas . In the event we just had pie and champagne. Party poppers the lot.

Back at the dump afterwards, the night long party was the best I can ever remember. A lot of us ended the night covered in mud and trifle along with our posh Fat Finger caving gear. Mama Cas wasn't too pleased seeing the abuse of her gorgeous trifles, which she'd spent many hours arranging, but eventually (as you would expect after a wine or two) saw the funny side of it and joined in. Despite rumours to the contrary I recollect it was evil Ian Wellock that started chucking it – I just retaliated and the rest joined in – he says it was me!

Tom Paxton wrote a brilliant song called "Wasn't that a party" which I always associate with this event. The first verse goes like this:-
"Could have been the whiskey - might have been the gin
could have been the three or four six packs I don't know
but look at the mess I'm in
Head like a football – think I'm going to die
But won't you tell me me oh my
Wasn't that a party!

Someone had a grapefruit – wore it like a hat
I saw someone under the kitchen table talking to an old tom cat
He was talking about football – the cat was talking back
Just about then everything went black
But wasn't that a party!

Our illustrious digging team went on to scale great heights (sic) or is that lows? With discoveries of Losers Pot, Henslers Pot, Corky's Pot, Generator Pot, Christmas Cracker, Pay Sank and Klondyke to name a few. These discoveries gave us (nearly the whole club contributed) the opportunity to write our Tratman Award winning book (bragging) along

with my good friend John Cordingley, Adventures Underground. It took five years to put it together and get it into print but they were some of the most enjoyable, exciting experiences Di, John and I have ever had and that's saying something.

Greengates Pot:- There were quite a few incidents and accidents, near misses and laughs associated with our digging adventures so I thought I'd include just a handful for posterity. It was shock horror and heart stopping when Garth slipped off the scaffolding at the top when we were digging Greengates Pot and dived head first onto a sloping rock fifteen feet down. Luckily the sloping slab of rock broke his fall as he collided with it hands first and we were all amazed to see him immediately stand up and start laughing, as first thoughts were "that's a horrific fall" - he didn't have a scratch on him.

Ragnar and I have been having fun recalling some of the hilarious incidents and near misses we enjoyed during our happy digging days and have decided to record them here for posterity.

Ragnar writes:-

Mud Mine, Ingleborough:- We discovered a hitherto unknown geological phenominum called 'detached solid' rock at this dig. We found solid rock ten feet down which turned out to be 'detached solid' and very unstable. We abandoned it as we realised it would be quicker and safer to dig it as a trench from the surface and then put a roof on it!

Fat Finger, Penyghent:- Dave and I were digging a pitch in New Year's Inlet. Dave was down about shoulder height when what we thought was a solid wall we were digging against became another "detached solid" the size of a slop stone sink heading fast down to Dave. I jammed myself across the pitch, Dave climbed over me and jammed whilst I climbed over him and so on til we got out, which was just in time to miss tons of mobile shit burying us alive. We then retired to the pub and got pissed celebrating a near miss!

Winners Pot, Penyghent:- The dig at Winner's was looking too dodgy to continue so we decided to pull out all the scaffolding we'd inserted and fill it back in again 'we dig the holes and then we fill them in' Dave and I were having 'words' (a pretty rare occurrence) as to how it should be achieved with safety. Dave wanted to remove the last piece of scaffolding at the bottom first and he had his maverick head on and wanted to do it. We compromised and tied a rope around it and after loosening the bolt Dave, Ged and I stood at the top of the hole and hauled on the rope. The piece of scaffolding came away alright and all the rest of it immediately started disappearing downwards with a low rumble along with tons of boulders, mud and bits of shoring – just like when they show an explosion in slow motion on television and the cooling tower crumbles. Spectacular – we all fell about laughing as the self filling hole did it's stuff.

Good job the voice of reason prevailed eh Ragnar – Dangerous Dave lives again.

Woodland Creatures:- we were exploring, with a view to digging, a well known short cave which shall remain nameless. Dave and his mate Stewart Davis, a fellow BPC member, were with me on this occasion (Ged was with us on future trips) We spotted a small hole in the floor, which had a strong draught, so we enlarged it until I suddenly fell through to a sort of bedding plain with a small chamber below. I crawled flat out to investigate the chamber and why there were tufts of dead grass in it, and something else in the lower areas of the chamber which stunk. Bugger! We'd tunnelled into a badger set and I'd just fallen through the roof of its toilet.

We never got any recognition from the caving world for this unique achievement, but I did receive the much coveted Pillock of the Year Award from the BPC.

Just for the record I stunk so badly they made me sit in the car boot all the way back to the dump where I was immediately hosed down.
Now Dave writes:-

Generator Pot:- Mendip (Carol) was hauling up the bucket whilst I dug at the bottom one hot day at Generator Pot on Ingleborough. She'd tied the arms of her furry suit around her in an effort to keep cool. I shouted 'bucket ready' and looked up just in time to see her suit fall down to her ankles as she hauled up the bucket bollock naked so to speak – we all wet ourselves laughing as usual.

Fat Finger:- Ged and I were digging at the bottom of New Year inlet when we both started to feel light headed and unwell. Ged.com said 'there's no oxygen, we're getting carbon dioxide poisoning' We both shot out just in the nick of time. Later Fred Rat made us the ARSE machine referred to earlier which worked well, but we had to abandon this dig as the ongoing sump passage got too tight and we couldn't get the water away.

I would love to have related the story of Ged in Klondyke Pot in Adventures Underground but PC prevented it so here it is now:- Ged decided to just drill a hole and stick in a det without bang to widen a passage – this way there are no fumes, so you only have to get out of the way and then you can carry on. Ged went round two bends and fired it, but the cartridge ricocheted and shot Ged through the thigh. It nearly shot his bollocks off which necessitated a trip to Airedale, where he had a real job convincing the doctors that he hadn't been in a shoot out with somebody. He's still alive to tell the tale but I thought I'd beat him to it. Some mates!

Footnote; Restaurant Review – 'The Bothy'
A chance find situated on the slopes of scenic Ingleborough Mountain. The decor is an adventurous mix of early medieval squalor juxtaposed with a daring modernist installation of aluminium tubing from the hands of the artist Ark' Wright. I was welcomed by attentive staff, clad in unusual green designer outfits. An eclectic range of foods was on offer, cooked al-fresco at your table on a wood burning stove. Your critic enjoyed

Quiche and baked potatoes, with a side dish of roast chestnuts – the Lamb Chops looked especially appetising. The service deteriorated and the staff became quite abusive when I refused to accompany them down an adjacent hole – at this point your critic made his excuses and left. Limited parking, bring your own wine.
Roland the Gourmand

SECTION 2.17 – THE TRUE STORY OF THE SHOOT-OUT AT THE KLONDIKE CORRAL, OCTOBER 8TH 2005. – GERALD BENN.

It is now 15 years since this famous occurrence and I have decided to tell the true story rather than the massaged version which circulated at the time. The regulations for the control and use of explosives had just been tightened up and cavers had only just managed to retain the right to use explosives. It had been touch and go, hence the need to play down the incident.

Back in 2005 whilst at an Explosives Users Group meeting in South Wales I was talking to a guy about Hilti capping. He told me about a similar technique using detonators. This involved drilling an 8mm hole and inserting an electric detonator, this could then be fired more remotely than the case with Hilti capping.

Shortly afterwards whilst obtaining my "digging supplies" I was given some"free" detonators and I thought that this was an opportunity to try out det capping. At the time we were digging in the bottom of Klondike in a small passage with a protruding ridge of rock along the left-hand wall. Removal of this ridge would allow progress to be made. Conventional blasting would have meant relatively little rock could be removed at a time and since time had to be allowed for the fumes to clear progress would be very slow. Using det capping would allow multiple shots to be fired hence speeding up progress.

It must be explained at this point that the "free" detonators were not our normal instantaneous type but delay ones used when driving tunnels in solid rock where successive rings of charges have to be fired in sequence. The delays are only of the order of tens of milliseconds which is irrelevant to normal single shot use. The detonators themselves were about twice the length of a normal one, the extra length containing a delay element. At the time I was unaware of the nature of these delay elements and the consequences of their use in det capping!

Back in Klondike I drilled the first hole, inserted the detonator and retired to the end of the det wire (about 3m) lying with my feet toward the det. My reasoning for doing this rather than extending the wire was that the rock would come off sideways and hit the opposite wall rather than flying along the passage. I fired the det and a reasonable lump

of rock was removed. I repeated the exercise twice more with good results. A fourth hole was drilled and the shot was fired. This time I felt something hit my leg with considerable force – very much like a massive dead-leg that youngsters give to each other. After a short while lying there wondering what had happened I told Fred, who was back up the passage, that I needed to get out. When I lifted myself up off the floor I found a cylindrical bit of metal which I put in my pocket with the assumption that this was what had hit me. By this time the sensation had eased off a bit and I crawled back to the bottom of Goldrush Pitch which had a 15m ladder. With a good lifeline I managed to 'hop' my way up, my injured left leg being rather stiff.

Out on the surface I took off my oversuit but because there didn't appear to be any significant bleeding I kept on my fleece until I could get somewhere to examine the damage. I managed to limp off down to Ingleborough Cave without too much problem apart from on the steep bits. At the Cave I went into the toilets to inspect my leg. All along the only pain I was aware of was at the front of my thigh and sure enough there was a wound which fortunately was not bleeding. It was only then that I found out there was another wound at the back of my thigh and a bit lower down!! Surprisingly there was no pain from this wound! It was immediately obvious that rather than just hitting my leg the projectile had actually gone through it!!

It was clear at this point that I had to go to A & E so I got a lift down to Clapham and John Robinson took me down to Airedale. On the way there I did wonder what I was going to tell them about what had happened. This was very much like a gunshot injury and I hoped that the police were not going to get involved because this could have had repercussions for the caving use of explosives. After booking in at reception I sat down and not long after was aware that a couple of policemen were at the reception desk – panic!! Fortunately they were there because of an RTA on the main road – what a let off! After triage I was put on a trolley whilst they decided what to do. They insisted on carrying out an X-ray despite the fact that I could tell them that there was nothing left inside. There was then a discussion about treatment. One junior medic wanted to put some stitches in but the more experienced one said to just dress it after cleaning it up. The junior guy washed the wounds with saline, squirting half a bottle at each one. I think he hoped to squirt it right through but the muscle had closed up the channel so he was disappointed! All the while this was going on there was a succession of medics coming to have a look, I would have thought that gunshot wounds were quite common in the Keighley area but they were all quite fascinated!

This being the night of the Diggers' Dinner at the Station at Ribblehead there was now a mad dash back and when we arrived a great cheer went up, we were just in time for pie & peas and a pint!

There followed a couple of weeks hobbling around, initially with a stick, but not long after I was back up the hill and had the pleasure of blasting the bottom of Pay Sank and getting through into Grange Rigg. As the wounds healed, on a couple of occasions, I did find tufts of blue fluff in the scabs. These were from my fleece that had been carried through my leg!

For the record, the delay element that went through me was a piece of cylindrical metal 6.5mm diameter X 34mm long. It had a hole through it for the delay composition and it was flat-ended. Although about the size of a rifle bullet it had been propelled out of the shot hole like a rifle barrel but because it was driven by high explosive rather than gun propellant it would have been travelling much, much faster. This presumably accounted for the lack of pain at the entry site. The trauma I felt was all at the exit site which was hard on the floor I was lying on. I think its speed cauterised the flesh hence the lack of bleeding. The metal has a distinct burr on one end where it hit the rock under me. It is beside me now as I type this article!

Beware of free gifts there might be price to pay after all!!

2.18   THE CASTLEDEN CHRONICLES.

Early days

So how did you get into caving with the BPC? As usual a long story but I will try and make it shorter. As a lad I was relatively feral and wondered far and wide with my pals Chris Whelan and Jon Parkinson. One day at the age of 13 I discovered a large cave at the bottom of a local quarry and was keen to explore, the cave was full of water so I traversed along the wall, all went well until the wall detached and I fell backwards into the water still clutching the wall! Fortunately I managed to get clear before I drowned and emerged soaking wet and managed the mile or so home without dying of hyperthermia and equally fortunately managed to get my clothes dry before mother came home from work.

The following day I told my pals at school and Parky mentioned that he knew about a cave at St Ives near Bingley, so at the weekend off the 3 of us went to explore, no helmets of course and a bike light each. Now for those of you who have not had the pleasure of exploring Pan Holes can I say you have been very fortunate? It amounts to a muddy flat out crawl for a couple of metres followed be a decent sized rift which closes very quickly, but still very exciting. Now that could have been the end of my caving career but this time mother found out about my caving exploits, primarily due to the state of my clothes which were of course covered in mud. Being very concerned she confided in my much older sister who offered to solve the problem by introducing me to one of her neighbours in Clayton. The neighbour was Don Leach a member of the Bradford Pothole Club who was seriously crippled with Rheumatoid Arthritis, the result my sister assumed of getting wet in those terrible caves, this was designed to put me off the idea of caving permanently, wrong!

Don may have been crippled but he was full of enthusiasm producing photos and surveys to wet my appetite. He also suggested that I should join the Bradford on one of their monthly bus meets and the rest as they say is history.

The Old Dump

By the age of 15 I was a regular on the bus trips to the Dales and eventually discovered the Dump, situated behind the Flying Horse Shoes at Clapham Station. Unlike the current dump this place really was a dump! A tiny 2 story building at the end of some outhouses, adjacent to the pub. Downstairs

there was a small washing up sink and a stove for heat in the winter which filled the place with smoke. Upstairs we had some World War 2 steel framed 3 tier army bunks, with 2 inch wide steel bands, no springs, and sadly very few mattresses. The skill to sleeping was firstly a lot of beer and secondly placing a hip bone into the 4 inch square of fresh air between the steel straps, not the most comfortable arrangement but that's life! Not long after we acquired another room, at the end of the out buildings, which was a great improvement, at least you did not get asphyxiated by the fumes from the stove. One of my favourite recollections is of Alan Brittain, one of the older members, wiring the bunks we were sleeping on together to produce a resistance when he was charging his old CEAG miners light with a charger designed for a motor bike.

The place at the time seemed full of strange and eccentric characters, ATMB who looked like something out of the Bible, black malley who liked explosions and talked about the IRA, Kenny Heseltine young and strong who one night managed to throw an axe across the room into the door and Mike Boon, probably the hardest caver I have ever met quite a baptism of fire for a young impressionable lad!

Weekends were always fun, trips down Car Pot which had not been done for many years with the Baptistry crawl half full of debris must have been a highlight together with numerous other explorations, all this with Chris and Parky and latterly Raymond Stoyles known to everyone as farmer. Socially it worked well the pub seemed blind to our under aged drinking and our singing was the same as now with both folk songs and the inevitable rugby songs. This did get us into a bit of an event one night when an equally raucous group of Geordies seemed to want to sing their songs in competition with ours, this resulted in a bar room brawl and I still recall jumping onto the back of one big lad who flicked my 9 stone to one side without any effort whilst he battled with another BPC member. Fortunately before anyone was really damaged we made the peace and all had a great night together.

Fortunately at the start of the 1960s the great and good of the Club, who incidentally rarely if ever stayed at the Dump, decided to find a new HQ and after much work and deliberation found our current abode at Bracken bottom.

The new Dump

Sheer luxury! But still very basic by 2020 standards, no heating or hot water, rough floors and no showers. It did hold one surprise, in what is now the men only dorm, commonly known as the Kremlin, a bath, right in the middle of the floor, and totally unusable. Still there was lots of space, particularly in the bedrooms, which we filled with the same old ex-army 3 tier steel bunks but by some miracle they now all had mattresses.

The member's bedroom had a fire place which is still there to this day and on one particularly freezing night we lit a coal fire, sheer joy and went to bed with the flicker of flames and warmth what could be better? Sadly the committee heard of this and the very next week Dicky Dobson, builder by trade came and walled up the fireplace. Well as they say they can't take away what you have already had. Now the people are the same as ever but with one particularly memorable character.

Mike boon was probably the hardest caver I have ever known; whilst most of the Club were involved in sport caving Mike was strictly exploration. Together with Pete Livesey he effectively rediscovered Mossdale with trips to the far reaches and various banging trips opening the way for ULSA who then started the laborious work of surveying.

Personally I had a couple of trips one in the middle of the night was to Hammer Pot on Fountains Fell, an exciting episode starting at midnight to avoid the farmer who had imposed a ban on cavers over many years. When we arrived at the hole it was completely blocked but undaunted we dug it out and manged to get underground just as it started raining. This was a bit daunting when you realise that the entrance crawl is a stream way and sludge crawl can be wet and awful, needless to say Mike got to the bottom whilst I called it a day at the start of sludge crawl and did not return for several years.

The most eventful trip was the second, Mike and Pete wanted to explore the Hunt Pot inlet in Penygent pot, so recruited me, a mere 17year old and Neil Thorpe who was even younger to act as Sherpas for the vast amount of ladder and rope needed to get down the 10th pitch in Penygent. We arrived at the hole, Neil and me donned our usual woollies etc. Mike and Pete appeared with wet suits, the first time I had ever seen one of these and realised how good they would be in wet conditions. Almost on que as we were about to descend it started to rain and to this day I remember Mike saying let's get down before it rains properly!

The trip down was uneventful and Neil and me took up our positions at the top of the tenth whilst the other two ventured into the aqueous regions of the Hunt Pot inlet. All was well a comfortable spot and we spent the time trying to eat a tin of sardines without an opener, great fun! Then the water started to rise at a frightening speed, we must have waited an hour with thoughts that the other two could easily be dead. We had just decided to head out when thankfully Mike and Pete arrived having spluttered their way out before the water from hunt pot really arrived. The trip out was exciting to say the least, by the time we got up the big pitch I was mentally and physically exhausted and crawled into a hole with no intention of ever coming out. Mike then taught me a lesson in motivation, he talked nicely to persuade me but having failed resorted to more direct action and attacked me with his boots at which point I jumped up and had him by the throat! Ok says Mike if you have that much energy you can get up the next pitch, brilliant.

That problem resolved we set off for the crawl, wow the entire roof was covered in froth, so what to do stay and wait or go for it with the possibility that it was still raining. Decision made with heart in mouth and bounding with adrenaline we set off out and survived. On the way down the hill we bumped into the CRO coming to get us. With the storm above some of the BPC walked up to the hole and found it had disappeared and been replaced by a small lake, realising that the water in the crawl was by now going through under pressure they feared the worst and ran down for the CRO. For some strange reason that was the last trip I ever did with Boon!

Still the members were the same and also the rules, i.e. no women allowed. Although this did weaken a bit to, no women sleeping in the dump, which allowed Mike Boon to bring Dorothy Clegg, widow of Alan Clegg, for one of our regular drunken evenings. A pot of tea had a dead mouse submerged in it, Mike and Dorothy took turns to drink and see who got the mouse first, Dorothy succeeded and promptly threw up over the common room floor! Probably thought the mouse was just a joke, what a mistake.

Taking a step backwards our Easter meet at Easegill in 1964, which I was privileged to lead at a very early age, proved a challenge with seven of the regulars wanting to go but in those days transport was at a premium and no one had a car. With no options available and mountains of ropes, ladders and camping gear we rang the local taxi company and managed to hire their luxury wedding car which was big enough for 5 people and the gear. Raymond Stoyles, alias Farmer, and I got there on my old Lambreta scooter, complete with cushions from the settee for the floor of our tent. Needless to say Farmer ended up having to push the scooter up some of the steepest parts of the road to Bull Pot Farm.

Saturday we woke to a beautiful clear day camped out in the snow, Alan Clegg, a big lad, arrived with his wife Dorothy and Mike Boon, who intended to dive the downstream sump in Lancaster. I was getting changed and Alan promptly picked up a 9 stone Cas and dropped me in a snow drift then disappeared towards Lancaster laughing merrily, it was the last time I saw him alive. He died in the pool at the end of the dive still in view of Mike and more to the point Dorothy. Late that night, I recall pulling his body out of the entrance to Lancaster, a terrible contrast and an experience which prevented me from ever contemplating becoming a cave diver.

Obviously a full history would be a book in its self but apart from the amazing work carried out on the dump in those days it is interesting to note the social changes that occurred in those early years.
To start with it was the same rough and ready group of men and boys, mostly from practical back grounds and to the best of my knowledge none of the regular dump dwellers had a degree between them.

Also the dump was fairly basic and far from clean and tidy. Things started to change when we decided to allow women to become members, I remember being against the idea at the time, primarily due to a concern that it would no longer be the tight knit group, and totally change the interpersonal behaviour of the regular dump dwellers. However good sense prevailed and it was not long before we voted in our first female members.

OK I have to admit that this was not only one of the most important decisions we have made in the history of the club but in my opinion it has been the making of the BPC. Prior to female members and guests the average active caving life of members was about 5 years, wives and girlfriends were not impressed by their men folk disappearing every weekend without them. But once women could be involved all that changed and now there seems no limit. The average age on trips seems to continuously increase from early 20s in the 1960s to 40 plus at the present time.

The other big social change was the invasion of the teachers, starting with Brian Smith and closely followed by our past President Ian Wilkinson and also the likes of Cedric Binns Dicky Mcalindon etc. This resulted in the club organisation improving no end with regular Summer Trips to Europe etc.

To this date we continue to evolve and the Club is going from strength to strength. The BPC has been the one continuous and important social institution in the the lives of myself and Carol and many others, whatever happens there is always the BPC who accept your flaws and all no matter what else is happening in life.
Viva the BPC
CAS

SECTION 2.19– GET KNOTTED. MICHAEL RILEY – 2007.

[*The tale of a man suffering a guilt induced, delusional episode where he anthropomorphises a rope*]

After an absence of some 12 years from BPC trips abroad, Brian Rhodes, John Perry and myself decided that it was time to prove that we still had got what it takes. The proposed trip from T1 entrance to Santa Elena in the Aranonera system ticked all of the correct boxes, apparently being not too long or taxing and with a top and bottom entrance. With teams of the more keen and practised cavers of the Club on hand to do all that pesky rigging, we planned on a relaxing holiday, letting others do all the hard work before making a quick effortless abseil through the cave and out of the bottom entrance.

John and myself had a last minute panic regarding our ability to ascend and descend single ropes and just managed to fit in trips down Sell Gill and Jingling Pot in between torrential downpours to prove we could remember what to do. The rain-lashed Yorkshire Dales proved something of a contrast when we arrived soon after in the Spanish Pyrenees, where the sun bore down on us relentlessly for the best part of 2 weeks, (cruelly forcing me out of bed before 10am. some mornings). The 'C' team had a trip into Santa Elena, the bottom entrance of the system whilst the top pitches were being rigged and this provided us with a good 3 - 4 hour trip up a large streamway. This provides interesting caving with plenty of climbing over and through slippery boulder blockages and traversing around or through deep (and cold) pools. The water presented no real hazards but I wouldn't like to be there in flood as it drains a large area of mountainside with many entrances. We eventually reached an old fixed rope that marked where the horizontal section of cave ends. All that was required now was a trip to the top entrance where we would make our rapid descent through the pre-rigged system and conclude our triumphant return to continental caving. Thus we expected to have the caving out of the way by Tuesday of the first week allowing plenty of time to enjoy everything else that the region offers.

Back at the campsite our cunning plan started to unravel as the rigging of the upper series was proving to be slower than expected and the C team, perhaps overcome by too much sun, found themselves volunteering to complete the job. Next morning I proved that I definitely did have too much sun by just managing to stagger the 2 hours up to the entrance, merrily vomiting all the way, [not a hangover in case that is what you are thinking] I spent the rest of the day horizontal on the campsite whilst John and Brian continued with the rigging, although they too had to come back out of the top entrance, leaving a team of the Club's young tigers to complete the rigging of the last big pitch and make the first through trip.

Several days later everyone had done the trip bar the C team and we decided we would get clever and derig the bottom pitches of the cave whilst making our trip through. We left early, before 7am, so we would avoid the heat of the sun and be out of the cave by late afternoon, thus allowing plenty of time for the celebration in the evening. We geared up in pleasant morning sunshine before the shock of entering the cave. The first few pitches are cold and icy and have a couple of tricky moves swinging from one shaft into another. A long descent down an inclined ramp lands in a large horizontal dry section of passage where the nature of the cave changes completely, with the icy draught disappearing and things becoming much more pleasant.

We travelled quickly along to a short rising traverse where the passage narrows to the fateful point where we re-rigged a couple of short pitches and pulled the ropes after us. This was the first stage of our cunningly thought out master plan.

Then to the big pitch - this is a pair of magnificent parallel shafts totalling about 100m of descent. A straight abseil descent lands in a sump pool - however by clipping into an in-situ line, a diagonal descent is made to reach a large ledge, from where the second 50m descent is made to reach the passage that quickly leads to the streamway and sweet, sweet daylight

John descended to the bottom of both pitches and Brian to the big ledge halfway, where he removed the rebelays. From a rather mind-blowing position, hanging from some reassuringly large bolts, I pulled up the rope and rigged the rope for the pull through. I let the full length of rope hang down the pitch, then pulled it through and knotted the ends together. Keeping the knot I pulled everything through again so I had definitely got the middle of the rope on the bolt and then carefully fed the rest of the rope down the pitch (or so I thought). In the darkness below strange forces were afoot; loops of rope were twisting around each other. Sensing something was wrong I started pulling up the rope. As I peered down the shaft I saw big twisted loops of rope fall onto each other creating my nemesis - 'BFK', loosely translated as 'big frigging knot'. I hauled up BFK and shouted down to my companions that I had a slight problem.

A rough summary of the next 16 hours is as follows (the timings are approximate):-

14.00 BFK is proving to be a tough adversary. Dangling over the pitch, I pull loops through loops, trying to keep lengths untwisted and separate.

15.30 I assure the others that the rope is nearly sorted.

15.35 BFK recoils itself. Brian and John maintain lonely vigils.

16.30 I assure the others that the rope is nearly sorted.

16.35 BFK recoils itself. Brian and John maintain lonely vigils.

17.30 I assure the others that the rope is nearly sorted. I have the rope in a single length down the pitch.

17.35 I carefully pull the doubled rope through the big bolt. Below me the ropes twist around each other again - BFK has returned.

17.36 I start to despair.

17.37 I pull myself together and continue my manful struggle with BFK.

18.30 John finally departs to get help. I am convinced we will be out before midnight.

19.00 I have a big tantrum, swear a lot and feel much better.

19.30 Brian suggests that I go back up the passage a bit. This is a good idea as I have been hanging from the bolts pulling 100m of rope up and down the pitch for five hours and I am getting knackered. It is like doing mental arithmetic and aerobics at the same time and BFK is outwitting me. Me and BFK take up residence in the small passage. My strategy now is to pass each end of the rope through the mass of BFK and keep the ends separate - this means passing 100m of rope through itself countless times.

20.00 There is a small but noticeable draught in the small passage - I start to get cold.

20.30 I almost cry but give myself a good talking to. BFK looks smug. I notice it is fighting a rearguard action and my carefully stacked piles of rope are actually twisting into loops before my very eyes. I get into a full-blown argument with the rope and slap it about a bit.

21.00 I realise I am very knackered and thirsty. My forearms are pumped up like Popeye's but I am consoled that if I die at least my pecs will be nice and toned.

21.15 BFK is now begging for mercy.

21.30 At last BFK is no more - with only a faint 'see you in hell baby' he disappears. Relay the joyous news to Brian who has had eight lonely hours without even a big knot to talk to.

21.35 I rig the pitch very, very carefully - I am mentally and physically wrecked.

21.40 Finally convinced the rope is hanging free and untwisted. I clip in my descender, clip a cowstail into the guide rope, check everything a thousand times and gingerly start my descent, several times.

21.45 I arrive on the ledge. In a state of euphoria I declare 'J'arrive!' (*as proclaimed by a professional French caver after freeing a rope on a pull through on a BPC trip many years ago*). I clip my cowstail into a bolt, relax and undo my descender from the rope.

21.46 Brian calmly informs me that the rope is now 9m away across the shaft. It is the revenge of BFK.

21.47 I await a justified beating from Brian, who accepts the situation with more humour and composure than I deserve.

21.47 I calm down and we assess the situation. There is an ancient rope on the pitch below - which we immediately discount. When the party split, most of the emergency kit was in the bag John took down and is either 75m below us or out of the cave altogether. We have one foil blanket and not much food. We settle down under the blanket that just manages to cover us if we huddle very close together. Every time we move, an extremity is exposed and we immediately feel the cold, but otherwise it is just bearable. We continue to spoon each other for the next 7 hours, even managing some sleep in which BFK tormented me in my dreams. The rest of the time I replay the seconds where I undid the descender, over and over again. I resolve to give up caving, take up crown green bowling and possibly assume a new identity.

22.00 As we have not reappeared on surface a rescue plan is formulated. Simon acts as surface controller and John and Cas re-enter the bottom entrance, hoping to meet us coming out.

01.00 Roger and Steve depart for upper entrance together with Sherpas John and Oliver Robbo to await instructions.

02.00 John, unaware of BFK's revenge, arrives back at bottom of the pitch and establishing we are well- and-truly stuck, turns around and returns back down the streamway, leaving some food and equipment at the bottom of the pitch.

03.30 John, completing a superhuman effort, reaches the surface yet again and radios the team at the upper entrance to enter the cave. Roger and Steve race through the upper series with spare ropes to re rig where necessary.

05.30 We can hear them at the top of the pitch - (Brian has now been here 16 hours)

05.45 Steve and Roger arrive and we are carefully shepherded to the bottom of the pitch where a stove is fired up and we are force fed food and drink.

The trip through the streamway is uneventful and at 09.30 we are back on the surface.

Some conclusions and observations;-

1. Following constant analysis over several anguished months my main conclusion still remains the same - 'I am a f**kwit'. How can I have possibly let go of the rope? I had just completed the hardest eight hours work that I have ever done (seriously) but it is no real excuse.

2. I will think long and hard before doing a pull through in such a cave again. The decision to do the pull through to ease the de-rigging was mainly mine and was not a good one in retrospect, but how many continental caves have we done like this?

3. Why did the rope tangle so much? Can it really have taken me eight hours to untangle it? I have never seen anything like it in 25 years of caving. It was a 9mm rope and receives infrequent use on foreign trips. Had it been used with figure of eights descenders on a gorge trip perhaps?

4. In future, make sure that personal survival gear stays on your person and is not put in a group tackle bag that ends up somewhere else when it is required. I will make sure a survival bag stays in my furry suit pocket at all times in future. Foil Blankets are not a good idea, and a survival bag that can keep out draughts should be carried.

5. I am a f**kwit. Have I already mentioned that? Brian is blameless.

6. John Robbo's pocket radios saved hours of time in our rescue and should be considered mandatory for future foreign trips.

7. Our rescue was speedy, faultless, professional and selfless. A reduced team on the campsite meant that people had to do things when they didn't really want to. To everyone who contributed through a sleepless night, including surface control, cooking meals, carrying gear and those who came underground, and doing it with such good grace and humour, thanks - you are my heroes.

8. I am a f**kwit. I think I might have already mentioned that.

Postscript: A few days later, John and Brian (both surprisingly still talking to me) and myself were in a small tent on Monte Perdido as a full blown alpine storm hit us; thunder and lightning raged for hours, wind driven spray was lashed through the tent walls and several inches of water ran through one side of the tent and out of the other, threatening to fill our Goretex bivi bags and dissolving our sandwiches.

Perhaps someone up there doesn't like us.

Picture Courtesy Russell Brooks

Above – April 19th 1947 – Bill Porteus [left] and Dan Hutton [*No record of Dan's membership has been found – Ed*] on the long sought for traverse between Rift Pot and Long Kin East. Eric Barraclough had just carved his initials with 'BPC' and are clearly visible with the date. The other initials are those of the CPC chaps who found the traverse. Picture Arnold Patchett and Frank Moulson.

Left - 1966 - Pete Livesey and friends dived the sumps in Langstroth cave and were then stopped by this 45 foot pitch. After others failed to organise the climb Pete took control and climbed up this and seven others to almost reach the surface. Now recorded as a BSA find, with the help of the CDG. In reality the BPC divers and sherpas dragged the scaling poles through the sumps and, after many dives, successfully climbed all the pitches and surveyed the whole cave. Pete actually got hauled before the committee, during this time, to explain why he had kept so many ladders booked out for so long. Nowadays little thought is given to those lads back in the 60's who showed their peers and future generations what hard work and determination can achieve.
Picture – 2013 Nicola Brooks looking back up at the rub point as she prussiks up this beautiful shaft.

Five potholers are found dead

Others may be missing

FROM A STAFF REPORTER—Grassington, June 25

The bodies of five members of the Leeds University Potholing Club were found deep in the Mossdale caverns near here tonight. Hundreds of rescuers had worked through the day in an attempt to save them.

Late tonight police said it was feared that a sixth potholer, Michael Ryan, aged 17, of Dene Close, Bradford, might be trapped in the flooded cave.

"We have information which suggests that he went down, but we have found no trace of him", a police spokesman said. "There have been a number of reports that even more potholers might have entered the cave, but we cannot be certain of this."

A member of the rescue team said the cavern was "one of the biggest and hardest systems of the country". It is more than four miles long and floods frequently filling most of the passages to the roof.

The five potholers were members of a party of nine who entered the cave at 2.30 p.m. on Saturday. Four of the party emerged at 5 p.m., but their companions decided to go on. They were due out at 11 p.m.

One of the rescuers emerges from the entrance to the Mossdale cavern.

Rising water

When they failed to appear, one of the four, Miss Morag Forbes, who had been perturbed by the rising water in a stream feeding the cave, ran two miles across country to the village of Conistone to give the alarm.

The dead men were named tonight as:—

William Frakes, of Southway, Eldwick, Yorkshire; Colin Vickers, of Kenley Mount, Moor Avenue, Bradford; David Adamson, of Lofthouse Place, Leeds; Jeffrey Boireau, of Fernlea Crescent, Swinton, Manchester; and John Ogden, of Quernden Street, Colne, Lancashire.

Miss Forbes, of Blandford Gardens, Leeds, was engaged to Mr. Adamson, the leader of the party. They were to be married in six weeks' time.

Police said the rescuers were ordered out of the cavern before they could recover the bodies because it was too dangerous to carry on.

Police frogmen

Taking part in the massive rescue operation today were cave rescue teams from all over the north of England, as well as police frogmen and R.A.F. mountain rescue units. Rescuers stripped to the waist with picks and shovels to divert the stream running into the cavern.

Michael Ryan, the missing potholer, is a member of the Bradford Pothole Club and a friend of Colin Vickers and William Freakes, two of the dead men.

He left his home in Dean Close, Allerton, Bradford, on Friday Late last night his father, Mr. John Ryan, said he had been told by police that his son was believed to be dead.

Cave rescuers' burden, page 2.

1967 – Mossdale. How the World found out about the Mossdale Tragedy and due to the confused facts, why to this day, even cavers think the fatalities were all ULSA men. Of the six that died, three were members of the BPC.

Right – The plaque mounted on Mossdale Scar serving as a reminder of the young lives lost on that terrible day in 1967. It also serves to raise questions in the minds of people about to descend this hole that has such a reputation. To this day the word Mossdale always causes cavers to think for a moment, or is that just the older generation?

Engineers say 'there is no such thing as an accident' but we will never know all the circumstances leading to the decision to descend on that day. We know they heard the weather forecast, perhaps that was inadequate, as it didn't suggest that they might be in danger. It is hard to think of another failing, other than perhaps their somewhat arrogant belief in their own abilities. It will probably take a worse disaster happening to let us forget Mossdale; do we want to forget at such a high cost?

IN EVERLASTING MEMORY
FROM THE FAMILIES OF
DAVID ADAMSON
AGED 26
GEOFFREY WARREN BOIREAU
AGED 24
WILLIAM FRAKES
AGED 19
JOHN OGDEN
AGED 20
MICHAEL JOHN RYAN
AGED 17
COLIN RICHARD VICKERS
AGED 23
WHO REST HERE IN MOSSDALE CAVERNS
WHERE THEY DIED
24th JUNE, 1967.
will lift up mine eyes unto the hills:
from whence cometh my strength

1967 Provatina – Above - Russell Cox keeping a sensible distance behind the back end of a donkey on the walk up to the Astraka plateau, some 3000 feet high, in searing heat. Jim Eyre's wife, Rose, clearly found walking too hot and chanced riding a donkey. [*The expedition was led by Jim Eyre whose motivational shout was "If yer not 'ard yer shouldn't 'ave come!", to which some retorted "I'm not 'ard and I'm beginnin' to wish I 'adn't" – Ed*]
The four BPC members on the trip were Peter Faulkner, Russell Cox, Alan Brittain and Carl Pickstone.
Below – The entrance with what looks like somthing being lowered down the shaft.

Above – Russell Cox, Bill? and Jim Newton assembling the sophisticated life lining winch, it had two drive handles and a belt brake with 1000' [305M] of wire,
Right – The view up the shaft from the ice shelf at -570' [174M]
Below – Left Ian Carruthers or Dave Stevenson Stepping onto the ladder at the ice shelf ready for the long climb.
Below - Right – The view into the abyss below, they thought at the time that there was another 1000' below them [*It turned out to be only 768' [234M] – Ed*]

All 6 pictures Pete Faulkner

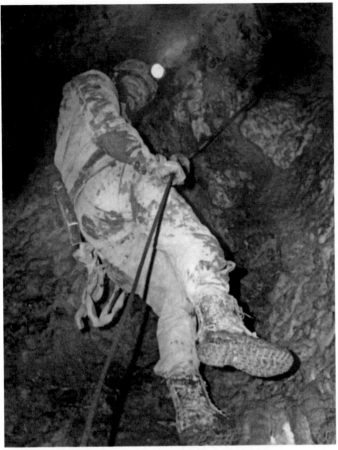

Picture – Brian Sellars

1974 – Left - Brian Smith abseiling in the Chourun des Aiguilles on the final trip to this cave. Some members had visited the cave some years before the 1973 expedition which made the successful 1974 trip the fourth visit by the BPC. It is this trip that accelerated the club's transition to SRT, most UK clubs were messing with the concepts but the BPC took the bull by the horns and created a working system with equipment available in the UK at that time. The derived system was then used to demonstrate its viability by bottoming the third deepest cave in 6 hours. We were the first British team to bottom the system and we were just one club, the second Ghar Parau expedition used SRT two years earlier but that was a heavily funded team selected from across the UK. British clubs were largely trying to learn SRT independently. It is a little strange that the club has never considered returning to this classic system.

Below left – Brian Sellers in the Meandre aux Boutons.
Below right – Raymond Lee in the Chateau de Cartes. [*The gear of the time seems quaint by modern standards – Ed*]

Picture – Brian Smith

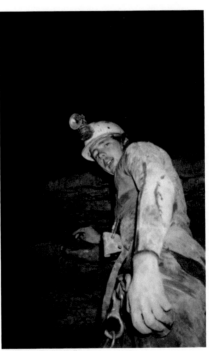

Picture – Brian Sellars

Some of the successful 1974 team looking like an inherently unsuccessful boy band.
Left to Right – Jim Abbott, Raymond Lee, Brian Smith, Brian Sellers, Dick McLindon, Ian Wilkinson.

1979 – Sofa Rugby
A rare picture showing a sofa rugby match in progress. The venue for this match was the BEC's Belfry which was about to have a complete window frame pushed out by the force of a BPC advance.

186

1979 - Like a shattered cold war relic, the SGCIF 'Fighiera' Refugio on top of Monte Corchia as it is today. Looking as if it eventually succumbed to the forces of nature, rather like the team it saved over 40 years ago. [*You can actually see Jim Abbott's handhold that he used as a straining bar before we entered the cave – quarter of the way up the right hand edge. We should perhaps get the remains of this hut removed and shipped back to the dump as a monument to the older generation of BPC - Ed*]

Left - Saturday 28th May 1983? - Geoff Yeadon about to abseil down main shaft on his way to Ingleborough Cave? Jerry Wooldridge taking a last shot from above while Geoff Crossley waits his turn along with some sherpas. The problem with this shot is there is no winch, which featured heavily on the through trip day getting all the film gear down to main chamber. This is a staged re-enactment after the actual event so that Sid Perou could capture missing footage for the television programme.

Below - 1985 – BPC divers Geoff Crossley and Jim Abbott were invited, along with the BBC, to help dive and film the underground outflow from Lake Glom Dahl below the Svartisen Glacier in Arctic Norway.
Left – Right Geoff Crossley, Russell England, Mike Pitts, Jim Abbott, Stein-Eric Lauritzen, Lesley James, Iain Schroder, Andy Ive.

Left - Circa 1997
Dave Ryall diving
in the Doux de
Coly

Picture Courtesy Gavin Newman

Below Left - Bryan Schofield [Scoff] diving in the Doux de Coly.
Below Right -Scoff and Dave Celebrating an empty line reel at El Manadero, Spain.
Bottom Right- Scoff at Hurtle Pot 1984.

Picture Courtesy Gavin Newman

Picture Courtesy Rowena Schofield

Photo – Fred Rattray?.

Circa 2003, some of the Green Man [*and women*] digging team in 'Corky's Bothy'. The wood burning stove is a luxury to make life bearable in the winter; a tarpaulin roof is added when it is raining or particularly cold and or windy. This picture captures the moment when Roland the Gourmand [*Mick Riley*] visited to sample the delights of this alternative, al fresco dining venue. Clockwise from left – Tim Sullivan, Dave Ryall, Alyson Brook, Fred Rattray, Janet Packwood, Bob Arkright, Jude Harrison, Dave Haigh, Mick Riley.

Left – 2014. The thought provoking, dramatic resurgence of Guires Mort near Chartreuse. The club had visited the Trou Du Glaz and this cave several times in the preceeding years. Picture Terry Devaney.

Waiting for a tracter with backs to the wall a chill wind blows on GG11 de-tackle day. Only Carol Castleden seems to have noticed the camera and be unaware of the cold. [*She appears to be still wearing her Tina Turner tribute hair from the last night in the beer tent – Ed*]

SECTION 3
BPC MEMBERSHIP
WHO'S WHO.

3.1 This section is a list of every member that appears in the club records; obviously the club records from 1933 are very 'patchy' and largely nonexistent in areas such as membership details. However by cross referencing other sources, there is now reasonable confidence that we have listed the huge majority from the early days. As time moves forward so does the quality of records but that doesn't mean there won't be some mistakes in the subsequent years.

3.2 The data supplied against every member is derived from five sources;

i] Every contactable member has been asked to fill in a short questionnaire this was hoped to confirm the full name and date of birth then go on to list their version of which trips they were on, what they got up to and what they think they would like to be remembered for and what they will probably be remembered for. Less than 8% of current members submitted this data. Past members have been asked, where they have been found, to complete the task for all living past members remains a major objective for the centenary up issue of this document.

ii] Every member's original application form has been studied to confirm the spellings and dates. The three trips required for member ship application have been included in the information section if available, the application forms, at times, did not record the trips. Less than half of the applicants completed the details in their form and in more cases than you would think they never achieved membership.

Iii] The BPC Committee meeting minutes have been studied for the new members section and these were cross referenced with the names in this section. It was surprising how many names appeared as accepted at the meeting and their names never appear anywhere else. This data is also cross referenced with the membership lists that used to be published every few years.

iv] Every BPC Bulletin has been studied for names, dates, locations, anecdotes and strategic events for the history of the club.

v] Every BPC newsletter has also been studied for names, dates, locations, anecdotes and strategic events for the history of the club.

3.3 There are several reasons why there may be no references against a person's name.

i] If they were a very early member and membership was not recorded there were no published trip records.

ii] If they didn't join in club meets or those that were recorded with a report in the newsletter or bulletin. This is probably true for the majority of cases as very few meets were reported and those that were rarely had the names of those that were on it.

Iii] We have simply lost the records, most of the Dump log books have not been found, if they ever turn up we can access the data and a subsequent update will be required.

iv] A surprisingly high percentage of people join the club yet remain active for only one or two years which limits their opportunity to make a lasting name for themselves, which this text could save for posterity. Some people join the club more for the social attractions and after a couple of caving trips get engaged to be married and reduce their activity or just help at GG or around the Dump and go walking, which is of course fine but doesn't leave a huge footprint in the records. They may go digging every week but that rarely gets reported as a meets report and their names are not noted for every trip.

3.5 It is estimated that as little as 5% of caving trips are recorded, higher for club meets, and of those only 50% have named all the people on the trip.

They use nicknames, first names or just initials and on at least one occasion a dark gloomy picture to identify the team. A lot of reports simply state the author's name and say there were 10 people on the trip or I can't remember who was on it. In all these cases the names of the team members have obviously been omitted.

3.6 Any errors or omissions should be reported, in writing, to the President.

3.7 – NICKNAME DICTIONARY

NB. Nicknames cannot be simple distortions of the actual name EG. Smithy or Wilky, discretion has been used.

Nickname	Real Name	Nickname	Real Name
1-Amp	Andrew Hainsworth	Ferdy	Fred Ackroyd
Abdul [the Bull]	Frank Croll	Frogman	Dave Ryall
Alt	Ian Wilkinson	Fuckwit Spice	Susan Ryall
Askey	Keith Asquith	Garth	William Frakes
Baby Bones	Christopher Sharp	Garth	Andrew Haigh
Basher	Martin Baines	Ged	Gerald Benn
Basher	Bob Booth 2	Gimmer	Adrian Laycock
Beaker	Peter Sykes	Gladys	Alan Ward
Beanz	Ian Greenwood	Gob	Adrian Laycock
Belay Briggs	Frank Briggs	Gobshite	David Miller
Bev	Deborah Last	Grass	Ian Ashwell
Billy Whizz	Martin Smith	Grassy	David Greenwood
Blunderwoman	Sharon Kelly	Gush 2 [Seep]	Karl Martin
Bog	Tony Brown	Handwound	Richard Elliot
Bon Jovi	Paul Wood	Hare [The]	Adam Spillane
Bones	Michael Sharp	Heavy Lemming	Geoffrey Flood
Boots	Peter Faulkner	Herr Flick	Peter Faulkner
Bowels	John Offord	His Royal Highness	Max Koval
Brave Duck	Dave Brook	Jekyl	Alan Charlton
Bump	Jon Holden	Jesse	Derek Jowett
Buzby	Geoff Crossley	Jim the Scott	James Brown
Buzzy	John Duckworth	Joe Berger	Joe Groves
Cabin Boy	Thomas Clifford	Joe Bones	Joseph Sharp
Cardboard Caver [The]	Tony Blick	Jonah	Urban Padmore Jones
Chemo Tim	Tim Sullivan	Jumbo	John Heale
Chuck	Charles Holder	Kermit	Richard Warman
Chucky	Ian Wilkinson	King Oaf	Max Koval
CJ	Christopher Sutton	Kiwi Pete	Peter Young
Corky	Colin Davenport	Knobbly Norbert	Nicholas Evans
Crispy	John Arcedeckna-Butler	Ladybird	Neil Dyson
Crispy Knees	Michael Jessop	Lefty	Ian Thorpe
Curly	Pauline Koval	Little Chicken	Ian Cross
Dad	Christopher Smith	Loftus	Tony Binns
Dad	Frank Moulson	Long Bob	William Riley
Daft Jonah	John Schofield	Long John	John Sunter
Dalek	Bob Bialek	Maclain	S. Cooper
Diesel	John Davis	Made in Hong Kong	Timothy Webster
Digger's Labourer [The]	Tim Sullivan	Martel	Andy Jackson
Digging Mistress [The]	Carole White	Max 2	Ian Johnson
Dr Lurv	Michael Riley	Mendip [Carole]	Carole White
Dreads	Stuart Coxon	Mendip [Jim]	Jim Abbott
Druggy John	John Bolton	Mick Steve Fuck Knows	Michael Marshall
Duchess [The]	Christine Davenport	Milkhead	Christopher Brown
Duds	Steve Dudley	Mini Prof	David Getling
Dusty	Brian Rhodes	Miss Whiplash	Kirsti Ashworth
Earthmother	Sharon Kelly	Moley	Peter Sykes
Eeny Weeny	Ian Wellock	Momma Cas	Carol Castleden
El Supremo	Colin Gates	Moose	Bryan Dobson
Farles	Charles Richardson	Mortuary Boots	Christopher Green
Farmer	Thomas Raymond Stoyles	Rusty Scooter	Ryszard Szkuta

Mr Bean	Mark Slater
Mr Dead	Michael Skinner
NikNik	Nick Cornwell-Smith
NJB	Janet Packwood
Nobby	John Clarke
Nolly	Noel Spencer
O'Malley	John Colau
Paparazzi Pete	Peter Monk
Parrot	David Cockfield
Phil Underpants	Philip Underwood
Plug	Andrew Graham
Poppit	Ian Lloyd
Prince of Darkness	Jim Abbott
Ragnar	Brian Simister
Ranting Roger	Roger Saxton
Red Ced	Cedric Binns
Red Dave	Dave Roberts
Ripcord	Robert Renshaw
Roaring Robinson	David Robinson
Roger Rabbit	Roger Adams
Roland the Gourmand	Michael Riley
Rotten	Dave Ryall
Runt	Titus Illingworth
Sandy	Andrew Wright
SAS Bob	Robin Arkwright
Scoff	Bryan Schofield
Sheppy	Arthur Shepherd
Silly	John Mitchell
Smeagle	Robert Jarvis
Smeg	William Booth
Smiley	Michael Riley
Snagglepuss	Kevin Murgatroyd
Snake	Raymond Lee
Sorcerer's Apprentice	Rodney McGhee
Spacy	Christopher Speight
Spotty Dog	Angie Rotherham
Stemple	Robert Jarvis
Suet	Anita Tempest
Swampy	David Haigh
Sweet Boy	Matt Mclaren
Thug	Andy France
Thumbprint	Colin Gates
Tigger	Christopher Epton
Tiny	Robert Atkin
Ug	Neil Griffin
Vincest	Vincent Buckley
Zippy	Graham Haydock

ABBOTT, James Hugh Stanton; AKA: Mendip Jim, The Prince of Darkness. *J1972, b1951,*
Probationary Meets; Flood-Stream Passage, Mendip Meet, Calf Holes-Browgill.
Member; BEC, CDG.
Main outdoor interests and activities; Caving, cave diving, exploration, walking, mountaineering, mountain biking, armchair research etc.
Foreign Expeditions; Reseau Des Aiguilles [Needles Pit], Devoluy France 1973 & 1974, 1974 was the first introduction of SRT for the BPC on the successful bottoming trip. Complesso Fighiera – Antro del Corchia, Toscany Italy, 1979, about 500m depth in Fighiera. Number of trips to Vercors starting in 1975 including Gouffre Berger bottomed twice in different years 1980 and 1992. Chartreuse, Jura. Massif d Arbas. Slovenia Tanne du Bel Espoir Grotte de La Diau, Parmelan, through trip 1981 and 1989. Pierre Saint Martin 1995 Tete Sauvage to Salle Verna. Bac Son Massif, Vietnam, 1992. Cave diving in Greece, Spring of Dracos and Island of Evia, 1982. Cave Diving in Glomdal, Norway, Caves of Marble, 1985. Cave Diving in the Dordogne, 1986.
Notable Achievements/Involvements; First exploratory dive in Hallucination Sump in Far Country, GG 1973, subsequently pushed through to Explore Troubled Waters with Geoff Crossley. Explored Far reaches of Dub Cote 1983 to 1985. Dived Pate Hole and pushed upstream sump for 135 metres, 1983? Involved in connection of GG to Ingleborough Cave and subsequent through trip with Geoff Yeadon, Geoff Crossley and Julian Griffiths 1983. Involved with the introduction of SRT as the main means of descent and ascent for club trips. Bottomed and explored Mossdale Caverns with Brian Judd 1974. Surveyed and radio located Little Neath River Cave 8 with Marco

Paganuzzi and Bob Machin 1987. Swildons 12 with Martin Bishop. Wookey 24 on two separate occasions with Geoff Crossley and others. Bottomed Langcliffe Pot with Dave and Thirza Hyde, Bob Bialeck, Mandy Glanville and Geoff Crossley.
Club Posts; Assistant Secretary, Librarian, Bulletin Editor, Chairman.
Remembered For; Giving a lift to numerous characters back from the Crown to the Dump, with unfortunately Jekyll and Harpic *[So named as he was clean round the bend - CPC member]* ending up in Douk Gill, well they were on the bonnet of the car until they fell off on one of the corners! Tied up in the winch chair by miscreant BPC members and thrown in the pond by the barn on route to GG-1988. [Because he was the Chairman-Miscreant]
Setting off fire extinguishers at dump, Jekyll was the main recipient. [All were replaced that week.] Woke up in communal tent [Sebastopol], to the smell of shit, someone had clearly shit themselves! I buried my head deeper in my sleeping bag to discover the smell got worse, it had to be me!! Subsequent investigations proved Chris Smith had crawled through a packet left by Bones and wiped the excess in my luxuriant beard whilst I was asleep. The beard subsequently became more luxuriant!
Stating categorically that "you don't need a wet suit in the Jura", and then nearly dying from hyperthermia along with five other members who were daft enough to believe him.
Bulletin References: *Black Shiver Pot, Oct 1972, Rift Pot Sept 1972,Chourum Des Aiguilles 1973, Diving sump below Hallucination Aven GG 1973, Diving Little Hull Nov 1973, Chourum Des Aiguilles 1974, Knucklebone Pot June 1975, Clapham*

Bottoms Roof Passage 1976, Potts Moor Cave, Clapham Bottoms Roof Passage 1976, Grotte de Bury 1976, Potts Moor Cave 1977, Newby Moss Sink May 1977, Newby Moss Sink 3rd Shaft 1977, Cartilage Cave 1977, Otter Hole 1977, Pasture Cave [Discovery] 1978, Rift Pot [Bolting] 1979, Mossdale Caverns [Digging] 1979, Hallucination Sump [Dive] 1979, Abbisa Fighiera 1979, Gouffre Berger Aug 1980, Ingleborough–GG connection May 1983. Cow Garth Cave [Exploration] 1982/84, Tanne Du Bel Espoir–Diau Aug 1984, Dub Cote Extensions 1984, Dub Cote Extensions [Diving] 1990, Tanne De Bel Espoir–La Diau Parmilan 1991, Gouffre Berger Aug 1992, Reseau de la Pierre Saint Martin-Tete Sauvage July 1995.

Newsletter References; Birks Fell April 1972, Swinsto Hole [Down & Up] June 1972, Pen-y-Ghent Pot Aug 1972, Birks Fell Cave April 1973, Little Neath River Cave June 1973, Pasture Gill Feb 1974, Chourum des Aiguilles [BP] July 1974, Lost John's Hole Aug 1974, Black Shiver Oct 1974, Swildons Oct 1974, Meregill April 1975, Stream Passage–Flood Entrance Feb 1975, Birks Fell Cave April 1975, Notts Pot March 1976, Scrafton Pot April 1976, Goyden Pot Feb 1976, Dale Head Pot April 1978, Cwm Dwr–OFD II April 1978, OFD I April 1978, Dan Yr Ogof April 1978, Hammer Pot Sept 1978, Gavel Pot Oct 1978,Simpsons Pot Jan 1979, Uamh nan Claig-ionn April 1979, Abbissa Fighiera Italy Aug 1979, Pippikin–Lancaster [Flood Pulse on Echo Aven] 1980, Goyden Pot [Diving] Feb 1980, Mossdale Caverns March 1980, Alum Pot June 1980, Gouffre Berger Aug 1980, Alum Pot March 1981, Lower Long Churn March 1981, New Goyden Pot April 1981, Magnetometer Pot March 1981, Mud Hall GG [BBC Filming Blue Peter] May 1981, Notts Pot Jan 1981, OFD 1 & 2 May 1981, Gaping Gill–Hallucination Aven [Dive] May 1981, Wookey Hole [Chamber 24] June 1981, Hurtle Pot [350'] June 1981, Tanne de Bel Espoir–Grotte de la Diau Aug 1981, Little Hull Pot [Dive Support] Oct 1981, Dub Cote Extension [Dive] Oct 1981, Ingleborough Cave Oct 1982, GG–Radagast's Revenge Ingleborough to clear dig for through trip Feb 1983, GG-Troubled Waters-Voice connection with Olympic Chamber in Clapham, Bottoms 1985, Magnetometer Pot Oct 1987, South Wales Nov 1988, King Pot Jan 1989, Gouffre Berger Aug 1992, Piaggia Bella July 1996, Walking Meet Sept 1997, White Scar Cave April 2001, Great/Little Douk Dec 2001, Milwr Tunnel June 2004, OFD 2 June 2004, Dufton–Garrigill Lakes Walk Sept 2005, Granett Bridge To ShapWalk Sept 2006, Committee Pot Dec 2006, Photographic Weekend Oct 2006, Short Drop-Gavel March 2007, White Scar Cave April 2007, Roundthwaite Common to Borrowdale Sept 2014, New Biggin on

Lune to Appleby Walking Meet Sept 2016, Lindale-Greenodd Walking Meet 2017.

ABBOTT, Richard George; J2018, b1955,
Probationary Meets; Wretched Rabbit-County Pot-Wretched Rabbit, Pippikin-Mistral, Notts 2, Lancaster-Wretched Rabbit.
Member; NUCC.
Newsletter References; County-Lancaster Jan 2019.

ABBOTT, Sheryl Jeanne; [née Haynes] J1973, b1953,
Probationary Meets; Outsleets Beck, South Wales, County Pot.
Bulletin References: Chourum Des Aiguilles 1973, GG Winch 1973, Chourum Des Aiguilles 1974, Grotte de Bury 1976, Abbisa Fighiera 1979, Gouffre Berger Aug 1980.
Newsletter References; Lockey Gill Cave June 1972, Birks Fell Cave April 1973,Chourum Des Aiguilles 1974, Great Whernside Walk Feb 1976, Mossdale Caverns [Surface Support] March 1980, Gouffre Berger [Surface Support] Aug 1980, Ingleborough Cave Oct 1982, County Pot-Top Sink April 1985.

ACKROYD, Frederick Oliver; AKA: Ferdy. J1937, b1909, d1989.
Bulletin References: On first Post War Caving trip Rift Pot April 7th 1946, Recorded as being the meet leader for the Upper Wharfedale meet on 29Th September 1946, Dowka Bottom 29th Sept 1946, Rift Pot-Long Kin East exchange April 20th 1947, Birks Cave, Buckden 11th May 1947, Calf Holes Aug 1947, Meregill 7th Sept 1947, Clapham Cave 11th April 1948, Birks Cave May 1948, Brow Gill & Calf Holes Oct 1948, Involved in the discovery of a dead body in what is now Body cave near Trow Ghyll, Aug 1947.

ACKROYD, John; [MBE] J1998, b1937,
Probationary Meets; Alum Pot, Short Drop, Rowten.
Newsletter References; County Pot-Lancaster March 1986, Marble Steps Dec 1998, Aygill Caverns Feb 1999, Easegill Jan 2000, Pikedaw Calamine Caverns March 2000, Coppice Cave April 2000, Long Kin West April 2000, Diccan Pot Oct 2000, Rowten Pot Dec 2000, Notts Pot Feb 2001, Swinsto Hole Jan 2002, Great/Little Douk Dec 2001, Swinsto-KMC Jan 2003, Notts Pot March 2004, Diccan Pot Feb 2005, Sell Gill Holes March 2012.

ACKROYD, John Colin; AKA: Jack. J1938, b1912, d1995.
BPC President 1964-72.

Bulletin References: *First Club trip to reach the sump in Meregill Sept 1946, Dowka Bottom 29th Sept 1946. Birks Cave, Buckden 11th May 1947, MereGill 7th Sept 1947, Birks Cave May 1948, Brow Gill & Calf Holes Oct 1948, Involved with BBC transmission from Alum Pot 7th May 1961,*

ACKROYD, John Michael; *J1955, b1938,*
Newsletter References; *Swinsto-KMC March 1999, King Pot March 1999,*

ADAMS, Roger; AKA Roger Rabbit. *J1986,*
Newsletter References; *Dow Cave April 1987, Ireby Fell Jan 1992, Rumbling Hole Jan 1992.*

ADDISON, Eric; *J1950, b1935,*
Bulletin References: *Quaking Pot April 1950.*

ADDISON, Paul; *J1953, b1935,*
Application for full membership 'left on the table'.

ALBRECHT, Rachel; *J2016, b1984,*
Probationary Meets; Long Churns, Skirwith Cave, KMC.
Newsletter References; *Skirwith Cave [Novice Trip] Jan 2016, Croesor Rhysydd Through Trip Oct 2016, OFD Top Ent Oct 2017.*

ALLSHORN, Sam; *J2010, b1983,*
Newsletter References; *Providence Pot-Dow Cave Nov 2009,*

AMBLER, Herbert; AKA; Bert. *J1939, d1972.*
Famous for; Disorganised personality especially at the top of a pitch, his rigging was to be avoided.
Bulletin References; *Pen-y-Ghent Long Churn-trapped by flood water for 27 hours October 1938.*

ANDERSON, Harry; *J1955, b1931,*

ANDERSON, Louise Jane; *J2014, b1992,*
Probationary Meets; Swinsto-KMC, GG18, Ireby Fell, Illusion Pot, Voldemort, Sell Gill.
Member; UNCC.
Newsletter References; *Tatham Wife Hole Jan 2020.*

ANDERTON, D; *J1979, b1942,*

ANDERTON, Peter Wightman; *J1959, b1942,*

ANDREWS, Neil Christopher; *J1969, b1952,*
Probationary Meets; Sell Gill, Sunset Hole, Lakes Walking Meet.
Newsletter References; *Lakes Walking Meet Nov 1969, Kingsdale Master Cave Dec 1969, Lancaster-*

County Pot Feb 1970, Lancaster–County Pot Dec 1971.

APPLEBY, Laura; *J2015, b1982,*
Probationary Meets; GG14/15, 2 x Slovenia Trips.
Member; DCC.
Newsletter References; *Grampian Meet Aug 2017, Hensler's Pot-Winch May 2017.*

ARCEDECKNA-BUTLER, John; AKA: Crispy. *J2008, b1969,*

ARCHER, Harold Wilfred; *J1957, b1935,*
Bulletin References: *Christmas Pot 1957.*

ARDOUREZ, Eric; *J1997, b1974.*

ARKWRIGHT, Robin; AKA: SAS Bob. *J1998, b1959,*
Probationary Meets; Alum Pot, Sell Gill.
Famous for; Stealth Walking. Amazing innovations /inventions, member of Balls to Craven/Little Green Men Digging team.
Bulletin References: *Hensler's Pot [Discovery] 1999-2003, Christmas Cracker Pot [Discovery] 2001, Losers Pot [Discovery] Mar 2002, Hensler's Pot [First Through Trip to GG] May 2003, Parkinson's Pot [Discovery] July 2003, Corky's Pot [Discovery] 2003-2005, Klondike Pot Digging /Exploration 2004-2007, Sell Gill Jan 2000, Alum Pot Jan 2000.*
Newsletter References; *Bull Pot March 2000, Pikedaw Calamine Caverns March 2000, KMC March 2000, Coppice Cave April 2000, Skirwith Cave July 2000, County-Lancaster Aug 2000, Bar Pot Nov 2000, Long Kin West Feb 2001, Bull Pot Jan 2001, Ingleborough Cave Digging 2001, Notts Pot Feb 2001, Great/Little Douk Dec 2001, Hensler's Pot Digging Dec 2001, Losers Pot [Discovery] Mar 2002, Sell Gill June 2002, Loser's Pot Dive Support July 2002, Sunset Hole Jan 2003, Corky's Digging Team 2004, Sell Gill Hole Dec 2004, Croll's Cavern Dec 2004, Hardrawkin Pot July 2006, Committee Pot July 2007, Notts Pot March 2008, Calf Holes/ Brow Gill Oct 2008, Helwith Bridge Show 2008, Long Churns July 2009.*

ARNOLD, James; *J1973,*

ARNOLD, Leslie; *J1973,*

ASHWELL, Ian; AKA: Grass. *J1971, b1955,*
Probationary Meets; Short Drop/Gavel, Sell Gill, Sunset Hole, Christmas Pot.
Re joined 2018.
Bulletin References; *Piaggia Bella 1975.*
Newsletter References; *Grange Rigg–Christmas Pot Jan 1972, Dow Cave Feb 1974, Agen Allwedd*

Mar 1974, Gingling Hole Sept 1974, Giants Hole Nov 1974, Gingling Hole June 1975, Stream Passage–Flood Entrance Pot March 1976.

ASHWORTH, Jeremy Robert; *J2003, b1960,*
Probationary Meets; Magnetometer Pot, Pippikin Pot, County Pot, GG03.
Member; NPC.
Bulletin References: *Hensler's Pot [Discovery] 1999-2003, Corky's Pot [Discovery] 2003-2005, Ingleborough Cave Digging 2001.*
Newsletter References; *Corky's Digging Team 2004, Corky's Digging Team 2004, Nettle Pot July 2009.*

ASHWORTH, Kirsti; [née Randall] AKA:Miss Whiplash. *J2000, b1971,*
Probationary Meets; GG00, Stream Passage, Bar Pot, Wade's Entrance, Notts Pot, Ingleborough Cave [Digging]
Member; SOC.
Bulletin References; *Hensler's Pot [Discovery] 1999-2003, Christmas Cracker Pot [Discovery] 2001, Corky's Pot [Discovery] 2003-2005.*
Newsletter References; *Bull Pot Jan 2001, Ingleborough Cave Digging 2001, Notts Pot Feb 2001, KMC Photographic Trip Nov 2002, Dan Yr Ogof/ OFD 2 June 2003, Robinson's Pot Oct 2003, Committee Pot Dec 2003, Corky's Digging Team 2004, Corky's Digging Team 2004, Simpson's-KMC Dec 2008, Aygill Caverns Jan 2009, Pikedaw Calamina Caverns Feb 2009, High Douk Holes Feb 2018.*

ASQUITH, Keith Bernard; AKA:Askey. *1954, b1936, d1960.*
Involved with the development of water tracing system using Rhodamine B, Suffered severe alkaline burns during a trip down Cat Holes Feb 1959.
Member of the Heath Grammar School contingent.
Bulletin References: *Clapham Cave March 1957, Rift Pot [Double rope failure]1957, Mendip Trip 1958, Newby Moss Pot 1961, Marble Steps Feb 1960, Lost John's March 1960, Involved with building electron ladders, 1950/60's.*
Newsletter References; *Washfold Pot July 1957, Lancaster Hole Oct 1957, Practice stretcher rescue Wade's entrance GG Nov 1957, Dow-Providence rescue Dec 1957, Alum Pot Sept 1957, Tackle testing Jan 1958, Bar Pot March 1958, Easter Camp April 1958, Lancaster Hole April 1958, Little Hull Pot April 1958, Little Hull Pot April 1958, Main Shaft to de-tackle Disappointment via Hensler's crawl [Hensler star] Whit 1958, Lancaster Hole June 1958, Tackle testing July 1958, St Cuthbert's Swallet Aug 1958, Eastwater Swallet Aug 1958,*

Swildon's Four Aug 1958, Bar Pot Oct 1958, St Cuthbert's Swallet March 1959, Leader Gaping Gill Members meet 1959, Inauguration Aven Aug 1959, Giant's Hole Nov 1959.

ATKIN, Robert J. H; AKA: Tiny. *J1938,b1913,d1958.*

ATKIN, Henry Harland; *J1938, b1916, d2002.*
BPC President 1953.

ATKINSON, A; *J1982,*

ATKINSON, Henry;

ATKINSON, P; *J1982,*

ATKINSON, Roy Ellison; *J1953,*
Membership refused - money returned.

ATTWATER, Merlyn; *J1973,*
Newsletter References; *Dow Cave Feb 1974,*

AVISON, Alison; *J2009, b1959,*
Probationary Meets; GG09, Bull Pot of the Witches, Brackenbottom Pot.
Member: CRO, UWFRA.

AYRE, Brendan; *J2013, b1974,*
Probationary Meets; Notts 2, Dolly Tubs, Wizards Chasm.
Member; CPC.

AYRE, D; *J1976,*

AYRTON, Colin; *J1965, b1949,*
Probationary Meets; Goyden Pot, Jackdaw Hole, Pen-y-Ghent Long Churn.

B

BABBINGTON, Michael Howard; *J1961, b1944,*
Probationary Meets; Bar Pot, Sell Gill, Sunset Hole.

BADDELEY, Louise; *J2019, b1995,*
Member, SUSS.

BAINES, Martell; [née Linsdell] *J2002, b1965,*
Bulletin References; *Ordessa National Park 2007.*
Newsletter References; *Easegill Feb 1997, Peak Cavern–Sumps Tour June 2001, Notts Pot Sept 2002, Sell Gill Hole Nov 2002, South Wales [Cwm Dwr & OFD 2] July 2002, Dan Yr Ogof/OFD2 June 2003, Brackenbottom Pot Dec 2003, Derbyshire Meet Jan 2004, OFD 2 June 2004, Peak Cavern Feb 2006, Ordessa National Park Spanish Pyrenees 2007, Hidden Earth Tewkesbury, Support Oct 2007, Helwith Bridge Show 2008, Cwm Dwr-OFD Top Ent June 2009, OFD Top Ent June 2009, Joint Hole [Diving experience] Jan 2010, Committee Pot March 2011, Long Churns March 2012, Long Churn-Alum [Novice Trip] July 2012, Old Ing+Birkwith Canal Aug 2014, Calf Holes-Browgill and Old Ing-Birkwith June 2015, GG Track repairs Feb 2017.*

BAINES, Martin Allen; AKA: Basher. *J1994, b1965,*
Probationary Meets; GG93, GG94, Simpsons-Swinsto, Large/Rift Pot.
Famous for; Sid Perou's DVD, resident DJ, motorcycle rides around the dales.
Bulletin References; *Carisbrooke Castle Well [Dive/Dig] 2002–2004, Pay Sank [Discovery] 2005, Created Sid Perou Retirement DVD for Hidden Earth 2010.*

Newsletter References; *Wretched Rabbit-Lancaster Hole March 1995, Malham Cove Abseil Sept 1995, Pool Sink-Lancaster Hole Dec 1995, Lancaster Hole-County Pot Oct 1995, Cherry Tree Hole Feb 1996, South Wales April 1996, Diccan Pot March 1996, Cow Pot July 1996, Lancaster Hole July 1996, Nettle Pot Oct 1996, Swinsto-Simpson's 1996, Hagg Gill 1996, Mistral Hole Nov 1996, Ireby Fell Rescue Feb 1997, Easegill April 1997, Alum Pot [Training Meet] July 1997, Easgill Aug 1997, Barclays Lode Wales July 1998, Nent Head-Brewery Shaft Oct 1998, Lost John's March 1999, Pay Sank Exploration Sept 2005, Hidden Earth Tewkesbury, Support Oct 2007, Helwith Bridge Show 2008, Joint Hole [Diving experience] Jan 2010, Committee Pot March 2011, Hunt Pot-Shrapnel Exchange April 2011, Spencer and Hoffman Lime Kilns March 2012, Long Churns March 2012, Long Churn-Alum [Novice Trip] July 2012, Old Ing+Birkwith Canal Aug 2014, Calf Holes-Browgill and Old Ing-Birkwith June 2015, Hoffman Kilns Stainforth Nov 2015.*

BAKER, Angela; *J1989, b1961,*
Member; OOPA.

BAKER, Sydney Arthur; *J1954, b1936,*

BAMBER, Kirsty, *J2009, b1982,*
Newsletter References; *Magnetometer Pot April 2010, KMC [Childrens Meet] June 2018.*

BAMBOROUGH, Louise Emma; *J1995, b1976,*
Probationary Meets; [12 Trips with Club?]

Newsletter References; *Lancaster Hole-County Pot Oct 1995.*

BANHAM, Geoffrey; *J1984, b1949,*
Member; CPC, WRCPC, UWFRA.
Notable Achievements; Involved with various cave rescues between 1976 and 1982. Involved with the exploration of extensions to Upper Heselden Cave2
Main Activities; Walking, Diving and World Travel.
Newsletter References; *Heron Pot Jan 1985, Sell Gill Hole Feb 1985, Sunset Hole & Southercales Pot June 1985, Pool Park Oct 1986, Pen-y-Ghent Pot March 1987, Coniston Mine July 1988, South Wales Nov 1988, South Wales Dec 1990, Easgill Aug 1997, Crackpot Cave [Photgraphic Meet] Jan 2003.*

BANKS, R. L; *J1959,*

BANKS, Sydney Arthur; *J1954, b1936,*

BARKER, Arnold; *J1948,*

BARKER, John Michael; *J1954, b1937,*
Fastest overall GG laddering times 8 mins down, 5 mins up – Aug 1961.
Resigned from committee Oct 1959 – Not Accepted.
Bulletin References; *Flood Entrance Pot March 1954, Juniper Gulf May 1954, Bull Pot of the Witches July 1955, Christmas Pot 1957, Lancaster Hole Oct 1957.*
Newsletter References; *Easter Camp April 1958, P5 April 1958, Little Hull Pot April 1958, Bar Pot May 1958, Lancaster Hole June 1958, Lancaster Hole June 1958, Alum Pot Aug 1958, Long Kin West Sept 1958, Juniper Gulf Nov 1958, Clapham Cave Nov 1958, Digging near Owl Hole Dec 1958.*

BARNES, Samantha Jane; *J2008, b1977,*
Probationary Meets; Alum Pot, Bull Pot, Sell Gill, KMC, Shuttleworth Pot, Tatham Wife Hole.
Bulletin References; *Pyrenees 2006, Ordessa National Park 2007, Doubs, France Aug 2009.*
Newsletter References; *Pyrenees Aug 2006, Ordessa National Park Spanish Pyrenees 2007, Les Arcs Aug 2008, Lost John's Oct 2008, Lancaster-Wretched Rabbit June 2009, Aquamole Pot Nov 2009, Marble Steps June 2010, Sell Gill May 2012, Committee Pot March 2013, Illusion Pot March 2013, Sell Gill April 2013, KMC/ToylandFeb 2016, Sell Gill April 2016, Sell Gill June 2016, Simpson's Pot Aug 2016, Death's Head-Big Meanie Sept 2016, Marble Steps Nov 2016, Bull Pot of the Witches Jan 2017, High Douk May 2019.*

BARRACLOUGH, Eric; *J1946,* *d1954.*

Bulletin References; *Recorded as taking part in first post war trip–Rift Pot 7th April 1946, involved in the first attempted Rift Pot-Long Kin East exchange April 28th 1946, Rift Pot 19th May 1946, Lost John's July/Aug 1946, Sleets Gill 29th Sept 1946. Rift Pot/Long Kin East exchange April 20th 1947. Calf Holes Aug 1947, Clapham Cave 11th April 1948, Brow Gill & Calf Holes Oct 1948, Great Douk, Sunset Hole April 1949, Flood Entrance July 1949, Rowten Pot Oct 1949, Quaking Pot April 1950.*

BARRACLOUGH, John Terrence; *J1959, b1932, d1999.*
Resigned Sept 1966.
Bulletin References; *Bull Pot Sept 1960.*
Newsletter References; *Clapham Cave Oct 1959, Clapham Cave Nov 1958.*

BARRETT, Peter; *J1961, b1940,*
Probationary Meets; Lost John's, Disappointment Pot, GG61, Easegill, Bull Pot.

BARRINGTON, Nicholas Robert; *J1954, b1935,*

BARTER, Timothy Bruce; *J1994, b1960,*
Probationary Meets; Most major UK caves, Expeditions to Clare, Cuba, Romania, France.
Member; WSG.
Bulletin References; *Tete Sauvage July 1995.*
Newsletter References; *Dan Yr Ogof June 2014.*

BATEMAN, Lloyd; *J2007, b1964,*
Newsletter References; *Committee Pot July 2007, Notts Pot March 2008, Sunset Hole Oct 2011, County Pot-Wretched Rabbit Feb 2012, Bull Pot of the Witches Jan 2013.*

BATEMAN, Steven; *J1994, b1968,*
Probationary Meets; [9 years experience?]

BATEMAN, Syrus; *J2009, b1968,*
Newsletter References; *Committee Pot July 2007.*

BATTENSBY, Emma; AKA: Battenberg. *J2013, b1983,*
Probationary Meets; GG15, Notts Pot.
Member; CUCC, TSG.
Newsletter References; *Grampian Meet Aug 2017, Treviso Aug 2017, OFD 1 Oct 2017.*

BEADNELL, Terry; *J1956, b1935,*
Suspended from club Dec 1959.
Newsletter References; *Washfold Pot July 1957.*

BEAUMONT, Carl; *J1958, b1941,*
Resigned Sept 1956.

Bulletin References; *Gaping Gill Meet 1960, Practice stretcher rescue Wade's entrance GG Nov 1957, Bar Pot March 1958.*
Newsletter References; *Little Hull Pot April 1958, Alum Pot Oct 1958, Bar Pot Oct 1958, OBJ Hole Nov 1958, Bar Pot Nov 1958, Little Hull Hole Aug 1959.*

BEAUMONT, Steven; *J1994, b1944,*
Newsletter References; *Wretched Rabbit-Lancaster Hole March 1995, Lancaster Hole-County Pot Oct 1995,Cherry Tree Hole Feb 1996, Marble Steps Jan 1997, Mongo Gill March 1997, Jingling Pot April 1997, Alum Pot [Training Meet] July 1997, Easgill Aug 1997.*

BEAZLEY, Gillian; *J2006, b1954,*
Newsletter References; *OFD 2 March 2007, Cwm Dwr March 2007.*

BEBBINGTON, Michael Howard; *J1961, b1944,*

BECK, Carl Simon; *J2008, b1979,*
Resigned 2010.
Probationary Meets; Hagg Gill, Sunset Hole, Top Sink-Lancaster, White Scar, Lancaster-Link, Heron Pot, Birks Fell Cave.
Bulletin References; *Alderley Edge Mines Sept 2009, Trapped in Hagg Gill several hours [Flood] Sept 2010.*
Newsletter References; *White Scar Cave April 2007, Alderley Edge Mines Sept 2009, Croesor Rhosydd [Through] Oct 2012.*

BECK, Ronald; *J1948,*

BEDFORD, A.D;
Expelled from club 1962 for non payment of subs.

BEDFORD, Bruce Leonard; *J1965, b1942,*

BEDFORD, Michael David; *J2005, b1954,*
Probationary Meets; Great Douk, Calf Holes, Dismal Hill, Browgill, Long Churns, Borrin's Moor.
Newsletter References; *Coppice Cave–Ling Gill Jan 2006.*

BEDFORD, Robert David; *J1960, b1943,*
Probationary Meets; Marble Steps, Lost John's, Rowten Pot.
Bulletin References; *Magnetometer Pot Nov 1960, Little Hull Pot Feb 1961.*

BENN, Alan David; *J1959, b1938, d2014.*
Committee member 1964.
Bulletin References; *Gaping Gill Meet 1960, Pen-y-ghent Pot July 1960, Gaping Gill–Whitsuntide 1961, Hard Level–Brandy Bottle [Mine Dig] 1964.*

Newsletter References; *Little Hull Hole Aug 1959, Diccan–Alum Exchange September 1959, Marble Steps Sept 1959.*

BENN, Anthony; AKA: Tony. *J1982,*
Newsletter References; *Sunset Hole July 1981.*

BENN, Christine; [née Davies] *J1971, b1945,*
BPC President 2014+5.
Probationary Meets; Pen-y-Ghent Pot, Gingling Pot, Birks Fell Cave.
Bulletin References; *Whitsun Series June 1968, September Rift GG, Sept 1971.*
Newsletter References; *Lancaster–County Pot Feb 1970, Lost John's Jan 1970, Marble Steps March 1970, Birks Fell Oct 1970, Heron Pot March 1971, Crackpot Cave March 1971 Grange Rigg–Christmas Pot Jan 1972, Lockey Gill Cave June 1972, Swinsto Hole-KMC June 1972, Gingling Hole Aug 1972, Birks Fell Cave April 1973, Short Drop–Gavel Pot1976, Scotland 1987, Smallcleugh Mine Aug 1989, Walking Meet Sept 1997, Boulby Potash Mine Jan 2016.*

BENN, Gerald Philip; AKA: Ged. *J1960, b1944,*
BPC President 1997+98.
Probationary Meets; Swinsto Hole, Scoska Cave, Marble Steps Pot.
Club expeditions; Chourum des Aiguilles 1970, Gouffre Berger 1992, Complexe de la Pierre St-Martin 1995, Gouffre Berger 2010.
Notable Achievements; Discovery of Whitsun Series Gaping Gill 1968, Excavation and discovery of Hensler's Pot, Corky's Pot, Pay Sank, Losers Pot, Christmas Cracker, OBJ connection to Wades Entrance [GG], Fat Finger Pot, Brackenbottom Pot, PoulaWillin Co Clare. Involved in the Connection of Ingleborough Cave to Gaping Gill 1983. On Committee continuously since 1963, roles include Asst Secretary, Bulletin Editor and Chairman. BPC President 1996-1998. Member of the Year 1994. [*One of first three recipients of 30 Year Awards along with P G Faulkner and M Hartland.*]
Main Activities; Caving, Walking, Climbing and Cave Digging.
Famous for; Involved in the Shoot out at the Klondike Corral! [Oct 8th 2005]
Bulletin References; *Gaping Gill Meet 1960, Pen-y-ghent Pot July 1960, Bar Pot Easter Sunday 1961, Simpson's Pot 16th April 1961-[Graham Shaw Accident] Gaping Gill-Whitsuntide 1961, Sunset Hole 1962, Hard Level-Brandy Bottle [Mine Dig] 1964, Ireby Fell Cavern April 1964, Lancaster Hole Jan 1966, Investigating various parts of Ingleborough Cave 1968, Involved in discovery of Whitsun Series GG 1968, Poulawillin [Clare] 1968, Lancaster Hole Digging in Graveyard Sept*

1968, Whitsun Series Whit 1969, Ingleborough Cave Nether Wallows 1969, Ingleborough Cave Rimstone East 1969, Trow Gill/Gour Aven Flood Test 1969, Hesleden Burgh Cave 1970, Straw Gallery Whitsun Series GG 1972, September Rift GG, Sept 1971, Digging Clapham Bottoms 1972/3, Clapham Bottoms Roof Passage 1976, Pippikin to Top Sink April 1980, Hard Level-Brandy Bottle [Mine] Dec 1991, Gouffre Berger Aug 1992, Tete Sauvage July 1995, Belfry [GG] Exploration May 1996, Christmas Cracker Pot [Discovery] 2001, Losers Pot [Discovery] Mar 2002, Hensler's Pot [Discovery] 1999-2003, Hensler's Pot [First Through Trip to GG] May 2003, Parkinson's Pot [Discovery] July 2003, Corky's Pot [Discovery] 2003-2005, Pay Sank [Discovery] 2005, Klondike Pot Digging/Exploration 2004-2007, Kalymnos Oct 2009, Buckden Gavel Lead Mines Mar 2010, OBJ Connection to GG May 2010, Witches Cave location and Dig Sept 2010, Restoration of Brown Hill Pot entrance Nov 2012-Feb 2013, Restoration of Clapham Bottoms Pot Entrance June 2013.

Newsletter References; Diccan-Alum Exchange September 1959, Lancaster-Easegill Feb 1969, Lost John's March 1969, Meregill June 1969, Bull Pot of the Witches July 1969, Pen-y-Ghent Pot Aug 1969, Lancaster Hole Sept 1969, Rumbling Hole Oct 1969, Juniper Gulf Nov 1969, Kingsdale Master Cave Dec 1969, Lancaster-County Pot Feb 1970, Lost John's Jan 1970, Marble Steps March 1970, Birks Fell Oct 1970, Lancaster Hole Nov 1970, Bull Pot March 1971, Meregill Hole Aug 1971, Lost John's Sept 1971, Black Shiver Pot Nov 1971, Lancaster-County Pot Dec 1971, Grange Rigg-Christmas Pot Jan 1972, Outsleets Beck Cave June 1972, Swinsto Hole [Down & Up] June 1972, Gingling Hole Aug 1972, Pen-y-Ghent Pot Aug 1972, Birks Fell Cave April 1973, Lancaster-Top Sink Oct 1973, Short Drop-Gavel Pot1976, Lost John's Sept 1978, Pippikin-Lancaster [Flood Pulse on Echo Aven] 1980, Meregill Feb 1980, Tom Taylor's Cave March 1980, Pippikin-Top Sink April 1980, Alum Pot June 1980, Gingling Hole July 1980, Black Shiver Sept 1980, Notts Pot Jan 1981, Birks Fell Cave July 1982, GG Main Chamber [Surveying Roof Stal] May 1982, Ingleborough Cave Oct 1982, GG–Radagast's Revenge Ingleborough to clear dig for through trip Feb 1983, Gingling Hole June 1983, Short Drop Caver Dec 1983, County Pot March 1984, New Goyden Pot April 1984, Ibbeth Peril July 1984, Sell Gill Feb 1985, Spectacle/Vesper Pot Mar 1985, Sunset Hole & Southercales Pot June 1985, Rift Pot April 1985, Gunnerside Gill Lead Mines June 1985, Ireby Fell Pot Oct 1986, Pippikin Pot Nov 1986, Scotland 1987, Coniston Mine July 1988, King Pot Jan 1989, Smallcleugh Mine Aug 1989, Rampgill Level Aug 1989, Pippikin Pot Oct 1989, Langstroth Pot & Cave [Diving] July 1989, Grange Rigg March 1990, Bird Watching Lakes Walk Sept 1990, Calf Holes, Browgill, Old Ing and Dismal Hill Jan 1991, Pen-y-Ghent Pot entrance restoration June 1991, Birks Fell Cave July 1991, Pikedaw Calamine Cavern March 1992, Vulcan Pot Feb 1992, Gouffre Berger Aug 1992, Pen-y-Ghent Pot July 1992, Swaledale Weekend Oct 1992, Ireby Fell Feb 1993, Grange Rigg-Christmas Pot March 1993, Easegill Caverns March 1993, Rift pot June 1993, Coniston Mines Weekend Sept 1993, Brown Hills Pot March 1994, Ireby Fell Caverns July 1994, Lost John's Jan 1995, Lakes Walking Meet Sept 1995, Malham Cove Abseil Sept 1995, Mongo Gill March 1995, Long Kin West March 1996, King Pot March 1996, Swinsto-Simpson's 1996, Marble Steps Jan 1997, Hunt Pot Feb 1997, Marble Steps March 1997, Lost John's Hole March 1997, Cherry Tree Hole April 1997, Alum Pot [Training Meet] July 1997, Walking Meet Sept 1997, Nent Head-Brewery Shaft Oct 1998, County-Wretched Rabbit Nov 1998, County-Pool Exchange Feb 1999, Lost John's March 1999, Fat Finger Millennium Party, Long Kin West April 2000, Christmas Cracker Sept 2000, Ingleborough Cave Digging 2001, Hensler's Pot Digging Dec 2001, Losers Pot [Discovery] Mar 2002, Hensler's High Aven voice connection June 2002, Corky's Digging Team 2004, Klondyke Pot Digging Team Jan 2005, Pay Sank Exploration Sept 2005, Pay Sank Breakthrough team Nov 2005, Committee Pot July 2007, Hidden Earth Tewkesbury, Support Oct 2007, Heron Pot Jan 2009, Pay Sank Feb 2009, Pikedaw Calamina Caverns Feb 2009, Aquamole Remediation March 2009, Stump Cross Caverns [Geoff Workman's 80th] April 2009, Nettle Pot July 2009, Gunnerfleet Caves Clear Up July 2009, Stile Repairs-Diccan and Long Churn 2010, Rebuild of stile at Browgill July 2010, Dig Capping Nov 2010, Fairy Holes April 2014, Hardrawkin Pot Fencing Conservation 2014, President's Meet Ribchester Walk June 2014, Skirwith Cave [Novice Trip] Jan 2016, Boulby Potash Mine Jan 2016, GG Track repairs Feb 2017, Devis Hole/Mine July 2017, Burtersett Quarry/Mine July 2017, Hartley Quarry Cave Jan 2018, Ingleborough Cave Oct 2018, Lancaster-Easegill June 2019.

BENN, Ian Michael; J1999, b1983,

Probationary Meets; GG94-99, Swinsto Hole-KMC, Old Ing [etc], Bull Pot, Bull Pot ot Witches, Alum Pot, Sunset Hole, County Pot–Wretched Rabbit. Extensive digging Owl, Fat Finger, Project X.

Newsletter References; Smallcleugh Mine Aug 1989, Ireby Fell Caverns July 1994, Walking Meet Sept 1997, Fat Finger Millennium Party, Ingleborough Cave Digging 2001, Committee Pot July 2007.

BENN, Ruth; *J1990, b1910, d2005.*
Elected as Honorary Member for secretarial services in 1960s. *[Mother of A. & G. Benn]*

BENNETT, Emma Louise; [Mrs Ug] *J1999, b1980,*
Probationary Meets; GG99,
Bulletin References; Deep Well *[Diving] 2000-2003.*
Newsletter References; *Charity work in Mexico 2003, Deep Well [Dive Support] GG04.*

BENNETTS, Mary; *J2016, b1983,*
Probationary Meets; County Pot, Bull Pot of the Witches, Tatham Wife Hole.
Newsletter References; *Otter Hole June 2016.*

BERG, P;

BERNAL, Elizabeth; AKA: Elisa. *J2003, b1966,*
Probationary Meets; Flood Entrance, Knots Pot, Wades Entrance, KMC.
Newsletter References; *Penygent House Pots and Cave April 2003, Dan Yr Ogof/ OFD2 June 2003, Ireby Fell Caverns Nov 2005.*

BERRY, Peter Jeffrey; *J1955, b1937,*
Bulletin References; *Lost John's March 1961, Pen-y-ghent Pot 1961, South Wales Easter 1963.*

BEST, Lorna Frances; *J2009, b1988,*

BEVITT, Norman; *J1975, b1945,*
Probationary Meets; Sunset Hole, GG75, Sell Gill, OFD, Gingling Hole.
Bulletin References; Slape Gill Cave III *[Discovery]* March 1980, Cow Garth Cave *[Exploration]* 1982-84.
Newsletter References; *Notts Pot March 1976, Scrafton Pot April 1976, Goyden Pot Feb 1976, Sleets Gill July 1976, Bull Pot of the Witches Nov 1977, Short Drop-Gavel Dec 1977, Kingsdale Master Cave Jan 1979, Lost John's Sept 1978, Scrafton Pot April 1980, Gingling Hole Oct 1985, Eden Valley-Teesdale Walking Meet Oct 1985.*

BIALEK, Robert John; AKA: Dalek, Bob. *J1978, b1955,*
Rejoined 1986.
Member; CPC, RRCPC.
Famous for; Asking how many miles of undiscovered cave there are? Arriving at a foreign expedition with his caving gear in his sleeping bag and a cooler box containing potatoes and several bottles of powdered milk.
Probationary Meets; Whitsun Series, GG78, Pippikin, Birks Fell, Lost John's, Otter Hole.

Had to be rescued from Pen-y-Ghent pot where he was caving without a permit-Oct 1988.
Bulletin References; *Otter Hole 1977, Gouffre Berger Aug 1980, Cow Garth Cave [Exploration] 1982/84, Cueva De La Marniosa Santander Aug 1982, Vercors Aug 1983, Climbing Stream Passage Pot May 1984, Trou De Glaz Aug 1989, Manchester Hole D/S Sump extension [Support] 1991, Deep Well [Diving support] May 1992, West Rift GG [Diving Support] 1992, Gouffre Berger Aug 1992, Albania 1992, Spluga Della Preta Sept 1992.*
Newsletter References; *Bull Pot of the Witches Nov 1977, Cwm Dwr-OFD II April 1978, OFD I April 1978, Dan Yr Ogof April 1978, Marble Sink June 1978, Rumbling Hole Aug 1978, Lancaster-Ease Gill Nov 1978, Meregill Feb 1980, King Pot Feb 1980, Scrafton Pot April 1980, Pen-y-Ghent Pot July 1980, Alum Pot June 1980, Gingling Hole July 1980, Black Shiver Sept 1980, Gouffre Berger Aug 1980, Ibbeth Peril Oct 1980, Lost John's Nov 1980, Magnetometer Pot March 1981, Notts Pot Jan 1981, Dow-Providence Sept 1981, Lancaster–County Pot Sept 1981, Cow Pot Oct 1981, Pippikin Pot Oct 1981, Lost John's Feb 1982, Alum Pot March 1982, Kingsdale Photographic meet April 1982, King Pot April 1982, Pen-y-Ghent Pot July 1982, Ingleborough Cave Oct 1982, Tatham Wife Hole Feb 1983, Simpsons-KMC April 1983, Hallucination Aven–Induction Location May 1983, Notts Pot March 1983, Pasture Gill Pot June 1983, Gingling Hole June 1983, Quaking Pot Aug 1983, South Wales Aug 1983, Rowten-Swinsto Exchange Nov 1983, Meregill Feb 1983, Rift Pot Feb 1984, County Pot March 1984, Langstroth Pot March 1984, Pool Sink-Lancaster Hole June 1984, Tatham Wife Hole Oct 1984, Sell Gill Hole Feb 1985, Marble Sink March 1985, Spectacle-Vesper Pot Mar 1985, County Pot-Top Sink April 1985, Sleets Gill June 1985, Langstroth Pot Sept 1985, Brezno, Leska, Babizop Rakov Scojan and the Pit of Bears Yugoslavia Aug 1985, Pool Park Oct 1986, County Pot-Lancaster March 1986, White Scar Cave July 1987, Top Sink-Link Feb 1988, Notts Pot Jan 1988, Weathercote Cave April 1988, Pippikin March 1988, Notts Pot Nov 1988, South Wales Nov 1988, Big Meanie-Death's Head Nov 1989, Out Sleets Beck Pot Dec 1989, Cow Pot-Wretched Rabbit Feb 1990, New Rift Pot Feb 1990, Large-Rift Pot March 1990, Hangman's Hole March 1990, Lakes Walk Sept 1990, Easegill Caverns Sept 1990, South Wales Dec 1990, Lost John's March 1991, Rumbling Hole Jan 1992, Out Sleets Beck Cave June 1992, Gouffre Berger Aug 1992, Lakes Meet June 1992.*

BICKERTON, James; *J1976, b1956,*
Probationary Meets; Little Hull, Ireby Fell, Meregill.

BICKNELL, Frank Rudley; *J1948,*
Bulletin References; *Birks Cave May 1948, Flood Entrance July 1949, Rowten Pot Oct 1949, Pen-y-Ghent Pot 2ⁿᵈ Rescue 11ᵗʰ June 1951 [A CPC member fell and sustained injuries]*

BINNS, Andrew; *J2011, b1973,*

BINNS, Cedric; AKA: Red Ced. *J1973,*
Famous for; Playing the guitar, girlfriend called Tony.
Probationary Meets; Knots Pot, Little Hull, Juniper Gulf.
Bulletin References; *Chourum Des Aiguilles 1973, Piaggia Bella 1975, Gouffre Berger Aug 1980,*
Newsletter References; *Juniper Gulf Dec 1974, County Pot Aug 1976, Bull Pot of the Witches Dec 1976, Gingling Hole July 1980, Sell Gill Hole 1980, Gouffre Berger Aug 1980, Bull Pot of the Witches {And assistance with the body recovery of Tracy Gibson from Top Sink] Oct 1980.*

BINNS, Toni; AKA: Loftus. *J1977, b1956,*
Bulletin References; *Bull Pot of the Witches Dec 1976, Gouffre Berger Aug 1980.*
Newsletter References; *Gouffre Berger Aug 1980.*

BLACKBURN, Peter; *J1957,*
Member; BTCPC.
Famous for; Being rescued from Dow-Providence Jan 1958, being left alone at GG Prelim 1958, tent burnt to the ground at members meet 1958.
Bulletin References; *Stream Passage Pot June 1962.*
Newsletter References; *Lancaster Hole Oct 1957, Practice stretcher rescue Wade's entrance GG [Victim] Nov 1957, Trapped with members of the Bradford Technical College Pothole Club in Dow-Providence Jan 1958, Lancaster Hole June 1959.*

BLACKER, Ian; *J1958, b1942,*
Bulletin References; *Clapham Bottoms dig Aug 1959, Involved with BBC transmission from Alum Pot 7ᵗʰ May 1961.*

BLAKELEY, Peter Rodney; *J1955, b1936, d2019.*
Famous for; Designing cover for 1960 newsletters.
Bulletin References; *Clapham Cave Aug 1955, Little Hull Hole Oct 1955, Clapham Cave March 1957, Clapham Cave Aug 1957, Stream Passage Pot June 1958, Goyden Pot Jan 1960, Involved with BBC transmission from Alum Pot 7ᵗʰ May 1961.*
Newsletter References; *Christmas Pot May 1957, Washfold Pot July 1957; Simpson's Pot Aug 1957, Swinsto Sept 1957, Rumbling Hole Oct 1957, Private meet Clapham Cave Nov 1957, Dow-Providence rescue Dec 1957, Bar Pot Dec 1957, Bar Pot May 1958, Involved with BBC Transmission from Alum Pot May 1958, Lancaster Hole June 1958, Alum Pot Aug 1958, Dow Cave Sept 1958, Disappointment Pot [Photographic trip] Oct 1958, Diccan-Alum Exchange September 1959, Clapham Cave Oct 1959, Antarctica [BAS] Dec 1961,*

BLAKELEY, Richard; AKA: Dick. *J1961, b1942,*
Probationary Meets; Sell Gill, Lost John's, Simpson's Pot.
Bulletin References; *Simpson's Pot 16ᵗʰ April 1961-[Graham Shaw Accident] Sunset Hole 1962, South Wales Easter 1963, Notts Pot Oct 1963, Lower Stream Passage Pot May 1965, Gouffre Berger Aug 1980.*
Newsletter References; *Bull Pot March 1971, Birks Fell April 1971, Lancaster-County Pot Dec 1971, Lancaster-Top Sink Oct 1973, Gouffre Berger Aug 1980, Lakes Walking Meet Oct 1987, Granett Bridge-ShapWalk Sept 2006.*

BLAKENEY, Helen; *J1985,*
Newsletter References; *Sleets Gill June 1985.*

BLANCHARD, Larry; *J2009, b1964,*
Probationary Meets; Aquamole,
Member; TSG [Sec], WSG.
Newsletter References; *Aquamole Pot Nov 2009, Marble Steps Jan 2010.*

BLICK, Anthony D; AKA: The Cardboard Caver. *J1960, b1944,*
Expelled from club 1962 for non payment of subs.
Probationary Meets; GG60, Alum Pot, Easegill.
Member ; CPC.
Re-joined 1966.
Bulletin References; *Dissapointment Pot Easter Meet 1961, Simpson's Pot 16ᵗʰ April 1961-[Graham Shaw Accident] Lost John's March 1961, Disappointment Pot Oct 1967, Poulawillin [Clare] 1968, Agen Allwedd 5ᵗʰ Choke April 1968.*
Newsletter References: *Lancaster-Easegill Feb 1969.*

BLOOM, Steven Mark; *J2008, b1953,*
Probationary Meets; Alum Pot, Heron Pot.
Member; PCC [2000-2005]
Other Expeditions; Caving in France & Russia [with PCC]

BLYTH, Helen Elizabeth; *J1998, b1973,*
Newsletter References; *White Scar Cave April 2001.*

BOLAM-PEEL, Adam; *J2006, b1971,*

Newsletter References; *New Rift Pot Nov 2006, Providence Pot-Dow Cave April 2007, Heron Pot Jan 2009, Wretched Rabbit-County Pot Nov 2010, Hunt Pot-Shrapnel Pot Nov 2011.*

BOLAM-PEEL, Thomas; *J2011, b1999,*
Newsletter References; *Wretched Rabbit-County Pot Nov 2010, Hunt Pot-Shrapnel Pot Nov 2011.*

BOLTON, John Philip; AKA: Druggy John. *J1972, b1952,*
Probationary Meets; Dow Cave, Birks Fell, Pen-y-Ghent Pot.
Motley - His doctor once said he had a body of a 50 year old-when he was in his 20's
Party Piece-Dance of the flaming arsehole [*This involved rolling a newspaper into a long cone and 'inserting' the narrow end then dancing around joyously shouting whilst naked. The open end of the cone is then set a light and the naked dance changes to more of a bent over run, like someone trying to run away from their own arse and the shouting turns to a higher pitched scream. When there is an accompanying smell of burning hair the dance usually comes quickly to an end. See picture - Ed*]
Bulletin References; *Black Shiver Pot, Oct 1972, Rift Pot Sept 1972, Chourum Des Aiguilles 1973, Diving sump below Hallucination Aven GG 1973, Newby Moss Sink May 1977, Mountain Hall [Scaling] 1980.*
Newsletter References; *Birks Fell April 1972, Pen-y-Ghent Pot Aug 1972, Dale Head Pot April 1978, Lancaster-Ease Gill Nov 1978, Simpsons Pot Jan 1979, Scrafton Pot April 1980.*

BONIFACE, Cyril; *J1949,*

BOOCOCK, Derek; *J1993, b1956,*
Member; DMMC [Instructor]

BOON, John Michael; *J1963, b1940, d2014.*
Member; SMCC, ASS, KRG-O, HWCPC, CDG.
Club expeditions; Jamaica 1965/6.
Notable Achievements; Bottomed Gouffre Berger 1963 with Ken Pearce. First cave diver to remove bottle to pass narrow passage. Published book [1966] on use of bottled compressed air as opposed to traditional use of oxygen re-breathers in UK sump diving, most active diver in UK [1962] and only one using waist mounted compressed air. Diving Langstroth Cave and climbing to pitch 8 before ULSA dug into Langstroth Pot and claimed discovery.
Main Activities; Caving, Cave Diving, Walking and Climbing.

Famous for; Digging in far reaches of Mossdale Caverns. Passing Swildon's 6 & 7. Passing sumps in Predjama-Slovenia. Solo exploration of Castleguard Cave-Canada, explorations in Mexico-Rio Iglesia–535m, Sotano de San Agustin –612m, Cueva San Agustin, Agua Carlota, Joya de Salas, Sotano de Tenejap, Sumidero de Chenalho, Cruz Pilal, Huixtan Resurgence [Mapachero], Sumidero Yochib,Guayateno, Sumidero Chicja, Sumidero de Agueyaco, Sumidero de Tenejapa, Xumula. Exploration of caves in Guatemala and Belize-The sinks of Chiquibul, El Sumidero [Rio Huista], Sumidero de San Ramon, Agua Escondida, explored in kayaks. In 1980 Boon wrote The Great San Agustin Cave Rescue, describing his involvement in the rescue of two injured Polish cavers. When he first arrived at the old Dump at the Shoe he was reknowned for scrounging food! He arrived with nothing at the beginning of the weekend and left at the end giving it away!
Bulletin References; *Pen-y-ghent Pot July 1960, Gaping Gill Meet 1960 [Diving Trip], Car Pot June 1963, Mossdale Caverns-Far Marathon Sept 1963, Cat Hole [Extension] Oct 1963, Pen-y-Ghent Pot Extensions Oct 1963, Notts Pot Oct 1963, Birks Fell Cave Dec 1963, Mossdale Caverns-High Level Mud Caverns Feb 1964, Hammer Pot July & September 1964, Climbing Circus Rift May 1964, Mossdale Caverns The Final Choke April 1965, Screen Hill-Legnabrocky Way Ireland Discovery Aug 1965, Mossdale Caverns Digging in far reaches April 1965, Ibbeth Peril 1966, Gingling Wet Sinks Oct 1966.*

BOOTH, David; *J1956,*

BOOTH, David Ian Robert; *J1978, b1954,*
Probationary Meets; GG78, Dale Head Pot, Bull Pot of the Witches.
Member; HCC.
Bulletin References; *Otter Hole 1977, Pasture Cave [Discovery] 1978.*
Newsletter References; *Dale Head Pot April 1978, A mine Nr Siegan Germany Feb 1981, Investigated a 90m deep sink hole in Germany 1982.*

BOOTH, Leslie Malcolm; *J1969, b1944,*
Probationary Meets; Swinsto-KMC, Langstroth, Dow Cave, Lancaster.
Newsletter Reference: *Lancaster-Easegill Feb 1969, Lost John's March 1969, Bull Pot of the Witches July 1969, Pen-y-Ghent Pot Aug 1969, Lancaster Hole Sept 1969.*

BOOTH, Robert Edwin; AKA: Basher, BB2. *J1978, b1946,*

Probationary Meets; Birks Fell, Lost John's, Short Drop Gavel.
Bulletin References; *Gouffre Berger Aug 1980.*
Newsletter References; *Short Drop–Gavel Dec 1977, Little Neath River Cave April 1978, Rumbling Hole Aug 1978, Lancaster-Ease Gill Nov 1978, Kingsdale Master Cave [Found old bang] Jan 1980, Alum Pot June 1980, Gouffre Berger Aug 1980, Swinsto–KMC April 1983, South Wales Aug 1983, Giant's Hole Sept 1983, Ibbeth Peril July 1984, Gunnerside Gill Lead Mines June 1985, Eden Valley-Teesdale Walking Meet Oct 1985, Scotland Easter 1986, Scotland 1987, Lakes Walking Meet Oct 1987, Lakes Walk Sept 1990, Bird Watching Lakes Walk Sept 1990, Calf Holes, Browgill, Old Ing and Dismal Hill Jan 1991, Lakes Meet June 1992, Alum Pot Nov 1993, Swaledale Weekend Oct 1992, Crooklands Walking Meet Sept 1993, Coniston Mines Weekend Sept 1993, Simpson's-Swinsto March 1994, Dowkabottom Feb 1995, Lancaster Canal Walk Meet 2001, Millenium Walk Sept 2002, Dufton–Garrigill Lakes Walk Sept 2005, Granett Bridge To ShapWalk Sept 2006, Ulverston-Coniston Walking Meet 2007, Lambrigg Fell–Tebay Walk Sept 2008, Salthill Quarry Geology Walk Nov 2008, Dunsop Bridge-Bilsborrow Walking Meet Sept 2009, Walking Meet Orton-Kirkby Thore Sept 2010, Cautley-Kirkby Stephen Walk Sept 2011, Crosby Ravensworth-AskhamWalking Meet Sept 2012, Roundthwaite Common to Borrowdale Sept 2014, Walking Meet 2015, New Biggin on Lune to Appleby Walking Meet Sept 2016, Lindale-Greenodd Walking Meet 2017, Cow Green Reservoir–Appleby Walking Meet 2018, Kirkby Lonsdale-Wharton Walking Meet Sept 2019.*

BOOTH, Robert George; AKA BB1. *J1968, b1949,*
Probationary Meets; Ingleborough Cave, Hunt Pot, Gaping Gill.
Bulletin References; *Chourum Des Aiguilles 1973, Grotte de Bury 1977.*
Newsletter References; *Tatham Wife March 1975, Notts Pot March 1976, Sunset Hole May 1976, Pippikin Hole Oct 1976, Lakes Walk Esk House March 1977, OFD I April 1978, Little Neath River Cave April 1978, Dan Yr Ogof April 1978, Swinst–KMC Jan 1981, Scotland Easter 1986, Scotland 1987, Lakes Meet June 1992, Derbyshire Meet Sept 1999, Granett Bridge-ShapWalk Sept 2006, Ulverston-Coniston Walking Meet 2007, Crosby Ravensworth-AskhamWalking Meet Sept 2012.*

BOOTH, William; AKA: Smeg. *J1987, b1966,*
Probationary Meets; Christmas Pot/Grange Rigg, GG86, [Main Shaft, Stream Passage, Whitsun Series] Pen-y-Ghent Pot.
Re Applied 2019 [Failed]

Newsletter References; *Pen-y-Ghent Pot March 1987.*

BORE, Kenneth; *J1981,*
Newsletter References; *Notts Pot Jan 1981.*

BOTCHERY, David; *J2019, b1997,*
Member; SUSS, CHECC.

BOTTALY, J; *J1982,*

BOTTOMLEY, John Francis; *J1982, b1958,*
Probationary Meets; Pippikin Pot, Vespers Pot, Big Meanie-Deaths Head, Knots Pot, Ingleborough Cave.
Member; CDG.
Bulletin References; *Cow Garth Cave [Exploration] 1982/84.*
Newsletter References; *Meregill Feb 1983.*

BOTTOMLEY, Lesley Ann Bernadette; *J1988, b1966,*
Probationary Meets; GG88, White Scar, Heron Pot, Sell Gill, Swinsto Hole.
Bulletin References; *Soca Valley [Diving] Aug 1990, Trou De Glaz Aug 1989, Remembrance Pot July 1994, Deep Well [Diving support] May 1992, Manchester Hole D/S Sump extension [Support] 1991, Albania 1992, Spluga Della Preta Sept 1992.*
Newsletter References; *Ireby Fell March 1990, Simpsons–KMC July 1990, Easegill Caverns Sept 1990, Eldon Hole & Oxlow Caverns Oct 1990, Calf Holes, Browgill, Old Ing and Dismal Hill Jan 1991, Lost John's March 1991, Magnetometer Pot July 1991, Ireby Fell Jan 1992, Pikedaw Calamine Caverns March 1992, Lakes Meet June 1992, 5 Caves Trip July 1993, Snatcher's Pot Nov 1993, Coniston Mines Weekend Sept 1993, Simpson's-Swinsto March 1994, Manchester By-pass-Wretshed Rabbit March 1995, Mongo Gill March 1997, GG Photographic Meet May 1998, Nent Head-Brewery Shaft Oct 1998, Fat Finger Millennium Party.*

BOWER, A.S; *J1956,*

BOWNESS, Natalie Anne; *J2016, b1988,*
Probationary Meets; Knots, Sell Gill, Heron Pot.
Newsletter References; *Lost John's-Notts 2 Sept 2015, Sell Gill Holes Sept 2015, Hagg Gill April 2016, Katnot Cave/Thorne Cave [Novice Trip] May 2016, Pool Sink June 2016, Simpson's Pot Aug 2016, Borrins Moor Cave Nov 2016, Croesor Rhysydd Through Trip Oct 2016, Bruntscar Cave Jan 2017, KMC May 2017, Calf Holes-Birkwith June 2017, Alum/Long Churns June 2017, Iron Kiln Sept 2017, Sunset Hole April 2019, High Douk May 2019.*

BRADBURY, Mark; *J1992, b1963,*
Member; OOPA.

BRADER, Thomas J; *J2013, b1992,*

BRADLEY, Holly; *J2010, b1983,*

BRADLEY, Terry; *J2010, b1963,*

BRADY, Patrick Richard; *J1995, b1966,*
Member; RPC [Dublin] Since 1989.
Bulletin References; *Tete Sauvage July 1995.*

BRAITHWAITE, John Cannon; *J1966, b1921,*
Probationary Meets; Gunnerfleet, Long Churn, Calf Holes-Brow Gill.

BRAITHWAITE, John Michael; *J1968, b1945,*
Probationary Meets; Alum Pot, Sell Gill, Smallclough Level.
Famous for; Sketch of HQ used on back of Bulletins, Vol 5 No2 - No 9.

BRATCHLEY, Joshua MBE; *J2016, b1991,*
Member; CDG.
Famous for; Member of the rescue of the Wild Boars football team from the Tham Luang cave system in Thailand's Chiang Rai province.
Newsletter References; *UK - Thai Cave rescue diver.*

BRATLEY, John; *J1971, b1949,*
Probationary Meets; GG71, Gingling Hole, Easegill.

BRAYBROOKE, Alan; *J2014,*
Newsletter References; *Titan Streamway March 2016.*

BREAR, Malcolm David; *J1960, b1944,*
Committee asked B. Dobson to talk to him regarding 'injudicious use of explosives and loose talk'.
Probationary Meets; Lost John's, Clapham Cave, Long Kin East.
Bulletin References; *Gaping Gill-Whitsuntide 1961.*

BREARLEY, Donald; *J1960, b1934,*
Probationary Meets; Easegill, Alum, Birkwith Cave.

BRIDGE, Malcolm; *J1972, b1945,*
Probationary Meets; Birks Fell, Outsleets Beck, Tatham Wife.
Memberships; EPC.
Main Activities; Caving, Cave photography,
Famous for; Winning best slide at BSA Conference 1963.

Bulletin References; *Recorded explaining new methods of cave photography 1961, Involved in the development of water tracing system using Rhodamine B. Easegill Caverns Aug 1959.*
Newsletter References; *Treak Cliff Cavern Oct 1959.*

BRIGGS, Antony Edmund; *J1957, b1933,*

BRIGGS, Colin; *J1959, b1942,*
Expelled from the club for non payment of subs Dec 1962.

BRIGGS, Frank Raymond; AKA: Belay Briggs. *J1950, b1922, d1984.*
Bulletin References; *Lost John's July 1951, Pen-y-Ghent Pot Rescue, young BSA member died of exhaustion 1951. Pen-y-Ghent Pot 2nd Rescue 11th June 1951 [A CPC member fell] Easter Camp GG 1951, Bull Pot of the Witches April 1951, Digging at Beck Head June 1951, Clapham Cave Sept 1951, Rowten Pot June 1951, Simpson's Pot July 1953, Flood Entrance Pot March 1954, Juniper Gulf May 1954, Clapham Cave June 1954, Lancaster Hole Oct 1954, Gaping Gill Meet 1960, Gaping Gill-Whitsuntide 1961.*
Newsletter References; *Pikedaw Calamine Mine Jan 1954, Leader Juniper Gulf May 1954, Swinsto Sept 1957, Dow-Providence rescue Dec 1957, Leader Bar Pot Dec 1957, Tackle testing Jan 1958, Little Hull Pot April 1958, Involved with BBC Transmission from Alum Pot May 1958, Tackle testing July 1958, Clapham Cave Nov 1958, Digging nr Owl Hole Dec 1958, Ingleborough Cave June 1959, Ingleborough Cave Survey Aug 1959, Diccan-Alum Exchange September 1959.*

BRIGGS, Harold Leslie; AKA: Leslie. *J1950,*

BRIGGS, Michael James; *J1949, b1933,*
Bulletin References; *Flood Entrance July 1949, Easter Camp-GG 1950.*

BRIGGS, William A; *J1936,*

BRILL, Douglas; *J1995, b1942, d2015.*
Probationary Meets; Lancaster-County Pot, Brackenbottom Pot, Lancaster –Pool Sink, Rowten Pot.
Newsletter References; *County-Lancaster Hole Oct 1995, Hunt Pot Feb 1998, Marble Steps Dec 1998, Lost John's March 1999, Pikedaw Calamine Caverns March 2000, Long Kin West April 2000, Christmas Cracker Sept 2000, Rowten Pot Dec 2000, Notts Pot Feb 2001, Diccan Pot Feb 2005, Sell Gill Holes March 2012.*

BRILL, Guy Hamilton; *J1995, b1972,*
Probationary Meets; Lancaster-County Pot, Brackenbottom Pot.
Member; FRCC, RAF Leuchars MRT.
Newsletter References; *County-Lancaster Hole Oct 1995, Lost John's March 1999.*

BRILL, Simon Alistair; *J1997, b1970,*
Probationary Meets; Lancaster-County, Lancaster-Pool, Brackenbottom Pot, Short Drop.
Member; FRCC, RAF Leuchars MRT, CSCA.
Newsletter References; *County-Lancaster Hole Oct 1995.*

BRITTAIN, Alan Tomline McLeod; AKA: ATMB. *J1961, b1939,*
Re-Joined 2007.
Probationary Meets; Grange Rigg Pot, Pen-y-Ghent Pot, Rumbling Hole.
["I thought being born was compulsory?-Anyway, I'm very annoyed with Adolf Hitler for upstaging me by invading Czechoslovakia"]
Member; BITPC, YGS *[Member 2017]*, Cave Research Group/BCRA, MCS *[Life Member N°5]*, BSAC *[Joined 1970, left after two boating accidents and some underwater scares, "I like to choose my own hazards"]*
Club expeditions; Provatina 1966, Chourum des Aiguilles 1973.
Other Expeditions; Expeditions with Nature Conservancy to Isle of Skye, Summer Islands, Lorne *[Found specimens of Liocareinus corrugoetus many miles north of its known range. One is now in the natural History Museum in London. Found an egg mass of Loligo forbesii in 20M of water-supposed to be much deeper]*
Notable Achievements; First time in a cave [Peak Cavern] circa 1948, first time down a mine circa 1954 [Anhydrite Mine-Billingham], One of a very few members to clock up 1000 bed nights at the old dump, first to sleep at Brackenbottom *[After we bought it but before we moved in]* First BPC member down Boulby Potash Mine *[Along with various Professors and PhDs]* Involved in various cave rescues in the 1960's. Chorister on bus meets and at GG. Very involved in the basic conversion of 'Bracken Hill Cottage' into the New Dump, mostly done during the foot and mouth epidemic of 1970. Spent a lot of time digging in Ingleborough Cave, Christmas Pot and Grange Rigg. On Birkbeck's Ledge at least 8 times. Involved in rope assessments for SRT. First person to get through the Font. BA Hons-OU [1980]
Main Activities; Caving, walking, diving, conservation.

Famous for; Inspiring Ian Wilkinson and a young John Edwards by demonstrating the window test to ascertain the cleanliness of underwear.
Bulletin References; *Lost John's March 1961, Little Hull Pot Feb 1961, Pen-y-Ghent pot 1961, Jockey Hole Feb 1962, Christmas Pot 1962, Stream Passage Pot June 1962, Ridge Scar Caves [Discovery] 1962, Long Kin West July 1962, Rowten Pot & Jingling Pot Nov 1962, Christmas/Grange/P5 April 1962, Christmas/Grange/P5 extensions May 1962, Car Pot June 1963, Lost John's July 1963, Pen-y-Ghent Pot Feb 1964, Buttertubs / Flood Entrance/ Sell Gill/ May 1964, Ashberry Windpit Aug 1964, Nick Pot Nov 1964, Provatina Abyss July/Aug 1967, Investigating various parts of Ingleborough Cave 1968, Involved in discovery of Whitsun Series GG 1968, Robin Hood's Well 1968, Poulawillin [Clare] 1968, Work in Ingleborough Cave 1968, Whitsun Series Whit 1969, Ingleborough Cave Nether Wallows 1969, Ingleborough Cave Insignificant Inlet 1969, Cold Streak Mine 1969, Lower Stream Passage Pot [Diving]1971, Rift Pot Sept 1972, Chourum Des Aiguilles 1973, Digging Clapham Bottoms 1972/3, Cartilage Cave 1977, White Scar Cave Dec 31 1977, Silurian Sea Cave 1980.*
Newsletter References; *Ryedale Easter 1965, Rumbling Hole July 1965, Wharfedale weekend Oct 1970, Grange Rigg-Christmas Pot Jan 1972, Lost John's Hole Aug 1974, Giants Hole Nov 1974, Juniper Gulf Dec 1974, Goyden Pot Feb 1976, Lakes Walk Esk House March 1977.*

BROADBENT, John B; *J1935, b , d1951.*
Club expeditions; *Brow Gill & Calf Holes Oct 1948, Rift Pot/Long Kin East exchange April 1949, Easter Camp-GG 1950.*
Main Activities; Caving, Walking.
Famous for; Attending the vast majority of club trips, always lagging behind on the walks to a cave.
Newsletter References; *Lancaster Hole June 1958.*

BROADBENT, Kate; *J2009,*

BROADBENT, Paul Desmond; *J1999, b1958,*
Member; WVCC [5 years]
Bulletin References; *Croesor-Rhosydd Feb 2009.*
Newsletter References; *Pippikin Pot Nov 1999, Great/Little Douk Dec 2001, Swinsto Hole Jan 2002, Derbyshire Meet Jan 2004, Swinsto Hole-KMC Feb 2004, Committee Pot Nov 2004, Gingling Hole July 2005, Long Kin West Dec 2005, Tatham Wife Hole March 2006, Lost John's Hole Sept 2006, Jingling Pot Dec 2006, Granett Bridge To ShapWalk Sept 2006, Committee Pot Dec 2006, Committee Pot July 2007, Ulverston-Coniston Walking Meet 2007, Bar Pot Dec 2007, Valley Entrance June 2008, Lost*

John's March 2009, Croesor-Rhosydd March 2010, Jingling Pot Dec 2011, Juniper Gulf March 2012, Croesor Rhosydd [Through] Oct 2012, Swinsto-KMC Feb 2016.

BROGAN, William Andrew; *J1976, b1958,*
Probationary Meets; Lancaster, Alum Pot, Sunset Hole, Bar Pot, Whitsun Series, Disappointment Pot.

BROOK, Alyson; AKA: Ally. *J2000, b1985,*
Probationary Meets; Easegill, GG, Heron Pot, KMC, At least 30 Digging Trips.
Club expeditions; Complexe de la Pierre St-Martin 2006.
Other Expeditions; Gouffre Berger 2012 [With WCC]
Notable Achievements; Member of the UWFRA from 2009. Involved in various digging exploits with the BPC BALLS digging team.
Main Activities; Running, walking, climbing & caving.
Bulletin References; *Losers Pot [Discovery] Mar 2002, Hensler's Pot [Discovery] 1999-2003, Carisbrooke Castle Well [Dive/Dig] 2002-2004, Parkinson's Pot [Discovery] July 2003,Corky's Pot [Discovery] 2003-2005, Deep Well [Dive support] 2004, Pay Sank [Discovery] 2005, Klondike Pot Digging/Exploration 2004-2007, Pyrenees 2006, Mallorca Dec 2007, Restoration of Brown Hill Pot entrance Nov 2012-Feb 2013, Walking Meet Sept 1997.*
Newsletter References; *Ingleborough Cave Digging 2001, Time Tunnel Dig Ingleborough Cave Dec 2001, Losers Pot [Discovery] Mar 2002, Sunset Hole Jan 2003, Alum Pot March 2004, Corky's Digging Team 2004, Deep Well Dive [Support] GG04, Jackpot P8 Feb 2006, Peak Cavern Feb 2006, Rumbling Hole July 2006, Hardrawkin Pot July 2006, Pyrenees Aug 2006, Upper & Lower Long Churn Nov 2006, Aquamole Pot Jan 2007, Derbyshire Meet Jan 2007, OFD 2 March 2007, Committee Pot July 2007, Hidden Earth Tewkesbury, Support Oct 2007, Ireby Fell Caverns [A grand day out-digging Whirlpool] Feb 2008, Brackenbottom Pot Digging Feb 2008, Notts Pot March 2008, Deep Well [Dive support] May 2008, Aygill Caverns Jan 2009, Dan Yr Ogof March 2009, OFD-Cwm Dwr March 2009, Notts Pot Sept 2009, Marble Steps June 2010, Dan Yr Ogof, Sept 2010, Death's Head Hole July 2012, Blue John Aug 2012.*

BROOK, David Christopher; AKA: Brave Duck.
J1961, b1944,
BPC President 2001 & 2.
Probationary Meets; Sell Gill, Magnetometer, Bar Pot.

Bulletin References; *Gaping Gill Main shaft on ladders 1961, Stonelands Cave Aug 1963, Notts Pot Oct 1963, Ireby Fell Cavern April 1964, South Wales Easter 1963, Three Peaks Dec 1963, Ashberry Windpit Aug 1964, Lower Stream Passage Pot May 1965, Investigating various parts of Ingleborough Cave 1968, Involved in discovery of Whitsun Series GG 1968, Poulawillin [Clare] 1968, Whitsun Series Whit 1969, Ingleborough Cave Rimstone East 1969, Trow Gill-Gour Aven Flood Test 1969, Investigating Grayrigg Sinks 1970, Straw Gallery Whitsun Series GG 1972, Digging Clapham Bottoms 1972/3, Newby Moss Sink 3rd Shaft 1977, Doline Cave [Discovery] 1990, Hard Level-Brandy Bottle [Mine] Dec 1991, Losers Pot [Discovery] Mar 2002, Parkinson's Pot [Discovery] July 2003, Hensler's Pot [Discovery] 1999-2003, Pay Sank [Discovery] 2005, Carisbrooke Castle Well [Dive/Dig] 2002-2004, Klondike Pot Digging/Exploration 2004-2007, Corky's Pot [Discovery] 2003-2005, , Restoration of Brown Hill Pot entrance Nov 2012-Feb 2013, Restoration of Clapham Bottoms Pot Entrance June 2013.*
Newsletter References; *Ireby Fell Nov 1965, Lakes Walk March 1969, Lancaster-County Pot Feb 1970, Marble Steps March 1970, Lockey Gill Cave June 1972, Birks Fell Cave April 1973, Gingling Hole Sept 1974, Giants Hole Nov 1974, Birks Fell Cave April 1975, Scrafton Pot April 1976, County Pot Aug 1976, Smallcleugh Mine Aug 1989, Rampgill Level Aug 1989, Lakes Walk Sept 1990, Swaledale Weekend Oct 1992, Lakes Walking Meet Sept 1995, Walking Meet Sept 1997, Barclays Lode Wales July 1998, Nent Head-Brewery Shaft Oct 1998, Ingleborough Cave Digging 2001, Time Tunnel Dig Ingleborough Cave Dec 2001, Losers Pot [Discovery] Mar 2002, Corky's Digging Team 2004, Pay Sank Exploration Sept 2005, Hidden Earth Tewkesbury, Support Oct 2007, Salthill Quarry Geology Walk Nov 2008, Gunnerfleet Caves Clear Up Aug 2009, Stile Repairs-Diccan and Long Churn 2010, Yordas Cave Conserervation Aug 2010, Dig Capping Nov 2010, President's Meet Ribchester Walk June 2014, Clearing Daimler Hole & Homeshaw Hole Sept 2014, Providence Pot Restoration Nov 2014, Whernside circular walk July 2015, GG Track repairs Feb 2017.*

BROOK, Kathryn; *J1995, b1979,*
Newsletter references; *Smallcleugh Mine Aug 1989, Ireby Fell Caverns July 1994, Lakes Walking Meet Sept 1995, Long Kin West March 1996, Swinsto-Simpson's 1996, Hunt Pot Feb 1997, County-Wretched Rabbit Nov 2000, Sell Gill June 2002.*

BROOK, Margaret Elizabeth; [née Payne] *J1971, b1946,*
BPC President 2016.
Probationary Meets; Heron, Marble Steps, Ingleborough Cave.
Newsletter References; *Heron Pot March 1971, Crackpot Cave March 1971, Lockey Gill Cave June 1972, Birks Fell Cave April 1973, Gingling Hole Sept 1974, Giants Hole Nov 1974, Birks Fell Cave April 1975, Scrafton Pot April 1976, Lakes Walk Sept 1990, Walking Meet Sept 1997.*

BROOKS, J; *J1978, b1970,*

BROOKS, Nicola; [Née Stock] *J2011, b1984,*
Probationary Meets; Jingling Pot.
Member; SWCC.
Bulletin References; *Gouffre Pont Du Gerbout Aug 2011, Gouffre De Heretiques Aug 2011, Felix Trombe 2011, Jingling Hole June 2011, Calf Holes-Browgill/Old Ing June 2011, Big Meanie-Death's Head Exchange Oct 2011, Lancaster-Wretched Rabbit Nov 2011, Shuttleworth Pot Feb 2012, Lost John's Cave July 2012, Dow Cave Oct 2012, KMC Toyland Nov 2012, White Keld Sump 5 Location [Diving Support] Feb 2013, Haw Bank or Wet Grooves Mine Feb 2013, Fells End Pots Feb 2013, Ibbeth Peril March 2013, Ibeth Peril April 2014, Dowkabottom Cave July 2014, Dowkabottom Cave July 2014, Swildon's Hole Feb 2015, St Cuthbert's Swallet Feb 2015, Goatchurch Aven Feb 2015, Grampian Meet Aug 2017.*

BROOKS, Russell Peter; *J2007, b1970,*
Probationary Meets; GG06-08, Digging Marylin, Bar Pot, Flood Entrance, Dyhedral, Clapham Bottoms, Brackenbottom Pot, Ireby Fell, Alum.
Member; WCC, UWFRA.
Bulletin References; *Mallorca Dec 2007.*
Newsletter References; *Ireby Fell Caverns [A grand day out-digging Whirlpool] Feb 2008, Dan Yr Ogof March 2009, OFD-Cwm Dwr March 2009, Notts Pot Sept 2009, SRT Training Ingleborough Hall Oct 2009, Joint Hole [Diving experience] Jan 2010, Long Churn/Dolly Tubs [Novice trip] Feb 2010, Hardrawkin Pot May 2010, Pen-y-Ghent Gill [Digging CPC/ULSA Dig] May 2010, Hurtle Pot [DivingSupport] May 2010, Joint Hole [Diving Support] May 2010, Dan Yr Ogof, Sept 2010, Pillar Holes Oct 2010, Sell Gill [Training Meet] Oct 2010, Hunt Pot-Shrapnel Exchange April 2011, Lancaster-Wretched Rabbit Nov 2011, Shuttleworth Pot Feb 2012, Lost John's Cave July 2012, Dow Cave Oct 2012, White Keld Sump 5 Location [Diving Support] Feb 2013, Haw Bank or Wet Grooves Mine Feb 2013, Fells End Pots Feb 2013, Illusion Pot March 2013, Ibbeth Peril [Twice] March 2013, Crackpot*

[Photographic Trip] April 2013, Ibeth Peril April 2014, First Lady Pot July 2014, Goatchurch Aven Feb 2015, GG Track repairs Feb 2017, Grampian Meet Aug 2017, Hartley Quarry Cave Jan 2018, Lost River Sump [Dive Support] May 2019, Hells Bells Hole [Dive Support] Feb 2020.

BROOKSBANK, Jean; *J2014, b1962,*
Probationary Meets; Illusion Pot, Shuttleworth Pot, County Pot, Tatham Wife Hole, Carlewalk Caverns, Calf Holes-Brow Gill.
Newsletter References; *Mistral Hole Nov 2014, Lancaster-County Pot Nov 2014, Lost John's-Notts 2 Sept 2015, Simpson's Pot Aug 2016, Iron Kiln Sept 2017, Mongo Gill Sept 2018.*

BROOMHALL, Charles; *J1979,*
Newsletter References; *Lost John's Sept 1978.*

BROTHERS, C; *J1936,*

BROWN, Anthony; *J2009, b1959,*
Newsletter References; *Hell Hole, Whitewell Cave& Pot Nov 2008, Cononley Mine Sept 2011 & Jan 2012, Scoska Cave April 2014.*

BROWN, Anthony James; AKA: Bog. *J2005, b1946,*
Probationary Meets; KMC, GG2000-08, Bar Pot, Wades Entrance, East Pasage, Corky's Pot, Alum Pot, Churns, Pay Sank, Xmas Cracker.
Member; LUCC [1965-1970], LCCC [1976-1981], NB [1981-Present]
Notable Achievements; Articles on Caves and Cave Conservation published in Descent, Speleologist and The British Caver. Produced YouTube caving videos including [Bog4053] 'A Blind Caver Tackles Yordas Pot' [Feb 2015]
Main Activities; Walking, caving, digging.
Famous for; Going down Marble Steps Pot in heavy rain and getting trapped beyond Stink Pot-1965.
Bulletin References; *Witches Cave location and Dig Sept 2010, Buckden Gavel Lead Mines Mar 2010, Restoration of Brown Hill Pot entrance Nov 2012-Feb 2013, Restoration of Clapham Bottoms Pot Entrance June 2013, Dinkling Green Mine Cave & Calamine Pit July 2019.*
Newsletter References; *Aquamole Remediation March 2009, Providence Pot Restoration Nov 2014, Shuttleworth/Witches 2 Conservation Feb 2015, Dinkling Green Mine Cave July 2019.*

BROWN, Christopher Peter; AKA: Milkhead. *J1984, b1946,*
Newsletter References; *Sell Gill Hole April 1981, Short Drop Caver Dec 1983, County Pot March 1984, Ibbeth Peril July 1984, Mud Pot [Aborted Dive] Dive support. May 1985, Short Drop Pot Nov*

1985, Scotland Easter 1986, Scotland 1987, Stile Repairs-Diccan and Long Churn 2010.

BROWN, Ian; *J1963, b1938,*
Probationary Meets; Christmas Pot, Car Pot.
Bulletin References; *Hammer Pot July 1964.*

BROWN, James; AKA; Jim the Scot. *J1999, b1957,*
Probationary Meets; Sunset Hole, Ribblehead Caves, Calf Holes/Brow Gill, GG00-GG2011.
Member; KMC [1976]
Notable Achievements; Climbed the Old Man of Hoy 1977, Solo ascent of Steall Falls 1981.
Main Activities; Caving, Walking.
Famous for;Being rescued from Stream Passage Pot 2000.
Newsletter References; *Alum Pot [Training Meet] July 1997, Being rescued from main chamber after sitting down clutching his chest, airlifted with a previous rescue.*

BROWN, James; *J1954, b1934,*
Newsletter References; *Bar Pot Dec 1957.*

BROWN, M; *J1981,*

BROWN, Neil; *J1951, b1934,*

BROWNE, Hugh; *J1936, b1909, d1972.*
BPC President 1957-60.
First Trip Goyden Pot with torches, RAF 1941-45, BPC Librarian 1938-56, BPC Chairman 1954-56, 1957 BPC President, Trapped down Penygent long churn October 1938, Last BPC hand winch meet GG main shaft July 1949, lowering sleeping bags and food down to campers, it got stuck, Hugh spent the night joining cable together to telephone below to explain why the supplies had not arrived. Bought, with Don Leach, the dural [?] poles for the gantry 1950.
Bulletin References; *Pen-y-Ghent Long Churn-trapped by flood water for 27 hours October 1938,Brow Gill & Calf Holes Oct 1948, Rift Pot/Long Kin East exchange April 1949, Flood Entrance July 1949, Easter Camp GG 1950, Simpson's Pot July 1953, Little Hull Pot July 1954, Old Ing Caves Aug 1954, Bull Pot of the Witches July 1955, Jackdaw Hole & Pen-y-Ghent Long Churn Nov 1955, Rift Pot [Double rope failure] 1957,* Gaping Gill Meet 1960, *Involved with BBC transmission from Alum Pot 7th May 1961.*
Newsletter References; *Leader Gaping Gill Whit 1954, Washfold Pot July 1957; Swinsto Sept 1957, Rumbling Hole Oct 1957, Lancaster Hole Oct 1957, Dow-Providence rescue Dec 1957, Bar Pot Dec 1957, Tackle testing Jan 1958, Easter Camp April 1958, Little Hull Pot April 1958, Involved with BBC*

Transmission from Alum Pot May 1958, Lancaster Hole June 1958, Treak Cliff Cavern Oct 1959.

BROWNE, Stephen Anthony; *J1965,b1944,*
Probationary Meets; Mongo Gill, Bull Pot, Echo Pot.

BRUMBY, Caitlin Isabelle; *J2010, b1991,*
Newsletter References; *Magnetometer Pot April 2010, Lost John's-Boxhead Pot Sept 2010, Hull Pot [Filming with the BBC] Oct 2010.*

BRYAN, Bethan; *J2015, b?,*
Bulletin References; *Doubs, France Aug 2009.*
Newsletter References; *Calf Holes-Browgill and Old Ing-Birkwith June 2015, Long Churn and Wilsons cave [Novice Trip] July 2015, Lindale-Greenodd Walking Meet 2017.*

BRYAN, Gwyn David; *J1979, b1957,*
Probationary Meets; Notts Pot, Gavel Rigg, Lancaster–County.
Motley. The only person that said he would go back to Albania at the time. Famous for falling down a storm drain on his way back from the bar in St Engrace on the 2013 PSM trip.
Bulletin References; *Mountain Hall [Scaling] 1980, Albania 1992, Tete Sauvage July 1995, Doubs, France Aug 2009, Croesor-Rhosydd Feb 2009, Reseau de la Pierre Saint Martin Aug 2013, Devis Hole/Mine July 2017,.*
Newsletter References; *Top Sink–Lancaster and Back! Oct 1978, Meregill Feb 1980, Scrafton Pot April 1980, Gavel Pot Dec 1980, Sunset Hole July 1981, Cow Pot Oct 1981, Pippikin Pot Oct 1981, South Wales Aug 1983, County Pot March 1984, Heron Pot Jan 1985, Brezno, Leska, Babizop Rakov Scojan and the Pit of Bears Yugoslavia Aug 1985, Notts Pot Feb 1986, Pool Park Oct 1986, Cliff Force Cave 1986, Coniston Mine July 1988, South Wales Nov 1988, Langstroth Pot & Cave [Diving] July 1989, Eldon Hole & Oxlow Caverns Oct 1990, South Wales Dec 1990, Mendip Weekend Sept 1991, Cow Pot March 1993, Coniston Mines Weekend Sept 1993, Easgill Aug 1997, Notts Pot Sept 2009, Link Pot Sept 2009, Dunsop Bridge-Bilsborrow Walking Meet Sept 2009, Dowkerbottom Cave Oct 2009, Sell Gill Nov 2009, Aquamole Pot Nov 2009, Marble Steps Jan 2010, Croesor-Rhosydd March 2010, Alum Pot Oct 2010, Wretched Rabbit-County Pot Nov 2010, Heron Pot Nov 2010, Heron Pot Nov 2010, Committee Pot March 2011, Oxlow Caverns March 2011, Peak CavernMarch 2011, Feizor-Moughton Walk July 2011, Darnbrook Pot [Novice Trip] Sept 2011, Robinson's Pot Oct 2011, Gillfield Level May 2012, Crosby Ravensworth-Askham Walking Meet Sept 2012,Giant's Hole April 2013,*

Wretched Rabbit-Lancaster Nov 2013, Calf Holes-Browgill and Old Ing-Birkwith June 2015, Long Churn and Wilsons cave [Novice Trip] July 2015, Alderley Edge Mines Oct 2015, New Biggin on Lune to Appleby Walking Meet Sept 2016, Devis Hole/Mine July 2017, Lindale-Greenodd Walking Meet 2017, Kirkby Lonsdale-Wharton Walking Meet Sept 2019.

BRYANT, William Thomas; AKA: Bill. *J1989, b1971,*
Probationary Meets; ["About 10 Trips" ?]
Member; CDG, TSG.
Bulletin References; *Digging unknown hole Langstrothdale 1991, New Rift Pot Feb 1990,*
Newsletter References; *Skirwith Cave July 2000.*

BUCKLEY, Vincent Eric; AKA: Vincest. *[Because he went to live with his sister] J1970, b1950,*
Probationary Meets; Puits des Banes, Creve Coeur, Chourum Des Aiguilles.
Bulletin References; *Little Hull Hole Aug 1971, Henslers Master Cave [Find in Disappointment final chamber] 1972, Newby Moss Sink May 1977, Newby Moss Sink 3rd Shaft 1977, Coast to Coast Plus July / Aug 1978.*
Newsletter References; *Kingsdale Master Cave Dec 1969, Lost John's Jan 1970, Marble Steps March 1970, Lancaster Hole Nov 1970, Bull Pot March 1971, Black Shiver Pot Nov 1971, Pippikin Pot Nov 1976, Cherry Tree Hole July 1978.*

BURDON, Guy Martin; *J1989, b1962,*
Probationary Meets; Bar Pot, Disappointment Pot, Snatchers Hole, Simpsons, Nenthead, Mongo Gill, OFD1-2.
Newsletter References; *South Wales Nov 1988, Smallcleugh Mine Aug 1989, Sunset Hole March 1990, Eldon Hole & Oxlow Caverns Oct 1990, Pen-y-Ghent Pot entrance restoration June 1991, Pippikin March 1992, Malham Cove Abseil Sept 1995, Top Sink-Pippikin Nov 1995, Hunt Pot Feb 1998, Rowten Pot Dec 1998, Langstroth Pot June 2000, County-Wretched Rabbit Nov 2000.*

BURGESS, Tom, *j before 1939,*

BURKE, Matt, *J2013, b1972,*

BURKE, Robbie; *J2000, b1979,*

BURNETT, Colin Charles; *J1995, b1966,*
Probationary Meets; GG95/96, Tatham Wife Hole.
Newsletter References; *Top Sink-Lancaster July 1996.*

BURN, William; *J2018, b1992,*

BUSHELL, Ian; *J1976,*
Newsletter References; *Scrafton Pot April 1976, Goyden Pot Feb 1976, Sleets Gill July 1976.*

BUSS, Gaby; *J2006, b1954,*
Probationary Meets; Hurnell Moss Pot, Long Churn, Alum Pot.
Newsletter References; *Hurnell Moss Pot Oct 2006, Brackenbottom Pot Feb 2008, Diccan Pot Oct 2010.*

BUTTERWORTH, David Charles; *J1961, b1941,*
Probationary Meets; Bull Pot of the Witches, Heron Pot, Marble Steps Pot.

BUTTERWORTH, David Edward; *J1966,*

BYCROFT, Michael; *J1968, b1946,*
Probationary Meets; Alum Pot, GG68 [Far East Passage, Bar Pot]
Bulletin References; *Involved in discovery of Whitsun Series GG [On his first club meet] 1968.*

BYWATER, Malcolm Geoffrey; AKA: Geoff. *J1953, b1934,*
Bulletin References; *Simpson's Pot July 1953.*

CALLAGHAN, Peter Joseph; *J1996, b1957,*

CALLAWAY, Reginald Dennis; AKA: Cab. *J1948, b1926,*
Bulletin References; *Recorded as being on a trip to Birks Cave May 1948, Flood Entrance July 1949, Rowten Pot Oct 1949, Easter Camp GG 1951.*

CANHAM, Harold; *J1946,*

CARR, Emma; *J2009, b1989,*
Probationary Meets; GG08, Calf Holes/Brow Gill, Long Churns.

CARROLL, Leslie; See Lloyd.

CARROLL, Michael Andrew; *J1989, b1956,*
Probationary Meets; GG88, Flood Entrance, Bar Pot, Alum Pot, Gingling Pot.
Bulletin References; Brackenbottom Pot, *[Dig / Exploration]* 1989, Trou De Glaz Aug 1989.
Newsletter References; *Juniper Gulf [Abandoned] Jan 1990, Large-Rift Pot March 1990, Simpsons–Kingsdale July 1990, Easegill Caverns Jan 1991, Lost John's March 1991.*

CARRY, C; *J1979,*

CARRYSFORTH, Dick; *J1935,*

CARSON, Karen P; *J2007, b1963,*
Probationary Meets; Old Ing.

CARTER, Ben; *J2011, b1977,*
Probationary Meets; Lancaster Hole-Wretched Rabbit.
Other Expeditions; Gouffre Berger 2012 *[With Wessex Cave Club]*
Notable Achievements; Member of the Calder Valley Search and Rescue Team since 2003-Team

Leader 2015-2020. Member of the Cave Rescue Organisation cavers list.
Main Activities; Running, mountain biking, mountaineering & caving.
Newsletter References; *Lancaster-Wretched Rabbit Jan 2011, KMC-Toyland Feb 2011, Committee Pot March 2011, Hunt Pot-Shrapnel Exchange April 2011, Yordas Pot April 2011, Long Churn [Novice Trip] June 2011, Illusion Pot June 2011, Big Meanie Sept 2011, Big Meanie-Death's Head Exchange Oct 2011, Foul Pot Nov 2011, Shuttleworth Pot Feb 2012, Juniper Gulf March 2012, Deaths Head Hole July 2012, Sell Gill April 2013.*

CARTER, Beverley Susan; *J1981, b1958,*

CARTER, C;

CARTEWRIGHT, Peter; *J1965,*

CASSON, Gillian; *J2012,*
Newsletter References; *Simpson's Pot Aug 2016, Devis Hole/Mine July 2017.*

CASTLE, Janice Lillian; *J1974, b1953,*
Probationary Meets; Sunset Hole, County Pot, Dow Cave, Grange Rigg/Christmas Pot.
Bulletin References; *Chourum Des Aiguilles 1973, Dow Cave Feb 1974.*
Newsletter References; *Chourum Des Aiguilles 1974, Gingling Hole Sept 1974, Swildons Oct 1974.*

CASTLEDEN, Carol Sylvia; AKA: Momma [Nanna] Cas. *J1972, b1946,*
BPC President 2017.
Member of the Year 2010.
Club Expeditions; Majority of club trips since Vercors 1983.

Notable achievements: Climbed Mont Blanc without guides 2000, was introduced to a book "Classic Treks of the World" in 1999, completed 24 out of 30 by 2020. Learned SRT at the age of 69 in order to cave with the BPC in Majorca for two successive years. Spent 15 years running the tea tent at Gaping Gill.

Main Activities: Could spend a lifetime listing this lot. Yes to all biking, caving, walking, climbing, skiing, back packing around the World and Trekking on every continent over a 20 year period.

Famous for: Good things will be organising soirees at GG and supporting Cas with workathons when he was Dump engineer for 17 years. Always being Mama, bossy, boozy but happy to help in all situations. Organising parties, helping with communal cooking and most of all being thrown into the campervan by different younger members of the Club whilst at the dump. (something to do with red wine).

Probationary Meets; Bar Pot, Tatham Wife Hole, County Pot.

Bulletin References; *Soca Valley [Diving] Aug 1990, Ordessa National Park 2007.*

Newsletter References; *Pen-y-Ghent Pot Aug 1972, Brezno, Leska, Babizop Rakov Scojan and the Pit of Bears Yugoslavia Aug 1985, Walking Meet Sept 1997, Dufton–Garrigill Lakes Walk Sept 2005, Ordessa National Park Spanish Pyrenees 2007, Walking Meet 2015, New Biggin on Lune to Appleby Walking Meet Sept 2016, Cow Green Reservoir–Appleby Walking Meet 2018.*

CASTLEDEN, Derek; AKA: Cas. *J1962, b1946,*
BPC President 2003 & 4.
Caved with the club since 14 years old.

Probationary Meets; Goyden Pot, Magnetometer Pot, Sell Gill.

Club Expeditions; Lots of club trips since Vercors 1983.

Other Expeditions; Albania 1992.

Notable Achievements; Detackling the bottom half of Berger in 1980 with three other members, Tete Sauvage-Verna-EDF through trip 1996, Member of the year 2003. Independantly climber Mont Blanc 2000, climbed Kilimanjaro, Mt Meru, & Mt Kenya 2008, Introduced to a book "Classic Treks of the World in 1999, completed 24 out of the 30 by 2020, Refurbishing the Dump over a 17 year period as Dump engineer, making the dump more female friendly by demolishing the communal showers and providing individual compartments, also removing the communal alpine bunks from the womens room and providing 6 individual bunks not to mention carpets on the floor etc. Removing the old war time 3 tier metal bunks from the men only dorm and replacing with solid wooden 2 tier bunks.

Renewing the foam and coverings on all the bunks in the main dorms. Installing heating in all the dorms except the members only dorm. Improving the family room with modern bunks etc.

Main Activities; Caving, biking, walking, climbing, skiing, back packing round the World (following retirement age 51 in 1997)

Famous for; First member to obtain a bang licence (same time as Ged Benn) but not as conscientiously applied. Decided to help dig the rubbish pit at Gaping Gill, dug 4 shot holes and placed 1 pound of explosive in each one before realising we only had about 5 mtrs of wire. Joined by Sandra Webb who loved blowing things up and retired to a small depression, could hardly call it a shake hole! The members all retired to a safe distance, scattered across the moor before we let rip!! When we detonated an enormous cloud of rocks and earth shot over the heads of me and Sandra we looked round to see the rest of the Club running in every direction as the shower descended upon them, a miracle that no one was killed or seriously injured.

Providing the members with beer for 25 years and creating an annual beer festival at Gaping Gill for many years.

Bulletin References; *Lost John's July 1963, Sell Gill Cave [Pushing] Nov 1963, Pen-y-Ghent Pot Extensions Oct 1963, Leader Pen-y-Ghent Pot Feb 1964, Hammer Pot July 1964, Nick Pot Nov 1964, Hull Pot April 1965, Lumphammer Hole Sept 1965, Explored through sump in GG which eventually led to Whitson series 1965.Whitsun Series Whit 1969, Henslers Master Cave [Find in Disappointment final chamber] 1972, Chourum Des Aiguilles 1973, Dog Tooth Inlet GG. [Digging] May 1975, Piaggia Bella 1975, Farrer Hall Choke 1976, Grotte de Bury 1976, Far SE passage [Digging] 1980, Gouffre Berger Aug 1980, Vercors Aug 1983, Krisna Jama Aug 1984, Leski Aug 1984, Trou De Glaz Aug 1989, Soca Valley [Diving] Aug 1990, 38 Parmilan Plateau Sept 1990, Tete Sauvage July 1995, Ordessa National Park 2007, Croesor-Rhosydd Feb 2009.*

Newsletter References; *Pen-y-Ghent Pot Aug 1972, Lancaster–Top Sink Oct 1973, Lost John's Hole Aug 1974, Lost John's September 1976, Pillar Holes Sept 1978, Hammer Pot Sept 1978, Pippikin-Link-Top Sink Oct 1979, Gouffre Berger Aug 1980, Sell Gill Hole April 1981, Hallucination Aven–Induction Location May 1983, South Wales Aug 1983, Birks Fell Cave July 1984, Brezno, Leska, Babizop Rakov Scojan and the Pit of Bears Yugoslavia Aug 1985, Top Sink-County Pot March 1986, Notts Pot Nov 1988, South Wales Nov 1988, Cow Pot–Pool Sink March 1989, Big Meanie-Death's Head Nov 1989, Langstroth Pot & Cave [Diving] July 1989, Black Shiver Pot Jan 1991, Dowbergill Passage Unknown*

1990, Pikedaw Calamine Cavern March 1992, Alum Pot Nov 1993, Ireby Fell Feb 1993, Grange Rigg-Christmas Pot March 1993, Death's Head-Big Meanie Nov 1993, Cherry Tree Hole Feb 1996, Mistral Hole Nov 1996, Walking Meet Sept 1997, Alum Pot July 2002, Aquamole Pot Dec 2003, Dufton–Garrigill Lakes Walk Sept 2005, Committee Pot July 2007, Ordessa National Park Spanish Pyrenees 2007, Croesor RhosyddMarch 2010, Feizor-Moughton Walk July 2011, Heron Pot [Novice Trip] Aug 2012, Trou du Garde-Creux de la Cavale - Bauges Aug 2012, President's Meet cycle pub crawl July 2015, Walking Meet 2015, New Biggin on Lune to Appleby Walking Meet Sept 2016, Devis Hole/Mine July 2017, Cow Green Reservoir–Appleby Walking Meet 2018.

CASTLEDEN, Jonathan Derek; J1992, b1976,
Probationary Meets; GG, Bar Pot, Flood Entrance.
Bulletin References; Vercors Aug 1983, Soca Valley [Diving] Aug 1990, Tete Sauvage July 1995.
Newsletter References; Brezno, Leska, Babizop Rakov Scojan and the Pit of Bears Yugoslavia Aug 1985, Alum Pot Nov 1993, Ireby Fell Feb 1993, Cherry Tree Hole Feb 1996, Mistral Hole Nov 1996, Easegill April 1997, Alum Pot Dec 1998.

CASTLEDEN, Ruth, Emma; [Ex; Skinner] J1997, b1973,
Probationary Meets; GG Since 1979, France, Czech Republic, Slovakia, Simpsons, Swinsto, Alum Pot, Calf Holes, Cherry Tree, Mistral, Pool Sink, Lancaster, Marble Steps, Sell Gill, Mongo Gill.
Member; Rock City Climbing Centre.
First Girl in Bargh's new bit [Mongo Gill]
Newsletter References; Pool Sink-Lancaster Hole Dec 1995, Cherry Tree Hole Feb 1996, Mistral Hole Nov 1996, Ireby Fell Rescue Feb 1997, Mongo Gill March 1997, Marble Steps March 1997, Easegill April 1997, Easgill Aug 1997, Alum Pot Dec 1998, Pippikin Pot Nov 1999, Lost John's March 2002, Rumbling Hole July 2002, Lost John's Pot July 2003, Milwr Tunnel June 2004, Short Drop-Gavel Pot Nov 2004, Committee Pot Nov 2004, Sell Gill Hole Dec 2004, Skirwith Cave [Novice Trip] Jan 2016, Simpson's Flooded Aug 2016, Devis Hole/Mine July 2017, Old Ing-Birkwith July 2017, Sell Gill Sept 2017.

CASWELL, Henry John Crosby; AKA: John. J1953, b1922,
Bulletin References; Notts Pot Sept 1953, Flood Entrance Pot March 1954, Clapham Cave June 1954, Old Ing Caves Aug 1954, Bull Pot of the Witches July 1955.
Newsletter References; Leader Little Hull Pot Aug 1954, Leader Grange Rigg Oct 1955.

CATAWAY, Christopher; J1962,

CHAMBERS, Michael Eric; J1979, b1953,
Member; LUES.
Other Expeditions; SULIS '75 Arctic Norway Expedition.
Probationary Meets; Dowbergill Passage, Simpsons-Swinsto, Gingling Hole, GG78.
Bulletin References; Slape Gill Cave III [Discovery] March 1980.
Newsletter References; Scrafton pot April 1980, Alum Pot March 1981.

CHAPMAN, Michael; AKA: Mick. J1970, b1950,
Probationary Meets; Marble Steps, Little Hull, GG70.
Bulletin References; Lower Stream Passage Pot [Diving] 1971, Earl Pot 1971, Maypoling Little Hull Pot 1972.
Newsletter References; Marble Steps March 1970, Lancaster Hole Nov 1970, Lost John's Sept 1978.

CHAPMAN, Steven; J2007, b1966,
Probationary Meets; Great Douk Cave.
Member; Achille Ralti Climbing Club.

CHAPPELOW, B. F; J1948,
Bulletin References; Flood Entrance July 1949.

CHARLESWORTH, G;

CHARLTON, Alan; AKA: Jekyll. J1971, b1942,
Probationary Meets; Tatham Wife Hole, Lost John's, Alum Pot.
Bulletin References; Black Shiver Pot, Oct 1972, Chourum Des Aiguilles 1973, Piaggia Bella 1975, White Scar Cave Dec 1977, Grotte de Bury 1976 & 1977, Cnoc Nan Uamh & Uamh Nan Claig-Ionn Easter 1978, Gouffre Berger Aug 1980.
Newsletter References; Tatham Wife Hole Aug 1971, Lost John's Sept 1971, Lancaster–County Pot Dec 1971, Grange Rigg–Christmas Pot Jan 1972, Gingling Hole Aug 1972, Pen-y-Ghent Pot Aug 1972, Little Neath River Cave June 1973, Dow Cave Feb 1974, Lost John's Hole Aug 1974, Flood Entrance-Stream Passage Pot Exchange Feb 1975, Black Shiver May 1976, Bull Pot of the Witches Dec 1976, Christmas Pot Feb 1977, Pen-y-Ghent Pot April 1977, Lakes Walk Esk House March 1977, Bull Pot of the Witches Nov 1977, Lost John's Sept 1978, Hall Pot Oct 1978, Top Sink–Lancaster and Back! Oct 1978, Lancaster–Ease Gill Nov 1978, Uamh nan Claig-ionn April 1979, Lancaster Hole [Maple Leaf Pitch Team] 1980, Black Shiver Sept 1980, Gouffre Berger Aug 1980, Ibbeth Peril Oct 1980, Mendip Oct 1980, Mendip weekend April 1983, Scotland

1987, Calf Holes Jan 1988, Millenium Walk Sept 2002, Walking Meet Orton-Kirkby Thore Sept 2010.

CHATBURN, R; *J1984,*

CHATTLE, Peter; *J2009, b1974,*
Probationary Meets; Disappointment-Bar Pot, Croeser-Rhoysdd.
Member; Burnley Caving Club.
Newsletter References; *Croesor-Rhosydd Feb 2009.*

CHEDGEY, Roisin; *J2018, b1993,*
Probationary Meets; GG18, Illusion Pot, Voldemort.
Newsletter References; *P5 [Radio Locating] June 2018.*

CHESHIRE, Graham George; AKA: George. *J1964, b1947,*
Probationary Meets; Lancaster Hole, Yordas Cave, Bull Pot of the Witches.
Bulletin References; *Alum Pot/Diccan Pot 1966, Investigating various parts of Ingleborough Cave 1968, Pay Sank [Discovery] 2005, Klondike Pot Digging/Exploration 2004-2007, Sorbas Almeria 2007.*
Newsletter References; *Millenium Walk Sept 2002, Corky's Digging Team 2004, OFD 2 June 2004, Runscar Cave Sept 2004, November Hole April 2006, Lambrigg Fell-Tebay Walk Sept 2008, Salthill Quarry Geology Walk Nov 2008, Walking Meet Orton-Kirkby Thore Sept 2010, Roundthwaite Common to Borrowdale Sept 2014, Walking Meet 2015.*

CHESHIRE, Steven; *J1968, b1952,*
Probationary Meets; GG68, Easegill, Sell Gill.
Newsletter References; *Lancaster-County Pot Feb 1970.*

CLARKE, A; *J?, b1954,*
Newsletter References; *Calf Holes Jan 1988.*

CLARKE, B.R; *J1979, b1936,*

CLARKE, Brenda; *J1987, b1948,*
Bulletin References; *The Haute Route 1990, Doline Cave [Discovery] 1990.*
Newsletter References; *Eden Valley-Teesdale Walking Meet Oct 1985, Calf Holes Jan 1988, New Goyden Pot Oct 1988, Short Drop Cave Nov 1989, Scrafton Pot June 1990, Lakes Walk Sept 1990, Easegill Caverns Sept 1990, Easegill Caverns March 1993, Bagshaw Caverns Oct 1993, Coniston Mines Weekend Sept 1993, Simpson's-Swinsto March 1994, Lost John's Jan 1995, Notts Pot Feb 1995,*

Wretched Rabbit-Lancaster Hole March 1995, Pikedaw Calamine Caverns Sept 1995, Giants Hole Nov 1995, Peak Cavern Nov 1995, Top Sink-Lancaster July 1996, Swinsto-Simpson's 1996, Mistral Hole Nov 1996, Marble Steps Jan 1997, Notts Pot Jan 1997, Nent Head-Brewery Shaft Oct 1998, Bull Pot March 2000, Bar Pot [Rope Ladder] May 2000, Land's End–John O Groats Charity Cycle Ride-2006.

CLARKE, Jane; *J1984, b1954,*
Member; BEC.
Probationary Meets; GG81-83, Tanne de Bel Espoir-Diau, Pool Sink.
One of 'The Bassets' [Also see Graham Wilton-Jones]
Newsletter References; *Tatham Wife Hole Oct 1984.*

CLARKE, John M; AKA: Nobby. *J1957, b1936,*
BPC President 1989-92.
Club expeditions; Norway; Caves around Mo I Rana 1958. Yugoslavia; Postojnia 1963. Vercours [France] Sornin Plateau and Vats of Sassenage 1978. Complexe De La Pierre Saint Martin 1995. Many trips to Ireland in conjunction with Irish Caving Club.
Other Expeditions; Caving in Cyprus [*National Service*] 1960-1962.
Notable Achievements; First caving trip –Bar Pot with rope ladders and hemp lifelines. Hand making electron ladders. First Dump Warden at the new dump after helping to raise the money to buy it 1963. Held other BPC committee offices of Hon.Photographer, Social Sec, Secretary and Chairman. Became a committee member of CNCC 1963, and later became the Treasurer until 1975. Rebuilt GG winch and converted it to hydraulic operation with Paul Turner 1978. Fitted new engine to GG winch and modified gearing 1991. Became BPC President for four consecutive years 1989-1993.
Main Activities; Caving, walking and cycling.
Famous for; Re-enacting a 1934 club meet to Alum Pot, complete with hand cart and rope ladders. Testing new rope ladders by laddering down GG main shaft before the filmed re-enactment of the 100th Anniversary of Martel's first descent 1995. Cycling 4200 miles across USA 2003. But will probably be best remembered for a Presidents meet in Deepdale when millions of midges descended upon us, or for singing an endless rap song rather than giving a Presidential speech.
Bulletin References; *Stream Passage Pot June 1962, Hardrawkin Pot Sept 1962, Juniper Gulf Dec 1962, Pen-y-Ghent Pot Extensions Oct 1963, Ireby Fell Cavern April 1964, Screen Hill-Legnabrocky*

Way Ireland Discovery Aug 1965, Lancaster Easegill 1966, The Haute Route 1990, Tete Sauvage July 1995, Doline Cave [Discovery] 1990.

Newsletter References; *Washfold Pot July 1957; Simpson's Pot Aug 1957, Swinsto Sept 1957, Lost John's Hole Aug 1965, Bradford Mine shaft collapses Aug 1965, Lancaster-County Pot Feb 1970, KMC-Swinsto June 1972, Heron Pot Jan 1985, Eden Valley-Teesdale Walking Meet Oct 1985, Calf Holes Jan 1988, New Goyden Pot Oct 1988, Short Drop Cave Nov 1989, Scrafton Pot June 1990, Lakes Walk Sept 1990, Easegill Caverns Sept 1990, Easegill Caverns March 1993, Bagshaw Caverns Oct 1993, Coniston Mines Weekend Sept 1993, Simpson's-Swinsto March 1994, Lost John's Jan 1995, Notts Pot Feb 1995, Wretched Rabbit-Lancaster Hole March 1995, Pikedaw Calamine Caverns Sept 1995, Giants Hole Nov 1995, Peak Cavern Nov 1995, Top Sink-Lancaster July 1996, Swinsto-Simpson's 1996, Marble Steps Jan 1997, Notts Pot Jan 1997, Nent Head-Brewery Shaft Oct 1998, Bull Pot March 2000, Bar Pot [Rope Ladder] May 2000, KMC Photographic Trip Nov 2002, Crackpot Cave [Photgraphic Meet] Jan 2003, Kings Cave Arran 2004, Calf Holes & Brow Gill Cave Feb 2006, Land's End–John O Groats Charity Cycle Ride- 2006, President's Meet cycle pub crawl July 2015.*

CLAY, E;

CLEAVEATER, *J1981,*

CLEET, Rowan, Thomas; *J2018, b1996,*
Newsletter References; *Long Churns+Borrins Moor Sept 2018, Calf Holes-Browgill Cave Nov 2018, Great Douk Jan 2019, Sell Gill Nov 2019.*

CLEKLESON, Paul; *J1953, b1935,*

CLIFFORD, Arthur David; *J1951, b1923, d2007.*
Bulletin References; *Lost John's July 1951, Rowten Pot, Simpson's Pot July 1953 [Leader], Juniper Gulf May 1954, Clapham Cave June 1954, Lost John's Sept 1954.*
Newsletter References; *Little Hull Pot Leader May 1953, Leader Lost John's Oct 1953, Auctioneer at the club Mock Auction Nov 1953, Leader Clapham Cave June 1954, Leader Lost John's Sept 1954, Disappointment Pot to Main Shaft winch June 1957, Bull Pot of the Witches Aug 1958.*

CLIFFORD, Thomas Christopher; AKA: Cabin Boy. *J1980, b1963,*
Probationary Meets; KMC, Meregill Hole, GG80.
Bulletin References; *Vercors Aug 1983.*
Newsletter References; *Top Sink De-tackle Jan 1980, Kingsdale Master Cave [Found old bang] Jan*

1980, Meregill Feb 1980, Bull Pot of the Witches [And assistance with the body recovery of Tracy Gibson from Top Sink] Oct 1980, Goyden Pot March 1981, Alum Pot March 1981, Lower Long Churn March 1981, Dow-Providence Sept 1981, Little Hull Pot [Dive Support] Oct 1981, Pippikin Pot Oct 1981, Lost John's Feb 1982, Alum Pot March 1982, Kingsdale Photographic meet April 1982, King Pot April 1982, Ireby Fell Caverns July 1982, Birks Fell Cave [Photographing] July 1982, Ingleborough Cave Oct 1982, Mendip weekend April 1983, Gingling Hole June 1983, Hurnel Moss Pot July 1983, Rowten-Swinsto Exchange Nov 1983, Short Drop Caver Dec 1983, County Pot March 1984, Diccan Pot March 1984, New Goyden Pot April 1984, Pool Sink-Lancaster Hole June 1984, Heron Pot Jan 1989.*

CLIFTON, Robert, *J2019,*

COATES, Graham A; *J2014, b1960,*
Probationary Meets; Cow Pot-Link Pot, Link-Serendipity, Bull Pot of the Witches.
Member; CPC.
Newsletter References; *Lancaster-County Pot Nov 2014, Lancaster-Wretched Rabbit Nov 2014, Bull Pot of the Witches Jan 2015, Link Pot March 2015, Lost John's-Notts 2 Sept 2015, Titan Streamway March 2016, Top Sink-Wretched Rabbit Jan 2018.*

COATES, Jack; *J1961, b1922, d1971.*
Resigned Oct 1966.

COBB, Quentin; *J1980,*
Bulletin References; *Gouffre Berger Aug 1980.*
Newsletter References; *Gouffre Berger Aug 1980, Swinsto-KMC Jan 1981.*

COBLEY, David A. E; *J1965, b1918,*
Dived Rowten sumps 1967.
Bulletin References; *Gingling Hole Dec 1964, Fornah Gill Cavern March 1965, Antler Pot Feb 1965, Screen Hill-Legnabrocky Way Ireland Discovery Aug 1965, Lumphammer Hole Sept 1965, Fermanagh Dec 1966.*

COCKFIELD, David; AKA: Parrot. *J1988, b1962,*
Probationary Meets; Tatham Wife, Nick Pot/Vulcan, Juniper Gulf.
Member; CPC.
Bulletin References; *Mosquito Plane [Midge Hole Support/ exploration] 1991.*
Newsletter References; *Nick Pot Nov 1987, Pippikin March 1988, Notts Pot Nov 1988, Simpsons–Kingsdale July 1990, Easegill Caverns Sept 1990, Pikedaw Calamine Cavern March 1992, 5 Caves Trip July 1993, Bull Pot of the Witches*

March 1993, Snatcher's Pot Nov 1993, Coniston Mines Weekend Sept 1993, Simpson's-Swinsto March 1994, Marble Steps March 1994.

COFFEY, T.A. *J1936,*

COFFEY, Leon A; *J1936,*

COLAU, Andrew John; AKA: O'Malley. *J1997, b1948,*
Probationary Meets; GG97, Stream Passage Pot,
Member; CRO [Since 1976]
Bulletin References; *Slit Pot [Discovery] 1979.*
Newsletter References; *Hunt Pot Feb 1998,*

COLL, John Alexander; *J1963, b1942,*

COLLIER, J; *J2002,*

COLLINGE, Adam P; *J2008, b1972,*
Probationary Meets; White Scar, Alum Pot, Lost John's.
Member; WRCPC, UWFRA.
Newsletter References; *Illusion Pot Dec 2011.*

COLLYER, Jane Sarah; *J2000, b1970,*
Member; RRCPC.

CONEY, George, Richard. *J2019, b1968,*
Newsletter References; *Bullpot Jan 2020, Sunset Hole Feb 2020.*

CONLON, Jason; AKA: Jaz. *J2012, b1978,*
Probationary Meets; Sunset Hole, Lancaster-Wretched Rabbit, Alum Pot, Bar Pot, Flood Entrance, Stream Passage Pot.
Newsletter References; *Sunset Hole Oct 2011, Bull Pot of the Witches Jan 2013.*

COOKE, John David; *J1960, b1940,*
Probationary Meets; Ribblehead, Alum Pot, Easegill-Lancaster.
Bulletin References; *Sunset Hole 1962, Pen-y-Ghent Long Churn Oct 1969.*
Newsletter References; *Lancaster Hole Nov 1970, Meregill Hole Aug 1971, Lost John's Sept 1971, Pasture Gill Hole Oct 1971, Grange Rigg-Christmas Pot Jan 1972, Birks Fell April 1972, Washfold Pot April 1972, Rift-Long Kin East Pot Sept 1972, Rowten Pot Dec 1972, Barbondale Pot Dec 1973, Pillar Holes Sept 1978.*

COOPER, Daniel; Temporary Member.

COOPER, Ellen; *J2016, b1991,*
Member; SWCC.

COOPER, John Edward; *J1973, b1948,*
Bulletin References; *Chourum Des Aiguilles 1974, Grotte de Bury 1976, Cnoc Nan Uamh Easter 1978, Jean Pot [Discovery] 1979.*
Newsletter References; *Chourum Des Aiguilles 1974, Birks Fell Cave April 1975, Bull Pot of the Witches Nov 1977, Scrafton Pot April 1980.*

COOPER, John Joseph; *J2009, b1989,*
Probationary Meets; Long Kin East.
Newsletter References; *GG10,*

COOPER, Linda; *J1988, b1963,*
Probationary Meets; Pippikin, Outsleets Beck, Easegill.
Member; UBPC.
Newsletter References; *Pippikin March 1988, Coniston Mine July 1988, Short Drop Cave Nov 1989, Out Sleets Beck Pot Dec 1989, Easegill Caverns Sept 1990,*

COOPER, S; AKA: McLain.

CORDING, Dave; *J1959, b1940,*
Resigned from club 1964 EGM dissatisfied when women allowed to stay at the club.
Bulletin References; *Pen-y-ghent Pot July 1960, Lancaster–Eastgill Aug 1960, Grange Rigg Easter 1961, Celebrations held in Flying Horse shoe to*
Bulletin References; *Pen-y-Ghent Pot July 1960, Lancaster-Easegill Aug 1960, Grange Rigg Easter 1961, Celebrations for Dave's 21st held in Flying Horseshoe Easter 1961, Bar Pot Easter Sunday 1961, Simpson's Pot 16th April 1961-[Graham Shaw Accident] Little Hull Pot Feb 1961, Testing old Courlene rope 1961, Pen-y-Ghent pot 1961, Cima Grande Ridge Aug 1962, Juniper Gulf Dec 1962, Lost John's July 1963, Notts Pot Oct 1963, Pen-y-Ghent Long Churn Nov 1963.*

CORNWELL-SMITH, Nicholas Brian; AKA: NikNik.
J1978, b1956,
BPC President 2020.
Probationary Meets; Lost John's, Lancaster-County Pot, GG78, Dan yr Ogof.
Member; QMCC [1974-1977], WSG [1977-1988], BEC [1988-2000], LSCC.
Club expeditions; Gouffre Berger 1980, Cervinia 1980, Scotland 1980, Ardeche 1981, Stelvio 1981, Ireland 1988 & 1989, Gaping Gill 1978-Present.
Other Expeditions; Norway [WSG] 1977.
Notable Achievements; Published 'They Words, They Words' a caving song book 1993. Sang on Radio Bristol in connection with song book. [*Copies still available*]
Main Activities; Caving, Skiing, Climbing / Walking, Scouts.

Famous for; Caving song book 1993.
Bulletin References; *Gouffre Berger Aug 1980, Wildcat Shuffle May 1994, Deep Well [Diving support] May 1992.*
Newsletter References; *Lost John's Sept 1978, Tom Taylor's Cave March 1980, Black Shiver Sept 1980, Sell Gill Hole 1980, Gouffre Berger Aug 1980, Canterbury Cave July 1982, Weathercote Cave April 1988, South Wales Dec 1990, Mendip Weekend Sept 1991, Snatcher's Pot Nov 1993.*

COULSON, Mathew James Douglas; *J1979, b1956,*
Probationary Meets; GG80, Bull Pot of the Witches, Pasture Ghyll.
Newsletter References; *Pasture Gill Cave Sept 1980, Bull Pot of the Witches [And assistance with the recovery of Tracy Gibson's body from Top Sink] Oct 1980, Mendip Oct 1980, Lower Long Churn March 1981.*

COULTON, Martin Andrew; *J1980, b1956,*
Probationary Meets; GG80, Lancaster/Easegill.
Newsletter References; *Alum Pot March 1981, New Goyden Pot April 1981, Gingling Hole Rescue July 1981, Pippikin Pot Oct 1981.*

COWELL, Aaron; *J2013,*
Newsletter References; *Skirwith Cave [Novice Trip] Jan 2016, Devis Hole/Mine July 2017, Burtersett Quarry/Mine July 2017.*

COWELL, Lian James; *J2010, b1999,*

COWELL, Mark Andrew; *J2012, b1968,*
Newsletter References; *Hidden Earth Tewkesbury, Support Oct 2007, Heron Pot Jan 2009, Pikedaw Calamina Caverns Feb 2009, Skirwith Cave [Novice Trip] Jan 2016.*

COWLEY, David Robert; *J1960, b1938,*

COX, Pauline; *J1971, b1949, d1995.*
Probationary Meets; Easegill, Crackpot Cave, Dow Cave.
Bulletin References; *One of the people who instigated sending hot drinks down to the main chamber queues during the winch meets.*
Newsletter References; *Crackpot Cave March 1971, Swildons Oct 1974, Giants Hole Nov 1974, Brezno, Leska, Babizop Rakov Scojan and the Pit of Bears Yugoslavia Aug 1985, Eden Valley-Teesdale Walking Meet Oct 1985.*

COX, Russell Perry; *J1964, b1942,*
BPC President 2010-11.
Other Expeditions; Provatina Expedition 1967.

Bulletin References; *Dan Yr Ogof Nov 1966, Alum Pot/Diccan Pot 1966, Ireland [Clare] March 1967, Provatina Abyss July/Aug 1967, Gouffre Berger Aug 1980, Vercors Aug 1983, Grotte De Ramats Aug 1985.*
Newsletter Reference: *Lancaster–Easegill Feb 1969, Bull Pot of the Witches July 1969, Rumbling Hole Oct 1969, Birks Fell April 1971, Meregill Hole Aug 1971, Lost John's Sept 1971, Crackpot Cave March 1971, Rift–Long Kin East Pot Sept 1972, Birks Fell Cave April 1973, Little Neath River Cave June 1973, Agen Allwedd Mar 1974, Swildons Oct 1974, Giants Hole Nov 1974, Meregill April 1975, Stream Passage–Flood Entrance Feb 1975, Birks Fell Cave April 1975, Pippikin Hole Oct 1976, Top Sink–Lancaster and Back! Oct 1978, Gouffre Berger Aug 1980, Ibbeth Peril Oct 1980, Gingling Hole June 1983, Quaking Pot Aug 1983, Nettle Pot Sept 1983, Peak Cavern Sept 1983, Pool Sink-Lancaster Hole June 1984, County Pot-Top Sink April 1985, Sell Gill July 1985, Lost John's Pot July 1985, Gunnerside Gill Lead Mines June 1985, Brezno, Leska, Babizop Rakov Scojan and the Pit of Bears Yugoslavia Aug 1985, Eden Valley-Teesdale Walking Meet Oct 1985, Salthill Quarry Geology Walk Nov 2008,*

COX, T; *J1973,*
Newsletter References; *Birks Fell April 1971.*

COXON, Barbara Jean; *J2017, b1957,*
Probationary Meets; KMC, Goyden Pot, Sell Gill, GG17, Stream Passage-Bar Pot.

COXON, Stuart; AKA: Dreads. *J2016, b1989,*
Probationary Meets; Sell Gill, Bull Pot, GG16, Stream Passage Pot, Flood Entrance, Bar Pot, Bruntscar Cave.
Newsletter References; *Bull Pot Feb 2017, Jingling Feb 2017, Devis Hole/Mine July 2017, Burtersett Quarry/Mine July 2017, Hartley Quarry Cave Jan 2018, Jingling Pot Feb 2018, P5 [Radio Locating] June 2018, Sunset Hole April 2019, Bull Pot Oct 2019, Silvestre to Marniosa Treviso [First Through Trip] Sept 2019.*

CRABTREE, Donald; *J1953,*

CRABTREE, Harry; *j1938,*

CRAMPTON, Michael; *J1971, b1946,*

CRAP, D; *J1973,*
Newsletter References; *County Pot Oct 1975, Lost John's Nov 1975,*

CRAVEN, Lawrence Stanley; *J1966, b1949,*

CRAVEN, Susan; *J1973?*
Newsletter References; *Dow Cave Feb 1974.*

CRAWLEY, Theo; *J2010,*

CRAWSHAW, James; *J2019, b1984,*
Newsletter References; *Great Douk Jan 2019.*

CRICK, Barry; *J1961, b1945, d2006.*
Probationary Meets; New Goyden Pot, Bar Pot, Magnetometer Pot.
Other Club Memberships; VMC.
Main Activities; Caving, Climbing, Walking, Bell Ringing and Morris Dancing.
Bulletin References; *Long Kin West July 1962, Car Pot June 1963, South Wales Easter 1963, Stonelands Cave Aug 1963, Lower Stream Passage Pot May 1965.*

CROFT, Paul; *J1989, b1960,*
Probationary Meets; Bull Pot of the Witches.
Newsletter References; *Pippikin Pot Oct 1989, New Rift Pot Feb 1990, Hangman's Hole March 1990, Lost John's Jan 1995.*

CROLL, Diana; *J1985,*
Newsletter References; *Lost John's Sept 1978, Sell Gill July 1985, Gunnerside Gill Lead Mines June 1985, Gingling Hole Oct 1985, Eden Valley-Teesdale Walking Meet Oct 1985, Calf Holes Nov 1985, Scotland 1987, New Goyden Pot Oct 1988, Short Drop Cave Nov 1989, Lakes Walk Sept 1990, Easegill Caverns Sept 1990, Gouffre Berger Aug 1992, Crooklands Walking Meet Sept 1993, Bagshaw Caverns Oct 1993, Lakes Walking Meet Sept 1995, Peak Cavern Nov 1995, King Arthur's Labyrinth May 1997, Black Combe-Foxfield Walk Sept 2003, Land's End–John O Groats Charity Cycle Ride 2006, Great Wall of China Charity Walk [Her group raised £40,000] 2008.*

CROLL, Frank Bracey; AKA: Abdul [the Bull] *J1956, b1936, d2007.*
BPC President 1985-88.
Member; BSG, RRCPC.
Bulletin References; *Christmas Pot 1957, Clapham Cave March 1957, Rift Pot [Double rope failure] 1957, Lost John's March 1960, Pen-y-ghent Pot April 1960, Rowten Pot April 1960, Gaping Gill Meet 1960, Pen-y-ghent Pot July 1960, Lancaster-Eastgill Aug 1960 [got Lost], Knots Pot Sept 1960, Simpson's Pot 16th April 1961 [Graham Shaw Accident] Lost John's March 1961, Little Hull Pot Feb 1961, Pen-y-Ghent pot 1961, Hardrawkin Pot Sept 1962, Lost John's July 1963, Ireby Fell Cavern April 1964, Grotte de Bury 1977, Antro del Corchia, 1978, Gouffre Berger Aug 1980, Krisna Jama Aug 1984, Brezno V Madvedovi Konti Aug 1984, Leski Aug 1984, Tanne Du Bel Espoir-Diau Aug 1984, Grotte De Ramats Aug 1985, Doline Cave [Discovery] 1990.*
Newsletter References; *Washfold Pot July 1957, Lancaster Hole Oct 1957, Easter Camp April 1958, Stream Passage Pot April 1958, Lancaster Hole April 1958, Little Hull Pot April 1958, Main Shaft to de-tackle Disappointment via Hensler's crawl [Hensler star] Whit 1958, Lancaster Hole June 1958, Alum Pot Aug 1958, Long Kin West Sept 1958, OBJ Hole Nov 1958, Digging near Owl Hole Dec 1958, Alum Pot April 1959, Lower Gunnerfleet Cave April 1959, Inauguration Aven June 1959, Measuring Depth of GG shaft Aug 1959, Little Hull Hole Aug 1959, Diccan-Alum Exchange September 1959, Brown Scar Cave Sept 1959, Lost John's Sept 1959, Clapham Cave Oct 1959, Leader Notts Pot Sept 1960, Leader Alum, Pot Oct 1960, Leader Little Hull Feb 1961, Leader Lost John's Mar 1961, Gaping Gill Main Shaft Aug 1961, KMC-Swinsto Hole June 1972, Rowten Pot Dec 1972, Flood-Bar SRT practice Feb 1975, Meregill April 1975, Nick Pot Oct 1975, Lost John's Sept 1978, Black Shiver Sept 1980, Gouffre Berger Aug 1980, Alum Pot March 1981, Notts Pot Jan 1981, Tanne de Bel Espoir-Grotte de la Diau Aug 1981, Heron Pot Jan 1985, Top Sink-County Pot April 1985, Wretched Rabbit Passage April 1985, Sell Gill July 1985, Lost John's Pot July 1985, Gunnerside Gill Lead Mines June 1985, Gingling Hole Oct 1985, Eden Valley-Teesdale Walking Meet Oct 1985, Calf Holes Nov 1985, Pool Park Oct 1986, Top Sink-County Pot March 1986, Pen-y-Gent Pot March 1987, Scotland 1987, Lakes Walking Meet Oct 1987, Notts Pot Nov 1988, New Goyden Pot Oct 1988, Short Drop Cave Nov 1989, Simpsons–KMC July 1990, Scrafton Pot June 1990, Lakes Walk Sept 1990, Easegill Caverns Sept 1990, Lost John's March 1991, Gouffre Berger Aug 1992, Crooklands Walking Meet Sept 1993, Bagshaw Caverns Oct 1993, Lakes Walking Meet Sept 1995, Peak Cavern Nov 1995, King Arthur's Labyrinth May 1997, Walking Meet Sept 1997, Black Combe-Foxfield Walk Sept 2003.*

CROLL, Rachel Jane; *J1995, b1970,*
Probationary Meets; Long Churns, KMC, Bar Pot, Calf Holes, GG97.
Member; YSS.
Newsletter References; *Bull Pot Dec 1996, Walking Meet Sept 1997.*

CROSS, Ian; AKA: Little Chicken, Iron Cross. *J1978, b1957,*
Probationary Meets; Rumbling Hole, Pillar Holes, Notts Pot.

Member; WSG [1977-1982], WASG [1980-1981], QMCCC [1976-1980], QMCMC [1 year]

Club expeditions; Gouffre Berger Expedition 1980, Vercors [France] 1989, Ireland County Clare 1988 & 1989 [Where he met his wife]

Other Expeditions; Kimberley Region-1980. [With the WASG]

Notable Achievements; Rescued from OFD II-Circa 1979 [QMCCC Trip] Discovered new caves [Lava Tubes] whilst caving in Washington State USA-2003 [With Williamette Valley Grotto [Oregon Chapter of National Speleological Society-USA] Held many positions on BPC committee, Member 1987 & 2006-2010 [Also chair], Photographer 1988 & 1993-1996, Secretary 2011-Present.

Main Activities; Caving, Walking, Motorcycling.

Famous for; Checked the petrol level in the digging generator at the bottom of the 1st pitch in Sell Gill whilst wearing a lit carbide lamp.

Bulletin References; *Gouffre Berger Aug 1980, Tanne De Bel Espoir-La Diau Parmilan 1991,*

Newsletter References; *Rumbling Hole Aug 1978, Pillar Holes Sept 1978, Hammer Pot Sept 1978, Tom Taylor's Cave March 1980, Sell Gill Hole 1980, Gouffre Berger Aug 1980, Mendip weekend April 1983, Meregill Feb 1983, Langstroth Pot Sept 1985, Gingling Hole Oct 1985, Calf Holes Nov 1985, Mendip Dec 1986, Top Sink-County Pot March 1986, Pen-y-Gent Pot March 1987, Dow Cave April 1987, Weathercote Cave April 1988, Coniston Mine July 1988, South Wales Nov 1988, Heron Pot Jan 1989, Haytime Hole 1990, Crooklands Walking Meet Sept 1993, GG Photographic Trip May 1993, Cherry Tree Hole Jan 1994, Ribblehead Caves Feb 1995, Lakes Walking Meet Sept 1995, Hagg Gill 1996, Bar Pot [Rope Ladder] May 2000, Skirwith Cave July 2000, White Scar Cave April 2001, Lancaster Canal Walk Meet 2001, Dismal Hill-Old Ing Jan 2006, Calf Holes July 2008, Haytime Hole March 2009, Crosby Ravensworth-Askham Walking Meet Sept 2012, Ibeth Peril April 2014, Scoska Cave April 2014, President's Meet Ribchester Walk June 2014, BCA Party June 2014, Dowkabottom Cave July 2014, Old Ing&Birkwith Canal Aug 2014, Roundthwaite Common to Borrowdale Sept 2014, BCRA 25th Cave Science Symposium Oct 2014, Providence Pot Restoration Nov 2014, High & Great Douk Dec 2014, Calf Holes-Browgill and Old Ing-Birkwith June 2015, Ribblehead Caves July 2015, Bruntscar Cave July 2015, Walking Meet 2015, Hoffman Kilns Stainforth Nov 2015, GG Track repairs Feb 2017, Devis Hole/Mine July 2017, Lindale-Greenodd Walking Meet 2017, Wildcat Rift May 2018, Long Churns&BorrinsMoor Sept 2018, Cow Green Reservoir–Appleby Walking Meet 2018, Kirkby Lonsdale-Wharton Walking Meet Sept 2019, Illusion Pot Sept 2019.*

CROSS, Pamela Johnson; *J1990, b1960,*

CROSSLEY, Geoffrey William; AKA: Buzby. *J1977, b1960,*

Probationary Meets; Long Kin West, GG77, Hurnel Moss.

Member; SCG, Hyperion.

Bulletin References; *Potts Moor Cave 1977, Winnats Head Cave 1978, Antro del Corchia, 1978, Hallucination Sump [Dive] 1979, Abbisa Fighiera 1979, Pippikin to Top Sink April 1980, Gouffre Berger Aug 1980, Ingleborough-GG connection May 1983, Vercors Aug 1983, Tanne Du Bel Espoir-Diau Aug 1984, Dub Cote Extensions 1984, Hurtle Pot [Dive extension] 1984, Dub Cote Extensions [Diving] 1990, Tanne De Bel Espoir-La Diau Parmilan 1991.*

Newsletter References; *Cwm Dwr-OFD II April 1978, Marble Sink June 1978, Rumbling Hole Aug 1978, Giants Hole Dec 1978, Gavel Pot Oct 1978, Pippikin-Link-Top Sink Oct 1979, Giants Hole Dec 1978, Abbissa Fighiera Italy Aug 1979, Lost John's Sept 1978, Pippikin-Lancaster [Flood Pulse on Echo Aven] 1980, Diccan-Main Shaft Jan 1980, King Pot Feb 1980, Goyden Pot [Diving] Feb 1980, Boreham Cave March 1980, Frakes Series [Diving] April 1980, Lancaster Hole [Maple Leaf Pitch] April 1980, Pippikin-Top Sink April 1980, Ingleborough Cave Secret Streamway April 1980, Alum Pot June 1980, Gouffre Berger Aug 1980, Wookey Hole [Dive to chamber 20] Oct 1980, Vobster Quarry [Dive] Oct 1980, Sell Gill Holes Oct 1980, Simpsons Pot-KMC Oct 1980, Lost John's Nov 1980, Stainforth Force [Dive] Nov 1980, Peak Cavern [Swine Hole Dive] Nov 1980, Lancaster-County Pot Nov 1980, Noxon Park Iron Mine [Dive] Dec 1980, Peak Cavern Treasury Sump [Dive] Dec 1980, Swinsto-KMC Jan 1981, Ingleborough Cave [Dive] Jan 1981, Helwith Bridge Quarry [Dive] Feb 1981, Boreham Cave [Dive] Feb 1981, Wookey Hole [Chamber 22] March 1981, Alum Pot March 1981, Hurtle Pot [Dive] April 1981, Hurtle Pot [Dive] March 1981, New Goyden Pot April 1981, Magnetometer Pot March 1981, Wookey Hole [Chamber 22] April 1981, Bridge Cave-Little Neath River Cave April 1981, Mud Hall GG [BBC Filming Blue Peter] May 1981, Notts Pot Jan 1981, Gaping Gill-Hallucination Aven [Dive] May 1981, Spout Tunnel May 1981, Wookey Hole [Chamber 24] June 1981, Longwood/August Swallet June 1981, Hurtle Pot [450'] June 1981, Hurtle Pot [500' @ 90'] July 1981, Tanne de Bel Espoir-Grotte de la Diau Aug 1981, Little Hull Pot [Dive Support] Oct 1981, Bull Pot Oct 1981, Dub Cote Extension [Dive] Oct 1981, Birkwith Cave 'Got lost in sump and later on moor' [CDG report] Nov 1981, Ingleborough Cave Oct 1982, Received Royal*

Humane Society Medal for involvement in rescue of Scout from Dido's Cave 1983, Welly Boot Connection between Gaping Gill and Ingleborough Cave Jan 1983, GG–Radagast's Revenge Ingleborough to clear dig for through trip Feb 1983, Mendip weekend April 1983, Wookey 20 Dive April 1983, Hallucination Aven-Induction Location May 1983, South Wales Aug 1983, Giant's Hole Sept 1983, GG-Troubled Waters, Discovery, Passed air bell sump [Lost dive line hence name], GG-Troubled Waters-Voice connection with Olympic Chamber in Clapham, Bottoms 1985, Gingling Hole Oct 1985, Scotland 1987.

CROSSLEY, Thomas; *J1946,*

CROSTON, Jeffrey Joseph; *J1993, b1948,*
Probationary Meets; Lancaster, Mongo Gill, Scrafton Pot, Tatham Wife, KMC, Brandy Bottle, Coniston Copper Mines.
Member; NMRS.
Bulletin References; *Alderley Edge Mines Sept 2009.*
Newsletter References; *Swaledale Weekend Oct 1992, Alum Pot [Training Meet] July 1997, Nent Head-Brewery Shaft Oct 1998, Skirwith Cave July 2000, Cherry Tree Hole Jan 2001, White Scar Cave April 2001, Robinson's Pot Sept 2002, Hagg Gill Oct 2002, Lancaster Hole Feb 2003, Sunset Hole Sept 2003, Robinson's Pot Oct 2003, Aquamole Pot Dec 2003, Long Kin East Nov 2003, Pikedaw Calamine Caverns Jan 2004, Bull Pot Dec 2003, Swinsto Hole-KMC Feb 2004, Sell Gill Holes March 2004,Ireby Fell Cavern June 2004, Gingling Hole July 2004, High Hull Cave Oct 2004, Dowkabottom Cave Oct 2004, Committee Pot Nov 2004, Lancaster Hole Dec 2004, Valley Entrance Dec 2004, Giant's Hole Jan 2005, Calf Holes & Dismal Hill & Old Ing Jan 2005, Lancaster Hole April 2005, HardwrakinPot April 2005, Pippikin-Mistral Sept 2005, Simpson's Pot Dec 2005, Jackpot P8 Feb 2006, Bull Pot Jan 2006, ConistonCopper Mines Oct 2006, Hunt Pot Nov 2006, Jingling Pot Dec 2006, Committee Pot Dec 2006, Top Sink-Lancaster Hole Feb 2007, White Scar Cave April 2007, Providence Pot-Dow Cave April 2007, Swinsto Hole June 2007, Heron Pot Sept 2007, Death's Head & Big Meanie Sept 2007, Hard Level-Brandy Bottle Incline Sept 2007, Great Expectations Dec 2007, Hard Level-Brandy Bottle Incline Nov 2007, Bull Pot of the Witches Jan 2008, Aygill Caverns Feb 2008, Sunset Hole April 2008, Lambrigg Fell-Tebay Walk Sept 2008, Brackenbottom Pot Oct 2008, Hell Hole, Whitewell Cave & Pot Nov 2008, Lower Long Churn Nov 2008, Bull Pot of the Witches Jan 2009, Stump Cross Caverns Dec 2008, Simpson's-KMC Dec 2008, Aygill Caverns Jan 2009, Pikedaw Calamina Caverns Feb 2009, New Goyden Pot March 2009, Link Pot April 2009, Stump Cross Caverns [Geoff Workman's 80th] April 2009, Nettle Pot July 2009, Heron Pot July 2009, Alderley Edge Mines Sept 2009, Ireby Fell Caverns Oct 2009, Pool Sink-Easegill Dec 2009, Tatham Wife Hole Feb 2010, Swinsto Hole Feb 2010, Magnetometer Pot April 2010, Mistral Hole June 2010, Roaring Hole May 2010, Alum Pot July 2010, Mistral Hole Aug 2010, Sell Gill Sept 2010, Committee Pot March 2011, Swinsto Hole Nov 2011, Jingling Pot Dec 2011, Lancaster-Wretched Rabbit Jan 2012, Shuttleworth Pot Feb 2012, Yordas Pot Feb 2012, Notts Pot March 2012, Sell Gill March 2012, Swinsto-KMC March 2012, Hardrawkin Pot April 2012, Sell Gill May 2012, Old Ing/Calf Holes-Browgill [Novice Trip] June 2012, Old Ing/Calf Holes-Browgill [Novice Trip] July 2012, White Scar Cave July 2012, Heron Pot [Novice Trip] Aug 2012, Committee Pot Sept 2012, Croesor Rhosydd [Through] Oct 2012, Link Pot Nov 2012, Aquamole Pot Dec 2012, Sell Gill Dec 2012, Calf Holes-Browgill Dec 2012, Bull Pot of the Witches Jan 2013, Swinsto-KMC Feb 2013, Top Sink-Lancaster Hole March 2013, Alum Pot April 2013, Titan-JH April 2013, Illusion Pot June 2013, GB Cave June 2013, Reservoir Hole [The Frozen Deep] June 2013, Heron Pot Sept 2013, Hardrawkin Pot Sept 2013, Sell Gill Holes Nov 2013, Mongo Gill Nov 2013, Magnetometer Pot Nov 2013, White Scar Cave July 2014, Fairy Holes Sept 2014, Nenthead Mines Sept 2014, Shuttleworth Pot Oct 2014, Mistral Hole Nov 2014, Sunset Hole Dec 2014, Bull Pot of the Witches Jan 2015, Pasture Gill Jan 2015, The Borehole-Boundary Pot Feb 2015, County Pot Feb 2015, Link Pot March 2015, Simpson's Pot May 2015, Link Pot-Cow Pot June 2015, Robinson's Pot July 2015, Lost John's-Notts 2 Sept 2015, Alderley Edge Mines Oct 2015, Heron Pot Nov 2015, County Pot Jan 2016, Swinsto-KMC Feb 2016, Darnbrook Pot March 2016, Hagg Gill April 2016, Pool Sink June 2016, Simpson's Pot Aug 2016, Pool Sink-County Pot Oct 2016, Simpson's Pot-KMC Dec 2016, Rift Pot-Long Kin East [Exchange] July 2016,County Pot Dec 2016, Bull Pot of the WitchesJan 2017, County Pot Feb 2017, Heron Pot [Novice trip] April 2017, Langstroth Cave April 2017, Calf Holes-Birkwith June 2017, Robinson's Pot Sept 2017, Iron Kiln Sept 2017, Wretched Rabbit-County Pot Sept 2017, Stump Cross Caverns Dec 2017, High Douk Holes Feb 2018, Darnbrook Pot June 2018, Voldemort Pot-Notts 2 Feb 2018, Stump Cross Cavertns July 2018, Mongo Gill Sept 2018, Cherry Tree Hole Oct 2018, Stump Cross Caverns Nov 2018,Wizard's Chasm Dec 2018, County Pot Dec 2018, Wretched Rabbit-County Pot March 2019, Heron Pot July 2019, Alum and Churns [Novice trip] Dec 2019, Pool Sink-Wretched Rabbit Feb 2020.*

CROWE, Emma; *J2009, b1984,*

CROWLEY, Desmond James; *J1987, b1955,*
Probationary Meets; Dow Cave, GG87, Alum Pot.
Bulletin References; *Rescued from Large-Rift Pot 1994, Deep Well [Diving support] May 1992, Gouffre Berger Aug 1992.*
Newsletter References; *Nick Pot Nov 1987, Weathercote Cave April 1988, Coniston Mine July 1988, Ireby Fell [Diving Support] Oct 1988, South Wales Nov 1988, King Pot Jan 1989, Pool Sink-Cow Pot March 1989, Bull Pot of the Witches April 1989, Langstroth Pot & Cave [Diving] July 1989, Cow Pot-Wretched Rabbit Feb 1990, Rift-Large Pot March 1990, Easegill Caverns Jan 1991, Marble Steps Pot Dec 1990, Sell Gill Training Meet Nov 1991, Gouffre Berger Aug 1992, Pen-y-Ghent Pot July 1992, Ireby Fell Feb 1993, Deep Well [Dive Support] May 1997, County-Wretched Rabbit Nov 1998, Lost John's March 1999, Darnbrook Pot Oct 2016.*

CROWLEY, Josephine; *J2002, b1947,*

CROWLEY, Russell; *J2000, b1985,*
Probationary Meets; Dyhedral, Heron Pot, Lancaster, Sell Gill, Easegill, Hardrawkin, Alum Pot.
CROWLEY, Theo; *J2010,*
Probationary Meets; GG09.

CROWTHER, Frederick; AKA: Freddy. *J1933, d1944.* [Died whilst on active service in WWII]

CULPAN, John Barrie; *J1958, b1937,*

CULPAN, John Terrance; AKA: Terry. *J1957, b1938,*
Newsletter References; *Swinsto Sept 1957, Lancaster Hole Oct 1957, Alum Pot Aug 1958.*

CULSHAW, Isaac;-See Wood.

CULSHAW, Poppy;-See Wood.

CUNNINGHAM, Caitlin; Temporary Member.

CUNNINGHAM, John; Temporary Member.

CURLEY, LYNN; *J2019, b1961,*
Probationary Meets; GG16-18, Great Douk, Morcambe Bay Walk.

CURRY, Christopher; *J2017, b1992,*
Probationary Meets; Brackenbottom Pot, Oxlow Caverns, Swinsto-KMC.

CURTIS, C; *J1984,*

CVETKOVA, Liama; *J2013, b1984,*

67

D

DACKA-POLAKOWSKA, Elzbieta; *J2017, b1981,*
Probationary Meets; Great Douk, Long Churns.
Member; UKMC.

DALE, Howard; *J1982,*
Newsletter References; *Ingleborough Cave Oct 1982.*

DARBON, Frank C; *J1959*
Member; BEC, WSG.
Bulletin References; *Mendip Trip 1958, Disappointment Pot Easter Meet 1961.*

DARWOOD, C; *J1936,*

DAVENPORT, Alan;
Bulletin References; *Reseau de la Pierre Saint Martin Aug 2013.*
Newsletter References; *Calf Holes & Brow Gill Cave Feb 2006, Long Churn [Novice Trip] June 2011.*

DAVENPORT, Christine A; [née Rosser] AKA: Duchess. *J1985,*
Bulletin References; *Tanne De Bel Espoir-La Diau Parmilan 1991, Reseau de la Pierre Saint Martin Aug 2013.*
Newsletter References; *Sell Gill Feb 1985, County Pot–Top Sink April 1985, Gunnerside Gill Lead Mines June 1985, Notts Pot Feb 1986, Pool Park Oct 1986, Pippikin Pot Nov 1986, County Pot-Lancaster March 1986, Scotland 1987, Top Sink–Link Feb 1988, King Pot Jan 1989, Cow Pot–Pool Sink March 1989, Great Douk Cave & Jan 1990, Simpson's-Swinsto March 1994, Dowkabottom Feb 1995, Lakes Walking Meet Sept 1995, Calf Holes & Brow Gill Cave Feb 2006.*

DAVENPORT, Colin Alan; AKA: Corky. *J1982, b1958, d2010.*
Probationary Meets; Alum Pot, Slit Pot, KMC.
Went through Calf Holes to Browgill with only sparklers for light, Tom Taylors through trip with only a box of matches!
Bulletin References; *Vercors Aug 1983, Brackenbottom Pot, [Dig/exploration] 1989, Tanne De Bel Espoir–La Diau Parmilan 1991, Wildcat Shuffle May 1994.*
Newsletter References; *Little Neath River Cave April 1978, Alum Pot June 1980, Alum Pot March 1982, Kingsdale Photographic meet April 1982, Birks Fell Cave [Photographing] July 1982, Ingleborough Cave Oct 1982, South Wales Aug 1983, Ibbeth Peril July 1984, Gunnerside Gill Lead Mines June 1985, Langstroth Pot Sept 1985, Brezno, Leska, Babizop Rakov Scojan and the Pit of Bears Yugoslavia Aug 1985, Scotland 1987, Weathercote Cave April 1988, Simpson's-Swinsto March 1994, Dowkabottom Feb 1995, Lakes Walking Meet Sept 1995, Calf Holes & Brow Gill Cave Feb 2006.*

DAVENPORT, Peter; *J2009, b2002,*
Bulletin References; *Reseau de la Pierre Saint Martin Aug 2013,*
Newsletter References; *Calf Holes & Brow Gill Cave Feb 2006, Long Churn [Novice Trip] June 2011.*

DAVEY, John; *J1959, b1940,*
Resigned 2009 [After disagreement in committee]
Member; BEC [1960-1968]
Member of the Heath Grammar School contingent.

Club expeditions; BPC/Red Rose coach trip to France [Pyrenees]
Notable Achievements; Organising trip to Pyrenees [*with Alan Kershaw and Alf Hurworth*] 1961. Significant, life saving, contributions to Graham Shaw rescue from Simpson's Pot 1961. Jointly with Nick Pratchet were the first to reach the bottom of Grange Rigg Pot after 'banging' blocked rift. First BPC member to free dive into Secret Stream passage and Arrow chamber in Clapham Cave [*With Bob Jarman*] Led GG Winch meets [*with Frank Briggs and Chris Dufton*] Much committee work carried out and helped John Clarke rebuild the Geoff Money Studio.
Main Activities; Caving.
Famous for; Having a chip pan in the 'Old Dump'. 'Bog' Supremo at GG Winch meet having constructed new style toilets. Singing rude songs.
Bulletin References; *Pen-y-ghent Pot April 1960, Pen-y-ghent Pot July 1960, Wharfedale Camp Aug 1960, Stonelands Cave July 1960, Alum Pot July 1960, Mendip Trip Sept 1960, Magnetometer Pot Nov 1960, Flood Entrance Pot Dec 1960, Grange Rigg Easter 1961, Celebrations held in Flying Horseshoe to celebrate John's 21st Easter 1961, Simpson's Pot 16th April 1961-[Graham Shaw Accident] Little Hull Pot Feb 1961, Hardrawkin Jan 1961, Newby Moss Pot 1961,Gaping Gill-Whitsuntide 1961, Alum Pot June 1961, Clapham Cave-First to do 'Round Trip' 1961, Calf Holes CRO rescue practice Dec 1961, Flood Entrance March 1962, Long Kin West July 1962, Little Hull Pot July 1962, Lost John's July 1963, Notts Pot Oct 1963.*
Newsletter References; *Swildon's Hole Sept 1959, Ingleborough Cave Survey Aug 1959, St Cuthberts Swallet Sept 1959, Measuring Depth of GG shaft Aug 1959, Gunnerfleet Caves Oct 1959, Leader Wharfedale Bank Holiday Camp July 1960, Leader Flood Entrance GG Dec 1960, Kingsdale Master Cave Dec 1969, Calf Holes Jan 1988, Pen-y-Ghent Pot entrance restoration June 1991.*

DAVEY, Leo; *J1950, b1932,*

DAVIDSON, William; *J1968, b1937,*
Newsletter References; *Great Douk Cave Jan 1990, Long Churn May 2010.*

Davies, Christine;-See Benn.

DAVIES, John Robert; *J1987, b1965,*
Member; SBHC.
Bulletin References; *Brackenbottom Pot 1989.*

DAVIES, J. S; *J1989, b1971.*

DAVIES, Peter James; *J1998, b1978,*

Probationary Meets; Bar Pot, Giants hole, Diccan, Top Sink-Wretched Rabbit, Big Meanie-Death's Head, Committee Pot.
Bulletin References; *Pyrenees 2006, Ordessa National Park 2007, Croesor-Rhosydd Feb 2009.*
Newsletter References; *Aygill Caverns Feb 1999, Out Sleets Beck Pot April 1999, Derbyshire Meet Sept 1999, White Scar Cave April 2001, James Hall Over-Engine Mine to Bitch Pitch Jan 2005, Giant's Hole Jan 2005, Lancaster Hole April 2005, Magnetometer Pot April 2005, Pen-y-Ghent Pot June 2005, Lost John's Hole Sept 2005, Simpson's Pot Dec 2005, Cow Pot [Lancaster] April 2006, Black Shiver Pot July 2006, Pyrenees Aug 2006, Committee Pot Dec 2006, Top Sink-Lancaster Hole Feb 2007, White Scar Cave April 2007, Providence Pot-Dow Cave April 2007, Ordessa National Park Spanish Pyrenees 2007, Swinsto Hole-KMC Dec 2007, Vesper Pot Jan 2008, King Pot Feb 2008, JH-Peak Cavern via White River Series March 2008, Otter Hole June 2008, Lost John's Oct 2008, Croesor-Rhosydd Feb 2009, Cow Pot April 2009, Large-Rift Pot Exchange July 2009, Rumbling Hole March 2010, Ireby Fell Cavern Jan 2011, Hunt Pot-Shrapnel Pot Nov 2016, Cow Pot March 2019, Illusion Pot Sept 2019,*

DAVIES, Tim R; *J1998, b1971,*

DAVIS, J. Kingsley; *J ?, b1940,*

DAVIS, John Stuart; AKA:Diesel. *J1974, b1940, d2002.*
Left the club a legacy in his will.
Member; BCRA, PDMHS.
Probationary Meets; Gingling Hole, Lost John's, Easegill.
Bulletin References; *Piaggia Bella 1975.*
Newsletter References; *Lost John's Hole Aug 1974, Birks Fell Cave April 1975, Dowkabottom Feb 1995, Ingleborough Cave Digging 2001, Loser's, Fat Finger, Hensler's Pot and Project X digging 2002.*

DAWBER, Emily Joanna; *J2012, b1981,*
Newsletterr References; *Juniper Gulf March 2012, Committee Pot Sept 2012, Runscar-Thistle [Novice Trip] Jan 2016.*

DAWSON, Charles William; *J1950, b1917,*
Bulletin References; *Eglin's Hole September 1950, Lost John's July 1951.*

DAYNES, Peter; *J1957, b1938,*
Suspended from club Dec 1959, expelled Dec 1962 for non payment of subs.
Newsletter References; *Lancaster Hole Oct 1957, Practice stretcher rescue Wade's entrance GG Nov*

1957, Tackle testing July 1958, Sunset Hole Aug 1958, Alum Pot Aug 1958,

DEACON, John Graham; *J1964, b1928,*
Probationary Meets; Sell Gill, Hardrawkin, Lost John's, Oxford Pot.

DEAN, Brian; *J1950, b1934,*
Bulletin References; *Bar Pot Feb 1951, Easter Camp GG 1951, Digging at Beck Head June 1951, Lost John's July 1951, Rowten Pot June 1951, Bar Pot April 1952.*

DEAN, Cyril; *J1955, b1934,*
Newsletter References; *Bar Pot Dec 1957.*

DEAN, John; *J1980, b1961,*
Member; MUPC.
Probationary Meets; Alum Pot, GG79, Pasture Gill, Little Hull Pot, Peak Cavern, Mossdale Caverns.
Newsletter References; *Scrafton Pot April 1980.*

DEELEY, Samuel; *J2016, b1990,*
Newsletter References; *Treviso Aug 2017.*

DEIGHTON, John; *J1999, b1959,*
Newsletter References; *Pippikin Pot Nov 1999, Rowten Pot Dec 2000.*

DENMAN, John; *J1951, b1918,*
Bulletin References; *Simpson's Pot July 1953.*

DENNSAN, John; *J1951, b1918,*

DENT, Stephen; *J1998, b1950,*
Probationary Meets; Joint Hole [Dive]
Member; WRCPC, CPC.

DEVANEY, Christopher James; *J2016, b1981,*
Probationary Meets; GG, Committee Pot, Robinson's Pot, Skirwith Cave.
Caved with scouts and WVCC - 1988-1999, GG99-19, Great Douk, Calf Holes, Browgill Cave, KMC, Dow Cave, Mistral, Hagg Gill.
Club Expeditions; Bauges Massif 2012, Complexe Pierre Saint Martin 2013, Chartreuse 2014, Vercors 2015, Jura/Doubs 2016, Reseau Felix Trombe 2017, Slovenia 2018, Vercors 2019, Sauze d'Oulx 2020.
Bulletin References; *Reseau de la Pierre Saint Martin Aug 2013.*
Newsletter References; *Daimler Hole Sept 2010, Croesor Rhysydd Through Trip Oct 2016, Devis Hole/Mine July 2017, OFD Top Ent Oct 2017, Stump Cross Caverns July 2018, Long Churns & Borrins Moor Sept 2018, Ingleborough Cave Oct 2018, Bull Pot of the Witches Jan 2019, Lancaster-Easegill*

June 2019, Kirkby Lonsdale-Wharton Walking Meet Sept 2019.

DEVANEY, Terry. *J1999, b1950,*
Probationary Meets; Large-Rift Pot, Red Moss, Skirwith Cave.
Member; MSCC [1963-1965] [with a teacher and Mike Hartland] BPC [1965-1967], BWCC [1967-Present], WVCC [1983-1999], BPC [1999-Present] [Initial BPC membership with a teacher, trips included: Upper and Lower Long Churns, Alum Pot, Notts Pot, Marble Steps Pot, Old Ing, Dowkabottom Cave, Bakers Pit, Pridhamsleigh Cavern, Gaping Gill Winch Meet 1965 or 1966. It rained a lot whichever year it was and there were 2 of us in a 6 x 4 x 3 ridge tent with no sewn in groundsheet]
Club Expeditions; Vercors [France] 2002, Reseau Felix Trombe 2003, Reseau Felix Trombe 2004, Chartreuse and Vercors 2005, Complexe Pierre Saint Martin 2006, Systema Aranonera [Spanish Pyrenees] 2007, Les Arcs Alps [Walking] 2008, Jura/Doubs 2009, Gouffre Berger 2010, Reseau Felix Trombe 2011, Bauges Massif 2012, Complexe Pierre Saint Martin 2013, Chartreuse 2014, Vercors 2015, Jura/Doubs 2016, Reseau Felix Trombe 2017, Slovenia 2018.
Other Expeditions; Vercors 1995. [With White Rose Pothole Club]
Notable Achievements; Organising most of the club expeditions above since 2002.
Main Activities; Caving, Cycling, Skiing, Walking, Climbing, Via Ferrata, Kayaking
Famous for; Committee Member and Meets Secretary from 2002, attending all and organising most of the Club Expeditions listed above.
Bulletin References; *Pyrenees Aug 2003, Pyrenees Aug 2004, Ordessa National Park 2007, Croesor-Rhosydd Feb 2009, Cwmorthin Slate Mine Feb 2009, Alderley Edge Mines Sept 2009, Trapped in Hagg Gill several hours [Flood] Sept 2010, Gouffre Pont Du Gerbout Aug 2011, Felix Trombe 2011, Reseau de la Pierre Saint Martin Aug 2013.*
Newsletter References; *Little Hull Pot July 1999, Bull Pot March 2000, Coppice Cave April 2000, Hagg Gill Pot June 2000, Christmas Cracker Sept 2000, Diccan Pot Oct 2000, Lancaster-County Aug 2000, Skirwith Cave July 2000, Rowten Pot Dec 2000, Long Kin West Feb 2001, Cherry Tree Hole Jan 2001, White Scar Cave April 2001, Ingleborough Cave Digging 2001, Notts Pot Feb 2001, Meregill Dec 2001, Swinsto Hole Jan 2002, Great/Little Douk Dec 2001, Short Drop-Gavel Jan 2002, Sell Gill June 2002, South Wales [Cwm Dwr & OFD 2] July 2002, Alum Pot July 2002, Rumbling Hole July 2002, Notts Pot Sept 2002, Robinson's Pot Sept 2002, Sell Gill Hole Nov 2002, KMC*

Photographic Trip Nov 2002, Lancaster Hole Feb 2003, Sunset Hole Jan 2003, Swinsto [Through] Jan 2003, Crackpot Cave [Photgraphic Meet] Jan 2003, Dan Yr Ogof/OFD 2 June 2003, Marble Steps July 2003, Lost John's Pot July 2003, Pool Sink Sept 2003, Great Douk Cave Sept 2003, Sell Gill Hole Sept 2003, Robinson's Pot Oct 2003, Bar Pot Dec 2003, Brackenbottom Pot Dec 2003, Committee Pot Dec 2003, Aquamole Pot Dec 2003, Pikedaw Calamine Caverns Jan 2004, Sell Gill Holes Feb 2004, Swinsto Hole-KMC Feb 2004, Alum Pot March 2004, Lancaster Hole April 2004, Washfold Pot April 2004, MilwrTunnel June 2004, OFD 2 June 2004, Runscar Cave Sept 2004, High Hull Cave Oct 2004, Old Ing/Dismal Hill Oct 2004, Short Drop-Gavel Pot Nov 2004, Committee Pot Nov 2004, Lancaster Hole Dec 2004, Valley Entrance Dec 2004, New Rift Dec 2004, James Hall Over-Engine Mine to Titan Shaft [Bottom] Jan 2005, Calf Holes & Browgill Cave Nov 2004, Calf Holes & Dismal Hill & Old Ing Jan 2005, Diccan Pot Feb 2005, Magnetometer Pot April 2005, Pen-y-Ghent Pot June 2005, Gingling Hole July 2005, Pippikin Sept 2005, Roaring Hole Sept 2005, Lost John's Hole Sept 2005, Heron Pot Nov 2005, Long Kin West Dec 2005, Ribblehead Caves Dec 2005, Simpson's Pot Dec 2005, Ireby Fell Caverns Nov 2005, Brackenbottom Pot Jan 2006, Coppice Cave–Ling Gill Jan 2006, Bull Pot Jan 2006, James Hall Mine Feb 2006, Peak Cavern Feb 2006, Calf Holes & Brow Gill Cave Feb 2006, Cow Pot [Lancaster] April 2006, November Hole April 2006, Rumbling Hole July 2006, Black Shiver Pot July 2006, Hurnell Moss Pot Oct 2006, Lost John's Hole Sept 2006, Pyrenees Aug 2006, Thistle & Runscar Caves Sept 2006, New Rift Pot Nov 2006, Hunt Pot Nov 2006, Jingling Pot Dec 2006, Nick Pot Dec 2006, Aquamole Pot Jan 2007, Committee Pot Dec 2006, Derbyshire Meet Jan 2007, Dismal Hill/Old Ing Feb 2007, Top Sink-Lancaster Hole Feb 2007, OFD 1 & 2 March 2007, Short Drop/Gavel March 2007, White Scar Cave April 2007, Providence Pot-Dow Cave April 2007, Darnbrook Pot June 2007, Rift Pot July 2007, Ordessa National Park Spanish Pyrenees 2007, High Hull Pot Sept 2007, High Hull Pot Sept 2007, Death's Head & Big Meanie Sept 2007, Washfold Pot Dec 2007, Bar Pot Dec 2007, Long Churns Training Meet Dec 2007, Great Expectations Dec 2007, Bull Pot of the Witches Jan 2008, Dismall Hill-Old Ing Jan 2008, Vesper Pot Jan 2008, Brackenbottom Pot Feb 2008, King Pot Feb 2008, Roger Kirk Caves Feb 2008, Heron Pot [High level route] March 2008, Coppice Cave April 2008, Otter Hole June 2008, Les Arcs Aug 2008, Brackenbottom Pot Oct 2008, Calf Holes/Brow Gill Oct 2008, Lost John's Oct 2008, Cherry Tree Hole Oct 2008, Bull Pot of the Witches Jan 2009, Heron Pot Jan 2009, Simpson's-KMC Dec 2008, Aygill Caverns Jan 2009, Pikedaw Calamina Caverns Feb 2009, Long Kin East March 2009, Peak Cavern April 2009, Titan Shaft April 2009, Lancaster-Wretched Rabbit June 2009, Cwm Dwr-OFD Top Ent June 2009, OFD Top Ent June 2009, Large-Rift Pot Exchange July 2009, Long Churns July 2009, Notts Pot Sept 2009, Link Pot Sept 2009, KMC Sept 2009, Alderley Edge Mines Sept 2009, Roger Kirk Caves Oct 2009, Ireby Fell Caverns Oct 2009, Dowkerbottom Cave Oct 2009, Death's Head Hole Nov 2009, Sell Gill Nov 2009, Aquamole Pot Nov 2009, Pool Sink-Easegill Dec 2009, Sell Gill Dec 2009, Lower Long Churn-Dolly Tubs Jan 2010, Calf Holes [Novice Trip] Jan 2010, Tatham Wife Hole Feb 2010, Croesor-Rhosydd March 2010, Cwmorthin Slate Mine March 2010, Magnetometer Pot April 2010, Hurnell Moss Pot April 2010, Alum Pot July 2010, Daimler Hole Sept 2010, Lost John's-Boxhead Pot Sept 2010, Alum Pot Oct 2010, Hull Pot [Filming with the BBC] Oct 2010, Diccan Pot Oct 2010, Lancaster Hole Oct 2010, Wretched Rabbit x County Pot Nov 2010 , Long Churns [Training Meet] Nov 2010, Rowten Pot Nov 2010, Ireby Fell Cavern Jan 2011, Committee Pot March 2011, Titan-Peak Cavern March 2011, Vesper Pot April 2011, Black Shiver Pot April 2011, Jingling Hole June 2011, Calf Holes-Browgill/Old Ing June 2011, Hunt Pot-Shrapnel Pot June 2011, Death's Head Sept 2011, Long Kin West Oct 2011, New Rift Pot Oct 2011, Swinsto Hole Nov 2011, Hunt Pot-Shrapnel Pot Nov 2011, Aquamole Pot Dec 2011, Jingling Pot Dec 2011, Wretched Rabbit-Lancaster Jan 2012, Simpson's Pot Jan 2012, Wizard's Chasm Jan 2012, Yordas Pot Feb 2012, Notts Pot March 2012, Excalibur Pot March 2012, Juniper Gulf March 2012, Sell Gill March 2012, Swinsto-KMC March 2012, Cullaun 2 April 2012, Pollnagollum April 2012, Hardrawkin Pot April 2012, Sell Gill May 2012, Old Ing/Calf Holes-Browgill [Novice Trip] June 2012, Old Ing/Calf Holes-Browgill [Novice Trip] July 2012, Long Churn-Alum [Novice Trip] July 2012, Boxhead-Lost John's July 2012, White Scar Cave July 2012, Committee Pot Sept 2012, Trou du Garde / Creux de la Cavale - Bauges Aug 2012, Rowten Pot Sept 2012, Little Hull Pot Sept 2012, Croesor Rhosydd [Through] Oct 2012, Brackenbottom Pot Nov 2012, Jingling Pot Nov 2012, Aquamole Pot Dec 2012, Sell Gill Dec 2012, Calf Holes-Browgill Dec 2012, Bull Pot of the Witches Jan 2013, Swinsto-KMC Feb 2013, Notts Pot [Twilight Zone] Feb 2013, Top Sink-Lancaster Hole March 2013, Alum Pot April 2013, Titan-JH April 2013, Illusion Pot June 2013, GB Cave June 2013, Reservoir Hole [The Frozen Deep] June 2013, Short Drop-Gavel Sept 2013, Heron Pot Sept 2013, Hardrawkin Pot Sept 2013, Hurnell Moss Pot Oct 2013, Sell Gill Holes Nov 2013, Mongo Gill Nov 2013, Boxhead-

Cracker Feb 2014, Greenside Mine April 2014, Bore Hole-Boudary Pot May 2014, White Scar Cave July 2014, Dowkabottom Cave July 2014, Fairy Holes Sept 2014, Nenthead Mines Sept 2014, Shuttleworth Pot Oct 2014, Mistral Hole Nov 2014, Aquamole Dec 2014, Bull Pot of the Witches Jan 2015, Pasture Gill Jan 2015, County Pot Feb 2015, Link Pot March 2015, Simpson's Pot May 2015, Sunset Hole July 2015, Robinson's Pot July 2015, Lost John's-Notts 2 Sept 2015, Sell Gill Holes Sept 2015, Alderley Edge Mines Oct 2015,Water Icicle Oct 2015, Heron Pot Nov 2015, Alum-Diccan Pot Nov 2015, Boulby Potash Mine Jan 2016, KMC/Toyland Feb 2016, Lost John's-Boxhead Pot March 2016, Wretched Rabbit-County Pot April 2016, County Pot-Boundary Pot April 2016, Meregill Hole May 2016, Hole May 2016, Voldemort-Committee Pot July 2016, Death's Head-Big Meanie Sept 2016, County Pot-Pool Sink Oct 2016, Croesor Rhysydd Through Trip Oct 2016, Simpson's Pot-KMC Dec 2016, Marble Steps Nov 2016, Bull Pot of the Witches Jan 2017, Bull Pot Feb 2017, Short Drop-Gavel Pot March 2017, Black Shiver May 2017, KMC May 2017, Devis Hole/Mine July 2017, Alum/Long Churns June 2017, Sunset Hole [Novice trip] Sept 2017, Short Drop-Gavel Pot Nov 2017, Lancaster Hole Oct 2017, Brackenbottom Pot Dec 2017,Jingling Pot/Bull Pot [CPC joint trip] April 2018, Darnbrook Pot June 2018, Stump Cross Cavertns July 2018, Long Churns & BorrinsMoor Sept 2018, Alum Pot Oct 2018, Ingleborough Cave Oct 2018, Death's Head Nov 2018, Vulcan Pot Oct 2018, Calf Holes-Browgill Cave Nov 2018, Bull Pot of the Witches Jan 2019, Pikedaw Calamine Cavern Dec 2018, County-Lancaster Jan 2019, Committee Pot Feb 2019,Wretched Rabbit-County Pot March 2019, Sunset Hole April 2019, Lancaster-Easegill June 2019, Kirkby Lonsdale-Wharton Walking Meet Sept 2019, Bull Pot Oct 2019, Sell Gill Nov 2019, Aquamole Pot Nov 2019, Bullpot Jan 2020, Pool Sink-Wretched Rabbit Feb 2020.

DE VILLE, Tyrrian J; J2011, b1972,
Probationary Meets; Upper & Lower Long Churns, Calf Holes, Browgill, Runscar Caves.
Newsletter References; Committee Pot March 2011, Cautley-Kirkby Stephen Walk Sept 2011, Yordas Pot Oct 2011, Sell Gill Holes March 2012, Poll Dugh April 2012, Cullaun 2 April 2012, Skosca Cave Feb 2013, President's Meet Ribchester Walk June 2014, Roundthwaite Common-Borrowdale Sept 2014, Sunset Hole [Novice trip] Sept 2017.

DEWISON, Jack; J2018, b1994,
Member; SUSS.
Newsletter References; High Douk May 2019.

DIAHI, K; J1953,

DICKINSON, Donald; AKA: Dick. J1948,
Resigned 1954.
Bulletin References; Bar Pot Feb 1951, Bull Pot of the Witches April 1951, Bar Pot April 1952,

DICKSON, William Basil; J1950,
Bulletin References; Little Hull Hole Oct 1955, Clapham Cave Aug 1955, Stream Passage Pot June 1958, Gaping Gill Meet 1960.
Newsletter References; Simpson's Pot Aug 1957, Involved with BBC Transmission from Alum Pot May 1958.

DIXON, David Robert; J2005, b1974,
Re-joined 2011.
Newsletter References; Heron Pot Nov 2005, Brackenbottom Pot Jan 2006, Dismal Hill-Old Ing Jan 2006, Jackpot P8 Feb 2006, Peak Cavern Feb 2006, Calf Holes & Brow Gill Cave Feb 2006, Tatham Wife Hole March 2006, Hunt Pot Nov 2006, Photographic Weekend Oct 2006, Mistral Hole Aug 2010, Illusion Pot Dec 2011.

DIXON, Kevin; J2013, b1965,
Probationary Meets; GG08, GG14, Corky's Pot, Stream Passage Pot, Long Henslers, Booth Parsons-Long Henslers, Queensbury Pot [Inc Avens], Northern Line..
Member; YUCPC, CPC.
Famous for; 3D Scanning survey of GG.
Newsletter References; Providence Pot Restoration Nov 2014, Clapham Bottoms [Survey] Feb 2015, Bar Pot [Photographic Trip] March 2015, Bar Pot [Graveyard Inlet Surveying] Jan 2016, GG Track repairs Feb 2017, Rat Hole May 2017, Nick Gymer rescue CPC winch meet Aug 2017, North West Extension Aug 2017, Mallorca [Broken ligament] Feb 2018, Dawn Chamber GG May 2017, Ingleborough Cave [Surveying] May 2018, Spout Tunnel May 2019, Ingleborough Cave Circus Rift Sept 2019, Far Waters Nov 2019.

DIXON, Peter; J1981, b1954,
Probationary Meets; Gouffre Berger, Swinsto, Notts Pot.
Bulletin References; Gouffre Berger Aug 1980,
Newsletter References; Gouffre Berger Aug 1980, Lost John's Nov 1980, Peak Cavern [Swine Hole Dive] Nov 1980, Swinsto-KMC Jan 1981, Lancaster-County Pot Nov 1980.

DIXON, Roy Cecil; J1959, b1934, d2004.
Rejoined 1986.
Founder member of WRCPC.

Main Activities; Caving, Climbing, walking.
Notable Achievements; Climbed many of the high Austrian Peaks.
Bulletin References; Pen-y-ghent Pot 1961, Lancaster Easegill 1966.
Newsletter References; *Clapham Cave Oct 1959, Little Hull Hole Aug 1959, Leader Dowber Gill Passage Oct 1960, Bradford Mine shaft collapses Aug 1965, Ireby Fell Nov 1965.*

DOBBY, J. L; *J1983,*

DOBSON, Bryan Edgar; AKA: Moose. *J1953, b1932, d1957.*
First Aid box in Dump and modified Neil Robertson stretcher bought by his memorial fund.
Bulletin References; *Simpson's Pot July 1953, Notts Pot Sept 1953, Flood Entrance Pot March 1954, Old Ing Caves Aug 1954, Marble Steps Nov 1954, Bull Pot of the Witches July 1955, Little Hull Hole Oct 1955, Jackdaw Hole & Pen-y-Ghent Long Churn Nov 1955, Clapham Cave Aug 1955, Christmas Pot 1957.*
Newsletter References; *Leader Meregill Camp Aug 1955, Rumbling Hole Oct 1957, Lancaster Hole Oct 1957, Practice stretcher rescue Wade's entrance GG Nov 1957, Dow-Providence rescue Dec 1957, Bar Pot Dec 1957, Calf Holes & Browgill Sept 1957.*

DOBSON, Howard; *J Before 1938,*

DOBSON, Richard; AKA: Dick. *J1960, b1944,*
Probationary Meets; Lost John's, Clapham Cave, Long Kin East.
Bulletin References; *Flood Entrance Pot Dec 1960, Lost John's March 1961, Gaping Gill 1961, Pen-y-Ghent pot 1961, Jockey Hole Feb 1962, Stream Passage Pot June 1962, Long Kin West July 1962, Sell Gill July 1962, Rowten Pot & Jingling Pot Nov 1962, Juniper Gulf Dec 1962, Notts Pot Oct 1963, Ireby Fell Cavern April 1964.*

DODSWORTH, Andrew; *J2014, b1967,*

DODSWORTH, Connor Mathew; *J2014, b2006,*

DOUGLAS, Geoffrey; *J1985, b1948,*
Bulletin References; *36 Parmilan Plateau Sept 1990, Deep Well [Diving support] May 1992, Gouffre Berger Aug 1992, Gingling Hole June 1983, Pippikin Pot Oct 1989, Langstroth Pot & Cave [Diving] July 1989, South Wales Dec 1990, Sell Gill Training Meet Nov 1991, Dan Yr Ogof June 1991, Gouffre Berger Aug 1992, Lakes Meet June 1992, Simpson's-Swinsto March 1994, Swinsto-Simpson's 1996, Walking Meet Sept 1997, Nent Head-Brewery Shaft Oct 1998, Dufton–Garrigill Lakes*

Walk Sept 2005, Granett Bridge To ShapWalk Sept 2006, Ulverston-Coniston Walking Meet 2007, Lambrigg Fell-Tebay Walk Sept 2008, Cautley-Kirkby Stephen Walk Sept 2011, Crosby Ravensworth-Askham Walking Meet Sept 2012, Roundthwaite Common to Borrowdale Sept 2014, Walking Meet 2015, New Biggin on Lune to Appleby Walking Meet Sept 2016, Lindale-Greenodd Walking Meet 2017, Cow Green Reservoir–Appleby Walking Meet 2018, Kirkby Lonsdale-Wharton Walking Meet Sept 2019.

DOUGLAS, Robert; *J2018,*
Probationary Meets; Lancaster Hole-Wretched Rabbit, Cupcake, Pool Sink-Boundary Pot.
Newsletter References; *Wizard's Chasm Dec 2018, Calf Holes-Browgill Cave Nov 2018, Lancaster Hole-Wretched Rabbit Nov 2018, Bull Pot of the Witches Jan 2019, Pikedaw Calamine Cavern Dec 2018, Great Douk Jan 2019, Long Churns Feb 2019, Cow Pot March 2019, County Pot-Lancaster Hole June 2019, Bull Pot Oct 2019, Pool Sink-Boundary Pot Nov 2019.*

DOUGLAS, Stephen John; *J1993, b1972,*

DOUGLAS, Valmai Reynolds; [née Williams] *J1991, b1941,*
Probationary Meets; GG91, Stream Passage, Bar Pot, Lancaster-Wretched Rabbit, OFD.
Bulletin References; *Deep Well [Diving support] May 1992, Gouffre Berger Aug 1992, South Wales Dec 1990, Sell Gill Training Meet Nov 1991.*
Newsletter References; *Dan Yr Ogof June 1991, Gouffre Berger Aug 1992, Lakes Meet June 1992, Simpson's-Swinsto March 1994, Swinsto-Simpson's 1996, Walking Meet Sept 1997, Nent Head-Brewery Shaft Oct 1998, Dufton–Garrigill Lakes Walk Sept 2005, Granett Bridge To ShapWalk Sept 2006, Ulverston-Coniston Walking Meet 2007, Lambrigg Fell–Tebay Walk Sept 2008, Cautley-Kirkby Stephen Walk Sept 2011, Crosby Ravensworth-AskhamWalking Meet Sept 2012, Roundthwaite Common to Borrowdale Sept 2014, Walking Meet 2015, Lindale-Greenodd Walking Meet 2017, Cow Green Reservoir–Appleby Walking Meet 2018, Kirkby Lonsdale-Wharton Walking Meet Sept 2019.*

DOWNTON, Alan; *J1990, b1963,*
Probationary Meets; Ireby Fell.
Member; BEC, CDG.
Bulletin References; *Mosquito Plane [Midge Hole Support/ exploration] 1991, Soca Valley [Diving] Aug 1990, Ireby Fell March 1990.*

DRACUP, Charles William; *J1963, b1946, d198?*

Climbing partner to Roger Sutcliffe.
Bulletin References; *Notts Pot Oct 1963, Pen-y-Ghent Long Churn Nov 1963, The Fellsman Hike May 1963.*

DRAKE, Keith William; *J1953, b1932,*
Bulletin References; *Juniper Gulf May 1954, Old Ing Caves Aug 1954.*

DRAPER, A;

DREW, S; *J1981,*

DRIFFILL, Peter Royston; *J1951, b1929,*
Bulletin References; *Lost John's July 1951, Bull Pot June 1952.*

DUCK, Colin; Temporary Membership.

DUCKHAM, Andrew Frederick; *J1949,*
Bulletin References; *Quaking Pot April 1950, Bull Pot of the Witches Aug 1950, Sunset Hole Oct 1950, Bar Pot Feb 1951, Easter Camp GG 1951, Bull Pot of the Witches April 1951, Lost John's July 1951, Rowten Pot June 1951, Bar Pot April 1952.*

DUCKWORTH, Andrew John; *J1988, b1968,*
Probationary Meets; Pippikin, Stream-Bar, Lancaster-Wretched Rabbit, Pool Sink-WR, Alum Pot, Notts Pot, Gingling Pot, GG Short & Mud Henslers.

DUCKWORTH, Kevin John; AKA: Buzzy. *J1993, b1946, d2001.*
Probationary Meets; Gouffre Berger, GG92, Lancaster.
Bulletin References; *Gouffre Berger Aug 1992, Losers Pot [Discovery] Mar 2002, Hensler's Pot [Discovery] 1999-2003.*
Newsletter References; *Gouffre Berger Aug 1992, Lakes Meet June 1992, Easgill Aug 1997, Nent Head-Brewery Shaft Oct 1998, Grange Rigg [Surface Locating] March 1999, Fat Finger Millennium Party.*

DUDLEY, Steven Charles; AKA: Duds. *J1973, b1953,*
Probationary Meets; Magnetometer Pot, Lost John's, Pasture Gill.
Bulletin References; *Otter Hole 1977, Coast to Coast Plus July/Aug 1978, Soca Valley [Diving] Aug 1990.*
Newsletter References; *Magnetometer Pot Sept 1973, Pasture Gill Feb 1974, Lost John's Hole Aug 1974, Tatham Wife March 1975, Meregill April 1975, Birks Fell Cave April 1975, County Pot Oct 1975, Lost John's Nov 1975, Short Drop–Gavel Pot*

1976, Pasture Gill Cave July 1976, Lost John's September 1976, Pippikin Pot Nov 1976, Lakes Walk Esk House March 1977, Short Drop–Gavel Dec 1977, Rumbling Hole Aug 1978, Lost John's Sept 1978, Boreham Cave [Diving Support] March 1980, Scrafton Pot April 1980, Pasture Gill Cave Sept 1980, Ibbeth Peril Oct 1980, Gavel Pot Dec 1980, Ingleborough Cave [Dive Support] Jan 1981, Lancaster–County Pot Sept 1981, Pippikin Pot Oct 1981, Kingsdale Photographic meet April 1982, Birks Fell Cave July 1982, Hallucination Aven–Induction Location May 1983, South Wales Aug 1983, Giant's Hole Sept 1983, Peak Cavern Sept 1983, Langstroth Pot March 1984, Gunnerside Gill Lead Mines June 1985, Gingling Hole Oct 1985, New Rift Pot Jan 1986, South Wales Nov 1988, Birks Fell Cave July 1991, Grange Rigg-Christmas Pot March 1993, Easegill Caverns March 1993,

DUFTON, Christopher James; *J1955, b1935,*
BPC President 1980-84.
Bulletin References; *Bull Pot of the Witches July 1955, Little Hull Hole Oct 1955, Christmas Pot 1957, Clapham Cave Aug 1955, Clapham Cave Sept 1956, Clapham Cave March 1957, Clapham Cave Aug 1957, Clapham Cave Dec 1957, Gaping Gill Meet 1960, Lost John's March 1961, Involved with BBC transmission from Alum Pot 7th May 1961, Pen-y-ghent Pot 1961, Christmas Pot 1962, Helvelyn Dec 1965, Tete Sauvage July 1995, Gouffre Berger Aug 1992.*
Newsletter References; *Leader Calamine Shaft Aug 1956, Leader Dow Cave Nov 1956, Newby Moss Hole May 1957, Washfold Pot July 1957, Simpson's Pot Aug 1957, Swinsto Sept 1957, Rumbling Hole Oct 1957, Lancaster Hole Oct 1957, Practice stretcher rescue Wade's entrance GG Nov 1957, Private meet Clapham Cave Nov 1957, Dow-Providence rescue Dec 1957, Bar Pot Dec 1957, Leader Stump Cross Jan 1958, Main Shaft to detackle Disappointment via Hensler's crawl [Hensler star] Whit 1958, Involved with BBC Transmission from Alum Pot May 1958, Lancaster Hole June 1958, Tackle testing July 1958, Alum Pot Aug 1958, Dow Cave Sept 1958, Disappointment Pot [Photographic trip] Oct 1958, Inauguration Aven July 1959, Diccan–Alum Exchange September 1959, Whernside Walk Feb 1976, Alum Pot June 1980, Lost John's Nov 1980, Gavel Pot Dec 1980, Notts Pot Jan 1981, Eden Valley-Teesdale Walking Meet Oct 1985, Scotland 1987, Calf Holes Jan 1988, Lakes Walk Sept 1990, Gouffre Berger Aug 1992, Ireby Fell Feb 1993, Land's End–John O Groats Charity Cycle Ride-2006.*

DUNS, Bruce Stuart; *J1960, b1940,*

Probationary Meets; GG60, Ribblehead Caves, Alum Pot.

DUXBURY, Andrew John; *J1999, b1960,*
Probationary Meets; GG99.
Member; YRC, Fell & Rock Climbing Club.

DUXBURY, John Stephen; *J2017, b1970,*
Probationary Meets; Alum Pot, Hurtle, Jingle, Midge [Dives]
Member; UKMC.
Newsletter References; *Old Ing-Birkwith July 2017, Top Sink-Wretched Rabbit Jan 2018, High Douk Holes Feb 2018, Jingling Pot/Bull Pot [CPC joint trip] April 2018, Alum Pot Oct 2018, Mongo Gill Sept 2018, Oxlow-Maskhill Mine Oct 2018, Wretched Rabbit-Lancaster Hole Dec 2018, Bull Pot of the Witches Jan 2019, Pikedaw Calamine Cavern Dec 2018.*

DWYER, John D; *J1982,*
Newsletter References; *KMC Photographic Meet April 1982, Jingling Pot Feb 2018,*

DWYER, Stephanie; *J2010, b1984,*
Re-joined 2016 + 2019.
Bulletin Reference; *Foul Pot Nov 2011.*
Newsletter References; *Ireland May 2010, Bull Pot Oct 2010, Pillar Holes Oct 2010, Rowten Pot Nov 2010, Lancaster-Wretched Rabbit Jan 2011,Titan-Peak Cavern March 2011, Hunt Pot-Shrapnel Exchange April 2011, Illusion Pot June 2011, Foul Pot Nov 2011, Pollnagollum April 2012, Marble Arch [Diving-Vickers Choke] Easter 2012.*

DYSON, Neil Ross; AKA: Ladybird. *J1962, b1944,*
Probationary Meets; Calf Holes, Marble Steps, Goyden Pot.
Bulletin References; *South Wales Easter 1963, Three Peaks Dec 1963, The Fellsman Hike May 1963, Yugoslavia 1964, Four Inns Walking Competition April 1965, Lyke Wake Walk June 1965, Grotte Hercules [Morocco] 1966, Kilnsey to*

Brackenbottom 1966, Lyke Wake Walk Dec 1968, Peak Marathon Walk 1969, Jenny Twig and her daughter Tib [Two Grit Pillars] 1969, Rather Standard Walk 1970, Investigating Grayrigg Sinks 1970, Lions Head [South Africa] 1972, Mount Malanje [Africa] 1972, The Dales Way 1973, Kendal Charter Walk 1975, Cnoc Nan Uamh & Uamh Nan Claig-Ionn Easter 1978, Weekend Ramble No 16, Peakland Hundred May 1980, Mallerstang Marathon 1984, The North York Moors Crosses Walk 1985, Kielder Forest Festival Event 1991, Mount Baker USA 1992, A'Mhaighjdean May 1994, Glenkiln 1994, Beinn Mheadhoin 1995, Seana Bhraigh May 2011.
Newsletter References; *Lakes Walking Meet Nov 1969, Heron Pot March 1971, Crackpot Cave March 1971, Birks Fell April 1971, Tatham Wife Hole Aug 1971, Grange Rigg–Christmas Pot Jan 1972, Gingling Hole Aug 1972, Rowten Pot Dec 1972, Giants Hole Nov 1974, Lakes Walk Esk House March 1977, Short Drop–Gavel Dec 1977, Uamh nan Claig-ionn April 1979, Kingsdale Photographic meet April 1982, Smallcleugh Mine Aug 1989, Crooklands WalkingMeet Sept 1993, Lakes Walking Meet Sept 1995, Walking Meet Sept 1997, Lancaster Canal Walk Meet 2001, Millenium Walk Sept 2002, Black Combe-Foxfield Walk Sept 2003, Walking Meet Sept 2004, Dufton–Garrigill Lakes Walk Sept 2005,Granett Bridge To ShapWalk Sept 2006, Ulverston-Coniston Walking Meet 2007, Lambrigg Fell–Tebay Walk Sept 2008, Dunsop Bridge-Bilsborrow Walking Meet Sept 2009, Walking Meet Orton-Kirkby Thore Sept 2010, Cautley-Kirkby Stephen Walk Sept 2011, Crosby Ravensworth-Askham Walking Meet Sept 2012, President's Meet Ribblesdale Walk June 2014, Roundthwaite Common to Borrowdale Sept 2014, Walking Meet 2015, New Biggin on Lune to Appleby Walking Meet Sept 2016, Lindale-Greenodd Walking Meet 2017, Cow Green Reservoir–Appleby Walking Meet 2018, Kirkby Lonsdale-Wharton Walking Meet Sept 2019.*

26

EASTON, Edward; *J2005, b1944,*
Probationary Meets; Balls Digging Team 17 trips 2004/5.
Member; MPC, NB.
Bulletin References; *Pay Sank [Discovery] 2005, Klondike Pot Digging/Exploration 2004-2007, Restoration of Brown Hill Pot entrance Nov 2012-Feb 2013, Restoration of Clapham Bottoms Pot Entrance June 2013.*
Newsletter References; *Klondyke Pot Digging Team Jan 2005, Pay Sank breakthrough team Nov 2005, Gunnerfleet Caves Clear Up July 2009, Long Churn May 2010, Rebuild of stile at Browgill July 2010, Yordas Cave Conserervation Aug 2010, Dig Capping Nov 2010, Yordas Pot Feb 2012, Yeadon Tarn [Artificial Cave] Nov 2013, Scoska Cave April 2014, Hardrawkin Pot Fencing Conservation 2014, Bore Hole-Boudary Pot May 2014, Providence Pot Restoration Nov 2014.*

EASTON, Kay; *J2011, b1953,*
Member; MPC, NB.
Probationary Meets; Churns, Dowkabottom, Old Ing.
Bulletin References; *Restoration of Brown Hill Pot entrance Nov 2012-Feb 2013.*
Newsletter References; *Gunnerfleet Caves Clear Up July 2009, Long Churn May 2010, Rebuild of stile at Browgill July 2010, Yordas Cave Conserervation Aug 2010, Ribblehead Caves Jan 2012, Yeadon Tarn [Artificial Cave] Nov 2013, Scoska Cave April 2014, Hardrawkin Pot Fencing Conservation 2014, Providence Pot Restoration Nov 2014.*

EASTWOOD, Ben; *J1946,*
Bulletin References; *On first recorded caving trip after WW2, Rift Pot April 7th 1946, MereGill 7th Sept 1947, Birks Cave May 1948,*

EASTWOOD, Harry; *J1955, b1939,*
Bulletin References; *Little Hull Hole Oct 1955.*

EASTWOOD, James Bernard; *J1951, b1914,*

EATON, Annie; *J2017, b1992,*
Probationary Meets; Brackenbottom Pot, Alum Pot, KMC.
Newsletter References; *North West Extension Aug 2017.*

EAVES, Beverley Susan; *J1981, b1958,*
Probationary Meets; New Goyden, Magnetometer, Link Pot.

ECCLES, Jack; *J1966,*
Newsletter References; *Goyden Pot March 1981, Alum Pot March 1981, Lower Long Churn March 1981, Sell Gill Hole April 1981, Link Pot Sept 1981, Pippikin Pot Oct 1981, Lost John's Feb 1982, Ingleborough Cave Oct 1982, Scotland 1987.*

EDWARDS, Gareth J.E; *J2010, b1979,*
Member; SWCC, MUSC, SUI.
Bulletin References; *Reseau de la Pierre Saint Martin Aug 2013, Doubs, France Aug 2009.*
Newsletter References; *Magnetometer Pot April 2010, Blue John Aug 2012, Dow Cave Oct 2012, Fells End Pots Feb 2013.*

EDWARDS, John; *J1979, b1956,*
Probationary Meets; Otter Hole, Fighiera Italy, County-Lancaster, Notts Pot.
Member; NCCC [1974-1979]
Active on club and private meets in 70's, 80's & 90's
Club Expeditions; Abissa Fighiera 1979 [See Section 2], Jura-Doubs [Ornans] Grotte Sarrazine, Chauveroche, Diau system, Gouffre Des Biefs Boussets, Baume Des Cretes etc. 1985 & 1987 & 1991, Tan de Belle Espoir/Diau 1986, 3β [Parmilan Plateau] weekend trip 1988, Vercours France 1989 [Christian Gathier, Scialet de L'Appel, Gournier, Trou qui Souffle etc.] Tanne de Belle Espoir-Grotte de la Diau 1991, Organised British Caving Expedition to Albania 1992. Reseau de La Pierre Saint Martin, Pyrenees Tete Sauvage 1995.
Other Expeditions; Organised rafting trip down Alaskan Yukon 1994. Organised expedition to the Ice caves of Patagonia 1997/8 [*Moulins in Glacier Grey-Chile*]
Notable Achievements; BPC Committee member 1992-1996 and Secretary 1994 & 5. Conceived and edited this book, BPC Calendars and Pillock of the year awards [Made the figure of 4 descender as the original award [Now lost, in S. Kelly's house]- Half the weight, half the price, half as good] Initiated the Robinson's adventure weekends, involved with Wilky's mountain biking underground photo shoot. Found a large warm pool full of naked young ladies in a lava tube in Iceland June/July 1981.
Main Activities; Caving, walking and a bit of climbing in early days. New route to name-Hairy Crack, Odin Rake Derbyshire [Now destroyed]
Famous for; Having a ladder break 40' up Lancaster entrance pitch [Not a BPC ladder] Surviving a grizzly bear attack at night - Mature female [10 feet tall] charged after we unavoidably got between her and her cub, we were only seconds away from a wolf pack attack when we escaped the bear-Alaska 1995. Obliviously carrying boxes of beer with Jim Abbott down the street in Ornans and ignoring crouching armed policemen gesturing us over. We were unaware that there was an armed bank robbery in progress on the other side of the road; we were eventually bungled off the road by an armed SWAT team [1985] Turning Dan Yr Ogof Bakerloo streamway red after a brief interface with underwater flake and right knee.
Bulletin References; *Abbisa Fighiera 1979, Trou De Glaz [No Recollection of this] Aug 1989, Albania 1992, Alum/Long Churn on Mountain Bikes Dec 1994, Alaska 1995, Tete Sauvage July 1995, Ice Caves of Patagonia 1997/8.*

Newsletter References; *Abbissa Fighiera Italy Aug 1979, Lancaster Hole [Maple Leaf Pitch Team] in flood 1980, Alum Pot June 1980, Jingling Pot March 1981, Little Hull Pot [Dive Support] Oct 1981, Ingleborough Cave Oct 1982, Meregill Feb 1983, Hurnel Moss Pot July 1983, Nettle Pot Sept 1983, Peak Cavern Sept 1983, Heron Pot Jan 1985, Eldon Hole & Oxlow Caverns Oct 1990, Ireby Fell Jan 1992, Derbyshire Meet Sept 1999.*

EDWARDS, Paul David; *J1978, b1954,*
Probationary Meets; France 1977, Lost John's, GG79.
Bulletin References; *Grotte de Bury 1977, Gouffre Berger Aug 1980, 3B Parmilan Plateau Sept 1990,*
Newsletter References; *Douk Ghyll May 1979, Slasher Hole extension [Dug/explored]Aug 1978, Pen-y-Ghent Pot July 1980, Gouffre Berger Aug 1980, Keay Hole Feb 1981, Tatham Wife Hole Feb 1983.*

EDWARDS, Peter Martin; *J1998, b1981,*
Probationary Meets; GG87-98, Grotte de Gournier, Stream Passage Pot., PSM [Salle Verna], Carlswalk Cavern.
Main activities: Climbing, Winter mountaineering, Biking, Caving.
Famous for; Escaping a lightning storm near top of the Diamond on Longs Peak at ~4000m via simul ab to sit under boulder drinking whiskey until storm passed.
Club Expeditions; PSM [Salle Verna] 1995.
Other Expeditions; Bloody Sunday E4 6a (Huntsman's leap, Pembroke); Cruel sister E3 5c (Pavey Ark, Lakes); Widowmaker E3 5c (Mowingword, Pembroke); Wendigo E2 5b (Red Walls, Gogarth); Pervertical Sanctuary 5.11a (The Diamond, Longs Peak, Co); Chouinard-Herbert 5.11c (Sentinal Rock, Yosemite); Lightning Bolt Cracks 5.11 (North Six Shooter, Indian Creek, Utah); Southern Arete 5.10+ R (Black Canyon of the Gunnison, Co); Contamine Route TD 6a+ (Mont Blanc du Tacul); Poachers fall V 5 (Liathach, Torridon); Nordwand direct IV 5 (Ben Nevis); All Mixed Up WI IVR (Thatchtop, Co).

EGAN, Chris; *J2009, b1968,*

EGAN, Joe; *J2007, b1986,*
Probationary Meets; KMC, Ireby Fell, Mallorca, GG08, Brackenbottom Pot, Notts Pot.
Bulletin References; *Mallorca Dec 2007.*
Newsletter References; *Ireby Fell Caverns [A grand day out-digging Whirlpool] Feb 2008, Brackenbottom Pot Digging Feb 2008, Notts Pot March 2008, Helwith Bridge Show 2008, Roaring Hole [Diving Support] May 2010, Hardrawkin Pot*

May 2010, Hull Pot [Filming with the BBC] Oct 2010, Bull Pot Oct 2010, Pillar Holes Oct 2010, Long Churns [Training Meet] Nov 2010.

ELLERTON, Peter Stuart; *J1963, b1947,*
Probationary Meets; Alum Pot, Sunset Hole, Goyden Pot.
Resigned Sept 1965, dispute over club getting a loan to buy Brackenbottom.

ELLIOT, David; *J2003, b1946,*

ELLIOT, John Raymond; *J1989, b1949,*
Probationary Meets; Mongo Gill, Ireby Fell, Snatchers, Pool Sink, BPOTW, GG89, Marble Steps, Meregill, Birks Fell, Trou de Glaz.
Bulletin References; *Brackenbottom Pot, [Dig/exploration]1989, Trou De Glaz Aug 1989, Dig above Hagg Gill Pot 1991, Sludge Cave [Discovery] Aug 1993.*
Newsletter References; *Pool Sink-Cow Pot March 1989, Big Meanie-Death's Head Nov 1989, New Rift Pot Feb 1990, Grange Rigg March 1990, Grange Rigg-Christmas Pot March 1993, Bagshaw Caverns Oct 1993, Peak Cavern Nov 1995.*

ELLIOT, Richard Alexander; AKA: Handwound. *J1960, b1941,*
Dick used the handle to manually bring the chair up after an engine failure and earned his nickname Handwound [GG61]
Probationary Meets; Easegill, Bull Pot, Lost John's.
Bulletin References; *Gaping Gill Meet 1960, Lost John's March 1961, GG61, Stonelands Pot June 1961.*

ELLIS, Richard William; AKA: Dick. *J1987, b1945,*
Probationary Meets; Magnetometer Pot, Dan Yr Ogof, Ogof Craig y Fynnon.
Member; White Rose CPC 1962-5, NCC 1965-9, HWCPC 1969-73, NCC 1979-87.
Entered Big Plonka on application form as a medical condition.
Newsletter References; *Magnetometer Pot Oct 1987, South Wales Nov 1988, Photographic Weekend Oct 2006.*

ELOY, Michael; *J1998, b1975,*
Probationary Meets; GG98, Nettle Pot, Fat Finger.
Member of a French Club [?]

ELSWORTH, Alan; *J1961, b1943,*
Probationary Meets; Easegill Caverns, Lost John's, Notts Pot, Magnetometer Pot.

EMMETT, John Barry; AKA: Barry. *J1972, b1940,*

Probationary Meets; Outsleets Beck, Birks Fell Cave, GG72, Heron Pot.
Bulletin References; *Chourum Des Aiguilles 1973.*

EMSAL, David;
Newsletter References; *Sunset Hole May 1976.*

EPTON, Christopher; AKA: Tigger. *J2011, b1985,*
Newsletter References; *Long Churn [Novice Trip] June 2011, Calf Holes-Browgill/Old Ing June 2011, Hunt Pot-Shrapnel Pot June 2011, Death's Head Sept 2011, Robinson's Pot Oct 2011, Sunset Hole Oct 2011, Swinsto Hole Nov 2011, Yordas Pot Oct 2011, Hunt Pot-Shrapnel Pot Nov 2011, Lancaster-Wretched Rabbit Nov 2011, Aquamole Pot Dec 2011, Sell Gill March 2012, Jingling Pot Nov 2012, Wizard's Chasm Jan 2013.*

EVANS, Nicholas John; AKA: Knobbly Norbert. *J2010, b1953,*
Probationary Meets; GG08, GG09, GG10, GG11, Stream Passage Pot, Bar Pot, Corky's.
Member; ULSA, LUSS, VMC.
Other Expeditions; Vercors [ULSA], Treviso [LUSS] 1981.
Newsletter References; *KMC & Bar Pot [Blind Novice Trips] May 2011, Wizard's Chasm Jan 2013, Illusion Pot March 2013, Sunset Hole [Novice trip] Sept 2017, KMC [Novice Trip] Jan 2018.*

EYRE, David; *J1976, b1957,*
Probationary Meets; County Pot, Cherry Tree Hole, Birks Fell.
Newsletter References; *County Pot Aug 1976.*

50

F

FAIRCLOUGH, Helen; *J2019, b1993,*
Probationary Meets; GG18, Henslers, Marylin, Cow Pot, Hammer Pot, Far Waters, Tresviso.
Member; DCRO, SUSS.
Newsletter References; *Hells Bells Hole [Dive Support] Feb 2020.*

FARLEY, Derrik Gordon; *J1953, b1933,*
Bulletin References; *June 1951, Simpson's Pot July 1953.*

FARNSWORTH, Mark David; *J2000, b1964,*
Probationary Meets; County-Lancaster, Sell Gill, Alum Pot.

FARRAR, John David; *J1957, b1940,*
[Not of Clapham]
Newsletter Rerferences; *Simpson's Pot Aug 1957, Swinsto Sept 1957, Lancaster Hole Oct 1957, Bar Pot May 1958, Lancaster Hole June 1958.*

FARRER [MCQUAT], Jane;
Elected Honarary Member 2017.

FARRER, John Anson [Dr]; AKA: Doc. *J1960's b1921, d2014.*
Elected Honarary Member 1960's.

FARRER, John Peter [Dr]; *J1968, b1948, d2016.*
Elected Honarary Member 2015.
Bulletin References; *Lancaster Hole Jan 1966.*

FARRER, Annie; *J2017, b1948,*
Elected Honarary Member 2017.

FARTINGTON, Keith; *J1987,*

FAULKNER, Kathleen; [née O'Brien] *J1971, b1948,*
Probationary Meets; Easegill, GG70, Disappointment Pot.
Newsletter References: *Lancaster–Easegill Feb 1969, Heron Pot March 1971, Crackpot Cave March 1971.*

FAULKNER, Paul George; *J1992, b1975,*
Probationary Meets; President;'s Meets 1988-92.

FAULKNER, Peter George; AKA: Boots, Hier Flick. *J1960, b1940,*
BPC President 1999 & 2000.
Probationary Meets; Lost John's, Alum Pot, Lancaster-Easegill.
Notable Achievements: Being at the heart of the club, at the Dump, in committee and actively for over 50 years.
Famous for; Being teleported naked to a stranger's front room after a session in the Queen's Arms at Littondale. Innocently exposing himself to a group of girl guides whilst asleep. Greeting new visitors to the Dump wearing just his string underwear and asking "Who the F*#K are You?"
Club Expeditions; Chourum Des Aiguilles 1973/74, Piaggia Bella 1975, Grotte de Bury 1976/77, Gouffre Berger 1980.
Other Expeditions; Maritime Alps BPC/RRCPC 1962, Provatina Abyss 1967.
Bulletin References; *Bull Pot Sept 1960, Pen-y-ghent pot 1961, Long Kin West July 1962, Maritime Alps BPC/RRCPC trip July/Aug 1962, Cat Hole [Extension] Oct 1963, Pen-y-Ghent Pot Extensions Oct 1963, Pen-y-ghent Pot Feb 1964, Provatina Abyss July/Aug 1967, Chourum Des Aiguilles 1973, Chourum Des Aiguilles 1974, Piaggia Bella 1975,*

Grotte de Bury 1976 & 1977, Gouffre Berger Aug 1980.

Newsletter References; *Grange Rigg-Christmas Aug 1965,* Lancaster-Easegill Feb 1969, *Rumbling Hole Oct 1969, Lancaster Hole Nov 1970, Crackpot Cave March 1971, Bull Pot March 1971, Grange Rigg-Christmas Pot Jan 1972, Swinsto Hole –KMC June 1972, Little Neath River Cave June 1973, Agen Allwedd Mar 1974,* Chourum des Aiguilles [BP] July 1974, *Lost John's Hole Aug 1974, Gingling Hole Sept 1974, Juniper Gulf Dec 1974, Flood Entrance-Stream Passage Pot Exchange Feb 1975, Meregill April 1975, Lost John's September 1976, Rumbling Hole Dec 1976, Lakes Walk Esk House March 1977 [Pete's Dog Sam refused to go to the top and had to be found shelter from the wind] Lakes Walk Esk House March 1977, Top Sink-Pool Sink Sept 1977, Short Drop-Gavel Dec 1977, Cherry Tree Hole July 1978, Rumbling Hole Aug 1978, Alum Pot June 1980, Gouffre Berger Aug 1980, Eden Valley-Teesdale Walking Meet Oct 1985, Scotland 1987, Crooklands WalkingMeet Sept 1993, Lakes Walking Meet Sept 1995, Walking Meet Sept 1997, Lancaster Canal Walk Meet 2001, Millennium Walk Sept 2002, Dufton-Garrigill Lakes Walk Sept 2005, Granett Bridge To Shap Walk Sept 2006.*

FAWCET,?; *J1959,*

FAWTHROP, Gorden Leslie; *J1960, b1944,*
Probationary Meets; Bull Pot, Alum Pot, Easegill.

FAWTHROP, T;

FEARNLEY, Frank; *J1936, [Died on active service in WWII]*

FEARNLEY, Philip; *J1995, b1962,*
Probationary Meets; Jingling, BPOTW, Sunset, Heron, Flood Entrance, Sell Gill, Hagg Gill, Calf Holes, Swinsto, Yordas, Great Douk.
Newsletter References; *Diccan Pot March 1996.*

FENNESSEY, Frederick Herbert; *J1951, b1914, d1998.*

FERN, Timothy James; *J1995, b1963,*

FIELDEN, Hubert; *J1946,*
Bulletin References; *Recorded as taking part in the first attempted Rift Pot/ Long Kin East exchange April 28th 1946. Recorded as down Rift Pot 19th May 1946, Flood Entrance July 1949.*

FILBY, J;

FINCHAM, Alan; *J1953,*

FINNIE, Amy; *J2011, b1974,*
Newsletter References; *Committee Pot March 2011, Link Pot-Wretched Rabbit June 2011, Long Churn [Novice Trip] June 2011, Swinsto-KMC Nov 2011.*

FIRM, Dean; *J1998, b1968,*

FIRTH, David Booth; *J1956, b1938,*
FITZGERALD, Lee Thomas; *J2000, b1966,*
Probationary Meets; County Pot, Black Shiver, Pool Sink, Disappointment Pot, Alum Pot, Diccan, Great Douk, Meregill, P8, Giants, White Scar, Bar Pot.
Newsletter References; *Bar Pot Nov 2000, White Scar Cave April 2001.*

FLEMING, Brian; *J1960, b1942,*
Expelled from club for non payment of subs Dec 1962.
Probationary Meets; Jingling Cave, Rowten pot, Bar Pot, GG60+.

FLEMING, John; *J1946,*
Bulletin References; *Rift Pot/ Long Kin East exchange April 20th 1947. [His son life lined at Rift Pot]*

FLOOD, Geoffrey Michael; AKA: Heavy Lemming. *J1983, b1962,*
Probationary Meets; Lost John's, GG82, Stream Passage, Swildon's .
Newsletter References; *Lost John's [Fell off near the bottom of a pitch-not seriously injured] Feb 1982, Kingsdale Photographic meet April 1982, Hallucination Aven-Induction Location May 1983.*

FLOOD, Mark Andrew; AKA: Andy. *J1982, b1964,*
Probationary Meets; Pippikin, GG82, Lancaster Hole.
Newsletter References; *Alum Pot March 1981, Magnetometer Pot March 1981, Gaping Gill-Hallucination Aven [Dive support] May 1981, Pippikin Pot Oct 1981, Ireby Fell Caverns July 1982, LKE-Rift Exchange Feb 1992, Pen-y-Ghent Pot July 1992.*

FLOYD, Jack Christopher; *J1989, b1973,*
Probationary Meets; GG89, Swinsto, Marble Steps, Sunset.

FORD, Beverley Jane; *J2012, b1963,*

FORDER, John; *J1964, b1946,*
Probationary Meets; Heron Pot, Lost John's, Ireby Fell.

Bulletin References; *Picos de Europa [OUCC] July 1967.*

FOREMAN, Peter Campton; *J1961, b1932,*
Probationary Meets; Clapham cave, Bar Pot, Easegill.

FOSTER, Michael Grieveson; *J1965, b1944,*
Probationary Meets; Mongo Gill, Goyden Pot, Bar Pot.

FOSTER, PAUL; *J1967, b1947,*
Rejoined 1986.
Probationary Meets; Disappointment Pot, Ireby Fell, Little Hull Pot.
Bulletin References; *Investigating various parts of Ingleborough Cave 1968, Lancaster Hole Jan 1966, Whitsun Series Whit 1969, Ingleborough Cave Nether Wallows 1969, Ingleborough Cave Insignificant Inlet 1969, Ingleborough Cave Rimstone East 1969.*
Newsletter Refernces; *Meregill June 1969, Pen-y-Ghent Pot Aug 1969, Lancaster Hole Sept 1969, Marble Steps March 1970, Ireby Fell Pot Oct 1986.*

FOSTER, Lionel; *J1981, b1947,*
Newsletter References; *Gingling Hole July 1980, Pasture Gill Cave Sept 1980, Bull Pot of the Witches [And assistance with the body recovery of Tracy Gibson from Top Sink] Oct 1980.*

FOWLEY, H; *J1984,*

FOX, John, Renshaw; *J2004, b1976,*
Probationary Meets; Sell Gill, Sunset Hole, Notts Pot, Simpsons Pot, Runscar Cave, Thistle Cave, Pen-y-Ghent Pot, High Hull, Short Drop.
Newsletter References; *Notts Pot March 2004, Runscar Cave Sept 2004, Lancaster Hole Dec 2004, Gingling Hole July 2005, Simpson's Pot Dec 2005, Lost John's Hole Sept 2006, White Scar Cave April 2007.*

FOX, S; *J1980,*

FOXALL, William; *J2017, b1994,*
Probationary Meets; Meregill, Ireby Fell, Illusion Pot, GG17.
Member; UNCC, Speleo ?
Newsletter References; *Lost River Sump [Dive Support] May 2019, Aquamole Pot Nov 2019.*

FOXTON, David George; *J1998, b1973,*
Member; LUCC.
FOYLE, Rita; *J2015, b1957,*

FRAKES, John; AKA: Jack. *J1962, b1921, d1987.*

Probationary Meets; Bull Pot, Goyden Pot.
Father of William
Bulletin References; *Long Kin West July 1962.*

FRAKES, William; AKA: Garth. *J1963, b1947, d1967.*
Probationary Meets; Lost John's, Marble Steps, GG62.
Died in Mossdale 1967.
Bulletin References; *Long Kin West July 1962, Hardrawkin Pot Aug 1964, Lumphammer Pot Sept 1965, Ibbeth Peril 1966, Fermanagh Dec 1966, Gingling Wet Sinks Oct 1966, Screen Hill-Legnabrocky Way Ireland Discovery Aug 1965.*
Newsletter References; *Practice Cave Rescue Alum [Jumped in to show the water was deeper than he was tall] May 1965, Rumbling Hole July 1965.*

FRAMPTON, Michael; *J1971, b1946,*

FRANCE, Andrew Michael; AKA: Andy Thrance, Thug. *J1981, b1963,*
Probationary Meets; Juniper Gulf, GG80, Pippikin Pot.
Famous for; Fire walking in the glowing embers of the Dump plot night fire. Eating a dead shrew with discarded lettuce and chips in the New Inn beer garden, to the horror of some tourists.
Bulletin References; *Gavel Pot Dec 1980, Brackenbottom Pot [Dig] 1985, M5 Pot [Dig] July 1984.*
Newsletter References; *Alum Pot March 1981, Lower Long Churn March 1981, Sell Gill Hole April 1981, Lancaster-County Pot Sept 1981, Pippikin Pot Oct 1981, Kingsdale Photographic meet April 1982, Little Neath River Cave, Porth Yr Ogof and OFD April 1983, Simpsons-Valley Entrance April 1983, Mendip weekend April 1983, Hallucination Aven-Induction Location May 1983, Link Pot July 1983, South Wales Aug 1983, Swinsto-Rowten Exchange Nov 1983, Rift Pot Feb 1984, Scotland 1987, Bird Watching Lakes Walk Sept 1990.*

FREELAND, Denis R; *J1978, b1954,*
Member; QMCCC, SACC.
Probationary Meets; Dan Yr Ogof, Little Neath, Washfold, Lost John's, GG78, Whitsun Series, Disappointment Pot.
Bulletin References; *Antro del Corchia Aug 1978.*

FROUDE, Simon; *J1993, b1960,*
Member; SPCC, WSG, ACC,
Bulletin References; *Tete Sauvage July 1995, Pyrenees 2006, Ordessa National Park 2007.*
Newsletter References; *Marble Steps March 1997, Lancaster-Wretched Rabbit Jan 1999, Rowten Pot Dec 2000, Peak Cavern - Sumps Tour June 2001,*

Short Drop-Gavel Jan 2002, South Wales [Cwm Dwr & OFD 2] July 2002, Notts Pot Sept 2002, KMC-Toyland Oct 2002, Sell Gill Hole Nov 2002, Dan Yr Ogof/OFD2 June 2003, Great Douk Cave Sept 2003, Robinson's Pot Oct 2003, Brackenbottom Pot Dec 2003, Aquamole Pot Dec 2003, Derbyshire Meet Jan 2004, OFD 2 June 2004, New Rift Dec 2004, James Hall Over-Engine Mine to Titan Shaft [Bottom] Jan 2005, Pippikin Sept 2005, Simpson's Pot Dec 2005, Brackenbottom Pot Jan 2006, James Hall Mine Feb 2006, Peak Cavern Feb 2006, Rumbling Hole July 2006, Black Shiver Pot July 2006, Pyrenees Aug 2006, Aquamole Pot Jan 2007, Derbyshire Meet Jan 2007, Top Sink-Lancaster Hole Feb 2007, OFD 2 March 2007, Cwm Dwr March 2007, Ordessa National Park Spanish Pyrenees 2007, Hidden Earth Tewkesbury, Support Oct 2007, Long Churns Training Meet Dec 2007, King Pot Feb 2008.

FROUDE, Katie; *J2002, b1987,*
Bulletin References; *Pyrenees 2006,*
Newsletter References; *Robinson's Pot Oct 2003, New Rift Dec 2004, Rumbling Hole July 2006,*
Pyrenees Aug 2006, Hidden Earth Tewkesbury, Support Oct 2007.

FROUDE, Robert; *J2002, b1990,*
Bulletin References; *Ordessa National Park 2007.*
Newsletter References; *Ordessa National Park Spanish Pyrenees 2007.*
NG; AKA: Mandy. *J2012, b1984,*
Newsletter References; *Alderley Edge Mines Nov 2012.*

FULCINI, Peter; *J2004, b1970,*
Bulletin References; *Pyrenees Aug 2004.*
Newsletter References; *Brackenbottom Pot Dec 2003, Derbyshire Meet Jan 2004, Sell Gill Holes Feb 2004, Swinsto Hole-KMC Feb 2004, Alum Pot March 2004, MilwrTunnel June 2004, Gingling Hole July 2004, Lancaster Hole Dec 2004,Giant's Hole Jan 2005, Yordas Pot & Cave Dec 2004, Calf Holes & Dismal Hill & Old Ing Jan 2005, Diccan Pot Feb 2005.*

FURLONG, Imogen; *J2011, b1971,*
Member; SUSS, GSG.

45

G

GAFFNEY, Martin John; *J1983, b1955,*
Probationary Meets; Gouffre Berger, Notts Pot.
Member; ACC, Speleo Club de Skerabeck.

GARDNER, John; *J2009, b1948,*
Bulletin References; *Reseau de la Pierre Saint Martin Aug 2013, Croesor-Rhosydd Feb 2009.*
Newsletter References; *Croesor-Rhosydd March 2010, Lost John's-Boxhead Pot Sept 2010, Link Pot-Wretched Rabbit June 2011, Trou du Garde/Creux de la Cavale-Bauges Aug 2012, Rowten Pot Sept 2012, Little Hull Pot Sept 2012, Deaths Head-Notts Oct 2012, Croesor Rhosydd [Through] Oct 2012, White Scar Cave July 2014, Shuttleworth Pot Oct 2014, Lancaster-County Pot Nov 2014, Lancaster-Wretched Rabbit Nov 2014, Fairy Holes Sept 2015, Jingling Pot Dec 2015, Wretched Rabbit-County Pot April 2016, County Pot-Boundary Pot April 2016, Pool Sink-County Pot Oct 2016, Alum Pot Dec 2016, Short Drop-Gavel Pot March 2017, Lancaster Hole Oct 2017, OFD Top Ent Oct 2017, Wretched Rabbit-Top Sink Jan 2018, Notts Pot Sept 2018, Ingleborough Cave Oct 2018, Oxlow-Maskhill Mine Oct 2018, Lancaster Hole [Magic Roundabout Series] Nov 2018, Lancaster Hole-Wretched Rabbit Nov 2018, Lancaster Hole-Wretched Rabbit Dec 2018, Bull Pot of the Witches Jan 2019, Magnetometer Pot Sept 2019, Pool Sink-Boundary Pot Nov 2019.*

GARGETT, Michael; AKA: Mick. *J1999, b1970,*
Newsletter References; *Lancaster-Wretched Rabbit Jan 1999.*

GARGSFORTH, R. H; *J1935,*

GARTHWAITE, David John; *J1978, b1954,*
Probationary Meets; Gavel Pot, Lost john's, Notts Pot.
Member; UNCC.
Newsletter References; *Top Sink-Pool Sink Sept 1977, Rumbling Hole Aug 1978, Pillar Holes Sept 1978, Gavel Pot Oct 1978, Lost John's Sept 1978.*

GATES, Colin; AKA: Thumbprint, El Supremo. *J1975, b1952,*
Probationary Meets; Tatham Wife, Langdale Horseshoe, Birksfell Master Cave.
Motley [*Resigned from Motleys 1981*]
Bulletin References; *Mountain Hall [Scaling] 1980, Gouffre Berger Aug 1980, Cueva De La Marniosa Santander Aug 1982, Krisna Jama Aug 1984, Brezno V Madvedovi Konti Aug 1984, Leski Aug 1984, Gouffre Berger Aug 1992.*
Newsletter References; *Tatham Wife March 1975, Birks Fell Cave April 1975, Lost John's September 1976, Bull Pot of the Witches Dec 1976, Pen-y-Ghent Pot April 1977, Rumbling Hole Aug 1978, Simpsons Pot Jan 1979, Hammer Pot Sept 1978, Top Sink-Lancaster and Back! Oct 1978, Lost John's Sept 1978, Meregill Feb 1980, Scrafton Pot April 1980, Gouffre Berger Aug 1980, Pasture Gill Cave Sept 1980, Gavel Pot Dec 1980, New Goyden Pot April 1981, OFD 1 & 2 May 1981, Sunset Hole July 1981, Lancaster-County Pot Sept 1981, Cow Pot Oct 1981, Pippikin Pot Oct 1981, Rift Pot& Long Kin East Jan 1982, Alum Pot March 1982, Birks Fell Cave July 1982, Mendip weekend April 1983, Hallucination Aven Location May 1983, South Wales Aug 1983, Rift Pot Feb 1984, Diccan Pot March 1984, Top Sink-County Pot April 1985, Gunnerside Gill Lead Mines June 1985, Brezno, Lèska, Babizop Rakov Scojan and the Pit of Bears*

Yugoslavia Aug 1985, Eden Valley-Teesdale Walking Meet Oct 1985, Scotland Easter 1986, Pool Park Oct 1986, Cliff Force Cave 1986, Scotland 1987, Top Sink-Link Feb 1988, Nick Pot Nov 1987, Coniston Mine July 1988, South Wales Nov 1988, Smallcleugh Mine Aug 1989, Langstroth Pot & Cave [Diving] July 1989, Eldon Hole & Oxlow Caverns Oct 1990, South Wales Dec 1990, Gouffre Berger Aug 1992, Crooklands Walking Meet Sept 1993, Coniston Mines Weekend Sept 1993.

GETLING, David; AKA: Mini Prof. *J1983,*
Bulletin References; *Notts Pot March 1983, Mendip weekend April 1983, Vercors Aug 1983.*

GIBSON, J. W; *J1973,*
Bulletin References; *Clint Cave Extension May 1974, Grotte de Bury 1977.*

GILL, Alan; *J1956, b1930, d2010.*
Famous for; Member of Wally Herbert's team that were the first to walk to the North Pole.
Bulletin References; *Was a member of Wally Herbert's polar Expedition in 1961-3620 miles from Point Barrow, Alaska, to Blackboard Island, February 21st-29th May. [Also Fritz Koener and Ken Hedges] Now recognised as the first time walking to the North Pole was accomplished. Little Hull Hole Oct 1955, Christmas Pot 1957, Clapham Cave March 1957.*
Newsletter References; *Newby Moss Hole May 1957, Swinsto Sept 1957, Granted Honorary Membership of the BPC in recognition of having dedicated his life to Polar Exploration-March 2000.*

GILL, C; *J1983,*

GILMOUR, Christopher Thomas; *J1966,*

GLANDHILL, R. M; *J1979,*

GLANVILL, Cary Amanda Jane;AKA: Mandy. *J1978, b1957,*
Probationary Meets; Birks Fell, Otter Hole, GG78, Disappointment-Main Shaft.
Member; CSS, AAC.
Bulletin References; White Scar Cave Dec 31 1977, Gouffre Berger Aug 1980, Pippikin to Top Sink April 1980, *Rumbling Hole Aug 1978.*
Newsletter References; *Pippikin-Top Sink April 1980.*
GLEDHILL, Colin; *J1951, b1923,*

GLEDHILL, Philip Haigh; *J1950, b1923,*
Bulletin References; *Pen-y-Ghent Pot Rescue, young BSA member died of exhaustion 1951. Bull*

Pot of the Witches April 1951, Clapham Cave Sept 1951.

GLEDHILL, R. M; *J1980,*

GLEW, J; *J1959,*

GLOVER, Richard R; *J1972, b1930,*
Bulletin References; *Involved in discovery of Whitsun Series GG 1968.*

GOLDSBROUGH, H; *J1936, b1920,*

GOFF, Maurice; *J1946,b1915,d1993.*

GOMERSAL, G; *J1959,*

GORMAN, Aaron; *J2003, b1991,*

GORMAN, Jamie; *J2003, b1988,*

GOTT, William; AKA: Bill. *J1933, b1902, d1998.*
Founder Member
Bulletin References; *Recorded as down Sleets Gill 29th Sept 1946.*

GRAHAM, Andrew; AKA: Plug.*J1998, b1968,*
Probationary Meets; GG98, Goyden, Manchester Hole, Eglins Hole, New Goyden.

GRAIS, Roy Peter; *J1996, b1946,*
Probationary Meets; GG96 [+ CPC GG96]

GRANT, David; *J1979, b1955,*
Probationary Meets; Bull Pot, Lancaster-Easegill, Notts Pot, Peak Cavern.
Newsletter References; *Top Sink Oct 1978, Gingling Hole July 1980, Pasture Gill Cave Sept 1980.*

GRASS, Martin; *J1987, b1955,*
Member; BEC.
Claims to have taught Geoff Crossley to dive.
Newsletter References; *Boreham Cave March 1980, Mossdale Caverns March 1980, Wookey Hole [3-9] March 1981, Wookey Hole [Chamber 20] June 1981, Pine Tree Hole June 1981, Top Sink-County Pot April 1985, South Wales Nov 1988, Mendip Weekend Sept 1991, Dan Yr Ogof June 1991, Peak Cavern Feb 2006, Reservoir Hole [The Frozen Deep] June 2013, Fairy Holes Sept 2014, Swildon's Hole Feb 2015.*

GREEN, Christopher; AKA: Mortuary Boots. *J1998, b1964,*
Newsletter References; *Easegill Jan 2000, Lancaster Round Trip March 2000, Bull Pot Jan*

2001, Great/Little Douk Dec 2001,Sunset Hole Jan 2003, Swinsto –KMC Jan 2003.

GREEN, Daniel; *J2009,*

GREEN, John Anthony; *J1957, b1936,*
Newsletter References; *Rumbling Hole Oct 1957, Lancaster Hole Oct 1957, Dow-Providence rescue Dec 1957, Tackle testing July 1958, Sunset Hole Aug 1958.*

GREEN, Peter Nicholl; *J1957, b1936,*
Bulletin References; *Blencathra March 1968, Bowfell Buttress 1968.*
Newsletter References; *Simpson's Pot Aug 1957, Swinsto Sept 1957.*

GREENE, John Willoughby; *J1961, b1942,*
Probationary Meets; Magnetometer Pot, Sell Gill, Stream Passage.
Bulletin References; *Involved in discovery of Whitsun Series GG 1968, Whitsun Series Whit 1969, Disappointment Pot Oct 1967, Poulawillin [Clare] 1968, Lower Stream Passage Pot [Diving] 1971, Juniper Gulf [Bolting] 1974, Marble Sink May 1976, Piaggia Bella 1975, Far SE passage [Digging] 1980, Gouffre Berger Aug 1980, Vercors Aug 1983, Cow Garth Cave [Exploration] 1982 / 84, Tanne Du Bel Espoir-Diau Aug 1984, Grotte De Ramats Aug 1985.*
Newsletter References; *Leader Tatham Wife Hole January 1969, Meregill June 1969, Lost John's Jan 1970, Wharfedale weekend Oct 1970, Birks Fell April 1971, Black Shiver Pot Nov 1971, Lancaster-County Pot Dec 1971, Washfold Pot April 1972, Lancaster–Top Sink Oct 1973, Lost John's Hole Aug 1974, Gingling Hole Sept 1974, Flood Entrance–Stream Passage Pot Exchange Feb 1975, Lost John's Nov 1975, Pippikin Pot Nov 1976, King Pot Feb 1980, Mossdale Caverns March 1980, Gouffre Berger Aug 1980, New Goyden Pot April 1981, Tanne de Bel Espoir–Grotte de la Diau Aug 1981, Dowkabottom Cave Dec 1981, Rift Pot& Long Kin East Jan 1982, Pasture Gill Pot June 1983, South Wales Aug 1983, Marble Sink March 1985, South Wales Nov 1988, Simpson's-Swinsto March 1994, Lakes Walking Meet Sept 1995, Lancaster Canal Walk Meet 2001, Millenium Walk Sept 2002, Black Combe-Foxfield Walk Sept 2003, Dufton–Garrigill Lakes Walk Sept 2005, Granett Bridge To ShapWalk Sept 2006, Ulverston-Coniston Walking Meet 2007, Salthill Quarry Geology Walk Nov 2008, Feizor-Moughton Walk July 2011.*

GREENE, Margeret; *J1989, b1955,*

GREENWOOD, David Austin; AKA: Grassy. *J1958, b1941,*

Resigned from club 1964, rejoined 1965.
Member of the Heath Grammar School contingent.
Bulletin References; *Lower Stream Passage Pot May 1959, Lower Stream Passage Pot May 1965, Pen-y-Ghent Pot April 1960, Pen-y-ghent Pot July 1960, Alum Pot July 1960, Lancaster-Eastgill Aug 1960, Long Kin West July 1962, Little Hull Pot July 1962, Lost John's July 1963, Sunset Hole Aug 1958, Discovery Lower Stream Passage Pot April 1959.*
Newsletter References; *Swildon's Hole Sept 1959, Ingleborough Cave Survey Aug 1959, Measuring Depth of GG shaft Aug 1959, Little Hull Hole Aug 1959, St Cuthberts Swallet Sept 1959, Memories Sept 2013.*

GREENWOOD, Ian Paul; AKA: BEANZ. *J1981, b1960,*
Expelled from club for unacceptable behaviour 1995.
Probationary Meets; Pippikin, Cow Pot, Pool Sink, Link Pot.
Newsletter References; *Alum Pot March 1981, Sunset Hole July 1981, Gingling Hole Rescue July 1981, Dow-Providence Sept 1981, Link Pot Sept 1981, Cow Pot Oct 1981, South Wales Aug 1983, Rift Pot Feb 1984, County Pot March 1984, Diccan Pot March 1984, Heron Pot Jan 1985, Top Sink-County Pot April 1985, Brezno, Leska, Babizop Rakov Scojan and the Pit of Bears Yugoslavia Aug 1985, Eden Valley-Teesdale Walking Meet Oct 1985, Notts Pot Feb 1986, Scotland Easter 1986, Pool Park Oct 1986, Mendip Dec 1986, Scotland 1987, South Wales Nov 1988, Smallcleugh Mine Aug 1989, Langstroth Pot & Cave [Diving] July 1989.*

GREENWOOD, June; See Smith.

GREENWOOD-Sole, Natalie; *J2017, b1995,*
Probationary Meets; Lancaster-County Pot.

GRENFELL, Stephen D; *J2000, b1957,*
Newsletter References; *Rowten Pot Dec 2000, White Scar Cave April 2001, Great/Little Douk Dec 2001, Short Drop-Gavel Jan 2002, Hagg Gill Oct 2002, KMC-Toyland Oct 2002, Sunset Hole Sept 2003, Brackenbottom Pot Dec 2003, Long Kin East Nov 2003, Bull Pot Dec 2003, Sell Gill Holes March 2004, Ireby Fell Cavern June 2004, Short Drop-Gavel Pot Nov 2004, Committee Pot Dec 2006.*

GREGORY, J;
Newsletter References; *Washfold Pot July 1957;*

GRIFFIN, Neil Richard; AKA: Ug. *J1996, b1974,*

Probationary Meets; Sunset, GG96-98, Brackenbottom Pot, Swinsto, Mongo Gill, Coppice Cave, Far Country.
Rejoined 2017.
Bulletin References; *Deep Well [Diving] 2000-2003,*
Newsletter References; *Deep Well [Dive Support] May 1997, GG Photographic Meet May 1998, Lancaster Round Trip March 2000, Great/Little Douk Dec 2001, Sell Gill Holes Feb 2004, Deep Well Dive[Support] GG04, James Hall Mine Feb 2006, Peak Cavern Feb 2006, Old Ing-Birkwith July 2017, Long Churn [Childrens Meet] April 2018, KMC [Childrens Meet] June 2018.*

GRIFFITHS, William Frederick; *J1964, b1945,*
Probationary Meets; 1963+4 Ingleton YHA / BPC course.

GROVE, Joe; AKA: Joe Berger. *J1992, b1965,*
Probationary Meets; Flood Entrance, Top Sink, Diccan-Alum Pot, Little Hull, Ireby Fell.
Legend has it that having got to the bottom of Gouffre Berger he turned to Gerald Benn and Wilki and asked them which jammer he should move first when he got to the rebelay and they each gave him a different answer!
Bulletin References; *Deep Well [Diving support] May 1992, Gouffre Berger Aug 1992, Top Sink-County Pot Nov 1991, Ireby Fell Jan 1992, Little Hull Dec 1991.*
Newsletter References; *Gouffre Berger Aug 1992, Pen-y-Ghent Pot July 1992.*
GROVE, Peter C; *J1990, b1940,*
Probationary Meets; Pen-y-Ghent Pot, Diccan-Alum, Little Hull, LKE, Marble Steps, Far Country, BPC 3 Peaks 1997.
Re joined 1997.
Newsletter Rerferences; *Easegill Caverns Sept 1990, Sell Gill Training Meet Nov 1991, Top Sink-County Pot Nov 1991, Ireby Fell Jan 1992, Little Hull Dec 1991, Rift-LKE Exchange Feb 1992, Pen-y-Ghent Pot July 1992, Rowten Pot Nov 1993, Death's Head/Big Meanie Nov 1993.*

GROVES, B;
Newsletter Rerferences; *Simpson's Pot Aug 1957, Swinsto Sept 1957, Lancaster Hole Oct 1957.*

GRUNDY, Samuel; *J1937,*
Went to Jamacia to live and work then went to Northern Canada, sent interesting related articles back to the BPC.

GUDGEON, Derrick; *J1952, b1934,*

GUEST, Peter Midgley; *J1951, b1924,*

H

HADFIELD, Rosie; *J2012, b1989,*
Probationary Meets; Brackenbottom Pot [Digging],
GG12, Austria [BPC Members Trip] 2009, China
[BPC Members Trip] 2011.
Member; SUSS, TSG.

HAIGH, Andrew; AKA: Garth. *J1987, b1981,*
Probationary Meets; Alum Pot, Mistral, Lancaster
Hole, Bull Pot.
Bulletin References; *Hensler's Pot [Discovery]
1999-2003, Pyrenees 2006, Ordessa National Park
2007, Doubs, France Aug 2009.*
Newsletter References; *Bull Pot Dec 1996, Mistral
Hole Nov 1996, Hunt Pot Feb 1997, Mongo Gill
March 1997, Lost John's Hole March 1997, Alum
Pot [Training Meet] July 1997, Batty Wife Cave Aug
1997, Easgill Aug 1997, Rowten Pot/Jingling Pot
July 1997, Hunt Pot Feb 1998, Simpson's & Swinsto
March 1998, GG Photographic Meet May 1998,
Wades-Bar Feb 1998, Barclays Lode Wales July
1998, Nent Head-Brewery Shaft Oct 1998, Diccan
Rescue Nov 1998, Rowten Pot Dec 1998, Alum Pot
Dec 1998, County-Pool Exchange Feb 1999,
Swinsto-KMC March 1999, King Pot March 1999,
New Rift April 1999, Grange Rigg [Locating] March
1999, Lost John's March 1999, Derbyshire Meet
Sept 1999, Notts Pot August 1999, Birks Fell June
1999, Fat Finger Millennium Party, GG-Mill Hill
[Dive support] May 2000, Ingleborough Cave Aug
2000, County-Wretched Rabbit Nov 2000, Losers
Pot [Discovery] Mar 2002, Lost John's Hole Sept
2005, Pyrenees Aug 2006, Ordessa National Park
Spanish Pyrenees 2007, Bull Pot April 2008, Deep
Well [Dive support] May 2008, Les Arcs Aug 2008,
Lambrigg Fell-Tebay Walk Sept 2008, Lost John's
Oct 2008, Bull Pot of the Witches Jan 2009,*

*Lancaster-Wretched Rabbit June 2009,
Dowkerbottom Cave Oct 2009, Aquamole Pot Nov
2009, Pen-y-Ghent Gill [Digging CPC/ULSA Dig]
May 2010, Hardrawkin Pot May 2010, Hurtle Pot
[Diving Support] May 2010, Joint Hole [Diving
Support] May 2010, Marble Steps June 2010,
Committee Pot March 2013, Lost River Sump [Dive
Support] May 2019, Kirkby Lonsdale-Wharton
Walking Meet Sept 2019, Bullpot Jan 2020.*

HAIGH, David [Dr]; *J1983, b1960,*
Member; ULSA.
Probationary Meets; Simpson's Pot, Pen-y-Ghent
Pot, Mongo Gill.
Newsletter Rerferences; *Ireby Fell Caverns July
1982, Birks Fell Cave July 1982.*

HAIGH, David Anthony; AKA: Swampy. *J1963,
b1943,*
BPC President 2005.
Probationary Meets; Marble Steps, Sunset Hole,
Goyden Pot.
Famous for; Discovery of Losers pot, Henslers Pot,
Parkinsons Pot, Corky's Pot, Pay Sank, Klondyke
Pot, Fat Finger and Christmas Cracker by digging.
Being rescued from Alum Pot in flood as a novice
and getting stuck and rescued from Nettle Pot
when he should have known better. An incoherent
speech involving a stuffed parrot at 2020 AGM.
Bulletin References; *Pen-y-Ghent Pot Extensions
Oct 1963, Notts Pot Oct 1963, Pen-y-Ghent Long
Churn Nov 1963, Pen-y-Ghent Pot Feb 1964,
Buttertubs/Flood Entrance/Sell Gill May 1964,
Antler Pot Feb 1965, Losers Pot [Discovery] Mar
2002, Hensler's Pot [Discovery] 1999-2003,
Hensler's Pot [First Through Trip to GG] May 2003,*

Parkinson's Pot [Discovery] July 2003, Corky's Pot [Discovery] 2003-2005, Pay Sank [Discovery] 2005, Klondike Pot Digging/Exploration 2004-2007.
Newsletter References; *Bradford Mine shaft collapses Aug 1965, Simpsons-Valley Entrance April 1983, Tatham Wife Hole Sept 1983, Swinsto-Rowten Exchange Nov 1983, Ibbeth Peril July 1984, Brezno, Leska, Babizop Rakov Scojan and the Pit of Bears Yugoslavia Aug 1985, Gingling Hole Oct 1985, New Rift Pot Jan 1986, Pen-y-Gent Pot March 1987, Dow Cave April 1987, Weathercote Cave April 1988, Heron Pot Jan 1989, Calf Holes, Browgill, Old Ing and Dismal Hill Jan 1991, Dowkabottom Feb 1995, GG Photographic Meet May 1998, Diccan Rescue Nov 1998, Fat Finger Millennium Party, KMC March 2000, Christmas Cracker Sept 2000, Ingleborough Cave Aug 2000, Ingleborough Cave Digging 2001, Hensler's Pot Digging Dec 2001, Losers Pot [Discovery] Mar 2002, Loser's Pot June 2002, Hensler's High Aven voice connection June 2002, Corky's Digging Team 2004, Klondyke Pot Digging Team Jan 2005, Croll's Cavern Dec 2004, Pay Sank Exploration Sept 2005, Pay Sank Breakthrough team Nov 2005, Salthill Quarry Geology Walk Nov 2008, Winner of Ghar Parau Foundation Tratman Award for literary excellence [writing 'Adventures Underground' with John Cordingley] Nov 2018.*

HAIGH, Diana; [née Readman] *J1987, b1942,*
Newsletter References; *Dow Cave April 1987, Weathercote Cave April 1988, Calf Holes, Browgill, Old Ing and Dismal Hill Jan 1991.*

HAIGH, Harry H; *J1981, b1946,*
Probationary Meets; Pool Sink, Vespers Pot, Rift-Long Kin East.
Bulletin References; *Losers Pot [Discovery] March 2002,*
Newsletter References; *Kingsdale Photographic meet April 1982, Pen-y-Ghent Pot July 1982, Tatham Wife Hole Feb 1983, Notts Pot March 1983, Link Pot July 1983, Hurnel Moss Pot July 1983, Swinsto-Rowten Exchange Nov 1983, Tatham Wife Hole Oct 1984, Top Sink-County Pot April 1985, Lost John's Pot July 1985, Coniston Mine July 1988, Ireby Fell March 1990, Scrafton Pot June 1990, Swaledale Weekend Oct 1992, Ireby Fell Feb 1993, Mongo Gill March 1997, Nent Head-Brewery Shaft Oct 1998, County-Wretched Rabbit Nov 1998, Bar Pot [Rope Ladder] May 2000, Christmas Cracker Sept 2000, Ingleborough Cave Aug 2000, Ingleborough Cave Digging 2001, Milwr Tunnel June 2004, Fairy Holes Sept 2014, Nenthead Mines Sept 2014.*

HAIGH, Jeffrey; *J1958, b1941,*

Suspended from club Dec 1959.
Newsletter References; *Lancaster Hole June 1958, Newby Moss Dig Nov 1958.*

HAIGH, L. A; *J1981, b1968,*

HAIGH, Michael; *J2000, b1986,*
Re-joined in 2003.
Bulletin References; *Losers Pot [Discovery] Mar 2002, Christmas Cracker, Christmas Cracker Sept 2000, Ingleborough Cave Digging 2001, MilwrTunnel June 2004.*

HAIGH, Peter Anthony; *J1958, b1941,*
Bulletin References; *Involved with building electron ladders, 1950/60's, Lower Stream Passage Pot May 1959, Pen-y-ghent Pot July 1960, Simpson's Pot 16th April 1961-[Graham Shaw Accident] Long Kin West July 1962.*
Newsletter References; *Little Hull Pot April 1958, Discovery Lower Stream Passage Pot April 1959.*

HAIGH, Peter David; AKA: Dave Haigh II. *J1984, b1968,*
Probationary Meets; County Pot, GG84, Ibbeth Peril.
Newsletter References; *Rift Pot Feb 1984, Birks Fell Cave July 1984, Ibbeth Peril July 1984, Heron Pot Jan 1985, Top Sink-County Pot April 1985, Sleets Gill June 1985, Lost John's Pot July 1985, Sell Gill April 1985, Brezno, Leska, Babizop Rakov Scojan and the Pit of Bears Yugoslavia Aug 1985, Gingling Hole Oct 1985, Calf Holes Nov 1985, New Rift Pot Jan 1986, Pen-y-Gent Pot March 1987, Short Drop Cave Nov 1989, Easegill Caverns Sept 1990, Pool Sink-Lancaster Hole Dec 1995.*

HAINSWORTH, Andrew; AKA: 1-Amp. *J2006, b1984,*
Famous for; Heroically attempting to recover a tackle bag from the depths of Lake Cadoux in the Gouffre Berger. Performing a rescue of fellow members from the Berger during flood conditions. Leaving his camera on top of his wheelie bin before setting off to France. On the same trip he stuffed 500 Euros behind his sun visor only to open his window whilst at speed and then pull down his visor to see all his money distributed across the French autoroute.
Bulletin References; *Pyrenees 2006, Reseau de la Pierre Saint Martin Aug 2013, Trapped in Hagg Gill several hours [Flood] Sept 2010, Croesor-Rhosydd Feb 2009, Dachstein Hallstatt Expedition 2010.*
Newsletter References; *Sunset Hole July 2006, Hurnell Moss Pot Oct 2006, Lost John's Hole Sept 2006, Thistle & Runscar Caves Sept 2006, New Rift Pot Nov 2006, Hunt Pot Nov 2006, Upper & Lower*

Long Churn Nov 2006, Nick Pot Dec 2006, Aquamole Pot Jan 2007, Committee Pot Dec 2006, Photographic Weekend Oct 2006, Great Douk Feb 2007, Derbyshire Meet Jan 2007, OFD 2 March 2007, White Scar Cave April 2007, Darnbrook Pot June 2007, Rift Pot July 2007, High Hull Pot Sept 2007, Death's Head & Big Meanie Sept 2007, Vesper Pot Jan 2008, King Pot Feb 2008,Roger Kirk Caves Feb 2008, Bull Pot April 2008, Deep Well [Dive support] May 2008, Brackenbottom Pot Oct 2008, Lost John's Oct 2008, Stump Cross Caverns Dec 2008, Cow Pot April 2009, Lancaster-Wretched Rabbit June 2009, Aquamole Pot Nov 2009, Pool Sink-Easegill Dec 2009, Sell Gill Dec 2009, Lower Long Churn-Dolly Tubs Jan 2010, Croesor-Rhosydd March 2010, Magnetometer Pot April 2010, Hurnell Moss Pot April 2010, Pen-y-Ghent Pot May 2010, Shrapnel Pot July 2010, Dachstein-Hallstatt Aug 2010, Long Churns [Training Meet] Nov 2010, Ireby Fell Cavern Jan 2011, Vesper Pot April 2011, Long Churn [Novice Trip] June 2011, Death's Head Sept 2011, Darnbrook Pot [Novice Trip] Sept 2011, Sunset Hole Oct 2011, Sell Gill May 2012, Far Coutry via Marilyn May 2012, Old Ing/Calf Holes-Browgill [Novice Trip] June 2012, White Scar Cave July 2012, Heron Pot [Novice Trip] Aug 2012, Bull Pot of the Witches Jan 2013, Notts Pot [Twilightt Zone] Feb 2013, Lost John's-Notts Pot March 2013, Illusion Pot March 2013, Aquamole Dec 2014, Link Pot-Cow Pot June 2015, Goyden Sept 2015.

HAINSWORTH, Bernard; J1951, b1929,
Bulletin References; Simpson's Pot 1952, Simpson's Pot July 1953, Flood Entrance Pot March 1954, Old Ing Caves Aug 1954, Marble Steps Nov 1954, Bull Pot of the Witches July 1955, Jackdaw Hole & Pen-y-Ghent Long Churn Nov 1955.
Newsletter References; Leader Great Douk Feb 1954, Leader Ribbleshead July 1956, Leader Lancaster Ease Gill Oct 1956.

HAINSWORTH, Diane Elaine; J1998, b1964,
Probationary Meets; Alum Pot, Calf Holes, Great Douk, Goyden, Dow Cave.

HAINSWORTH, Katie; J2015, b?,

HAINSWORTH, Robert Richard; J1951, b1929,

HALEY, Colin; J1959, b1939,

HALL, Colin David; J2008, b1939,

HALL, David; J2011, b1959,
Probationary Meets; Fell Close, Long Churn, Calf Holes.

Newsletter References; Calf Holes-Browgill/Old Ing June 2011, Old Ing/Calf Holes-Browgill [Novice Trip] July 2012.

HALL, David; J1961, b1944,
Resigned Sept 1965.
Probationary Meets; Bar Pot, Clapham Cave, Lost John's, Alum Pot.
Bulletin References; Calf Holes CRO rescue practice Dec 1961 [Rescuee], Stream Passage Pot June 1962, Sunset Hole 1962, Maritime Alps BPC/RRCPC trip July/Aug 1962, Christmas/Grange/P5 extensions May 1962, P5 Pushing Trip Aug 1962 Christmas/Grange/P5 extensions May 1962, Goyden Pot Feb 1963, Carlswalk Cavern May 1963, South Wales Easter 1963, Agen Allwedd April 1963, Car Pot June 1963, Crackpot Cave Dec 1963, Notts Pot Oct 1963, Little Hull Dec 1991, Rift-LKE Exchange Feb 1992, Death's Head/Big Meanie Nov 1993.

HALL, David Stephen; J1990, b1961,
Probationary Meets; GG93, Easegill, Heron Pot.
Newsletter References; Easegill Caverns Sept 1990, Top Sink-County Pot Nov 1991, Ireby Fell Jan 1992, Snatcher's Pot Nov 1993, Ribblehead Caves Jan 2012, Great Douk April 2012, Gillfield Level May 2012, Thistle, Runscar & Gunnerfleet Nov 2013, Old Ing-Birkwith July 2017.

HALL, Edward Malcolm; J1964, b1944,
Probationary Meets; Sell Gill, Bull Pot of the Witches, Sunset Hole.

HALL, Joseph William; J2008, b1984,

HALL, Stephan; J1984, b1961,
Probationary Meets; Simpson's Pot, GG83, Link Pot.
Bulletin References; Gouffre Berger Aug 1992, Simpsons-Valley Entrance April 1983, Link Pot July 1983, Langstroth Pot Sept 1985, Eden Valley-Teesdale Walking Meet Oct 1985, Rift/Large Pot Oct 1985, Spectacle-Vespers Feb 1990, Easegill Caverns Jan 1991.
Newsletter References; Gouffre Berger Aug 1992, Pen-y-Ghent Pot July 1992, Rowten Pot Nov 1993, Coniston Mines Weekend Sept 1993, Swinsto Hole-KMC Feb 2004.

HALL, Stephen Andrew; J1976, b1957,
Probationary Meets; Lancaster-Easegill, Alum Pot, Sunset Hole, KMC-Rowten Sumps, Bar pot.

HALLS, Katie; J2016, b1990,

HALSAY, F. R; J1979, b1956,

HALSAY, Malcolm G.S; *J1977, b1956,*
Probationary Meets; Cherry Tree Hole, Christmas-Grange Rigg, Top Sink-Lancaster.
Member; CMCCC.
Bulletin References; *Gouffre Berger Aug 1980.*
Newsletter References; *Pippikin-Link-Top Sink Oct 1979, Alum Pot June 1980, Gouffre Berger Aug 1980, Lancaster-County Pot Nov 1980, Wookey Hole [3-9] March 1981, Notts Pot Jan 1981.*

HALSAY, Ruth; *J1980, b1956,*
Member; CMCCC.
Probationary Meets; Dowbergill Passage, Top Sink-Lancaster, GG78.
Bulletin References; *Gouffre Berger Aug 1980.*
Newsletter References; *Top Sink-Lancaster and Back! Oct 1978, Alum Pot June 1980, Gouffre Berger Aug 1980, County Pot-Lancaster Nov 1980, Notts Pot Jan 1981.*

HAMBLIN, Susan; *J2006, b1964,*
Newsletter References; *OFD 2 March 2007, Cwm Dwr March 2007.*

HANDSCOMBE, Malcolm Stewart; *J1953,*
Bulletin References; *Simpson's Pot July 1953, Juniper Gulf May 1954, Little Hull Pot July 1954.*

HANLON, Leo Vincent; *J1960, b1938,*
Probationary Meets; Scoska Cave, Bar Pot [GG60], Lancaster Hole.

HARDACRE, Philip; *J1999, b1958,*

HARDING, R.A.J;

HARDY, Chris; *J1984,*
Newsletter References; *Birks Fell Cave July 1984, Tatham Wife Hole Oct 1984, Lost John's Pot July 1985, Gingling Hole Oct 1985, Top Sink / County Pot March 1986.*

HARE, Christopher; *J1986,*
Newsletter References; *Sell Gill Hole Feb 1985, Brezno, Leska, Babizop Rakov Scojan and the Pit of Bears Yugoslavia Aug 1985, Notts Pot Feb 1986, Pool Park Oct 1986.*

HARGATE, Raymond Peter; *J1987, b1960,*
Probationary Meets; Calf Holes-Brow Gill.
Newsletter References; *Calf Holes Jan 1988.*

HARGREAVES, Harry; *J1933, b????, d1958,*
Founder Member

HARPER, Denis; *J1956, b1926,*

HARPER, Edwin; AKA: Ted. *J1946,*
Bulletin References; *Recorded as taking part in first attempted Rift Pot-Long Kin East exchange April 28th 1946.*

HARRISON, Gordon; *J1952, b1933,*

HARRISON, Judith; AKA: Jude. *J2004, b1963,*
Newsletter References; *Helwith Bridge Show 2008.*

HARRISON, Peter A.O; *J1959, b1933,*

HARRISON, Robert; AKA: Bob. *J1980,*
Newsletter References; *Alum Pot June 1980.*

HART, Jessica Rose; *J2003, b1960,*
Probationary Meets; Sunset Hole.
Bulletin References; *Pyrenees Aug 2003, Pyrenees Aug 2004, Corky's Pot [Discovery] 2003-2005, Pay Sank [Discovery] 2005, Klondike Pot Digging/Exploration 2004-2007, Pyrenees 2006, Mallorca Dec 2007.*
Newsletter References; *Dan Yr Ogof/ OFD2 June 2003, Giant's Hole Jan 2004, Pikedaw Calamine Caverns Jan 2004, Sell Gill Holes Feb 2004, Corky's Digging Team 2004, Washfold Pot April 2004, Milwr Tunnel June 2004, OFD 2 June 2004, James Hall Over-Engine Mine to Titan Shaft [Bottom] Jan 2005, Roaring Hole Sept 2005, Pay Sank Breakthrough team Nov 2005, Titan Shaft Feb 2006, Peak Cavern Feb 2006, Cow Pot [Lancaster] April 2006, Pyrenees Aug 2006, Photographic Weekend Oct 2006, Great Douk Feb 2007, OFD 2 March 2007, Cwm Dwr March 2007, Hidden Earth Tewkesbury, Support Oct 2007, Heron Pot [High level route] March 2008, Valley Entrance June 2008, SRT Training Ingleborough Hall Oct 2009, Hull Pot [Filming with the BBC] Oct 2010.*

HART, Terrance; *J1966,*

HARTLAND, Michael W; *J1959, b1940,*
BPC President 1994-95.
Bulletin References; *Alum Pot July 1960, Pen-y-Ghent Long Churn Nov 1963, Clachaig Gully [Summer] 1966, Lancaster Easegill 1966, Sell Gill 1966, Giant's Hole & P8 Rescue 1966, Alum Pot/Diccan Pot 1966, Blencathra March 1968, Bowfell Buttress 1968, Lyke Wake Walk 1968, Gavel Pots, Bishopdale 1972, September Rift GG, Sept 1971, The Dales Way 1973, The Lairig Ghru [Winter] 1975, The Littondale Horseshoe March 1975, Mallerstang Marathon 1984, Beinn Mheadhoin 1995, Pay Sank [Discovery] 2005, Klondike Pot Digging/Exploration 2004-2007.*

Newsletter References; *Leader Lost John's Aug 1965, Sunset Hole Jan 1969, Lake District Walk March 1969, Lancaster Hole Sept 1969, Short Drop -Gavel Oct 1969, Lakes Walking Meet Nov 1969, Lancaster-County Pot Feb 1970, Marble Steps March 1970, Short Drop Cave Oct 1971, Dufton-High Force Walking Meet Oct 1971, Sell Gill Hole Oct 1971, Sunset Hole Nov 1971, Grange Rigg–Christmas Pot Jan 1972, Rift–Long Kin East Pot Sept 1972, Rowten Pot Dec 1972, Little Neath River Cave June 1973, Sunset Hole March 1974, Lancaster Hole Sept 1974, Swildons Oct 1974, Whernside Walk Feb 1976, Lost John's Sept 1978, Gunnerside Gill Lead Mines June 1985, Eden Valley-Teesdale Walking Meet Oct 1985, Short Drop Pot Nov 1985, Short Drop Cave Nov 1989, Easegill Caverns Sept 1990, Pen-y-Ghent Pot entrance restoration June 1991, Crooklands Walking Meet Sept 1993, Millenium Walk Sept 2002, Klondyke Pot Digging Team Jan 2005, Calf Holes & Browgill Cave Nov 2004, Pay Sank Exploration Sept 2005, Dufton–Garrigill Lakes Walk Sept 2005, High Douk, Middle Washfold & Great Douk June 2006, Ulverston-Coniston Walking Meet 2007, Lambrigg Fell–Tebay Walk Sept 2008, Dunsop Bridge-Bilsborrow Walking Meet Sept 2009, Walking Meet Orton-Kirkby Thore Sept 2010, Feizor-Moughton Walk July 2011, Cautley-Kirkby Stephen Walk Sept 2011, Crosby Ravensworth-Askham Walking Meet Sept 2012, President's Meet Ribblesdale Walk June 2014, Walking Meet 2015, New Biggin on Lune to Appleby Walking Meet Sept 2016, Cow Green Reservoir–Appleby Walking Meet 2018.*

HARTLEY, Fay Deirdre; *J2006, b1946,*
Member; *CUCC, MCC, BCC, MUSS, RDCC, DCC, PDMHS, JCG, FICC, CCG, PCC, NZSS, LC, WRCPC.*
Bulletin References; *Pyrenees 2006, Ordessa National Park 2007, Gouffre Pont Du Gerbout Aug 2011, Trapped in Hagg Gill several hours [Flood] Sept 2010, Gouffre De Heretiques Aug 2011, Doubs, France Aug 2009, Croesor-Rhosydd Feb 2009, Felix Trombe 2011, Alderley Edge Mines Sept 2009, Washfold Pot April 2004, Rumbling Hole July 2006, Black Shiver Pot July 2006, Lost John's Hole Sept 2006, Pyrenees Aug 2006, Derbyshire Meet Jan 2007, Top Sink-Lancaster Hole Feb 2007, OFD 1& 2 March 2007, White Scar Cave April 2007, Providence Pot-Dow Cave April 2007, Heron Pot Sept 2007, Ordessa National Park Spanish Pyrenees 2007, Hidden Earth Tewkesbury, Support Oct 2007, Hard Level-Brandy Bottle Incline Nov 2007, Vesper Pot Jan 2008, King Pot Feb 2008, Notts Pot March 2008, Bull Pot April 2008, Notts Pot [With Antares CC] Sept 2008, Dowkabottom Cave Sept 2008, Meregill Hole Dec 2008, Robinsons Pot Sept 2008, Pay Sank Feb 2009, Cow Pot April 2009, Nettle Pot July 2009, Large-Rift Pot Exchange July 2009, Notts Pot Sept 2009, Link Pot Sept 2009, Alderley Edge Mines Sept 2009, Rift-LKE Oct 2009, SRT Training Ingleborough Hall Oct 2009, Lost John's Hole Nov 2009, Hunt Pot Dec 2009, Croesor-Rhosydd March 2010, Wretched Rabbit-County Pot Nov 2010, Ireby Fell Cavern Jan 2011, Wretched Rabbit-Lancaster Jan 2012, Bull Pot of the Witches Jan 2013, Titan-JH April 2013, Giant's Hole April 2013, Pen-y-ghent Pot May 2013, Roger Kirk Cave Oct 2013, Hurnell Moss Pot Oct 2013, Sell Gill Holes Nov 2013, Mongo Gill Nov 2013, Magnetometer Pot Nov 2013, Boxhead-Cracker Feb 2014, Aquamole Dec 2014, Pasture Gill Jan 2015, The Borehole-Boundary Pot Feb 2015, Simpson's Pot May 2015, Otter Hole July 2015, Fairy Holes Sept 2015, Alderley Edge Mines Oct 2015, Water Icicle Oct 2015, Jingling Pot Dec 2015, Ireby Fell Caverns Jan 2016, JH Mine March 2016, Wretched Rabbit-County Pot April 2016, Meregill Hole May 2016, Simpson's Pot Aug 2016, Simpson's Pot Aug 2016, Voldemort-Committee Pot July 2016, Pool Sink-County Pot Oct 2016, Hunt Pot-Shrapnel Pot Nov 2016, Bruntscar Cave Jan 2017, Bull Pot Feb 2017, Heron Pot [Novice trip] April 2017, Link Pot April 2017, Black Shiver May 2017, Short Drop-Gavel Pot Nov 2017, Lindale-Greenodd Walking Meet 2017, Lancaster Hole Oct 2017, Brackenbottom Pot Dec 2017, Wretched Rabbit-Top Sink Jan 2018, Jingling Pot Feb 2018, Jingling Pot/Bull Pot [CPC joint trip] April 2018, Notts Pot Sept 2018, Ingleborough Cave Oct 2018, Death's Head-Lost John's-Committee Pot Nov 2018, Oxlow-Maskhill Mine Oct 2018, Vulcan Pot Oct 2018, Wretched Rabbit-Lancaster Hole Dec 2018, Lancaster Hole-Wretched Rabbit Nov 2018, Bull Pot of the Witches Jan 2019,Pikedaw Calamine Cavern Dec 2018, Cow Pot March 2019, Heron Pot July 2019, Kirkby Lonsdale-Wharton Walking Meet Sept 2019, Bull Pot Oct 2019, Pool Sink-Boundary Pot Nov 2019, Bullpot Jan 2020, Pool Sink-Wretched Rabbit Feb 2020.*

HASLAM, Ben; *J2018, b1993,*
Member; *Another Club.[idiot]*
Newsletter References; *Darnbrook Pot June 2018, Voldemort Pot-Notts 2 Feb 2018.*

HASLAM, Helen; *J2018, b1962,*
Member; *Another Club [idiot]*
Newsletter Reference; *Ibbeth Peril caves April 2018, Darnbrook Pot June 2018, Long Churns Feb 2019, Sell Gill Nov 2019.*
HASLAM, Scott; *J2018, b1997,*
Member; *Another Club.[idiot]*
Newsletter References; *Top Sink-Wretched Rabbit Jan 2018, Darnbrook Pot June 2018, Voldemort Pot-Notts 2 Feb 2018, Oxlow-Maskhill Mine Oct*

2018, Wizard's Chasm Dec 2018, Sunset Hole Feb 2020.

HASSLEDEN, K; *J1959,*

HATTON, John Geoffrey; *J1956, b1938,*

HAWKINS, Graham; *J1964, b1948,*
Probationary Meets; GG64 [CPC], Lancaster Hole, Sleets Ghyll.

HAYDOCK, Graham David; AKA: ZIPPY. *J2004, b1976,*
Re-Joined 2017.
Probationary Meets; Brow Gill-Calf Holes, Dow Cave, Birkwith, Old Ing, Upper Eglin, Long Churns.
Newsletter References; *Old Ing-Birkwith July 2017, Long Churns [Childrens Trip] April 2018, KMC [Childrens Trip] June 2018.*

HAYNES, Sheryl Jeanne; See Abbott.

HAYWOOD, S;

HAZELL, James; *J2001, b1984,*
Probationary Meets; Nenthead Mines, Notts Pot, Shuttleworth Cave.

HEALE, John; AKA: Jumbo. *J2004, b1959,*
Probationary Meets; Jackdaw Hole, Flood Entrance, Stream Passage, Lost John's, Runscar Cavbes.
Member; WSG.
Newsletter References; *Old Ing/Dismal Hill Oct 2004, Gingling Hole July 2005, Ireby Fell Caverns Nov 2005, Rumbling Hole July 2006, Karwendel Mountains June 2006.*

HEALEY, Dyson; *J1993, b1976,*
Probationary Meets; Alum Pot,

HEAP, David; *J1956, b1940,*

HEATH, Bruce Michael; *J1961, b1943,*
Probationary Meets; Sell Gill, Sunset Hole, Lost John's.

HEATON, Sam I; *J2009, b1985,*

HEMMINGWAY, Herman; *J1961, b1917,*
Probationary Meets; Sell Gill Holes, Easegill Caverns.

HENDY, John; *J1992,*
Probationary Meets; GG92.
Newsletter References; *Alum Pot Nov 1993.*

HENDY, Peter; *J1992,*
Probationary Meets; GG92.
HEPWORTH, Brian George; *J1967, b1946,*
Probationary Meets; GG67, 3 Private Meets.

HERBERT, S. I; *J1981,*

HERON, Emma; *J2010, b1976,*
Probationary Meets; GG11, Hardwarkin, Dub Cote.
Member; WCC, CDG.
Bulletin References; *Gandara through trip Ason Gorge Spain, May 2014, Picos de Europa, Cueva Barbancho July 2011.*
Newsletter References; *Langdale-Stickle Tarn walk March 2012, Providence-Dow Cave April 2012, Rana/Claonite, Smoo Caves Oct 2012, White Keld Sump 5 Location [Diving] Feb 2013.*

HESELTINE, John Stuart; *J2009, b1945,*
Bulletin References; *Reseau de la Pierre Saint Martin Aug 2013, Gouffre Pont Du Gerbout Aug 2011, Gouffre De Heretiques Aug 2011, Felix Trombe 2011, OBJ Connection to GG May 2010.*
Newsletter Rerferences; *Pay Sank Feb 2009, Lost John's March 2009, Cow Pot April 2009, Lancaster-Wretched Rabbit June 2009, Large-Rift Pot Exchange July 2009, Notts Pot Sept 2009, Link Pot Sept 2009, Ireby Fell Caverns Oct 2009, SRT Training Ingleborough Hall Oct 2009, Death's Head Hole Nov 2009, Lost John's Hole Nov 2009, Providence Pot-Dow Cave Nov 2009, Pool Sink-Easegill Dec 2009, Marble Steps Jan 2010, Tatham Wife Hole Feb 2010, Swinsto Hole Feb 2010, Rumbling Hole March 2010, Magnetometer Pot April 2010, Hurnell Moss Pot April 2010, Marble Steps June 2010, Alum Pot July 2010, Easter Grotto Photo Trip July 2010, Lost John's-Boxhead Pot Sept 2010, Alum Pot Oct 2010, Diccan Pot Oct 2010, Juniper Gulf Oct 2010, Wretched Rabbit-County Pot Nov 2010, Rowten Pot Nov 2010, Cherry Tree Hole Jan 2011, Committee Pot March 2011, Titan-Peak Cavern March 2011, Black Shiver Pot April 2011, Link Pot-Wretched Rabbit June 2011, Jingling Hole June 2011, Big Meanie Sept 2011, Long Kin West Oct 2011, Robinson's Pot Oct 2011, New Rift Pot Oct 2011, Swinsto Hole Nov 2011, Hunt Pot-Shrapnel Pot Nov 2011, Wretched Rabbit-Lancaster Jan 2012, Simpson's Pot Jan 2012, Excalibur Pot March 2012, Juniper Gulf March 2012, Cow Pot March 2012, Washfold Pot April 2012, Sell Gill May 2012, Old Ing/Calf Holes-Browgill [Novice Trip] July 2012, Boxhead-Lost John's July 2012, Committee Pot Sept 2012, Trou du Garde / Creux de la Cavale-Bauges Aug 2012, Rowten Pot Sept 2012, Little Hull Pot Sept 2012, Deaths Head-Notts Oct 2012, Croesor Rhosydd [Through] Oct 2012, Brackenbottom Pot Nov 2012, Jingling Pot Nov*

2012, Aquamole Pot Dec 2012, Sell Gill Dec 2012, Bull Pot of the Witches Jan 2013, Swinsto-KMC Feb 2013, Notts Pot [Twilightt Zone] Feb 2013, Notts Pot-Lost John's March 2013, Top Sink-Lancaster Hole March 2013, JH-Titan April 2013, Pen-y-ghent Pot May 2013, Illusion Pot June 2013, Boxhead-Cracker Feb 2014, Marble Steps April 2014, Bore Hole-Boudary Pot May 2014, White Scar Cave July 2014, Lancaster-Wretched Rabbit July 2014, Notts 2 Sump 2 By-pass Aug 2014, Juniper Gulf Oct 2014, Mistral Hole Nov 2014, Lancaster-County Pot Nov 2014, Lancaster-Wretched Rabbit Nov 2014, Aquamole Dec 2014, Bull Pot of the Witches Jan 2015, The Borehole-Boundary Pot Feb 2015, Link Pot March 2015, Simpson's Pot May 2015, Gingling Hole July 2015, Fairy Holes Sept 2015, Alum-Diccan Pot Nov 2015, Jingling Pot Dec 2015, Ireby Fell Caverns Jan 2016, Titan Streamway March 2016, County Pot-Wretched Rabbit April 2016, County Pot-Boundary Pot April 2016, Meregill Hole May 2016, Voldemort-Committee Pot July 2016, Pool Sink-County Pot Oct 2016, Marble Steps Nov 2016, Alum Pot Dec 2016, Cow Pot Jan 2017,Short Drop-Gavel Pot March 2017, Link Pot April 2017, Black Shiver May 2017, Lancaster Hole Oct 2017, Top Sink-Wretched Rabbit Jan 2018, Notts Pot Sept 2018, Alum Pot Oct 2018, Death's Head-Lost John's-Committee Pot Nov 2018, Oxlow-Maskhill Mine Oct 2018, Lancaster Hole [Magic Roundabout Series] Nov 2018, Wretched Rabbit-Lancaster Hole Dec 2018, Bull Pot of the Witches Jan 2019, Cow Pot March 2019, Magnetometer Pot Sept 2019, Pool Sink-Boundary Pot Nov 2019, Bullpot Jan 2020, Pool Sink-Wretched Rabbit Feb 2020.

HESELTINE, Tom; *J1951, b1928,*
Bulletin References; *Lost John's July 1951.*

HESLOP, Michael; *J1969, b1950,*
Newsletter References; *Bull Pot of the Witches July 1969.*

HESSELDEN, Kenneth; *J1964,*
Bulletin References; *Lost John's March 1961, Little Hull Pot Feb 1961, Jockey Hole Feb 1962, Stream Passage Pot June 1962, Long Kin West July 1962.*

HEYLINGS, Ian George; *J1969, b1950,*
Probationary Meets; Alum Pot.
Newsletter References; *Kingsdale Master Cave Dec 1969.*

HEYLINGS, John Falkner; *J1969, b1948,*
Probationary Meets; Alum Pot.
Newsletter References; *Kingsdale Master Cave Dec 1969.*

HICK, Roger Geoffrey Andrew; *J1960, b1944,*
Probationary Meets; GG60, Lancaster-Easegill, Bull Pot.
Bulletin References; *Pen-y-ghent pot 1961.*

HICKMAN, Joanne; *J2016, b1978,*
Probationary Meets; Slovenia 2015, KMC, Notts 2, Goyden.
Newsletter References; *KMC [Novice Trip] Jan 2016, Notts 2 Jan 2016, Browgill Jan 2016, KMC/Toyland Feb 2016, Katnot Cave/Thorne Cave [Novice Trip] May 2016, Sell Gill June 2016, Marble Steps Nov 2016, Devis Hole/Mine July 2017, Alum/Long Churns June 2017, Grampian Meet Aug 2017, Sell Gill Sept 2017, Stump Cross Caverns Nov 2018.*

HIGGINS, John; *J1966, b1937,*
Probationary Meets; Sunset, Bar Pot, Calf Holes.

HIGGINS, Martin; *J1985, b1937,*
Newsletter References; *Top Sink-County Pot April 1985, Lost John's Pot July 1985.*

HILL, Elaine Alais Susanna; *J2010, b1963,*
Probationary Meets; Rumbling Hole, Gouffre Berger, Easegill, Oxlow, Nentheadf Mines, Trou qui Souffle, Great Douk.
Member; KCC, CPC, CDG, TSG, NPC.
Club Expeditions; Gouffre Berger 2010, Ardeche, Dordogne 2010.
Bulletin References; *New Zealand Jan 2011.*
Newsletter References; *Rumbling Hole March 2010, Ireland May 2010, Daimler Hole Sept 2010, Su Bentu [Sardinia] Oct 2010, Su Palo [Sardinia] Oct 2010, Rampgill Level Oct 2010, Smallcleugh Mine Oct 2010, Wretched Rabbit-County Pot Nov 2010, Heron Pot Nov 2010, Cherry Tree Hole Jan 2011, Oxlow Caverns March 2011, Peak Cavern March 2011, Vesper Pot April 2011, Middle Earth Green link System New Zealand North Island Feb 2011, Ogof Llyn Parc Sept 2011, Lancaster-Wretched Rabbit Jan 2012, Shuttleworth Pot Feb 2012, Notts Pot March 2012, Box Freestone Mine March 2012, Charterhouse Cave March 2012,Gillfield Level May 2012, Mongo Gill May 2012, White Scar Cave July 2012, Foux de Lauret [Herault]Sept 2012, Grotte du Banquier [Herault] Sept 2012, Pikedaw Calamine Caverns Sept 2013, Short Drop-Gavel Sept 2013, Roger Kirk Cave Oct 2013, Clayton-le-Woods Victorian underground Reservoir Oct 2013, Magnetometer Pot Nov 2013, Scoska Cave April 2014, Pikedaw Calamine Caverns Feb 2015, Bruntscar Cave July 2015, Water Icicle Oct 2015, Sell Gill Feb 2016, Great Douk Sept 2016, Stump Cross Caverns July 2018.*

HILL, Keith Ian; *J1988, b1958,*

HINCHCLIFFE, Nicholas B; *J2005, b1964,*
Probationary Meets; Yordas, Calf Holes, Roger Kirk Cave.
Member; TCC, YMC, FRCC, TC.
Club expeditions; Slovenia 2018.
Notable Achievements; Makes no claims of notoriety but has featured on page three of the Sun.
Main Activities; Walking, Climbing, Caving & Biking -"all badly"
Famous for; Featuring on page three of the Sun [Really]
Bulletin References; *Eagle Ridge Feb 1985, Alderley Edge Mines Sept 2009.*
Newsletter References; *Yordas Pot & Cave Dec 2004, Calf Holes & Dismal Hill & Old Ing Jan 2005, Lancaster Hole April 2005, Ireby Fell Caverns Nov 2005, Jackpot P8 Feb 2006, Peak Cavern Feb 2006, Tatham Wife Hole March 2006, Lost John's Hole Sept 2006, Pyrenees Aug 2006, Coniston Copper Mines Oct 2006, Dismal Hill/Old Ing Feb 2007, Cwm Dwr March 2007, Short Drop/Gavel March 2007, Committee Pot July 2007, Swinsto Hole June 2007, Heron Pot Sept 2007, Long Churns Training Meet Dec 2007, Hard Level-Brandy Bottle Incline Nov 2007, Aygill Caverns Feb 2008, Cherry Tree Hole Oct 2008, KMC Sept 2009, Alderley Edge Mines Sept 2009, Committee Pot March 2011, Robinson's Pot Oct 2011, Swinsto Hole Nov 2011, Keld Bank Sink Nov 2011, Illusion Pot Dec 2011, Sell Gill Holes March 2012, Long Churns March 2012, Gillfield Level May 2012, Blue John Aug 2012, Committee Pot Sept 2012, Yordas Pot Oct 2014, Calf Holes-Browgill and Old Ing-Birkwith June 2015, Lost John's-Notts 2 Sept 2015, Old Ing-Birkwith July 2017, Long Churns & BorrinsMoor Sept 2018, Ingleborough Cave Oct 2018, Stump Cross Caverns Nov 2018, Great Douk Jan 2019, Long Churns Feb 2019, Sunset Hole April 2019, High Douk May 2019, Illusion Pot Sept 2019.*

HINCHCLIFFE, Rose; *J1984,*
Newsletter References; *Sleets Gill June 1985, Eden Valley-Teesdale Walking Meet Oct 1985.*

HINDLE, Joanne; *J2018, b1967,*

HINDLE, Melvin J; *J1959, b1942,*
Probationary Meets; Long Kin West 1958.
Bulletin References; *Pen-y-ghent Pot April 1960, Alum Pot July 1960, Lancaster-Eastgill Aug 1960, Bull Pot Sept 1960, Flood Entrance Pot Dec 1960, Involved with building electron ladders, 1960's,*
Newsletter References; *Swinsto Hole Oct 1959.*

HIRST, J; *J1958,*

HITT, Malcolm Rodney; *J1960, b1944,*
Probationary Meets; Clapham Cave, Alum Pot, Lancaster Hole.
Bulletin References; *Lancaster-Eastgill Aug 1960, Bar Pot Easter Sunday 1961, Oxlow Caverns June 1961, Alum Pot Aug 1958.*

HITT, Peter Dennis Pearson; *J1958, b1939,*
Bulletin References; *Lancaster Hole June 1958, Gaping Gill Meet 1960, Pen-y-Ghent Pot Feb 1964.*
Newsletter References; *Alum Pot Aug 1958, Dowbergill Passage April 1959, GG members meet 1959, Marble Steps Sept 1959.*

HOBBS, John Christopher; *J1960, b1943,*
Probationary Meets; Goyden Pot, Marble Steps, Lost John's.

HOBKIRK, Eddie; *J before 1938,*

HODGE, Gillian; *J2012, b*

HODGSON, Andrea; *J1993, b1960,*
Probationary Meets; Pen-y-Ghent Pot, Lancaster-Wretched Rabbit, Swinsto.
Member; UBUPC.

HOFFMAN, Sarah; *J2019, b1983,*
Probationary Meets; Swinsto, Lost John's, Bull Pot, Alum Pot.

HOGGARTH, Laura Bethany; See Myers.

HOLDEN, Jon; AKA: Bump. *J2014, b1972,*
Probationary Meets; GG14, GG15, GG16, Long Churn, Marble Steps, Lancaster Hole, Ireby Fell, Hunt Pot.
Member; RFDCC, MNRC.

HOLDEN, Thirza; See Hyde.

HOLDER, Charles David; AKA: Chuck. *J2010, b1984,*
Probationary Meets; GG-Stream Passage Pot, Lost John's Hole, Rowten Pot.
Member; YUCPC, YCC, EUSS.
Newsletter References; *Lost John's-Boxhead Pot Sept 2010, Hull Pot [Filming with the BBC] Oct 2010, Rowten Pot Nov 2010, Calf Holes-Browgill/Old Ing June 2011, Darnbrook Pot [Novice Trip] Sept 2011, Wretched Rabbit-Lancaster Jan 2012, Sell Gill March 2012, Gillfield Level May 2012, Mongo Gill May 2012, Hurnell Moss Pot Oct 2013, Greenside Mine April 2014, The Borehole-Boundary Pot Feb 2015, County Pot Feb 2015,*

Clapham Bottoms [Survey] Feb 2015, Link Pot-Cow Pot June 2015, Sunset Hole July 2015, Calf Holes [Novice Trip] July 2015, Lost John's-Notts 2 Sept 2015, Alum-Diccan Pot Nov 2015, KMC [Novice Trip] Jan 2016, CNCC SRT Workshop Feb 2016, Lost John's-Boxhead Pot March 2016, Wretched Rabbit-County Pot April 2016, Pillar Holes April 2016, Otter Hole June 2016, Simpson's Pot Aug 2016, Notts Pot Feb 2017, Jingling Pot/Bull Pot [CPC joint trip] April 2018, Bull Pot Oct 2019, Pool Sink-Boundary Pot Nov 2019, Aquamole Pot Nov 2019.

HOLDER, Mary; [née Bennetts] *J2016, b1983,*

HOLDING, Stephen;
Newsletter References; *Goyden Pot Feb 1976,*

HOLLAND, Roy; *J1960, b1930,*
Probationary Meets; Alum Pot, Easegill, Bull Pot.
Bulletin References; *Bull Pot Sept 1960, Lost John's March 1961.*

HOLMES, John; *J1989, b1956,*
Member; PMC, LUCC, CPC, BCRA, NMRS, RGS [Fellow]

HOLMES, Jack, Luther; *J1978, b1944,*
Probationary Meets; Bull Pot o t Witches, Short Drop-Gavel, Sleets Gill [Flooded]
Main Activities; Caving, Climbing, Mountaineering [Snow and Ice]
Newsletter References; *Lancaster–Ease Gill Nov 1978.*

HOLMES, Nichola Jane; *J1993, b1971,*
Probationary Meets; Simpson's Pot.
Member; NUCC.

HOLYOAKE, Emmaline; *J2017, b1974,*

HOOD, Carl Richard; *J1999, b1955,*
Newsletter References; *Pippikin Pot Nov 1999.*

HOOD, Stuart Norman; *J1963, b1947,*
Probationary Meets; Stonelands Cave, Clapham Cave, Dow Cave.
Bulletin References; *Batty Cave Jan 1964, Oxlow Caverns Feb 1964.*

HOOL, James Richard; *J1973, b1944, d2004.*
Probationary Meets; Simpson's, Mongo Gill, Gingling Hole.
Famous for; 1st ever caving trip, Tatham Wife, fell and broke his foot, PGF made him climb out on his own then had an accident bottle walking, bad cuts to hands, arms and face, then crashed his car.

Bulletin References; *Newby Moss Sink 3rd shaft 1977, Cnoc Nan Uamh & Uamh Nan Claig-Ionn Easter 1978, Grotte de Bury 1976, Gouffre Berger Aug 1980.*
Newsletter References; *Lost John's Hole Aug 1974, Gingling Hole Sept 1974, Bar Pot March 1975, Stream Passage-Flood Entrance Pot March 1976, Sunset Hole May 1976, Bull Pot of the Witches Dec 1976, Christmas Pot Feb 1977, Gouffre Berger Aug 1980, Mendip weekend April 1983, Sunset Hole & Southercales Pot June 1985, Scotland Easter 1986.*

HOOPER, Catherine Ruth; *J2018, b1985,*
Probationary Meets; GG17, GG18, Stream Passage Pot, Sell Gill.

HOPKINS, Donald; *J1987, b1950,*
Probationary Meets; South Wales, GG87, Mines of Coniston.
Bulletin References; *Deep Well [Diving support] May 1992, Ireby Fell [Diving Support] Oct 1988, Scrafton Pot June 1990, Lakes Walk Sept 1990, Easegill Caverns Sept 1990, Calf Holes, Browgill, Old Ing and Dismal Hill Jan 1991, Easegill Caverns Jan 1991, Marble Steps Pot Dec 1990, Ribblehead Caves Sept 1991, Sell Gill Training Meet Nov 1991, Pikedaw Calamine Caverns March 1992, Ireby Fell Feb 1993, Bull Pot of the Witches March 1993,*

HOPKINS, Hester Catherine; *J1990, b1960,*
Probationary Meets; Great Douk, GG13, Main Chamber-Stream Passage, Long Churns.
Member; OOPA, Chadderton Sub-Aqua Club, Oldham Canoe Club, Milnrow Tennis Club.
Newsletter References; *Yordas Pot Oct 2014, Burtersett Quarry/Mine July 2017, Grampian Meet Aug 2017, Sell Gill Sept 2017.*

HOPKINS, Malcolm; *J1956, b1935,*
Resigned Aug 1958.
Newsletter References; *Christmas Pot May 1957, Washfold Pot July 1957, Alum Pot Aug 1958.*

HOPKINS, Malcolm; *J2014, b1973,*

HOPKINS, Zoe; *J1990, b1975,*
Probationary Meets; Scrafton Pot, Easegill, Calf Holes-Brow Gill, Birkwith, Old Ing.
Newsletter References; *Scrafton Pot June 1990, Easegill Caverns Sept 1990, Calf Holes, Browgill, Old Ing and Dismal Hill Jan 1991, Easegill Caverns Jan 1991, Marble Steps Pot Dec 1990, Sell Gill Training Meet Nov 1991, Pikedaw Calamine Caverns March 1992, Bull Pot of the Witches March 1993.*

HOPKINSON, Barry; *J1960, b1941,*

Probationary Meets; Lost John's, Rift Pot, Stream Passage Pot.
Bulletin References; *Gaping Gill Meet 1960, Wharfedale Camp Aug 1960, Magnetometer Pot Nov 1960, Lost John's March 1961, Pen-y-ghent pot 1961, Recorded for describing the mountaineering in North West Scotland 1961, Goyden Pot Feb 1962, Jockey Hole Feb 1962, Flood Entrance March 1962, Stream Passage Pot June 1962, Juniper Gulf Dec 1962, Notts Pot Oct 1963.*
Newsletter References; *Bradford Mine shaft collapses Aug 1965, Land's End–John O Groats Charity Cycle Ride-2006.*

HOPWOOD, G.W; *J1981,*

HORKNEY, A; *J1983,*

HORN, Philip John; *J1963, b1944,*
Probationary Meets; Little Hull, Sunset Hole, Rowten Pot.

HORNE, Malcolm Ernest; *J1956, b1933,*
Membership lapsed 1962.
Newsletter References; *Washfold Pot July 1957.*

HORSMAN, Donald; *J1950, b1928, d1988.*
Started the Digger's Dinner with Barry Dixon.
Bulletin References; *Simpson's Pot July 1953, Juniper Gulf May 1954, Clapham Cave June 1954, Little Hull Pot July 1954, Old Ing Caves Aug 1954 [Trapped by floodwater], Bull Pot of the Witches July 1955, Clapham Cave Aug 1955, Involved with BBC transmission from Alum Pot 7th May 1961, Sell Gill & Bar Pot 1966.*
Newsletter References; *Leader-Easter Camp 1954, Leader Sell Gill July 1954, Leader Bar Pot Jan 1955, Leader Alum Pot Feb 1956, Leader Easter Camp Kingsdale Easter 1956, Simpson's Pot Aug 1957, Involved with BBC Transmission from Alum Pot May 1958.*

HORTON, Richard John Adair; *J1969, b1942,*
Probationary Meets; Agen Allwedd.

HOUNSLOW, N; *J1973,*

HOWDEN, Donald; *J1949,*
Bulletin References; *Flood Entrance July 1949.*

HOWE, Chris; *J1986,*

HOWE, David William; *J1965, b1945,*
Probationary Meets; YHA Caving Adventure Holiday-Ingleton.

Bulletin References; *Member of Swansea College of Education Speleological Society Llethrid Swallett 1968,*

HOWORTH, John Halstead; *J1953, b1934,*

HUDSON, Edward; *J1960, b1939,*
Probationary Meets; Marble Steps, Lost John's, Rift Pot.
Bulletin References; *Lost John's March 1960, Gaping Gill Meet 1960 [Dye testing], Pen-y-ghent Pot July 1960.*

HUDSON, Richard; *J2009, b1968,*
Newsletter References; *Long Churn/Dolly Tubs [Novice trip] Feb 2010, Keld Head [Diving] May 2010, Dan Yr Ogof [Far North] Sept 2010, OFD 1 Sept 2010, Wizard's Chasm Jan 2012, Providence-Dow Cave April 2012, Meregill Hole May 2016, Lancaster-County Jan 2019.*

HUGGAN, David; *J1959, b1937,*
Bulletin References; *Gaping Gill Meet 1960, Ingleborough Cave June 1959, Ingleborough Cave Sept 1959, Brown Scar Cave Sept 1959.*

HUGHES, Malcolm; *J1999, b1958,*
Bulletin References; *Doubs, France Aug 2009.*
Newsletter References; *Pippikin Pot Nov 1999, Bull Pot March 2000, Church Pot April 2000, Hagg Gill Pot June 2000, Christmas Cracker Sept 2000, Lancaster-County Aug 2000, Skirwith Cave July 2000, Rowten Pot Dec 2000, Long Kin West Feb 2001, Cherry Tree Hole Jan 2001, White Scar Cave April 2001, Ingleborough Cave Digging 2001, Swinsto Hole Jan 2002, Short Drop-Gavel Jan 2002, Hagg Gill Oct 2002, KMC-Toyland Oct 2002, Lancaster Hole Feb 2003, Sunset Hole Sept 2003, Robinson's Pot Oct 2003, Aquamole Pot Dec 2003, Giant's Hole Jan 2004, Pikedaw Calamine Caverns Jan 2004, Bull Pot Dec 2003, Swinsto Hole-KMC Feb 2004, Sell Gill Holes March 2004, Milwr Tunnel June 2004, Ireby Fell Cavern June 2004, Gingling Hole July 2004, High Hull Cave Oct 2004, Dowkabottom Cave Oct 2004, Old Ing-Dismal Hill Oct 2004, Short Drop-Gavel Pot Nov 2004, Committee Pot Nov 2004, Lancaster Hole Dec 2004, Valley Entrance Dec 2004, New Rift Dec 2004, Giant's Hole Jan 2005, Skirwith Cave Nov 2004, Yordas Pot & Cave Dec 2004, Calf Holes & Browgill Cave Nov 2004, Calf Holes & Dismal Hill & Old Ing Jan 2005, Lancaster Hole April 2005, Hardrakin Pot April 2005, Gingling Hole July 2005, Pippikin-Mistral Sept 2005, Heron Pot Nov 2005, Simpson's Pot Dec 2005, Jackpot P8 Feb 2006, Peak Cavern Feb 2006, Calf Holes & Brow Gill Cave Feb 2006, Coniston Copper Mines Oct 2006, Hunt Pot Nov 2006,*

Jingling Pot Dec 2006, Committee Pot Dec 2006, Top Sink-Lancaster Hole Feb 2007, Providence Pot-Dow Cave April 2007, Swinsto Hole June 2007, Heron Pot Sept 2007, Death's Head & Big Meanie Sept 2007, Hard Level-Brandy Bottle Incline Sept 2007, Swinsto-KMC Dec 2007, Great Expectations Dec 2007, Hard Level-Brandy Bottle Incline Nov 2007, Bull Pot of the Witches Jan 2008, Aygill Caverns Feb 2008, Heron Pot March 2008, Notts Pot March 2008, Sunset Hole April 2008, Bull Pot of the Witches June 2008, Valley Entrance June 2008, Lambrigg Fell–Tebay Walk Sept 2008, Dowkabottom Cave Sept 2008, Brackenbottom Pot Oct 2008, Hell Hole, Whitewell Cave& Pot Nov 2008, Lower Long Churn Nov 2008, Bull Pot of the Witches Jan 2009, Stump Cross Caverns Dec 2008, Aygill Caverns Jan 2009, Pay Sank Feb 2009, Pikedaw Calamina Caverns Feb 2009, New Goyden Pot March 2009, Link Pot April 2009, Stump Cross Caverns [Geoff Workman's 80th] April 2009, Nettle Pot July 2009, Heron Pot July 2009, Pool Sink-Easegill Dec 2009, Tatham Wife Hole Feb 2010, Swinsto Hole Feb 2010, Magnetometer Pot April 2010, Mistral Hole June 2010, Roaring Hole May 2010, Mistral Hole Aug 2010, Sell Gill Sept 2010, Illusion Pot Dec 2011, Lancaster-Wretched Rabbit Jan 2012, Sell Gill May 2012, Croesor Rhosydd [Through] Oct 2012, Link Pot Nov 2012, Calf Holes-Browgill Dec 2012, Bull Pot of the Witches Jan 2013, Top Sink-Lancaster Hole March 2013, Titan-JH April 2013, Illusion Pot June 2013, GB Cave June 2013, Reservoir Hole June 2013, Heron Pot Sept 2013, Sell Gill Holes Nov 2013, Mongo Gill Nov 2013, Lancaster-Wretched Rabbit Nov 2013, Magnetometer Pot Nov 2013, Marble Steps April 2014, Bore Hole-Boudary Pot May 2014, Fairy Holes Sept 2014, Nenthead Mines Sept 2014, Shuttleworth Pot Oct 2014, Yordas Pot Oct 2014, Mistral Hole Nov 2014, Lancaster-County Pot Nov 2014, Pasture Gill Jan 2015, County Pot Feb 2015, Simpson's Pot May 2015, Roaring Hole June 2015, Robinson's Pot July 2015, Alderley Edge Mines Oct 2015, Water Icicle Oct 2015, Heron Pot Nov 2015, County Pot Jan 2016, Hagg Gill April 2016, Pool Sink June 2016, Simpson's Pot Aug 2016, Simpson's Pot-KMC Dec 2016, Darnbrook Pot Oct 2016, County Pot Dec 2016, County Pot Feb 2017, Heron Pot [Novice trip] April 2017, Langstroth Cave April 2017, Robinson's Pot Sept 2017, Iron Kiln Sept 2017, Wretched Rabbit-County Pot Sept 2017, Stump Cross Caverns Dec 2017, High Douk Holes Feb 2018, Darnbrook Pot June 2018, Voldemort Pot-Notts 2 Feb 2018, Stump Cross Cavertns July 2018, Mongo Gill Sept 2018, CherryTree Hole Oct 2018, Stump Cross Caverns Nov 2018, Wizard's Chasm Dec 2018, Pikedaw Calamine Cavern Dec 2018, Wretched Rabbit-County Pot March 2019,

Heron Pot July 2019, Pool Sink-Wretched Rabbit Feb 2020.

HUGHS, John W;
Newsletter References; Goyden Pot Feb 1976,

HUMPHREY, Brian; J2003, b1948,
Probationary Meets; Top Sink-Wretched Rabbit, Ireby Fell.
Bulletin References; Pennine Way June 2002.
Newsletter References; Derbyshire Meet Jan 2004, Swinsto Hole-KMC Feb 2004, Committee Pot Nov 2004, Tatham Wife Hole March 2006, Lost John's Hole Sept 2006, Committee Pot July 2007, Bar Pot Dec 2007, Valley Entrance June 2008, Lost John's March 2009, Jingling Pot Dec 2011, Juniper Gulf March 2012.

HURST, Jack; J1957, b1935,
Suspended from club Dec 1959.
Newsletter References; Bar Pot March 1958,

HURWORTH, Alfred; J1955, b1926, d2013.
Resigned from club in protest June 1966.
Made a Honourary Member 2012.
Bulletin References; Bull Pot of the Witches July 1955, South Wales Easter 1963, Stream Passage Pot June 1958, Christmas Pot 1957, Clapham Cave Aug 1955, Clapham Cave Aug 1955, Clapham Cave March 1957, Clapham Cave Aug 1957, Clapham Cave Dec 1957, Hammer Pot March 1960, Gaping Gill Meet 1960, Bull Pot Sept 1960, Magnetometer Pot Nov 1960, Flood Entrance March 1962, Christmas Pot 1962, Long Kin West July 1962, Agen Allwedd April 1963.
Newsletter References; Recorded as sitting at the top of first pitch in Meregill to life line for nine hours! Aug 1955, Leader Marble Steps April 1956, Leader GG June 1957, Leader Main Shaft Laddering with RRCPC June 1957, Simpson's Pot Aug 1957, Rumbling Hole Oct 1957, Lancaster Hole Oct 1957, Practice stretcher rescue Wade's entrance GG Nov 1957, Private meet Clapham Cave Nov 1957, Bar Pot Dec 1957, Easter Camp April 1958, Digging near Owl Hole April 1958, Involved with BBC Transmission from Alum Pot May 1958, Lancaster Hole June 1958, Tackle testing July 1958, Alum Pot Aug 1958, OBJ Hole Nov 1958, Norway Sept/Oct 1958, Clapham Cave Nov 1958, Inauguration Aven June 1959, Ingleborough Cave Diving trip, new rift discovered July 1959, Ingleborough Cave Survey Aug 1959, Little Hull Hole Aug 1959, Diccan-Alum Exchange September 1959, Ingleborough Cave the Wallows beddings Sept 1959, Ingleborough Cave Oct 1959, Swinsto Hole Oct 1959, Leader Juniper Gulf Oct 1960, Dowber Gill Passage Oct 1960, Jnr Leader Chapel le Dale Jan 1961, Leader Stream

Passage Pot Jan 1961, Leader South Wales Camp Easter 1961, Eden Valley-Teesdale Walking Meet Oct 1985.

HUTCHINSON, Martin G; *J1956, b1940,*
Unorthodox application form.

HUTCHINSON, Peter; *J1959, b1924,*

HUTTON, J.G; *J1956,*

HYDE, David; *J1982, b1954,*
Member; GSS.
Probationary Meets; Rowten Pot, Jingling Pot, Dowbergill Passage, Dow Cave, Langstroth Pot.
Found a new carbide lamp in Dow Cave
Bulletin References; *Cow Garth Cave [Exploration] 1982/84, Vercors Aug 1983, Climbing Stream Passage Pot May 1984, Kamniski Alps Aug 1988, Dub Cote Extensions [Diving] 1990, Tanne De Bel Espoir-La Diau Parmilan 1991.*
Newsletter References; *Dow-Providence Sept 1981, Ingleborough Cave Oct 1982, Meregill Feb 1983, Gingling Hole June 1983, Pippikin-Link July 1983, Quaking Pot Aug 1983, County Pot March 1984, Langstroth Pot March 1984, Lost John's Pot July 1985, Langstroth Pot Sept 1985, Gingling Hole Oct 1985, Eden Valley-Teesdale Walking Meet Oct 1985, Pool Park Oct 1986, County Pot-Lancaster March 1986, Lakes Walking Meet Oct 1987, Magnetometer Pot Oct 1987, Ireby Fell [Diving] Oct 1988, South Wales Nov 1988, King Pot Jan 1989, Langstroth Pot & Cave [Diving] July 1989, Lakes Walk Sept 1990, Bird Watching Lakes Walk Sept 1990, Easegill Caverns Jan 1991, Lakes Meet June 1992.*

HYDE, Thirza; [née Holden] *J1982, b1959,*
Member; GSS.
Probationary Meets; Rowten Pot, Jingling Pot, Dowbergill Passage, Dow Cave, Langstroth Pot.
Rescued from Dowber Gill and Birks Fell Pot Nov 1978.
Bulletin References; *Cow Garth Cave [Exploration] 1982 / 84, Vercors Aug 1983, Kamniski Alps Aug 1988, Tanne De Bel Espoir-La Diau Parmilan 1991.*
Newsletter References; *Dow-Providence Sept 1981, Ingleborough Cave Oct 1982, Pasture Gill Pot June 1983, Gingling Hole June 1983, Quaking Pot Aug 1983, County Pot March 1984, Langstroth Pot March 1984, Lost John's Pot July 1985, Pool Park Oct 1986, County Pot-Lancaster March 1986, Lakes Walking Meet Oct 1987, South Wales Nov 1988, Langstroth Pot & Cave [Diving] July 1989, Lakes Walk Sept 1990, Bird Watching Lakes Walk Sept 1990, Lakes Meet June 1992.*

5

I

ILLINGWORTH, Titus; AKA: Runt. *J1933, b1905, d1964.*
Founder Member
Bulletin References;
Recorded as down Dowka Bottom 29th Sept 1946.

INGHAM, Alfred Pearson; *J before 1938,*

INGHAM, Stuart Frederick; *J2011, b1946, d2012.*
Member; ULCC, ULSA, LCCC, NB,
Newsletter References; *Digging in Cupcake, Clapham Bottoms and Shuttleworth Pot. Whilst digging 'The Pot With No Name' in Clapham Bottoms he demonstrated his prodigious strength by dispatching some of the huge boulders which were pulled out of the shaft. Stuart was a regular member of Andrew Hinde's Cave Conservation Volunteers and had been on most of the fencing, tree planting, stile building and cave entrance stabilisation projects over the previous couple of years.*

IRVING, Marcus; *J2010, b1975,*
Newsletter References; *Pool Sink-Easegill Dec 2009, Lower Long Churn-Dolly Tubs Jan 2010, Kalymnos Climbing July 2011.*

IBSON, Andrew Kevin; *J1961, b1944,*
Probationary Meets; Sunset Hole, Long Kin East Pot, Sell Gill.

41

J

JACKSON, Andrew Mark; AKA: Martell. *J1989, b1969,*
Probationary Meets; Notts Pot, Lost John's, King Pot.
Bulletin References; *Giggle Rav Pot, [Dig/exploration] 1989, Brackenbottom Pot, [Dig/exploration] 1989, Dig above Hagg Gill Pot 1991, Trou De Glaz Aug 1989, Brackenbottom Pot 1989, Remembrance Pot July 1994, Short Gill Rising [Dive/dig] 1981, Digging unknown hole Langstrthdale 1991, Manchester Hole D/S Sump extension [Diving] 1991, Deep Well [Diving support] May 1992, Albania 1992, Spluga Della Preta Sept 1992, Sludge Cave [Discovery] Aug 1993, Belfry [GG] Exploration May 1996, Lechuguilla Cave USA 1998, Nguom Lang Van & Nguom Chiem Vietnam 2003, Mallorca Dec 2007, The Bob Graham Round [22:49] 2011.*
Newsletter References; *King Pot Jan 1989, Langstroth Pot & Cave [Diving] July 1989, Ireby Fell March 1990, Simpsons–KMC July 1990, Easegill Caverns Sept 1990, Eldon Hole & Oxlow Caverns Oct 1990, Black Shiver Pot Jan 1991, Calf Holes, Browgill, Old Ing and Dismal Hill Jan 1991, Lost John's March 1991, Pen-y-Ghent Pot entrance restoration June 1991, Marble Steps Pot Dec 1990, Magnetometer Pot July 1991, Birks Fell Cave July 1991, Sell Gill Training Meet Nov 1991, Ireby Fell Jan 1992, Pikedaw Calamine Caverns March 1992, Lakes Meet June 1992, KMC Oct 1993, Alum Pot Nov 1993, Rowten Pot Nov 1993, Ireby Fell Feb 1993, 5 Caves Trip July 1993, Cow Pot March 1993, Bull Pot of the Witches March 1993, Snatcher's Pot Nov 1993, Bagshaw Caverns Oct 1993, Coniston Mines Weekend Sept 1993,GG Photographic Meet May 1993, Cherry Tree Hole Jan 1994, Simpson's-Swinsto March 1994, Manchester By-pass-Wretched Rabbit March 1995, Mongo Gill March ·*

1995, Deaths Head-Big Meanie Jan 1996, Simpson's-Swisto Feb 1996, Diccan Pot March 1996, Swinsto-Simpson's 1996, Notts Pot Jan 1997, Mongo Gill March 1997, Lost John's Hole March 1997, Rowten Pot/Jingling Pot July 1997, GG Photographic Meet May 1998, Barclays Lode Wales July 1998, Nent Head-Brewery Shaft Oct 1998, Fat Finger Millennium Party, Bar Pot [Rope Ladder]May 2000, Langstroth Pot June 2000, Hidden Earth Tewkesbury, Support Oct 2007, Ireby Fell Caverns [A grand day out-digging Whirlpool] Feb 2008.

JACKSON, Leslie Ann Bernadette; See Bottomley.

JACKSON, Richard; AKA: Dick. *J?, b1922,*
Newsletter Reference: *Lancaster-Easegill Feb 1969.*

JACKSON, John Michael; *J1950,*

JACKSON, Lesley H; *J1962,*

JACKSON, Sydney Hardisty; *J1962, b1922, d2007.*
Probationary Meets; GG61, Bar Pot, Lancaster Hole, Pikedaw Mine, Goyden Pot,
Lancaster Hole Jan 1966.
Newsletter Reference: *Lancaster-Easegill Feb 1969.*

JAGGER, Elaine Margeret; *J1987, b1959,*
Rejoined 1993.
Probationary Meets; GG87, Tatham Wife, Little Neath, Swinsto, Sell Gill.
Newsletter References; *Sell Gill Hole Feb 1985.*

JAGGER, Mathew; *J2010, b1982,*

Probationary Meets; Stream Passage Pot, Marilyn, Flood Entrance, Bar Pot, Simpson's Pot.
Re-joined 2013.
Newsletter References; *Cwm Dwr-OFD Top Ent June 2009, Alum Pot April 2013, Titan-JH April 2013.*

JAKUSCZ, J;
Newsletter References; County Pot Aug 1976.

JAMES, Mathew; *J1979,*

JARMAN, Robert Alfred; *J1957, b1934,*
Bulletin References; *Lost John's March 1960, Gaping Gill Meet 1960 [Diving Trip], Involved with BBC transmission from Alum Pot 7th May 1961, Lost John's March 1961, Stonelands Pot June 1961, Clapham Cave 1961, Grange Rigg Easter 1961, Clapham Cave-Diving Feb 1962, Ingleborough Cave Diving Dec 1962.*
Newsletter References; *Simpson's Pot Aug 1957, Swinsto Sept 1957, Rumbling Hole Oct 1957, Lancaster Hole Oct 1957, Practice stretcher rescue Wade's entrance GG Nov 1957, Dow-Providence rescue Dec 1957, Bar Pot Dec 1957, Alum Pot Sept 1957, Tackle testing Jan 1958, Easter Camp April 1958, Stream Passage Pot April 1958, Beck Head April 1958, Flood Entrance Pot April 1958, Little Hull Pot April 1958, Involved with BBC Transmission from Alum Pot May 1958, Lancaster Hole June 1958, Swildon's Hole Aug 1958, Alum Pot Aug 1958, Alum Pot Oct 1958, English Electric Trip-Alum Pot Nov 1958, Bar Pot Nov 1958, Clapham Cave Nov 1958, Digging near Owl Hole Dec 1958, Alum Pot April 1959, Lower Gunnerfleet Cave April 1959, Ingleborough Cave June 1959, Diccan-Alum Exchange September 1959, Ingleborough Cave Sept 1959, Brown Scar Cave Sept 1959, Ingleborough Cave Oct 1959, Bar Pot Nov 1959.*

JARVIS, Colin Philip; AKA: Big Col. *J1999, b1962,*
Probationary Meets; Alum Pot.
Newsletter References; *Great/Little Douk Dec 2001, Sell Gill Holes Feb 2004, Long Churn [Childrens Meet] April 2018.*

JARVIS, Emma; *J2009, b1988,*

JARVIS, Neil; *J2016, b1966,*
Probationary Meets; Great Douk.
Newsletter References; *Katnot Cave/Thorne Cave [Novice Trip] May 2016, Ibbeth Peril Caves April 2018.*

JARVIS, Robert; AKA: Stemple, Smeagle. *J2004, b1988,*

Probationary Meets; Flood Entrance-Stream Passage Pot, Hensler's, De-rig Flood Entrance.
Newsletter References; *Sell Gill Holes Feb 2004, James Hall Mine Feb 2006, Peak Cavern Feb 2006, Rumbling Hole July 2006, Upper & Lower Long Churn Nov 2006, Aquamole Pot Jan 2007, Derbyshire Meet Jan 2007, Link Pot Nov 2012, Sunset Hole July 2015, Simpson's Pot Aug 2016, County Pot-Pool Sink Oct 2016, Dawn Chamber GG May 2017, Dawn Chamber GG May 2018.*

JARVIS, Wendy; *J1981, b1950,*
Rejoined *J2011.*
Newsletter References; *Short Drop Pot Nov 1985, Scotland Easter 1986, Scotland 1987, Weathercote Cave April 1988.*

JEFFCOCK, Mathew; *J2009, b1991,*

JEFFIES, R;

JEFFS, Peter; *J1954, b1938,*

JEMINSON, Philip Martin; *J1989, b1968,*

JENKINS, Rhianwen H; *J2003, b1964,*
Probationary Meets; OFD, Goyden & Manchester Hole, Calf Holes, GG03, Long Churns.
Newsletter References; *OFD 2 June 2003, Great Douk Cave Sept 2003, Sell Gill Holes Feb 2004.*

JENNINGS, Victoria; *Temporary Membership.*

JENSEN, Lotte Gerner; *Temporary Membership.*

JEPPS, Simon Philip; *J2010, b1982,*
Bulletin References; *Coast to Coast Plus July / Aug 1978.*

JEPSON, Arnold; *J1935,*

JESSOP, Michael John; AKA: Crispy Knees. *J1973, b1949,*
Probationary Meets; GG73, Goyden Pot, KMC.

JEWELL, Chris; *J2009, b1982,*
Probationary Meets; Wookey Hole [Diving], Short Gill Rising [Digging], Roaring Hole.
Newsletter References; *Notts Pot Sept 2009, Roaring Hole [Diving] Extended sump by 70 Meters [@30Meters] May 2010, Ellerbeck Hole [Digging] May 2010.*

JOHNSON, Ian; AKA: Max 2. *J2005, b1971,*
Probationary Meets; Lost John's, Notts Pot, Robinson's Cave, GG04/5.
Rejoined 2012.

Newsletter References; *Heron Pot [Abandoned Photo Meet] Nov 2003, Long Kin East Nov 2003, Derbyshire Meet Jan 2004, Swinsto Hole-KMC Feb 2004, Notts Pot March 2004, Washfold Pot April 2004, Lancaster Hole April 2005.*

JOHNSON, Kate M; *J2007, b1963,*
Probationary Meets; Heron Pot, Long Churns, Calf Holes-Brow Gill.

JOHNSON, Pamela Ann; *J1990, b1960,*
Probationary Meets; Fisherstreet Cave, Dow Cave, Old Ing, Birkwith, Calf Holes, Long Churns.

JOLLEY, Kenneth; *J1951, b1917,*

JONES, Christopher Michael; *J2011, b1964,*

JONES, David Nigel; *J1965,*

JONES, Gemma Danielle [Dr]; *J2003, b1978,*
Newsletter References; *Robinson's Pot Sept 2002, Hagg Gill Oct 2002, Heron Pot [Abandoned Photo Meet] Nov 2003, Long Kin East Nov 2003, Short Drop-Gavel Pot Nov 2004.*

JONES, Katherine; *J2010, b1963,*

JONES, Robert Sydney; *J1958, b1940,*
Newsletter References; *Washfold Pot July 1957; Simpson's Pot Aug 1957, Swinsto Sept 1957.*

JONES, Steven; *J2010, b1961,*
[Initiated the Caving Film Night at the Kendal Film Festival Oct 2013]

JONES, Urban Padmore; AKA: Jonah. *J1958, b1907,*
Famous for; Refusing three offers of marriage from three Irish women, including a Dublin business woman, on a trip to Ireland 1968.
Bulletin References; *Gaping Gill Meet 1960, Simpson's Pot 16th April 1961 [Graham Shaw Accident], Lost John's March 1961, Gaping Gill-Whitsuntide 1961, Pen-y-Ghent pot 1961, Lower Gunnerfleet Cave June 1959.*
Newsletter References; *Swildon's Four Aug 1958, Marble Steps Sept 1959, Lost John's Sept 1959, August Hole Aug 1959, Longwood Swallet Aug 1959, Swildon's Hole Aug 1959, Goatchurch Hole Aug 1959, Lamb Lear Aug 1959, Stoke Lane Slocker Aug 1959, Swinsto Hole Oct 1959, Kirkdale Cave April 1965.*

JONES, W.B; *J1958, b1907,*

JONKINSON, S;

JOWETT, Christopher Paul; *J1988, b1960,*
Member; LPPS.

JOWETT, Derek; AKA: Jesse. *J1955, b1938,*
Resigned forom club Sept 1966 *[But wanted to keep getting newsletters]*
Famous for; Hanging on a ladder for 20 minutes after having two life lines break on the last [big] pitch in Rift Pot July 1957.
Bulletin References; *Little Hull Hole Oct 1955, Christmas Pot 1957, Rift Pot [Double rope failure] 1957, Long Kin West 1958, Xmas Pot Easter 1960, Gaping Gill Meet [Diverting P5 water] 1960, Rowten Pot April 1960, Pen-y-ghent Pot July 1960, Grange Rigg Easter 1961.*
Newsletter References; *Washfold Pot July 1957; Simpson's Pot Aug 1957, Leader Rumbling Hole Oct 1957, Lancaster Hole Oct 1957, Practice stretcher rescue Wade's entrance GG Nov 1957, Dow-Providence rescue Dec 1957, Alum Pot Sept 1957, Tackle testing Jan 1958, Leader Easter Camp April 1958, P5 April 1958, Flood Entrance Pot April 1958, Little Hull Pot April 1958, Bar Pot May 1958, Tackle testing July 1958, Eastwater Swallet Aug 1958, Swildon's Four Aug 1958, Alum Pot Aug 1958, Long Kin West Sept 1958, Bar Pot Nov 1958, Clapham Cave Nov 1958, Digging nr Owl Hole Dec 1958, Grange Rigg March 1959, Assisted with Ingleborough Cave survey June 1959, Little Hull Hole Aug 1959, Diccan-Alum Exchange September 1959, Brown Scar Cave Sept 1959, Lost John's Sept 1959, August Hole Aug 1959, Longwood Swallet Aug 1959, Swildon's Hole Aug 1959, Goatchurch Hole Aug 1959, Lamb Lear Aug 1959, Stoke Lane Slocker Aug 1959, Clapham Bottoms dig Aug 1959, Clapham Cave Oct 1959.*

JOWETT, John Andrew; *J1974, b1957,*
Probationary Meets; Pasture Gill, Far Waters, Gingling Hole.
Newsletter References; *Gingling Hole Sept 1974, Giants Hole Nov 1974, Tatham Wife March 1975.*

JUDD, Brian Robert; *J1973, b1954,*
Probationary Meets; Pasture Gill, Agen Allwedd. Sunset, Top Sink-Lancaster, Whitsun Series.
Bulletin References; *Chourum Des Aiguilles 1974, Farrer Hall Extension May 1974, Knucklebone Pot June 1975, Clint Cave Extension May 1974, John Campbell's Hole March 1975, Skosca Moor Pot IV [Digging Discovery] Feb 1975, Dog Tooth Inlet GG. [Digging] May 1975, Piaggia Bella 1975, Trou Qui Souffle 1975, Clapham Bottoms Roof Passage 1976, Potts Moor Cave April 1977, White Scar Cave Dec 1977, Rift Pot [50' Extension] 1979, Mossdale Caverns [Digging] 1979, Keay Hole Extension April*

1981, Gouffre Berger Aug 1980, Brackenbottom Pot, [Dig/exploration] 1989, Dub Cote Extensions [Diving] 1990.

Newsletter References; *Chourum des Aiguilles [BP] July 1974, Black Shiver Oct 1974, Juniper Gulf Dec 1974, Lost John's September 1976, Pippikin-Lancaster [Flood Pulse on Echo Aven] 1980, Pen-y-Ghent Pot July 1980, Gouffre Berger Aug 1980, Lost John's Nov 1980, Kaey Hole March 1981, New Goyden Pot April 1981.*

JUPP, Thomas; Temporary Member.

KARVIK, Eric; *J2009, b1994,*

KARVIK, Jan; *J2008, b1963,*
Probationary Meets; High Hull Pot, Heron Pot, Bull Pot of the Witches, Dismal Hill-Old Ing, Simpsons-KMC, Bar Pot, Stream Passage Pot, Otter Hole, Miss Graces Lane Cave.
Member; RFDCC.
Newsletter References; *High Hull Pot Sept 2007, Bull Pot of the Witches Jan 2008, Dismall Hill-Old Ing Jan 2008, Otter Hole June 2008, Miss Graces Lane June 2008, Hell Hole, Whitewell Cave & Pot Nov 2008, P8 April 2009, Hurnell Moss Pot April 2010, Daimler Hole Sept 2010, Lost John's-Boxhead Pot Sept 2010, Shuttleworth Pot Feb 2012, Otter Hole July 2015.*

KARVIK, Nina; *J2009, b1995,*

KEIGHLEY, Frank Silvester; *J1933, b1908, d1978.*
Founder Member
Bulletin References; *Dowka Bottom 29th Sept 1946.*

KEIGHLEY, Harold Gordon; AKA: Gordon. *J1959, b1930, d2002.*
Bulletin References; *Lost John's March 1960.*
Newsletter References; *Ingleborough Cave Oct 1959.*

KEIGHLEY, John; *J1938,*

KEIGHLEY, John; *J1948,*
Bulletin References; *Rift Pot/Long Kin East exchange April 1949, Rowten Pot Oct 1949, Easter Camp GG 1951, Bull Pot of the Witches April 1951, Digging at Beck Head June 1951, Pikedaw Calamine Mine Aug 1953, Clapham Cave 1951, Lost John's July 1951, Old Ing Caves Aug 1954 [Trapped by*

floodwater], Involved with BBC transmission from Alum Pot 7th May 1961.

KELLET, D;

KELLEY, Steven Robin; *J1969, b1949,*
Probationary Meets; Disappointment Pot, Marble Steps, Little Hull.
Newsletter References; *Kingsdale Master Cave Dec 1969.*

KELLY, Jayne; *J2010, b1976,*

KELLY, Sharon Anne; AKA: Shaz, Blunder Woman, Earthmother. *J1984, b1961,*
A rather young Sharon Kelly woke at the Dump one Sunday morning to find her car had a puncture, lacking the necessary skills she called on the young men of the club to help her out. They duly obliged showing her the necessary technique and she was able to put her spare wheel on. This was thirsty work so she went inside to make a brew. What followed was like a Formula One pit stop as the spare wheel was quickly replaced with the punctured one. She was not impressed when she returned!
Bulletin References; *Giggel Rav Pot, [Dig/exploration] 1990, Brackenbottom Pot, [Dig/exploration] 1989, Trou De Glaz Aug 1989, Giggel Rav Pot 1989, Brackenbottom Pot 1989, Tanne De Bel Espoir-La Diau Parmilan 1991, Sima de las Tainas de Mattarubia, Sima del Carlista, Simas M-21 & CJ-3. Sept 2001, Kamniski Alps Aug 1988, Tete Sauvage July 1995, Deep Well [Diving support] May 1992, Gouffre Berger Aug 1992, Albania 1992, Hensler's Pot [Discovery] 1999-2003, Hensler's Pot [First Through Trip to GG] May 2003, Pyrenees Aug 2003, Reseau de la Pierre Saint Martin Aug 2013, Doubs, France Aug 2009.*

Newsletter References; *Sell Gill Hole Feb 1985, Spectacle-Vesper Pot Mar 1985, County Pot-Top Sink April 1985, Sleets Gill June 1985, Lost John's Pot July 1985, Rift Pot April 1985, Gunnerside Gill Lead Mines June 1985, Langstroth Pot Sept 1985, Calf Holes Nov 1985, Pool Park Oct 1986,County Pot-Lancaster March 1986, Pen-y-Gent Pot March 1987, Scotland 1987, White Scar Cave July 1987, Matienzo July/Aug 1987, Top Sink-Link Feb 1988, Nick Pot Nov 1987, Weathercote Cave April 1988, Coniston Mine July 1988, South Wales Nov 1988, Dow-Providence July 1989, Smallcleugh Mine Aug 1989, Death's Head-Big Meanie Nov 1989, Pippikin Pot Oct 1989, Rift-Large Pot March 1990, Lakes Walk Sept 1990, Easegill Caverns Sept 1990, Bird Watching Lakes Walk Sept 1990, Eldon Hole Oct 1990, South Wales Dec 1990, Black Shiver Pot Jan 1991, Easegill Caverns Jan 1991, Marble Steps Pot Dec 1990, Dan Yr Ogof June 1991, Birks Fell Cave July 1991, Mendip Weekend Sept 1991, Sell Gill Training Meet Nov 1991, Top Sink-County Pot Nov 1991, Little Hull Dec 1991, Ireby Fell Jan 1992, Vulcan Pot Feb 1992, Rumbling Hole Jan 1992, LKE-Rift Exchange Feb 1992, Pippikin March 1992, Out Slets Beck Cave June 1992, Pen-y-Ghent Pot July 1992, Lakes Meet June 1992, Simpson's Pot Oct 1993, Alum Pot Nov 1993, Death's Head-Big Meanie Nov 1993, Snatcher's Pot Nov 1993, Coniston Mines Weekend Sept 1993, Simpson's-Swinsto March 1994, Brown Hills Pot March 1994, Pikedaw Calamine Caverns Sept 1995, Top Sink-Pippikin Nov 1995, Easegill April 1997, Deep Well [Dive Support] May 1997, Out Sleets Beck Pot Jan 1998, Sunset Hole/Great Douk July 1998,Heron Pot July 1998, Nent Head-Brewery Shaft Oct 1998, Swinsto-KMC March 1999, King Pot March 1999, Grange Rigg [Locating] March 1999, Lost John's March 1999, Derbyshire Meet Sept 1999, Birks Fell June 1999, Rumbling Hole Oct 1999, Pippikin Pot Nov 1999, Langstroth Pot June 2000, El Manadero [Support] Aug 2000, County-Lancaster Aug 2000, County-Wretched Rabbit Nov 2000, Bull Pot Jan 2001, Peak Cavern - Sumps Tour June 2001, Peak Cavern-Speedwell Via Colostomy June 2001, Peak Cavern-White River Series July 2001, Lost John's Hole Sept 2005, Trou du Garde/Creux de la Cavale - Bauges Aug 2012, Wildcat Rift May 2018, Lancaster-Easegill June 2019.*

KEMP, P; *J1980, b1952,*

KEMP, Trevor Ian; *J1969, b1952, d1994.*
Probationary Meets; Lancaster Hole, Little Hull, Sell Gill.
Bulletin References; *Henslers Master Cave [Find in Disappointment final chamber] 1972, Gavel Pots, Bishopdale 1972, Diving Bransgill Cave Feb 1975,*

Piaggia Bella 1975, Sell Gill Hole [Attempted Dive] April 1981, Kingsdale Photographic meet April 1982.
Newsletter References; *Lancaster-County Pot Feb 1970, Lost John's Jan 1970, Marble Steps March 1970, Lancaster Hole Nov 1970, Bull Pot March 1971, Sell Gill Hole Oct 1971, Pasture Gill Hole Oct 1971, Pen-y-Ghent Pot Aug 1972, Magnetometer Pot Sept 1973, Lost John's Hole Aug 1974, Black Shiver Oct 1974, Flood-Bar SRT practice Feb 1975, County Pot Oct 1975, Nick Pot Oct 1975, Short Drop-Gavel Pot 1976, Sleets Gill July 1976, Lost John's September 1976, Rumbling Hole Dec 1976, Notts Pot March 1983, Gingling Hole Oct 1985, Simpson's-Swinsto March 1994.*

KENDALL, Harry; *J2000, b1994.*

KENDALL, Laura; *J2000, b1990.*

KENDALL, Richard Graham; *J1984, b1960,*
Probationary Meets; Black Shiver, Rowten-Swinsto, Pasture Gill.
Bulletin References; *Vercors Aug 1983, Krisna Jama Aug 1984, Brezno V Madvedovi Konti Aug 1984, Leski Aug 1984, Leski Aug 1984, Nettle Pot [Dig] July 1984, Albania 1992, Tete Sauvage July 1995.*
Newsletter References; *Alum Pot March 1981, Sunset Hole July 1981, Pasture Gill Pot June 1983, Gingling Hole June 1983, South Wales Aug 1983, Peak Cavern Sept 1983, Swinsto-Rowten Exchange Nov 1983, County Pot March 1984, Brezno, Leska, Babizop Rakov Scojan and the Pit of Bears Yugoslavia Aug 1985, Ireby Fell Jan 1992, Alum Pot Nov 1993, Piaggia Bella July 1996, Grotta del Calgeron Aug 1997.*

KENDALL, Sarah; *J2000, b1993,*

KERMAN, Andrew John; *J2005, b1982,*
Probationary Meets; Bar Pot, Top Sink-Wretched Rabbit, Death's Head-Big Meanie.
Rejoined 2013 & 2016.
Bulletin References; *Pyrenees 2006.*
Newsletter References; *Magnetometer Pot April 2005, Gingling Hole July 2005, Lost John's Hole Sept 2005, Heron Pot Nov 2005, Ribblehead Caves Dec 2005, Simpson's Pot Dec 2005, Ireby Fell Caverns Nov 2005, Dismal Hill-Old Ing Jan 2006, Bull Pot Jan 2006, James Hall Mine Feb 2006, Peak Cavern Feb 2006, Rumbling Hole July 2006, Pyrenees Aug 2006, Hunt Pot Nov 2006, Otter Hole June 2008, Haytime Hole March 2009, Cwm Dwr-OFD Top Ent June 2009, Alum Pot April 2013, Sell Gill Sept 2017, Long Churns & Borrins Moor Sept 2018.*

KERNOT, Roy M; *J1967, b1948,*
Probationary Meets; Christmas-Grange Rigg, Diccan-Alum, Hunt Pot.
Bulletin References; *Alum Pot/Diccan Pot 1966.*

KERR, Brian Andrew; *J1965, b1937,*

KERSHAW, Alan; *J1959, b1935, d2009.*
Alan and Dick Elliot were operating the winch when the engine broke down so Dick used the handle to manually bring the chair up. Last trip underground GG92.
Bulletin References; *Gaping Gill Meet 1960, Pen-y-ghent Pot July 1960, Jnr Leader Little Hull Feb 1961, Gaping Gill-Whitsuntide 1961.*

KHAN, April S; *J2009, b1973,*

KHAN, Mumtaz Begum; *J2011, b1973,*
Probationary Meets; Yordas Cave, GG11.
Newsletter References; *Yordas Pot April 2011, Illusion Pot June 2011, Sunset Hole June 2011.*

KIMBERLEY, N; *J1981,*

KINCH, Peter Frank; *J1978, b1956,*
Probationary Meets; Lost John's, Bull Pot of the Witches, Short Drop.
Newsletter References; *Short Drop-Gavel Dec 1977.*

KING, Christopher James Douglas; *J1997, b1980,*

KING, David John; *J1973,*
Probationary Meets; Ireby Fell, Bull Pot, Gingling Hole.
Bulletin References; *Marble Sink May 1976, Clapham Bottoms Roof Passage 1976, Farrer Hall extension 1980, Farrer Hall Choke 1970-76, White Scar Cave Dec 1977, Cow Garth Cave [Exploration] 1982/84.*
Newsletter References; *Lost John's Hole Aug 1974, Gingling Hole Sept 1974, Giants Hole Nov 1974, Tatham Wife March 1975, Meregill April 1975, Short Drop–Gavel Pot 1976, Goyden Pot Feb 1976, Pippikin Pot Nov 1976, Scrafton Pot April 1980, Gingling Hole Oct 1985, Calf Holes Nov 1985, Pool Park Oct 1986, Dow Cave April 1987, South Wales Nov 1988, Millenium Walk Sept 2002.*

KING, Philip John; *J1997, b1973,*

KING, William Anthony; *J1950,*

KIRK, Gillian Louise; *J1999, J1964,*
Probationary Meets; Swinsto-Simpson's, GG98, Disappointment Pot.

Newsletter References; *Pippikin Pot Nov 1999.*

KITCHEN, Gary; *J1961, b1944,*

Expelled from club Dec 1962 for non payment of subs.
Probationary Meets; Bar Pot, Disappointment Pot, Giant's Hole.
Newsletter References; *Little Hull Pot April 1958.*

KJELSTRUP-JOHNSON, Kristian; *J2018, b1989,*
Member; WCMS.

KLAUSETH, Malvin; *J1964, b1942,*
['Residential difficulties' attending meets - lives in Norway]

KNIGHT, Ian Gordon; *J1961, b1945,*
Probationary Meets; Lost John's, Notts Pot, Sunset Hole, Disappointment Pot.
Bulletin References; *Christmas Pot 1962.*

KNIGHTINGALE, Helen; *J2014, b1980,*

KNOWLES, Liam Raymond; *J2015, b1990,*
Newsletter References; *Pikedaw Calamine Caverns Feb 2015, KMC/Toyland Feb 2016, Hagg Gill April 2016, County Pot-Wretched Rabbit April 2016, Voldemort-Committee Pot July 2016, Bruntscar Cave Jan 2017, Jingling Feb 2017, Old Ing-Birkwith July 2017, Sell Gill Sept 2017, Ibbeth Peril caves April 2018.*

KNOWLES, Stacey; *J2016, b1990,*
Newsletter References; *KMC/Toyland Feb 2016.*

KOVAL, Max; AKA: HRH, King Oaf. *J1971, b1947,*
Probationary Meets; Calf Holes, Tatham Wife Hole, Easegill.
Newsletter References; *Heron Pot March 1971, Tatham Wife Hole Aug 1971, Lost John's Sept 1971, Lancaster–County Pot Dec 1971, Grange Rigg–Christmas Pot Jan 1972, Gingling Hole Aug 1972, Pen-y-Ghent Pot Aug 1972, New Rift Pot Jan 1986, Bull Pot of the Witches April 1989, Heron Pot March 1993, Crooklands WalkingMeet Sept 1993, Dowkabottom Feb 1995, Hagg Gill 1996, Lancaster Canal Walk Meet 2001, Millenium Walk Sept 2002, Black Combe-Foxfield Walk Sept 2003, Derbyshire Meet Jan 2004, Granett Bridge To ShapWalk Sept 2006, Ulverston-Coniston Walking Meet 2007, Lambrigg Fell–Tebay Walk Sept 2008, Dunsop Bridge/Bilsborrow Walking Meet Sept 2009, Walking Meet Orton-Kirkby Thore Sept 2010, Cautley/Kirkby Stephen Walk Sept 2011, Crosby Ravensworth-AskhamWalking Meet Sept 2012,Roundthwaite Common to Borrowdale Sept*

2014, New Biggin on Lune to Appleby Walking Meet Sept 2016, Lindale-Greenodd Walking Meet 2017, Cow Green Reservoir–Appleby Walking Meet 2018, Kirkby Lonsdale-Wharton Walking Meet Sept 2019.

KOVAL, Pauline Anne; [née Shepley] AKA: Curly.
J1974, b1951,
Famous for; *falling off GG tracter and breaking a leg 1973, putting up with Max.*

66

L

LABADIE, Paul Richard; *J1987, b1943,*
Probationary Meets; Alum Pot, Pippikin, Nidderdale, Magnetometer, Tatham Wife.
Newsletter References; *Magnetometer Pot Oct 1987, Hull Pot [Filming with the BBC] Oct 2010.*

LABADIE, Susan; [née Stevens] *J1984, b1960,*

LACKENBY, Sandra Pauline; *J1992, b1954,*
Probationary Meets; GG85-92, Sand Caverns, Mud Hall.

LAKE, Colin; *J1959, b1944,*

LAKE, Paul George; *J1961, b1944,*
Probationary Meets; Magnetometer, Bar Pot, Sunset Hole.
Bulletin References; *Magnetometer Pot Nov 1960, Simpson's Pot April 1961 - [Graham Shaw Accident], Simpson's Pot May 1962.*

LAKE, Susan Carolyn; *J1993, b1971,*
Member; EDSS, DSS.

LANCASTER, John Anthony; *J1961, b1943,*
Probationary Meets; Magnetometer, Clapham Cave, Great Douk/Middle Washfold.
Bulletin References; *Batty Cave Jan 1964, Oxlow Caverns Feb 1964.*

LAND, Geoffrey Michael; *J1965, b1943,*
Probationary Meets; Grange Rigg, Mongo Gill, Goyden Pot.

Bulletin References; *Lyke Wake Walk June 1965, Lyke Wake Walk Dec 1966.*

LANE, John Michael; *J1959, b1938,*
Bulletin References; *Lost John's March 1960, Wharfedale Camp Aug 1960, Involved with building electron ladders, 1960's.*

LANGLEY, Jaqueline Marie; *J1996, b1969,*

LAST, Deborah; AKA: Bev. *J2010, b1982,*
Probationary Meets; Rumbling Hole, Little Hull Pot, Gouffre Berger, Magnetometer Pot.
Member; RRCPC, MUSC, YUCPC.
Club Expeditions; Gouffre Berger 2010.
Newsletter References; *Rumbling Hole March 2010, Magnetometer Pot April 2010, Hurnell Moss Pot April 2010, Marble Steps June 2010, Shrapnel Pot July 2010, Alum Pot Oct 2010, Pillar Holes Oct 2010, Sell Gill [Training Meet] Oct 2010, Hunt Pot-Shrapnel Exchange April 2011, Big Meanie Sept 2011, Big Meanie-Death's Head Exchange Oct 2011, Sell Gill April 2013, Marble Steps April 2014, Simpson's Pot Aug 2016.*

LATIMER, Andrew; *J2016, b1971,*
Newsletter References; *Alum-Diccan Pot Nov 2015,*

LATIMER, Daisy May; *J2016, b2015,*

LATIMER, John; *J2015, b1979,*

Probationary Meets; Sell Gill, Aquamole, Alum Pot, GG15.
Member; EPC.

LATIMER, Judith Clare; *J2013, b1984,*
Newsletter References; *Skirwith Cave [Novice Trip] Jan 2016, Runscar-Thistle [Novice Trip] Jan 2016, Dyhedral [With Graham Owen (blind) and filmed by ITV with Ben Fogle]*

LATIMER, Rupert Sean; *J2015, b2014,*
Newsletter References; *Sell Gill & Notts [Pre-natal trips] Skirwith Cave [Novice Trip] Jan 2016.*

LATIMER, Simon Tarquin; *J2015, b1967,*
Member; Another Club [EPC ?]

LATIMER, Susan; *J2015, b1971,*

LAUGHTON, Guy Jamal; *J1987, b1963,*

LAWLESS, Padraic; *J2018, b1990,*
Member; UCDCPC, SUI, ICRO.

LAWRENCE, Bethany Heather; *J2010, b2004,*
Probationary Meets; Goyden Hole, Manchester Hole, Goatchurch Cavern, Swildons, GG10.
Bulletin References; *Reseau de la Pierre Saint Martin Aug 2013, Doubs, France Aug 2009.*
Newsletter References; *Skosca Cave Feb 2013, Skirwith Cave Feb 2015, Yordas/KMC March 2015, Great and High Douk June 2015, Calf Holes-Browgill and Old Ing-Birkwith June 2015, Long Churn and Wilson's cave [Novice Trip] July 2015, Calf Holes [Novice Trip] July 2015, Katnot Cave/Thorne Cave [Novice Trip] May 2016, Grampian Meet Aug 2017.*

LAWRENCE, Carol Phyllis; *J2009, b1973,*
Probationary Meets; Brackenbottom Pot.
Bulletin References; *Reseau de la Pierre Saint Martin Aug 2013.*
Newsletter References; *Lost John's Oct 2008, Stump Cross Caverns Dec 2008, Aygill Caverns Jan 2009, Pay Sank Feb 2009, Link Pot April 2009, Link Pot Sept 2009, Roger Kirk Caves Oct 2009, Dowkerbottom Cave Oct 2009, Excalibur Pot March 2012, Dan Yr Ogof April 2012, Cullaun 2 April 2012, Hardrawkin Pot April 2012, Washfold Pot April 2012, Old Ing/Calf Holes-Browgill [Novice Trip] June 2012, Brackenbottom Pot, June 2012, Croesor Rhosydd [Through] Oct 2012, Link Pot Nov 2012, KMC Toyland Nov 2012, Ireby Fell Cavern June 2013, Magnetometer Pot Nov 2013, Skosca Cave Feb 2013, White Scar Cave July 2014, Dowkabottom Cave July 2014, Fairy Holes Sept 2014, Nenthead Mines Sept 2014, Simpson's Pot-*

KMC Sept 2014, High & Great Douk Dec 2014, Swildon's Hole Feb 2015, Swildon's Hole Feb 2015, Goatchurch Aven Feb 2015, Skirwith Cave Feb 2015, Yordas/KMC March 2015, Sell Gill June 2015, Great and High Douk June 2015, Calf Holes-Browgill and Old Ing-Birkwith June 2015, Poll Dudh June 2015, St Catherine's1-Fisher St June 2015, Faunarooska June 2015, Long Churn and Wilsons cave [Novice Trip] July 2015, Long Churn and Wilsons cave [Novice Trip] July 2015, Calf Holes [Novice Trip] July 2015, Fairy Holes Sept 2015, Goyden Sept 2015, Nenthead Mines Sept 2015, KMC [Novice Trip] Jan 2016, Notts 2 Jan 2016, Browgill Jan 2016, KMC High Traverse in Flood Feb 2016, P8 March 2016, Pillar Holes April 2016, Rowten Pot & Cave April 2016, Katnot Cave/Thorne Cave [Novice Trip] May 2016, Simpson's Pot Aug 2016, Croesor Rhysydd Through Trip Oct 2016, Rift Pot-Long Kin East [Exchange] July 2016, Bull Pot of the WitchesJan 2017, Alum/Long Churns June 2017, Grampian Meet Aug 2017, Sell Gill Sept 2017, Ingleborough Cave {Surveying] May 2018, Mongo Gill Sept 2018,

LAWRENCE, Joseph; *J2010,*
Newsletter References; *Skosca Cave Feb 2013, Croesor Rhysydd Through Trip Oct 2016,*

LAWRENCE, Stanley; *J1949,*

LAWRENSON, Peter; *J2011, b1959,*
Probationary Meets; Upper & Lower Long Churns, Bar Pot, Heron Pot, Calf Holes, KMC.
Newsletter References; *Sunset Hole Oct 2011, County Pot-Wretched Rabbit Feb 2012.*

LAWSON, A; *J1982, b1954,*

LAWSON, Timothy Mark; *J1994, b1954,*
Probationary Meets; Dowbergill Passage,

LAYCOCK, Adrian Stephen; AKA: Gob, Gimmer. *J1981, b1963,*
Probationary Meets; Tatham Wife, Lost John's, GG80.
Famous for; Drove up a tree and demolished a dry stone wall in December 1982. *[Whats black, got three wheels and sits on walls? Adrians Van]* Scoff had bet Adrian a gallon of beer that he would write off his Mini van within one year, it took just over 10 months. Section of wall since referred to as 'Adrians Wall'.
Bulletin References; *Vercors Aug 1983, Brezno V Madvedovi Konti Aug 1984, Leski Aug 1984, Wildcat Shuffle May 1994.*
Newsletter References; *Bull Pot of the Witches [And assistance with the body recovery of Tracy*

Gibson from Top Sink] Oct 1980, Goyden Pot March 1981, Pippikin Pot Oct 1981, Rift Pot& Long Kin East Jan 1982, Lost John's Feb 1982, Alum Pot March 1982, Ireby Fell Caverns July 1982, Birks Fell Cave July 1982, Providence-Dow Cave July 1982, Ingleborough Cave Oct 1982, Tatham Wife Hole Feb 1983, Little Neath River Cave, Porth Yr Ogof and OFD April 1983, Swinsto-Valley Entrance April 1983, Mendip weekend April 1983, Hallucination Aven-Induction Location May 1983, Link Pot July 1983, South Wales Aug 1983, Rowten-Swinsto Exchange Nov 1983, Rift Pot Feb 1984, Diccan Pot March 1984, Scotland Easter 1986, Scotland 1987, Weathercote Cave April 1988, Heron Pot Jan 1989, Heron Pot March 1993, Cherry Tree Hole Jan 1994, Calf Holes-Browgill and Old Ing-Birkwith June 2015, Wildcat Rift May 2018.

LEACH, Charles Henry; *J1936, b1906, d1997.*
BPC President 1933-36.
Bulletin References; *First President of Bradford Moor Cave Club.*

LEACH, Francis Donald; AKA: Don. *J1949, b1922, d1967.*
Bulletin References; *Easter Camp-GG 1950, Pen-y-Ghent Pot Rescue , young BSA member died of exhaustion 1951. Bull Pot of the Witches April 1951, Clapham Cave Sept 1951, Rowten Pot June 1951, Simpson's Pot July 1953, Flood Entrance Pot March 1954, Old Ing Caves Aug 1954, Marble Steps Nov 1954, Don was awarded a posthumous award by the Scout Association in recognition of his courage and devotion to duty under great suffering.[He suffered greatly from Arthritis in later life-Ed] Donald was the designer of the BPC Gaping Gill gantry and probably provided the initial momentum to create a winch at all .*
Newsletter References; *Leader Flood Entrance March 1954, Leader Marble Steps Nov 1954, Leader Littondale Jan 1955, Leader GG June 1957, Lancaster Hole Oct 1957, Leader-Practice stretcher rescue Wade's entrance GG Nov 1957, Dow-Providence rescue Dec 1957,Narrowly survived boulder fall in Rift Pot Aug 1957,Calf Holes& Browgill Sept 1957, Easter Camp April 1958, Digging near Owl Hole April 1958, Bar Pot May 1958, Bull Pot of the Witches Aug 1958, Leader Marble Steps Oct 1958, Digging nr Owl Hole Dec 1958, GG members meet 1959, Clapham Cave Oct 1959, Joint Leader GG 1960.*

LEACOCK, William Llewellyn; *J1963, b1946,*
Probationary Meets; Heron Pot, Stream Passage, Dow Cave.

LEADBETTER, Gareth Jack; *J1995, b1968,*

Probationary Meets; County Pot, Bar Pot, Pierre Saint Martin.

LEAKE, D. S; *J1973,*

LEATHER, Lydia Clare; *J2019, b1998,*
Member; NUCC.
Newsletter References; *Lost River Sump [Dive Support] May 2019, Silvestre to Marniosa Treviso [First Through Trip] Sept 2019.*

LEDGER, Frank; *J1948,*
Bulletin References; *Flood Entrance July 1949.*

LEE, Barry Edward; *J1970, b1947,*
Probationary Meets; Notts Pot, GG70, Gingling Hole.
Newsletter References; *Lancaster Hole Nov 1970, Bull Pot March 1971.*

LEE, Brian; *J1959, b1938,*
Newletter References; *Measuring Depth of GG shaft Aug 1959, Clapham Bottoms dig Aug 1959.*

LEE, Carmel; *J1987, b1947,*
Newsletter References; *Brezno, Leska, Babizop Rakov Scojan and the Pit of Bears Yugoslavia Aug 1985, Eden Valley-Teesdale Walking Meet Oct 1985, Scotland Easter 1986, Scotland 1987, Lakes Walk Sept 1990, Bird Watching Lakes Walk Sept 1990.*

LEE, Raymond; AKA: Snake. *J1967, b1949,*
BPC President 2012 & 13.
Probationary Meets; Lost John's, Marble Steps, GG67.
Bulletin References; *Disappointment Pot Oct 1967, Whitsun Series Whit 1969, Trow Gill/Gour Aven Flood Test 1969, September Rift GG, Sept 1971, Little Hull Hole Aug 1971, Lower Stream Passage Pot [Diving] 1971, Henslers Master Cave [Find in Disappointment final chamber] 1972, Maypoling Little Hull Pot 1972, Gavel Pots, Bishopdale 1972, Black Shiver Pot, Oct 1972, Chourum Des Aiguilles 1973, Chourum Des Aiguilles 1974, Juniper Gulf [Bolting] 1974, Piaggia Bella 1975, New Entrance to Newby Moss Cave Dec 1976, Farrer Hall Choke 1970-76, Clapham Bottoms Roof Passage 1976, Potts Moor Cave 1977, Newby Moss Sink May 1977, Newby Moss Sink 3rd Shaft 1977, Rift Pot [Bolting] 1979, Jean Pot [Discovery] 1979, Abbisa Fighiera 1979, Pillar Holes [Digging] June 1980, Far SE passage [Digging] 1980, Mountain Hall [Scaling]1980,Gouffre Berger Aug 1980, Cow Garth Cave [Exploration] 1982/84, M5 Pot [Dig] July 1984, Nettle Pot [Dig] July 1984, Tanne Du Bel Espoir–Diau Aug 1984, Brackenbottom Pot,*

[Dig/exploration] 1989, Trou De Glaz Aug 1989, Brackenbottom Pot 1989, Giggel Rav Pot, [Dig/exploration] 1990.

Newsletter References; *Lost John's March 1969, Meregill June 1969, Bull Pot of the Witches July 1969, Pen-y-Ghent Pot Aug 1969, Rumbling Hole Oct 1969, Juniper Gulf Nov 1969, Kingsdale Master Cave Dec 1969, Lancaster–County Pot Feb 1970, Lost John's Jan 1970, Marble Steps March 1970, Birks Fell [Trapped by a dropped boulder in a crawl] Oct 1970, Bull Pot March 1971, Birks Fell April 1971, Lost John's Sept 1971, Pasture Gill Hole Oct 1971, Black Shiver Pot Nov 1971, Lancaster-County Pot Dec 1971, Grange Rigg-Christmas Pot Jan 1972, Birks Fell April 1972, Washfold Pot April 1972, Pen-y-Ghent Pot Aug 1972, Agen Allwedd Mar 1974, Chourum des Aiguilles [BP] July 1974, Lost John's Hole Aug 1974, Black Shiver Oct 1974, Juniper Gulf Dec 1974, Bar Pot March 1975, Short Drop–Gavel Pot 1976, Stream Passage–Flood Entrance Pot March 1976, Lost John's September 1976, Christmas Pot Feb 1977, Pillar Holes Sept 1978, Abbissa Fighiera Italy Aug 1979, Gingling Hole July 1980, Sell Gill 1980, Gouffre Berger Aug 1980, Sell Gill Hole April 1981, Tanne de Bel Espoir–Grotte de la Diau Aug 1981, Brezno, Leska, Babizop Rakov Scojan and the Pit of Bears Yugoslavia Aug 1985, Eden Valley-Teesdale Walking Meet Oct 1985, Scotland Easter 1986, Pool Park Oct 1986, New Rift Pot Jan 1986, Scotland 1987, Magnetometer Pot Oct 1987, Haytime Hole 1990, Lakes Walk Sept 1990, Bird Watching Lakes Walk Sept 1990, Brackenbottom Pot April 1992, Committee Pot March 2011.*

LEEDAL, Geoffrey, Philip; *J1946,*

LEGGETT, Richard Anthony; *J1995, b1948,*
Probationary Meets; GG95.

LEONE, Francis; *J1994, b1967,*

LEPORT, Anne; *J2008, b1982,*

Li, Laura; Temporary Member.

LIA, Thomas; *J2014, b1989,*
Member; CUCC.

LINSDELL, Jonathan Simon; *J2008, b1985,*
Probationary Meets; Calf Holes, Bar Pot, Small Mammal, Gournier.
Newsletter References; *Cwm Dwr-OFD Top Ent June 2009, OFD Top Ent June 2009.*

Linsdell, Martell; See Baines.

LISTER, Harold; *J1946,*
Bulletin References; *Lost John's July/Aug 1946. Great Douk, Sunset Hole April 1949.*

LITTLEWOOD, Gary Stephen; *J1998, b1976,*
Probationary Meets; Fat Finger, Losers Pot, Green Gates.

LIVESEY, Michael Peter; AKA: Peter. *J1961, b1943, d1998.*
Club Expeditions; Jamaica 1965/6.
Main Activities; Climbing, Caving, Fell Running, Athletics, Canoeing and Orienteering.
Probationary Meets; Lost John's/Notts Pot, Pen-y-Ghent pot, Bar Pot.
Famous for; Raising the standard of UK rock climbing in Britain during the 1970s. As one of the best climbers the United Kingdom has ever produced, he had an international reputation for hard routes. He was one of the first climbers to implement a hard training regime, enabling him to ascend his difficult new routes such as Footless Crow [on Goat Crag in the Lake District] and Downhill Racer [at Froggatt in the Peak District] There is a certain irony in his first free ascent of Clink in 1972. As an avid reducer of aid in his climbing, Clink was over bolted in 2004. Livesey was not only a top rock climber but also a fell-runner, athlete, caver, canoeist and orienteer. He took up orienteering in his 40s and within two years was topping the M45 rankings in Britain. He also had a remarkable record as a fell runner, including four consecutive top ten placings in the Karrimor International Mountain Marathon [KIMM]
Bulletin References; *Little Hull Pot Feb 1961, Christmas Pot 1962, Little Hull Pot July 1962, Hardrawkin Pot Sept 1962, Rowten Pot & Jingling Pot Nov 1962, Ingleborough Cave Sherpaing Dec 1962, Christmas-Grange/P5 April 1962, Christmas-Grange-P5 extensions May 1962, Juniper Gulf Dec 1962, Goyden Pot Feb 1963, Old Cote Pot April 1963, South Wales Easter 1963, Agen Allwedd April 1963, Mossdale Caverns-Far Marathon Sept 1963, Skell Gill Cave [Solo] Nov 1963, Pen-y-Ghent Pot Extensions Oct 1963, Notts Pot Oct 1963, Birks Fell Cave Dec 1963, Mossdale Caverns-High Level Mud Caverns Feb 1964, Ireby Fell Cavern April 1964, Little Hull Sump Jan 1964, Hammer Pot 1964, , Nick Pot Nov 1964, Gingling Hole Dec 1964, Fornah Gill Cavern March 1965, Vector Climb 1965, Antler Pot Feb 1965, Lumphammer Hole Sept 1965, Screen Hill-Legnabrocky Way Ireland Discovery Aug 1965, Ibbeth Peril 1966, Jamaica 1965/66, Trolltind Wall Norway [Second Ascent] June 1968, Pen-y-Ghent Long Churn Oct 1969, Caving in Andy Good*

Mountain [Canada] 1972, Old Ing-Birkwith July 2017.

LODALE, R. J; *J1957, b*

Newsletter References; *Washfold Pot July 1957; Simpson's Pot Aug 1957, Swinsto Sept 1957.*

LODGE, Gillian; *J2012,*
Newsletter References; *Sell Gill April 2016,*

LLOYD, Brian Arthur; *J1974, b1952,*
Probationary Meets; Pen-y-Ghent Pot, Lost John's, Black Shiver Pot.
Bulletin References; *Skosca Moor Pot IV [Digging/Discovery] Feb 1975, Grotte de Bury 1977, Nettle Pot 1980, Moss Pot 1980, Gouffre Berger Aug 1980, Strawberry Pot May 1980, Keay Hole Extension April 1981, Alderley Edge Mines Sept 2009.*
Newsletter References; *Lost John's Hole Aug 1974, Black Shiver Oct 1974, Birks Fell Cave April 1975, County Pot Oct 1975, Sleets Gill July 1976, Pippikin Hole Oct 1976, Ogof Hesp alyn March 1977, Eglyws Faen June 1977, Cwm Dwr–OFD II April 1978, Little Neath River Cave April 1978, Douk Ghyll May 1979, Slasher Hole extension [Dug/explored] Aug 1978, Meregill Feb 1980, Pen-y-Ghent Pot July 1980, Gouffre Berger Aug 1980, Keay Hole Feb 1981, Kaey Hole March 1981,Tatham Wife Hole Feb 1983,Rift/Large Pot Oct 1985,Grotte Casteret Aug 1987, South Wales Nov 1988, MilwrTunnel June 2004, Skirwith Cave Nov 2004, Giant's Hole Jan 2005, Alderley Edge Mines Sept 2009.*

LLOYD, Lesley; [née Carroll] *J1989, b1954,*
Bulletin References; *Trou De Glaz Aug 1989,*
Newsletter References; *Bird Watching Lakes Walk Sept 1990, Peak Cavern Nov 1995, Alum Pot [Training Meet] July 1997.*

LLOYD, Ian Marriott; AKA: Poppit. *J1992, b1955,*
Probationary Meets; Pikedaw Calamine Cavern.
Member; CDG, BSC.
Declared Medical Condition; Schizophrenic /Psychosis & Acute Sclerosis of Liver.
Bulletin References; *Short Gill Rising [Dive/ dig] 1981, Manchester Hole D/S Sump extension [Diving] 1991, Deep Well [Dive support] May 1992, Alum/Long Churn on Mountain Bikes Dec 1994.*
Newsletter References; *Pikedaw Calamine Caverns March 1992, Pen-y-Ghent Pot July 1992, Lancaster Hole March 1995, Manchester By-pass-Wretshed Rabbit March 1995, Malham Cove Abseil Sept 1995, Giants Hole Nov 1995, Peak Cavern Nov 1995, Lancaster Hole-County Pot Oct 1995, South Wales April 1996, King Pot March 1996, Diccan Pot*

March 1996, Lancaster Hole July 1996, Swinsto-Simpson's 1996, Mongo Gill March 1997, Easegill April 1997, Cherry Tree Hole April 1997, Deep Well [Dive] May 1997, Alum Pot [Training Meet] July 1997, Derbyshire Meet Sept 1999, Langstroth Pot June 2000, Cherry Tree Hole Jan 2001, Notts Pot Feb 2001, Rumbling Hole July 2002, KMC-Toyland Oct 2002, Wretched Rabbit-County Pot Nov 2010, Link Pot Nov 2012, Simpson's Pot-KMC Dec 2016, Jingling Feb 2017, Notts Pot Feb 2017, County Pot-Lancaster Hole June 2019.

LOFTUS, Anthony; AKA: Tony. *J1977, b1956,*
Probationary Meets; Bull Pot o t Witches, Short Drop-Gavel, Birks Fell.
Bulletin References; *Piaggia Bella 1975,* County Pot Aug 1976.

LONG, Catherine Pamela; *J2017, b1992,*
Probationary Meets; Great Douk, Heron Pot, Yordas, Brunt Scar, GG17.
Newsletter References; *Borrins Moor Cave Nov 2016, Bruntscar Cave Jan 2017, KMC May 2017, Calf Holes-Birkwith June 2017, Alum/Long Churns June 2017, Old Ing-Birkwith July 2017, Iron Kiln Sept 2017.*

LONG, Jeremy James; AKA: Jim. *J1997, b1957,*
Probationary Meets; Dow Cave, Long Churns, Goyden, Crackpot, Runscar.
Newsletter References; *Alum Pot [Training Meet] July 1997.*

LONG, Yvonne Lesley; *J1997, b1963,*
Probationary Meets; Marble Steps, Calf Holes.
Newsletter References; *Alum Pot [Training Meet] July 1997.*

LONGSTAFF, J; *J1959,*

LOUGLIN, A; *J1980,*

LOUGLIN, L; *J1980,*

LOXAM, John; *J2008, b1958,*
Probationary Meets; Great Douk.
Member; ARCC.

LUBELSKI, Andrew; *J1988, b1972,*

LUCAS, Neville; *J2017,*
Newsletter References; *Pool Sink-Wretched Rabbit Feb 2020.*

LUMB, Martin Russell; *J1966,*

LUPTON, Jonathan; *J1989, b1972,*

LUPTON, Michael; AKA: MICK. *J1989, b1945,*
Probationary Meets; Bar Pot, Swinsto, Flood Entrance, KMC, Great Douk, Ireby Fell, Alum Pot, Sell Gill.
Newsletter References; *New Goyden Pot Oct 1988, Short Drop Cave Nov 1989, Easegill Caverns Sept 1990, Millenium Walk Sept 2002, Crackpot Cave [Photgraphic Meet] Jan 2003, Land's End– John O Groats Charity Cycle Ride-2006, Dunsop Bridge-Bilsborrow Walking Meet Sept 2009, President's Meet cycle pub crawl July 2015, New Biggin on Lune- Appleby Walking Meet Sept 2016.*

MACHNICKI, M; *J1972,*

MALE, Christopher David; *J2012, b2002,*

MALE, Henry James; *J2012, b2001,*

MALIR, J;

MANGEOLLES, James; *J1961, b1940,*
Probationary Meets; Marble Steps, Flood Entrance, Bar Pot.

MARKHAM, Michael John; AKA: Mark. *J1987, b1933,*
Re-Joined 2017.
Probationary Meets; GG87-91, Dowkabottom, New Goyden.
Newsletter References; *Sleets Gill June 1985, Eden Valley-Teesdale Walking Meet Oct 1985, Scotland Easter 1986, Scotland 1987, Pikedaw Calamine Caverns March 1992.*

MAROCHOP, M; *J1981,*

MARSH, Norman William Almond; *J1969, b1940,*

MARSH, Robert; *J1956,*
Bulletin References; *Great Douk, Sunset Hole April 1949.*   .

MARSH, Stuart; *J1987,*
Newsletter References; *Gingling Hole Oct 1985.*

MARSHALL, Joshua Paul; *J2014, b1996,*
Probationary Meets; *Dyhedral, Calf Holes, Radio Locating [with J. Rattray]*
Famous for; being rescued with his dad from the Gouffre Berger canals after a storm flood. Getting stuck on Dyhedral. Created BPC Facebook page.

Bulletin References; *Gouffre Berger Canals beyond Camp 1 [Aged 14] Aug 2010, Cwmorthin Slate Mine Feb 2009, Croesor-Rhosydd Feb 2009.*
Newsletter References; *Sunset Hole July 2006, Croesor-Rhosydd March 2010, Cwmorthin Slate Mine March 2010, Ireby Fell Cavern Jan 2011, Boulby Potash Mine Jan 2016.*

MARSHALL, Michael; AKA: Mick Steve Fuck Knows. *J1985,*
Bulletin References; *Gouffre Berger Aug 2010.*
Newsletter References; *Tatham Wife Hole Feb 1983, Top Sink-County Pot April 1985, Gingling Hole Oct 1985, Eden Valley-Teesdale Walking Meet Oct 1985, Ireby Fell [Diving Support] Oct 1988.*

MARSHALL, Paul David; *J1998, b1970,*
Famous for; being rescued with his son from the Gouffre Berger canals after a storm flood.
Newsletter References; *Aygill Caverns Feb 1999, Out Sleets Beck Pot April 1999, Pen-y-Ghent Pot July 2000, Rowten Pot Dec 2000, Rowten Pot Dec 2000, White Scar Cave April 2001, Loser's Pot June 2002, Bar Pot Jan 2005, Sunset Hole July 2006, Cwmorthin Slate Mine March 2010, Ireby Fell Cavern Jan 2011, Titan-Peak Cavern March 2011, Boulby Potash Mine Jan 2016.*

MARSTON, Terence K; *J1956, b1937,*
Bulletin References; *Little Hull Hole Oct 1955, Bar Pot 1958, Involved with building electron ladders, 1950/60's, Pen-y-ghent Pot July 1960, Lost John's March 1960, Gaping Gill Meet 1960, Alum Pot July 1960, Lancaster-Eastgill Aug 1960, Disappointment Pot Easter Meet 1961, Dye Test P5 Water Easter 1961, Simpson's Pot 16th April 1961- [Graham Shaw Accident] Pen-y-Ghent Long Churn Oct 1969, Gaping Gill-Whitsuntide 1961, Lower Stream Passage Pot May 1959.*

Newsletter References; *Rumbling Hole Oct 1957, Lancaster Hole Oct 1957, Dow-Providence rescue Dec 1957, Easter Camp April 1958, Lancaster Hole April 1958, Alum Main Shaft April 1958, Lancaster Hole June 1958, St Cuthbert's Swallet Aug 1958, Eastwater Swallet Aug 1958, Swildon's Hole Aug 1958, Alum Pot Aug 1958, Newby Moss Dig Nov 1958, Norway Sept/Oct 1958, Clapham Cave Nov 1958, Swildon's Hole New Year 1959, Lower Gunnerfleet Cave June 1959, Inauguration Aven June 1959, Ireland Aug 1959, Diccan-Alum Exchange September 1959, Marble Steps Sept 1959, Treak Cliff Cavern Oct 1959, Oxlow Caverns Nov 1959, Reported for National Service-Rejected 1960 Terminal Sump Ingleborough Cave Inauguration series Aug 1960, Leader Long Kin East Oct 1960, Leader Pen-y-Ghent Long Churn Oct 1960, Jnr Leader Easter Camp Clapham 1961.*

MARTIN, Callum; *J2013, b2002,*
Newsletter References; *Calf Holes-Browgill and Old Ing-Birkwith June 2015, Darnbrook Pot June 2018,Wildcat Rift May 2018, Lancaster Hole-Wretched Rabbit Nov 2018.*

MARTIN, Eric; *J1964, b1948,*
Probationary Meets; Sunset Hole, Bull Pot, Sell Gill.

MARTIN, Karl Bernard; AKA; Gush 2. *J1997, b1967,*
Probationary Meets; Easegill, Milwur Tunnel, Alum pot, Easegill, Swinsto Hole.
Member; SUSS, GCC, NWCRO.
Bulletin References; *Reseau de la Pierre Saint Martin Aug 2013.*
Newsletter References; *Easgill Aug 1997, Hunt Pot Feb 1998, GG Photographic Meet May 1998, Barclays Lode Wales July 1998, Rowten Pot Dec 1998, Alum Pot Dec 1998, Swinsto-KMC March 2012, Croesor Rhosydd [Through] Oct 2012, Lancaster-Wretched Rabbit Nov 2013, Pikedaw Calamine Caverns Feb 2015, Calf Holes-Browgill and Old Ing-Birkwith June 2015, Simpson's Flooded August 2016, Simpson's-KMC Aug 2016, Darnbrook Pot June 2018, Wildcat Rift May 2018, Ingleborough Cave Oct 2018, Cherry Tree Hole Oct 2018, Lancaster Hole-Wretched Rabbit Nov 2018, Coast to Coast [Mountain Bike in 13.25 hours] July 2019.*

MARTIN, Liam; *J2013, b2003,*
Newsletter References; *Calf Holes-Browgill and Old Ing-Birkwith June 2015, Wildcat Rift May 2018, Lancaster Hole-Wretched Rabbit Nov 2018.*

MARTIN, Rachel; [née Storry] *J2004, b1973,*

Newsletter References; *Short Drop-Gavel Pot Nov 2004, Skirwith Cave Nov 2004, Yordas Pot & Cave Dec 2004, Lancaster Hole April 2005, Gingling Hole July 2005, Pippikin Sept 2005, Calf Holes & Brow Gill Cave Feb 2006, High Douk, Middle Washfold & Great Douk June 2006, Thistle & Runscar Caves Sept 2006, Photographic Weekend Oct 2006, Great Douk Feb 2007, Dismal Hill/Old Ing Feb 2007, Committee Pot July 2007, Bull Pot of the Witches Jan 2008, Heron Pot March 2008, Coppice Cave April 2008, Bull Pot of the Witches June 2008,Valley Entrance June 2008, Dowkabottom Cave Sept 2008, Salthill Quarry Geology Walk Nov 2008, Lower Long Churn Nov 2008, Bull Pot of the Witches Jan 2009, Long Churns July 2009, Gunnerfleet Caves Clear Up Aug 2009, Stile Repairs-Diccan and Long Churn 2010, Ribblehead Caves April 2010, Long Churn May 2010, Brow Gill-Calf Holes [and back] May 2010, Alum Pot July 2010, Mistral Hole Aug 2010, Yordas Cave Conserervation Aug 2010, Wretched Rabbit-County Pot Nov 2010, Dig Capping Nov 2010, KMC-Toyland Feb 2011, Illusion Pot April 2011, Sleets Gill April 2011, Yordas Pot April 2011, Illusion Pot June 2011, Sunset Hole June 2011, Sell Gill July 2011, Feizor-Moughton Walk July 2011, Jingling Pot Dec 2011, Shuttleworth Pot Feb 2012, Yordas Pot Feb 2012, Notts Pot March 2012, Hardrawkin Pot April 2012, White Scar Cave July 2012, Wizard's Chasm Jan 2013, Illusion Pot March 2013, Wretched Rabbit-Lancaster Nov 2013, Thistle, Runscar & Gunnerfleet Nov 2013, Nenthead Mines Sept 2014, KMC Sept 2014, Shuttleworth Pot Oct 2014, Alum Pot March 2015, Yordas/KMC March 2015, Great and High Douk June 2015, Robinson's Pot July 2015, Sell Gill Holes Sept 2015, Goyden Sept 2015, Ireby Fell Caverns Jan 2016, Skirwith Cave [Novice Trip] Jan 2016, KMC/Toyland Feb 2016, County Pot-Pool Sink Oct 2016, KMC [Novice Trip] Dec 2016, Bruntscar Cave Jan 2017, Notts Pot Feb 2017, Sell Gill Sept 2017, Short Drop-Gavel Pot Nov 2017, KMC [Novice Trip] Jan 2018, Jingling Pot Feb 2018, Long Churn [Childrens Meet] April 2018, Sunset Hole April 2019, Heron Pot July 2019,*

MARTIN, Stewart; *J1990, b1948,*
Probationary Meets; Mongo Gill, King Pot, Marble Steps, Lancaster-Wretched Rabbit, Lost John's, Meregill Hole, Magnetometer.
Member; Nottingham Climbing Club, Alpine Club, MAoM, MR-Cumbria-Central Fells.
Newsletter References; *Ireby Fell Jan 1992, Rumbling Hole Jan 1992.*

MARVEL, M; *J1983,*

MARVELL, Wayne; *J1988, b1968,*

MASON, Edward Ian; *J1965, b1937,*
Newsletter References; *Lancaster Hole Oct 1957, Bar Pot Dec 1957, Bar Pot May 1958, Lancaster Hole June 1958, Digging nr Owl Hole Dec 1958, Lancaster Hole June 1959.*

MASON, Michael Arthur; *J1965, b1945,*
Probationary Meets; Lost John's, Clapham Cave, Washfold Pot.
Bulletin References; *Lancaster Easegill 1966, Investigating various parts of Ingleborough Cave 1968, Grange Rig Pot 1968.*

MASSIADER, D; *J1979,*

MATTHEWS, David; *J1973, b1947,*
Probationary Meets; Gingling Hole, Lost John's, Lancaster-Top Sink.
Member; BMC.
Bulletin References; *Chourum Des Aiguilles 1974, Juniper Gulf [Bolting] 1974, Piaggia Bella 1975, Grotte de Bury 1976, Cow Garth Cave [Exploration] 1982/84.*
Newsletter References; *Chourum Des Aiguilles 1974, Gingling Hole Sept 1974, Giants Hole Nov 1974, Juniper Gulf Dec 1974, Lost John's Nov 1975, Nick Pot Oct 1975, Pippikin Hole Oct 1976, Bull Pot of the Witches Dec 1976, Bull Pot of the Witches Nov 1977, Link Pot Oct 1978, Alum Pot June 1980, Ireby Fell Caverns July 1982, Meregill Feb 1983, Spectacle-Vesper Pot Mar 1985, Gingling Hole Oct 1985, Pool Sink-Cow Pot March 1989, Crosby Ravensworth-AskhamWalking Meet Sept 2012, Providence Pot Restoration Nov 2014, Bull Pot of the Witches Jan 2015, County Pot Feb 2015, Shuttleworth/Witches 2 Conservation Feb 2015, Ribblehead Caves July 2015, Gingling Hole July 2015, Lost John's-Notts 2 Sept 2015, Sell Gill Holes Sept 2015, Walking Meet 2015, Alderley Edge Mines Oct 2015, Ireby Fell Caverns Jan 2016, KMC/Toyland Feb 2016, Hagg Gill April 2016, Meregill Hole May 2016, Sell Gill June 2016, Pool Sink June 2016, Simpson's Pot Aug 2016, Marble Steps Nov 2016, County Pot Dec 2016, Alum Pot Dec 2016, Heron Pot [Novice trip] April 2017, Calf Holes-Birkwith June 2017, Alum/Long Churns June 2017, Sunset Hole [Novice trip] Sept 2017, Iron Kiln Sept 2017, Wretched Rabbit-County Pot Sept 2017, Lancaster Hole Oct 2017, Ibbeth Peril caves April 2018, Cherry Tree Hole Oct 2018, Pikedaw Calamine Cavern Dec 2018.*

MATUSEWICZ, Jakub; *J2017, b1987,*
Probationary Meets; Darnbrook, Hagg Gill, Long Churns, Hurtle-Jingle Pot [Dive]
Member; UKMC.

Newsletter References; *Darnbrook Pot March 2016, Hagg Gill April 2016.*

MCDONALD, J; *J1982,*

MCGAVIN, Brian; *J2010, b1986, d2016.*
Probationary Meets; Little Hull, Gouffre Berger, Swinsto Hole.
Bulletin References; *Reseau de la Pierre Saint Martin Aug 2013.*
Newsletter References; *Illusion Pot June 2011, Cullaun 2 April 2012.*

MCGHEE, Jack; *J1958, b1922, d2003.*
BPC President 1975-1977.
Famous for his magic tricks especially 'the rings'.
Newsletter References; *The Rings appeared at the 1982 AGM.*

MCGHEE, Rodney Stuart Jack; AKA: Sorcerer's Apprentice. *J1961, b1943,*
Son of Jack.
Probationary Meets; Magnetometer, Bar Pot, Long Kin East Pot.
Famous for; Getting his foot stuck on a tight pitch in Penyghent Long Churn when flooding rapidly.
Bulletin References; *Oxlow Caverns June 1961, Flood Entrance March 1962, Pen-y-Ghent Pot Extensions Oct 1963, Notts Pot Oct 1963.*
Newsletter References; *Lancaster–County Pot Feb 1970.*

MCLAREN, Matthew Gavin; AKA: Sweet Boy. *J1993, b1972,*
Probationary Meets; Birks Fell, Swinsto-Simpson's, New Rift Pot.
Member; SUCPC, BCG, San Francisco Bay Grotto of the National Speleological Society Western Region, USA: 2002 to 2006. Cave Diving Section of the National Speleological Society USA: 2013/14.
Speleo Netherlands Limburg Group from 2010, Speleological Union of Ireland from 2019.
Club Expeditions; Pierre Saint Martin August 1995. Dordogne Cave Diving August 1995. Vercors August 1997, Italian/Swiss Alps September 1998, Summitted the Breithorn [4164M], Vercors, September 1998, Discovery of El Manadero and connection of Cueva Del Lago to the Manadero resurgence Ucero, Soria, Spain September 2000, Exploration of El Manadero to ~450m September 2001, South Doubs, France 2009, Gouffre Berger August 2010, Trou de Glaz, Chartreuse, August 2014, Vercors, France, August 2015, Vercors, France, July/August 2019.
Other Expeditions; Gouffre Berger September 1993, Joint University: South Wales University [Speleo Caerdydd], Salford [SUCPC], Reading

[RUCC], Croydon CC to Picos du Europa July/Aug 1997, exploration of Pozo Trasllambrian [LL8], Joint Spanish/Belgian [Military]/British expedition to Italian/Swiss Alps July 1999 Summitted Pollux [4092M], Castor [4228M], Rimpfischhorn [4199M], Mount Shasta (4322M) Northern California 2006, Gouffre Berger August 2016 with Speleo Netherlands, Mallorca Cave Diving May 2019.

Notable Achievements; Digging of Brackenbottom Pot 1993-1994. Part of the rescue team that recovered Trevor Kemp from Birkwith 9/10th July 1994 President's Meet. Several Radio Location efforts in GG94/95/98. Also supporting GG dives in Troubled Waters [1994], Deep Well [1999] and Mill Hill Sump [2000] Digging of Fat Finger with Dave Haigh and many others 1997-98. Including the famous incident recorded in Dave Haigh's book on 21st March 1997 where we thought the whole thing was about to collapse around us-never have 2 cavers exited a cave faster. First diver to connect Cueva Del Lago to the Manadero resurgence 17th September 2000. Part of the team to explore El Manadero in Soria, Spain, September 2001 with Scoff and Dave Ryall [+ surface support from Rowena Schofield, Sue Ryall, Cleona McLaren, Sharon Kelly, Mark Slater, Dennis Wray] as recorded in Scoff's Memoirs. Qualified Full Cave Diver PSA International, May 2010. NAUI Open Water Diving Instructor March 2014. Certificate A [Brevet A] for SRT and Cave competency awarded by the Verbond van Vlaamse Speleologen Belgium October 2015. Pushed upstream [dive] Wolves Hole in Cong, Co. Galway, Ireland 70m; 17th July 2017 [supported by Brendan and Alex McLaren]

Main Activities; Caving, digging, cave diving, open water diving, alpine climbing, walking, mountain biking.

Famous for: Coming to the dump [and other meets] for years on a small motorcycle with all my gear. Living next door to Richard Kendall on Via Mateo, San Jose, California, 7000 miles from the dump.

Remembers; Falling off my Honda 100cc motorcycle twice on my way to a Kettlewell meet on a very wet, miserable day in July 1993. The second time caused by a rear tyre blow out, only for the next car along to be a BPC member [Mark] driving a van with full motorcycle transport equipment on board. I was safely escorted to a garage in Kettlewell, left the bike to be repaired and went caving in Birksfell Cave. Proper BPC spirit. Testing Scoff's bog-O-zep to destruction in El Manadero in 2001. The buoyancy tubes imploded 25 mins into the dive @-25m, causing me to nose dive into the mud killing all visibility. After that it was not balanced in the water so undriveable. Not wanting to abandon it I spent the next hour

dragging it out of the cave system [under water] to arrive back much later than anticipated and to the consternation of at least some.

Bulletin References; *Death's Head/Big Meanie Nov 1993, Simpson's-Swinsto March 1994, Ribblehead Caves Feb 1995, Tete Sauvage July 1995, Mongo Gill March 1997, Marble Steps March 1997, Boxhead Pot March 1997, Belfry Survey [GG] June 1998, Barclays Lode Wales July 1998, El Manadero [Diving Exploration], Sima de las Tainas de Mattarubia, Sima del Carlista, Simas M-21 & CJ-3 Sept 2001, Doubs France Aug 2009.*

Newsletter References; *El Manadero Aug 2000.*

MCLINDON, Richard John; AKA: Dick. *J1975, b1951,*
Probationary Meets; Chourum Des Aiguilles 73&74, Pen-y-Ghent Pot, GG78.
Bulletin References; *Chourum Des Aiguilles 1973, Chourum Des Aiguilles 1974, Piaggia Bella 1975, Trou Qui Souffle 1975, Newby Moss Sink 3rd Shaft 1977, Gouffre Berger Aug 1980.*
Newsletter References; *Chourum Des Aiguilles 1974, Short Drop-Gavel Pot1976, Goyden Pot Feb 1976, Sleets Gill July 1976, Bull Pot of the Witches Dec 1976, Cherry Tree Hole July 1978, Sleets Gill July 1980, Gouffre Berger Aug 1980.*

MCNAMARA, Michael William; *J1989, b1950,*
Probationary Meets; Ireby Fell, Notts Pot, GG89. Rejoined 2005.
Bulletin References; *Trou De Glaz Aug 1989, Gouffre Berger Aug 1992.*
Newsletter References; *Ireby Fell [Diving Support] Oct 1988, Notts Pot Nov 1988, Dow-Providence July 1989, Out Sleets Beck Pot Dec 1989, Langstroth Pot & Cave [Diving] July 1989, Grange Rigg March 1990, Vulcan Pot Feb 1992, Rumbling Hole Jan 1992, Nick Pot Jan 1992, LKE-Rift Exchange Feb 1992, Gouffre Berger Aug 1992, Lancaster Hole April 2005, Long Kin West Dec 2005, Bull Pot Jan 2006, Peak Cavern Feb 2006, Tatham Wife Hole March 2006, Jingling Pot Dec 2006.*

MCQUAT-FARRER, Jane; *J2007,*
Elected Honarary Member 2017.

MELLOR, Joseph; *J2013, b1965,*
Probationary Meets; Brackenbottom Pot [Digging]
Member; WCC.

MELLOR, S;

MERRITT, John David; *J1971, b1947,*
Probationary Meets; Ireby Fell, Short Drop-Gavel.

MEUNIER, Andre; *J2002, b1952,*

MEUNIER, Katrina; *J2002, b1986,*

MIDDLETON, F.Norman; *J1938, b1901, d1985.*
Often referred to as a founder member this is not true, he did not join until 1938. He was the club book keeper for many years.
Main Activities; Caving, Walking.

MIDDLETON, Robert; *J2011, b1985,*
Member; SUSS 2004-Present, CDG 2014-Present.
Club Expeditions; Tresviso [Spain] 2015 & 2018.
Other Expeditions; Crete 2006, 2008, 2009 & 2010 [SUSS], Mulu [Malaysia] 2009, 2013, 2015 & 2017, China 2012, Peru 2012.
Notable Achievements; Derbyshire Cave Rescue Organisation Leader 2013-Present. Found new cave in Dub Cote, Foul Pot and Peak Cavern.
Main Activities; Caving, Cave Diving, Climbing and Running.
Famous for; Drinking too much.
Newsletter References; *Hells Bells Hole [Diving] Feb 2020.*

MIDGLEY, Graham Derek; *J1968, b1951,*
Probationary Meets; Alum Pot, Disappointment Pot, Bar Pot.
Involved in discovery of Whitsun Series GG 1968,

MIDWINTER, Jennifer; *J1996, b1960,*
Probationary Meets; GG97, Flood Entrance, Stream Passage, Bull Pot, Alum Pot.
Member; CPC, *YSS.*
Club photographer for several years.
Bulletin References; *Losers Pot [Discovery] March 2002.*
Newsletter References; *Bull Pot Dec 1996, Alum Pot [Training Meet] July 1997, Easgill Aug 1997, GG Photographic Meet May 1998, Swinsto-KMC March 1999, Birks Fell June 1999, Fat Finger Millennium Party, Lancaster Round Trip March 2000, Skirwith Cave July 2000, Cherry Tree Hole Jan 2001, Ingleborough Cave Digging 2001, Great/Little Douk Dec 2001, Losers Pot [Discovery] Mar 2002, Sell Gill June 2002, South Wales [Cwm Dwr & OFD 2] July 2002, Alum Pot July 2002, Rumbling Hole July 2002, Pippikin-Mistral Through June 2002, Crackpot Cave [Photgraphic Meet] Jan 2003, Dan Yr Ogof/ OFD2 June 2003.*

MIERS, Andrew Jose; *J2019, b1996,*

MILLER, David James; AKA: Gobshite. *J1989, b1967,*
Probationary Meets; Bull Pot o t Witches, GG89-91, Alum Pot, Trou de glaz.
Member; BOPC.

Bulletin References; *Mountain Hall [Scaling] 1980, Nochobueno Fin [Mexico] Feb 1993, Gouffre Berger Aug 1992, Out Sleets Beck Pot Dec 1989, Pippikin Pot Oct 1989, New Rift Pot Feb 1990, Grange Rigg March 1990, Pikedaw Calamine Caverns March 1992, Gouffre Berger Aug 1992, Swaledale Weekend Oct 1992, Ireby Fell Feb 1993,Hodge Close Sept 1993, Snatcher's Pot Nov 1993, Cherry Tree Hole Feb 1996, Ulverston-Coniston Walking Meet 2007.*

MILLER, John; *J1951, b1926,*
Bulletin References; *Lost John's July 1951, Caving in the Timavo Valley-Yugoslavia 1953. Wharfedale Camp Aug 1960, Stonelands Cave July 1960.*
Newsletter References; *Assisted with survey of Ingleborough Cave June 1959.*

MILLER, Michael; AKA: Mick. *J1978, b1953,*
Rejoined 1987.
Probationary Meets; Simpson's Pot, Gingling, Notts Pot.
Motley.
Newsletter References; *Rumbling Hole Aug 1978, Simpsons Pot Jan 1979, Hammer Pot Sept 1978, Top Sink-Lancaster and Back! Oct 1978, Lost John's Sept 1978, Scrafton Pot April 1980, Pasture Gill Cave Sept 1980, Alum Pot March 1981, New Goyden Pot April 1981, Sunset Hole July 1981, Sunset Hole July 1981, Gingling Hole Rescue July 1981, Dow–Providence Sept 1981, Link Pot Sept 1981, Pippikin Pot Oct 1981, King Pot April 1982, Providence–Dow Cave July 1982, Link Pot July 1983, County Pot March 1984, Weathercote Cave April 1988, Pippikin March 1988, South Wales Nov 1988.*

MILLWARD, Alan; *J1990, b1946,*
Probationary Meets; Providence Pot, Dowbergill Passage, Diccan-Alum, Rumbling Hole, Nick Pot-Vulcan.
Member; CPC [1989-1991]
Notable Achievements; Made the CRO call out for the 'Des Crowley rescue'.
Main Activities; Caving, Walking, Cycling.
Newsletter References; *Birks Fell Cave July 1991, Vulcan Pot-Nick exchange Feb 1992, Pikedaw Calamine Caverns March 1992, Rumbling Hole Jan 1992, Pippikin March 1992, Simpson's-KMC April 1992, Brackenbottom Pot April 1992, Pen-y-Ghent Pot July 1992, Swaledale Weekend Oct 1992, Rowten Pot Feb 1994, Marble Steps March 1994, Pool Sink-Lancaster Hole Dec 1995, Long Kin West March 1996, Diccan Pot March 1996, Top Sink-Lancaster July 1996, Hunt Pot Feb 1997, Alum Pot [Training Meet] July 1997.*

MINTOW, G; *J1982,*

MITCHELL, Albert; *J1936,*

MITCHELL. Derek; *J1966,*

MITCHELL, Grahame; *J1963, b1944, d2001.*
Probationary Meets; Sunset Hole, Marble Steps, Jingling Pot.
Lived near and caved with Pete Livesey, left a substantial legacy to the club.
Bulletin References; *South Wales Easter 1963, Notts Pot Oct 1963.*

MITCHELL, James Gordon; *J1960, b1932,*
Probationary Meets; Clapham Cave, Sleets Gill, Dowkabottom, GG60, Easegill.

MITCHELL, John; AKA: SILLY. *J1996,*

MITCHELL, John; *Joined before 1938,*

MONEY, Jeffrey; *J1971, b1929, d1987.*
Probationary Meets; GG69-71.
Responsible for the introduction of draught beer at GG. Once set his hair on fire with a candle at a Christmas Dinner, very festive.
Bulletin References; *Cartilage Cave 1977.*

MONK, Peter; AKA: Paparazzi Pete: *J2011, b1947,*
Member; NB.
Bulletin References; *Witches Cave location and Dig Sept 2010, Buckden Gavel Lead Mines Mar 2010, Dinkling Green Mine, Restoration of Brown Hill Pot entrance Nov 2012-Feb 2013, Restoration of Clapham Bottoms Pot Entrance June 2013, Cave & Calamine Pit July 2019.*
Newletter References; *Stile Repairs-Diccan and Long Churn 2010, Scoska Cave April 2014, Hardrawkin Pot Fencing Conservation 2014, Providence Pot Restoration Nov 2014, Dinkling Green Mine Cave July 2019.*

MOODY, Catherine Laura; AKA: Cat. *J2013, b1985,*
Probationary Meets; Little Hull Pot, Lost John's Hole, Illusion Pot, JH-Titan, Corky's-Main Chamber, Dyhedral-Stream Passage.
Member; YUCPC 2008-16, YCC 2010-16.
Expeditions; Gouffre Berger 2011, Durmitor 2012, 13, 14, 16 [YUCPC], Mulu Caves Project & China Caves Project 2015.
Notable Achievements; BPC Editor from 2015.
Main Activities; Caving, Via Ferrata.
Newsletter References; *Illusion Pot March 2013, Simpson's Pot-KMC Sept 2014, Bar Pot [Photographic Trip] March 2015, Link Pot-Cow Pot June 2015, Poll Dudh June 2015, St Catherine's1-Fisher St June 2015, Faunarooska June 2015, Otter*

Hole June 2016, Death's Head-Big Meanie Sept 2016, County Pot-Pool Sink Oct 2016, Marble Steps Nov 2016, Link Pot April 2017, Hensler's Pot-Winch May 2017, Notts Pot Sept 2018, Long Churns & BorrinsMoor Sept 2018.

MOORCROFT, James P; *J2012, b1991,*
Newsletter References; *Sunset Hole June 2013.*

MOORE, Brian Paul; *J1995, b1969,*
Member, RPC.
Bulletin References; *Tete Sauvage July 1995.*

MOORE, John; *J2012, b1979,*

MOORE, Paul; *J2018,*
Newsletter References; *Top Sink-Wretched Rabbit Jan 2018.*

MORGAN, Simon; *J2000, b1973,*
Probationary Meets; County-Wretched Rabbit, Pippikin-Mistral, Sell Gill, Alum Pot, Notts Pot.
Newsletter References; *County-Wretched Rabbit Nov 2000.*

MORRIS, Kevin Mark; *J1980, b1960,*
Probationary Meets; Dow-Providence, Lost John's, Simpson's KMC.
Newsletter References; *Lost John's Sept 1978, King Pot Feb 1980.*

MOULSON, Arthur; *J1937, b1911, d1960.*

MOULSON, Frank; AKA: Dad. *J1937, b1907, d1980.*
BPC President 1973-74.
Notable Achievements; Main Activities; Caving, Walking
Famous for; The Frank Moulson Annual Photographic Award.
Bulletin References; *Recorded as taking part in first post war trip–Rift Pot 7th April 1946. Also involved in the first attempted Rift Pot/ Long Kin East exchange April 28th 1946, Rift Pot/ Long Kin East exchange April 20th 1947, Birks Cave, Buckden 11th May 1947, Calf Holes Aug 1947, MereGill 7th Sept 1947, Calf Holes / Brow Gill Exchange 1948, Clapham Cave 11th April 1948, Birks Cave May 1948, Brow Gill & Calf Holes Oct 1948, Great Douk, Sunset Hole April 1949, Bull Pot of the Witches July 1955.*
Newsletter References; *Leader Alum Pot Open Aug 1954, Dow-Providence rescue Dec 1957, Calf Holes& Browgill Sept 1957.*

MOULTON, Hannah; *J2011, b1986,*
Rejoined 2019.
Member; SUSS, OCC.

Newsletter References; *Rift-LKE Oct 2009, Treviso Aug 2017.*

MULLER, Mark Antony Alan Jules; *J1996, b1968,*
Newsletter References; *Cherry Tree Hole Feb 1996, Mistral Hole Nov 1996, Great/Little Douk Dec 2001, Runscar Cave Sept 2004.*

MULLINS, Carol; *J1987, b1959,*
Probationary Meets; Sunset, Dan Yr Ogof, Tatham Wife.
Lady Motley.
Bulletin References; *Doubs, France Aug 2009, Felix Trombe 2011, Alderley Edge Mines Sept 2009,*
Newsletter References; *Weathercote Cave April 1988, Pippikin March 1988, South Wales Nov 1988, November Hole April 2006, Great Douk July 2006, Robinsons Pot Sept 2008, Alderley Edge Mines Sept 2009, Hull Pot [Filming with the BBC] Oct 2010, Heron Pot Nov 2010, Heron Pot Nov 2010, KMC-Toyland Feb 2011, Committee Pot March 2011, Oxlow Caverns March 2011, Crosby Ravensworth-AskhamWalking Meet Sept 2012, Roundthwaite Common to Borrowdale Sept 2014, Walking Meet 2015, New Biggin on Lune to Appleby Walking Meet Sept 2016, Devis Hole/Mine July 2017, Lindale-Greenodd Walking Meet 2017.*

MURGATROYD, David; *J1985, b1963,*
Probationary Meets; GG86, Swinsto, Sell Gill.

MURGATROYD, Derek Ernest; *J1951, b1933,*
Bulletin References; *Lost John's July 1951.*

MURGATROYD, Kevin Stuart; AKA: Snagglepuss. *J1976, b1953,*
Probationary Meets; Flood Entrance-Bar Pot, Lost John's, Short Drop-Gavel.
Member; WSG, SSSS.
Bulletin References; *Otter Hole 1977, Grotte de Bury 1977.*
Newsletter References; *County Pot Oct 1975, Lost John's Nov 1975, Short Drop–Gavel Pot 1976, Stream Passage–Flood Entrance Pot March 1976, Pasture Gill Cave July 1976, Lost John's September 1976, Rumbling Hole Dec 1976, Pen-y-Ghent Pot April 1977.*

MURPHY, Zita Marie; *J1998, b1975,*
Probationary Meets; County Pot.
Member; QUCC.

MUSIRI, Lloyd; *J2018, b1985,*
Probationary Meets; GG18, Bar Pot, Aquamole, Lancaster, Bull Pot, Sell Gill, Long Churns, KMC.
Newsletter References; *Alum Pot Oct 2018, Death's Head Nov 2018, Sunset Hole Feb 2020.*

MUTIAH, Nur; *J2005, b1965,*
Probationary Meets; GG4/5, KMC.

MYERS, Derrick; *J1951, b1924,*
Bulletin References; *Lost John's July 1951.*

MYERS, Gerald Garnett; AKA: Gerry. *J1994, b1945,*
Newsletter References; *Manchester By-pass-Wretched Rabbit March 1995, Lancaster Hole-County Pot Oct 1995, Easegill April 1997, Lost John's Hole March 1997, GG Photographic Meet May 1998, County-Wretched Rabbit Nov 1998, Lancaster-Wretched Rabbit Jan 1999, Derbyshire Meet Sept 1999, KMC Photographic Trip Nov 2002, Lancaster Hole Feb 2003, Crackpot Cave [Photgraphic Meet] Jan 2003, Giant's Hole Jan 2004, Diccan Pot Feb 2005, HardwrakinPot April 2005, Rumbling Hole July 2006, Salthill Quarry Geology Walk Nov 2008, Link Pot Sept 2009.*

MYERS, Lara Berthany; [née Hoggarth] *J1997, b1968,*
Probationary Meets; Lancaster Hole, Gingling,Skirwith, Calf Holes, Short Drop-Gavel, Roger Kirk, GG99, Bar Pot, Mongo Gill, Sell Gill, Easegill.
Member; LUG, LUCC, NUCC.
Bulletin References; *Restoration of Brown Hill Pot entrance Nov 2012-Feb 2013, Reseau de la Pierre Saint Martin Aug 2013.*
Newsletter References; *Easegill April 1997, Lost John's Hole March 1997, County-Wretched Rabbit Nov 1998, Lancaster-Wretched Rabbit Jan 1999, Derbyshire Meet Sept 1999, KMC Photographic Trip Nov 2002, Lancaster Hole Feb 2003, Crackpot Cave [Photgraphic Meet] Jan 2003, Giant's Hole Jan 2004, Diccan Pot Feb 2005, HardwrakinPot April 2005, Rumbling Hole July 2006, Link Pot Sept 2009.*

MYERS, Lily-Ann; *J2017, b2012,*

MYERS, Peter; *J1953,*

N

NASH, George Trevor; AKA: Trevor. *J1958, b1936,*
Bulletin References; *Mendip Trip 1958, Lost John's March 1960 [Fell 15' unhurt], Lost John's March 1961, Silozwane Cave [Rhodesia] 1966.*
Newsletter References; *Sunset Hole Aug 1958, Bar Pot Nov 1958, St Cuthbert's Swallet March 1959, Measuring Depth of GG shaft Aug 1959, Clapham Bottoms dig Aug 1959, Ireland Aug 1959, Giant's Hole Nov 1959.*

NASH, Philip; *J1958, b1942,*
Bulletin References; *Calf Holes 1958, Old East Passage GG 1960, Flood Entrance Pot Dec 1960, Little Hull Pot Feb 1961, Gunnerfleet Caves Oct 1959.*

NAYLOR, Alec Thomas; *J1949,*
Bulletin References; *Flood Entrance July 1949,*

NAYLOR, Peter S; *J1963, b1945,*
Probationary Meets; Magnetometer Pot, Little Hull, Carlswark Caverns.
Bulletin References; *Old Cote Pot April 1963, Notts Pot Oct 1963.*

NEEDHAM, George David; *J1955, b1936,*
Resigned Aug 1958.

NELLIS, Claire; *J2009, b1976,*
Probationary Meets; KMC, Long Churns, Upper Hackersgill, Heron Pot.
Newsletter References; *SRT Training Ingleborough Hall Oct 2009, Sell Gill Nov 2009, Illusion Pot June 2011.*

NELSON, David George; *J1988, b1965,*
Probationary Meets; Wales, Pippikin, Mongo Gill.
Newsletter References; *South Wales Nov 1988.*

NEMETH, Viktoria; *J2018, b1995,*
Member; BCRA.

NEWMAN, David; *J1967, b1932,*

NEWMAN, Joanne; *J2019, b1993,*

NICHOL, Alan; *J1936,*
Bulletin References; *Pen-y-Ghent Long Churn-trapped by flood water for 27 hours October 1938.*

NICHOLSON, Michael Edward Charles; *J1950,*
Bulletin References; *Bull Pot of the Witches Aug 1950, Sunset Hole Oct 1950, Pen-y-Ghent Pot Rescue, young BSA member died of exhaustion 1951. Bar Pot Feb 1951, Easter Camp GG 1951, Lost John's July 1951.*

NIGHTINGALE, Helen; *J2014, b1980,*
Probationary Meets; White Scar,
Member; WCMS.
Newsletter References; *White Scar Cave July 2014.*

NIXON, Kenneth; *J1996, b1942,*
Probationary Meets; Sell Gill.

NOBLE, Peter; *J1962, b1938,*
Probationary Meets; Ribblehead Caves, Marble Steps, Alum Pot.
Peter was voted as a member of the committee before someone pointed out he wasn't actually a member of the Club.
Bulletin References; *Lost John's March 1960, Jockey Hole Feb 1962.*

NOLAN, John Gordon; AKA: Gordon. *J1959, b1932,*
Bulletin References; *Gaping Gill Meet 1960, Grange Rigg Easter 1961, Stonelands Pot June 1961, Clapham Cave 1961, Christmas Pot April 1962, Ingleborough Cave Diving Dec 1962, Christmas/Grange/P5 extensions May 1962.*
Newsletter References; *Carried out survey of Ingleborough Cave June 1959, Ingleborough Cave Survey Aug 1959, Ingleborough Cave Sept 1959, Ingleborough Cave the Wallows beddings Sept*

1959, Ingleborough Cave Oct 1959, Bar Pot Nov 1959, Leader Easter Camp Clapham 1961.

NORTH, D.I; [Recorded as a member in 1950]

NORTH, Fred H; J1959,

NORTH, Geoffrey Denis; AKA: Denis. J1948,
Bulletin References; Recorded as taking part in first post war trip-Rift Pot 7th April 1946, and involved in the first attempted Rift Pot/Long Kin East exchange April 28th1946, Rift Pot 19th May 1946, Lost John's July/Aug 1946, Birks Cave May 1948, Great Douk, Sunset Hole April 1949, Quaking Pot April 1950, Pen-y-Ghent Pot Rescue, young BSA member died of exhaustion 1951, Easter Camp GG 1951.

NORTH, John Fred; AKA: Fred. J1946, b1917,
Bulletin References; Recorded as taking part in first Rift Pot-Long Kin East exchange April 28th 1946. Rift Pot 19th May 1946, Recorded as taking part in Lost John's trip Jan 1947, Lost John's July/Aug 1946, Birks Cave 5th Oct 1947, Great Douk, Sunset Hole April 1949, Quaking Pot April 1950, Pen-y-Ghent Pot Rescue, young BSA member died of exhaustion 1951. Easter Camp GG 1951.

NORTH, J. H; J1946,
Bulletin References; June 1951, Bull Pot June 1952, Simpson's Pot July 1953.

NUTTON, Clive Robert; J2003, b1969,
Re-joined 2015.
Main Activities; Caving, Walking, Climbing, Kayaking, Sailing.
Notable Achievements; Newsletter Editor and committee member.
Probationary Meets; Goyden Pot, Robinson's Pot, Committee Pot, Long Kin East, Aquamole, Bar Pot, Bull Pot, Pikedaw Calamine, Darnbrook Pot, Giant's Hole, Swinsto Hole, Sunset Hole.
Bulletin References; Deep Well [Diving Support] 2000-2003, Pyrenees Aug 2004.
Newsletter References; Swinsto-KMC Jan 2003, Lancaster Hole Feb 2003, Crackpot Cave [Photgraphic Meet] Jan 2003, Pool Sink Sept 2003, Great Douk Cave Sept 2003, Sell Gill Hole Sept 2003, Robinson's Pot Oct 2003, Heron Pot [Abandoned Photo Meet] Nov 2003, Bar Pot Dec 2003, Long Kin East Nov 2003, Giant's Hole Jan 2004, Pikedaw Calamine Caverns Jan 2004, Bull Pot Dec 2003, Swinsto Hole-KMC Feb 2004, Alum Pot March 2004, Washfold Pot April 2004, Deep Well [Dive Support] GG04, MilwrTunnel June 2004, Gingling Hole July 2004, Dowkabottom Cave Oct 2004, New Rift Dec 2004, Bar Pot Jan 2005, Yordas Pot & Cave Dec 2004, Calf Holes & Browgill Cave Nov 2004, Pen-y-Ghent Pot June 2005, Pippikin Sept 2005, Simpson's Pot Dec 2005, Coppice Cave-Ling Gill Jan 2006, James Hall Mine Feb 2006, Peak Cavern Feb 2006, Hurnell Moss Pot Oct 2006, Hunt Pot Nov 2006, Great Expectations Dec 2007, Katnot Cave/Thorne Cave [Novice Trip] May 2016, Borrins Moor Cave Nov 2016, Bruntscar Cave Jan 2017, Red Moss Pot [Novice Trip] April 2017, Long Churns & Borrins Moor Sept 2018, Ingleborough Cave Oct 2018, Death's Head Nov 2018, Wizard's Chasm Dec 2018, Lancaster Hole-Wretched Rabbit Nov 2018, Lancaster-County Jan 2019, Sunset Hole April 2019, Sunset Hole Feb 2020.

16

O'BRIEN, Kathleen; See Faulkner.

O'BYRNE, Donal; *J2010, b1981,*
Club Expeditions; *Gouffre Berger 2010.*

O'BYRNE, Peter Charles; *J1991, b1951,*

O'CONNOR, Erin; *J2009, b2003,*
Newsletter Rererences; *Ribblehead Caves April 2010, Upper Long Churn June 2010.*

O'CONNOR, Leanne; *J2002, b1973,*

O'CONNOR, Matthew, James; *J1986, b1965,*
Probationary Meets; Ireby Fell, Pool Sink-Cow Pot, Bull Pot of the Witches.
Newsletter References; *Lost John's Pot July 1985, Ireby Fell [Diving Support] Oct 1988, Rift-Large Pot March 1990, Lancaster Hole-County Pot Oct 1995, Easegill April 1997, Deep Well [Dive Support] May 1997, Ribblehead Caves April 2010, Upper Long Churn June 2010, County Pot-Lancaster Hole June 2019.*

OFFORD, John; AKA: Bowels. *J1977, b1955,*
Probationary Meets; GG76, Bull Pot o t Witches, Dow Cave, Disappointment Pot.
Bulletin References; *Cnoc Nan Uamh & Uamh Nan Claig-Ionn Easter 1978, Gouffre Berger Aug 1980.*
Newsletter References; Top Sink-Lancaster and Back! Oct 1978, *Gouffre Berger Aug 1980.*

OLEJNIK, Jozef; AKA: Joe Oilyneck. *J1976, b1957,*
Probationary Meets; Lancaster-Easegill, Nick Pot, Wade's-Bar Pot.

Member; CHGS.
Bulletin References; *West Rift GG [Exploration] 1989 / 1990,*
Newsletter References; *Nick Pot Oct 1975, Stream Passage-Flood Entrance Pot March 1976, OFD I April 1978, Top Sink Oct 1978, Lost John's Sept 1978, Ingleborough Cave Oct 1982, Dow-Providence July 1989, Ireby Fell March 1990, South Wales Dec 1990, Bar Pot [Rope Ladder] May 2000.*

OLEJNIK, Ruairidh; AKA: Rory. *J2000,*
Newsletter References; *Bar Pot [Rope Ladder] May 2000.*

OLIVER, T; *J1978,*

O'MALLEY, Barry Richard; *J1990, b1970,*

OPENSHAW, Antony Wilson; *J1958, b1942,*
Newsletter References; *Little Hull Pot April 1958,*

OTTIWELL, David; *J1999, b1974,*
Probationary Meets; GG98, South Wales, Easegill.

OWEN, Graham; *J2013, b1962,*
Probationary Meets; GG11, GG12, GG13.
Newsletter References; *Sunset Hole April 2019.*

OWEN, Gwyneth Olwen; *J1993, b1959,*
Probationary Meets; GG90/91.

OWEN, Tracy; *J2013, b1970,*
Probationary Meets; GG11, GG12, GG13.

OWENS, A; *J197*

71

P

PACKWOOD, Janet Susan; AKA: NJB. *J2008, b1960,*
Probationary Meets; GG07 [Bar Pot, Flood
Entrance, Stream Passaage Pot], GG08, GG09.
Member; VMC [1990 to Present], WRCPC [1996-2000]
Club expeditions; Gouffre Berger 2010.
Main Activities; Previously SRT, Climbing, Walking
and Cycling. Presently Driving, Gear Cleaning and
general Dogsbody. Involved in taking blind caver
Graham Owen underground 2011-2.
Famous for; Onion Bhajis at Gaping Gill.
Bulletin References; *Croesor-Rhosydd Feb 2009.*
Newsletter References; *Rumbling Hole March
2010, Croesor-Rhosydd March 2010, Hurnell Moss
Pot April 2010, Alum Pot July 2010, KMC & Bar Pot
[Blind Novice Trips] May 2011, Hurnell Moss Pot
Oct 2013, Mongo Gill Nov 2013.*

PAGE, C. F;

PALEY, Derek; *J1958, b1942,*
Newsletter References; *Lancaster Hole June 1958,
GG members meet 1959, Assisted with survey of
Ingleborough Cave June 1959, Clapham Bottoms
dig Aug 1959.*

PALFREMAN, Bernard; *J1934,*

PARKER, Alan; *J1953, b1939*

PARKER, Anthony; *J1975, b1956,*
Probationary Meets; Lancaster Hole, Nick Pot, Lost
John's.
Newsletter References; *Lancaster Hole June 1958,
Lost John's Nov 1975, Nick Pot Oct 1975, Stream
Passage-Flood Entrance Pot March 1976, Lancaster
Hole [Maple Leaf Pitch Team] 1980, Top Sink-
County Pot April 1985.*

PARKER, Hugh; *J2008, b1989,*

PARKINSON, John; *J1962, b1945,*
Probationary Meets; Lancaster Hole, Alum Pot,
Sunset Hole, GG13, GG14.
Rejoined 2012 & 2015.
Bulletin References; *Lost John's July 1963, Pen-y-
Ghent Pot Extensions Oct 1963, Hammer Pot July &
September 1964, Giants Hole Jan 1964, Gautries
Pot Nov 1964, Antler Pot Feb 1965.*
Newsletter References; *Crackpot Cave Aug 1965,
KMC-Swinsto June 1972.*

PARRINGTON, John; *J1982, b1964,*
Rejoined 2007.
Probationary Meets; Pippikin Pot, Gingling Pot,
Lost John's.
Bulletin References; *Vercors Aug 1983, Pippikin
Pot Oct 1981.*
Newsletter References; *Ireby Fell Caverns July
1982, Birks Fell Cave July 1982, Providence-Dow
Cave July 1982, Ingleborough Cave Oct 1982,
Swinsto-Valley Entrance April 1983, Mendip
weekend April 1983, Hallucination Aven Location
May 1983, Notts Pot March 1983, Pasture Gill Pot
June 1983, Gingling Hole June 1983, Pippikin-Link
July 1983, Quaking Pot Aug 1983, South Wales Aug
1983, Short Drop Caver Dec 1983, Langstroth Pot
Sept 1985.*

PARTINGTON, Keith; *J1987, b1945,*
Probationary Meets; GG87, Alum Pot, White Scar.
Newsletter References; *White Scar Cave July 1987,
Nick Pot Nov 1987, Rumbling Hole March 1988,
Pippikin March 1988, Notts Pot Nov 1988, King Pot
Jan 1989, Pool Sink-Cow Pot March 1989, Big
Meanie-Death's Head Nov 1989, Ireby Fell March
1990, Black Shiver Pot Jan 1991.*

PARTINGTON, John; *J1982, b1945.*
Bulletin References; *Brackenbottom Pot [Dig] 1985.*
Newsletter References; *Lost John's Feb 1982.*

PATCHETT, Arnold; *J1936, b1905, d2004.*
BPC President 1954-56.
Member; YRC, BS, RSSG [Life Member]
Other expeditions; The Anglo–French Expedition to Labouiche River cave Pyrenees with Norbet Casteret-June 1955.
Main Activities; Caving, Walking.
Famous for; Attending 50th Anniversary Dinner 1983. Recorded as taking part in an Anglo-French expedition to Labouiche [Limoge] June 1955. Met Norbert Castet and found large extension including a chamber later named after him by Norbert Casteret.
Bulletin References; *Recorded as taking part in first post war trip-Rift Pot 7th April 1946. Also involved in the first attempted Rift Pot/Long Kin East exchange April 28th 1946, Lost John's July/Aug 1946, Dowka Bottom 29th Sept 1946, First Club trip to reach the sump in Meregill Sept 1946, Rift Pot/Long Kin East exchange April 20th 1947, Birks Cave, Buckden 11th May 1947, Birks Cave 5th Oct 1947, Clapham Cave 11th April 1948, Clapham Cave 11th April 1948, Rift Pot-Long Kin East exchange April 1949, Lost John's July 1951, Involved with BBC transmission from Alum Pot 7th May 1961.*
Newsletter References; *Bar Pot Dec 1957, Involved with BBC Transmission from Alum Pot May 1958.*

PATCHETT, Harry; *J1949,*

PATERSON, Martyn William; *J1998, b1961,*

PATTINSON, Adrian; *J1965, b1947,*
Probationary Meets; Rumbling Hole, Crackpot Cave.

PAWSON, David George; AKA: Dave. *J1971, b1948,*
Probationary Meets; Ireby Fell, Little Hull, Tatham Wife.
Bulletin References; *Gavel Pots, Bishopdale 1972, September Rift GG, Sept 1971, Little Hull Hole Aug 1971.*
Newsletter References; *Tatham Wife Hole Aug 1971, Sell Gill Hole Oct 1971, Pasture Gill Hole Oct 1971, Black Shiver Pot Nov 1971, Birks Fell April 1972, Washfold Pot April 1972, Swinsto Hole [Down & Up] June 1972, Gingling Hole Aug 1972, Flood-Bar SRT practice Feb 1975.*

PAYNE, L; *J2002,*

PAYNE, Margaret, Elizabeth;-See Brook.

PAYNE, P; *J1957, b1946.*

PAYNE, Robert Frederick; *J1964, b1933,*
Probationary Meets; Sell Gill, Bull Pot of the Witches.

PEAKE, D; *J1981,*

PEARCE, John Swinside; *J1958, b1940,*
Newsletter References; *Lost John's Sept 1959.*

PEARSON, Karen; *J2007, b1963,*

PEARSON, Mark; *J1994, b1967,*
Probationary Meets; Birks fell, Spectacle-Vespers, Alum-Diccan.
Newsletter References; *King Pot [Support] March 1999, Langstroth Pot June 2000.*

PEDDER, John William; *J1966, b1946,*
Probationary Meets; Dow Cave, GG66, Calf Holes.

PEEL, A; *J1980,*

PEEL, C;

Newsletter References; *Washfold Pot July 1957; Simpson's Pot Aug 1957, Swinsto Sept 1957.*

PEGRAM, David Methley; *J1959, b1938,*
Expelled from club non payment of subs Dec 1962.

PEIRCE, J. S; *J1958,*

PEIRSON, Jack M; *J1957, b1942,*
Newsletter Refernces; *Brown Scar Cave Sept 1959.*

PEIRSON, John Warwick; *J1959, b1942,*
Member; BPC Heavy Gang 2014, 'The Twats' 1990.
Club expeditions; BPC Bus meet-Pyrenees 1961-La Grotte Casteret, Lascaux [Shortly after this trip Lascaux was closed permanently and replaced with a fibre glass copy]
Other Expeditions; Molde Norway 1965, Surveyed Trollkirkegrotten with Peter Livesey.
Notable Achievements; Climbed Matterhorn via Zimut Ridge with two friends and a German guide book 1962. Dived entrance passage Stonelands cave, Littondale-25th June 1961 [Claiming possible first underground use of an aqualung by a BPC member?]
Main Activities; Walking [Hill Bagging-Nuttall's >2K' guide], Archaeology [Bronze Age & Neolithic, Cup & Ring markings etc], Locating WWII aircraft wreck sites.

Famous for; being one of the first Dump Wardens and once changed the Dump door lock and issued 20 new keys without testing first, several members had to spend a rough night sleeping in the woodshed.

Bulletin References; *Pen-y-ghent Pot July 1960, Wharfedale Camp Aug 1960, Stonelands Cave July 1960, Lost John's March 1961, Stonelands Pot June 1961, Pen-y-Ghent pot 1961, Flood Entrance March 1962, Stream Passage Pot June 1962, Long Kin West July 1962, Little Hull Pot July 1962, Hardrawkin Pot Sept 1962, Juniper Gulf Dec 1962, Hardrawkin Pot Aug 1964, Nick Pot Nov 1964.*

Newsletter References; *Lakes Walk Sept 1990, Millenium Walk Sept 2002, Black Combe-Foxfield Walk Sept 2003, Ulverston-Coniston Walking Meet 2007, Lambrigg Fell-Tebay Walk Sept 2008, Salthill Quarry Geology Walk Nov 2008, Dunsop Bridge-Bilsborrow Walking Meet Sept 2009, Cautley-Kirkby Stephen Walk Sept 2011, Crosby Ravensworth-Askham Walking Meet Sept 2012, Roundthwaite Common to Borrowdale Sept 2014.*

PELL, Andrew Charles; *J1966, b1954, d2019.*
Rejoined 1980 +2016.
Member; BCOAS.
He left his sons alone in main chamber and they were messing about leaving their light on the empty chair as long as they dare, Daniel left his too long and was hoisted many feet in the air before the cable pulled out of the headset and he fell to the floor. Luckily he escaped with only broken wrists.
Probationary Meets; Mongo Gill, Bull Pot of the Witches, GG80.
Newsletter References; *GG Interim week May 1981.*

PENDRED, Philip Roger William; *J1969, b1943,*
Famous for; Making cine films [recently restored onto DVD and presented to the club archive]
Bulletin References; *September Rift GG, Sept 1971, Little Hull Hole Aug 1971, Rift Pot Sept 1972, Newby Moss Sink May 1977, Gouffre Berger Aug 1980, Gouffre Berger Aug 1992.*
Newsletter References; *Pen-y-Ghent Pot Aug 1969, Rumbling Hole Oct 1969, Kingsdale Master Cave Dec 1969, Lancaster-County Pot Feb 1970, Lost John's Jan 1970, Meregill Hole Aug 1971, Sell Gill Hole Oct 1971, Pasture Gill Hole Oct 1971, Birks Fell April 1972, Washfold Pot April 1972, Swinsto-KMC June 1972, Gingling Hole Aug 1972, Pen-y-Ghent Pot Aug 1972, Rowten Pot Dec 1972, Sunset Hole March 1974, Pasture Gill Feb 1974, Lancaster Hole Sept 1974, Giants Hole Nov 1974, Juniper Gulf Dec 1974, Lost John's September 1976, County Pot Oct 1978, Meregill Feb 1980, Gingling Hole July 1980,*

Gouffre Berger Aug 1980, Lost John's Nov 1980, Gavel Pot Dec 1980, Goyden Pot March 1981, Alum Pot March 1981, New Goyden Pot April 1981, Notts Pot Jan 1981, Sunset Hole July 1981, Rift Pot& Long Kin East Jan 1982, Gingling Hole June 1983, Swinsto-Rowten Exchange Nov 1983, Diccan Pot March 1984, Gingling Hole Oct 1985, Top Sink-County Pot March 1986, Calf Holes Jan 1988, Short Drop Cave Nov 1989, Calf Holes, Browgill, Old Ing and Dismal Hill Jan 1991, Sell Gill Training Meet Nov 1991, Pikedaw Calamine Caverns March 1992, Gouffre Berger Aug 1992, Simpson's Pot Oct 1993, Alum Pot Nov 1993, Ireby Fell Feb 1993, Simpson's-Swinsto March 1994, Lakes Walking Meet Sept 1995, Walking Meet Sept 1997.

PERCY, Nicholas; *J1959, b1938,*
Bulletin References; *Bull Pot Sept 1960, Pen-y-Ghent Long Churn Oct 1969, Flood Entrance Pot Dec 1960, Pen-y-Ghent Pot 1961.*

PERCY, Richard; *J1964, b1944,*
Probationary Meets; Ireby Fell, GG64, Ingleborough Cave.
Bulletin References; *Buttertubs/Flood Entrance/Sell Gill May 1964, Hammer Pot September 1964, Ashberry Windpit Aug 1964, Nick Pot Nov 1964, Ibbeth Peril 1966, Ryedale Easter 1965, Grange Rigg-Christmas Aug 1965.*

PEROU, Sidney Alan Bruce; *J1997, b1937,*
Bulletin References; *Lechiguilla Cave 1998,*

PERRY, Denyse Janet; *J2009,*

PERRY, John Arthur; AKA: Big John. *J1988, b1957,*
Probationary Meets; GG88, Stream Passage, Flood Entrance, Bar Pot.
Famous for; Prussiking up a pitch with an old Italian hand grenade inside his suit - Albania 1992.
Bulletin References; *Giggel Rav Pot, [Dig/exploration]1990, Brackenbottom Pot, [Dig/exploration] 1989, Trou De Glaz Aug 1989, Tanne De Bel Espoir-La Diau Parmilan 1991, Giggel Rav Pot 1989, Brackenbottom Pot 1989, Gouffre Berger Aug 1992, Albania 1992, Ordessa National Park 2007, Doubs, France Aug 2009, Croesor-Rhosydd Feb 2009.*
Newsletter References; *Birks Fell Cave July 1982, Gingling Hole June 1983, Scotland 1987, White Scar Cave July 1987, Magnetometer Pot Oct 1987, Dale Head Pot Oct 1987, Coniston Mine July 1988, South Wales Nov 1988, Dow-Providence July 1989, Smallcleugh Mine Aug 1989, Langstroth Pot & Cave [Diving] July 1989, Bird Watching Lakes Walk Sept 1990, Eldon Hole & Oxlow Caverns Oct 1990, South Wales Dec 1990, Birks Fell Cave July 1991, Mendip*

Weekend Sept 1991, Dan Yr Ogof June 1991, Gouffre Berger Aug 1992, Lakes Meet June 1992, Ireby Fell Feb 1993, Rumbling Hole Oct 1999, Derbyshire Meet Sept 1999, Darnbrook Pot June 2007, Ordessa National Park Spanish Pyrenees 2007, Otter Hole June 2008, Miss Graces Lane June 2008, Croesor-Rhosydd Feb 2009, Burtersett Quarry/Mine July 2017, Grampian Meet Aug 2017, Sell Gill Sept 2017, Lancaster-Easegill June 2019.

PERRY, Mark Stephen; *J1980, b1955,*
Probationary Meets; Lost John's, King Pot.
Famous for; Stitching my knee up with Wato sat on me and biting his seat belt [Alegro] Dan Yr Ogof.
Bulletin References; *Gouffre Berger Aug 1980, Pippikin to Top Sink April 1980, Cueva De La Marniosa Santander Aug 1982, Tanne Du Bel Espoir-Diau Aug 1984.*
Newsletter References; *Hall Pot Oct 1978, Alum Pot June 1980, Gouffre Berger Aug 1980, Tanne de Bel Espoir-Grotte de la Diau Aug 1981, Dow-Providence Sept 1981, King Pot April 1982, Tatham Wife Hole Sept 1983, County Pot March 1984, Diccan Pot March 1984.*

PERRY, Rebekah Sarah; *J2018, b1995,*
Newsletter References; *Stump Cross Cavertns July 2018, Notts Pot Sept 2018, Cow Pot March 2019, High Douk May 2019, Heron Pot July 2019, Illusion Pot Sept 2019.*

PESTER, Anthony Stuart; *J1961, b1944,*
Probationary Meets; Sell Gill, Lost John's, Simpson's Pot.
Bulletin References; *Simpson's Pot 16ᵗʰ April 1961-[Graham Shaw Accident]*

PETTITT, Trevor Charles William; *J1988, b1950,*
Probationary Meets; Sell Gill, Nick Pot, Rift Pot.
Member; HCC.
Newsletter References; *Ireby Fell [Diving Support] Oct 1988, Notts Pot Nov 1988.*

PETTY, Michael Lee; *J1958, b1941,*
Expelled from club non payment of subs Dec 1962.
Bulletin References; *Pen-y-ghent Pot July 1960, OBJ Hole Nov 1958.*

PEVISON, J; *J1936,*

PHILLIPS, Jane Rhian; *J2008, b1985,*

PHILLIPS, Seaton Clifford Laybourne; *J1962, b1928,*

PICKLES, Ernest Rodney, AKA Rodney. *J1959, b1940,*

Newsletter References; *Clapham Cave Oct 1959, Treak Cliff Cavern Oct 1959.*

PICKLES, George Frederick; *J1959, b1915,*
Newsletter References; *Treak Cliff Cavern Oct 1959.*

PICKSTONE, Carlton; AKA: Carl. *J1966, b1939,*
Member; WCC.
Bulletin References; *Lancaster Hole Jan 1966, Provatina Abyss July/Aug 1967, Involved in discovery of Whitsun Series GG 1968, Work in Ingleborough Cave 1968, Poulawillin [Clare] 1968, Ingleborough Cave Rimstone East 1969.*
Newsletter Reference: *Lancaster-Easegill Feb 1969, Lakes Walk March 1969.*

PILKINGTON, Gary; *J1966, b1947,*
Member; WCC.
Famous for; Twice telling the BPC committee about the advantages of SRT before 1970.
Bulletin References; *Disappointment Pot Oct 1967, Sotano Del San Agustin Mexico 1967, Tatham Wife Hole [Solo] 1968, Greenbrier County USA1968, Juniper Gulf Nov 1969.*

PITMAN, Edward Roderick; AKA Rod. *J1985, b1954,*
Probationary Meets; Lost John's, Alum Pot, GG Main Shaft, Simpson's.
Newsletter References; *Lost John's Feb 1982, Alum Pot March 1982, Mendip weekend April 1983, Pippikin-Link July 1983.*

PITTARD, Michael Harold; *J1953, b1933,*
Resigned – moving away Feb 1953.
Bulletin References; *Simpson's Pot July 1953.*

PLATT, Rachel; *J2008, b1984,*
Probationary Meets; Tatham Wife Hole, GG09.
Member; LSCT.

PLUMMER, Stephen Kenneth; *J1983, b1953,*
Probationary Meets; Birks Fell, Mongo Gill, Tatham Wife.
Newsletter References; *Birks Fell Cave July 1982, Tatham Wife Hole Feb 1983, Tatham Wife Hole Sept 1983, Lost John's Pot July 1985, Top Sink-County Pot March 1986.*

POCKLINGTON, M. A; *J1959,*

POLAKOWSKI, Daniel Patryk; *J2015, b2003,*
Newsletter References; *Long Churn and Wilsons cave [Novice Trip] July 2015, Calf Holes [Novice Trip] July 2015, Alum/Long Churns June 2017, Old Ing-Birkwith July 2017.*

POLAKOWSKI, Tomasz; *J2012, b2003,*
Newsletter References; *Old Ing/Calf Holes-Browgill [Novice Trip] June 2012, Old Ing/Calf Holes-Browgill [Novice Trip] July 2012, Long Churn-Alum [Novice Trip] July 2012, Brackenbottom Pot Nov 2012, Committee Pot March 2013, Long Churn and Wilsons cave [Novice Trip] July 2015, Calf Holes [Novice Trip] July 2015, Darnbrook Pot March 2016, Alum/Long Churns June 2017, Old Ing-Birkwith July 2017.*

POLTORAK, Taras Nikolaevich; *J2013, b1976,*

POPHAM, Edward George; AKA: Ted. *J1975, b1947,*
Probationary Meets; *Juniper Gulf, Black Shiver, Gingling Hole, Italy 1975.*
Bulletin References; *Piaggia Bella 1975, White Scar Cave Dec 31 1977, Grotte de Bury 1976.*
Newsletter References; *Black Shiver Oct 1974, Juniper Gulf Dec 1974, Birks Fell Cave April 1975, Short Drop-Gavel Pot1976, Notts Pot March 1976, Lost John's September 1976, Pippikin Hole Oct 1976, Short Drop-Gavel Dec 1977, Dale Head Dec 1989.*

POPLE, D; *J1974,*

PORTEOUS, William; AKA: Bill. *J1946,*
Bulletin References; *Recorded as down Rift Pot 19th May 1946, Lost John's July/Aug 1946. Rift Pot/ Long Kin East exchange April 20th 1947. Calf Holes Aug 1947, Meregill 7th Sept 1947, Rift Pot-Long Kin East exchange April 1949.*

PORTER, Barry; *J2010, b1944,*
Newsletter References; *County Pot-Wretched Rabbit Feb 2012.*

POTTER, Melanie Jane; See Scatliffe.

POTOLZNIAK, Peter; *J2012,*
Newsletter References; *Old Ing/Calf Holes-Browgill [Novice Trip] July 2012, Long Churn-Alum [Novice Trip] July 2012, Brackenbottom Pot Nov 2012.*

PRATCHETT, Nicholas; AKA: Nick. *J1954, b1933,*
Resigned – moving away Sept 1965.
Bulletin References; *Clapham Cave June 1954, Ease Gill Caverns Oct 1954, Lancaster Hole Oct 1954, Bull Pot of the Witches July 1955, Little Hull Hole Oct 1955, Jackdaw Hole & Pen-y-Ghent Long Churn Nov 1955, International Expedition-Sump 1 Gouffre Berger 1956, Stream Passage Pot June 1958, Goyden Pot Jan 1960, Grange Rigg Easter 1961, Christmas Pot April 1962 [He found the connection to Grange Rigg on this trip], Christmas/Grange/P5 April 1962, Christmas/Grange/P5 extensions May 1962.*
Newsletter References; *Lost john's Sept 1956, Leader Notts Pot May 1957, Disappointment Pot to Main Shaft winch June 1957, Rumbling Hole Oct 1957, Got his Bang Licence Oct 1957, Leader Lancaster Hole Oct 1957, Practice stretcher rescue Wade's entrance GG Nov 1957, Lancaster Hole June 1958, Tackle testing July 1958, St Cuthbert's Swallet Aug 1958, Alum Pot Aug 1958, Long Kin West Sept 1958, Leader Simpsons-Swinsto Exchange with RRCPC Sept 1958, Grange Rigg [Blasting boulder choke] Aug 1961.*

PREECE, D;
Newsletter References; *Notts Pot March 1976, Scrafton Pot April 1976.*

PREST, Robert; *J1936,*

PRESTON, James; *J1955, b1938,*
Bulletin References; *Little Hull Hole Oct 1955.*

PROCTER, David Thomas; *J1962, b1942,*
Member; UWFRA.
Bulletin References; *Old Cote Pot April 1963,*

PURCELL, Alan James; *J2015, b1971,*
Probationary Meets; Great Douk, High Douk, Sunset Hole, Skirwith Pot, KMC, Sell Gill, Illusion Pot, Yordas Pot, Bull Pot of the Witches, Alum Pot, Peak Cavern, P8, Oxlow Caverns, Holme Bank Chert Mine, Sell Gill Holes Feb 2015.
Newsletter References; *Calf Holes-Browgill and Old Ing-Birkwith June 2015, Sunset Hole Oct 2015, Heron Pot Nov 2015, Grampian Meet Aug 2017.*

PURDEY,?; *J1980,*

PURNELL, Richard; *J2009, b1964,*
Probationary Meets; Disappointment Pot, Long Churns.
Newsletter References; *Wretched Rabbit-County Pot Nov 2010, Rowten Pot Nov 2010, Vesper Pot April 2011, Hunt Pot-Shrapnel Pot June 2011, Big Meanie Sept 2011, Long Kin West Oct 2011, Juniper Gulf March 2012, Committee Pot Sept 2012.*

8

R

RADLEY, P; *J1981,*

RAISON, Hazel; *J2018, b1981,*
Probationary Meets; Sunset Hole, Old Ing, Sell Gill.
Newsletter References; *High Douk Holes Feb 2018 Jingling Pot/Bull Pot [CPC joint trip] April 2018, Calf Holes-Browgill Cave Nov 2018.*

RAISTRICK, D;

RALPHS, John; *J1976, b1946,*
Probationary Meets; Lost John's, Tatham Wife, Meregill, Top Sink-Lancaster, Cherry Tree Pot.
Member; HEG, DCC.
Club Expeditions; Abbisa Fighiera 1979.
Other Expeditions; France with EPC.
Bulletin References; *Abbisa Fighiera 1979.*
Newsletter References; *Pen-y-Ghent Pot April 1977 [Cut his hand], Dale Head Pot April 1978, Rumbling Hole Aug 1978, Giants Hole Dec 1978, Abbissa Fighiera Italy Aug 1979.*

RALPHS, Stephanie J; *J1977,*
Club Expeditions; Fighiera trip 1979.

RAMSDEN, Clifford; *J1945,*

RAMSDEN, Thomas B; *J1950,*

RANDALL, Kirsti-See Ashworth.

RATCLIFFE, Bert; *d1945.* Died on active service WWII.

RATTRAY, Alexandra Helen; *J2000, b1990,*

RATTRAY, Frederick; AKA: Fred Ratbag. *J1999, b1964,*
Probationary Meets; Bar Pot, Clapham Bottoms, Fat Finger, GG90/99.
Member; NB.
Club Expeditions; Gouffre Berger 2010.
Famous for; Digging Caves and Radio Location of same.
Remembers; The lighting of the Bonfire at the Dump with a rocket on a guide line and a gas filled exploding Guy Fawkes caver in a green chemical suit.
Bulletin References; *Losers Pot [Discovery] Mar 2002, Hensler's Pot [Discovery] 1999-2003, Parkinson's Pot [Discovery] July 2003, Corky's Pot [Discovery] 2003–2005, Pay Sank [Discovery] 2005, Klondike Pot Digging/Exploration 2004-2007, Kalymnos Oct 2009, Doubs, France Aug 2009, Witches Cave location and Dig Sept 2010, Buckden Gavel Lead Mines Mar 2010, OBJ Connection to GG May 2010, Ireland Radio Locating Oct/Nov 2011, Restoration of Brown Hill Pot entrance Nov 2012– Feb 2013, Restoration of Clapham Bottoms Pot Entrance June 2013,*
Newsletter References; *Grange Rigg [Surface Locating] March 1999, Ingleborough Cave Digging 2001, Corky's Digging Team 2004, Klondyke Pot Digging Team Jan 2005, Pay Sank Exploration Sept 2005, Pay Sank Breakthrough Team Nov 2005, Hardrawkin Pot July 2006, Committee Pot July 2007, Hidden Earth Tewkesbury, Support Oct 2007, Pay Sank Feb 2009, Nettle Pot July 2009, Heron Pot July 2009, Gunnerfleet Caves Clear Up July 2009, Stile Repairs-Diccan and Long Churn 2010, Alum Pot July 2010, Rebuild of stile at Browgill July 2010, Yordas Cave Conserervation Aug 2010, KMC & Bar*

Pot [Blind Novice Trips]May 2011, Long Churn [Novice Trip] June 2011, Wizard's Chasm Jan 2012, Yordas Pot Feb 2012, Spencer and Hoffman Lime Kilns March 2012, Long Churns March 2012, Great Douk April 2012, Old Ing/Calf Holes-Browgill [Novice Trip] June 2012, Old Ing/Calf Holes-Browgill [Novice Trip] July 2012, Long Churn-Alum [Novice Trip] July 2012, Lost John's Cave July 2012, Blue John Aug 2012, Wizard's Chasm Jan 2013, White Keld Sump 5 Location [Dive Support] Feb 2013, Haw Bank or Wet Grooves Mine Feb 2013, Fells End Pots Feb 2013, Committee Pot March 2013, Illusion Pot March 2013, Ibbeth Peril March [Twice] 2013, Crackpot [Photographic Trip] April 2013, Fairy Holes April 2014, First Lady Pot July 2014, Providence Pot Restoration Nov 2014, High Frequency communication experiments GG15, Lost John's-Notts 2 Sept 2015, KMC [Novice Trip] Jan 2016, Skirwith Cave [Novice Trip] Jan 2016, Bruntscar Cave Jan 2017, Devis Hole/Mine July 2017, Hartley Quarry Cave Jan 2018, P5 [Radio Locating] June 2018, Stump Cross Cavertns July 2018, Hells Bells Hole [Dive Support] Feb 2020.

RATTRAY, James; AKA: Jimmy Ratbag. J1973, b1947,
Member; CPC.
Bulletin References; Digging Clapham Bottoms 1972/3, M5 Pot [Dig] July 1984, Brakenbottom Pot [Dig] 1985, Giggel Rav Pot, [Dig/exploration] 1985, Losers Pot [Discovery] Mar 2002, Croesor-Rhosydd Feb 2009.
Newsletter References; Hallucination Aven-Surface Location May 1983, Bull Pot April 1986, Ireby Fell Pot Oct 1986, Pippikin Pot Nov 1986, Matienzo July/Aug 1987, Haytime Hole 1990, GG Photographic Meet May 1998, Grange Rigg [Surface Locating] March 1999, Rumbling Hole March 2010, Croesor-Rhosydd March 2010, Hurnell Moss Pot April 2010, Alum Pot July 2010, KMC & Bar Pot [Blind Novice Trips] May 2011, Hurnell Moss Pot Oct 2013, High Frequency communication experiments GG15.

RATTRAY, June M; J1985,
Newsletter References; Hallucination Aven-Surface Location May 1983, Matienzo July/Aug 1987.

RAYNERD, Paul; J2015, b1970,
Member; KCC.
Newsletter References; Sunset Hole Dec 2014, Bull Pot of the Witches Jan 2015, The Borehole-Boundary Pot Feb 2015.

RAYTON, Jonathon Nicholas; J1996, b1968,

RECKERT, John Nicholas Adam; AKA: Nicholas. J1974, b1951,
Member; WSG, CUCC.
Probationary Meets; Gingling Hole.
Newsletter References; Black Shiver Oct 1974.

REDFERN, Thomas Brian; J1966, b1951,
Probationary Meets; Bar Pot, Little Hull, Alum Pot.

REED, Robert George; J1966, b1947,
Probationary Meets; Lost John's, Marble Steps, Magnetometer Pot.
Bulletin References; Alum Pot/Diccan Pot 1966.
Newsletter Reference: Lakes Walk March 1969, Bull Pot of the Witches July 1969, Pen-y-Ghent Pot Aug 1969.

RELTON, F. J; J1957,

RENNIE, Tam; J2011, b1980,
Probationary Meets; Black Shiver Pot.
Re-joined 2019.
Member; LCC, EPC.
Other Expeditions; Slovenia, Felix Trombe, Vercors, Mallorca, Ireland.
Newsletter References; Black Shiver Pot April 2011, Simpson's Pot Jan 2012, It's a Cracker-Lost John's-Deaths Head July 2012, White Scar Cave July 2012, Titan-JH April 2013, Skosca Cave Feb 2013, Boxhead-Cracker Feb 2014, Lost John's-Notts 2 Sept 2015, Lost John's-Boxhead Pot March 2016, Link Pot April 2017, Black Shiver May 2017.

RENSHAW, John; J2004, b1976,

RENSHAW, Robert; AKA: Bob, Ripcord. J1966, b1948,
Probationary Meets; Calf Holes, Lost John's, Clapham Cave.
Bulletin References; Agen Allwedd 5th Choke April 1968.
Newsletter Reference: Lancaster–Easegill Feb 1969, KMC Dec 1969.

RHODEN, Gerik; J2003, b1958,
Member; YSS.
Bulletin References; Gouffre Pont Du Gerbout Aug 2011, Reseau de la Pierre Saint Martin Aug 2013, Gouffre De Heretiques Aug 2011, Doubs, France Aug 2009, Croesor-Rhosydd Feb 2009, Cwmorthin Slate Mine Feb 2009, Felix Trombe 2011, Alderley Edge Mines Sept 2009, Aquamole Pot Jan 2007.
Newsletter References; Pool Sink Sept 2003, Long Kin West Dec 2005, Ireby Fell Caverns Nov 2005, Bull Pot Jan 2006, Cow Pot [Lancaster] April 2006, Black Shiver Pot July 2006, Hunt Pot Nov 2006, Jingling Pot Dec 2006, Top Sink-Lancaster Hole Feb

2007, Darnbrook Pot June 2007, Rift Pot July 2007, High Hull Pot Sept 2007, Bar Pot Dec 2007, Brackenbottom Pot Feb 2008, King Pot Feb 2008, Bull Pot April 2008, Otter Hole June 2008, Miss Graces Lane June 2008, Robinsons Pot Sept 2008, Lost John's Oct 2008, Hell Hole, Whitewell Cave & Pot Nov 2008, Lower Long Churn Nov 2008, Pay Sank Feb 2009, Croesor-Rhosydd Feb 2009, Lost John's Hole March 2009, Peak Cavern April 2009, Cow Pot April 2009, Notts Pot Sept 2009, Link Pot Sept 2009, Alderley Edge Mines Sept 2009, Aquamole Pot Nov 2009, Joint Hole [Diving experience] Jan 2010, Marble Steps Jan 2010, Calf Holes [Novice Trip] Jan 2010, Tatham Wife Hole Feb 2010, Croesor-Rhosydd March 2010, Cwmorthin Slate Mine March 2010, Keld Head [Diving] May 2010, Short Gill Rising [Digging] May 2010, Joint Hole [Diving] May 2010, Shrapnel Pot July 2010, Dan Yr Ogof [Far North] Sept 2010, OFD 1 Sept 2010, Alum Pot Oct 2010, Bull Pot Oct 2010, Pillar Holes Oct 2010, Lancaster Hole Oct 2010, Heron Pot Nov 2010, Lancaster-Wretched Rabbit Jan 2011, Cherry Tree Hole Jan 2011, Committee Pot March 2011, Voldemort Pot March 2011, Titan-Peak Cavern March 2011, James Hall Mine-Titan March 2011, Jingling Hole June 2011, Ogof Llyn Parc Sept 2011, Big Meanie-Death's Head Exchange Oct 2011, Hunt Pot-Shrapnel Pot Nov 2011, Lancaster-Wretched Rabbit Nov 2011, Aquamole Pot Dec 2011, Tatham Wife Hole Dec 2011, Shuttleworth Pot Feb 2012, Box Freestone Mine March 2012, Washfold Pot April 2012, Gillfield Level May 2012, Mongo Gill May 2012, It's a Cracker-Lost John's-Death's Head July 2012, White Scar Cave July 2012, Foux de Lauret [Herault] Sept 2012, Grotte du Banquier [Herault] Sept 2012, KMC Toyland Nov 2012, Aquamole Pot Dec 2012, Illusion Pot March 2013, Top Sink-Lancaster Hole March 2013, Pen-y-ghent Pot May 2013, Ireby Fell Cavern June 2013, Pikedaw Calamine Caverns Sept 2013, Short Drop-Gavel Sept 2013, Magnetometer Pot Nov 2013, Skosca Cave Feb 2013, Boxhead-Cracker Feb 2014, Scoska Cave April 2014, President's Meet Ribchester Walk June 2014, Dan Yr Ogof June 2014, First Lady Pot July 2014, Dowkabottom Cave July 2014, Fairy Holes Sept 2014, Simpson's Pot-KMC Sept 2014, Shuttleworth Pot Oct 2014, Pasture Gill Jan 2015, Swildon's Hole Feb 2015, Goatchurch Aven Feb 2015, Skirwith Cave Feb 2015, Yordas/KMC March 2015, Poll Dudh June 2015, St Catherine's1-Fisher St June 2015, Faunarooska June 2015, Long Churn and Wilsons cave [Novice Trip] July 2015, Calf Holes [Novice Trip] July 2015, Fairy Holes Sept 2015, Alderley Edge Mines Oct 2015, Water Icicle Oct 2015, KMC [Novice Trip] Jan 2016, Notts 2 Jan 2016, Browgill Jan 2016, CNCC SRT Workshop Feb 2016, KMC High

Traverse in Flood Feb 2016, Lost John's-Boxhead Pot March 2016, Titan Streamway March 2016, P8 March 2016, Pillar Holes April 2016, Rowten Pot & Cave April 2016, Death's Head-Big Meanie Sept 2016, Croesor Rhysydd Through Trip Oct 2016, Marble Steps Nov 2016, Bull Pot of the WitchesJan 2017, Devis Hole/Mine July 2017, Grampian Meet Aug 2017, Wildcat Rift May 2018, Ingleborough Cave Oct 2018, Stump Cross Caverns Nov 2018.

RHODES, Brian; J1983, b1956,
Probationary Meets; Mongo Gill, Ingleborough Cave, Pool Sink.
Famous for; Being stuck for many hours on a ledge with Michael Riley after a misunderstanding with a rope. [See Section 2]
Bulletin References; Vercors Aug 1983, Krisna Jama Aug 1984, Brezno V Madvedovi Konti Aug 1984, Leski Aug 1984, M5 Pot [Dig] July 1984, Tanne De Bel Espoir-La Diau Parmilan 1991, Deep Well [Diving support] May 1992, Gouffre Berger Aug 1992, Tete Sauvage July 1995, Ordessa National Park 2007, Doubs, France Aug 2009, Croesor-Rhosydd Feb 2009, Reseau de la Pierre Saint Martin Aug 2013.
Newsletter References; Alum Pot March 1982, Ingleborough Cave Oct 1982, Tatham Wife Hole Feb 1983, Simpsons-Valley Entrance April 1983, Mendip weekend April 1983, Hallucination Aven-Induction Location May 1983, Gingling Hole June 1983, Pippikin-Link July 1983, South Wales Aug 1983, Swinsto-Rowten Exchange Nov 1983, Rift Pot Feb 1984, County Pot March 1984, Diccan Pot March 1984, Pool Sink-Lancaster Hole June 1984, Sell Gill Hole Feb 1985, Brezno, Leska, Babizop Rakov Scojan and the Pit of Bears Yugoslavia Aug 1985, Eden Valley-Teesdale Walking Meet Oct 1985, Rift-Large Pot Oct 1985, Notts Pot Feb 1986, Scotland Easter 1986, Pool Park Oct 1986, Mendip Dec 1986, Cliff Force Cave 1986, Scotland 1987, Dale Head Pot Oct 1987, Notts Pot Jan 1988, Nick Pot Nov 1987, Rumbling Hole March 1988, Weathercote Cave April 1988, Coniston Mine July 1988, Notts Pot Nov 1988, South Wales Nov 1988, King Pot Jan 1989, Cow Pot–Pool Sink March 1989, Dow-Providence July 1989, Death's Head-Big Meanie Nov 1989, Ireby Fell March 1990, Lakes Walk Sept 1990, South Wales Dec 1990, Sell Gill Training Meet Nov 1991,Top Sink-County Pot Nov 1991, Black Shiver Pot Jan 1991,Notts Pot March 1992, Little Hull Dec 1991, Rift-LKE Exchange Feb 1992, Gouffre Berger Aug 1992, Pen-y-Ghent Pot July 1992, Lakes Meet June 1992, Coniston Mines Weekend Sept 1993, Piaggia Bella July 1996, Bull Pot Dec 1996, Darnbrook Pot June 2007, Ordessa National Park Spanish Pyrenees 2007, Helwith Bridge Show 2008, Croesor-Rhosydd Feb 2009,

Roundthwaite Common to Borrowdale Sept 2014, Goyden Sept 2015, Nenthead Mines Sept 2015, Darnbrook Pot March 2016, New Biggin on Lune to Appleby Walking Meet Sept 2016, Lindale-Greenodd Walking Meet 2017, Cow Green Reservoir–Appleby Walking Meet 2018, Lancaster-Easegill June 2019.

RHODES, Brian Kenneth; AKA: Dusty. *J1955, b1937,*
Expelled from club non payment of subs Dec 1962.
Newsletter References; *Swinsto Sept 1957, Easter Camp April 1958, Digging near Owl Hole April 1958, Little Hull Hole Aug 1959, Diccan-Alum Exchange September 1959, Langstroth Pot Sept 1985.*

RHODES, Christine, [née Edwards] *J1984, b1956,*
Bulletin References; *Krisna Jama Aug 1984, Leski Aug 1984, M5 Pot [Dig] July 1984, Ordessa National Park 2007, Doubs, France Aug 2009, Ingleborough Cave [Dive Support] Jan 1981,*
Newsletter References; *Mendip weekend April 1983, Wookey 20 [Dive Support] April 1983, South Wales Aug 1983, Langstroth Pot Sept 1985, Brezno, Leska, Babizop Rakov Scojan and the Pit of Bears Yugoslavia Aug 1985, Scotland Easter 1986, Mendip Dec 1986, Scotland 1987, Gouffre Berger Aug 1992, Lakes Meet June 1992, Coniston Mines Weekend Sept 1993, Ordessa National Park Spanish Pyrenees 2007, Helwith Bridge Show 2008.*

RHODES, Kerry; *J2000, b1988,*
Newsletter References; *Gouffre Berger Aug 1992, Sunset Hole / Great Douk July 1998, Heron Pot July 1998.*

RHODES, Neville, *J1953, b1936,*

RICE, Lionel Peter; *J1998, b1962,*
Probationary Meets; Easegill Caverns, Red Moss Pot.
Newsletter References; *Out Sleets Beck Pot April 1999.*

RICHARDSON, C. V;

RICHARDSON, D; *J1980, b1961,*

RICHARDSON, D. Charles; AKA: Farles. *J1979, b1959,*
Newsletter References; *Lost John's Sept 1978,*

RICHARDSON, Jillian; *J1989, b1959,*
Probationary Meets; Heron Pot, Yordas,

RICHARDSON, Stephen John; *J1987, b1961,*

Probationary Meets; Magnetometer Pot, Sunset, Ireby Fell, Scotland.

RICHER, John; *J1946,*
Bulletin References; *Rift Pot 19th May 1946.*

RICHMOND, Norman Henry; *J1956, b1930,*
Newsletter References; *Dow-Providence rescue Dec 1957, Tackle testing Jan 1958, Lancaster Hole June 1958, Treak Cliff Cavern Oct 1959.*

RIDER, Anthony Herbert; AKA: Tony. *J1961, b1940,*
Probationary Meets; Little Hull, Newby Moss, Lost John's.
Bulletin References; *Lost John's March 1961, Little Hull Pot Feb 1961, Oxlow Caverns June 1961, Jockey Hole Feb 1962, Stream Passage Pot June 1962, Ridge Scar Caves [Discovery] 1962, Prospecting near Birkwith May 1962.*

RIED, Alexander Christian Andreas; *J2017, b1990,*
Probationary Meets; Heron Pot, Marilyn, Henslers Mud-Whitsun Series-Flood Entrance, Ireby Fell Caverns [Duke St 2-Jupiter Series]
Member; NUCC, TSG.
Newsletter References; *Dawn Chamber [Bolting] GG May 2017, Ingleborough Cave {Surveying} May 2018, High Douk May 2019.*

RILEY, E; *J1959,*

RILEY, Michael John; AKA: Smiley Riley, Dr Lurv, Roland the Gourmand. *J1984, b1960,*
Famous for; The knot incident in Spain [See section 2]
Bulletin References; *Kamniski Alps Aug 1988, Gouffre Berger Aug 1992, Tete Sauvage July 1995, Ordessa National Park 2007, Doubs, France Aug 2009, Croesor-Rhosydd Feb 2009, Reseau de la Pierre Saint Martin Aug 2013.*
Newsletter References; *Tatham Wife Hole Feb 1983, Simpsons–Valley Entrance April 1983, Link Pot July 1983, Sleets Gill June 1985, Langstroth Pot Sept 1985, Brezno, Leska, Babizop Rakov Scojan and the Pit of Bears Yugoslavia Aug 1985, Eden Valley-Teesdale Walking Meet Oct 1985, Rift-Large Pot Oct 1985, Pool Park Oct 1986, Mendip Dec 1986, New Rift Pot Jan 1986, Pen-y-Gent Pot March 1987, Scotland 1987, Matienzo July/Aug 1987, Weathercote Cave April 1988, Notts Pot Nov 1988, South Wales Nov 1988, Death's Head-Big Meanie Nov 1989, Spectacle-Vespers Feb 1990, Rift-Large Pot March 1990, Lakes Walk Sept 1990, Bird Watching Lakes Walk Sept 1990, South Wales Dec 1990, Marble Steps Pot Dec 1990, Ireby Fell Jan 1992, Little Hull Dec 1991, Dan Yr Ogof June 1991,*

Vulcan Pot Feb 1992, LKE-Rift Exchange Feb 1992, Gouffre Berger Aug 1992, Pen-y-Ghent Pot July 1992, Lakes Meet June 1992, Simpson's Pot Oct 1993, Alum Pot Nov 1993, Rowten Pot Nov 1993, Grange Rigg-Christmas Pot March 1993, Top Sink-Pippikin Nov 1995, Rumbling Hole Oct 1999, Diccan Pot Oct 2000, Peak Cavern Sumps Tour June 2001, Long Kin East Nov 2003, Pikedaw Calamine Caverns Jan 2004, Swinsto Hole-KMC Feb 2004, Alum Pot March 2004, Committee Pot Nov 2004, Giant's Hole Jan 2005, Lost John's Hole Sept 2005, Ireby Fell Caverns Nov 2005, Ordessa National Park Spanish Pyrenees 2007, Pay Sank Feb 2009, Croesor-Rhosydd Feb 2009.

RILEY, William Robert; AKA: Long Bob. *J2016, b1951,*
Re-joined 2016.
Newsletter References; *Meregill Hole Dec 2008, Rift-LKE Oct 2009, Voldemort-Committee Pot July 2016, Alum Pot Dec 2016, GG Track repairs Feb 2017, Cow Pot Jan 2017, Link Pot April 2017, OFD Top Ent Oct 2017, Top Sink-Wretched Rabbit Jan 2018, Jingling Pot/Bull Pot [CPC joint trip] April 2018, Notts Pot Sept 2018, Death's Head-Lost John's-Committee Pot Nov 2018, Oxlow-Maskhill Mine Oct 2018, Lancaster Hole-Wretched Rabbit Nov 2018, Bull Pot of the Witches Jan 2019, Pikedaw Calamine Cavern Dec 2018, County-Lancaster Jan 2019, Cow Pot March 2019, Sunset Hole April 2019, County Pot-Lancaster Hole June 2019, Magnetometer Pot Sept 2019, KMC Jan 2020, Pool Sink-Wretched Rabbit Feb 2020.*

RIMMER, Maria Theresa; *J1995, b1974,*
Probationary Meets; Dowbergill Passage, County Poy.
Newsletter References; *County-Lancaster Hole Oct 1995, Big Meanie-Deaths Head Jan 1996, Lost John's Hole Nov 2009.*

RIPLEY, Norman Francis; *J1951, b1934,*

ROBERTS, David; AKA: Red Dave. *J1987, b1951,*
Probationary Meets; Magnetometer, Sunset Hole, Ireby Fell, Dale Head, Scotland 1987.
Bulletin References; *36 Parmilan Plateau Sept 1990, Gouffre Berger Aug 1992,*
Newsletter References; *Eden Valley-Teesdale Walking Meet Oct 1985, Scotland 1987, Dale Head Pot Oct 1987, Simpsons–KMC July 1990, Black Shiver Pot Jan 1991, Dowbergill Passage Unknown 1990, Gouffre Berger Aug 1992, Lakes Meet June 1992.*

ROBERTS, David; *J1957, b1938,*
Suspended from club Dec 1959.

Newsletter Rerferences; *Simpson's Pot Aug 1957, Lancaster Hole Oct 1957.*

ROBERTS, Kenneth Roy; *J1957, b1922,*

ROBERTS, Richard John; *J1962, b1943,*

ROBERTS, Samuel; *J2014, b1991,*
Probationary Meets; Tatham Wife Hole, Marble Steps Pot, Ireby Fell Caverns, Swinsto-KMC.
Newsletter References; *Marble Steps April 2014, Yordas Pot Oct 2014, Lancaster-County Pot Nov 2014, Large Pot Dec 2014, Pasture Gill Jan 2015, Juniper Gulf Feb 2015, Ireby Fell Caverns Jan 2016.*

ROBERTSHAW, Barrie; *J1966, b1946,*
Probationary Meets; Calf holes, Alum Pot, Lost John's.

ROBERTSHAW, Graham William; *J1953, b1926,*
Bulletin References; *Flood Entrance Pot March 1954, Juniper Gulf May 1954,*
Newsletter References; *Disappointment Pot to Main Shaft winch June 1957.*

ROBERTSHAW, Jack; *J1947,*
Bulletin References; *Rift Pot/ Long Kin East exchange April 20th 1947.*

ROBINSON, B; *J1959, b1938,*

ROBINSON, Christopher; *J1983, b1961,*
Probationary Meets; Pool Sink, Tatham Wife, Notts Pot.
Newsletter References; *Tatham Wife Hole Feb 1983, Notts Pot March 1983, Calf Holes Nov 1985, Mendip Dec 1986, Scotland 1987, Millenium Walk Sept 2002, Granett Bridge To ShapWalk Sept 2006, Walking Meet Orton-Kirkby Thore Sept 2010, Sunset Hole July 2015, Lindale-Greenodd Walking Meet 2017.*

ROBINSON, David; AKA Roaring Robinson. *J1959, b1936,*
Bulletin References; *Pen-y-Ghent Pot April 1960, Lost John's March 1960, Gaping Gill Meet 1960, Magnetometer Pot Nov 1960, Grange Rigg Easter 1961, Simpson's Pot 16th April 1961-[Graham Shaw Accident]Lost John's March 1961, Stonelands Pot June 1961, Pen-y-Ghent pot 1961.*
Newsletter References; *Lost John's Sept 1959, Clapham Cave Oct 1959.*

ROBINSON, Harold; *J1936,*
Bulletin References; *Pen-y-Ghent Long Churn-trapped by flood water for 27 hours October 1938, see section 2.*

ROBINSON, James Barry; *J1954, b1936,*
Suspended from club Dec 1959.
Bulletin References; *Bull Pot of the Witches July 1955, Dow-Providence rescue Dec 1957.*

ROBINSON, John Stephen; AKA: Robbo. *J1966, b1946,*
BPC President 2008 +2009.
Probationary Meets; Calf Holes, Alum Pot, Sell Gill.
Bulletin References; *Chourum Des Aiguilles 1973, Vercors Aug 1983, Krisna Jama Aug 1984, Tete Sauvage July 1995, Ordessa National Park 2007, Reseau de la Pierre Saint Martin Aug 2013, Doubs, France Aug 2009, Alderley Edge Mines Sept 2009.*
Newsletter References; *Lakes Walking Meet Nov 1969, Kingsdale Master Cave Dec 1969, Marble Steps March 1970, Wharfedale weekend Oct 1970, Heron Pot March 1971, Crackpot Cave March 1971, Tatham Wife Hole Aug 1971, Grange Rigg-Christmas Pot Jan 1972, Lockey Gill Cave June 1972, Swinsto-KMC June 1972, Pen-y-Ghent Pot Aug 1972, Gingling Hole Sept 1974, Short Drop-Gavel Pot 1976, Dowkabottom Cave Dec 1981, Kingsdale Photographic meet April 1982, Top Sink-County Pot April 1985, Wretched Rabbit Passage April 1985, Gunnerside Gill Lead Mines June 1985, Brezno, Leska, Babizop Rakov Scojan and the Pit of Bears Yugoslavia Aug 1985, Calf Holes Nov 1985, Pool Park Oct 1986, Scotland 1987, Calf Holes Jan 1988, Weathercote Cave April 1988, Coniston Mine July 1988, Heron Pot Jan 1989, Short Drop Cave Nov 1989, Easegill Caverns Sept 1990, Sell Gill Training Meet Nov 1991, Pikedaw Calamine Caverns March 1992, Swaledale Weekend Oct 1992, Crooklands Walking Meet Sept 1993, 5 Caves Trip July 1993, Coniston Mines Weekend Sept 1993, GG Photographic Meet May 1993, Lakes Walking Meet Sept 1995, Peak Cavern Nov 1995, Hagg Gill 1996, Piaggia Bella July 1996, Cherry Tree Hole April 1997, Grotta del Calgeron Aug 1997, Walking Meet Sept 1997, Nent Head-Brewery Shaft Oct 1998, County-Wretched Rabbit Nov 1998, Fat Finger Millennium Party, Bar Pot [Rope Ladder] May 2000, Hagg Gill Pot June 2000, Ingleborough Cave Digging 2001, Lancaster Canal Walk Meet 2001, Millenium Walk Sept 2002, KMC Photographic Trip Nov 2002, Crackpot Cave [Photgraphic Meet] Jan 2003, Black Combe-Foxfield Walk Sept 2003, Dismal Hill-Old Ing Jan 2006, Peak Cavern Feb 2006, Calf Holes & Brow Gill Cave Feb 2006, High Douk, Middle Washfold & Great Douk June 2006, Granett Bridge To ShapWalk Sept 2006, Photographic Weekend Oct 2006, Great Douk Feb 2007, OFD 2 March 2007, Ordessa National Park Spanish Pyrenees 2007, Hidden Earth Tewkesbury, Support Oct 2007, Valley Entrance June 2008,* Heron Pot Jan 2009, Dunsop Bridge-Bilsborrow Walking Meet Sept 2009, Alderley Edge Mines Sept 2009, Calf Holes [Novice Trip] Jan 2010, Walking Meet Orton-Kirkby Thore Sept 2010, Peak Cavern March 2011, Long Churn [Novice Trip] June 2011, Calf Holes-Browgill/Old Ing June 2011, Feizor-Moughton Walk July 2011, Cautley-Kirkby Stephen Walk Sept 2011, Great Douk April 2012, Poll Dugh April 2012, Cullaun 2 April 2012, Old Ing/Calf Holes-Browgill [Novice Trip] July 2012, White Scar Cave July 2012, Crosby Ravensworth-Askham Walking Meet Sept 2012, President's Meet Ribblesdale Walk June 2014, Roundthwaite Common to Borrowdale Sept 2014, Yordas Pot Oct 2014, Walking Meet 2015, Alderley Edge Mines Oct 2015, Boulby Potash Mine Jan 2016, Great Douk Sept 2016, Heron Pot [Novice trip] April 2017, Devis Hole/Mine July 2017, Burtersett Quarry/Mine July 2017, Lindale-Greenodd Walking Meet 2017, Cow Green Reservoir–Appleby Walking Meet 2018, Kirkby Lonsdale-Wharton Walking Meet Sept 2019.*

ROBINSON, N; *J1956,*

ROBINSON, Peter; *J1961, b1938,*
Probationary Meets; Magnetometer Pot, Bar Pot, Sunset Hole.

ROBINSON, Peter; *J1990, b1949,*

ROBINSON, Roland; *J1936, b1908,*

ROBSHAW, Trevor; *J1969, b1950,*
Probationary Meets; Lancaster, Lost John's, Cherry Tree Hole.
Bulletin References; *Lower Stream Passage Pot [Diving] 1971, Earl Pot 1971, Lancaster Hole Nov 1970.*
Newsletter Reference: *Lancaster-Easegill Feb 1969, Meregill June 1969, Pen-y-Ghent Pot Aug 1969, Juniper Gulf Nov 1969, Marble Steps March 1970.*

ROBSON, D; *J1959,*

ROE, Chris; *J1980, b1959,*
Probationary Meets; Langstroth Pot, Pippikin, Lost John's, Swinsto-Simpson's, Birks Fell.
Newsletter References; *Lost John's Sept 1978, Pippikin-Top Sink April 1980, Alum Pot June 1980, Gingling Hole July 1980, Simpsons Pot-KMC Oct 1980.*

ROE, Martin; *J1992, b1964,*
Probationary Meets; Jingling Hole, Simpson's Pot, Alum Pot, Sell Gill.
Member; MCE, EMRG.

Newsletter References; *Hodge Close Sept 1993, 5 Caves Trip July 1993, Coniston Mines Weekend Sept 1993.*

ROSE, Christopher Peter; *J1999, b1978,*
Probationary Meets; GG89.

ROSSER, Christine; See Davenport.

ROSS, Bryan C; *J before 1950.*
Bulletin References; *Bull Pot of the Witches April 1951, Clapham Cave Sept 1951.*

ROSS, Thomas Stuart; *J2019, b1983,*
Newsletter References; *Great Douk Jan 2019, Long Churns Feb 2019, Committee Pot Feb 2019.*

ROTHERHAM, Angela Maxine; AKA: Angie, Spotty Dog. *J1978, b1954,*
Probationary Meets; Grotte de Bury, Lost John's Pool Sink.
Joined as Sharp.
Bulletin References; *Short Drop-Gavel Pot1976, Clapham Bottoms Roof Passage 1976, Grotte de Bury 1977, Gouffre Berger Aug 1980, Abbisa Fighiera 1979, Gouffre Berger Aug 1980,*
Newsletter References; *Stream Passage-Flood Entrance Pot March 1976.*

ROTHERY, Richard Anthony; *J1998, b1956,*
Rejoined 2010.
Probationary Meets; Lancaster Hole, Alum Pot, Outsleets Beck.
Member; WRCPC.
Bulletin References; *Reseau de la Pierre Saint Martin Aug 2013.*
Newsletter References; *Diccan Rescue Nov 1998, Marble Steps Dec 1998, Lancaster-Wretched Rabbit Jan 1999, New Rift April 1999, Derbyshire Meet Sept 1999, Notts Pot August 1999, Dismall Hill-Old Ing Jan 2008, Valley Entrance June 2008, Nettle Pot July 2009, Long Churn May 2010, Sleets Gill April 2011.*

ROUNDTREE, R; *J1983,*

ROWBOTTOM, R; *J1978,*

ROWE, John; *J1980, b1957,*
Member; PCG.
Probationary Meets; Hunt Pot, Moss Pot, Marble Steps.
Newsletter References; *Gouffre Berger Aug 1980, Pippikin to Top Sink April 1980, Pen-y-Ghent Pot July 1980, Gingling Hole July 1980, Gouffre Berger Aug 1980.*

ROWLEY, Geoffrey; *J1959, b1942,*

ROWSELL, Philip John; AKA: Mad Phil. *J2012, b1966,*
Probationary Meets; GG12.

RUSHWORTH, R;

RUSSUM, John Trevor; *J1965, b1943,*
Bulletin References; *Mickle Fell [2591'] 1966.*

RYALL, David; AKA: Rotten, Frogman. *J1997, b1965,*
Member; CDG, CCC, RRCPC, GSV.
Rejoined 2014, 2018.
Bulletin References; *El Manadero [Diving Exploration] Sept 2001, Losers Pot [Discovery] Mar 2002, Hensler's Pot [Discovery] 1999-2003, Hensler's Pot [First Through Trip to GG] May 2003, Carisbrooke Castle Well [Dive/Dig] 2002–2004, Parkinson's Pot [Discovery] July 2003, Deep Well [Diving] 2000–2004, Corky's Pot [Discovery] 2003–2005, Pay Sank [Discovery] 2005, Klondike Pot Digging/Exploration 2004-2007, Hornstrandir Iceland 2006.*
Newsletter References; *Alum Pot [Training Meet] July 1997, Simpson's & Swinsto March 1998, Nent Head-Brewery Shaft Oct 1998, Diccan Rescue Nov 1998, Swinsto-KMC March 1999, New Rift April 1999, Grange Rigg [Locating] March 1999, Lost John's March 1999, Derbyshire Meet Sept 1999, Notts Pot August 1999, Fat Finger Millennium Party, Lancaster Round Trip March 2000, GG-Mill Hill [Dive] May 2000, Langstroth Pot June 2000, El Manadero [Dive/Exploration] Aug 2000, Peak Cavern-Sumps Tour June 2001, Peak Cavern-Speedwell Via Colostomy June 2001,Peak Cavern-White River Series July 2001, Hensler's Pot Digging Dec 2001, Hensler's High Aven voice connection June 2002, Loser's Pot Dive July 2002, Crackpot Cave [Photgraphic Meet] Jan 2003, Corky's Digging Team 2004, Committee Pot Nov 2004, Giant's Hole Jan 2005, Pay Sank Exploration Sept 2005, Pay Sank Breakthrough team Nov 2005, Peak Cavern Feb 2006, Darnbrook Pot June 2007, Hidden Earth Tewkesbury, Support Oct 2007, Ireby Fell Caverns [A grand day out-digging Whirlpool] Feb 2008, Deep Well [Diving 320M] May 2008, Helwith Bridge Show 2008, Jackdaw Hole March 2009, Matienzo April 2009, Titan Shaft April 2009, Lancaster-Wretched Rabbit June 2009, Dob Dale Cave [Dive/explore]July 2009, Ibbeth Peril [Twice] March 2013, Lost River Sump [Dive Support] May 2019, Bull Pot Oct 2019.*

RYALL, Susan; [née Smith] AKA: Fuckwit Spice. *J1997, b1966,*

Member; CCC, RRCPC, GSV.
Re-joined 2018.
Bulletin References; *Carisbrooke Castle Well [Dive/Dig] 2002-2004, Hornstrandir Iceland 2006.*
Newsletter References; *Alum Pot [Training Meet] July 1997, Rowten Pot/Jingling Pot July 1997, GG Photographic Meet May 1998, Wades-Bar Feb 1998, Sunset Hole/Great Douk July 1998, Nent Head-Brewery Shaft Oct 1998, Diccan Rescue Nov 1998, Short Gill Cave Jan 1999, Swinsto-KMC March 1999, King Pot March 1999, Grange Rigg [Surface Locating] March 1999, Lost John's March 1999, Derbyshire Meet Sept 1999, Notts Pot August 1999, Birks Fell June 1999, Fat Finger Millennium Party, El Manadero [Support] Aug 2000, Crackpot Cave [Photgraphic Meet] Jan 2003, Granett Bridge To ShapWalk Sept 2006, Darnbrook Pot June 2007, Rift Pot July 2007, High Hull Pot Sept 2007, Hidden Earth Tewkesbury, Support Oct 2007, Ireby Fell Caverns [A grand day out-digging Whirlpool] Feb 2008, Deep Well [Dive support] May 2008, Lambrigg Fell-Tebay Walk Sept 2008, Helwith Bridge Show 2008, Matienzo April 2009, Titan Shaft April 2009, Lancaster-Wretched Rabbit June 2009.*

RYCROFT, R; *J1936,*

RYE, Michael; *J1987, b1962,*
Probationary Meets; Pippikin, Long Kin East, GG87.
Newsletter References; *Pippikin Pot Nov 1986, Matienzo July/Aug 1987.*

132

S

SALISBURY, Charles Albert; *J1948,*
Famous for; First recorded use of abseiling - Pikedaw Calamine mine Aug 1953.
Bulletin References; *Brow Gill & Calf Holes Oct 1948, Rowten Pot Oct 1949, Pikedaw Mine March 1950, Easter Camp-GG 1950, Ierby Fell Cavern Nov 1950, Lost John's July 1951, Pen-y-Ghent Pot Rescue, young BSA member died of exhaustion 1951, Digging at Beck Head June 1951, Pikedaw Calamine Mine Aug 1953, Lost John's July 1951, Simpson's Pot 1952.*

SALISBURY, Charles H; J1952, b1904, d1966.

SALT, Peter; *J2009, b1957,*
Newsletter References; *Hard Level-Brandy Bottle Incline Nov 2007, Lost John's March 2009, Long Churn/Dolly Tubs [Novice trip] Feb 2010, Hardrawkin Pot May 2010.*

SAVAGE, David; AKA: Dave. *J1970, b1942,*
Newsletter References; *Birks Fell April 1971,*

SAXTON, Edwin Charles; *J1967, b1939,*
Probationary Meets; Disappointment Pot, Rumbling Hole, Ireby Fell.

SAXTON, Robert; *J1958, b1938,*
Expelled from club non payment of subs Dec 1962.
Newsletter References; *Eastwater Swallet Aug 1958, Swildon's Four Aug 1958.*

SAXTON, Roger; AKA: Ranting Rog. *J2004, b1968,*

Bulletin References; *Deep Well [Diving]2000-2003, Pyrenees Aug 2004, Pyrenees 2006, Ordessa National Park 2007, Doubs, France Aug 2009, Croesor-Rhosydd Feb 2009.*
Newsletter References; *Bar Pot Dec 2003, Derbyshire Meet Jan 2004, Pikedaw Calamine Caverns Jan 2004, Swinsto Hole-KMC Feb 2004, Alum Pot March 2004, Lancaster Hole April 2004, Notts Pot March 2004, Washfold Pot April 2004, Deep Well Dive [Support] GG04, MilwrTunnel June 2004, Runscar Cave Sept 2004, High Hull Cave Oct 2004, Committee Pot Nov 2004, Lancaster Hole Dec 2004, Bar Pot Jan 2005, James Hall Over-Engine Mine to Titan Shaft [Bottom] Jan 2005, Titan Shaft Jan 2005, James Hall Over-Engine Mine to Titan Shaft [Bottom] Jan 2005, Yordas Pot & Cave Dec 2004, Lancaster Hole April 2005, Gingling Hole July 2005, Lost John's Hole Sept 2005, Long Kin West Dec 2005, Ireby Fell Caverns Nov 2005, Coppice Cave-Ling Gill Jan 2006, Dismal Hill-Old Ing Jan 2006, Bull Pot Jan 2006, Calf Holes & Brow Gill Cave Feb 2006, Rat Hole March 2006, Cow Pot [Lancaster] April 2006, Black Shiver Pot July 2006, Lost John's Hole Sept 2006, Pyrenees Aug 2006, Coniston Copper Mines Oct 2006, Committee Pot Dec 2006, Derbyshire Meet Jan 2007, Dismal Hill-Old Ing Feb 2007, Top Sink-Lancaster Hole Feb 2007, OFD 1& 2 March 2007, Providence Pot-Dow Cave April 2007, Ordessa National Park Spanish Pyrenees 2007, Washfold Pot Dec 2007, Swinsto Hole-KMC Dec 2007, Vesper Pot Jan 2008, Brackenbottom Pot Feb 2008, King Pot Feb 2008, JH-Peak Cavern via White River Series March 2008,*

Coppice Cave April 2008, Notts Pot March 2008, Deep Well [Dive support] May 2008, Otter Hole June 2008, Overhanging Bastion Sept 2008, Simpson's-KMC Dec 2008, Aygill Caverns Jan 2009, Croesor-Rhosydd Feb 2009, Dan Yr Ogof March 2009, OFD-Cwm Dwr March 2009, Cow Pot April 2009, Scafell Central Buttress July 2009, Notts Pot Sept 2009, Pool Sink-Easegill Dec 2009, Rumbling Hole March 2010, Diccan Pot Oct 2010, Long Churn [Novice Trip] March 2011, Swinsto Hole Nov 2011, Shuttleworth Pot Feb 2012, Short Drop-Gavel Pot Nov 2017, Lancaster-County Jan 2019.

SCARGILL, Ian; J1966,

SCATLIFFE, Martin Howard A; J1973, b1945, d2015.
Probationary Meets; GG73, Goyden, Gunnerfleet [Photo Meet]
Famous for; A very eccentric character who was at the centre of club activities through the 70's and 80's. He once drove the Gaping Gill winch in full top hat and tails. He would recite Kipling such as 'The Road to Samarkand' and 'Snarler Yowl'. He would perform The Sand Dance while singing The Old Bazaar in Ciaro; he could also recite many of the old music hall monologues. Martyn could sing the 3rd, 4th & 5th verses etc. of almost any Methodist hymn. He owned a mummy's leg and could take massive amounts of snuff in one snort as a party trick. He also arranged a wine and cheese party in Sand Cavern where attendees were required to wear a tie over their caving gear, and he had taken down a wind up gramophone to provide music. He also collected wax cylinder recordings including one of Florence Nightingale and one of the bugler who sounded the charge for the Light Brigade. Once successfully represented several club members in court and got the case dismissed.
Bulletin References; Chourum Des Aiguilles 1973, Coast to Coast Plus July/Aug 1978, Slit Pot [Discovery] 1979, Gouffre Berger Aug 1980.
Newsletter References; Magnetometer Pot Sept 1973, Tatham Wife March 1975, Birks Fell Cave April 1975, Short Drop-Gavel Pot1976, Lakes Walk Esk House March 1977, Kingsdale Master Cave [Found old bang] Jan 1980, Gouffre Berger Aug 1980, Ibbeth Peril Oct 1980, Ingleborough Cave [Dive Support] Jan 1981, Helwith Bridge Quarry [Dive Support] Feb 1981, GG Interim week May 1981, Kingsdale Photographic meet April 1982, Ingleborough Cave Oct 1982, Gunnerside Gill Lead Mines June 1985.

SCATLIFFE, Melanie, Jane; [née Potter] J1983, b1966,

Probationary Meets; Birks Fell, Otter Hole, GG83.
Newsletter References; Birks Fell Cave July 1982, Ingleborough Cave Oct 1982, Gunnerside Gill Lead Mines June 1985.

SCHOFIELD, Bryan; AKA: Scoff. J1981, b1956, d2017.
Member; WSG, WCC.
Probationary Meets; Lost John's, KMC, Long Churns, Alum Pot, Magnetometer Pot, Jingling Pot, GG81.
Famous for; Wearing very brightly coloured jumpers and clogs. A large personality and a truely honourable man.
Bulletin References; Short Gill Rising [Dive/ dig] 1981, Vercors Aug 1983, Krisna Jama Aug 1984, Leski Aug 1984, Skocjanske Jame Aug 1984, Brakenbottom Pot [Dig]1985, M5 Pot [Dig] July 1984, Nettle Pot [Dig] July 1984, Giggel Rav Pot, [Dig/exploration]1990, Soca Valley [Diving]Aug 1990, Dub Cote Extensions [Diving] 1990, Manchester Hole D/S Sump extension [Support] 1991, Digging unknown hole Langstrthdale 1991, Doux De Coly [Diving] July/Aug 1991, Mosquito Plane [Midge Hole Diving/ exploration] 1991, Brants Gill Head [Dive/Dig] 1988-1991, Dig above Hagg Gill Pot 1991, Deep Well [Diving] May 1991&1992, Growling Swallet System [Tasmania] 1995, Belfry [GG] Exploration May 1996, Cook Islands 1992, El Manadero [Diving Exploration] Sept 2001, Carisbrooke Castle Well [Dive/Dig] 2002-2004, Lava Tubes of Iceland 2006.
Newsletter References; Alum Pot March 1981, Lower Long Churn March 1981, Sell Gill Hole April 1981, GG Interim week May 1981, Lancaster-County Pot Sept 1981, Link Pot Sept 1981, Dowkabottom Cave Dec1981, Rift Pot& Long Kin East Jan 1982, Lost John's Feb 1982, Alum Pot March 1982, Kingsdale Photographic meet April 1982, Birks Fell Cave[Photographing] July 1982, Pen-y-Ghent Pot July 1982, Ingleborough Cave Oct 1982, GG–Radagast's Revenge Ingleborough to clear dig for through trip Feb 1983, Little Neath River Cave, Porth Yr Ogof and OFD April 1983, Simpsons-Valley Entrance April 1983, Mendip weekend April 1983, Notts Pot March 1983, Link Pot July 1983, South Wales Aug 1983, Nettle Pot Sept 1983, Peak Cavern Sept 1983, Rowten-Swinsto Exchange Nov 1983, Rift Pot Feb 1984, Mud Pot [Aborted Dive] May 1985, South East Pot Dive May 1985, Hurtle Pot [8 Dives] Upstream Extension July/Aug 1985, Langstroth Pot Sept 1985, Brezno, Leska, Babizop Rakov Scojan and the Pit of Bears Yugoslavia Aug 1985, Scotland Easter 1986, Mendip Dec 1986, Scotland 1987, International Cave Diving Expedition-Dordogne Summer 1987, Weathercote Cave April 1988, Simpsons–KMC July

1990, 5 Caves Trip July 1993, South Wales April 1996, Swinsto-Simpson's 1996, Lost John's Hole March 1997, GG Photographic Meet May 1998, Diccan Rescue Nov 1998, Grange Rigg [Surface Locating] March 1999, Lost John's March 1999, GG-Mill Hill [Dive support]May 2000, El Manadero [Dive/Exploration] Aug 2000, Peak Cavern-Sumps Tour June 2001, Lost John's March 2002, Notts Pot March 2004, Hidden Earth Tewkesbury, Support Oct 2007, Notts Pot March 2008, Bull Pot April 2008, Helwith Bridge Show 2008, Joint Hole [Diving] Jan 2010, Keld Head [Diving] May 2010, Hurtle Pot [Diving] May 2010, Committee Pot March 2011, Yordas Pot March 2015, Aquamole Pot March 2015, Lost John's-Boxhead Pot March 2016.

SCHOFIELD, David; *J1963, b1946,*
Probationary Meets; Short Drop-Gavel Pot, Stonelands Cave, Clapham Cave.
Newsletter References; *Batty Cave Jan 1964, Oxlow Caverns Feb 1964.*

SCHOFIELD, Jack; *J1957, b1933,*
Bulletin References: *South Wales Easter 1963, Lost John's March 1960, Flood Entrance Pot Dec 1960, Oxlow Caverns June 1961, Pen-y-Ghent Pot Feb 1964, Tackle testing Jan 1958.*
Newsletter References; *Marble Steps Sept 1959, Easegill Caverns Aug 1959, Jnr Leader Pen-y-Ghent Long Churn Oct 1960, Leader Bar Pot GG Dec 1960, Jnr Leader Stream Passage Pot Jan 1961.*

SCHOFIELD, John Stewart; AKA: Daft Jonah. *J1964, b1939,*
BPC President 2006 + 7.
Member; NSG.
Bulletin References; *Lost John's March 1960, Pen-y-Ghent Pot Extensions Oct 1963, Bar Pot Dec 1957.*
Newsletter References; *Great Douk July 2006.*

SCHOFIELD, Rowena; [née Hill] *J2002, b1963,*
Elected Honorary Membership 2017
Bulletin References; *Carisbrooke Castle Well [Dive/Dig] 2002-2004, Lava Tubes of Iceland 2006, Scotland Easter 1986.*
Newsletter References; *El Manadero [Support] Aug 2000, Black Combe-Foxfield Walk Sept 2003, Helwith Bridge Show 2008.*

SCHOFIELD, S; *J1982,*
Newsletter References; *Dowkabottom Cave Dec 1981,*

SCOWCROFT, Alan E; *J2008, b1956,*

Probationary Meets; GG09, Lancaster-Wretched Rabbit, Brackenbottom pot.
Member; UWFRA, CCCC, PPCC.
Newsletter References; *Lancaster-Wretched Rabbit June 2009, Brackenbottom Pot Nov 2012.*

SCURR, Robert Adrian; *J1974, b1957,*
Probationary Meets; Far Waters, GG74, Pen-y-Ghent Pot, County-Lancaster.
Newsletter References; *Gingling Hole Sept 1974, Giants Hole Nov 1974, Stream Passage Pot–Flood Entrance Feb 1975, Christmas Pot Feb 1977.*

SELLERS, Brian Hugh; *J1975, b1950,*
Probationary Meets; GG71, Lost John's, Lancaster-Easegill, Needles Pit [1974], Pen-y-Ghent Pot.
Famous for; Enjoying a non-politically correct fag while climbing the entrance pitch to Magnetometer Pot sometime in 1981 He was suddenly inundated with several helmets full of water by Wilky. He got the strong impression at that moment that he wasn't keen on his indulging in the "noxious weed" underground. On the Piaggia Bella trip in Italy in 1975 we camped near the local caving club hut which was half way up a mountain and a three hour trek uphill from where we could park the expedition land-rovers. One of our members was so keen to get caving once he had ferried his kit up to camp that unable to curb his enthusiasm, he immediately donned his wetsuit, helmet and harness slung a rope down the large pothole entrance near the hut and vanished from sight, only to rapidly prussik out a few minutes later having made a record first descent for the BPC down what our host caving club termed their "Abisso Rubbish Dump", which in those non-environmentally friendly times was liberally covered at the bottom of this blind pitch with rusting tin cans, empty bottles and other unsavoury items.
Bulletin References; *Chourum Des Aiguilles 1974, Piaggia Bella 1975, Mossdale Caverns [Digging] 1979, Gouffre Berger Aug 1980, Tanne Du Bel Espoir-Diau Aug 1984.*
Newsletter References; *Lancaster-County Pot Dec 1971, Chourum des Aiguilles [BP] July 1974, Pen-y-Ghent Pot July 1980, Gouffre Berger Aug 1980, Lancaster-County Pot Nov 1980, New Goyden Pot March1981, Magnetometer Pot March 1981, Notts Pot Jan 1981, OFD 1 & 2 May 1981, Tanne de Bel Espoir-Grotte de la Diau Aug 1981.*

SELLERS, John Andrew; *J1981, b1948,*
Member; LUSS [1969-71]
Probationary Meets; Tatham Wife, Lancaster Hole, New Goyden.

Bulletin References; *Tatham Wife Hole 1980, New Goyden Pot April 1981.*

SENELL, D;

SENIOR, Richard Charles; *J1992, b1948,*
Bulletin References; *Trou De Glaz Aug 1989, Gouffre Berger Aug 1992, Rumbling Hole Jan 1992.*
Newsletter References; *Gouffre Berger Aug 1992, Alum Pot Nov 1993.*

SETCHFIELD, Matthew Robert; *J2000, b1967,*
Probationary Meets; LKW, Short Drop-Gavel, Nick Pot, Gingling, Meregill, White Scar, Mongo Gill, Rumbling Hole, Growling Hole, Brown Hill, Sell Gill, Stream Passage, Notts Pot, Buckden Gard Mine, Dyhedral, Aygill Caverns, Lost John's, Rowten Pot, Coppice Cave, Wades Entrance, Cow Pot, Thistle Cave, Scar Top Cave, Batty Wife Cave.
Member; WSG.
Bulletin References; *Reseau de la Pierre Saint Martin Aug 2013.*
Newsletter References; *Coppice Cave April 2000, Lost John's March 2002, Notts Pot Sept 2002, Sell Gill Hole Nov 2002, Penygent House Pots and Cave April 2003, DanYr Ogof/OFD2 June 2003, Slanting Cave Oct 2003, Nettle Pot Jan 2004, High Hull Cave Oct 2004, Old Ing-Dismal Hill Oct 2004, James Hall Over-Engine Mine-Titan Shaft [Bottom] Jan 2005, Gingling Hole July 2005, Nippikin Pot Dec 2005, Ireby Fell Caverns Nov 2005, Rumbling Hole July 2006, Hurnell Moss Pot Oct 2006, Karwendel Mountains June 2006, Darnbrook Pot June 2007, High Hull Pot Sept 2007, Hard Level-Brandy Bottle Incline Nov 2007, Vesper Pot Jan 2008, Robinsons Pot Sept 2008, Heron Pot Jan 2009, Aygill Caverns Jan 2009, New Goyden Pot March 2009, Haytime Hole March 2009, Jackdaw Hole March 2009, Lancaster-Wretched Rabbit June 2009, Aquamole Pot Nov 2009, Rumbling Hole March 2010, Marble Steps June 2010, Lancaster Hole Oct 2010, Sell Gill [Training Meet] Oct 2010, Wretched Rabbit-County Pot Nov 2010, Long Churns [Training Meet] Nov 2010, KMC-Toyland Feb 2011, Committee Pot March 2011, Voldemort Pot March 2011, Hunt Pot-Shrapnel Exchange April 2011, Illusion Pot April 2011, Long Kin West Oct 2011, New Rift Pot Oct 2011,Wizard's Chasm Jan 2012, Notts Pot March 2012, Dan Yr Ogof April 2012, Far Coutry via Marilyn May 2012, Old Ing/Calf Holes-Browgill [Novice Trip] June 2012, Brackenbottom Pot, June 2012, It's a Cracker-Lost John's-Deaths Head July 2012, White Scar Cave July 2012, Link Pot Nov 2012, KMC Toyland Nov 2012, Lost John's-Notts Pot March 2013, Pen-y-ghent Pot May 2013, Sunset Hole June 2013, Ireby Fell Cavern June 2013, Magnetometer Pot Nov 2013, Dan Yr Ogof June 2014, Shuttleworth Pot Oct 2014, Juniper Gulf Oct 2014, Yordas Pot Oct 2014, Great and High Douk June 2015, Poll Dudh June 2015, St Catherine's1-Fisher St June 2015, Faunarooska June 2015, Gingling Hole July 2015, Bruntscar Cave July 2015, Fairy Holes Sept 2015, Nenthead Mines Sept 2015, Hoffman Kilns Stainforth Nov 2015, Pillar Holes April 2016, Rowten Pot + Cave April 2016, Death's Head-Big Meanie Sept 2016, Unterstein Tennessee 2016, Rift Pot-Long Kin East [Exchange] July 2016, Sell Gill Sept 2017, Špilja Šipun, Cavtat [Croatia] July 2017, Darnbrook Pot June 2018, Magnetometer Pot Sept 2019, Illusion Pot Sept 2019, Bull Pot Oct 2019, Pool Sink-Boundary Pot Nov 2019, Sell Gill Nov 2019.*

SEWELL, Adam. J; *J2000, b1970,*
Rejoined 2009.
Probationary Meets; GG99/00, Dig Oil Well Pot, Radio locate Henslers High Aven, Dig Hensler's Pot, KMC, Heron Pot.
Bulletin References; *Tete Sauvage July 1995. [This could be a separate A. Sewell? – Ed]*

SHACKLETON, Milton; *J1933, b1903, d1989.*
Founder Member
BPC President 1952.
Notable Achievements; Founder member-BPC [1933]
Main Activities; Caving, Climbing
Bulletin References; *East Passage 1934, Sleets Gill 29th Sept 1946, Surveying at Beck Head June 1951.*

SHACKLETON, Vincent; *J1933, b1913, d2008.*
Founder Member
BPC President 1978-79.
Other Club Memberships; The Magic Circle.
Notable Achievements; Founder member-BPC [1933]
Main Activities; Caving, Climbing, Magic, Punch & Judy.
Bulletin References; *Involved in the rescue from Pen-y-Ghent Long Churn October 1938.*

SHARP, Angela Maxine; See Rotherham.

SHARP, Colin Edward; *J1961, b1941,*
Probationary Meets; GG61, Lost John's, Alum Pot.
Bulletin References; *Maritime Alps BPC/RRCPC trip July/Aug 1962.*

SHARP, Christopher; AKA: Baby Bones. *J1990, b1969,*
Probationary Meets; Goyden Pot, Great Douk, Grange Rigg.
Rejoined 2013.

Newsletter References; *Langstroth Pot & Cave [Diving] July 1989, Great Douk Cave +Jan 1990, Sunset Hole March 1990, Grange Rigg March 1990, Simpsons–Kingsdale July 1990, Easegill Caverns Sept 1990, Black Shiver Pot Jan 1991, Calf Holes, Browgill, Old Ing and Dismal Hill Jan 1991, Marble Steps Pot Dec 1990, Ribblehead Caves Sept 1991, Ireby Fell Jan 1992, LKE-Rift Exchange Feb 1992, Out Slets Beck Cave June 1992, KMC Oct 1993, Alum Pot Nov 1993, Cherry Tree Hole Jan 1994, Simpson's-Swinsto March 1994, Dowkabottom Feb 1995, Wretched Rabbit-Lancaster Hole March 1995, Black Combe-Foxfield Walk Sept 2003, Roger Kirk Cave Oct 2013, Lancaster-Wretched Rabbit Nov 2013, Sell Gill Holes April 2014, The Borehole-Boundary Pot Feb 2015, President's Meet cycle pub crawl July 2015, Lost John's-Notts 2 Sept 2015, Swinsto-KMC Feb 2016, OFD 1 Oct 2017, Great Douk Jan 2019, Pool Sink-Wretched Rabbit Feb 2020.*

SHARP, Donald; *J1959, b before 1938,*
Newsletter References; *Dowbergill Passage April 1959.*

SHARP, John; *J1948,*

SHARP, Joseph; AKA: Joe Bones. *J2011, b1992,*
Probationary Meets; Heron Pot, Bar Pot, Stream Passage Pot, Disappointment Pot, Tatham Wife Hole, Committee Pot, Calf Holes, Crackpot.
Bulletin References; *Reseau de la Pierre Saint Martin Aug 2013, Gouffre Pont Du Gerbout Aug 2011, Gouffre De Heretiques Aug 2011, Felix Trombe 2011. Coniston Mines Weekend Sept 1993.*
Newsletter References; *Calf Holes & Browgill Cave Nov 2004, Heron Pot Nov 2005, Tatham Wife Hole March 2006, Committee Pot July 2007, Pen-y-Ghent Gill [Digging CPC/ULSA Dig] May 2010, Heron Pot Nov 2010, Heron Pot Nov 2010, Death's Head Sept 2011, Darnbrook Pot [Novice Trip] Sept 2011, Lancaster-Wretched Rabbit Jan 2012, Simpson's Pot Jan 2012, Shuttleworth Pot Feb 2012, Cow Pot March 2012, Cullaun 2 April 2012, Pollnagollum April 2012, Lost John's Cave July 2012, Trou du Garde/Creux de la Cavale-Bauges Aug 2012, Illusion Pot March 2013, Top Sink-Lancaster Hole March 2013, Black Shiver May 2017, Alum/Long Churns June 2017, Hensler's Pot-Winch May 2017, Lindale-Greenodd Walking Meet 2017, OFD 1 Oct 2017, Far Waters May 2017, Voldemort Pot-Notts 2 Feb 2018, Mongo Gill Sept 2018, Aquamole Pot Nov 2019.*

SHARP, Michael; AKA: Bones. *J1974, b1956,*
BPC President 2019.

Probationary Meets; Pen-y-Ghent Pot, Agen Allwedd, Pasture Gill.
First reference to nickname was having "Oud Bones" down a flooding Pen-y-Ghent, before full membership.
Club Expeditions; Grotte de Bury 1977, Abissa Figiera 1979, Gouffre Berger 1980 & 1992, Leski 1984, Tanne de Bel Espoir-Diau 1986, Pierre Saint Martin 1995 & 2013, Felix Tromme 2011.
Other Expeditions; Mexico 1985.
Notable Achievements; Significant contribution to Ingleborough /GG connection.
Main Activities; Caving, walking, scuba diving, mountain biking.
Famous for; Unique renditions of 'Barnicle Bill the sailor' after sufficient inducement.
Bulletin References; *Dog Tooth Inlet GG. [Digging] May 1975, Clapham Bottoms Roof Passage 1976, Otter Hole 1977, Grotte de Bury 1977, Abbisa Fighiera 1979 [See Section 2], Pippikin to Top Sink April 1980, Gouffre Berger Aug 1980, Leski Aug 1984, Tanne De Bel Espoir–La Diau Parmilan 1991, Gouffre Berger Aug 1992, Gouffre Pont Du Gerbout Aug 2011, Reseau de la Pierre Saint Martin Aug 2013, Gouffre De Heretiques Aug 2011, Felix Trombe 2011, Lancaster-Wretched Rabbit Jan 2012.*
Newsletter References; *Pen-y-Ghent Pot Aug 1972, Tatham Wife March 1975, Birks Fell Cave April 1975, County Pot Oct 1975, Pasture Gill Cave July 1976, Little Neath River Cave April 1978, Abbissa Fighiera Italy Aug 1979, Lost John's Sept 1978, Pippikin–Lancaster [Flood Pulse on Echo Aven] 1980, Diccan-Main Shaft Jan 1980, Lancaster Hole [Maple Leaf Pitch] April 1980, Pippikin–Top Sink April 1980, Gouffre Berger Aug 1980, Lost John's Nov 1980, Lancaster–County Pot Nov 1980, Jingling Pot March 1981, Alum Pot March 1981, Kingsdale Photographic meet April 1982, GG–Radagast's Revenge Ingleborough to clear dig for through trip Feb 1983, Mendip weekend April 1983, Giant's Hole Sept 1983, Peak Cavern Sept 1983, Mendip Dec 1986, South Wales Nov 1988, Bull Pot of the Witches April 1989, Lakes Walk Sept 1990, Gouffre Berger Aug 1992, Coniston Mines Weekend Sept 1993, Calf Holes & Browgill Cave Nov 2004, Heron Pot Nov 2005, Tatham Wife Hole March 2006, Committee Pot July 2007, Heron Pot Nov 2010, Heron Pot Nov 2010, Death's Head Sept 2011, Darnbrook Pot [Novice Trip] Sept 2011, Long Kin West Oct 2011, Robinson's Pot Oct 2011, Swinsto Hole Nov 2011, Simpson's Pot Jan 2012, Shuttleworth Pot Feb 2012, Cow Pot March 2012, Washfold Pot April 2012, Lost John's Cave July 2012, Trou du Garde-Creux de la Cavale - Bauges Aug 2012, Crosby Ravensworth-Askham Walking Meet Sept 2012, Croesor Rhosydd [Through] Oct*

2012, Wizard's Chasm Jan 2013, Illusion Pot March 2013, Lancaster-Wretched Rabbit Nov 2013, Roundthwaite Common to Borrowdale Sept 2014, The Borehole-Boundary Pot Feb 2015, Walking Meet 2015, Croesor Rhysydd Through Trip Oct 2016, Lindale-Greenodd Walking Meet 2017, OFD 1 Oct 2017, Far Waters May 2017, Cow Green Reservoir–Appleby Walking Meet 2018.

SHARP, Paul; J1999, b1969,

SHARP, Rosie; J2003, b1994,
Bulletin References; Reseau de la Pierre Saint Martin Aug 2013.
Newsletter References; Calf Holes & Browgill Cave Nov 2004.

SHARP, Sally; J1992, b1960,
Bulletin References; Reseau de la Pierre Saint Martin Aug 2013, Mendip Dec 1986, South Wales Nov 1988.
Newsletter References; Lakes Walk Sept 1990, Coniston Mines Weekend Sept 1993, Calf Holes & Browgill Cave Nov 2004, Crosby Ravensworth-Askham Walking Meet Sept 2012, Roundthwaite Common to Borrowdale Sept 2014, Walking Meet 2015, Cow Green Reservoir–Appleby Walking Meet 2018.

SHAW, Graham; J1958, b1941,
Member of the Heath Grammar School contingent.
Bulletin References; Pen-y-ghent Pot July 1960, Mendip Trip Sept 1960, Involved with building electron ladders, 1950/60's, Simpson's Pot 16th April 1961-Graham Shaw Accident, Discovery Lower Stream Passage Pot April 1959.

SHAW, Peter Raymond; J1957, b1934,

SHAW, Ronald; J1961, b1943,
Probationary Meets; Easegill, Notts Pot, Clapham Cave.
Bulletin References; Magnetometer Pot Nov 1960, Flood Entrance Pot Dec 1960.

SHEPHERD, Arthur; AKA: Sheppy. J1938, b1915, d1995.
BPC President 1961-63.
Bulletin References; Part in first post war trip-Rift Pot 7th April 1946. And involved in the first attempted Rift Pot/ Long Kin East exchange April 28th 1946. First Club trip to reach the sump in Meregill Sept 1946 Rift Pot/ Long Kin East exchange April 20th 1947. Birks Cave, Buckden 11th May 1947. MereGill 7th Sept 1947. Birks Cave 5th Oct 1947, Birks Cave May 1948, Rift Pot/Long

Kin East exchange April 1949, Great Douk, Sunset Hole April 1949.
Newsletter References; Auctioneer at the club Mock Auction Nov 1953.

SHEPLEY, Pauline; See Koval.

SILSON, Geoffrey Riley; J1958, b before 1937,
Bulletin References; Gaping Gill Meet 1960, Bull Pot Sept 1960, Magnetometer Pot Nov 1960, Flood Entrance Pot Dec 1960, Disappointment Pot April 1961, Lost John's March 1961.
Newsletter References; Lancaster Hole June 1958, Dow Cave Sept 1958, Disappointment Pot [Photographic trip] Oct 1958, English Electric Trip-Alum Pot Nov 1958, Dowbergill Passage April 1959, Diccan-Alum Exchange September 1959, Bull Pot Aug 1959, Clapham Cave Oct 1959, Bar Pot Nov 1959, Joint Leader GG 1960, Leader Alum, Pot Oct 1960, Leader Magnetometer Pot Nov 1960.

SIMISTER, Brian; AKA: Ragnar. J1992, b1946,
Probationary Meets; GG91.
Member; OOPA
Bulletin References; Hensler's Pot [Discovery] 1999-2003.
Newsletter References; GG Photographic Meet May 1998, Fat Finger Millennium Party, KMC March 2000, Losers Pot [Discovery] Mar 2002, Millenium Walk Sept 2002, Great Douk July 2006.

SIMISTER, Thia; J2005, b1965,
Newsletter References; Great Douk July 2006.

SIMISTER, Pauline; J1998, b1950,

SIMMONS, Michael George; J1958, b1937,
Resigned 2013.
Bulletin References; Recorded as caving in Cyprus 1959 Akrotiri Potholing Club [RAF]

SIMPSON, Andrew; J2004, b1983,
Bulletin References; Pyrenees 2006, Ordessa National Park 2007, Doubs, France Aug 2009.
Newsletter References; Skirwith Cave July 2000, Old Ing/Dismal Hill Oct 2004, Short Drop-Gavel Pot Nov 2004, Lancaster Hole Dec 2004, Diccan Pot Feb 2005, Magnetometer Pot April 2005, Gingling Hole July 2005, Pippikin Sept 2005, Roaring Hole Sept 2005, Long Kin West Dec 2005, Dismal Hill-Old Ing Jan 2006, Titan Shaft Feb 2006, Peak Cavern Feb 2006, Rat Hole March 2006, Rumbling Hole July 2006, Hurnell Moss Pot Oct 2006, Lost John's Hole Sept 2006, Pyrenees Aug 2006, New Rift Pot Nov 2006, Aquamole Pot Jan 2007, Top Sink-Lancaster Hole Feb 2007, OFD 1& 2 March 2007, Short Drop-Gavel March 2007, White Scar Cave April 2007,

Heron Pot Sept 2007, Darnbrook Pot June 2007, Ordessa National Park Spanish Pyrenees 2007, High Hull Pot Sept 2007, Death's Head & Big Meanie Sept 2007, King Pot Feb 2008, JH–Peak Cavern via White River Series March 2008, Notts Pot March 2008, Heron Pot Jan 2009, Pay Sank Feb 2009, Lost John's March 2009, Long Kin East March 2009, Cow Pot April 2009, Large-Rift Pot Exchange July 2009, Ireby Fell Caverns Oct 2009, Pool Sink-Easegill Dec 2009, Sell Gill Dec 2009, Marble Steps Jan 2010, Tatham Wife Hole Feb 2010, Pen-y-Ghent Pot May 2010, Juniper Gulf Oct 2010, Ireby Fell Cavern Jan 2011, Black Shiver Pot April 2011, Notts Pot March 2012, It's a Cracker-Lost John's-Deaths Head July 2012, Sell Gill Dec 2012, Bull Pot of the Witches Jan 2013, Lost John's-Notts Pot March 2013, JH-Titan April 2013, Pen-y-ghent Pot May 2013, Sell Gill Holes Nov 2013, Greenside Mine April 2014, Fairy Holes Sept 2014, Nenthead Mines Sept 2014, Otter Hole July 2015.

SIMPSON, Colin John; *J2004, b1952,*
Rejoined 2013.
Newsletter References; *Skirwith Cave July 2000, Old Ing-Dismal Hill Oct 2004, Dismal Hill-Old Ing Jan 2006, Sunset Hole July 2006, Dismal Hill-Old Ing Feb 2007, OFD 2 March 2007, Short Drop-Gavel March 2007, White Scar Cave April 2007, Sunset Hole April 2008, Long Kin East March 2009, Tatham Wife Hole Feb 2010, Short Drop-Gavel Sept 2013.*

SIMPSON, John; *J2004, b1983,*
Bulletin References; *Pyrenees 2006, Ordessa National Park 2007, Doubs France Aug 2009.*
Newsletter References; *Skirwith Cave July 2000, Diccan Pot Feb 2005, Magnetometer Pot April 2005, Gingling Hole July 2005, Pippikin Sept 2005, Roaring Hole Sept 2005, Titan Shaft Feb 2006, Peak Cavern Feb 2006, Rumbling Hole July 2006, Black Shiver Pot July 2006, Lost John's Hole Sept 2006, Pyrenees Aug 2006, New Rift Pot Nov 2006, Aquamole Pot Jan 2007, Top Sink-Lancaster Hole Feb 2007, White Scar Cave April 2007, Heron Pot Sept 2007, Ordessa National Park Spanish Pyrenees 2007, High Hull Pot Sept 2007, Brackenbottom Pot Feb 2008, King Pot Feb 2008, JH-Peak Cavern via White River Series March 2008, Pay Sank Feb 2009, Lost John's March 2009, Long Kin East March 2009, Peak Cavern April 2009, Titan Shaft April 2009, Large-Rift Pot Exchange July 2009, Pool Sink-Easegill Dec 2009, Sell Gill Dec 2009, Marble Steps Jan 2010, Tatham Wife Hole Feb 2010, Juniper Gulf Oct 2010, Rowten Pot Nov 2010, Heron Pot Nov 2010, Heron Pot Nov 2010, Ireby Fell Cavern Jan 2011, Black Shiver Pot April 2011, Notts Pot March 2012, Sell Gill Dec 2012, Top Sink-Lancaster Hole March 2013, JH-Titan April 2013, Pen-y-ghent Pot*

May 2013, Greenside Mine April 2014, Otter Hole July 2015.

SIMPSON, John David; *J2010, b1962,*
Probationary Meets; GG10,

SIMPSON, Graham; *J1965, b1945,*
Probationary Meets; Jackdaw Pot, Pen-y-Ghent Pot, Bar Pot.

SINCLAIR, John Cameron; *J1954, b1934,*
Bulletin References; *Flood Entrance Pot March 1954.*

SIZER, Karen; AKA: Kaz. *J2010,*

SKILLERNE DE BRISTOWE, Bernard J; *J1968, b1946,*
Famous for; being hung-up on a KMC pitch when his wetsuit pulled into his descender.
Bulletin References; *Ingleborough Cave Nether Wallows 1969.*

SKINNER, Emily; *J2015, b2009,*
Probationary Meets; The Churns, KMC, Yordas, Skirwith, Great Douk, Old Ing, Birkwith, Grotte de Gournier, GG15.
Newsletter References; *Old Ing & Birkwith Canal Aug 2014, Skirwith Cave [Novice Trip] Jan 2016,*

SKINNER, Eve Charlotte; *J2018, b2012,*
Newsletter References; *Skirwith Cave [Novice Trip] Jan 2016.*

SKINNER, Michael D; Mr Dead. *J1998, b1970,*
Probationary Meets; Disappointment Pot-Hensler's High Aven-Winch, Dyhedral-Stream Passage Pot, Stream-Flood Entrance, Henslers, Bar Pot.
Newsletter References; *Pippikin Pot Nov 1999, Lost John's March 2002, Alum Pot July 2002, Rumbling Hole July 2002, Marble Steps July 2003, Lost John's Pot July 2003, Robinson's Pot Oct 2003, Aquamole Pot Dec 2003, Milwr Tunnel June 2004, Short Drop-Gavel Pot Nov 2004, Committee Pot Nov 2004, Sell Gill Hole Dec 2004, Hunt Pot-Shrapnel Pot June 2011, Notts Pot March 2012, Old Ing-Birkwith Canal Aug 2014, Skirwith Cave [Novice Trip] Jan 2016, Simpson's Pot Aug 2016, Voldemort-Committee Pot July 2016, Death's Head-Big Meanie Sept 2016, Simpson's Flooded August 2016, Simpson's-KMC Aug 2016, Simpson's Pot-KMC Dec 2016, Heron Pot [Novice trip] April 2017, Red Moss Pot [Novice Trip] April 2017, Link Pot April 2017, Black Shiver May 2017, Hensler's Pot-Winch May 2017, Brackenbottom Pot Dec 2017, Wretched Rabbit-Top Sink Jan 2018, Dawn Chamber GG May 2017, Wildcat Rift May 2018,*

Notts Pot Sept 2018, Mongo Gill Sept 2018, Lancaster-County Jan 2019, Cow Pot March 2019, Lancaster-Easegill June 2019, Heron Pot July 2019, Pool Sink-Boundary Pot Nov 2019.

SKINNER, Ruth Emma; See Castleden

SKIPSEY, James Barker; *J1949,*

SLATER, John Dudley; *J1959, b1941,*

SLATER, Mark Andrew; AKA: Mr Bean. *J1992, b1960,*
Probationary Meets; Ireby Fell, Easegill, Grange Rigg.
Bulletin References; *Sima de las Tainas de Mattarubia, Sima del Carlista, Simas M-21 & CJ-3. Sept 2001, Losers Pot [Discovery] Mar 2002 Hensler's Pot [Discovery] 1999-2003, Hensler's Pot [First Through Trip to GG] May 2003, Grange Rigg-Christmas Pot March 1993, Heron Pot March 1993, Rift pot June 1993, Hodge Close Sept 1993, Snatcher's Pot Nov 1993, Coniston Mines Weekend Sept 1993, Rowten Pot Feb 1994, Simpson's-Swinsto March 1994, Brown Hills Pot March 1994, Wretched Rabbit-Lancaster Hole March 1995, Manchester By-pass-Wretshed RabbitMarch 1995, Malham Cove Abseil Sept 1995, Top Sink-Pippikin Nov 1995, Pool Sink-Lancaster Hole Dec 1995, County-Lancaster Hole Oct 1995, Deaths Head-Big Meanie Jan 1996, Cherry Tree Hole Feb 1996, King Pot March 1996, Diccan Pot March 1996, Cow Pot July 1996, Top Sink-Lancaster July 1996, Nettle Pot Oct 1996, Swinsto-Simpson's 1996, Notts Pot Jan 1997, Easegill April 1997, Jingling Pot April 1997, Deep Well [Dive Support] May 1997, Pippikin Hole Sept 1997, Out Sleets Beck Pot Jan 1998, GG Photographic Meet May 1998, Wades-Bar Feb 1998, Heron Pot July 1998, Marble Steps Dec 1998, Short Gill Cave Jan 1999, Lancaster-Wretched Rabbit Jan 1999, County-Pool Exchange Feb 1999, Swinsto-KMC March 1999, King Pot March 1999, Grange Rigg [Locating] March 1999, Out Sleets Beck Pot April 1999, Lost John's March 1999, Derbyshire Meet Sept 1999, Birks Fell June 1999, Pippikin Pot Nov 1999, Easegill Jan 2000,Bull Pot March 2000, Coppice Cave April 2000, Rumbling Hole Oct 1999, GG-Mill Hill [Dive support]May 2000, Hagg Gill Pot June 2000, Langstroth Pot June 2000, Pen-y-Ghent Pot July 2000, County-Lancaster Aug 2000, Skirwith Cave July 2000, County-Wretched Rabbit Nov 2000, Long Kin West Feb 2001, Cherry Tree Hole Jan 2001, Cherry Tree Hole Jan 2001, Bull Pot Jan 2001, Coppice Cave Feb 2001, Peak Cavern-Sumps Tour June 2001, Peak Cavern-Speedwell Via Colostomy June 2001, Peak Cavern-White River Series July 2001, Notts Pot Feb*

2001, Losers Pot [Discovery] Mar 2002, Lost John's March 2002, Loser's Pot Dive Support July 2002, Pippikin-Mistral Through June 2002.

SLATER, Nicholas James Douglas; *J1992, b1969,*
Probationary Meets; GG92.
Newsletter Rererences; *Simpson's Pot Oct 1993.*

SMALLWOOD, Keri; *J2001, b1982,*
Probationary Meets; Nenthead Mines, Notts Pot, Shuttleworth Cave.

SMITH, A; J?   *b1986,*

SMITH, Brian Junior; *J1972, b1944, d2014.*
Elected Honorary Membership 2012.
Probationary Meets; Black Shiver, Grange Rigg, Stream Passage-Flood Entrance.
Bulletin References; *Chourum Des Aiguilles 1973, Chourum Des Aiguilles 1974, Dog Tooth Inlet GG. [Digging] May 1975, Piaggia Bella 1975, Trou Qui Souffle 1975, New Entrance to Newby Moss Cave Dec 1976, Newby Moss Sink 3rd Shaft 1977, Cartilage Cave 1977, Strawberry Pot-May 1980, Farrer Hall extension 1980, Farrer Hall Choke 1970-76, Otter Hole 1977, Cnoc Nan Uamh & Uamh Nan Claig-Ionn Easter 1978, White Scar Cave Dec 31 1977, Grotte de Bury 1976 & 1977, Antro del Corchia, 1978, Gouffre Berger Aug 1980, Vercors Aug 1983, Leski Aug 1984, Tanne Du Bel Espoir-Diau Aug 1984, Grotte De Ramats Aug 1985, Mosquito Plane [Midge Hole Diving/ exploration] 1991, Soca Valley [Diving] Aug 1990, Kamniski Alps Aug 1988, Doux De Coly [Diving] July/Aug 1991.*
Newsletter References; *Black Shiver Pot Nov 1971, Grange Rigg-Christmas Pot Jan 1972, Swinsto Hole-KMC June 1972, Lancaster-Top Sink Oct 1973, Chourum des Aiguilles [BP] July 1974, Lost John's Hole Aug 1974, Swildons Oct 1974, Giants Hole Nov 1974, Juniper Gulf Dec 1974, Flood Entrance-Stream Passage Pot Exchange Feb 1975, Meregill April 1975, Birks Fell Cave April 1975, Short Drop-Gavel Pot 1976, Stream Passage-Flood Entrance Pot March 1976, Notts Pot March 1976, Black Shiver May 1976, Sleets Gill July 1976, Lost John's September 1976, Pippikin Hole Oct 1976, Christmas Pot Feb 1977, Swildons Hole April 1977, Top Sink-Pool Sink Sept 1977, Bull Pot of the Witches Nov 1977, Dale Head Pot April 1978, Rumbling Hole Aug 1978, Lost John's Sept 1978, Pillar Holes Sept 1978, Hall Pot Oct 1978, Top Sink-Lancaster and Back! Oct 1978, Lancaster-Ease Gill Nov 1978, Giants Hole Dec 1978, Uamh nan Claig-ionn April 1979, Lancaster Hole [Maple Leaf Pitch Team] 1980, Alum Pot June 1980, Gingling Hole July 1980, Black Shiver Sept 1980, Gouffre Berger Aug 1980, Ibbeth Peril Oct 1980, Mendip Oct 1980, Wookey Hole*

[Chamber20] June 1981, Pine Tree Hole June 1981, Longwood/August Swallet June 1981, Tanne de Bel Espoir-Grotte de la Diau Aug 1981, GG Main Chamber [Surveying Roof Stal] May 1982, Mendip weekend April 1983, Wookey 20 Dive April 1983, Giant's Hole Sept 1983, Peak Cavern Sept 1983, Short Drop Caver Dec 1983, Top Sink-County Pot April 1985, Mud Pot [Aborted Dive] May 1985, South East Pot Dive May 1985, Clapham, Bottoms-Voice connection with GG-Troubled Waters from Olympic Chamber in 1985, Sunset Hole & Southercales Pot June 1985, Hurtle Pot [8 Dives] Upstream Extension July/Aug 1985, Langstroth Pot Sept 1985, Brezno, Leska, Babizop Rakov Scojan and the Pit of Bears Yugoslavia Aug 1985, Gingling Hole Oct 1985, Eden Valley-Teesdale Walking Meet Oct 1985, Scotland Easter 1986, Scotland 1987, International Cave Diving Expedition-Dordogne Summer 1987, Lakes Walking Meet [Alternative Route] Oct 1987, Weathercote Cave April 1988, Coniston Mine July 1988, Ireby Fell [Diving] Oct 1988, Ireby Fell March 1990, Crooklands Walking Meet Sept 1993, Piaggia Bella July 1996, Grotta del Calgeron Aug 1997, Sunset Hole/Great Douk July 1998.

SMITH, Christopher; AKA: Smithy, Dad. *J1972, b1946,*

Member; WRCPC.

Probationary Meets; Christmas Pot, Flood Entrance-Stream Passage, Birks Fell.

Bulletin References; *Black Shiver Pot, Oct 1972, Juniper Gulf [Bolting] 1974, Marble Sink May 1976, Potts Moor Cave 1977, Newby Moss Sink 3rd Shaft 1977, Farrer Hall Choke 1970-76, Jean Pot [Discovery] 1979, Gouffre Berger Aug 1980, Abbisa Fighiera 1979, Cow Garth Cave [Exploration] 1982/84, M5 Pot [Dig] July 1984, Nettle Pot [Dig] July 1984, Giggel Rav Pot, [Dig/exploration]1990, Brackenbottom Pot, [Dig/exploration] 1989, 3B Parmilan Plateau Sept 1990, Doline Cave [Discovery] 1990, Giggel Rav Pot 1989.*

Newsletter References; *Grange Rigg-Christmas Pot Jan 1972, Birks Fell April 1972, Swinsto Hole [Down & Up] June 1972, Pen-y-Ghent Pot Aug 1972, Rift-Long Kin East Pot Sept 1972, Lancaster-Top Sink Oct 1973, Barbondale Pot Dec 1973, Lost John's Hole Aug 1974, Lancaster Hole Sept 1974, Gingling Hole Sept 1974, Juniper Gulf Dec 1974, Flood Entrance-Stream Passage Pot Exchange Feb 1975, Lost John's Nov 1975, Scrafton Pot April 1976, Pippikin Hole Oct 1976, Pippikin Pot Nov 1976, Short Drop-Gavel Dec 1977, Rumbling Hole Aug 1978, Pippikin-Link-Top Sink Oct 1979, Abisso Fighiera Italy Aug 1979, King Pot Feb 1980, Mossdale Caverns March 1980, Black Shiver Sept 1980, Gouffre Berger Aug 1980, Pasture Gill Pot*

June 1983, South Wales Aug 1983, County Pot March 1984, Langstroth Pot March 1984, Marble Sink March 1985, Rift Pot April 1985, Langstroth Pot Sept 1985, Rift-Large Pot Oct 1985, Pool Park Oct 1986, Magnetometer Pot Oct 1987, Haytime Hole 1990, South Wales Dec 1990, Gouffre Berger Aug 1992, Lakes Meet June 1992, Rowten Pot Feb 1994, Simpson's-Swinsto March 1994.

SMITH, Colin Geoffrey; *J2000, b1959,*

SMITH, Duncan; *J2007, b1955,*

Probationary Meets; Top Sink-Lancaster, OFD1&3, Lancaster-Link, Spain 07, Birks Fell, Vespers Pot.

Bulletin References; *Pyrenees 2006, Ordessa National Park 2007, New Zealand Jan 2011, Reseau de la Pierre Saint Martin Aug 2013, Sardinia Oct 2010, Doubs, France Aug 2009, Croesor-Rhosydd Feb 2009, Alderley Edge Mines Sept 2009.*

Newsletter References; *Rumbling Hole July 2006, Pyrenees Aug 2006, OFD 1&2 March 2007, Providence Pot-Dow Cave April 2007, Ordessa National Park Spanish Pyrenees 2007, Vesper Pot Jan 2008, King Pot Feb 2008, Notts Pot March 2008, Les Arcs Aug 2008, Lambrigg Fell—Tebay Walk Sept 2008, Overhanging Bastion Sept 2008, Helwith Bridge Show 2008, Robinsons Pot Sept 2008, Croesor-Rhosydd Feb 2009, Cow Pot April 2009, Lancaster-Wretched Rabbit June 2009, Scafell Central Buttress July 2009, Large-Rift Pot Exchange July 2009, Link Pot Sept 2009, Pool Sink-Easegill Dec 2009, Rumbling Hole March 2010, Keld Head [Diving] May 2010, Short Gill Rising [Digging] May 2010, Ireland May 2010, Daimler Hole Sept 2010, Su Bentu [Sardinia] Oct 2010, Su Palo [Sardinia] Oct 2010, Rampgill Level Oct 2010, Smallcleugh Mine Oct 2010, Wretched Rabbit-County Pot Nov 2010, Rowten Pot Nov 2010, Heron Pot Nov 2010, Lancaster-Wretched Rabbit Jan 2011, Committee Pot March 2011, Voldemort Pot March 2011, Peak Cavern March 2011, Middle Earth Green link System New Zealand North Island Feb 2011, Ogof Llyn Parc Sept 2011, Lancaster-Wretched Rabbit Jan 2012, Shuttleworth Pot Feb 2012, Notts Pot March 2012, Juniper Gulf March 2012, Box Freestone Mine March 2012, Swinsto-KMC March 2012, Boxhead-Lost John's July 2012, Croesor Rhosydd [Through] Oct 2012, Foux de Lauret [Herault] Sept 2012, Grotte du Banquier [Herault] Sept 2012, Aquamole Pot Dec 2012, Bull Pot of the Witches Jan 2013, Lost John's-Notts Pot March 2013, Pen-y-ghent Pot May 2013, Short Drop-Gavel Sept 2013, Clayton-le-Woods Victorian underground Reservoir Oct 2013, Lancaster-Wretched Rabbit Nov 2013, Magnetometer Pot Nov 2013, Dan Yr Ogof June 2014, Mistral Hole Nov 2014, The Borehole-Boundary Pot Feb 2015,*

Swildon's Hole Feb 2015, Lost John's-Notts 2 Sept 2015, Alderley Edge Mines Oct 2015, Water Icicle Oct 2015, Jingling Pot Dec 2015, Lost John's-Boxhead Pot March 2016, JH Mine-Peak Cavern March 2016, County Pot-Wretched Rabbit April 2016, Pool Sink-County Pot Oct 2016, Bull Pot of the Witches Jan 2017, Cow Pot Jan 2017, Short Drop-Gavel Pot Nov 2017, Lancaster Hole-Wretched Rabbit Nov 2018, Bull Pot of the Witches Jan 2019, County-Lancaster Jan 2019, Committee Pot Feb 2019, Wretched Rabbit-County Pot March 2019, County Pot-Lancaster Hole June 2019, Magnetometer Pot Sept 2019.

SMITH, Edward James; *J2012, b1970,*
Probationary Meets; *Yordas Pot, GG12, Calf Holes, Hurnell Moss Pot, Croesor Rhosydd.*
Bulletin References; *Reseau de la Pierre Saint Martin Aug 2013.*
Newsletter References; *Illusion Pot Dec 2011, Yordas Pot Feb 2012, Brackenbottom Pot, June 2012, Old Ing/Calf Holes-Browgill [Novice Trip] July 2012, Croesor Rhosydd [Through] Oct 2012, Link Pot Nov 2012, KMC Toyland Nov 2012, Titan-JH April 2013, Sell Gill April 2013, Skosca Cave Feb 2013, White Scar Cave July 2014, Dowkabottom Cave July 2014, Fairy Holes Sept 2014, Nenthead Mines Sept 2014, High & Great Douk Dec 2014, Goatchurch Aven Feb 2015, Skirwith Cave Feb 2015, Yordas/KMC March 2015, Sell Gill June 2015, Great and High Douk June 2015, Poll Dudh June 2015, St Catherine's1-Fisher St June 2015, Faunarooska June 2015, Calf Holes [Novice Trip] July 2015, Goyden Sept 2015, Alderley Edge Mines Oct 2015, KMC [Novice Trip] Jan 2016, Notts 2 Jan 2016, Boulby Potash Mine Jan 2016, Bull Pot of the Witches Jan 2017, Grampian Meet Aug 2017, Mongo Gill Sept 2018.*

SMITH, Emma; *J2000, b1986,*
Newsletter References; *Scotland 1987, Lakes Walking Meet [Alternative Route] Oct 1987, Gouffre Berger Aug 1992, Crooklands WalkingMeet Sept 1993, Sunset Hole / Great Douk July 1998.*

SMITH, Gordon; *J1964, b1939,*
Probationary Meets; Giant's Hole, Dow-Providence, Lancaster.

SMITH, John Michael; *J1959, b1941,*
Expelled from club – non payment of subs Dec 1962.
Bulletin References; *Antler Pot Feb 1965.*

SMITH, J. R; *J1965,*

Smith, Jordan; Temporary Membership 18-03-2013. Sell Gill Dec 2012.

SMITH, June; [née Greenwood] *J1974, b1950.*
Probationary Meets; Dow Cave, Sunset Hole, GG74.
Bulletin References; *Chourum Des Aiguilles 1973, Chourum Des Aiguilles 1974, Grotte de Bury 1976 & 1977, Gouffre Berger Aug 1980, Brants Gill Head [Dive/Dig] 1988-1991.*
Newsletter References; *Dow Cave Feb 1974, Chourum Des Aiguilles 1974, Lost John's Hole Aug 1974, Gingling Hole Sept 1974, Swildons Oct 1974, Giants Hole Nov 1974, Lost John's September 1976, Bull Pot of the Witches Dec 1976, Lakes Walk Esk House March 1977, Top Sink-Pool Sink Sept 1977, Rumbling Hole Aug 1978, Gouffre Berger Aug 1980, Brezno, Leska, Babizop Rakov Scojan and the Pit of Bears Yugoslavia Aug 1985, Eden Valley-Teesdale Walking Meet Oct 1985, Scotland Easter 1986, Scotland 1987, Lakes Walking Meet [Alternative Route] Oct 1987, Calf Holes Jan 1988, Gouffre Berger Aug 1992, Crooklands Walking Meet Sept 1993.*

SMITH, Lawrence William; *J1951, b1924,*
Bulletin References; *Clapham Cave 1951, Lost John's July Simpson's Pot 1952.*

SMITH, Malcolm; *J2009, b1955,*
Newsletter References; *Long Churns July 2009, Roger Kirk Caves Oct 2009, Dowkerbottom Cave Oct 2009, Sell Gill Nov 2009, Tatham Wife Hole Feb 2010, Swinsto Hole Feb 2010, Hurnell Moss Pot April 2010, Easter Grotto Photo Trip July 2010, Lost John's-Boxhead Pot Sept 2010, Sell Gill [Training Meet] Oct 2010, Rowten Pot Nov 2010, Yordas Pot April 2011, Illusion Pot June 2011, Sunset Hole June 2011, Hunt Pot-Shrapnel Pot June 2011, Sell Gill July 2011, Swinsto Hole Nov 2011, Yordas Pot Oct 2011, Shuttleworth Pot Feb 2012, Yordas Pot Feb 2012, Notts Pot March 2012, Sell Gill Holes March 2012, Great Douk April 2012, Hardrawkin Pot April 2012, Boxhead-Lost John's July 2012, Committee Pot Sept 2012, Hardrawkin Pot/High Douk [Solo] Sept 2012, Aquamole Pot Dec 2012, Sell Gill Dec 2012, Great Douk [Novice Trip] March 2013, Top Sink-Lancaster Hole March 2013, Giant's Hole April 2013, Short Drop-Gavel Sept 2013, Heron Pot Sept 2013, Skosca Cave Feb 2013, Sell Gill Holes April 2014, Dowkabottom Cave July 2014, Shuttleworth Pot Oct 2014, Yordas Pot Oct 2014, Aquamole Dec 2014, High & Great Douk Dec 2014, Bull Pot of the Witches Jan 2015, Pasture Gill Jan 2015, County Pot Feb 2015, Sell Gill Holes Feb 2015, Yordas Pot March 2015, Alum Pot March 2015, Aquamole Pot March 2015, Sell Gill June 2015, Sunset Hole Oct*

2015, Darnbrook Pot March 2016, Katnot Cave/Thorne Cave [Novice Trip] May 2016, Sell Gill June 2016, Bull Pot of the Witches Jan 2017, Old Ing-Birkwith July 2017, Sell Gill Sept 2017, High Douk Holes Feb 2018, High Douk May 2019.

SMITH, Martin David; AKA: Billy Whizz. J1992, b1955,
Member; OUCC.
Probationary Meets; GG92, Flood Entrance-Jib Tunnel, Hurnel Moss, Washfold Pot, LKW.
Bulletin References; Tete Sauvage July 1995, Helgeland [Norway] 1992/94. Losers Pot [Discovery] Mar 2002, Hensler's Pot [Discovery] 1999-2003, Hensler's Pot [First Through Trip to GG] May 2003, Christmas Cracker Pot [Discovery] 2001, Parkinson's Pot [Discovery] July 2003, Corky's Pot [Discovery] 2003–2005, DeepWell [Diving]2000–2003, Pay Sank [Discovery] 2005, Klondike Pot Digging/Exploration 2004-2007, Pyrenees 2006, Doubs, France Aug 2009,
Newsletter References; Pikedaw Calamine Caverns March 1992, Alum Pot Nov 1993, Ireby Fell Feb 1993, Bagshaw Caverns Oct 1993, Brown Hills Pot March 1994, Cherry Tree Hole Feb 1996, South Wales April 1996, Bull Pot Dec 1996, Boxhead Pot March 1997, Deep Well [Dive Support] May 1997, Pippikin Hole Sept 1997, Out Sleets Beck Pot Jan 1998, Wades-Bar Feb 1998, Short Gill Cave Jan 1999, County-Pool Exchange Feb 1999, King Pot March 1999, Allt Nan Uamh Feb 1999, Birks Fell June 1999, Fat Finger Millennium Party, Pippikin Pot Nov 1999, Lancaster Round Trip March 2000, GG-Mill Hill [Dive support] May 2000, Long Kin West Feb 2001, Ingleborough Cave Digging 2001, Hensler's Pot Digging Dec 2001, Losers Pot [Discovery] Mar 2002, Lost John's March 2002, Hensler's High Aven voice connection June 2002, Notts Pot Sept 2002, Crackpot Cave [Photgraphic Meet] Jan 2003, Corky's Digging Team 2004, Deep Well Dive [Support] GG04, Croll's Cavern Dec 2004, Pay Sank Exploration Sept 2005, Coppice Cave-Ling Gill Jan 2006, Pyrenees Aug 2006, Helwith Bridge Show 2008, Trou du Garde-Creux de la Cavale - Bauges Aug 2012.

SMITH, Philip George; J1976, b1957,
Probationary Meets; Lancaster, Alum Pot, Heron Pot, Sunset Hole, GG76, Whitsun Series, Bar Pot.

SMITH, Rachel P; J2010, b1976,
Probationary Meets; Bar Pot, Rowten Pot, Stream Passage Pot, Flood Entrance, Disappointment Pot, Corky's, Dyhedral.

SMITH, Ronald Henry; J1965, b1941,

Probationary Meets; Calf Holes, Old Ing, Dow Cave.

SMITH, Stephen; J1974, b1954,
Probationary Meets; Lost John's, Lancaster, Agen Allwedd, Pasture Gill, Pen-y-Ghent Pot, County Pot.
Newsletter References; Birks Fell Cave April 1975, County Pot Oct 1975, Pasture Gill Cave July 1976.

SMITH, Susan;-See Ryall.

SMITHSON, Paul; J2000, b1969,
Probationary Meets; Brackenbottom Pot.
Member; DCC.
Newsletter References; Rowten Pot Dec 2000.

SMYTH, Stephen Andrew; J2004, b1964,
Bulletin References; Ordessa National Park 2007,
Newsletter References; Sell Gill Holes Feb 2004, Swinsto Hole-KMC Feb 2004, Runscar Cave Sept 2004, Dowkabottom Cave Oct 2004, Committee Pot Nov 2004, Bar Pot Jan 2005, Giant's Hole Jan 2005, Lancaster Hole April 2005, Ireby Fell Caverns Nov 2005, Bull Pot Jan 2006, Coniston Copper Mines Oct 2006, Hunt Pot Nov 2006, Jingling Pot Dec 2006, Committee Pot Dec 2006, Aquamole Pot Jan 2007, Derbyshire Meet Jan 2007, OFD 2 March 2007, Ordessa National Park Spanish Pyrenees 2007, Washfold Pot Dec 2007, Aygill Caverns Feb 2008, Robinsons Pot Sept 2008, Lower Long Churn Nov 2008, Simpson's-KMC Dec 2008, Aygill Caverns Jan 2009, OFD Top Ent June 2009, Link Pot Sept 2009, SRT Training Ingleborough Hall Oct 2009, Sell Gill Nov 2009, Calf Holes [Novice Trip] Jan 2010, Tatham Wife Hole Feb 2010, Rumbling Hole March 2010, Alum Pot July 2010, Long Churns [Training Meet] Nov 2010, Titan-Peak Cavern March 2011, Peak Cavern March 2011, Long Churn [Novice Trip] March 2011, Notts Pot March 2012, Fairy Holes Sept 2014, Lancaster-County Jan 2019.

SNAPE, Noel; J2010, b1983,

SOLIMAN, Martyn John; J2013, b1956,
Member; CCPC, WRCPC.
Bulletin References; Reseau de la Pierre Saint Martin Aug 2013, Death's Head-Lost John's-Committee Pot Nov 2018.

SOWERBY, Gillian; J1991, b1962,
Probationary Meets; Dow Cave, GG89, St Catherines-Doolin.

SPARKES, A; J1982,

SPARKES, C; J1983, b1964.

SPARKES, Gary S; AKA: Sparkey. *J1983, b1964,*
Probationary Meets; Ireland, Swinsto, Link Pot.
Newsletter References; *Gavel Pot Dec 1980, Ingleborough Cave Oct 1982, Swinsto-Valley Entrance April 1983, Gingling Hole June 1983, Link Pot July 1983, Hurnel Moss Pot July 1983, Short Drop Caver Dec 1983, County Pot March 1984, New Goyden Pot April 1984, Sell Gill July 1985, Pippikin Pot Nov 1986.*

SPEIGHT, Christopher; AKA: Spacy. *J1991, b1958,*
Probationary Meets; GG91/2, France-91, Trois Beta, Trou de Glaz, Stream Passage, Disappointment Pot, Bar Pot.
Bulletin References; *36 Parmilan Plateau Sept 1990, Deep Well [Diving support] May 1992, Albania 1992.*
Newsletter References; *Dowbergill Passage Unknown 1990, Pippikin March 1992, Out Slets Beck CaveJune 1992, Lakes Meet June 1992, Rift pot June 1993, Cow Pot March 1993.*

SPEIGHT, Kevin; *J2011, b1982,*

SPENCER, Noel; AKA: Nolly. *J1958, b1941,*
Bulletin References; *Gaping Gill Meet 1960, Pen-y-ghent Pot July 1960,*
Newsletter References; *Digging near Owl Hole Dec 1958, Clapham Bottoms dig Aug 1959, Lost John's Sept 1959.*

SPILLANE, Adam Dominic; AKA: The Hare. *J2009, b1972,*
Probationary Meets; OFD Top-1, Giants Hole, Brackenbottom Pot, GG10, Rowten Pot, Lancaster Hole-Wretched Rabbit.
Member; SUSS [1990-Present], NCC [1996-Present]
Expeditions; Slovenia-SUSS, Crete-SUSS [x2] China-Chongqing, Malasia-Mulu, Papua New Guinea-Nakanai, Australia-Nulllabor, New Zealand-Mount Arthur, Indonesia-East Kalimantan. Vietnam-Quang Binh [x11], Ha Giang, Central Provinces. Matienzo [x2], Dachstein [x2], Tresviso
Holidays; Vercors [x4], Complexe De La Pierre Saint Martin, Slovenia.
Notable Achievements; Original explorer of Hang Son Doong [Phong Nha-Kẻ Bàng National Park-Vietnam] 2009. Member of Derbyshire Cave Rescue Organisation, Committee member BPC.
Main Activities; Caving, Walking, Road Cycling, Scuba Diving.
Famous for; Making a career out of caving.
Newsletter References; *Long Churn/Dolly Tubs [Novice trip] Feb 2010, Hull Pot [Filming with the BBC] Oct 2010, Pillar Holes Oct 2010, Rowten Pot Nov 2010, Lancaster-Wretched Rabbit Jan 2011, Dow Cave Oct 2012, Brackenbottom Pot Nov 2012,*
Wizard's Chasm Jan 2013, White Keld Sump 5 Location [Diving Support] Feb 2013.

SPILLETT, Peter; *J1986, b1961,*
Rejoined 2013.
Member; UWFRA.
Bulletin References; *Giggel Rav Pot, [Dig/Exploration] 1990, Brackenbottom Pot, [Dig/Exploration] 1989, Trou De Glaz Aug 1989, Giggel Rav Pot 1989, Brackenbottom Pot 1989, Tanne De Bel Espoir-La Diau Parmilan 1991, Doline Cave [Discovery] 1990, Deep Well [Diving support] May 1992, Albania 1992, Spluga Della Preta Sept 1992, Lava Tubes Tenerife 1992.*
Newsletter References; *Pippikin Pot Nov 1986, Pen-y-Gent Pot March 1987, Matienzo July/Aug 1987, Coniston Mine July 1988, Big Meanie-Death's Head Nov 1989, Pikedaw Calamine Cavern March 1992, Swaledale Weekend Oct 1992, Coniston Mines Weekend Sept 1993, Easegill April 1997, Deep Well [Dive Support] May 1997, Rowten Pot Dec 1998, Marble Steps Dec 1998, Lancaster-Wretched Rabbit Jan 1999, Swinsto-KMC March 1999, Grange Rigg [Locating] March 1999.*

SPILLETT, Sara; *J1986, b1965,*
Rejoined 2013.
Member; UWFRA.
Bulletin References; *Giggel Rav Pot, [Dig/exploration] 1990, Brackenbottom Pot, [Dig/exploration] 1989, Trou De Glaz Aug 1989, Giggel Rav Pot 1989, Brackenbottom Pot 1989, Tanne De Bel Espoir-La Diau Parmilan 1991, Doline Cave [Discovery] 1990, Deep Well [Diving support] May 1992, Albania 1992, Spluga Della Preta Sept 1992, Lava Tubes Tenerife 1992.*
Newsletter References; *Ireby Fell Pot Oct 1986, Pippikin Pot Nov 1986, Pen-y-Gent Pot March 1987, Matienzo July/Aug 1987, Coniston Mine July 1988, Big Meanie-Death's Head Nov 1989, Pikedaw Calamine Cavern March 1992, Swaledale Weekend Oct 1992, Coniston Mines Weekend Sept 1993, Cherry Tree Hole Jan 1994, Easegill April 1997.*

SPOORS, Mark; *J2000, b1958,*

SPOORS, Nigel; *J1997, b1958,*

SPROATES, Samantha; *J2009, b1972,*
Probationary Meets; Churns, Dow Cave, KMC.
Member; Herts Canoe Club.
Bulletin References; *Alderley Edge Mines Sept 2009.*
Newsletter References; *Alderley Edge Mines Sept 2009.*

SQUIRE, Jamie; *Temporary Membership 28-07-2012.*

STABLES, Brendan; *J1997, b1939,*

STACEY, Paul; *J1952, b1936, d2005.*
Suspended from club Dec 1959.
Bulletin References; *Simpson's Pot July 1953, Notts Pot Sept 1953.*
Newsletter References; *Disappointment Pot to Main Shaft winch June 1957, Leader Main Shaft to de-tackle Disappointment via Hensler's crawl [Hensler star] Whit 1958.*

STAFFORD, Matthew William; **AKA: Matt.** *J2000, b1974,*
Probationary Meets; Bull Pot, LKW, Coppice Cave.
Newsletter References; *Bull Pot March 2000, Coppice Cave April 2000, Long Kin West April 2000, Peak Cavern Sumps Tour June 2001, Lost John's March 2002, KMC Photographic Trip Nov 2002, Swinsto [Through] Jan 2003, Crackpot Cave [Photgraphic Meet] Jan 2003, Bull Pot of the Witches Jan 2008, Magnetometer Pot April 2010, Hurnell Moss Pot April 2010.*

STAMP, Maria Ellen; AKA: Maz. *J1998, b1959,*
Probationary Meets; GG03, Bar Pot.
Rejoined 2015.
Notable Achievements; Holding up the roof in Fat Finger Dig.
Main Activities; Caving.
Famous for; Having a very loud domestic argument with Col [*her husband, see below*] while they were both wedged tight and incapable of moving in Horrock's Crawl [*GG*] It is still unclear if the argument was regarding Col wearing a white laboratory coat [*as part of a soap powder experiment*] or their mutual inability to offer assistance. Horrock's Crawl was subsequently always referred to as Tourettes Passage.
Newsletter References; *Pippikin Pot Nov 1999, Sell Gill Jan 2000, Alum Pot Jan 2000, Bull Pot March 2000, Bar Pot Nov 2000, Bull Pot Jan 2001, Coppice Cave Feb 2001, Ingleborough Cave Digging 2001, Loser's Pot June 2002, Sunset Hole Jan 2003, Sunset Hole July 2006, Magnetometer Pot April 2010, Ribblehead Caves April 2010, Hull Pot [Filming with the BBC] Oct 2010, Hoffman Kilns Stainforth Nov 2015.*

STAMP, Raymond Colin; *J1997, b1956,*
Probationary Meets; GG98, Stream Passage Pot, Bar Pot, Flood Entrance, Alum Pot, Pippikin Pot, Swinsto Hole.
Rejoined 2015.

Notable Achievements; Digging in Fat Finger, and Losers N° 6 [*New cave*]
Main Activities; Caving.
Famous for; Having a very loud domestic argument with MAZ [*his wife, see above*] while they were both wedged tight and incapable of moving in Horrock's Crawl [*GG*] It is still unclear if the argument was regarding Col wearing a white laboratory coat [*as part of a soap powder experiment*] or their mutual inability to offer assistance. Horrock's Crawl was subsequently always referred to as Tourettes Passage.
Newsletter References; *Alum Pot [Training Meet] July 1997, Wades-Bar Feb 1998, Pippikin Pot Nov 1999, Sell Gill Jan 2000, Alum Pot Jan 2000, Bull Pot March 2000, Bar Pot Nov 2000, Bull Pot Jan 2001, Coppice Cave Feb 2001, Ingleborough Cave Digging 2001, Sunset Hole Jan 2003, Sunset Hole July 2006, Magnetometer Pot April 2010, Ribblehead Caves April 2010, Hull Pot [Filming with the BBC] Oct 2010, Hoffman Kilns Stainforth Nov 2015*

STANSFIELD, Ernest Alan; *J1958, b1940,*
Member of the Heath Grammar School contingent.
Bulletin References; *Lower Stream Passage Pot May 1959, Involved with building electron ladders, 1950/60's.*

STEAD, Graham; *J2000, b1959,*
Newsletter References; *Lancaster Round Trip March 2000.*

STELCEL, Wayne Hugh; *J1996, b1956,*

STEPHENSON, P. T; *J1982,*

STEVENS, Susan; *J1989, b1960,*

STEWART, Andy; *J2006, b1964,*
Newsletter References; *Long Kin West Dec 2005, Titan Shaft Feb 2006, New Rift Pot Nov 2006, Nick Pot Dec 2006, Derbyshire Meet Jan 2007, King Pot Feb 2008, JH-Peak Cavern via White River Series March 2008, Otter Hole June 2008, Lost John's March 2009, Large-Rift Pot Exchange July 2009, Simpson's Pot Jan 2012, JH-Titan April 2013, Lancaster-County Pot Nov 2014, Lancaster-Wretched Rabbit Nov 2014, The Borehole-Boundary Pot Feb 2015, Vulcan Pot Oct 2018.*

STEWART, Kirsty; [née Bamber] *J2012, b1982,*

STEWART, William; *J2012, b1981,*
Newsletter References; *Magnetometer Pot April 2010.*

STOCK, Joseph; *J2015,*

STOCK, Nicola; See Brooks.

STOCKDALE, Alan Jerry; *J1962,*
Member; UWFRA.

STORRY, Amber; *J2013, b2007,*
Newsletter References; *Salthill Quarry Geology Walk Nov 2008, Brow Gill-Calf Holes [and back] May 2010, Wretched Rabbit-Lancaster Nov 2013, KMC Sept 2014, Yordas/KMC March 2015, Great and High Douk June 2015, Goyden Sept 2015, Skirwith Cave [Novice Trip] Jan 2016, [Novice Trip] Dec 2016, Bruntscar Cave Jan 2017, KMC [Novice Trip] Jan 2018, Long Churn [Childrens Meet] April 2018.*

STORRY, Caitlin; *J2007, b2000,*
Bulletin References; *Reseau de la Pierre Saint Martin Aug 2013,*
Newsletter References; *Thistle & Runscar Caves Sept 2006, Great Douk Feb 2007, Dismal Hill/Old Ing Feb 2007, Heron Pot March 2008, Valley Entrance June 2008, Dowkabottom Cave Sept 2008, Salthill Quarry Geology Walk Nov 2008, Lower Long Churn Nov 2008, Ribblehead Caves April 2010, Brow Gill-Calf Holes [and back] May 2010, Mistral Hole Aug 2010, Wretched Rabbit-County Pot Nov 2010, Sleets Gill April 2011, Long Churn [Novice Trip] June 2011, Shuttleworth Pot Feb 2012, Yordas Pot Feb 2012, White Scar Cave July 2012, Lancaster-Wretched Rabbit Nov 2013, KMC Sept 2014, Sell Gill Holes Sept 2015, Goyden Sept 2015, Skirwith Cave [Novice Trip] Jan 2016.*

STORRY, Jeremy Nicholas; *J2006, b1961,*
Probationary Meets; Heron Pot, Marilyn, KMC.
Newsletter References; *Thistle & Runscar Caves Sept 2006, Great Douk Feb 2007, Dismal Hill-Old Ing Feb 2007, Heron Pot March 2008, Salthill Quarry Geology Walk Nov 2008, Long Churns July 2009, Brow Gill-Calf Holes [and back] May 2010, Long Churn [Novice Trip] June 2011, Lancaster-Wretched Rabbit Nov 2013.*

STORRY, Rachel; See Martin.

STOTT, Christopher; *J2008, b1960,*
Probationary Meets; Bull Pot o t Witches, Old Ing, Dismal Hill, Birkwith, Simpson's-KMC, Sell Gill, Bar Pot, Stream Passage Pot, Miss Graces Lane Cave, Hell Hole, Whitemore, Brackenbottom Pot.
Newsletter References; *Washfold Pot July 1957 ?, Bull Pot of the Witches Jan 2008, Dismall Hill-Old Ing Jan 2008, Miss Graces Lane June 2008, P8 April 2009, Hurnell Moss Pot April 2010, Daimler Hole*

Sept 2010, Lost John's-Boxhead Pot Sept 2010, Shuttleworth Pot Feb 2012.

STOYLES, Thomas Raymond; **AKA: Farmer.** *J1964, b1945, d2012.*
Probationary Meets; Lancaster, Marble Steps, Bar Pot.
Bulletin References; *Buttertubs /flood Entrance/ Sell Gill/ May 1964, Ashberry Windpit Aug 1964, Jamaica 1965/66, Work in Ingleborough Cave 1968, Cold Streak Mine 1969, Chourum Des Aiguilles 1973, M5 Pot [Dig] July 1984,*
Newsletter References; *Kirkdale Cave April 1965, Ryedale Easter 1965, Heron Pot March 1971, Crackpot Cave March 1971, Hallucination Aven-Surface Location May 1983, Scotland Easter 1986, Scotland 1987, Crooklands WalkingMeet Sept 1993.*

STRACHEN, Ian Barry; *J1963, b1947,*
Probationary Meets; Short Drop, Pen-y-Ghent Long Churn, Stump Cross Cavern.

STURGESS, Jessica M; *J2017, b1996,*
Probationary Meets; Meregill, Illusion Pot, Ireby Fell Cavern, GG17.
Member; UNCC.
Newsletter References; *P5 [Radio Locating] June 2018, Lost River Sump [Dive Support] May 2019, Aquamole Pot Nov 2019.*

SULLIVAN, Timothy Patrick; **AKA: Digger's Labourer, Chemo Tim.** *J2003, b1941,*
Probationary Meets; GG03-09, Generator Pot [Digging x 30]
Member; NB.
Bulletin References; *Parkinson's Pot [Discovery] July 2003, Corky's Pot [Discovery] 2003-2005, Pay Sank [Discovery 2005, Klondike Pot Digging/Exploration 2004-2007, Restoration of Brown Hill Pot entrance Nov 2012-Feb 2013, Restoration of Clapham Bottoms Pot Entrance June 2013, Witches Cave location and Dig Sept 2010, OBJ Connection to GG May 2010.*
Newsletter References; *Corky's Digging Team 2004, Klondyke Pot Digging Team Jan 2005, Pay Sank Exploration Sept 2005, Pay Sank Breakthrough team Nov 2005, Committee Pot July 2007, Hidden Earth Tewkesbury, Support Oct 2007, Pay Sank Feb 2009, Aquamole Remediation March 2009, Nettle Pot July 2009, Gunnerfleet Caves Clear Up July 2009, Stile Repairs-Diccan and Long Churn 2010, Rebuild of stile at Browgill July 2010, Yordas Cave ConserervationAug 2010, Blue John Aug 2012, Haw Bank or Wet Grooves Mine Feb 2013, Fells End Pots Feb 2013, Ibbeth Peril [Twice] March 2013, Fairy Holes April 2014, Providence Pot Restoration*

Nov 2014, GG Track repairs Feb 2017, Hartley Quarry Cave Jan 2018, Hells Bells Hole [Dive Support] Feb 2020.

SUNDERLAND, Norman; *J1987, b1945,*
Probationary Meets; Pippikin, GG87/8.
Newsletter References; *South Wales Nov 1988,*

SUNTER, John Robert; AKA: Long John. *J1981, b1950,*
Member; LDSA.
Probationary Meets; Simpson's-Swinsto, Derbyshire Meet, Goyden/New Goyden, Alum-Diccan Pot.
Motley.
Newsletter References; *Scrafton Pot April 1980, Alum Pot March 1981, New Goyden Pot April 1981, Mud Hall GG [BBC Filming Blue Peter] May 1981, Sunset Hole July 1981, Gingling Hole Rescue July 1981, Dow–Providence Sept 1981, Link Pot Sept 1981, Lost John's Feb 1982, King Pot April 1982, Providence–Dow Cave July 1982.*

SUTCLIFFE, Michael Preston; *J1957, b1938, d2010.*
Newsletter References; *Bar Pot Dec 1957.*

SUTCLIFFE, Walter Preston; *J1950, b1906, d1961.*
Bulletin References; *Lost John's July 1951.*
Newsletter References; *Beck Head Stream Passage 1951, Bar Pot Dec 1957.*

SUTTON, Christopher; AKA: CJ. *J2013, b1993,*

SWAINE, Lawrence; *J1949,*
Bulletin References; *Flood Entrance July 1949.*

SWALE, Eric H; *J1949, b1923,*
Probationary Meets; Alum Pot, Marble Steps.
Bulletin References; *Pen-y-Ghent Pot 2ⁿᵈ Rescue 11ᵗʰ June 1951, CPC member fell and sustained injuries. Eglin's Hole September 1950, Easter Camp GG 1951, Bull Pot of the Witches April 1951, Pikedaw Calamine Mine Aug 1953, Clapham Cave Sept 1951, Lost John's July 1951, Simpson's Pot July 1953, Flood Entrance Pot March 1954.*

SWALLOW, Andrew; *J2009, b1972,*
Probationary Meets; Bar Pot, Sell Gill, Juniper Gulf, GG09, Lancaster Hole.
Newsletter References; *Bull Pot of the Witches Jan 2013.*

SWEET, Alan Elliot; *J1949,*
Bulletin References; *Flood Entrance July 1949, Clapham Cave Sept 1951.*

SYKES, Andrew William; *J2010, b2000,*

Notable Achievements; First Caving trip Crackpot Cave August 2008, First SRT trip Short Drop-Gavel September 2013.
Main Activities; Caving [Assistant leader Scout caving trips]
Famous for; Being over enthusiastic moving beer barrels and boxes at GG meets.

SYKES, Anthony; *J1981, b1965,*
Newsletter References; *Lost John's Sept 1978, Mendip Oct 1980, KMC Sept 2014, Bull Pot of the Witches Jan 2015, Goyden Sept 2015, Heron Pot Nov 2015, Sell Gill April 2016, Marble Steps Nov 2016, Red Moss Pot [Novice Trip] April 2017, Sell Gill Sept 2017, Brackenbottom Pot Dec 2017, Ingleborough Cave Oct 2018, CherryTree Hole Oct 2018, Stump Cross Caverns Nov 2018.*

SYKES, Peter John; AKA: Moley, Beaker. *J1993, b1965,*
Probationary Meets; GG93, Crackpot Hole, Cherry Tree Hole, Gingling, Langstroth Pot.
Member; NWCC-1995-1997, GCC-1996-2004, CSCA 1994-2008.
Club expeditions; Complexe de la Pierre Saint Martin 1995.
Notable Achievements; First caving trip-Long Churn Feb 1992, Des Crowley rescue from Large-Rift Pot April 1994, Discovered Ogof Siamber Wen [With GCC] 1996.
Main Activities; Caving [Assistant leader Scout caving trips]
Famous for; Unsubtle when drunk, The Cliona incident. Remembrance Pot July 1994, Tete Sauvage July 1995.
Newsletter References; *Hodge Close Sept 1993, Lost John's Jan 1995, Lancaster Hole March 1995, Peak Cavern Nov 1995, Pool Sink-Lancaster Hole Dec 1995, County-Lancaster Hole Oct 1995, Big Meanie-Deaths Head Jan 1996, Cherry Tree Hole Feb 1996, Long Kin West March 1996, South Wales April 1996, Diccan Pot March 1996, Cow Pot July 1996, Top Sink-Lancaster July 1996, Nettle Pot Oct 1996, Swinsto-Simpson's 1996, Bull Pot Dec 1996, Mistral Hole Nov 1996, Hunt Pot Feb 1997, Marble Steps March 1997, Easegill April 1997, Boxhead Pot March 1997, Red Moss Pot April 1997, Deep Well [Dive Support] May 1997, Alum Pot [Training Meet] July 1997, Batty Wife Cave Aug 1997, Easgill Aug 1997, Rowten Pot/Jingling Pot July 1997, Wades-Bar Feb 1998, Barclays Lode Wales July 1998, Nent Head-Brewery Shaft Oct 1998, Allt Nan Uamh Feb 1999, Christmas Cracker Pot Oct 2001, Lost John's Hole March 2002, Lost John's Hole Sept 2005, Aquamole Pot Nov 2009, KMC Sept 2014, Juniper Gulf Oct 2014, Bull Pot of the Witches Jan 2015, The Borehole-Boundary Pot Feb 2015, Goyden Sept*

2015, Heron Pot Nov 2015, County Pot-Wretched Rabbit April 2016, Sell Gill April 2016, Death's Head-Big Meanie Sept 2016, Simpson's Pot-KMC Dec 2016, Marble Steps Nov 2016, Alum Pot Dec 2016, Heron Pot [Novice trip] April 2017, Red Moss Pot [Novice Trip] April 2017, Devis Hole/Mine July 2017, Burtersett Quarry/Mine July 2017, Alum/Long Churns June 2017, Sell Gill Sept 2017, Robinson's Pot Sept 2017, Short Drop-Gavel Pot Nov 2017, Lancaster Hole Oct 2017,
Brackenbottom Pot Dec 2017, Top Sink-Wretched Rabbit Jan 2018, Jingling Pot Feb 2018, Voldemort Pot-Notts 2 Feb 2018, Notts Pot Sept 2018, Ingleborough Cave Oct 2018, Cherry Tree Hole Oct 2018, Stump Cross Caverns Nov 2018, Wizard's Chasm Dec 2018, Wretched Rabbit-Lancaster Hole Dec 2018, Pikledaw Calamine Cavern Dec 2018, Lancaster-County Jan 2019, Lost River Sump [Dive Support] May 2019, Bull Pot Oct 2019, Pool Sink-Boundary Pot Nov 2019, Sell Gill Nov 2019, Aquamole Pot Nov 2019, Pool Sink-Wretched Rabbit Feb 2020, Sunset Hole Feb 2020.

SZKUTA, Ryszard A. J; AKA: Rusty Scooter. *J1977, b1953,*
Newsletter References; *Lost John's Nov 1975, Short Drop–Gavel Dec 1977, Winner of the 1983 Christmas Dinner Golden Headgear prize.*

T

TAYLOR, David Christopher; *J1998, b1980,*
Probationary Meets; GG98, Digging.
Newsletter References; *Pen-y-Ghent Pot April 1977.*

TAYLOR, Julie; *J2006, b1969,*
Probationary Meets; Old Ing, Birkwith.

TAYLOR, Neil; *J1958, b1940,*
Bulletin References; *Digging in Owl Hole Dig N° 2 1958, Gaping Gill Meet [Diverting P5 water] 1960.*
Newsletter References; *Bar Pot Nov 1958.*

TAYLOR, Teena Douglas; *J2014, b1962,*

TEALE, A. L; *J1954,*

TEALE, Trevor;

TEMPEST, Anita Susan; AKA: Suet. *J2008, b1954,*
Claims no achievements underground, always in surface support at Gaping Gill, now more a social member than an active member.

TEMPEST, David Brandon; *J1997, b1982,*
Probationary Meets; Easegill.
Rejoined 2013.
Newsletter References; *Easgill Aug 1997.*

TEMPEST, Kayrine Helen; *J2013, b1985,*
Probationary Meets; GG12, GG13.

TEMPEST, Roy; *J1997, b1947,*
Newsletter References; *Alum Pot [Training Meet] July 1997, Easgill Aug 1997, Notts Pot August 1999, Bull Pot of the Witches Jan 2013.*

TENNANT, Lynn Diane; *J1994, b1955,*

TERRY, J. A; *J1981,*

TETLEY, Conrad M; *J2007,*
Newsletter References; *Dismal Hill/Old Ing Feb 2007, Cwm Dwr March 2007, Heron Pot March 2008, Valley Entrance June 2008, Dowkabottom Cave Sept 2008, Cherry Tree Hole Oct 2008.*

THERL, B. A; *J1955,*

THOMAS, Alan; *J1963, b1943,*
Resigned Sept 1965.
Probationary Meets; Little Hull Pot, Carlswark Caverns, South Wales.
Bulletin References; *Old Cote Pot April 1963.*

THOMAS, Caroline Rachel; *J2010 b1978,*

THOMAS, Michael; *J1960, b1944,*
Probationary Meets; Alum Pot, Bull Pot, Sell Gill.
Re joined in 1965.
Bulletin References; *Helvelyn Dec 1965, Alum Pot/Diccan Pot 1966, The Dales Way 1973.*
Newsletter References; *Short Drop / Gavel Oct 1969.*

THOMAS, Vaughan; *J1985, b1978,*
Denied full membership Oct 1986.
Newsletter References; *Sunset Hole & Southercales Pot June 1985, Langstroth Pot Sept 1985,*

THOMPSON, Alan Philip; *J1960, b1940,*
Probationary Meets; Lost John's, Rift Pot-Long Kin East, Rowten Pot.

Bulletin References; *Lost John's March 1960.*

THOMPSON, Christopher; *J2018, b1988,*
Newsletter References; *Old Ing-Birkwith July 2017.*

THOMPSON, John Derek; *J1954, b1928, d2015.*
Famous for the architectural design of the changes to Brackenbottom 1963.
Bulletin References; *Clapham Cave June 1954 Survey Team Leader], Little Hull Pot July 1954, Bull Pot of the Witches July 1955, Bull Pot [Kingsdale] Aug 1955, Little Hull Hole Oct 1955, Jackdaw Hole & Pen-y-Ghent Long Churn Nov 1955, Christmas Pot 1957, Clapham Cave Aug 1955, Rift Pot [Double rope failure] 1957, Lancaster-Eastgill Aug 1960, [Architect] Created development plans for Toll Bar Cottage as well as Brackenbottom. Magnetometer Pot Nov 1960, Easter South Wales Meet 1961, Lost John's March 1961, Ingleborough Cave Sherpaing Dec 1962, Christmas/Grange/P5 April 1962.*
Newsletter References; *Leader Bull Pot of the Witches July 1955, Leader Old Ings Farm. Leader Washfold Pot July 1957, Simpson's Pot Aug 1957, Swinsto Sept 1957, Rumbling Hole Oct 1957, Lancaster Hole Oct 1957, Dow-Providence rescue Dec 1957, Tackle testing Jan 1958, Easter Camp April 1958, Little Hull Pot April 1958, Tackle testing July 1958, St Cuthbert's Swallet Aug 1958, Eastwater Swallet Aug 1958, Swildon's Four Aug 1958, Jnr Leader Magnetometer Pot Nov 1960, Jnr Leader Lost John's Mar 1961.*

THOMPSON, Michael Murray; *J1961, b1933,*
Diver
Bulletin References; *Gaping Gill Meet 1960 [Diving Trip], Clapham Cave Dive Aug 1960.*

THOMPSON, Richard James; *J1988, b1958,*
Member; LSS.
Newsletter References; *Pippikin March 1988.*

THORNDIKE, Geoffrey; *J1956, b1937, d2015.*
BPC President 1993/4.
Bulletin References; *Rift Pot [Double rope failure] 1957, Pen-y-Ghent Pot April 1960, Rowten Pot April 1960, Pen-y-ghent Pot July 1960, Alum Pot July 1960, Bull Pot Sept 1960, Bull Pot Sept 1960, Simpson's Pot 16th April 1961-[Graham Shaw Accident] Lost John's March 1961, Little Hull Pot Feb 1961, Helvelyn Dec 1965.*
Newsletter References; *Washfold Pot July 1957; Simpson's Pot Aug 1957, Swinsto Sept 1957, Rumbling Hole Oct 1957, Lancaster Hole Oct 1957, Practice stretcher rescue Wade's entrance GG Nov 1957, Bar Pot Dec 1957, Tackle testing Jan 1958, Easter Camp April 1958, Main Shaft to de-tackle Disappointment via Hensler's crawl [Hensler star]*

Whit 1958, Leader Hull Pot [BSA extensions] Oct 1960, Leader Chapel le Dale Jan 1961, Eden Valley-Teesdale Walking Meet Oct 1985, Lakes Walk Sept 1990, Crooklands Walking Meet Sept 1993, Lancaster Canal Walk Meet 2001.

THORNHILL, Hugh; *J1959,*

THORNTON, John; *J1934,*

THORPE, Ian; AKA: Lefty. *J1985, b1947,*
Newsletter References; *Pippikin Pot Nov 1986.*

THORPE, Neil; *J1963, b1947,*
Probationary Meets; Stream Passage Pot, Sell Gill, Dow Cave.
Bulletin References; *Pen-y-Ghent Pot Extensions Oct 1963, Notts Pot Oct 1963, Pen-y-Ghent Pot Feb 1964, Lancaster Easegill 1966, explored through sump in GG which eventually led to Whitson series 1965. Screen Hill-Legnabrocky Way Ireland Discovery Aug 1965.*
Newsletter References; *Leader Rowten Pot [Didn't turn up] July 1965.*

THORPE, Percy D; *J1948,*
Bulletin References; *Rift Pot/Long Kin East exchange April 1949, Flood Entrance July 1949, Easter Camp-GG 1950.*

THWAITES, William. G;
Newsletter References; *Sunset Hole May 1976.*

TIDSWELL, Kenneth Brian; AKA: Ken. *J1958, b1940,*
Re-joined March 1974.
Member of the Heath Grammar School contingent.
Bulletin References; *Lancaster-Eastgill Aug 1960, Bull Pot Sept 1960, Lost John's March 1961, Dive support 'sherpa' Ingleborough Cave 1962, Juniper Gulf Dec 1962, Notts Pot Oct 1963.*
Famous for; being first member to abseil Bar Pot on a donated 'paratrooper rope'.
Newsletter References; *Discovery Lower Stream Passage Pot April 1959, Kingsdale Master Cave Dec 1969, Skirwith Cave July 2000.*

TIDSWELL, Peter Lee; *J1963, b1944, d2018.*
Member of the Heath Grammar School contingent.
Probationary Meets; Pen-y-Ghent Pot, Swinsto, Juniper Gulf.
Bulletin References; *Pen-y-ghent Pot 1961, Juniper Gulf 1962, Swinsto 1962, Notts Pot Oct 1963.*
Newsletter References; *Discovery Lower Stream Passage Pot April 1959.*

TIDSWELL, Hannah; *J2000,*

Newsletter References; *Skirwith Cave July 2000.*

TIDSWELL, Mark; *J2000,*
Newsletter References; *Skirwith Cave July 2000.*

TIERNAY, Leslie; *J1987, b1968,*

TILLOTSON, Anthony; *J2012, b1979,*
Newsletter References; *Old Ing/Calf Holes-Browgill [Novice Trip] July 2012.*

TODD, Peter; *J2008, b1981,*

TOLSON, Brian; *J1958, b1939,*
Suspended from club Dec 1959.
Newsletter References; *Easter Camp April 1958, Flood Entrance Pot April 1958, Little Hull Pot April 1958.*

TOMLINSON, Paul; *J1952, b1933,*

TOMLINSON, T. R;

TOMLINSON, Theresa; AKA: Taz. *J2002, b1959,*
Newsletter References; *Great/Little Douk Dec 2001, Runscar Cave Sept 2004.*

TOOES, Michael; *J2009,*
Newsletter Rerences; *Providence Pot-Dow Cave April 2007, Bar Pot Dec 2007, Dismall Hill-Old Ing Jan 2008, Vesper Pot Jan 2008.*

TOOKEY, M. A; *J1979,*

TOWERS, Denis; *J1957, b1936,*

TREWITT, D; *J1959,*
Bulletin References; *Magnetometer Pot Nov 1960, Flood Entrance Pot Dec 1960.*

TROTT, Elizabeth; *J2010, b2005,*

TROTT, John Raymond; *J1965, b1948,*
Probationary Meets; Magnetometer, Pot, Mary's Fell Hole.
Bulletin References; *Gingling Wet Sinks Oct 1966, Work in Ingleborough Cave 1968, Grange Rig Pot 1968, Cold Streak Mine 1969.*

TROTT, Joseph; *J2009, b1948,*

TROTT, Kristofer; *J2010, b2005,*

TURNER, H. A; *J1982, b1935,*

TURNER, Ian; *J1999, b1964,*
Probationary Meets; GG98/9.

TURNER, John Lawrence; *J1954, b1933,*

TURNER, Paul Robert; *J1969, b1945,*
Probationary Meets; Easegill, Sell Gill, Alum Pot.
Club expeditions; Chourum des Aiguilles 1973, Matienzo 1973.
Notable Achievements; Due to his engineering background worked closely with the conversion of the GG winch to a hydraulic drive, including making the chair and sliding plank for the gantry. Tackle secretary for 12 years.
Main Activities; Caving, Walking, some Climbing, Green Lane motor cycling with Ian 'Grass' Ashwell and latterly, Photography.
Famous for; A spontaneous round of applause from other members when the sliding plank system was seen to work very well making the planking job much easier. Being present when Allan Brittain, due to incompetence, fell headlong into a bramble filled ditch in Spain, his last words were heard to be "You're all pissed".
Newsletter References; Leader *Bull Pot of the Witches Dec 1976, Bull Pot of the Witches Nov 1977, Bull Pot of the Witches [And assistance with the body recovery of Tracy Gibson from Top Sink] Oct 1980.*

TYAS, Philip Lee; *J1949,*
Member; CPC.
Famous for; Being abandoned down Car Pot by CPC. Tyas Ledge in entrance shaft named after him after this incident in 1948/9. Joined BPC as a result.
Bulletin References; *Ierby Fell Cavern Nov 1950,*
Newsletter References; *Bull Pot March 1971, Lockey Gill Cave June 1972.*

U

UNDERWOOD, Philip Alexander; AKA: Phil Underpants. *J1999, b1965,*
Probationary Meets; Sell Gill, GG00, Pen-y-Ghent Pot.
Newsletter References; *Lost John's Jan 1995, Wretched Rabbit-Lancaster Hole March 1995, Pippikin Pot Nov 1999, Pen-y-Ghent Pot July 2000, Bull Pot Jan 2001, Swinsto [Through] Jan 2003, Lost John's March 2009, Ireby Fell Cavern Jan 2011, Notts Pot March 2012, Juniper Gulf March 2012.*

UNSWORTH, Sally; *J1988, b1960,*

UPFOLD, Martin; *J2014, b1960,*
Member; WCMS, CCC.
Newsletter References; *KMC Sept 2014.*

UPSALL, Jack; *J2020,*